the Outlaw Bible of
american literature

The
Outlaw Bible
of
american literature

EDITED BY

Alan Kaufman,

Neil Ortenberg,

&

Barney Rosset

THUNDER'S MOUTH PRESS
New York

THE OUTLAW BIBLE OF AMERICAN LITERATURE

Thunder's Mouth Press
An Imprint of Avalon Publishing Group Inc.
245 West 17th Street • 11th Floor
New York, NY 10011

AVALON
publishing group incorporated

Library of Congress Cataloging-in-Publication Data is available.

ISBN: 1-56025-550-1

9 8 7 6 5 4 3 2 1

Book design by Simon M. Sullivan
Printed in the United States of America
Distributed by Publishers Group West

contents

Acknowledgments   xiii

Introduction   xvii

Prologue: Voices from Outlaw Heaven

The Sexual Outlaw	John Rechy	1
The House on Mango Street	Sandra Cisneros	4
Live from Death Row	Mumia Abu-Jamal	5
Ballad of Easy Earl	Barry Gifford	6
The Basketball Diaries	Jim Carroll	8
Psychotic Reactions and Carburetor Dung	Lester Bangs	11
Complete	Patti Smith	13
*L'Anarchie Flier	Patti Smith	14

American Renegades

Paradoxia	Lydia Lunch	15
Fight Club	Chuck Palahniuk	20
Tropic of Cancer	Henry Miller	25
Ask Dr. Mueller	Cookie Mueller	31
Pimp	Iceberg Slim	37
Close to the Knives	David Wojnarowicz	39
What Did I Do?	Larry Rivers	40
*American Splendor Anthology	Harvey Pekar	45
Don Quixote	Kathy Acker	53
Last Exit to Brooklyn	Hubert Selby Jr.	54
Tin Pan Alley	Barney Rosset	59

An American Dream	Norman Mailer	63
Jew Boy	Alan Kaufman	68
The Journal of Albion Moonlight	Kenneth Patchen	78
The Sheltering Sky	Paul Bowles	83
Cool for You	Eileen Myles	86
Junky	William S. Burroughs	89
Leaving Las Vegas	John O'Brien	94

Holy Goofs

Jan and Jack	Neil Ortenberg	101
Baby Driver	Jan Kerouac	103
On the Road	Jack Kerouac	105
Minor Characters	Joyce Johnson	111
The First Third	Neal Cassady	117
Off the Road	Carolyn Cassady	119
Go	John Clellon Holmes	125
An Accidental Autobiography	Gregory Corso	130
Rolling Thunder Logbook	Sam Shepard	133

Road Dogs and Queens of Heart

*Paintings	Dee Dee Ramone	135
On Dee Dee Ramone	Neil Ortenberg	136
Legend of a Rock Star	Dee Dee Ramone	138
E.A.R.L.	DMX	142
Interview with Tupac Shakur	Larry Hester for *Vibe* Online	145
Tarantula	Bob Dylan	148
Miles	Miles Davis	151
Tha Doggfather	Snoop Dogg	154
James Brown:		
The Godfather of Soul	James Brown	155
To Do the Right Thing	Lou Reed	160
Please Kill Me	Legs McNeil and Gillian McCain	163
The Vulture	Gil Scott-Heron	170

Please Don't Let Me Be Misunderstood	Eric Burdon	173
The Old, Weird America	Greil Marcus	178

Fists in the Air

Ripening	Meridel Le Sueur	181
The Woman Rebel	Margaret Sanger	189
Thelma & Louise	Callie Khouri	192
SCUM Manifesto	Valerie Solanas	198
The Illegal Days	Grace Paley	205
Living My Life	Emma Goldman	210
Intercourse	Andrea Dworkin	221
*The Birth of Feminism	Guerrilla Girls	224

Chainwhipped

Hell's Angel	Ralph "Sonny" Barger	225
Street Justice	Chuck Zito	232
Troia	Bonnie Bremser	237
Freewheelin Frank	Frank Reynolds as told to Michael McClure	242
The Electric Kool-Aid Acid Test	Tom Wolfe	251
Outlaw Woman	Roxanne Dunbar-Ortiz	260

Bad Ass

Always Running	Luis Rodriguez	267
If He Hollers Let Him Go	Chester Himes	270
Push	Sapphire	275
Never Die Alone	Donald Goines	280
Sweet Sweetback's Baadasssss Song	Melvin Van Peebles	286
The Scene	Clarence Cooper Jr.	290
The White Boy Shuffle	Paul Beatty	297

Down These Mean Streets	Piri Thomas	301
Rope Burns	F. X. Toole	303

Riding the Rods

*Weird Self Portrait at Sea	Jack Kerouac	311
Sister of the Road	Boxcar Bertha	312
Bound for Glory	Woody Guthrie	316
Grand Central Winter	Lee Stringer	320
You Can't Win	Jack Black	323
Beggars of Life	Jim Tully	328
Midnight Cowboy	James Leo Herlihy	331
Black Fire	Nelson Peery	342

Nuclear Family Nightmares

Diary of an Emotional Idiot	Maggie Estep	347
The Bell Jar	Sylvia Plath	352
Requiem for a Dream	Hubert Selby Jr.	356
The Passionate Mistakes and Intricate Corruption of One Girl in America	Michelle Tea	359
In the City of Sleep	Wanda Coleman	361
Complete	Patti Smith	366
A Different Kind of Intimacy	Karen Finley	367
Whoreson	Donald Goines	371
Shock Value	John Waters	377
A Heartbreaking Work of Staggering Genius	Dave Eggers	382
Monkey Girl	Beth Lisick	385
Dogeaters	Jessica Tarahata Hagedorn	387
Geek Love	Katherine Dunn	390

OBEY

Fahrenheit 451	Ray Bradbury	399
The Lost	Jack Ketchum	404
Sales Pitch	Philip K. Dick	408
The Hellbound Heart	Clive Barker	410
Naked Lunch	William S. Burroughs	416
Drawing Blood	Poppy Z. Brite	424
The Manchurian Candidate	Richard Condon	426

Hardboiled

The Grifters	Jim Thompson	429
The Big Kill	Mickey Spillane	434
Taxi Driver	Paul Schrader	436
Thieves' Market	A. I. Bezzerides	443
Dark Passage	David Goodis	447
Really the Blues	Mezz Mezzrow	450
Angels of Catastrophe	Peter Plate	453
The Man with the Golden Arm	Nelson Algren	457
The Big Hunger	John Fante	461
The Asphalt Jungle	W. R. Burnett	464
The Getaway Man	Andrew Vachss	467

White Line Fever

Dogs of God	Pinckney Benedict	471
Escape from Houdini Mountain	Pleasant Gehman	476
The Car	Harry Crews	477
Drugstore Cowboy	James Fogle	481
This Outlaw Shit	Waylon Jennings	485
Love All the People	Bill Hicks	490
The Way It Has to Be	Breece D'J Pancake	492
American Skin	Don De Grazia	496
The Ceremony	Weldon Kees	502
Terminal Lounge	John Sayles	506

The Joint

*Sketch	Ken Kesey	511
On the Yard	Malcolm Braly	512
Soul on Ice	Eldridge Cleaver	521
In the Belly of the Beast	Jack Henry Abbott	523
Sketches	Ken Kesey	526
Life in Prison	Stanley "Tookie" Williams	527
Cool Hand Luke	Donn Pearce	531
The Family	Ed Sanders	534
Introduction to Short Eyes	Marvin Felix Camillo	537
Short Eyes	Miguel Piñero	539

XXX Hardcore

The Sexual Outlaw	John Rechy	545
Hardcore from the Heart	Annie Sprinkle	553
Candy	Terry Southern and Mason Hoffenberg	557
Period	Dennis Cooper	564
City of Night	John Rechy	564
Shirts & Skin	Tim Miller	569
Now Dig This	Terry Southern	574
Public Sex	Pat Califia	577

Playing in the Apocalypse

One Flew Over the Cuckoo's Nest	Ken Kesey	585
Nigger	Dick Gregory	593
Assata	Assata Shakur	598
The Delicious Grace of Moving One's Hand	Timothy Leary	599
The Autobiography of Malcolm X	Malcolm X	606
How to Talk Dirty and Influence People	Lenny Bruce	607
My Acid Trip with Groucho Marx	Paul Krassner	611
The Teachings of Don Juan	Carlos Castaneda	617

The Abortion	Richard Brautigan	618
Fear and Loathing in Las Vegas	Hunter S. Thompson	624
*Vintage Dr. Gonzo	Ralph Steadman	629

*Cover and Inside Cover of Evergreen Review
Statement in Support of the Freedom to Read   630

Contributors	633
Permissions	657
About the Editors	663

Acknowledgments

Alan Kaufman would like to thank God, Moses, Buddha, for always being there; the Rutherfurds (Elizabeth, Lewis, Marcelle, Jacqueline, and Hugo) and the Tannenbaums (Allen, Rina, Sarah, and Emmanuel) for taking me into their respective families; Fred Jordan, my great editor, for mentoring my literature; Joe Herlisy for making me a writer; and Wendy Merrill, Astrid Meyers, Herb Gold, John Lane, Thane Rosenbaum, Erik Laprade, Mike Gates, Ben Gardner, Corinna Gardner, Barbara Gabriel, David Carlson, Paul (Bean) Kirk, Kira Rosenberger, David and Erin Newman, Matt Gonzales, and James Sullivan for unstinting friendship. I want to especially thank Neil Ortenberg, a true outlaw and editorial giant, for his inspired collaboration and loyal camaraderie, and Barney Rosset, the greatest editor of all time, for his counsel, mentorship, and extraordinary example. Many thanks also to Dan O'Connor and Avalon's Catheline Jean-François.

Neil Ortenberg would like to thank Karen Chen for inspiration, patience, boundless love, and editorial savvy; Catheline Jean-François whose superb support helped make this book possible; Dan O'Connor for being at my side in publishing for a decade, and working on both *Outlaw* books; Glenn Thompson, a true outlaw publisher and departed friend; Alan Kaufman for his brilliant writing and creative editorial instinct; Barney Rosset for being a mentor and friend; and Erik Kahn for introducing me to Dee Dee Ramone.

Barney Rosset would like to thank Astrid Meyers for her love and support.

"For every man was secretly against the law in his heart . . . and it was the heart that mattered."

—Nelson Algren, *The Man with the Golden Arm*

Introduction

LIKE ITS HIGHLY ACCLAIMED companion and predecessor, *The Outlaw Bible of American Poetry*, *The Outlaw Bible of American Literature* is a document of revolt against a landscape dominated by a literary dictatorship of tepid taste, political correctness, and sheer numbing banality. But there is another authentic American literature that cuts to the bone. Works produced by such legendary authors as Hubert Selby Jr., Jack Kerouac, Kathy Acker, Norman Mailer, Eldridge Cleaver, David Wojnarowicz, Henry Miller, and John Rechy are examples of just a few of the giants contained in this collection. These visionaries produced such roguish masterpieces as *Last Exit to Brooklyn, On the Road, Blood and Guts in High School, An American Dream, Soul on Ice, Close to the Knives, Tropic of Cancer,* and *The Sexual Outlaw.* We do not claim to present here the entirety of countercultural American prose but only a vivid sampling and for every author included, ten were left out. The ones we've chosen are representative of larger cultural trends and are intended as sign pointers for the dreamers and seekers who find themselves upon this road.

It is in the Orwellian nature of our contemporary society that not only is the Outlaw past disclaimed but actually effaced from memory, as though it had never been. Like some ancient extinct civilization the Outlaw tradition in literature is just a legend, a rumor, a buried Atlantis. A new culture coming of age in the grip of Google and Wal-Mart might never know that Dick Gregory or Malcolm Braly, Boxcar Bertha, Nelson Algren, Lee Stringer, or Emma Goldman had ever existed. Know that some of our nation's great writing, a representative cross section of which is contained in this book, is a New India of underground prose, a spice route encompassed by mysteries and monsters, and comprises a fresh new canon sprung not from reality shows, Botox, or IPOs, but the streets, prisons, highways, trailer parks, and back alleys of the American Dream. The authors in this collection are not greeted with book club appearances and White House invitations, but often lead lives of state pen incarceration, suicide, drug addiction, street hustling, exile, martyrdom, and even murder at the hands of strangers. These rich stories, candid oral histories, letters, graphic testimonies, and autobiographical accounts of human burden come together as an unbroken circle of alternative/outsider literature.

Take the case of Donald Goines, author of seventeen books, but largely unknown to the mainstream. He is the father of a whole genre of Black film and fiction, an original American Dostoyevskian genius who lived the criminal life portrayed in such best-selling underground classics as *Whoreson, Never Die Alone*, and *Black Gangster*. Goines, at the age of thirty-seven, was shot at his own typewriter by an unknown assailant in what may have been an underworld hit.

Or take Richard Brautigan, America's psychedelic Chekhov, author of such singular works as *The Tokyo-Montana Express* and *The Abortion*. At the height of his fame, he blew out his brains with a shotgun.

Or take Breece D'J Pancake, who managed only one extraordinary collection before taking his own life.

Or F. X. Toole—arguably the greatest writer on boxing to appear since Hemingway—who published his first collection to rave acclaim after years of neglect at the absurd age of seventy, only to die a year later. You will not find these authors listed in the registry of the American Academy of Arts and Letters.

Some of our best, our fiercest, our most volcanic prose is not a tongue-twisted Henry Jamesian labyrinth of "creative writing" but an outraged American songline of tear-stained revelation from explorers like William S. Burroughs, who in his classic book *Junky* traveled to the edge of heroin addiction and preserved in deathless prose what he found there. Or like Iceberg Slim, author of *Pimp*, who ran whores before turning his hand to books, or Luis Rodriguez who gangbanged his way out of self-destruction through grueling literary mastery, or Ken Kesey who captured the American heart in great epic novels before transforming its society through Merry Prankster revolution.

Along the way, you'll hear Lydia Lunch on copulation at knife-point; John O'Brien of *Leaving Las Vegas* fame on non-stop black-out drinking; DMX on how he got payback with a shotgun taped to his leg. You'll read about Paul Krassner dropping acid with Groucho Marx, browse for guitars with Dee Dee Ramone, and ride through the inferno with Hell's Angels' president Sonny Barger.

These are Songs of Experience. The voices of nightmare and love that may not exactly kill you but demand a toll in dangerous emotion as the price for listening. These writers have forged new forms to corral incoherence, make a song of ugliness, and map new territories of distress. They have restored meaning to our human predicament through the power of their language.

Alan Kaufman
Neil Ortenberg
Barney Rosset

Prologue: Voices from Outlaw Heaven

JOHN RECHY

The Sexual Outlaw

5:02 P.M. HOLLYWOOD BOULEVARD. SELMA.

BEHIND THE THIN SHROUD of smog, the California sun scorches coldly white. Hollywood Boulevard is crowded with tribes of outlaws—hustlers, sex-hunters, queens.

Jim hugs each desiring glance on his shirtless body. Leaving the movie arcade earlier, he suddenly needed to sell his body.

"What's happenin?"

The blond hustler stands outside the Gold Cup Coffee Shop.

"Not much—with you?"

"Making it, making it."

The announcement of continuing survival.

Smiling, they separate. Ignoring a man who looks too much like a cop, Jim moves on to Selma.

He stands studying that terribly unextraordinary-looking street.

So much of his life, here. So many memories. They surface like ghosts. Ghosts . . .

The man who dialed numbers on his telephone while lying on the floor, Jim standing over him; the man dialing, hanging up, dialing again—then speaking hoarsely into the receiver: "Right this minute, I'm lying on the floor, and this muscular hustler is going to jerk off on me, and he'll force me to eat

1

his hot cum—and—and—. . . . Oh, oh!" The phone dropped on the cradle. Later Jim asked him, "You always call your friends when you're making it?" "Friends!" the man said. "Oh, no, I just dial at random until I reach anyone!"

And the gentle man who wanted to send Jim to school.

And the tough young kid with bulging arms; he drove a defiant, jacked-up car. He looked like a hustler himself, but he bought hustlers. He cuddled in his car with Jim, and came.

And the impeccable little man who merely wanted to massage Jim's body, and offered him more if he "fell asleep."

And the man who—. . . .

So many others, remembered, forgotten, remembered. Nights. Mornings. Afternoons.

And one particularly desolate night.

FLASHBACK: *CHRISTMAS EVE. TWO YEARS AGO. SELMA.*

A cold Texas-dusty night. To crush memories, Jim was hustling. The wind flung palmtree leaves on the streets. The day had been fiercely orange.

A man in a car kept circling the block, not stopping. Finally he parked a few feet away from Jim, got out, and approached him as if to study him better. They spoke for a few seconds, making arrangements. They drove to the man's home. What happened, Jim doesn't know—but it festers like a permanent cut.

Suddenly, after leaving the room for a short while—and before he had even touched Jim—the man returned and said he had just found a note from the man he worked for to pick him up in a few minutes. As strange as that, as abrupt. Jim felt an iron-fisted depression. The man gave him half the agreed amount of money—"for wasting your time"—and drove him back to the palm-littered streets. Moments later, when Jim had almost managed to force himself to believe the man's strange story, he saw the same man circling the block.

5:08 P.M. SELMA.

Jim speaks briefly to hustlers he recognizes; they warn him about cops or "weirdos" on the streets today. Two other shirtless hustlers sit on the steps of the Baptist church. As he passes the phone booth on the corner, he hears it ring. Curious, he answers it.

The voice asks: "How big is your cock?"

Jim laughs, hangs up.

A prissy, slightly effeminate old man with a pampered hairdo and impossibly even white teeth has parked a few feet ahead and is standing on the sidewalk staring at Jim. Jim touches his own chest. The man moves over to him: "What a beautiful body you have!" Jim feels a delicious warmth. "And thank God you're a *man* and not one of those skinny boys," the little man goes on. Because that stirred the specter of aging—though a compliment—Jim's warmth decreases slightly, returns fully when the man continues: "Too few masculine men are left. Oh, what a body! I adore muscles!"

They agree on twenty dollars, and that Jim will "do nothing." The man's name is Roo. He was once a chorus boy—"singing, dancing, camping"—oh, long, long ago "when Hollywood was *really* Hollywood!" Now he gives singing lessons.

5:25 P.M. ROO'S HOME.

A neat, inexpensive house—a piano draped with an old-fashioned fringed shawl, flower-embroidered. A photograph on it, a small bronze statue.

In the equally ordered bedroom, Roo asks Jim to put on a posing strap. "Like in the *really* sexy magazines, before they had to show *everything!*"

Jim does.

"Beautiful!" the man applauds.

For Jim, nothing further would be needed. Roo paid him even before they got here, is now admiring his body. Jim could leave now, fully satisfied by this scene. But he knows Roo wants more.

There's a loud knock on the front door.

"How rude!" Roo closes the bedroom door behind him.

Jim hears excited talk:

A rough voice: "Listen to me, Roo, I need twenty bucks right away. *Now*, dammit, I need it bad, and I'm in a hurry, Roo!"

Roo's voice is deliberately controlled—but tinged with agitation, and fear: "No, no! I don't have any money. And I have someone with me," he warns.

"Dammit, Roo!" The voice gets rougher.

"I said no!"

"You wanna blow me? I got a few minutes; you wanna blow me for the twenty bucks?"

"I told you, I'm with someone— . . ."

"Roo— . . . Motherfucker— . . ."

"All right. I'll give you a check. They'll cash it at that corner store."

"And give me some cigarettes, I'm outta cigarettes."

"All right, all right—just go away. *Please!*" A few seconds later: "Here."

The door slams.

Flushed, Roo returns to Jim in the bedroom.

"You're gorgeous," Roo resumes, his breathing slightly uneven. He kneels before Jim. "Shut your eyes, don't look at me." Jim closes his eyes. He feels Roo's suddenly toothless mouth on his cock.

Jim didn't come. Roo came secretly, trying to disguise even his quickened breathing.

Jim goes to the shower, the water harsh and cold on his body. Through, he stands wrapped in a towel; stands by the living room door looking at Roo's skinny form at the piano. Now Jim sees the photograph—a faded picture of an old white-haired woman—and the bronzed object—bronzed baby shoes tarnished with age.

The tiny, shriveled, used form of Roo sits at the piano and sings—beautifully—an old romantic song.

Sandra Cisneros

The House on Mango Street

I DON'T REMEMBER WHEN I first noticed him looking at me—Sire. But I knew he was looking. Every time. All the time I walked past his house. Him and his friends sitting on their bikes in front of the house, pitching pennies. They didn't scare me. They did, but I wouldn't let them know. I don't cross the street like other girls. Straight ahead, straight eyes. I walked past. I knew he was looking. I had to prove to me I wasn't scared of nobody's eyes, not even his. I had to look back hard, just once, like he was glass. And I did. I did once. But I looked too long when he rode his bike past me. I looked because I wanted to be brave, straight into the dusty cat fur of his eyes and the bike stopped and he bumped into a parked car, bumped, and I walked fast. It made your blood freeze to have somebody look at you like that. Somebody looked at me. Somebody looked. But his kind, his ways. He is a punk, Papa says, and Mama says not to talk to him.

And then his girlfriend came. Lois I heard him call her. She is tiny and pretty and smells like baby's skin. I see her sometimes running to the store for him. And once when she was standing next to me at Mr. Benny's grocery she was barefoot, and I saw her barefoot baby toenails all painted pale pale pink, like little pink seashells, and she smells pink like babies do. She's got big girl hands, and her bones are long like ladies' bones, and she wears makeup too. But she doesn't know how to tie her shoes. I do.

Sometimes I hear them laughing late, beer cans and cats and the trees talking to themselves: wait, wait, wait. Sire lets Lois ride his bike around the block, or they take walks together. I watch them. She holds his hand, and he stops sometimes to tie her shoes. But Mama says those kinds of girls, those girls are the ones that go into alleys. Lois who can't tie her shoes. Where does he take her?

Everything is holding its breath inside me. Everything is waiting to explode like Christmas. I want to be all new and shiny. I want to sit out bad at night, a boy around my neck and the wind under my skirt. Not this way, every evening talking to the trees, leaning out my window, imagining what I can't see.

A boy held me once so hard, I swear, I felt the grip and weight of his arms, but it was a dream.

Sire. How did you hold her? Was it? Like this? And when you kissed her? Like this?

MUMIA ABU-JAMAL

Live from Death Row

IN THE MIDST OF darkness, this little one was a light ray. Tiny, with a Minnie Mouse voice, this daughter of my spirit had finally made the long trek westward, into the bowels of this man-made hell, situated in the south-central Pennsylvania boondocks. She, like my other children, was just a baby when I was cast into hell, and because of her youth and sensitivity, she hadn't been brought along on family visits until now.

She burst into the tiny visiting room, her brown eyes aglitter with happiness; stopped, stunned, staring at the glassy barrier between us; and burst into tears at this arrogant attempt at state separation. In milliseconds, sadness and shock shifted into fury as her petite fingers curled into tight fists, which banged and pummeled the Plexiglas barrier, which shuddered and shimmied but didn't shatter.

"Break it! Break it!" she screamed. Her mother, recovering from her

Prologue: Voices from Outlaw Heaven

shock, bundled up Hamida in her arms, as sobs rocked them both. My eyes filled to the brim. My nose clogged.

Her unspoken words echoed in my consciousness: "Why *can't* I hug him? Why *can't* we kiss? Why *can't* I sit in his lap? *Why can't we touch?* Why not?" I turned away to recover.

I put on a silly face, turned back, called her to me, and talked silly to her. "Girl, how can you breathe with all them boogies in your nose?" Amid the rolling trail of tears, a twinkle started like dawn, and before long the shy beginnings of a smile meandered across her face as we talked silly talk.

I reminded her of how she used to hug our cat until she almost strangled the poor animal, and Hamida's denials were developing into laughter. The three of us talked silly talk, liberally mixed with serious talk, and before long our visit came to an end. Her smile restored, she uttered a parting poem that we used to say over the phone: "I love you, I miss you, and when I see you, I'm gonna kiss you!" The three of us laughed and they left.

Over five years have passed since that visit, but I remember it like it was an hour ago: the slams of her tiny fists against that ugly barrier; her instinctual rage against it—the state-made blockade raised under the rubric of security, her hot tears.

They haunt me.

November 1994

BARRY GIFFORD

Ballad of Easy Earl

"EARL, MY MAN, IT'S a goddamn good thing you got a big dick," Easy Earl Blakey said aloud, as he sat alone in his car on the side of the road by Irish Bayou, " 'cause you sure must have a tiny motherfuckin' brain."

He had no idea what time it was, but Earl figured it had to be well past midnight by now. He had been driving aimlessly around the city since fleeing Alfonzo's Mexicali, and finally pulled over due to fatigue. What had gone down back there? he asked himself. All he could remember was that there had been some kind of an argument at the other end of the bar, and then the gun spinning along the mahogany into his hand. He had heard someone coming up behind him, turned and saw two guns pointed in his direction. After that, Earl's mind was blank. He knew he had fired the revolver, though, even if he could not clearly recall having done so. Something in his brain had just snapped when he'd seen those pistols pushed toward his face.

He took a deep breath, then lit up a Kool. There was so little traffic out here, he thought, looking up at the crescent moon. If he shot himself, it might be two or three days, maybe a week, before his body would be discovered. Earl sat and smoked. When he had had enough of it, he tossed the butt out the window, then picked up the revolver and got out of the car. Earl walked over to the bayou and threw the gun into the water. He stood there for a minute, listening. All he heard were airplane engines droning overhead. Earl went back to the Mercury, got in and cranked it up. Where to? he wondered, and started driving.

For some reason, the image of Willie Wong entered Earl's mind. Willie Wong had been a boyhood pal of Earl's. They had grown up together in the Eighth Ward and remained friends until Willie's death at the age of twenty-one. Willie had been a normal Chinese-American kid; he had studied hard in school and worked regularly at various jobs to help support himself and his parents, who owned a small grocery store on St. Claude Avenue. Then, when Willie was eighteen, he saw the movie *The Wild One*, which starred Marlon Brando as a devil-may-care, hardcase motorcycle gang leader. Willie fell in love with the image personified by Brando, and he bought a thirdhand Triumph Bonneville, allowed his lank black hair to grow long, wore a leather jacket, engineer boots and oily Levi's. He also started smoking, something else he never had done before, and it was rare to see him riding around on his bike without an unfiltered Lucky Strike dangling from his lips. Willie even invented his own nickname, "the Wild Wong," and encouraged everyone he knew to call him that. Only his parents refused to honor this request, continuing to address him as they always had, by his Chinese name, Zhao.

The Wild Wong was killed on a wet Thursday evening when a drunken driver in a brand-new SAAB sedan cut too closely in front of Willie's Triumph on Chef Menteur Highway and clipped the front wheel, catapulting the Wild Wong headfirst into a roadside ditch, breaking his back and neck. At Willie's funeral, Earl had been surprised to see that the Wong family had dressed their son in his biker clothes to be viewed in an open casket. He had been certain that the Wongs would have cut Willie's hair and put him into a suit. As he passed the casket, Earl had noticed that an unsealed package of Lucky Strike cigarettes had been placed in Willie's left hand.

Why he thought at this difficult moment in his own life of the Wild Wong, Earl did not know. Something had happened to Willie when he'd seen that movie, and his life had been changed irrevocably. Now, Easy Earl knew, nothing would be the same for him, either. That was it, he supposed. Something a person never could imagine took place and then the world looked completely different.

The image of Willie Wong lying in his coffin twenty-five years ago would not go away, and Earl drove fast on the deserted road in his Monarch with the headlights off.

"Whoooeeee! Willie Wild Wong, you dumb motherfucker!" Earl shouted. "I'm comin' to find you, brother, ready or not!"

Jim Carroll

The Basketball Diaries

Winter 65

My Marxist pal, Bunty, from my new school, finally talked me into going to one of his Communist Party meetings today. It was in this sleazy place on 11th St. called Webster Hall. All the girls looked like reformed Mary Magdalenes. Everyone moans a lot and plays folk songs, one of the requirements seems to be that you have to be ugly. I was wearing my seediest clothes and I still came off looking like Arnold Palmer or something. I dig these motherfuckers, but the speeches bored the shit out of me. I went home and told my old man how the government suppresses the proletariat from his due. "I am the proletariat, you dumb bastard," he said, "and I think those motherfuckers are off their rockers. Now get the hell inside and do your homework."

Spring 66

I spent a good fucking sick morning trying to cop dope today but not a soul in the neighborhood is holding. "Just got my wakeup shot for the morning and this evening," is all I hear. "Heard there's been a big bust on 134th and nothing's happening at all." And that's the line I hear from every dealer I see, which wasn't too many 'cause sixteen saps got busted last night either in the pool room or in front of the candy store or in the projects, narcs just breezing right on into every other pair of pockets they could find. Steaming hot around here, like someone got busted and is feeding out names to save his own ass like a homing pigeon in heat. So for me it's back to the subway and down to the Village where on E. 2nd Street I spot amigo Kookie and his chick Diamond. They had the same story but did have methadone to sell, insisting it was good. I'm good friends with both, we been through a lot of N.Y. scenery together hunting a bag in winter midnights. I trust them as much as you can a junkie which ain't much no matter who it is but no time to be picky anyway. I've had methadone before and I have a very high natural tolerance to it but two hundred milligrams can do the trick so I give them eleven bucks, a good deal for that amount, and down the bottle, right on the spot. That's the shit with methadone, it's cut with Tang or O.J. so dealers can easily cut the shit, but this stuff was bitter enough so I figured it was OK. Of course the other hassle is you can't shoot the stuff and it takes a good hour at least to hit before you feel them warm oats settling down your sick belly. You bet that's a long hour too, with them cold flashes shooting up from your crotch right out your skull and your muscles feeling like wood and your energy to a sad eyed drip. Yep, I'm good and sick without that fix now and my rap of being the one who can keep it all under control is in that breeze cluttered with the same raps a million times run down by a million other genius wise ass cats walking like each other's ghosts around these same sick streets in my same sick shoes. So then the methadone is pumping that warmth back in me by now and I'm together again, but I ain't high worth one short nod, the high is all in the past . . . I'm just another normal body now functioning like all the other faces I pass going back uptown though they ain't laying out bread to get that way. But fuck all that 'cause once Mr. Jones got you by the back even self pity ain't worth shit, though it's about all most junk heads got left. More money equals less head. And that's the way it is and you know and you know.

Summer 66

I'm familiar with just about every junk pusher from 190th St. up to 225th St. Jimmy Mancole, out of his junkie necessity, probably knows even more. But today we must have knocked on every door and checked out every street corner among all these possibilities and not one dealer was holding a single bag. This is equal to walking down Fifth Avenue at lunchtime on a weekday afternoon and finding the entire street abandoned. I was a mixture of stoned disappointment and anger because I was planning a pleasant day in nod land, but Mancole was in complete sickness and hugging his last nerves. By the time we had exhausted all possible sources he had considered suicide close to fourteen times and must have stopped on every third corner to puke.

"It's those fucking Russians," he kept muttering, "the big bomb's coming at 3 this afternoon, something's happening man, someone's doing this to me." It was a bit rare, I thought.

So we hopped onto the "A" train and made it down to my old neighborhood on 29th to see if I could muster something up but the one guy I was sure of scoring off, Herbie Hemslie, was in the clink now for six months already for pushing some dude off a roof one night. I used to play ball with him less than three years ago, and now here he is up the river on a murder rap, it made me wonder a bit where I was heading. "Chinatown," Mancole yelled, "that's it, there's always someone on the street down there." Super, I thought, total intrigue, maybe we even get to smoke the old opium in the back of some laundry.

By this time Mancole was reeling in total madness, in the cab down there he kept singing, "Motherfucker, sisterfucker, blue ball bitch," then he'd look at me with this insane smile and whisper, almost sing it in fact, "A bitch is a female dog, a bitch is a female dog . . ." etc.

Then we hit Mott St. and bolt the cab because it was some old man driving and he didn't even bother to chase us. After a few minutes wait, we were out on the street sniffing around for this young chink cat Jimmy dealt with a year or two ago. Out of the blue come three long haired chinks who pull us aside and mutter, "You people looking to cop?" You bet your oriental asses we are, we implied in a quick nod and followed them into some obscure alley. "This must be the backdoor to the opium den," I whisper to Jimmy. "Oh, fuck you with your opium dens what the hell you think this is, a Charlie Chan movie, let's just get some H and head back up town." At this point one of the guys faces us and asks how much we got to spend. I told him I just wanted $10 worth figuring he was doing fivers and I was planning on getting two anyway, Mancole told him he had $75. "Well, we got excellent crackers, skyrockets like you never seen and very cheap cherry bombs." We look at each other in complete astonishment. These motherfuckers are selling *FIREWORKS*.

After we recover from this lame adventure we hit the streets again and hope to find John Tom, or at least the poolroom where he holds a mild reputation as the hustler top-notch south of Grand St. Finally we stumble onto the place, a real dive with only eight tables dimly lit and seedy and once again me sure the back room is flooded with opium hookahs. John Tom wasn't around at the time but the owner, crusty and looking straight out of a codeine medicine bottle, assures us he'll be about any minute now. Jimmy hits the bathroom and coughs up his fifth Italian ice, both his and my diet for the day. I do in a few chumps at nine ball (not a very cool move judging from the ill looks that start closing in) and finally in steps Tom. Hordes of nodding orientals stare up and make it over to him assuring us he's carrying. After he deals out his wrappers to the regulars he spots Mancole and struts over to see what we want. Jimmy hands over his seventy-five beans and pockets twenty-five bags amid various ohs and ahs from the onlookers. I get three, using my nine ball winning for a joy bag. Within five minutes we're back on the subway and heading up to Headquarters cooking up in an instant and leaning back against the chipped plaster tuning our nods in and out of a crumby George C. Scott drama. I hope for Mancole's sake that the same ordeal ain't gonna pop up tomorrow, but that's a long ways off from where we're at now.

LESTER BANGS

Psychotic Reactions and Carburetor Dung

I CALLED HER. RIGHT in the middle of the conversation, she said: "What do you feel like doing right now?" I replied, automatically, same tone of voice as one might say "I could go for a tuna sandwich on rye," I said: "I wanna fuck." A second of silence. Then: "Okay," she said, just as casually. "Come on over." I got there fast. She met me at the door in a frowzy black slip, hair all a mess, no makeup, barefoot, half-asleep, emotionally neutral to the world. I thought she was the sexiest thing I'd ever seen in my life. Especially in that ratty old black slip. I couldn't believe I was about to be holding something as magnificent as this in my arms, such a hunk of *woo*-man, such a primal Earth Goddess, such a lush juicy creation of the Almighty God in Heaven or Hell I didn't care which and she had a brain besides! I had it made. Life couldn't get any better than this! Like Swamp Dogg once sang: "If I die tomorrow / I've lived tonight!" Damn straight! Who cared if Western civilization was sinking into entropy or gearing up for Armageddon, I never could decide which? All my philosophy was gibberish, and Western civilization was a bucket of shit in the first place! So who cared! I wanted to fuck this woman in the mud of a ditch while a firestorm of whitehot PLO and Israeli bullets

Prologue: Voices from Outlaw Heaven

whizzed over our heads! I wanted to take her down to the Everglades and throw her down in the swamp and do dirty things to her till she screamed like a polecat tangled up in an electrified fence for "More! More! More! Stop! Stop! Stop! No, don't! Eat me! Kill me! Break me! Fuck me!" And then I'd push her down so deep in the mud and the green slime and rotting tropical overgrowth it almost buried both of us in our faces and hair and mouths and we'd love like reptiles slither down lower than the gutter our screaming bellies pounding together in the muck from which all life sprang before we or the media or New York magazine careers or anything else amounted to shit! Alligators would come slogging over, take one look at the likes of us and turn right around and hightail it the other way! Water moccasins cowered at the bottom of the river, scared we'd bite 'em and then they'd die! Because we are death as well as life! We are jungle fever, beri-beri, Mau Maus ravenous for each other after which we'll go machete and bar-bee-cue us some missionaries! We have become one with the primordial ooze! Beats the Upper East Side for shitsure! Then I yank her up from the slime and jet nonstop to Cambodia. I want to fuck her on top of a pile of bleached bones, mountains of skulls, hundreds of rotting carcasses! I want to feel death all around me, that's how alive I feel just looking at her, and TO BE INSIDE . . . yeah I want death from sea to shining sea, mountains of it blotting out the horizon, I want to scream with wild dog joy in the pit of a smoking charnel house! In Makindye Prison, Kampala, Uganda! On top of spilled organs of the dead a foot deep! I want Idi Amin to see us! He's been around a bit, I know, but he's never seen this! Might learn something! I want to fuck death, I want death to know that it ain't shit, I can lick it, because what I am holding in my arms right now and am about to carry into the bedroom and to which I will deliver up my body and soul deep in the center of her belly, the center of *her*, I'm serving notice right now is the final and absolute inarguable rebuttal that shoots death down forever!

Patti Smith

Complete

I HAVEN'T FUCKED MUCH with the past, but i've fucked plenty with the future over the skin of silk are scars from the splinters of stations and walls i've caressed. a stage is like each bolt of wood, like a log of helen, is my pleasure. i would measure the success of a night by the way by the way by the amount of piss and seed i could exude over the columns that nestled the PA some nights i'd surprise everybody by skipping off with a skirt of green net sewed over with flat metallic circles which dazzled and flashed. the lights were violet and white i had an ornamental veil, but i couldn't bear to use it. when my hair was cropped i craved covering, but now my hair itself is a veil, and the scalp inside is a scalp of a crazy and sleepy comanche lies beneath this netting of the skin. i wake up. i am lying peacefully. i am lying peacefully and my knees are open to the sun. i desire him, and he is absolutely ready to seize me. in heart i am moslem in heart i am an american. in heart i am moslem. in heart i'm an american artist and i have no guilt. i seek pleasure. i seek the nerves under your skin. the narrow archway; the layers; the scroll of ancient lettuce. we worship the flaw, the belly, the belly, the mole on the belly of an exquisite whore. he spared the child and spoiled the rod. i have not sold myself to god.

Reprinted courtesy of The Yipster Times *(March-April, 1977). A subscription to* The Yipster Times *is only $6/yr. to P.O. Box 392, Canal Street Station, New York, NY 10013. The Patti Smith Group's new record is* Radio Ethiopia *on Arista Records. Patti says: "Radio Ethiopia goes beyond the wax into a disc of light. Fight the good fight."*

You Can't Say "Fuck" in Radio Free America

BY PATTI SMITH

New Year's Eve, Patti Smith gave a concert at NYC's Palladium. WNEW-FM refused to air the concert on their station due to her using the word "fuck" on an interview with the station last November. Upon hearing of this decision, Patti wrote this heavy condemnation of "progressive" rock radio as we hear it now.

Fuck the word...fuck the word
fuck the word the word is dead
is re-defined...the bird in the (womb)
is expelled by the propelling
motion of fuck of fucking

On November 29, Patti Smith delivered an address on WNEW-FM in New York City. Because of the content of this message, the Patti Smith Group will not be aired live in the future on Metromedia. A transcript is available to the people, for the people who support free communication to decide what programming they want to hear on their radio. (S.s.a.e. to Radio Ethiopia, P.O. Box 188, Mantua, New Jersey 08051).
THE RESISTANCE
We believe in the total freedom of communication and we will not be compromised. The censorship of words is as meaningless as the censorship of musical notes; we cannot tolerate either. Freedom means exactly that: no limits, no boundaries...rock and roll is not a colonial power to be exploited, told what to say and how to say it. This is the spirit in which our music began and the flame in which it must be continued. Radio Ethiopia is a symphony of experience...each piece a movement...14 movements...14 stations.

There is silence on my radio...
—Stones
They are trying to silence us, but they cannot succeed. We cannot be "trusted" not to pollute the airwaves with our idealism and intensity. W(New) York radio has proved unresponsive at best to the new rock and roll being born under its ears...a music having worldwide cause and effect...injecting a new sense of urgency and imperative. Radio has consistently lagged behind the needs of the community it is honor-bound to serve. We do not consider paternalistic token airplay and passive coverage to be enough. FM radio was birthed in the 1960's as an alternative to

restrictive playlisting and narrow monopolistic visions. The promise is being betrayed.

We Want The Radio And We Want It Now
1977...the celebration of 1776-1976 ends tonight... we end with the same desires of individual and ethnic freedom of concept...the freedom of art...the freedom of work...the freedom/flow of energy that keeps rebuilding itself with the nourishment of each generation. The political awareness of the 1960's was a result of the political repression of the 1950's. The 70's have represented the merging of both...political-artistic/activism-expression.
The colonial year is dead. Rock and roll is not a colonial art. We colonize to further the freedom of space.

We must dedicate ourselves to the future...in the sixties the DOG was GOD...the underdogs rose up and merged and fought for political freedom... we of 1977 are Rat/Art.
—Radio Ethiopia, 1977

suspended in relics (art)...The guardians of ritual salute all that heralds and redefines civilization into a long streaming system of tongues...salute then spit on those who left us the ruins of much broken ground then move on...

dedicated to the future we are thus fasting...we rip into the past/perfect like raw meat...we do not accept the past as the summit of creation...we rise and pierce the membrane of mire and waste...the stagnation of rust...

1977. We the people of the neo-army are spewing JUST LUST...The absolute motion into the future... To fight the good fight...the fight for feedom of expression...The fight against fat and Roman satisfaction.

WE DON'T WANT NO SATISFACTION
!!THE ART/RAT DAWNS!!
(THE AWAKENING GRAIN)

RAISE UP/ TAKE POSITION/ DUO-SONIC THE SYSTEM OF GOD. ILLUMINATED WEAPONS POISED LIKE MALLOTS LIKE 2-SOUND PICK-UPS BAYONETING THE FLESH OF THE EVE...A GRAIN OF SAND THRU THE OPTIC NERVES OF HE THAT SEIZE ALL...A-R (rasive) AND STONED AND IRRATED BY A SPECT(RE) SO CUNNING HE EVENTUALLY SHOWS HIS PHASE HE EVENTUALLY WAKES UP) (SHARP AND ROUGH AND DELICATELY CUT THE AWAKENING GRAIN DOES ITS WORK! THE ART/RAT DAWNS AGAIN! ART/RAT KNAWS THRU SPACE/ RUSHING TADPOLES/ A BLACK STREAK ACROSS THE WHITE HOTEL. THE GLASS THAT SEPARATES HIM FROM SOCIETY IS THE TRUE PRISON OF LIGHT...ART/RAT IN THE SHAPE OF A BOY DRESSED IN A COAT OF MILK...ACTION PAINTER...RUBEDO HAIR OF THE ONE WHO SOARS AND SLASHES THRU THE AVIATOR BACK/FLAP W/OUT BARING THE SENCE OF PURE TONGUE RYTHUM... ART/RAT POSSESING THE NOBEL CONCEIT OF THE FUTURE AWAITS HIGH ORDERS TO SPEW THE TONGUE OF LOVE THAT UTTERS THE MOST PRECIOUS COMMAND THE WORDS OF LOVE THAT TURN US ON (THE PHYSICAL HIEROGLYPHICS))(THE 14 POSITIONS) ARE "FUCK ME FUCK ME FUCK ME FUCK ME...FUCK THE WORD/ THE WORD IS DEAD/ FUCK IS DEAD ON THE RADIO/ THE WORD IS DEAD/ IN A WAVE OF SOUND/ TO BE UNBOUND AND WAVED AND DEFILED LIKE A BANNER OUTSIDE SOCIETY OVER THE BLACK RIVER...CITIZENS ARISE! SPIT–BALL INTO*THE SKY! THE AWAKENING GRAIN AWAKENING A–WAKE UP W

Patti Smith L'Anarchie *Flier*

American Renegades

Lydia Lunch

Paradoxia

Los Angeles, an endless sprawl of suburban subdivisions spread out in a massive grid encircling Hollywood, the fraudulent Mecca of egotistical schemers. Everyone's got a grift in Hollywood, or working hard on devising one. The city is paved with broken hearts, shattered dreams, dashed hopes. Everyone expects their fifteen minutes, not realizing their minor brush with greatness will pollute the rest of their tortured lives, creating an almost unbearable torment whose mantra cries out for what could have been, what should have been, what will never be.

Its history of random violence, drive-by shootings, highway snipers, serial killers, religious cults, countless casualties, revolves around the eternal possibility that something greater is almost within reach of every leech, loser and low-life. Hollywood has created Sodom with the help of a corporate machine that feeds on the bruised bones of sacrificial offerings. Its obscene wealth, undeserved fame, untold riches reside side by side with a desperate poverty whose scope is forever overlooked, avoided, ignored. The root of all the sickness swelling inside its soured belly.

I went out to L.A. with a dream on my sleeve too. A dream of escaping the asshole who was obsessing my life back in New York. Just a small vacation, three or four days to clear my head. I put a call in to Pleasant, a hot Hollywood fixture. Part belly dancer, all ghost of Jayne Mansfield. A luscious redhead who knew where to score what from who, whenever. I knew her from New York, a friend of a friend. Suggested she shake some titty at the Wild West Saloon.

Even lent her some panties. She thought she was returning the favor when she suggested I hit a party that was happening on my first night in the City of Lights. Told me to look for Marty; a speedway freak who played hairdresser by day down in Malibu. She claimed he was my type, which I took to mean a little bit twisted. Said he grew up in Topanga, had a thing for Charlie, surrounded himself with chicks with Sexy Sadie fantasies. She was sure I'd be amused.

The party was a bust, full of Valley chicks, jocks and rockabillies. Disappeared into the kitchen looking for something stronger than liquor. There was a small bowl of quaaludes propped demurely behind a jar of powdered vitamin C. I popped one, stuck three in my pocket for later. After all, I was going to be out there for a few days.

Someone cranked the stereo up a few notches, the strains of early Carl Perkins wobbled the posterboard walls. I could see a wide circle form in the living room, as a greasy biker took center stage and slicked his hair back, threw one hip forward and began a hilariously awful Elvis impersonation. I knew it must be Marty. The gathering crowd clapped along, encouraging obscene gyrations, offset by hoots and howls. I was vaguely repulsed.

I decided to check out the master bedroom and bath, in search of a small token to justify my journey. A small tray of cheap jewellery sat on the dresser, I bypassed that and opened the top drawer. More costume crap and a fat rubber band of credit cards. I popped the Mastercard into my pocket, more as a memento. Rifled through the bathroom cabinets. Slipped a handful of ten milligram valium into my pocket. Felt much better. Thought I'd return and make the rounds once more before departure. Opened the bathroom door to find Marty cleaning his nails with a small switchblade. "Axle grease," he admitted under his breath. I could smell it on him. It turned me on. Like the smell of gasoline. Like my first real fuck with some blond-haired blue-eyed kid whose father was a two-bit mechanic in Upstate. "I'll be right back," he whispered undoing his belt buckle, a tarnished grim reaper. I headed out to the balcony, figuring he'd come looking.

I scanned the L.A. skyline, a neon blur of late night commerce. Scattered numbers in my head trying to size up the population, wondering how many dollars were spent every minute in vulgar pursuit of the next big thing, big star, major motion picture, scam, scheme, rip-off, rape. Wondering how many living rooms were under siege by drunken day laborers taking out the boss's bullshit on the wife and kids, how many punches were being thrown in alleys at the back of dirty bars, how many shots were being fired from Mexican gang bangers, how many kids were undergoing their first hustle with some stinking John in any make of car cruising down Hollywood Blvd., Santa Monica Blvd., Crenshaw Blvd.

I didn't hear him come out. Felt his breath on the back of my neck. "Creepy Crawl?" he questioned, an invitation I knew I somehow, somewhere would take him up on.

Marty was a mongrel mix of Cherokee/Black Irish. Trouble, in other words. He spoke in a strange dialect more Blue Ridge Mountains than Southern Californian. Spent his formative years racing dirt bikes in the backyard of the Manson Family down in the snakepit of Topanga Canyon. Watched the mudslides come and go, wiping out the hippies, hillbillies and dirt farmers who had set up camp in ill-constructed shacks which formed the valley near enough to Malibu, yet still light years away. Said he stayed there because he respected Mother Nature's mean streak, and besides what's a little mud. The place he shared with his brother, a lowbrow surf freak, had just withstood four feet of thick sludge seeping in and back out of its four shit-stained walls. Said he'd move when the place collapsed. I dug his gumption. Easy going nature. Devil may care attitude. Invited him to my hotel the next night, told him to come by when he was through re-styling the hair of would-be B-movie actresses who frequented the upscale yet still gritty salon he managed four days a week a few blocks from the beach.

I prepared for our date by swallowing a couple of quaaludes washed down with Jack Daniels. I slipped into sheer black, applied some lipstick, put on my pumps while dimming the lights. Opened the door, hair-line fracture crack, popped a matchbook flap under the dead bolt with "TRUE CONFESSIONS" stamped seductively in fire engine red, its 900 number torn in two. Knew he'd know exactly what to do. Stimulated myself with moistened fingertips dipped in drink. The stinging skin contracting and twitching as I twisted the tender flesh between index and forefinger. Felt so good I slipped into slumber. Woke to scissors pressed firmly to throat. The smell of hair gel and axle grease a pungent intoxicant. The mute TV transmitting a dead station whose black and white shadows tango'd upon the bed. "Will you die for me?" he purred, quoting Manson's headtrip played on Tex Watson a few months before the Tate/LaBianca murders. "I'd kill for you," I lied back, cementing the bond that would become a two year long, on again/off again love/hate, white trash romance.

The sex was a blur of unpronounced threats, deadly possibilities, future recall. *Badlands, Bonnie & Clyde, The Boston Strangler, I Want to Live.* Scattered dreamscapes melting in and out of consciousness. Trapped in a time-zone where minutes stretch into hours.

Woke up to find him gone. "Downstairs at 7" scrawled on the mirror in spunk.

• • •

He picked me up in a babyshit-brown '58 Ford Pickup. Cruised around Watts pulling up to Piggy's Fat Back, a Mississippi-style Bar-B-Q take-away consisting of a single battered countertop set against bullet-proof glass. The misspelled menu chicken-pecked in pencil near the low-hung, fly-specked ceiling. A tired overhead fan threatened collapse. Ordered Five Alarm pork tips, potato salad and spicy beans. The smell lingering hours after fingers are licked clean. A smell which will always remind me of his chipped, wolfen teeth, the way his hair hung down over one eye, the automatic rearranging of Levi jeans, the front of which swelled at random intervals. Our first near murder.

He asked if I'd come along on a money run. Claimed an ex-buddy was into him for twenty-five hundred. Owed him for refurbishing the tattered remains of a shell-shocked Vespa. We'd be out of there in no time. Take the money and run. Maybe stop on the way back from Inglewood to catch the late set by Eddie "CleanHead" Vincent who was doing three sets down in the Parisienne Room, a funky, rundown jazz club packed with older black couples who enjoyed a grind or two with their groove. Catch the eleven o'clock show if all went as planned.

I could smell something percolating. Knew better. Couldn't help myself. Had to see how he operated. We pulled into the underground garage, cut the lights and sat parked for a few minutes. Allowing our eyes to re-adjust. Deep breaths and a high-pitched hum from an electrical generator on the floor below book-ended the atmosphere scattering soundwaves bouncing around in the darkness. He snuck into the glove compartment and pulled out Mr. Rigid. A twelve-inch long, three-inch wide buck knife. He cleaned the blade with a soiled hanky, spat on and wiped the handle, set it in his lap. Slipped his still sticky fingers into worn leather racing gloves, picked up the buck and kissed it once for good luck. Slid it back into its sheath, snapped it onto his belt. A twisted smile from one corner of his mouth whispered "Let's do it . . ." Instructing me to leave the door open a crack, just enough so the light is out. Just enough for a smoother get away.

A massive hollow swallowed. Blind eyes, big cave, no fucking clue which way was even forward. Whispering "Marty . . . Marty . . ." He spat "Ssshh . . . c'mon . . ." allowing a small sliver of light to slip into the cavernous garage as he opened the stairwell door. My pulse already doing backflips. "Don't say my name again until we're back in the truck, keep your fucking mouth shut, don't even breathe hard," he threatened, spitting the words into my neck. He cocked his head toward the steps, took off up them, leaving me to lag behind, trying to get my boots to behave below my rubbered knees. Floor after floor, the hall entrances were locked. Seemed to make him more determined. He was smiling down at me as I hit level six, one hand slowly spinning the knob that allowed us entry. The other hand darting between my legs, rubbing leathered fingers against moistened jeans. He cocked his finger and pulled me into the hallway by my crotch. Eased the door shut. Holding finger to lips in a silent kiss, sniffing the remnants of nervous pussy. We found the interior stairway. Went back down to the second floor, circling around the hallway, stopped at apartment 9B. The entire Beatles *White Album* jumpcut in my head. He tried the door. Locked. Tapped boot to door jam. No answer. The lights were on, soft music lilting in the background. "Shit . . . we'll have to try the fire escape . . ." he grumbled, stroking the sheath the buck sat buckled in. I was so fucking high on adrenalin I couldn't think straight, much less make even a weak protest. I followed obediently as we once more mounted the interior stairs on the way to the roof. Just about ready to piss my pants, not knowing who we were stalking or what we would do to them once we found them. Exited onto the roof, half-moon glow, lit up with a backdrop of silver pinpricks, the irregular pattern of a dead star's radar mimicking my goosebumps. Marty slipped the door shut, pinning me against it. Unsnapped the sheath. As loud as a gunshot. Started to trace my outline, like a corpse at a crime scene, the thick blade slicing tar paper like cake icing. One hand around my throat, slow, heavy breath, hot on my face. Humid. With the tip of the blade he lifted my wrist from beside me, tracing close to my hip. Kicked my legs apart. Placed the buck between them, screwing it into the wall. Rubbed himself against the handle. Told me to close my legs, hold it in place with my pussy, make that pussy work for him. Unsnapped his jeans, shiny prick plops out, mossy aroma wafts mingling with sea breeze and gardenias, spanks it against the handle. Whimpers.

I beg for his fuck, beg to be power-slammed against the wall, squashed by his slippery prick, annihilated. Spins me against the tar paper, smooth cheek bitten by sand. Manhandles pants over ass, mutters "Ssshhh, ssshh," rubs his greasy prick between fat cheeks. Circling the bullseye.

Quick spastic jerk. Banging body parts off against twin receptors. Flood of relief as near panic is replaced with brutal focus. Slicing me open from behind like an engorged blood hound. Buck knife used as bind for breasts, edge flattens nipple in silent threat. Delirium.

Retreat to the pick-up. More alive the closer to Death. Our common bond a need for acceleration. Speed. Chaos. His ambition: to race dirt bikes as fast as possible on dirt tracks incurring a great many broken bones, a fractured skull, countless trips to the Emergency Room. An excuse for his behavior. My obsession: escalate blood pressure, overstimulate adrenal glands, taunt Death. Our marriage vows: a promise to scare the shit out of each other. Apathetic assholes that we were. We thrived on fear. Fear: the greatest of all aphrodisiacs.

Chuck Palahniuk

Fight Club

IT'S IN THE NEWSPAPER today how somebody broke into offices between the tenth and fifteenth floors of the Hein Tower, and climbed out the office windows, and painted the south side of the building with a grinning five-story mask, and set fires so the window at the center of each huge eye blazed huge and alive and inescapable over the city at dawn.

In the picture on the front page of the newspaper, the face is an angry pumpkin, Japanese demon, dragon of avarice hanging in the sky, and the smoke is a witch's eyebrows or devil's horns. And people cried with their heads thrown back.

What did it mean?

And who would do this? And even after the fires were out, the face was still there, and it was worse. The empty eyes seemed to watch everyone in the street but at the same time were dead.

This stuff is in the newspaper more and more.

Of course you read this, and you want to know right away if it was part of Project Mayhem.

The newspaper says the police have no real leads. Youth gangs or space aliens, whoever it was could've died while crawling down ledges and dangling from windowsills with cans of black spray paint.

Was it the Mischief Committee or the Arson Committee? The giant face was probably their homework assignment from last week.

Tyler would know, but the first rule about Project Mayhem is you don't ask questions about Project Mayhem.

In the Assault Committee of Project Mayhem, this week Tyler says he ran everyone through what it would take to shoot a gun. All a gun does is focus an explosion in one direction.

At the last meeting of the Assault Committee, Tyler brought a gun and the yellow pages of the phone book. They meet in the basement where fight club meets on Saturday night. Each committee meets on a different night:

Arson meets on Monday.

Assault on Tuesday.

Mischief meets on Wednesday.

And Misinformation meets on Thursday.

Organized Chaos. The Bureaucracy of Anarchy. You figure it out.

Support groups. Sort of.

So Tuesday night, the Assault Committee proposed events for the upcoming week, and Tyler read the proposals and gave the committee its homework.

By this time next week, each guy on the Assault Committee has to pick a fight where he won't come out a hero. And not in fight club. This is harder than it sounds. A man on the street will do anything not to fight.

The idea is to take some Joe on the street who's never been in a fight and recruit him. Let him experience winning for the first time in his life. Get him to explode. Give him permission to beat the crap out of you.

You can take it. If you win, you screwed up.

"What we have to do, people," Tyler told the committee, "is remind these guys what kind of power they still have."

This is Tyler's little pep talk. Then he opened each of the folded squares of paper in the cardboard box in front of him. This is how each committee proposes events for the upcoming week. Write the event on the committee tablet. Tear off the sheet, fold it, and put it in the box. Tyler checks out the proposals and throws out any bad ideas.

For each idea he throws out, Tyler puts a folded blank into the box.

Then everyone in the committee takes a paper out of the box. The way Tyler explained the process to me, if somebody draws a blank, he only has his homework to do that week.

If you draw a proposal, then you have to go to the import beer festival this weekend and push over a guy in a chemical toilet. You'll get extra favor if you get beat up for doing this. Or you have to attend the fashion show at the shopping center atrium and throw strawberry gelatin from the mezzanine.

If you get arrested, you're off the Assault Committee. If you laugh, you're off the committee.

Nobody knows who draws a proposal, and nobody except Tyler knows what all the proposals are and which are accepted and which proposals he throws in the trash. Later that week, you might read in the newspaper about an unidentified man, downtown, jumping the driver of a Jaguar convertible and steering the car into a fountain.

You have to wonder. Was this a committee proposal you could've drawn?

The next Tuesday night, you'll be looking around the Assault Committee meeting under the one light in the black fight club basement, and you're still wondering who forced the Jag into the fountain.

Who went to the roof of the art museum and snipered paint balls into the sculpture court reception?

Who painted the blazing demon mask on the Hein Tower?

The night of the Hein Tower assignment, you can picture a team of law clerks and bookkeepers or messengers sneaking into offices where they sat, every day. Maybe they were a little drunk even if it's against the rules in Project Mayhem, and they used passkeys where they could and used spray canisters of Freon to shatter lock cylinders so they could dangle, rappelling against the tower's brick façade, dropping, trusting each other to hold ropes, swinging, risking quick death in offices where every day they felt their lives end one hour at a time.

The next morning, these same clerks and assistant account reps would be in the crowd with their neatly combed heads thrown back, rummy without sleep but sober and wearing ties and listening to the crowd around them wonder, who would do this, and the police shout for everyone to please get back, now, as water ran down from the broken smoky center of each huge eye.

Tyler told me in secret that there's never more than four good proposals at a meeting so your chances of drawing a real proposal and not just a blank are about four in ten. There are twenty-five guys on the Assault Committee including Tyler. Everybody gets their homework: lose a fight in public; and each member draws for a proposal.

This week, Tyler told them, "Go out and buy a gun."

Tyler gave one guy the telephone-book yellow pages and told him to tear out an advertisement. Then pass the book to the next guy. No two guys should go to the same place to buy or shoot.

"This," Tyler said, and he took a gun out of his coat pocket, "this is a gun, and in two weeks, you should each of you have a gun about this size to bring to meeting.

"Better you should pay for it with cash," Tyler said. "Next meeting, you'll all trade guns and report the gun you bought as stolen."

Nobody asked anything. You don't ask questions is the first rule in Project Mayhem.

Tyler handed the gun around. It was so heavy for something so small, as if a giant thing like a mountain or a sun were collapsed and melted down to make this. The committee guys held it by two fingers. Everyone wanted to ask if it was loaded, but the second rule of Project Mayhem is you don't ask questions.

Maybe it was loaded, maybe not. Maybe we should always assume the worst.

"A gun," Tyler said, "is simple and perfect. You just draw the trigger back."

The third rule in Project Mayhem is no excuses.

"The trigger," Tyler said, "frees the hammer, and the hammer strikes the powder."

The fourth rule is no lies.

"The explosion blasts a metal slug off the open end of the shell, and the barrel of the gun focuses the exploding powder and the rocketing slug," Tyler said, "like a man out of a cannon, like a missile out of a silo, like your jism, in one direction."

When Tyler invented Project Mayhem, Tyler said the goal of Project Mayhem had nothing to do with other people. Tyler didn't care if other people got hurt or not. The goal was to teach each man in the project that he had the power to control history. We, each of us, can take control of the world.

It was at fight club that Tyler invented Project Mayhem.

I tagged a first-timer one night at fight club. That Saturday night, a young guy with an angel's face came to his first fight club, and I tagged him for a fight. That's the rule. If it's your first night in fight club, you have to fight. I knew that so I tagged him because the insomnia was on again, and I was in a mood to destroy something beautiful.

Since most of my face never gets a chance to heal, I've got nothing to lose in the looks department. My boss, at work, he asked me what I was doing about the hole through my cheek that never heals. When I drink coffee, I told him, I put two fingers over the hole so it won't leak.

There's a sleeper hold that gives somebody just enough air to stay awake, and that night at fight club I hit our first-timer and hammered that beautiful mister angel face, first with the bony knuckles of my fist like a pounding molar, and then the knotted tight butt of my fist after my knuckles were raw from his teeth stuck through his lips. Then the kid fell through my arms in a heap.

Tyler told me later that he'd never seen me destroy something so completely. That night, Tyler knew he had to take fight club up a notch or shut it down.

Tyler said, sitting at breakfast the next morning, "You looked like a maniac, Psycho-Boy. Where did you go?"

I said I felt like crap and not relaxed at all. I didn't get any kind of a buzz. Maybe I'd developed a jones. You can build up a tolerance to fighting, and maybe I needed to move on to something bigger.

It was that morning, Tyler invented Project Mayhem.

Tyler asked what I was really fighting.

What Tyler says about being the crap and the slaves of history, that's how I felt. I wanted to destroy everything beautiful I'd never have. Burn the Amazon rain forests. Pump chlorofluorocarbons straight up to gobble the ozone. Open the dump valves on supertankers and uncap offshore oil wells. I wanted to kill all the fish I couldn't afford to eat, and smother the French beaches I'd never see.

I wanted the whole world to hit bottom.

Pounding that kid, I really wanted to put a bullet between the eyes of every endangered panda that wouldn't screw to save its species and every whale or dolphin that gave up and ran itself aground.

Don't think of this as extinction. Think of this as downsizing.

For thousands of years, human beings had screwed up and trashed and crapped on this planet, and now history expected me to clean up after everyone. I have to wash out and flatten my soup cans. And account for every drop of used motor oil.

And I have to foot the bill for nuclear waste and buried gasoline tanks and landfilled toxic sludge dumped a generation before I was born.

I held the face of mister angel like a baby or a football in the crook of my arm and bashed him with my knuckles, bashed him until his teeth broke through his lips. Bashed him with my elbow after that until he fell through my arms into a heap at my feet. Until the skin was pounded thin across his cheekbones and turned black.

I wanted to breathe smoke.

Birds and deer are a silly luxury, and all the fish should be floating.

I wanted to burn the Louvre. I'd do the Elgin Marbles with a sledge-hammer and wipe my ass with the *Mona Lisa*. This is my world, now.

This is my world, my world, and those ancient people are dead.

It was at breakfast that morning that Tyler invented Project Mayhem.

We wanted to blast the world free of history.

We were eating breakfast in the house on Paper Street, and Tyler said, picture yourself planting radishes and seed potatoes on the fifteenth green of a forgotten golf course.

You'll hunt elk through the damp canyon forests around the ruins of Rockefeller Center, and dig clams next to the skeleton of the Space Needle leaning at a forty-five-degree angle. We'll paint the skyscrapers with huge totem faces and goblin tikis, and every evening what's left of mankind will retreat to empty zoos and lock itself in cages as protection against bears and big cats and wolves that pace and watch us from outside the cage bars at night.

"Recycling and speed limits are bullshit," Tyler said. "They're like someone who quits smoking on his deathbed."

It's Project Mayhem that's going to save the world. A cultural ice age. A prematurely induced dark age. Project Mayhem will force humanity to go dormant or into remission long enough for the Earth to recover.

"You justify anarchy," Tyler says. "You figure it out."

Like fight club does with clerks and box boys, Project Mayhem will break up civilization so we can make something better out of the world.

"Imagine," Tyler said, "stalking elk past department store windows and stinking racks of beautiful rotting dresses and tuxedos on hangers; you'll wear leather clothes that will last you the rest of your life, and you'll climb the wrist-thick kudzu vines that wrap the Sears Tower. Jack and the beanstalk, you'll climb up through the dripping forest canopy and the air will be so clean you'll see tiny figures pounding corn and laying strips of venison to dry in the empty car pool lane of an abandoned superhighway stretching eight-lanes-wide and August-hot for a thousand miles."

This was the goal of Project Mayhem, Tyler said, the complete and right-away destruction of civilization.

What comes next in Project Mayhem, nobody except Tyler knows. The second rule is you don't ask questions.

"Don't get any bullets," Tyler told the Assault Committee. "And just so you don't worry about it, yes, you're going to have to kill someone."

Arson. Assault. Mischief and Misinformation.

No questions. No questions. No excuses and no lies.

The fifth rule about Project Mayhem is you have to trust Tyler.

HENRY MILLER

Tropic of Cancer

I SUPPOSE I WOULD never have gotten out of Nanantatee's clutches if fate hadn't intervened. One night, as luck would have it, Kepi asked me if I wouldn't take one of his clients to a whorehouse nearby. The young man had just come from India and he had not very much money to spend. He was one of Gandhi's men, one of that little band who made the historic march to the sea during the salt trouble. A very gay disciple of Gandhi's I must say, despite the vows of abstinence he had taken. Evidently he hadn't looked at a woman for ages. It was all I could do to get him as far as the Rue Laferrière; he was like a dog with his tongue hanging out. And a pompous, vain little devil to boot! He had decked himself out in a corduroy suit, a beret, a cane, a Windsor tie; he had bought himself two fountain pens, a kodak, and some fancy underwear. The money he was spending was a gift from the merchants of Bombay; they were sending him to England to spread the gospel of Gandhi.

Once inside Miss Hamilton's joint he began to lose his *sang-froid*. When suddenly he found himself surrounded by a bevy of naked women he looked at me in consternation. "Pick one out," I said. "You can have your choice." He had become so rattled that he could scarcely look at them. "You do it for me," he murmured, blushing violently. I looked them over coolly and picked out a plump young wench who seemed full of feathers. We sat down in the reception room and waited for the drinks. The madam wanted to know why I didn't take a girl also. "Yes, you take one too," said the young Hindu. "I don't want to be alone with her." So the girls were brought in again and I chose one for myself, a rather tall, thin one with melancholy eyes. We were left alone, the four of us, in the reception room. After a few moments my young Gandhi leans over and whispers something in my ear. "Sure, if you like her better, take her," I said, and so, rather awkwardly and considerably embarrassed, I explained to the girls that we would like to switch. I saw at once that we had made a *faux pas*, but by now my young friend had became gay and lecherous and nothing would do but to get upstairs quickly and have it over with.

We took adjoining rooms with a connecting door between. I think my companion had in mind to make another switch once he had satisfied his sharp, gnawing hunger. At any rate, no sooner had the girls left the room to prepare themselves than I hear him knocking on the door. "Where is the toilet, please?" he asks. Not thinking that it was anything serious I urge him to do in the *bidet*. The girls return with towels in their hands. I hear him giggling in the next room.

As I'm putting on my pants suddenly I hear a commotion in the next room. The girl is bawling him out, calling him a pig, a dirty little pig. I can't imagine what he has done to warrant such an outburst. I'm standing there with one foot in my trousers listening attentively. He's trying to explain to her in English, raising his voice louder and louder until it becomes a shriek.

I hear a door slam and in another moment the madam bursts into my room, her face as red as a beet, her arms gesticulating wildly. "You ought to be ashamed of yourself," she screams, "bringing a man like that to my place!

He's a barbarian . . . he's a pig . . . he's a . . . !" My companion is standing behind her, in the doorway, a look of utmost discomfiture on his face "What did you do?" I ask.

"What did he do?" yells the madam. "I'll show you. . . . Come here!" And grabbing me by the arm she drags me into the next room. "There! There!" she screams, pointing to the *bidet*.

"Come on, let's get out," says the Hindu boy.

"Wait a minute, you can't get out as easily as all that."

The madam is standing by the *bidet*, fuming and spitting. The girls are standing there too, with towels in their hands. The five of us are standing there looking at the *bidet*. There are two enormous turds floating in the water. The madam bends down and puts a towel over it. "Frightful! Frightful!" she wails. "Never have I seen anything like this! A pig! A dirty little pig!"

The Hindu boy looks at me reproachfully. "You should have told me!" he says. "I didn't know it wouldn't go down. I asked you where to go and you told me to use that." He is almost in tears.

Finally the madam takes me to one side. She has become a little more reasonable now. After all, it was a mistake. Perhaps the gentlemen would like to come downstairs and order another drink—for the girls. It was a great shock to the girls. They are not used to such things. And if the good gentlemen will be so kind as to remember the *femme de chambre*. . . . It is not so pretty for the *femme de chambre*—that mess, that ugly mess. She shrugs her shoulders and winks her eye. A lamentable incident. But an accident. If the gentlemen will wait here a few moments the maid will bring the drinks. Would the gentlemen like to have some champagne? Yes?

"I'd like to get out of here," says the Hindu boy weakly.

"Don't feel so badly about it," says the madam. "It is all over now. Mistakes will happen sometimes. Next time you will ask for the toilet." She goes on about the toilet—one on every floor, it seems. And a bathroom too. "I have lots of English clients," she says. "They are all gentlemen. The gentleman is a Hindu? Charming people, the Hindus. So intelligent. So handsome."

When we get into the street the charming young gentleman is almost weeping. He is sorry now that he bought a corduroy suit and the cane and the fountain pens. He talks about the eight vows that he took, the control of the palate, etc. On the march to Dandi even a plate of ice cream it was forbidden to take. He tells me about the spinning wheel—how the little band of Satyagrahists imitated the devotion of their master. He relates with pride how he walked beside the master and conversed with him. I have the illusion of being in the presence of one of the twelve disciples.

During the next few days we see a good deal of each other; there are interviews to be arranged with the newspaper men and lectures to be given to the Hindus of Paris. It is amazing to see how these spineless devils order one another about; amazing also to see how ineffectual they are in all that concerns practical affairs. And the jealousy and the intrigues, the petty, sordid rivalries. Wherever there are ten Hindus together there is India with her sects and schisms, her racial, lingual, religious, political antagonisms. In the person of Gandhi they are experiencing for a brief moment the miracle of unity, but when he goes there will be a crash, an utter relapse into that strife and chaos so characteristic of the Indian people.

The young Hindu, of course, is optimistic. He has been to America and he has been contaminated by the cheap idealism of the Americans, contaminated by the ubiquitous bathtub, the five-and-ten-cent store bric-a-brac, the bustle, the efficiency, the machinery, the high wages, the free libraries, etc., etc. His ideal would be to Americanize India. He is not at all pleased with Gandhi's retrogressive mania. *Forward*, he says, just like a YMCA man. As I listen to his tales of America I see how absurd it is to expect of Gandhi that miracle which will deroute the trend of destiny. India's enemy is not England, but America. India's enemy is the time spirit, the hand which cannot be turned back. Nothing will avail to offset this virus which is poisoning the whole world. America is the very incarnation of doom. She will drag the whole world down to the bottomless pit.

He thinks the Americans are a very gullible people. He tells me about the credulous souls who succored him there—the Quakers, the Unitarians, the Theosophists, the New Thoughters, the Seventh-day Adventists, etc. He knew where to sail his boat, this bright young man. He knew how to make the tears come to his eyes at the right moment; he knew how to take up a collection, how to appeal to the minister's wife, how to make love to the mother and daughter at the same time. To look at him you would think him a saint. And he is a saint, in the modern fashion; a contaminated saint who talks in one breath of love, brotherhood, bathtubs, sanitation, efficiency, etc.

The last night of his sojourn in Paris is given up to "the fucking business." He has had a full program all day—conferences, cablegrams, interviews, photographs for the newspapers, affectionate farewells, advice to the faithful, etc., etc. At dinner time he decides to lay aside his troubles. He orders champagne with the meal, he snaps his fingers at the *garçon* and behaves in general like the boorish little peasant that he is. And since he has had a bellyful of all the good places he suggests now that I show him something more primitive. He would like to go to a very cheap place, order two or three girls at once. I steer him along the Boulevard de la Chapelle, warning him all the while to be careful of his pocketbook. Around Aubervilliers we duck into a cheap dive and immediately we've got a flock of them on our hands. In a few minutes he's dancing with a naked wench, a huge blonde with creases in her jowls. I can see her ass reflected a dozen times in the mirrors that line the room—and those dark, bony fingers of his clutching her tenaciously. The table is full of beer glasses, the mechanical piano is wheezing and gasping. The girls who are unoccupied are sitting placidly on the leather benches, scratching themselves peacefully just like a family of chimpanzees. There is a sort of subdued pandemonium in the air, a note of repressed violence, as if the awaited explosion required the advent of some utterly minute detail, something microscopic but thoroughly unpremeditated, completely unexpected. In that sort of half-reverie which permits one to participate in an event and yet remain quite aloof, the little detail which was lacking began obscurely but insistently to coagulate, to assume a freakish, crystalline form, like the frost which gathers on the windowpane. And like those frost patterns which seem so bizarre, so utterly free and fantastic in design, but which are nevertheless determined by the most rigid laws, so this sensation which commenced to take form inside me seemed also to be giving obedience to ineluctable laws. My whole being was responding to the dictates of an ambiance which it had never before experienced; that which I could call myself seemed to be contracting, condensing, shrinking from the stale, customary boundaries of the flesh whose perimeter knew only the modulations of the nerve ends.

And the more substantial, the more solid the core of me became, the more delicate and extravagant appeared the close, palpable reality out of which I was being squeezed. In the measure that I became more and more metallic, in the same measure the scene before my eyes became inflated. The state of tension was so finely drawn now that the introduction of a single foreign particle, even a microscopic particle, as I say, would have shattered everything. For the fraction of a second perhaps I experienced that utter clarity which the epileptic, it is said, is given to know. In that moment I lost completely the illusion of time and space: the world unfurled its drama simultaneously along a meridian which had no axis. In this sort of hair-trigger eternity I felt that everything was justified, supremely justified; I felt the wars inside me that had left behind this pulp and wrack; I felt the crimes that were seething here to emerge tomorrow in blatant screamers; I felt the misery that was grinding itself out with pestle and mortar, the long dull misery that dribbles away in dirty handkerchiefs. On the meridian of time there is no injustice: there is only the poetry of motion creating the illusion of truth and drama. If at any moment anywhere one comes face to face with the absolute, that great sympathy which makes men like Gautama and Jesus seem divine freezes away; the monstrous thing is not that men have created roses out of this dung heap, but that, for some reason or other, they should *want* roses. For some reason or other man looks for the miracle, and to accomplish it he will wade through blood. He will debauch himself with ideas, he will reduce himself to a shadow if for only one second of his life he can close his eyes to the hideousness of reality. Everything is endured—disgrace, humiliation, poverty, war, crime, *ennui*—in the belief that over-night something will occur, a miracle, which will render life tolerable. And all the while a meter is running inside and there is no hand that can reach in there and shut it off. All the while someone is eating the bread of life and drinking the wine, some dirty fat cockroach of a priest who hides away in the cellar guzzling it, while up above in the light of the street a phantom host touches the lips and the blood is pale as water. And out of the endless torment and misery no miracle comes forth, no microscopic vestige even of relief. Only ideas, pale, attenuated ideas which have to be fattened by slaughter; ideas which come forth like bile, like the guts of a pig when the carcass is ripped open.

And so I think what a miracle it would be if this miracle which man attends eternally should turn out to be nothing more than these two enormous turds which the faithful disciple dropped in the *bidet*. What if at the last moment, when the banquet table is set and the cymbals clash, there should appear suddenly, and wholly without warning, a silver platter on which even the blind could see that there is nothing more, and nothing less, than two enormous lumps of shit. That, I believe would be more miraculous than anything which man has looked forward to. It would be miraculous because it would be undreamed of. It would be more miraculous than even the wildest dream because *anybody* could imagine the possibility but nobody ever has, and probably nobody ever again will.

Somehow the realization that nothing was to be hoped for had a salutary effect upon me. For weeks and months, for years, in fact, all my life I had been looking forward to something happening, some extrinsic event that would alter my life, and now suddenly, inspired by the absolute hopelessness of everything, I felt relieved, felt as though a great burden had been lifted from my shoulders. At dawn I parted company with the young Hindu, after touching him for a few francs, enough for a room. Walking toward Montparnasse I decided to let myself drift with the tide, to make not the least resistance to fate, no matter in what form it presented itself. Nothing that had happened to me thus far had been sufficient to destroy me; nothing had been destroyed except my illusions. I myself was intact. The world was intact. Tomorrow there might be a revolution, a plague, an earthquake; tomorrow there might not be left a single soul to whom one could turn for sympathy, for aid, for faith. It seemed to me that the great calamity had already manifested itself, that I could be no more truly alone than at this very moment. I made up my mind that I would hold on to nothing, that I would expect nothing, that henceforth I would live as an animal, a beast of prey, a rover, a plunderer. Even if war were declared, and it were my lot to go, I would grab the bayonet and plunge it, plunge it up to the hilt. And if rape were the order of the day then rape I would, and with a vengeance. At this very moment, in the quiet dawn of a new day, was not the earth giddy with crime and distress? Had one single element of man's nature been altered, vitally, fundamentally altered, by the incessant march of history? By what he calls the better part of his nature, man has been betrayed, that is all. At the extreme limits of his spiritual being man finds himself again naked as a savage. When he finds God, as it were, he has been picked clean: he is a skeleton. One must burrow into life again in order to put on flesh. The word must become flesh; the soul thirsts. On whatever crumb my eye fastens, I will pounce and devour. If to live is the paramount thing, then I will live, even if I must become a cannibal. Heretofore I have been trying to save my precious hide, trying to preserve the few pieces of meat that hid my bones. I am done with that. I have reached the limits of endurance. My back is to the wall; I can retreat no further. As far as history goes I am dead. If there is something beyond I shall have to bounce back. I have found God, but he is insufficient. I am only spiritually dead. Physically I am alive. Morally I am free. The world which I have departed is a menagerie. The dawn is breaking on a new world, a jungle world in which the lean spirits roam with sharp claws. If I am a hyena I am a lean and hungry one: I go forth to fatten myself.

Cookie Mueller

Ask Dr. Mueller

Pink Flamingos

"What's the worst thing that can happen to me when I eat the dogshit?" Divine asked us, while we were sitting around the set waiting for John Waters, who was doing some exterior shots. Van Smith, the makeup man, was painting Divine's face. David Lockhary was arranging his blue hair and drinking coffee; Mink was putting her contact lenses in; Bonnie was reading the *Baltimore Sun*; I was trying to remember my lines.

There was no question that Divine would eat the dogshit. He was a professional. It was in his script, so he was going to do it.

"We'll find out what'll happen," I said.

It was a secret. Only a few people involved with *Pink Flamingos* knew about the shit-eating-grin scene at the end of the film. John wanted to keep it quiet. Maybe he was afraid some other filmmaker might beat him to it, steal the shit-pioneer award. Anyway too much word of mouth, now, would deplete the surprise for the filmgoer later.

"We'll talk to a doctor," Van said, pausing mid-stroke with the liquid eyeliner brush.

"I'll do it if it doesn't kill me," Divine said and laughed.

"Pretend it's chocolate," Bonnie suggested.

In the world there are many brave people: those who climb Mt. Everest, those who work in Kentucky coal mines, those who go into space as astronauts, those who dive for pearls. Few are as brave as actors who work with John Waters.

We didn't think he was asking too much. We didn't think he was crazy, just obsessed.

"Call a doctor right now," Mink said.

"Call a hospital. Call Johns Hopkins!" I said, and handed him the phone.

"Why belabor the situation? Why worry? Get it over with," said David.

"Dial the phone," said Mink.

"Call pediatrics. Tell them your son just ate dogshit. See what they say," Van suggested.

Divine started dialing the hospital and reached a doctor.

"My son just accidentally ate some dog feces," Divine said. "What's going to happen to him?"

"What's he saying?" Bonnie asked.

"Shh . . ." he said to Bonnie. "And then what?" Divine asked in the phone. "Hmmmhu, hmmmhu, okay, then. Thank you." He hung up.

"So?" asked David.

"He didn't sound too alarmed," Divine said. "I guess it's just a routine question for a doctor. He said all I have to be careful about is the white worm."

"What's that supposed to mean?" Mink asked.

"Tapeworms," Divine said, "that doesn't sound too dangerous."

"You don't have to swallow it anyway," Van said.

"He said to check out the dog. Take it to a vet," Divine said.

"John is doing that," I said.

"What kind of dog is it?" Mink asked.

"A miniature poodle," said Divine.

It was suggested to John to do the take in two shots, first the dog does his duty, then cut. Replace the real shit with fake shit. Divine eats it. Cut. But John knew, we all knew, that audiences wouldn't fall for that.

"No. NO. Everybody would know we replaced the real shit for fake. Divine's gotta scoop it right up still warm off the street," John had said a few days ago.

This was show biz. Divine didn't balk and he wasn't the only one. Mink Stole was going to do a big scene that called for her red hair to catch on fire. The dialogue would be: "Liar, liar, your hair's on fire." She didn't seem afraid at all.

"I'll do it. There'll be fire extinguishers there."

"You could use a wig," I said.

"Somebody already suggested that to John. No. Audiences want the truth," Mink said.

The day John was about to shoot the hair-on-fire scene, he changed his mind; he decided it would be too dangerous after all. They tested a piece of Mink's hair and it just smoked and sizzled and smelled awful. There'd be no dramatic effect; it wouldn't have burst into flames. John was a little disappointed but he'd think of something else. Mostly when John came up with these kinds of ideas for his actors, he was testing us or half joking; the actors were the ones who took him seriously, we were the hams. Actors know scenes like these make stars.

"Aren't you supposed to do some scene where you get fucked by a chicken?" Divine asked me.

"Fucked by a real chicken?" Mink asked me.

"How?" asked Bonnie.

"In the script it says Crackers cuts off the head of a chicken and he fucks me with the stump," I said.

"Oh that sounds easy," Divine said.

"Yeah, that's easy compared with what you have to do," I said to Divine.

"Chickens scratch pretty bad," David said. "Even without their heads."

"Bird wounds can be dangerous," Van said.

I thought about Hitchcock's *The Birds*, but those were seagulls and I knew just how powerful seagulls could be. Compared to them, chickens were jellyfish.

"I'm not worried about some little scratches," I said.

"But I don't think I can watch while the head's being cut off."

"Oh come on. Chickens don't know they're dying. They're not smart enough," David said.

There were a couple other scenes in the film we talked about.

"The whole trailer has to burn to the ground. That could get out of hand, couldn't it?" I asked.

"John's going to have a fire truck there," Van said.

"Doesn't Linda Olgeirson have to be artificially inseminated on camera? Down in the pit?" Mink asked.

"She'll have a stand-in," Bonnie said.

"It's a close-up beaver shot. Nobody will know it's not her. She doesn't want to expose her pussy for the audience. I wouldn't do that either," I said.

"No, I wouldn't either," said Mink.

We would all eat shit, catch on fire, fuck chickens, but we wouldn't do close-up crotch shots. There has to be a line drawn somewhere.

"I have to show my dick," David said.

"But you're going to have a turkey neck tied on it," Mink said. "That doesn't count."

"Elizabeth is going to expose her tits and her dick, David. So what are you complaining about?" Divine said, and we all agreed.

Making this film, we went to bed every night really excited for the next day's shoot. Perhaps there are other actors who can tell you that making films is really boring. This film wasn't. On big-budget sets, actors go into their private trailers, waiting for their camera time. Not on this set. We were all in the same room between takes, busy changing costumes, remembering lines, bitching about bit actors stealing scenes, layering makeup, getting ready to emote. There were no private trailers around.

Making low-budget films is work, but it's fun, it's more fun than working in big-budget films. If you're an actor, there is nothing more rewarding, despite the meager pay. On small films you get to know the whole cast and crew in a day, and all of these people are much more inventive because of the limited budget; they create effects that wouldn't have been born if there was more money. Necessity is the mother of invention; this is true. John is a master at this, his imagination runneth over.

Before we started shooting *Pink Flamingos,* I was living in Provincetown with two-month-old Max and Tom O'Connor, Max's stepfather of the moment. Max and I were staying with my mother in the Baltimore suburbs for the duration of the filming, but it wasn't turning out well living there with Mom and Dad.

My mother knew there was filming going on, but I didn't tell her Max was one of the stars, cast as the newborn infant bought by a lesbian couple, and I certainly didn't tell her I was going to have to fuck a chicken.

"Let me read the script," she'd say all the time.

"Ah . . . well . . . I don't have the script here. I left it on the set."

"Then tell me about the movie. About your part," she'd say.

"Not much to tell. It's the story of two rival families. I play the interme-diary, the spy," I said.

"What's the rivalry? Are they criminal families?" she asked.

"Not really, but sort of," I said. How in the world could I describe that film to my mother?

A few days later, when John came to pick up me and Max for the day's shoot, my mother stopped me from leaving.

"Where do you think you're going?" she demanded.

"I'm going to the set," I said.

"OH NO YOU'RE NOT," she screamed, "I FOUND THAT SCRIPT AND I READ IT AND YOU'RE NOT GOING ANYWHERE NEAR THAT SET!"

I sat down in the Victorian chair for a second. "Mom, it's not like you think. This movie's going to be funny. It's not porno. It's a whole other kind of film . . . it's art . . . it's . . ." I was at a loss for the right word, the label that would legitimize the film for her. How could she ever understand?

"ART?!?!?! ART!?!?! THIS ISN'T ART!!" she sputtered, and threw the script at me.

"Mom, hold on. Sit down," I said, but there was no calming her. She has quite a temper, that woman.

"AND YOU'RE GOING TO EXPOSE YOUR POOR DEAR LITTLE BABY TO ALL THIS NONSENSE?!?!? THIS GARBAGE?!??!" THIS IS THE SCRIBBLING OF THE DEVIL HIMSELF . . . THIS SCRIPT, THIS ART SCRIPT! HA! HA! ART!!!" She was really wild now.

All I could do was start packing. Fast.

I threw Max's clothes in his little bag, grabbed his Pampers box, stuffed my clothes into my suitcase, and put Max in my arms.

"WHERE DO YOU THINK YOU'RE GOING?!?!? PUT THAT CHILD DOWN!"

Outside, in the driveway, John innocently started beeping his car horn. I cringed.

"IS THAT MANIAC OUT THERE?!? I'M GOING TO GIVE HIM A PIECE OF MY MIND," she yelled and flew out the front door, me fol-lowing. I hopped in the car with Max and my bags before she reached it.

"Make tracks, John," I said to him. "My mother's on the warpath."

He sped down the driveway. My mother was standing on the front lawn flailing her arms around.

"YOU'RE BEELZEBUB," she screamed at John as we tore down the street.

"Did she read the script or something?" John asked. He was upset.

"She sure did," I said, looking back at her. She was still on the front lawn screaming.

"I guess she didn't exactly love it," he said and laughed.

"Not exactly."

"You shouldn't go back there. You can stay with me," John said.

"Yeah. I can't go back there. Did you hear her? She called you Beelzebub."

"Who's Beelzebub anyway?" John asked.

"One of the devil's footmen," I said.

"Was she serious?"

"She was brought up in the Deep South as a Southern Baptist. That was high drama. She's an actress," I told him.

"Maybe I ought to give her a part in the film," he laughed.

"I feel kinda bad just packing up and leaving so fast. You sure it's okay that I stay with you for awhile? I know you're under a lot of pressure with the film right now but Max doesn't cry much. I can put him in a dresser drawer. Dr. Spock says to put your infant in a drawer when you're traveling.

John started laughing, "You're joking."

"You're not supposed to close the drawer or anything," I said.

He just kept laughing.

We went to the farm from there and got ready to shoot the chicken scene in the chicken coop. It went well, but we had to reshoot four times, the chickens weren't too compliant. Danny (Crackers) had to kill eight or nine of them; I didn't watch him slice off the heads.

Just as David had said, even without heads they were a lively nasty bunch of fowl, flopping and kicking with all their might. I got completely scratched up by their sharp claws. I was getting hurt for real. I'd underestimated these chickens, even while I was feeling sorry for them.

In the next scene Max was great as Little Noodles. He upstaged even the bulldykes.

Later on, after we finished for the day, with the sun sinking beyond the horizon of winter's leafless trees, we roasted all those chickens, had a big feast for the whole cast and crew. Those chickens I'd felt so sorry for earlier sure were delicious.

Iceberg Slim

Pimp

I SAT ON A satin pillow in the corner near the glass door. I watched the show. I saw "Patch Eye" go and sit behind the bar. Everybody was in a big half-circle around the couch. It was like the couch was a stage, and "Sweet" the star. "Sweet" said, "Well how did you silly bastards like the fight. Did the Nigger murder that peckerwood or did his black ass turn shit yellow?"

A Southern white whore with a wide face and a sultry voice like "Bankhead's" drawled, "Mistah Jones, Ahm happy to repoat thet the Niggah run the white stud back intu his mammy's ass in thu fust round."

Everybody laughed except "Sweet." He was crashing together his mitts. I wondered what madness bubbled in his skull as he stared at her. A high-ass yellow broad flicked life back into the phonograph. "Gloomy Sunday," the suicide's favorite, dirged through the room. She stared at me as she came away.

"Sweet" said, "All right you freakish pigs. "Patch Eye's" got outfits and bags of poison. You got the go sign to croak yourselves."

They started rising from the satin pillows and velour ottomans. They clustered around "Patch Eye" at the bar.

The high-ass yellow broad came to me. She stooped in front of me. I saw black tracks on her inner thighs. The inside of her gaping cat was beef-steak red. She had a shiv slash on the right side of her face. It was a livid gully from her cheekbone to the corner of her twisted mouth. Smallpox craters covered her face. I caught the glint of a pearl-handled switch-blade in her bosom. Her gray eyes were whirling in her skull. She was high.

I was careful. I grinned. "Sweet" was digging us. He was shaking his head in disgust. I wondered if he thought I oughta slug her in the jib and maybe take that shiv in the gut.

She said, "Let me see that pretty dick, handsome."

I said, "I don't show my swipe to strange bitches. I got a whore to pamper my swipe."

She said, "Nigger, you ain't heard of me? I'm Red Cora" from Detroit. That red is for blood. You ain't hip I'm a thieving bitch that croaked two studs? Now I said show that dick. Call me Cora, little bullshit Nigger. Ain't you a bitch with one whore? You gonna starve to death, Nigger, if she's a chump flat-backer. Nigger, you better get hip and cop a thief."

A big husky broad with a spike in one hand and pack of stuff in the other took me off the hook. She kneed Cora's spine.

She said, "Bitch, I'm gonna shoot this dope. You want some? You can 'Georgia' this skinny Nigger later."

I watched Cora's rear end twist away from me. She and the husky broad went to the bar and got a spoon and a glass of water. I looked at "Sweet." He was giving me a cold stare.

I thought, "This track is too fast. I can't protect myself. With young soft bitches like the runt I'm a champ. These old, hard bitches, I gotta solve. I gotta be careful and not blow 'Sweet.' If I sucker out anymore tonight he'll freeze and boot me."

I sat in the corner bugeyed for two hours. My ears napped to the super-slick dialogue. I was excited by the fast-paced, smooth byplay between these wizards of pimpdom.

"Red Cora" kept me edgy. She went to the patio several times. She was "Hed" out of her skull. Each time she passed she cracked on me. She was sure panting to view my swipe.

Several of "Sweet's" whores came in. None of them had been at the "Roost" with him that first time I saw him. All of them were fine with low mileage. One of them was yellow and beautiful. She couldn't have been more than seventeen.

There was a giant black pimp from the "Apple." He had three of his whores with him. He had been boasting about how he had his swipe trained. He was one of the three at the party that didn't bang stuff. I had watched him snort "girl" and down a few mixed drinks. He had a glass in his hand standing over "Sweet" and "Top" on the couch.

He said, " 'Sweet,' ain't a bitch living can pop me off unless I want her to. I don't care if she's got velvet suction cups in her cat. Her jib can have a college degree, she ain't gonna make me pop against my will. I got the toughest swipe in the world. I got a 'C' note to back my crack."

"Sweet" said, "Sucker, I got a young bitch I turned out six months ago that could blow that tender sucker swipe of yours in five minutes. I ain't going to teach you no lesson for a measly 'C' note. If that 'C' note ain't all you got, put five bills in 'Top's' mitt and you got a bet."

The big joker snatched a roll from his side pocket. He plunked five "C" notes into "Top's" palm. "Sweet" eased a bale of "C" notes from the pocket of his smoking jacket. He covered the bet in "Top's" hand.

"Sweet" snapped his fingers. The beautiful yellow broad kneeled before the standing giant. She started to perform before the cheering audience. Within less than three minutes she had won the bet for "Sweet."

DAVID WOJNAROWICZ

Close to the Knives

HE'S GOT ME DOWN on my knees and I can't even focus on anything I have no time to understand the position of my body or the direction of my face I see a pair of legs in rough corduroy and the color of the pants are brown and surrounded by darkness and there's a sense of other people there and yet I can't hear them breathe or hear their feet or anything and his hand suddenly comes up against the back of my head and he's got his fingers locked in my hair and he's shoving my face forward and twisting my head almost gently but very violent in that gentleness and I got only half a breath in my lungs the smell of piss on the floorboards and this fleshy bulge in his pants getting harder and harder as my face is forced against the front of his pants the zipper tears my lips I feel them getting bruised and all the while he's stroking my face and tightening his fingers around the locks of my hair and I can't focus my eyes my head being pushed and pulled and twisted and caressed and it's as if I have no hands I know I got hands I had hands a half hour ago I remember lighting a cigarette with them lighting a match and I remember how warm the flame was when I lifted it toward my face and my knees are hurting from the floor it's a stone floor and my knees are hurting 'cause they banged on the floor when he dragged me down the cellar stairs I remember a door in the darkness and the breath of a dog his dog as it licked my hands when I reached out to stop my headlong descent its tongue licking out at my fingers and my face slams down and there's this electric blam inside my head and it's as if my eyes suddenly opened on the large sun and then went black with the switch thrown down and I'm shocked and embarrassed and his arms swing down he's lifting me up saying, lookin' for me?, and he buries his face in my neck and I feel the saliva running down into the curve of my neck and my arms are hanging loose and I can see a ceiling and a dim bulb tossing back and forth and suddenly I'm on my knees again and my face is getting mashed into his belly and sliding down across rough cloth and zippers and there's this sweet musty smell and his dick is slapping across my eyes and rubbing over my cheeks and bloody lips and suddenly it's inside my mouth and the hands twisted up in my hair and cradling my skull shove me forward and I feel his dick hit the back of my throat and I feel pain for the first time like the open pants are in focus and he's pulled his dick out of my mouth and I'm choking and he's running one hand over my face putting his fingers in my ears in my mouth dragging down my lower jaw and forcing his dick in between the fingers and the saliva and blood and shoving shoving in and out and pulling on my hair and everything goes out of focus my eyes moving around blindly the smell of basement water and sewage and mustiness and dirt and he's slapping my face like he wants to wake me up and I realize I'm crying and he tells me that he loves me and he lifts me up and puts his lips over mine and sticks his tongue in my mouth and buries his rough face down in my collar and licks and drags his tongue over my shoulder and neck and his hands are up inside my shirt and he's rubbing them back and forth across my belly and sides taking quick handfuls of flesh and twisting and rubbing and then they're inside my pants and he suddenly rips apart the opening of my pants I hear metal buttons hitting the floor and he punches me in the side of the head at the same time pulling my hair and pulling me back down to the floor and I'm on my belly I feel cold rough stone scratching my skin and he kneels down suddenly into the center of my back and it hurts and I try to yell but he's shoving my underwear into my mouth and I'm suddenly hit with such a feeling of intense claustrophobia and fear that it's hours before I realize that my hands and legs are tied together and that I'm lying on my side and the rag in my mouth is soaking wet and making small bubbling sounds each time I breathe.

LARRY RIVERS

What Did I Do?

A WRAP

AFTER SIX MONTHS OF family adventure mixed with sun, sea, and sand in Miami, I forgot why I was there. The anxiety about my heroin use in New York took a back seat to a number of other anxieties. I was beginning to feel that down in Miami my life was standing still. Who am I if I am not doing anything?—a question I still ask myself.

I wanted to be an artist, and I had to do it alone. This was a trip that did not include a partner, a lover, a woman and her sainted mother and children. I had to present myself in a characterless context, or a context I could make up as I went along. But four relatives with the Bronx emanating from their faces, clothes, and speech only spelled failure—not to mention the rows of Franco-American cans in the cupboard and the Heinz and Hormel on the table, and a wife who washed her hands ten times before serving and made her family wash their hands ten times before eating. Augusta's germ phobia was getting worse. I had to take so many baths before sex that I was developing a chapped body. She was getting tough to be around—literally. She began yelling at her mother for hovering over the stove or for allowing the kids to get away with a single washing before dinner. And the fact that she did this when I wasn't there made me see her in an unattractive light. I had to begin somewhere else.

I didn't want to live in a family apartment. My life was not going to be about living, it was going to be about art. I wanted a studio and paintings in that studio, and brushes, canvas, and paint to produce those paintings. I had to fulfill my desire to study art seriously, even if I might have fun doing it. I wanted to be an artist with all the trappings of the day. I wanted to replace the image of a musician—zoot suit, duck's ass haircut, hip talk—with dungarees, rope belts, zany shirts and sweaters, outfits and language that would be thought original and full of invention. I wanted to experience the actual act of painting. Smearing. I always found painting walls or boards with a wide brush physically pleasurable. I even wanted to learn to draw. I wanted to come by some serious avant-garde ideas, then put the results on a wall in a gallery on Fifty-seventh Street and read all about it in critical articles in magazines and newspapers.

Once More with Passion

Once back from Miami on Crescent Avenue with my four dependents, and not playing much horn, I began spending time downtown drawing at Nell Blaine's studio on Twenty-first Street. The subway ride back from Nell's up to the Bronx and my family was becoming a painful waste of time as my interest in that scene diminished. I was young and, as my uncle Morris said, had "a lot of time in the bank." I didn't want to squander it on the D train.

I would usually wait until late at night to return to Crescent Avenue after hanging out as long as there was Something Happening: probably smoking pot, listening to jazz, a little drinking, and long, uninformed talks about art and seduction; not much was Happening Sexually. Many nights we'd go to Times Square to see a foreign movie, foreign meaning French, with the great Jouvet, Arletty, and Jean-Louis Barrault. *Les Enfants du Paradis* was one of the most artistic experiences of my life, especially that scene at the film's end,

Barrault anxiously searching for the woman he loves in a crowded carnival street. The screenplay was by the poet Jacques Prévert. The love story inspired me to run out on Forty-second Street after the credits and look for the greatest love of my life. Having been told by friends and strangers that I resembled Barrault, I began to see myself as a thin, sensitive, odd-looking young man, disillusioned but still hoping to unite love and a life of art, for at least two hours after seeing the film.

My downtown friends and I would walk up to Times Square to see these films, and the buildings along the way were a show in themselves. The Flatiron Building, the Chrysler, the Georgian warehouses—every brick took on a new significance; we became sensible to seeing, we tried to cap each other in architectural observation. This was the first idea I had of new possibilities.

Augusta sensed that she was pretty far down on my People and Things to Think About list, which put her in a state of continual panic, confirming every negative view she intermittently held about herself. Her confrontations and accusations avalanched, leaving us little time for the fun of generalization. Augusta knew nothing about what interested me: jazz, art, old movies, fame (mainly in art, or anything else that might come along). She didn't have the social graces I began observing in women when I was downtown—not that we went anywhere to test them out. She was jealous and awkward. If a woman in the street, alone or with a date, looked at me for more than a moment as we strolled past the Paradise Theater on the Grand Concourse in the North Bronx, Augusta was capable of shouting at the innocent offender, "Hey! Like what you see? Turn your face!" I hovered between flattery and fear.

Sex with Augusta and guilt about leaving the children kept me on the D train up to the Bronx night after night. I liked my erotic sessions with Augusta—short as they were. I thought that part would improve, though I was convinced that the problem was more hers than mine. After all, I had the orgasm; she didn't!

But my sexual curiosity about different kinds of women was growing, and the world that would produce them for my omnivorous satisfaction lay waiting, I imagined, in a life of art and bohemianism. I went there.

I also found a way to leave those children to the wolves. I would continue to give what support I could by sending money. I would visit them, so that I wasn't completely neglecting them. And I'd be too busy to worry about them.

I never officially left. I never stood at the door, sax in one hand, bag in the other, delivering a farewell address. I never removed my clothes from the closet, my underwear and socks from the drawers. Nor did I peel the mural from the wall I painted. Sunday at 4:00 a.m. sharp, I would pay a visit wearing an outfit I hadn't changed in a week, and take a bath. The only space for me to sleep was in the bed with Augusta.

After a few months of the time between my homecomings lengthening, Augusta found a beau, one Aesop Gable, a handsome six-foot golf instructor. After Aesop's arrival on the scene, whenever I slipped under the covers in the dark, Augusta languorously pleaded with me not to try anything funny. She wanted to be faithful to Aesop. I made no immediate attempts to seduce her. I did try something funny. I stuck my middle finger up my ass and passed it under her nose. She jumped out of bed.

"Larry, you're impossible! I'm going to sleep on the floor."

"I'm sorry, let's just go to sleep."

So we tried to go to sleep. She turned on her side so that her more erotic parts, breast, belly button, mons veneris, and pubic hair, were the thickness of her body away from me. I would be hard put to try "anything funny" without having to climb over her. Well, I didn't need those parts in my hand to get aroused. I had this glass erection, my own, and it was difficult to fall asleep. Somehow tumescence and drowsiness are rarely experienced simultaneously. I waited till I heard her breathing evenly. In an extremely gentle and slow manner I put my cock at the opening in the natural turn of the thighs just below her ass. Taking my time and moving only on her exhale, I pressed my cock farther and farther into her vagina. After about twenty minutes I was all the way in. What I found surprising was how wet she was. I thought this occurred only after foreplay and vigorous fucking. Maybe she had just been laid by Aesop and hadn't dried out yet. My rhythm method worked. I fucked my wife while she was asleep. A few times she woke up a minute or so after I entered, and with great anger and strength pulled my cock out of her, and with a critical groan got up and went to sleep with Steven in his folding cot about five feet from our bed. Did he hear us? Does it matter now?

BRILLIANT IDEA

After the third angry removal of my cock, having spent a half hour of thrilling but difficult work, I was cured. I gave up necrophilia.

The next Saturday night I was downtown, stoned and drunk at a party deep in bohemia, probably Twenty-first Street, when I got the brilliant idea of fucking my mother-in-law. Fortunately phone calls are aural experiences; a visual one would have produced a fat gray-haired but large-breasted saint in a soiled housedress. I blubbered out my desires on the phone. Berdie, age fifty-six, said, "Oh, Larry, you're so funny. We miss you. Everybody's waiting to see you. Are you coming up?"

"Yeah, later."

I figured I'd stay at the party till it was certain that Augusta was off on her Saturday night date with Aesop, then sneak uptown to the arms of my wife's mother. I exhorted Berdie to be silent. "It goes without saying, Berdie, mum's the word."

"What do you mean, Larry?"

"Well, it might cause trouble."

"What kind of trouble, Larry?"

"Look, just don't tell Augusta."

An hour and a half later, I stepped off the D train at Fordham Road, walked around the corner to Crescent Avenue, poked my key in the lock, opened the door, and lurched toward Berdie, who was lying on the couch in the living room, her bed. I fell flat on top of her and said, "I love you."

The air was filled with shoes. Augusta stomped out of the closet and began pummeling me with a large black galosh. For five minutes I withstood her physical and verbal onslaught. I don't know what I said. But if something like this happened now, with the hindsight of a life in art, travel, reading, and psychoanalysis, I would say what I probably said that night. "I was only kidding. Let's go to bed." Which we did.

Harvey Pekar *American Splendor Anthology*

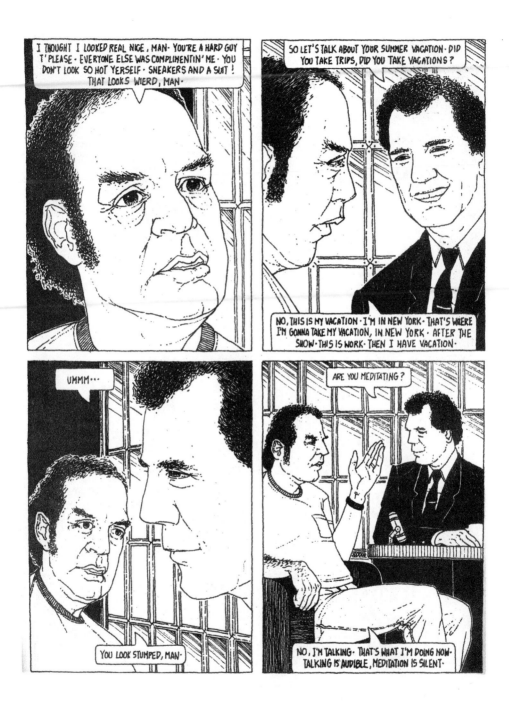

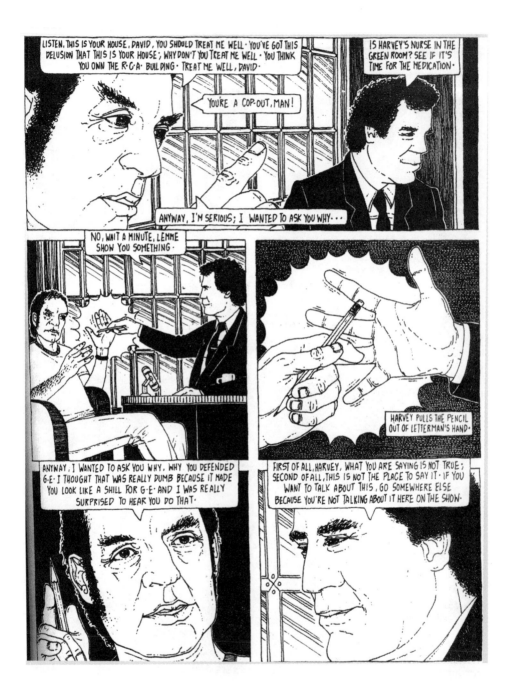

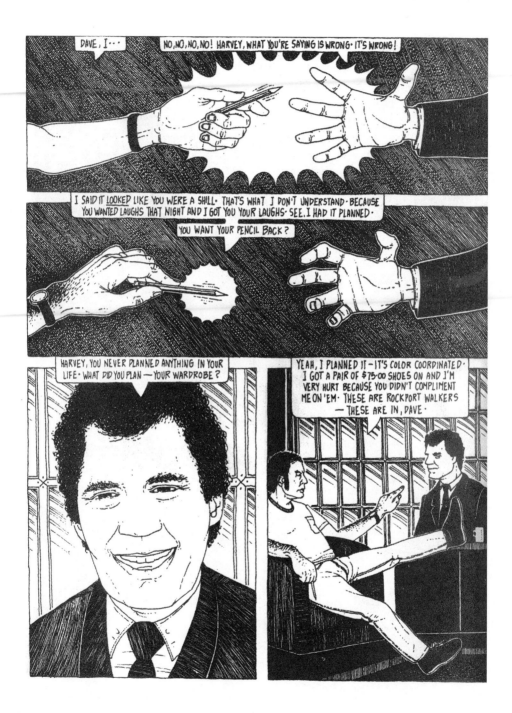

Kathy Acker

Don Quixote

I THINK PRINCE SHOULD be President of the United States because all our Presidents since World War II have been stupid anyway and are becoming stupider up to the point of lobotomy and anyway are the puppets of those nameless beings,—maybe they're human—demigods, who inhabit their own nations known heretofore as 'multi-nationals'. On the other hand: Prince, unlike all our other images or fakes or Presidents, stands for values. I mean: he believes. He wears a cross. President Reagan doesn't believe this crap he's handing out or down about happy families and happy black lynchings and happy ignorance. Worse: he might. Whereas The Prince believes in feelings, fucking, and fame. Fame is making it and common sense.

The Prince doesn't have any morals. Why? Because morals're part and parcel of a government which runs partly by means of the so-called 'have-nots' ' or bourgeoisie's cover-up, (via 'Culture'), of the 'haves' ' total control. Morality and 'Culture' are similar tools. The only culture that ever causes trouble is amoral. The Prince isn't moral: he doesn't give a shit about anybody but himself. The Prince wouldn't die for anyone, whereas Our President will always die for everybody while he's garnering in their cash.

Look at Prince's life. He's all-American because he's part black part white which is part good part evil. When he was thirteen, which is a magic number, he ran away from home just like Huckleberry Finn. He had nowhere to run to, cause there's nowhere to run to anymore. So he ran to a garage. He and his friend Cymone made music while they were screwing, sharing, and tying up girls. The Prince was the good boy because he didn't cuss and Cymone was the bad boy because he stole cars. Now Prince is twenty-six years old; he'll be thirty when he gets elected President of the United States. Thirty years old is the height of male cowboy American rock 'n roll energy.

Don't vote for a croaker again to run your life.

Does it matter that Prince doesn't know anything about governmental politics? I presume he doesn't. All political techniques, left and right, are the praxis and speech of the controllers. How can we get rid of these controllers, their praxis and speech or politics? Let the country go to Hell. By going to Hell, Prince, a good Catholic, might be able to save this country. Anyway, we'd have a lot more fun than now, now when we're slowly being turned into fake people who're alienated from themselves, or zombies. Our minds're floating in other bodies. The Prince is Dr Strange so he'll restore to us and restore us to those lowest of pleasures that are the only ones we Americans, being stupid, desire. Fucking, food, and dancing. This is the American Revolution.

It has been said that Prince presents nothing: he's dead, an image. But who do you think you are? Are you real? Such reality is false. You can only be who you're taught and shown to be. Those who have and are showing you, most of the controllers, are shits. Despite that, how can you hate you or the image? How can you be who you're not and how can you not be? Prince accepts his falsity. Prince uses his falsity. Prince, being conscious, can lead us. 'I'm not a lover. I'm not a man. I'm something you can understand. I'm not your leader. I'm not your friend.' We must be conscious in order to fight outside control. Make Prince who may be conscious the next President of the United States.

Hubert Selby Jr.

Last Exit to Brooklyn

THEY ATE IN A cafeteria and went to an allnight movie. The next day they got a couple of rooms in a hotel on the east side and stayed in manhattan until the following night. When they went back to the Greeks Alex told them some MPs and a detective were in asking about the guys who beat up a soldier the other night. They said he was in bad shape. Had to operate on him and he may go blind in one eye. Ain't that just too bad. The MPs said if they get ahold of the guys who did it theyd killem. Those fuckin punks. Whad the law say. Nottin. You know. Yeah. Killus! The creeps. We oughtta dumpem on general principles. Tralala laughed. I shoulda pressed charges fa rape. I wont be 18 for a week. He raped me the dirty freaky sonofabitch. They laughed and ordered coffeeand. When they finished Al and Tony figured theyd better make the rounds of a few of the bars and see what was doin. In one of the bars they noticed the bartender slip an envelope in a tin box behind the bar. It looked like a pile of bills on the bottom of the box. They checked the window in the MENS ROOM and the alley behind it then left the bar and went back to the Greeks. They told Tralala what they were going

to do and went to a furnished room they had rented over one of the bars on
1st avenue. When the bars closed they took a heavy duty screwdriver and
walked to the bar. Tralala stood outside and watched the street while they
broke in. It only took a few minutes to force open the window, drop inside,
crawl to the bar, pickup the box and climb out the window and drop to the
alley. They pried open the box in the alley and started to count. They almost
panicked when they finished counting. They had almost 2 thousand dollars.
They stared at it for a moment then jammed it into their pockets. Then Tony
took a few hundred and put it into another pocket and told Al theyd tell
Tralala that that was all they got. They smiled and almost laughed then
calmed themselves before leaving the alley and meeting Tralala. They took
the box with them and dropped it into a sewer then walked back to the room.
When they stepped from the alley Tralala ran over to them asking them how
they made out and how much they got and Tony told her to keep quiet that
they got a couple a hundred and to play it cool until they got back to the
room. When they got back to the room Al started telling her what a snap it
was and how they just climbed in and took the box but Tralala ignored him
and kept asking how much they got. Tony took the lump of money from his
pocket and they counted it. Not bad eh Tral? 250 clams. Yeah. How about
giving my 50 now. What for? You aint going no where now. She shrugged
and they went to bed. The next afternoon they went to the Greeks for coffee
and two detectives came in and told them to come outside. They searched
them, took the money from their pockets and pushed them into their car.
The detectives waved the money in front of their faces and shook their heads.
Dont you know better than to knock over a bookie drop? Huh? Huh, Huh!
Real clever arent you. The detectives laughed and actually felt a professional
amazement as they looked at their dumb expressions and realized that they
really didnt know who they had robbed. Tony slowly started to come out of
the coma and started to protest that they didnt do nothin. One of the detectives slapped his face and told him to shutup. For Christs sake dont give us
any of that horseshit. I suppose you just found a couple of grand lying in an
empty lot? Tralala screeched, a what? The detectives looked at her briefly
then turned back to Tony and Al. You can lush a few drunken seamen now
and then and get away with it, but when you start taking money from my
pocket youre going too far sonny. What a pair of stupid punks . . . OK sister,
beat it. Unless you want to come along for the ride? She automatically
backed away from the car, still staring at Tony and Al. The doors slammed
shut and they drove away. Tralala went back to the Greeks and sat at the
counter cursing Tony and Al and then the bulls for pickinem up before she
could get hers. Didn't even spend a penny of it. The goddamn bastards.

The rotten stinkin sonsofbitches. Those thievin flat-footed bastards. She sat drinking coffee all afternoon then left and went across the street to Willies. She walked to the end of the bar and started talking with Ruthy, the barmaid, telling her what happened, stopping every few minutes to curse Tony, Al, the bulls and lousy luck. The bar was slowly filling and Ruthy left her every few minutes to pour a drink and when she came back Tralala would repeat the story from the beginning, yelling about the 2 grand and they never even got a chance to spend a penny. With the repeating of the story she forgot about Tony and Al and just cursed the bulls and her luck and an occasional seaman or doggie who passed by and asked her if she wanted a drink or just looked at her. Ruthy kept filling Tralalas glass as soon as she emptied it and told her to forget about it. Thats the breaks. No sense in beatin yahead against the wall about it. Theres plenty more. Maybe not that much, but enough. Tralala snarled, finished her drink and told Ruthy to fill it up. Eventually she absorbed her anger and quieted down and when a young seaman staggered over to her she glanced at him and said yes. Ruthy brought them two drinks and smiled. Tralala watched him take the money out of his pocket and figured it might be worthwhile. She told him there were better places to drink than this crummy dump. Well, lez go baby. He gulped his drink and Tralala left hers on the bar and they left. They got into a cab and the seaman asked her whereto and she said she didnt care, anywhere. OK. Takeus to Times Square. He offered her a cigarette and started telling her about everything. His name was Harry. He came from Idaho. He just got back from Italy. He was going to—she didnt bother smiling but watched him, trying to figure out how soon he would pass out. Sometimes they last allnight. Cant really tell. She relaxed and gave it thought. Cant konkim here. Just have ta wait until he passes out or maybe just ask for some money. The way they throw it around. Just gotta getim in a room alone. If he dont pass out I/ll just rapim with somethin—and you should see what we did to that little ol . . . He talked on and Tralala smoked and the lampposts flicked by and the meter ticked. He stopped talking when the cab stopped in front of the Crossroads. They got out and tried to get in the Crossroads but the bartender looked at the drunken seaman and shook his head no. So they crossed the street and went to another bar. The bar was jammed, but they found a small table in the rear and sat down. They ordered drinks and Tralala sipped hers then pushed her unfinished drink across the table to him when he finished his. He started talking again but the lights and the music slowly affected him and the subject matter was changed and he started telling Tralala what a good lookin girl she was and what a good time he was going to show her; and she told him that she would show him the time of his life and didnt bother to hide a yawn.

He beamed and drank faster and Tralala asked him if he would give her some money. She was broke and had to have some money or she/d be locked out of her room. He told her not to worry that hed find a place for her to stay tonight and he winked and Tralala wanted to shove her cigarette in his face, the cheap sonofabitch, but figured she/d better wait and get his money before she did anything. He toyed with her hand and she looked around the bar and noticed an Army Officer staring at her. He had a lot of ribbons just like the one she had rolled and she figured hed have more money than Harry. Officers are usually loaded. She got up from the table telling Harry she was going to the ladies room. The Officer swayed slightly as she walked up to him and smiled. He took her arm and asked her where she was going. Nowhere. O, we cant have a pretty girl like you going nowhere. I have a place thats all empty and a sack of whiskey. Well . . . She told him to wait and went back to the table. Harry was almost asleep and she tried to get the money from his pocket and he started to stir. When his eyes opened she started shaking him, taking her hand out of his pocket, and telling him to wakeup. I thought yawere goin to show me a good time. You bet. He nodded his head and it slowly descended toward the table. Hey Harry, wakeup. The waiter wants to know if yahave any money. Showem ya money so I wont have to pay. He slowly took the crumpled mess of bills from his pocket and Tralala grabbed it from his hand and said I toldya he had money. She picked up the cigarettes from the table, put the money in her pocketbook and walked back to the bar. My friend is sleeping so I dont think he/ll mind, but I think we/d better leave. They left the bar and walked to his hotel. Tralala hoped she didnt make a mistake. Harry mightta had more money stashed somewhere. The Officer should have more though and anyway she probably got every-thing Harry had and she could get more from this jerk if he has any. She looked at him trying to determine how much he could have, but all Officers look the same. Thats the trouble with a goddamn uniform. And then she wondered how much she had gotten from Harry and how long she would have to wait to count it. When they got to his room she went right into the bathroom, smoothed out the bills a little and counted them. 45. Shit. Fuckit. She folded the money, left the bathroom and stuffed the money in a coat pocket. He poured two small drinks and they sat and talked for a few min-utes then put the light out. Tralala figured there was no sense in trying any-thing now, so she relaxed and enjoyed herself. They were having a smoke and another drink when he turned and kissed her and told her she had the most beautiful pair of tits he had ever seen. He continued talking for a few minutes, but she didnt pay any attention. She thought about her tits and what he had said and how she could get anybody with her tits and the hell with

Willies and those slobs, she/d hang around here for a while and do alright. They put out their cigarettes and for the rest of the night she didn't wonder how much money he had. At breakfast the next morning he tried to remember everything that had happened in the bar, but Harry was only vaguely remembered and he didn't want to ask her. A few times he tried speaking, but when he looked at her he started feeling vaguely guilty. When they had finished eating he lit her cigarette, smiled, and asked her if he could buy her something. A dress or something like that. I mean, well you know . . . Id like to buy you a little present. He tried not to sound maudlin or look sheepish, but he found it hard to say what he felt, now, in the morning, with a slight hangover, and she looked to him pretty and even a little innocent. Primarily he didnt want her to think he was offering to pay her or think he was insulting her by insinuating that she was just another prostitute; but much of his loneliness was gone and he wanted to thank her. You see, I only have a few days leave left before I go back and I thought perhaps we could— that is I thought we could spend some more time together . . . he stammered on apologetically hoping she understood what he was trying to say but the words bounced off her and when she noticed that he had finished talking she said sure. What thefuck. This is much better than wresslin with a drunk and she felt good this morning, much better than yesterday (briefly remembering the bulls and the money they took from her) and he might even give her his money before he went back overseas (what could he do with it) and with her tits she could always makeout and whatthehell, it was the best screwin she ever had . . . They went shopping and she bought a dress, a couple of sweaters (2 sizes too small), shoes, stockings, a pocketbook and an overnight bag to put her clothes in. She protested slightly when he told her to buy a cosmetic case (not knowing what it was when he handed it to her and she saw no sense in spending money on that when he could as well give her cash), and he enjoyed her modesty in not wanting to spend too much of his money; and he chuckled at her childlike excitement at being in the stores, looking and buying. They took all the packages back to the hotel and Tralala put on her new dress and shoes and they went out to eat and then to a movie. For the next few days they went to movies, restaurants (Tralala trying to make a mental note of the ones where the Officers hungout), a few more stores and back to the hotel. When they woke on the 4th day he told her he had to leave and asked her if she would come with him to the station. She went thinking he might give her his money and she stood awkwardly on the station with him, their bags around them, waiting for him to go on the train and leave. Finally the time came for him to leave and he handed her an envelope as she lifted her face slightly so he could kiss her. It was thin and she figured it might be a check. She put it in her pocketbook, picked up her bag and went to the waiting room and sat on a bench and opened the envelope. She opened the paper and started reading: Dear Tral: There are many things I would like to say and should have said, but—A letter. A god-damn LETTER. She ripped the envelope apart and turned the letter over a few times. Not a cent. I hope you understand what I mean and am unable to say—she looked at the words—if you do feel as I hope you do Im writing my address at the bottom. I dont know if I/ll live through this war, but—Shit. Not vehemently but factually. She dropped the letter and rode the subway to Brooklyn.

BARNEY ROSSET

Tin Pan Alley

IT MUST HAVE BEEN about 1946. The shabby streets had the murkiness that went with greasy half-wet black tar and glistening drops of oil, water drooled off the battered canopy outside of the bar, protruding into the deathly quiet, deserted Rush Street. A few bulbs among the dead ones hanging from the out-side fringe of the canopy were still burning in poor imitations of yellow and green and red, but their light was so dim that they had lost their garishness and slipped back into the realm of quiet, albeit foreboding, respectability.

There were few signs of light emanating from the interior; and only a dull red neon flickered in the windows, indicating that people might be within— that and the faraway sound of a piano that might be coming from this place named Tin Pan Alley.

To go in you had to walk under the canopy and then go down a flight of steps to the entrance, which was below the sidewalk level. One of the Chicago houses that had had to allow the cement to grow up around it and sink it into a half-subterranean world, the swamp from which the city had half emerged.

Chicago had a 4 A.M. closing law, and by 5 it was reasonable to suppose that most bars would be closed, and maybe they were. But not Jimmy's place. You could always get one more in this bar, and maybe even a little jazz to go with the bad bar whiskey, and Jimmy never seemed to notice.

Within the small confines of the canopy there were no lights, and as you walked down into this dive, you saw old music scores plastered over the walls, containing the songs of the twenties and early thirties half scraped off—trying to achieve a veneer of sentiment and not quite making it. Was this Jimmy's Chicago or was it his Sicily, or was it both finally joined at the heart?

Inside, the mazdas burned with about ten more watts than the half-moonlit night outside, and it was necessary to stop for a moment to allow the balls of the eyes to react and grasp the unfocused world of foul smokiness and deep reddish lights that swirled into each other, holding you there and snarling at you and choking you with the putridness of drying alcohol and dried life burnt out on a scarred bar top.

A Negro doorman stood inside the door instead of outside of it and he half opened the door for you and said, "Hello, ain't seen you for a long time, almost three hours, but maybe it was yesterday or tonight, or might have been last week when we saw that chick on the south side" and "gimme a piece of skin, man" and "when we gonna start that little bar of our own—only need about five hundred bucks." His name was Buck—just a poor tired guy looking for a buck bogged down into this pit for his pittance and "okay, Buck, I'll see you in a minute," and the 26 girl was still standing next to the door rolling the little cup of dice onto a tray before her and counting how they came up. If you had never seen her in the daylight, and probably you had not, she looked almost pretty. Her long black hair was falling down onto her shoulders framing the low-cut dress that showed her breasts as she bent over with a stub of pencil in her hand to write the numbers on the almost-concealed score sheet. And she or the dress or the light and maybe the bad whiskey kept the quarters rolling in, and sometimes her counting was not too accurate and 26 changed to 25, and who cared because the hair and the breasts were still there so close and not very close really.

The walls had been painted to make you think you were in Paris at a street cafe or watching an Apache dance or walking down a dark street or looking into a garish mirror with pink light. But you could never really quite decide, and maybe that poor slob of a painter had had his joke by not letting you know if you were sleeping through a nightmare of Paris or sinking into the cheapness of Chicago. But at least the bar was of secure solid stolid oak, and it was a refuge for the arms, and the ice in the glass was a spot of coolness.

Those self-isolating souls at the bar were the people you always saw. There was the young gay guy at the rear trying self-consciously to conceal his sweet girlishness and yet letting it ooze and drip out of him through his hands and his hair and his words of molten honey for the almost blind, huge black woman Laura Rucker, who was playing the piano in an almost perfunctory fashion yet still nurturing a little love for it as if it had once been her lover and part of her before she had lost him and grown blind and fat and now played only with her dreams grown stale. At her side was an elderly drummer, Baby Dodds, who was listlessly yet catlike pounding softly on the skin, and his eyes were maybe closed, and you did not know if there was any conscious effort on his part.

Two or three of the lost ones stood near the little upright piano asking Laura for this and that, and she tried to give it out but sometimes it was, "I'm sorry honey I just don't know it" and "please ask for something else." To Baby it did not matter much what it was. He followed in and pounded it out a little, and it did not matter much to those who listened either. Some things had the ring of familiarity—nice to hear the songs you once thought meant something, and in here you could still get the chance to feel important—name your song and hear it sung by a recording artist and a great jazz drummer who were playing some lost melody for you, corrupted out of themselves, but still it was only for you and maybe you had not even heard the songs before yours. You just wanted to hear the one played for you, and as soon as they methodically began grinding it out, you could forget it and turn back to the sad drink on the bar and watch the bartender try to cheat a little on the bonded stuff and maybe throw in a little of the bar whiskey to the drunk down at the end. And in this minuscule place the smoke deepened phantasmagorical-like and people sitting at the tables seemed isolated and a million lives away, crouched under the protective canopy of the Cafe de la Paix, only it was the painted canopy on the ceiling in the basement of the Tin Pan Alley, situated on Rush Street, Chicago. But the people must be real even if the canopy was not, and the smoke was making it hard to see their faces. This was important because someday she would be there. A girl would drift out of the smoke, and peering into it might materialize her. It had never happened but it might, and when the whiskeys mounted up the odds lessened and staying and waiting was made easier. The world contained itself in the off-red light and the *Chicago Tribune* ugliness stayed out, and the cold hard-boiled eggs sitting on the bar in their shells became the nourishment of the city. Up in front the door opened spasmodically with people moving in and out. Maybe the bar down the street would be better, but it never was and they always came back—out of the black maw of the night—through the door held by Buck, ready to give a piece of skin without the asking.

A guy strolled in with a big bulldog on a leash that ponderously, dignifiedly headed through the mist for a booth at the rear where he could crawl under the seat and wait for the other end of the leash to saturate and satisfy the cravings of the alones. The single girls who came in were not too appealing. That night there were two of them, but they were fond of each other and they made you know that their interests were in the drinks and each other and the deal was don't bother us please. But once in a while somebody different did wander in. A girl alone here, and you always wondered, and the wonderings were usually correct. The body had a price printed on it and the heart had atrophied beyond recognition. Yet there was always the lift of expectation when you pushed and maneuvered to the stool next to a female who might be attractive and who might be alone.

And when she wore a brown wool sweater and had long blond hair and wore horn-rimmed glasses it was new life. But finding the way to attract her was baffling because this did not happen here. A guy with failing eyesight and bad hearing could still tell that she was no stranger to this place even if she had never been here before. But there had been no better people and this was no place to question too deeply before you even savored the possibilities. And then you were talking and she had gone to Stanford and had later lived in San Francisco and you pretended you had too, and this became something you had created for sharing, and Telegraph Hill was your meeting place and more drinks brought that place on back to Chicago, and now her being close was real whether in Paris or California or Chicago, and the time for a move seemed nearing as you saw the bulldog retrace his way out of the gloom and you noticed that when Buck swung the door open the dawn stared back at you and then the dream snapped shut and you asked her if she would like a lift home and she said yes. The drink money was slid across the counter and the door to the dawn was open and the words were—I'll need twenty for this—and you mumbled something about that being a lot, but that was not what the disappointment was, and the dawn was cold and harsh, and Baby Dodds and Laura Rucker had long ago disappeared into the wall, and you wanted to die. But the night had been too long, and you got into the car and you closed the door and drove away without looking at her sitting there beside you.

NORMAN MAILER

An American Dream

"COME HERE, DARLING, AND give a kiss."

"I'd rather not."

"Tell me why not."

"Because I threw up a while ago and my breath is foul."

"Bad smells never bother me."

"Well, they bother me. And you've been drinking rum. You smell Godawful." It was true. When she drank too much, a stench of sweet rot lifted from her. "The Irish were never meant to go near rum," I said, "it brings out the odor of their fat."

"Do you talk this way to all your little girls?"

She did not know what I did with the days and weeks I spent away from her. This was forever agitating her rage. Once, years ago, she uncovered an affair I had been keeping in a corner. It had been with a rather ordinary young lady who (for compensation, no doubt) had been a burning wizard in bed. Otherwise, the girl was undeniably plain. Somehow, Deborah learned about her. The subsequent details are vicious, private detectives, so forth, but the indigestible issue was that Deborah had gone with the private detective to a restaurant where the girl always had lunch and studied her through a meal, all through a long meal the poor girl ate by herself. What a scene followed!

"I don't think I've been quite so marooned in all my beloved life," Deborah had said. "I mean, *figure-toi*, pet, I had to keep up a conversation with the detective, a *horrible* man, and he was laughing at me. All that money spent on fees, and for what, a poor wet little mouse. She was even afraid of the *waitresses*, and this was a *tea*-room. What a big boy you must be to take up with a sparrow."

The real part of her fury was that no intrigue had ensued; if the affair had been with one of her friends, or with some other woman of parts, then Deborah could have gone to war and fought one of her grand campaigns, hook and eye, tooth and talon, a series of parties with exquisite confrontations; but I had merely been piddling and that was the unforgivable sin. Since that time Deborah spoke only of my *little girls*.

"What do you say to them, pet?" asked Deborah now, "do you say, 'Please stop drinking so much because you smell like a piece of fat,' or do you say, 'Oh God, darling, I love your stink?'"

The mottling had spread in ugly smears and patches upon her neck, her shoulders, and what I could see of her breast. They radiated a detestation so palpable that my body began to race as if a foreign element, a poison altogether suffocating, were beginning to seep through me. Did you ever feel the malignity which rises from a swamp? It is real, I could swear it, and some whisper of ominous calm, that heavy air one breathes in the hours before a hurricane, now came to rest between us. I was afraid of her. She was not incapable of murdering me. There are killers one is ready to welcome, I suppose. They offer a clean death and free passage to one's soul. The moon had spoken to me as just such an assassin. But Deborah promised bad burial. One would go down in one's death, and muck would wash over the last of one's wind. She did not wish to tear the body, she was out to spoil the light, and in an epidemic of fear, as if her face—that wide mouth, fullfleshed nose, and pointed green eyes, pointed as arrows—would be my first view of eternity, as if she were ministering angel (ministering devil) I knelt beside her and tried to take her hand. It was soft now as a jellyfish, and almost as repugnant—the touch shot my palm with a thousand needles which stung into my arm exactly as if I had been swimming at night and lashed onto a Portuguese man o' war.

"Your hand feels nice," she said in a sudden turn of mood.

There was a period when we held hands often. She had become pregnant after three years of marriage, a ticklish pregnancy to conserve, for there had been something malformed about her uterus—she was never explicit—and her ducts had suffered from a chronic inflammation since Deirdre had been born. But we had succeeded, we wanted a child, there was genius between us we believed, and we held hands for the first six months. Then we crashed. After a black night of drink and a quarrel beyond dimension, she lost the baby, it came brokenly to birth, in terror, I always thought, of the womb which was shaping it, came out and went back in again to death, tearing by this miscarriage the hope of any other child for Deborah. What it left behind was a heart-land of revenge. Now, cohabiting with Deborah was like sitting to dinner in an empty castle with no more for host than a butler and his curse. Yes, I knelt in fear, and my skin lived on thin wire, this side of a profound shudder. All the while she stroked my hand.

But compassion, the trapped bird of compassion, struggled up from my chest and flew to my throat. "Deborah, I love you," I said. I did not know at that instant if I meant it truly, or was some monster of deception, hiding myself from myself. And having said it, knew the mistake. For all feeling departed from her hand, even that tingling so evil to my flesh, and left a cool empty touch. I could have been holding a tiny casket in my palm.

"Do you love me, pet?" she asked.

"Yes."

"It must be awful. Because you know I don't love you any more at all."

She said it so quietly, with such a nice finality, that I thought again of the moon and the promise of extinction which had descended on me. I had opened a void—I was now without center. Can you understand? I did not belong to myself any longer. Deborah had occupied my center.

"Yes, you're looking awful again," said Deborah. "You began to look all right for a little while, but now you look awful again."

"You don't love me."

"Oh, not in the least."

"Do you know what it's like to look at someone you love and see no love come back?"

"It must be awful," said Deborah.

"It's unendurable," I said. Yes, the center was gone. In another minute I would begin to grovel.

"It is unendurable," she said. "You do know?"

"Yes, I do."

"You have felt it?"

"There was a man I loved very much," she said, "and he didn't love me."

"You never told me that before."

"No, I didn't."

Before we married, she told me everything. She confessed every last lover— it had been her heritage from the convent: she had done more than tell me, she had gone to detail—we would giggle in the dark while she tapped my shoulder with one cultivated and very learned finger, giving me a sense of the roll and snap and lurch and grace (or lack of it) in each of her lovers, she had even given me a sense of what was good in the best of them, and I had loved her for it, painful as the news had sometimes been, for I had known at least what I was up against, and how many husbands could ever say that? It was the warrant of our love; whatever our marriage had been, that was our covenant, that had been her way of saying I was more valuable than the others.

And now she was inside me, fused at my center, ready to blow the rails.

"You don't mean it," I said.

"I do. There was one man I never told you about. I never told anyone about him. Although once, somebody guessed."

"Who was the man?"

"He was a bullfighter. Marvelous ripe man."

"You're lying."

"Have it your way."

"It wasn't a bullfighter."

"No, it wasn't. It was someone far better than a bullfighter, far greater." Her face had turned plump with malice, and the red mottling had begun to fade. "As a matter of fact, it was the finest and most extraordinary man I ever knew. Delicious. Just a marvelous wild feast of things. I tried to make him jealous once and lost him."

"Who could it be?" I asked.

"Don't bother to hop on one foot and then the other like a three-year-old who's got to go to the Lou. I'm not going to tell you." She took a sip of her rum, and jiggled the tumbler not indelicately, as if the tender circles of the liquor might transmit a message to some distant force, or—better—receive one. "It's going to be a bore not having you here once in a while."

"You want a divorce," I said.

"I think so."

"Like that."

"Not like *that*, darling. *After* all that." She yawned prettily and looked for the moment like a fifteen-year-old Irish maid. "When you didn't come by today to say goodbye to Deirdre . . ."

"I didn't know she was leaving."

"Of course you didn't know. How could you know? You haven't called in two weeks. You've been nuzzling and nipping with your little girls." She did not know that at the moment I had no girl.

"They're not so little any more." A fire had begun to spread in me. It was burning now in my stomach and my lungs were dry as old leaves, my heart had a herded pressure which gave promise to explode. "Give us a bit of the rum," I said.

She handed over the bottle. "Well, they may not be so little any more, but I doubt that, pet. Besides I don't care. Because I made a vow this afternoon. I said to myself that I would never . . ." and then she did not speak the rest of the sentence, but she was talking about something she had done with me and never with anyone else. "No," said Deborah, "I thought: There's no need for that any more. Never again. Not with Steve."

I had taught it to her, but she had developed a pronounced royal taste of her own for that little act. Likely it had become the first of her pleasures.

"Not ever again?" I asked.

"Never. The thought—at least in relation to you, dear sweet—makes me brush my gums with peroxide."

"Well, goodbye to all that. You don't do it so famously if the truth be told."

"Not so famously as your little girls?"

"Not nearly as well as five I could name."

The mottling came back to her neck and shoulders. A powerful odor of rot and musk and something much more violent came from her. It was like the scent of the carnivore in a zoo. This last odor was fearful—it had the breath of burning rubber.

"Isn't that odd?" asked Deborah. "I haven't heard a word of complaint from any new beau."

From the day of our separation she had admitted to no lover. Not until this moment. A sharp sad pain, almost pleasurable, thrust into me. It was replaced immediately by a fine horror.

"How many do you have?" I asked.

"At the moment, pet, just three."

"And you . . ." But I couldn't ask it.

"Yes, darling. Every last little thing. I can't tell you how shocked they were when I began. One of them said: 'Where did you ever learn to root about like that? Didn't know such things went on outside a Mexican whorehouse.' "

"Shut your fucking mouth," I said.

"Lately I've had the most famous practice."

I struck her open-handed across the face. I had meant—some last calm intention of my mind had meant—to make it no more than a slap, but my body was speaking faster than my brain, and the blow caught her on the side of the ear and knocked her half out of bed. She was up like a bull and like a bull she charged. Her head struck me in the stomach (setting off a flash in that forest of nerves) and then she drove one powerful knee at my groin (she fought like a prep-school bully) and missing that, she reached with both hands, tried to find my root and mangle me.

That blew it out. I struck her a blow on the back of the neck, a dead cold chop which dropped her to a knee, and then hooked an arm about her head and put a pressure on her throat. She was strong, I had always known she was strong, but now her strength was huge. For a moment I did not know if I could hold her down, she had almost the strength to force herself up to her feet and lift me in the air, which in that position is exceptional strength even for a wrestler. For ten or twenty seconds she strained in balance, and then her strength began to pass, it passed over to me, and I felt my arm tightening about her neck. My eyes were closed. I had the mental image I was pushing with my shoulder against an enormous door which would give inch by inch to the effort.

One of her hands fluttered up to my shoulder and tapped it gently. Like a gladiator admitting defeat. I released the pressure on her throat, and the door I had been opening began to close. But I had had a view of what was on the other side of the door, and heaven was there, some quiver of jeweled cities shining in the glow of a tropical dusk, and I thrust against the door once more and hardly felt her hand leave my shoulder, I was driving now with force against that door: spasms began to open in me, and my mind cried out then, "Hold back! you're going too far, hold back!" I could feel a series of orders whiplike tracers of light from my head to my arm, I was ready to obey. I was trying to stop, but pulse packed behind pulse in a pressure up to thunderhead; some blackbiled lust, some desire to go ahead not unlike the instant one comes in a woman against her cry that she is without protection came bursting with rage from out of me and my mind exploded in a fireworks of rockets, stars, and hurtling embers, the arm about her neck leaped against the whisper I could still feel murmuring in her throat, and *crack* I choked her harder, and *crack* I choked her again, and *crack* I gave her payment—never halt now—and *crack* the door flew open and the wire tore in her throat, and I was through the door, hatred passing from me in wave after wave, illness as well, rot and pestilence, nausea, a bleak string of salts. I was floating. I was as far into myself as I had ever been and universes wheeled in a dream. To my closed eyes Deborah's face seemed to float off from her body and stare at me in darkness. She gave one malevolent look which said: "There are dimensions to evil which reach beyond the light," and then she smiled like a milkmaid and floated away and was gone. And in the midst of that Oriental splendor of landscape, I felt the lost touch of her finger on my shoulder, radiating some faint but ineradicable pulse of detestation into the new grace. I opened my eyes. I was weary with a most honorable fatigue, and my flesh seemed new. I had not felt so nice since I was twelve. It seemed inconceivable at this instant that anything in life could fail to please. But there was Deborah, dead beside me on the flowered carpet of the floor, and there was no question of that. She was dead, indeed she was dead.

ALAN KAUFMAN

Jew Boy

I WAS PARANOID, PRIDEFUL, and newly arrived in San Francisco off a Greyhound bus with sixty-seven dollars in my pocket.

Carl Little Crow was half African-American, half Native American, a former back-alley drunk from Chicago with eighteen years of sobriety to his name. He was half my size and had a face like an alert animal. He wore an embroidered West African shaman's cap, a cowskin vest, baggy corduroys, and scuffed black shoes, and he carried a befeathered Native American tom-tom drum that he beat as he walked down Haight Street.

The things we did
1. Healing ceremonies atop Buena Vista Park in Haight-Ashbury. Carl claimed that a satanic sacrificial cult was operating in the area, abducting and murdering people, and that as spiritual human beings we must "cleanse" the area with our souls. For this ceremony, Carl's mentor, Roland, drove in from Arizona in a rusted brown station wagon. Also in attendance was Mike, sober ten years, known thereabouts as the Captain of Haight Street.

With only two months booze-free, I was the novice and appointed to carry the healing plant. The healing plant: a ratty-looking lobby shrub with withered leaves that Carl had salvaged from the trash outside a Tenderloin hotel. Carl took the plant home and fed it plant food, sunshine, Native American chants, water, and whispers of love until it was able to lift its head again. It still looked like a shitty plant from a flop hotel but vibrantly alive. And as I carried it, huffing, Carl led the way, chanting in a trance, beating the drum, walking in a slow procession up the slope to the top of the hill.

Deadheads and crack dealers watched us with interest. According to Carl, the devil worshippers were spying on us but chances were excellent that we wouldn't see them. It was strange, I thought, I'd shown up in San Francisco paranoid and delusional, clinging to my sobriety by bloody fingernails, gibbering about being pursued across the continent by devil worshippers, and here was Carl declaring that yes, they do exist, are a definite danger, and now once and for all we will rid the world of them. I felt both terrified and reassured.

Bringing up the rear was the Captain: tall, bone-lean, with a mean-looking handlebar mustache and a combative black beret set at a jaunty angle on his old gray skull. He had cold blue eyes and a big keyring jangling from his belt. He scanned the turf with sweeping looks, warning off anyone with the wrong idea. There's lots of such people around and they know Mike. While he may not beat you one-on-one the first time around, Mike will make it his religion to get even, even if it takes twenty years, and will not cease until you are effaced from the earth. His other hobbies are amateur photography, of which he is a very fine practitioner, and archiving local historical information and artifacts. For instance, he can show you, hidden near a drainage ditch covered over with dead leaves, a row of little white tombstones embedded like teeth into the cement that belong to a party of gold-mining

49ers killed in a drunken brawl " 'round these parts nigh a hunnert and fifty years ago," as Mike would say. Only the accent was an affectation, he was really a marvelously bright and well-educated man whom alcohol had laid low, like the rest of us.

Behind him, at a remove of ten paces, walked Roland, and I was surprised at how average-looking he seemed. Like any road dog you might come across in the Arizona desert. That hermit smile and blue eyes bleached kind by extreme loneliness. He wore just a plain old black T-shirt, stone-scrubbed blue jeans, and embossed leather cowboy boots. He was more a dude than a hierarchically royal medicine man of the Black Foot tribe. But I figured what the hell do I know about it anyway.

My job was to carry and I did. My arms grew heavy. I wanted to drop the damned plant. But I held on as we inched our way up, led by Carl's mournful voice and the boom-boom-boom of the tom-tom, and soon we were at the top, where we proceeded briskly to a ravine and slid down the slope to a wide shelf, which Carl declared to be our healing ground.

It was a godforsaken place of dead trees with amputated branches. We sat in a circle and Carl Little Crow said something in Native American tongue, and Roland nodded and smiled. Then they all looked at me. "What's your spirit animal?" Carl asked. Surprised, I shrugged. "I dunno," I said. Carl's eyes burned into mine. "Name it!" I couldn't think of any. We don't have animals in the Bronx. What should I say: cockroach? Rat? This is how I knew that I was really in California now. Someone named Carl Little Crow asking me to name my spirit animal. "I dunno," I said again. Once more he burned into me with his eyes and said: "Name it! Name it now!" Suddenly the word "hawk" popped into my brain, so I blurted out, "Hawk!" and Carl hissed: "Look up!" and I looked up, and O my God, O my ever-loving fucking God, right there, over us, circling, two of them, enormous, right here in Haight-Ashbury. What are hawks doing here anyhow? And right at this moment no less?! Now I felt the presence of what he called the Great Spirit, what others call God, or whatever they call it. I felt it. And it freaked the living daylights out of me. In a good way.

2. Walking down Haight Street together, Carl beating his drum, me holding onto his shirt, afraid to let go, that if I did I'd go drink. He led me up to trees and stood there talking to them, waving his hands with this ecstatic look on his animal-like face, and nodding his head vigorously with a look of delight, as though answering questions. "What're they saying, Carl?" I'd ask. "They're saying: 'Don't drink!' " he'd reply.

3. Take astral projection trips around the world. Actually, Carl took them while I sat there and watched. Usually we did this in the Café International on Haight and Fillmore. We sat at one of the scratched-up wooden tables embedded with hand-painted tiles, surrounded by electric paintings by young unknown geniuses, World Beat music playing, and Carl would close his eyes and begin to sway from side to side. It would seem as though the colors in the room were running together with acidlike intensity. You know how a GIF looks on your computer if the server crashes, like a kind of graphic ghost? Carl turned into that. If you'd clicked on him, nothing would have happened. He was elsewhere, transported by a spiritual metasearch engine into the hard drive of the Amazon jungle, or appearing on the interactive screen of the Himalayan Mountains. He was rapping with the Dalai Lama. He was reading poetry to the king of Sweden. Once he opened his eyes and I saw two white ghost buffaloes galloping in his eyeballs. When he did this it scared me but I preferred to stay by him rather than take my chances with my own mind, which was detoxing with d.t.'s and hallucinations that were trying to kill me. Each cell of my brain, my body, Carl had explained, had been perforated after years of drinking by a little hole that once I'd filled with alcohol but that now was empty, yearning, yawning, craving, desperate to be filled, an almost sexual need, and that I must fill it with something else now. I must fill it with my soul. I must fill it with the Great Spirit of the Universe. I must learn to know my spirit. That we were like two calling to each other across a great gulf. And that soon we would be reunited. So I sat and watched Carl Little Crow cavort with Dakota sandpainters and Ludwig van Beethoven. Ludwig, Carl informed me, was an abused child, like me.

4. Eat barbecue chicken wings. Carl had a shameless love of barbecue chicken wings. It surprised and disappointed me. I thought someone so spiritual would want to eat, say, a bowl of brown rice and drink a cup of green tea. Instead he'd take me over to Chicken Charlie's on Divisadero and order up big buckets of greasy, orange barbecue chicken wings and get all messed with juices and greases and bone smatterings on his grinning mouth, ecstatically cooing, "Yessss! Oh, yesssssss!" I'd take a nibble off one and smile happily despite myself. It just didn't fit the picture, him tearing at those chicken wings and slurping up a thirty-two-ounce Cherry Coke. He had a bit of a belly, too. But worse still, he had this ugly weal of a scar worming down the center of his chest where'd he'd had open-heart surgery, during which he'd died twice and been revived.

During the time he was dead he had floated above the table, smiling down at everyone, and then left for a few seconds to take an astral projection trip to New York City, where he danced, he said, with a señorita in Spanish Harlem. That too shocked me. I mean, that's all one can think to do at the moment of one's death? Dance with a woman? "Not just any woman," said Carl Little Crow, "a Puerto Rican woman." He jumped up and down in his seat laughing like a happy kid with the grease all over him and I said very gravely: "That shit's real bad for your heart, Carl, and seems like you already had one heart attack . . ."

Carl grew still and I fought back tears but lost and sobbed out: "And what if you die, man! What am I gonna do? How am I gonna stay sober!?" Carl's eyes grew moist and he said: "By helping another," he said. "Remember! It's always by helping another that we are healed ourselves."

And I am crying even now, seven and a half years later, to remember those words.

5. Eat a whole half-gallon of peach melba ice cream. Another of Carl's peculiar weaknesses. He'd have me at night seated on the floor of my tiny room near the Hayes Street projects in the Mo', as we called the Fillmore District, with the guns of battling crack gangs going pop-pop-pop outside our windows, and squealing tires and screaming voices, and a bundle of burning sage smoking in a bowl as we sat and breathed in and out, in and out, watching our breath, calming our bodies. Then we chanted a mantra: "God grant us the serenity to accept the things we cannot change, courage to change the things we can, and the wisdom to know the difference," and then he'd have me up on my feet dancing a slow spirit dance around the room, waving my hands, moving the energy fields around, as he put it. And when we were done, we then adjourned to the communal kitchen that I shared with a bunch of pot-heads and grunge maniacs, and took out a huge half-gallon of peach melba ice cream and two spoons!

The sugar wacked Carl out for sure. His eyes would get all red and he'd feel giddy and sway and stagger as he walked, and for a moment I could see eighteen years ago to the back-alley drunk he must have been, a little lethal menace. And it amazed me that he could have gone so long without a drink and I'd feel hope. Then he'd leave and I'd sometimes find a ten-spot on the bed, maybe his last, since he was always short of money and mostly unconcerned about it. I stretched out on the bed with my boots on, head pillowed on my hands, listening to the gunfire and the shouts and watching the fog roll over the last vestige of the San Francisco moon. I was flat broke, my welfare general assistance due to expire, and all that I had been, a father, a soldier, a lover, a boss, a highly touted this, and a well-regarded that, all lay behind me now. I remembered the park bench where I had laid down to die in Tompkins

Square on Avenue A in Alphabet City and from which I rose to live — damned if I understand to this day how or why — when every blood vessel in my flesh demanded booze and booze and more booze and when this disease I have, this disease of alcoholism, believed that it would continue to drink even after I had died. I found help in the rooms of recovery and, against the advice of the recovered drunks I met, board a bus with sixty-seven dollars in my pocket and a California sun rising in my addled, sleep-deprived, detoxing brain.

And this is what it means to be happy: to want nothing and to sit listening to the calm beating of your own heart as big wheels carry you off into a mystery lined with fast-food concession stands.

6. We got a man to detox. We happened upon him sitting on the steps of a Haight-Ashbury Victorian recovery home that had once been the residence of Janis Joplin, and just a few doors down from where novelist Kathy Acker once lived. (We'd see Kathy in her leather jacket hand-painted with skulls and roses and she, being a real dear woman under that tough exterior, always had a kind word.) He was dressed for business in a tie. He wore spectacles, his hair was thinning, and his hands were trembling violently. An overflowing suitcase lay open on the side-walk and he was staring at its contents and moaning, "Uhhhhhhhhhh, God, uuuuuhhhhhhhhh, oh, God." And Carl said, "What is it, my brother?" and he said, "You God?" and Carl Little Crow breathed out meditatively and said, "No. I am a drunk like you." And the man looked at him angrily, then at me, and snapped, "I'm no drunk!" and burst into tears. "I *am* a drunk! Oh, I am a *terrible* drunk!" he whined. "What happened?" I asked softly.

"My friend lent me his apartment for three days so I got permission to leave the recovery house on a pass and went there and dropped all his acid and drank all his brandy and smashed up the house and I ran back here and they saw that I'd gone out and they threw me into the street! Now I have no place to go! My friend's back by now. He's probably looking to kill me. What'll I do? What'll I do?"

"Go to detox," said Carl. The man looked at him, astonished.

"Detox? I can't go to detox!! I'm middle-class!" How well I understood that pretense. But booze strips us down to our essentials.

"It's your only option," said Carl. And the man nodded his head and sobbed and I went up the street to the phone booth to call the Mobile Assistance Patrol van to take him in. For hours we sat with the man, waiting. And I told him the story of my last run. There I was, I said, living in Park Slope, Brooklyn. Had a sixty-thousand-dollar-a-year job. Married to an English actress and had a one-year-old daughter, a little blonde and blue-eyed angel named Isadora who would say, "Da'ddy, Da'ddy," over and over to herself as though I were ambrosia to her little soul.

Had a garden out back where I'd sit at night in a lawn chair under a tree of heaven counting stars. Had sworn off the liquor for good, figuring that nothing, nothing, must ever spoil my chance for a beautiful life with this little girl, nothing on this earth! Belonged to a gym, too. Got into peak physical condition. Was up for a raise at work, bringing in a lot of new accounts and money. Inside I felt miserable but I thought: "What the hell, I've always been miserable, it's just the way it is for me."

One day on my way home from work, passing through the twilight streets of my little neighborhood, I passed a local tavern, a real nice place for a respectable clientele, and I thought: "Why not? Why the hell not? Don't I deserve it? Look at how beautiful my life is. It'll be the proverbial cherry on the pudding." A bartender dressed in a red Eisenhower jacket was toweling a tumbler dry by candlelight. "Good evening, sir," he said as I settled onto a plush red-leather bar stool and rested my elbows on the polished mahogany counter. "Evening." I smiled with a terse nod. "And what will you be having this evening?" I lifted a finger into the air: "Chivas Regal," I said, and as he turned I lifted a second finger: "Make it a double." When he brought it I held it up to the candlelight and swished it around in the brandy snifter, its golden elegance proclaiming the vigor and achievement of my adulthood. I slammed it down with a gasp and said: "Gimme another," and that came and no candlelit reflection now, just down the hatch, and another and another, the bulkhead filling fast. I don't remember anything after the sixth. I experienced a black roaring pain in my head and my eyes winced open to the vague chilly paleness of a Manhattan dawn sky. I was still dressed in my London Fog raincoat, still clutching my attaché. And I was lying in bushes in the projects on 23rd Street in Chelsea, covered with vomit, urine, and blood. I staggered to my feet to stumble off to work.

And now I tore through my little daughter's life with cyclonic ferocity, took to sleeping at the office on an inflatable Boy Scout mattress and spent the nights in Billy's Topless on Sixth Avenue and 24th Street, one of whose dancing girls was found decapitated and dismembered, her body parts boiled for soup and served up to the homeless in Tompkins Square Park. It was front page in all the papers. They found the killer, too, a local nutcase version of Charles Manson. I remember the girl, a sweet Swedish dancer. I had stuffed a few bills myself into her G-string. It was that kind of place, and those sorts of people. I'd go home only to stuff some of my cashed paycheck into a measuring cup in the cupboard and then leave again to ride the subway back into Manhattan to Billy's. Once, late at night, I came home to leave some money.

My wife didn't even bother to rise from bed. I put the money into the measuring cup and was heading for the door when I heard behind me the patter of little feet and turning saw Isadora, all of a year and a half, rush up and clasp my leg with her tiny arms and press her cheek to my shin and cling there, as if to say: "Please, Daddy, don't go." Never in my life had I ever loved anyone or anything as much as I loved her. I lifted her up, pressed her to me, kissed her cheeks with tears in my eyes, cradled her in my arms, and returned her to her place beside her mother, who lay there in the dark staring wordlessly at the ceiling. Then I turned and left. I went back to Billy's.

When I need to drink, nothing, no one, can stand in my way, I told the drunk on the stairs as we waited for the MAP van. It's not a thing that normies fathom. Nor should they have to. I am living proof that life is not fair, because if life were fair I'd be dead, slaughtered by the way I drank. Yet here I was, sober, and here was my friend and mentor Carl Little Crow with eighteen years. If we can do it, I told our middle-class friend, then so can you. And I knew that he believed me, as only one drunk can believe another who has been down the same road and lived to tell the tale.

7. From across the street a man with glowing eyes leered at me. Farther on a pair of tattooed and toothless motorcycle freaks eyeballed me, plotting my murder, as I hurried down Haight Street. Like the man with glowing eyes, they had been following me for days and were all part of the same conspiracy. So too was a tall black man with a shaved head and wire-rim spectacles who received a signal from them and registered my presence as I passed his Mercedes-Benz. I knew that he thought I was an FDA agent sent to spy on his cocaine-smuggling operation. His eyes promised me a slow, painful death. By the time I reached the corner of Church and Market, I was faint with fear. I looked around for shelter, spotted a shop called Aztec Taqueria, and made for it. But as I crossed the threshold of the steamy little shop, I realized that this was the headquarters of an Aztec sacrificial cult who knew that I knew what they were: I had tricked myself into the lion's lair. Now I was really doomed. I couldn't leave, though. Paralyzed with terror, I stood at the counter. "What'll you have?" asked the counter help, a Mexican with tired eyes. My eyes shifted nervously to the open door of an office near the kitchen. Someone in there was staring at me. There was a video screen monitoring traffic. So that's how they did it! I watched to see if someone would emerge to close the store's front door, trapping me. But the counterman's voice was adamant: "What's it gonna be, man?" "Burrito," I stuttered. "Refried or whole beans?" I didn't know what to answer to this obvious test. The wrong response would unleash hidden minions in white uniforms rushing out from every

corner to throw me onto the counter and hold me down for the high priest with the butcher knife. "For here or to go?" the counterman asked as he wrapped the burrito. He was looking at me strangely. Another test. "Here," I said. It was obviously the right answer. Only I had a plan. With shaking hands I received the burrito and paid him. A cauldron of white-hot panic boiled in my solar plexus as I made my way on wobbly legs to a table and sat down. I stared at the burrito without appetite, sure that a hundred eyes watched to see what I'd do. I must have looked white as a sheet. I just sat there. Had run out of steam. Felt ready to give up, stand, shout: "OK, then, murder me! Murder me!" It is what people who have completely snapped do in public with violent abruptness. Stand up on a bus or on a line, begin to shout about their crossover into the fifth dimension of insanity. Their way of saying that they hereby renounce their residency on Planet Normie. My plan was to sit thus until they, tired of their surveillance, looked away.

I waited, enveloped in sickening fear. Then I jumped up suddenly, burrito in hand, and ran out the door. I hurried down the street, sure they were on my heels, and halfway down the block my legs wobbled and lost all feeling and I sprawled over the sidewalk. I lay there, thirty-seven years old, paralyzed with terror, unable to walk, rise, or speak, certain of imminent execution, not wanting to die, and so alone, so very alone. "Carl," I whispered, "where are you Carl Little Crow? Help me. Help me." And I saw Carl Little Crow's face before my eyes. He said, Pray for help to whatever you call your Great Spirit—ask for protection. And so I did. I called upon the name of God in Hebrew, Elohim, remembered from my Bar Mitzvah, without a clue about what it named or meant. I called out that name in sorrow, anguish, and defeat. And my legs regained sensation. And I stood up. And I began to walk normally. I did not feel the need to hurry. I still felt threatened by death, but walked in the valley of its shadow without fear. This was on Church Street in San Francisco, where later I bought a Jewish prayer shawl for a buck off a junkie selling stolen goods.

8. Carl Little Crow, where are you? Often I think of those times we spent together. It's been over seven years and, can you believe it, I have gone that long without a drink and I have become a poet. It happened because you said to me one day as we walked down Haight Street: "What do you want to do with this great gift that you have been given?"

"You mean sobriety?" I said.

"Yes. How will you use this miracle for the benefit of others?"

I didn't know. I said: "Maybe I should get a good job and set myself up, you know, more comfortably."

And you stopped and looked hard at me. "What were you doing when you went on your last run?"

"Earning sixty grand," I said.

"And was this true to your real nature?"

"Nah," I said. "It wasn't. I knew it. I hated it. And I hated myself."

"And haven't you learned here, 'To thine own self be true?!' Is this not the motto of our recovery? *To thine own self be true!*"

"Yah," I replied.

"So what is it you would do with the gift that is true to your being? Because sobriety is the Great Spirit's gift to you, but what you do with it is your gift to the Great Spirit."

And I said: "Well . . . I've always had this fantasy to be a poet, ya know?"

And you jumped in the air, literally, finger pointing at my eyes, and howled: "Ho! Then that is what you must do! And never waver until the last breath of your life! And remember, the hawk is your spirit, in your work! Call upon him when you most need help!"

And I have done as you advised. Since then I have performed my work before audiences around the world. I live in a beautiful apartment with a woman named Diane, who is a kindergarten teacher. Last year, forgiven by her mother, I flew out to see Isadora, my daughter, so as not to be a phantom in her life: We got along like a house on fire.

Where are you, Carl? Last I heard you were crossing the Southwest on foot. I want you to know how I am. My life is so beautiful now that sometimes I sit in a chair in my study just listening to the sound of my heart. There's a garden outside my window where birds sing. Doves and hummingbirds and sparrows and blue jays and robins. And there's a garden inside of me. There is a pond in which a great blue carp rests at ease in the shadows, unmoving for days.

I miss you, Carl Little Crow. I want to show you this place that I have found within, because it is you who first led me to it and helped me to plant the first seed. I see you laughing with glee, slapping your sides, rolling on the ground. I see you whacking at a coffee can with an oar, trying to get it open because we couldn't find a can opener. I remember you as though you were in this room with me now, strolling like a warrior down Haight Street, the proudest man I have ever known. I remember how your head bobbed like a mongoose and your eyes fixed on me with unflinching compassion when I told you that my mother had been in the Holocaust and had beaten me as a child. You said: "She was wounded and passed her wound to you. But that wound is the flower from which all will grow, if only you don't drink, and instead turn your thoughts to love and service for others." I am crying now as

I write this, Carl Little Crow, unashamed of my feelings, another gift you gave to me. How your face, like a bust carved out of rock by a Mayan, would suddenly bear bright ribbons of tears caused by another's expression of pain.

Do you remember the trees you introduced me to in Golden Gate Park? There was the short black tree with white and yellow blossoms that you asked me to hug, and I did, in front of a group of Japanese tourists. There was the immense redwood that you slapped on the trunk with a shout "Ho! My brother!" and danced around while I stood by, bewildered by your energy and ignorant of your purpose. There was the eucalyptus whose leaves you snapped open under my nose to inhale and later brewed me tea from and told me of its healing properties. I remember how the little black birds that crowd the sidewalk outside the McDonald's on Haight Street would swarm over the sidewalk and sometimes land on your shoulder. Everyone around was too oblivious, consumed with their hamburgers, maybe consumed by them, to notice this extraordinary thing. "Yessssss, little brother," you sighed to the birds. "Ohhhhhhh, how are you, my friends? How is the food-gathering?" And you'd listen. I swear it seemed like they chirped back.

Kenneth Patchen

The Journal of Albion Moonlight

I AM TIRED OF writing on the air. I want to say something that will help you. We are animals together. I have no money. But I have made speeches in the mountains. I have held the body of a dying child in my arms. The road I have come hangs by a thin thread over a pit full of howling beasts. Let us consider. What is of importance? Why are you afraid? I will tell you what things are saddest for me. The cruelest thing of all is that we die. This is wrong. We die because we are animal organisms. Is there any reason for this? That is the heart of the trouble. We resent our human condition. Death is our color and our smell. It is sheer folly to be mortal. Why were we made only to die? Is there any purpose in this? No one has ever been able to find any. Why must we get sick? Why do our teeth ache? What rotten stuff are we made of that our arms and legs break; that our organs fill with pus and rot? But here we are. There is nothing we can do. On what day will you die? What about your head? What stops that? And then we set about slaughtering each other; we torture and debase these poor creatures. I have tried at times to think of man as something foreign to myself—like a bear or a toad; but then any possibility of understanding is lost; we must accept our horrible limitations, we must say, "I am a man-animal and I shall die." Within a century all men now living will be dead. We don't have much of it, do we? If I had been given a choice, I should have much preferred to be a horse or a deer. I tell you that I do not like the pain that is in me. If my thinking cannot alter the fact of our mortality, of what good is it? of what use? This war is important only to us; tomorrow's people will have a new war or a world without war. God grant that it may be easier to live then! War advertises death; death becomes the only player; everything else is forgotten.

We die.

But I have told you that I believe in angels.

I believe in the beautiful.

I am, in fact, an accomplished fool.

So, Roivas, have we found the world. If you are in touch with God, communicate these things to Him. Tell Him how it is with us.

For the sake of your records, I should like to list the following occurrences— or items, notes, observations, whatever—they may prove of use to you.

> (1) Jetter has had thirty-seven boils since we set forth.
> (2) We have spent on actual necessities $6,400.24.
> (3) We have spent on luxuries, such as tobacco, whiskey, talcum powder, taxi fares, whores, and lawyer fees—$2,871.65.
> (4) To date we have covered 21,000 miles—app.
> (5) Carol has had four abortions: three male embryos, one female.
> (6) We were held up and robbed of $700 by six masked gunmen just outside Scranton, Pa. We managed to kill two of them, a short man with a red wig and a very fat man who had a startling birthmark on his left shoulder-blade.
> (7) Billy Delian contracted syphilis in a place in Denver called *Maw Thompson's Haven.*
> (8) Mrs. Drew's condition is somewhat improved.
> (9) We have seen a horned rabbit, a hen's egg having five yolks, a goat that spoke passable French, and a king with a bottom constructed of steel and cork.

(10) Chrystle was murdered and raped by a person or persons unknown (as yet).

(11) We are wanted by the police.

(12) I found the body of a sparrow under an apple tree; its lungs had collapsed under the concussion of a great shell.

(13) Something snuffs upon the air above my head.

(14) Your wanderer taps at the invisible gate.

(15) My cathedral was so beautiful that the workmen who built it were moved to worship there.

(16) I have a blinding pain at the back of my head.

(17) What have men to do with goals? who spend their lives flying from themselves—their only goal.

(18) What will you say with your last breath?

(19) Be quiet in your heart and the noise of the world will die into nothingness.

(20) O everlasting confession! How we belly through the slime seeking—not a disease to kill the God Who put us there—but seeking to be pure in His ghoulish sight!

(21) We shall enter Galen on August 27th.

(22) Thomas Honey is quite blind now.

(23) I beheld you in a dream. You were singing a song made of blue satin and water lilies.

(24) The man with moss and nettles growing from his shoulders is bathed publicly every afternoon in a store window in Memphis.

(25) Jackeen wears a size 3A shoe.

(26) We shall have good things to tell you later of our trip to sea.

(27) Can you sew a dress without a seam? I asked Carol. So it wouldn't seem what? she answered.

(28) Our supply of salt is running low.

Allow me to interrupt this to say that we have just received word that Billy Delian has been elected President of the United States.

(29) I saw a beautiful woman in Houston, Texas. An enormous, rough wen grew from her cheek. She held out a penny and a little tin pig—"Take one," she offered.

(30) In my dream a drowned man sobbed out his love for the holy and luminous sea.

(31) The panther who broods with yellow tears on the unforgettable island where I shall go to my sleep . . .

(32) I am wide-awake! What a fantastic martyr I would make! Everlasting . . . eternal *doubt*. But I am amiable and shrunken under the leprous caresses of my parasites. Gentlemen! Ho! Ho! Heg!

(33) The hooded alleys and the monster in the pat of butter . . . I do not boast of my power. I shall murder out of tenderness; out of a frightful desire to be *charitable*.

(34) To those I have loved . . . this cruel glory. This stained contortion as a man stands upright—do you understand? do you hear? Great God do you hear me! The hand grows still and cold.

I tell you that I love Carol. She excites me with her art—she is an artist in making men suffer. This is her life, her possessed joy. Our courtship was carried on under the eyes of her husband, a dealer in flowered carpets and eccentric furniture. She despised him with all her heart; her first entry into my arms was made to torture him. The poor man was devoured by grief; he put a bullet through his head on a night when we were enchanting ourselves in her bed. He came into the room and stood above us with the revolver in his hand; she held me to my carnal position on her. "Get it over with," she told him; "kill me while I am like this." His eyes were full of tears. He smiled at her, then lifted the pistol to his head and fired. I attempted to rise; she would not suffer me to do so. A woman! Yes, Roivas, a woman . . . I felt remorse that I should have been an actor in that little farce. "He was always a fool," she said, stepping over his body to the chair where she had thrown her clothes.

The police declared his death a suicide; but it was the basest kind of murder. Her children were sent to a home for orphans.

She does not ask God for forgiveness. She lives for the night and a man in bed with her. Jetter . . . Billy Delian . . . *even the innkeeper* . . . (she confessed this herself) . . . she will call in a stranger from the street.

But she is pure and good, Roivas; this you must believe. She has been my comfort in time of terrible need. She is quite without jealousy; my possession of Jackeen would give her joy. It worries her that this is denied me. She even schemes that this dream of mine may succeed. Her ingenuity in this is surprising; she has a genius for intrigue. She has the winsomeness of a child as she attempts to persuade Jackeen into my arms. Secretly, she despises both of us. Her hatred of Joseph Gambetta is savage and sinister; she has a terror of that other world. News of Chrystle's death was honey on her heart.

She wears clothes with a style and dash that is the envy of all the women we have met on our journey. With a colored pin and a yard of wool she can gown herself like an empress. Her feet are large and the toes have a tendency to spread; one of her pleasures is to caress me with them—like a monkey's hand moving in ancient vice. Her aptitude for cleanliness is not strained; at times the gentle rain from heaven will furnish her only bath. Dirt has gathered under her fingernails, which she keeps long in order to ease the sting of bites from the colonies of bug-life with which she is infested. She eats noisily and in an uncouth manner; as a breaker of wind her finesse is deplorable. But she has a charm and manner that are completely winning; forest pools seem to lurk in the hollows where her eyes are. Her thighs are superbly rounded and firm; notwithstanding the presence of innumerable moles, her breasts display a beauty that is rare in this world.

Thomas Honey is drawn to her, but he will not permit himself so much as a kiss on the spine of her hand. He is content to give her tangerines and chocolate squares, which are a passion with her. There isn't a sloppy novel that she hasn't read; she cons the best-seller lists with an avidity that would do credit to a Maine schoolteacher. She especially likes the *How-to-do-it* books, but the particular one she'd like to see will probably never be published. It is scarcely necessary to say that she knows nothing of modern French and Spanish writers of the eclectic school. Similarly the formal architecture of a work of prose art is worse than lost on her. In her cultural ink-pot Stendhal does not exist. She sits in the gaudy shell of a protestant provincialism that is well-nigh blinding in its drabness.

But life will not fail her. Her heart is not with the dead. I rake the serpents out of her active fire and we feed on them together; as children, watching an idiot put a blue sleeve on his useless sex, are wont to say, "Now he has a metaphysical distinction, at least."—so Carol and I adorn ourselves in the winged and unimmaculate gloom. Ah, I feel so tender to her . . . *I could eat her.* Supposing she were laid in the ground—she will be dead with Shakespeare. Light! Light! I want light! I am sick of this darkness! My mother, gleaming in her talk, shakes her music in the grave . . . I thought how this life, the life I have in me, will go down below the gray wall where Beethoven lies, and I started a jig with a murdered gentleman whom I know, hands together, pit, pat, left foot—are you fond of Donatello? my sides ache! there they sit, the whole bloody shebang, drinking spider-milk from the hollow, wooden figure of a fatted calf—put a marinated star in my julep, Claude—and that Maid of Athens, did they wrap her in the winding sheet with the little pink bunnies on it? O Helas! Helas! I weep for John the Brown. The shadows begin to stir . . . crosses swing up with their horrible burdens . . . morning star, bring my love back to me . . . I am not to be hanged until the day breaks o'er yonder hill . . . then we can all go home and the bells tolling, tolling over our cold

graves. I shall put on my silver shoes and walk up and down out of the world.
Swing low, swift bomber . . . I thought how I would put flowers in her hair.
The lantern leans to the bitter end . . . SHEPHERD, WHY DO YOU KILL
YOUR SHEEP? *What do you want of me!*

PAUL BOWLES

The Sheltering Sky

AND SUDDENLY SHE STEPPED inside—a slim, wild-looking girl with great
dark eyes. She was dressed in spotless white, with a white turbanlike head-
dress that pulled her hair tightly backward, accentuating the indigo designs
tattooed on her forehead. Once inside the tent, she stood quite still, looking
at Port with something of the expression, he thought, the young bull often
wears as he takes the first few steps into the glare of the arena. There was
bewilderment, fear, and a passive expectancy in her face as she stared quietly
at him.

"Ah, here she is!" said Smaïl, still in a hushed voice. "Her name is
Marhnia." He waited a bit. Port rose and stepped forward to take her hand.
"She doesn't speak French," Smaïl explained. Without smiling, she touched
Port's hand lightly with her own and raised her fingers to her lips. Bowing,
she said, in what amounted almost to a whisper: *"Ya sidi, la bess âlik? Eglès,
baraka 'laou'fik."* With gracious dignity and a peculiar modesty of movement,
she unstuck the lighted candle from the chest, and walked across to the back
of the tent, where a blanket stretched from the ceiling formed a partial
alcove. Before disappearing behind the blanket, she turned her head to
them, and said, gesturing: *"Agi! Agi menah!"* The two men followed her
into the alcove, where an old mattress had been laid on some low boxes in
an attempt to make a salon. There was a tiny tea table beside the improvised
divan, and a pile of small, lumpy cushions lay on the mat by the table. The
girl set the candle down on the bare earth and began to arrange the cushions
along the mattress.

"Essmah!" she said to Port, and to Smaïl: *"Tsekellem bellatsi."* Then she
went out. He laughed and called after her in a low voice: *"Fhemtek!"* Port was
intrigued by the girl, but the language barrier annoyed him, and he was even

more irritated by the fact that Smaïl and she could converse together in his presence. "She's gone to get fire," said Smaïl. "Yes, yes," said Port, "but why do we have to whisper?" Smaïl rolled his eyes toward the tent's entrance. "The men in the other tent," he said.

Presently she returned, carrying an earthen pot of bright coals. While she was boiling the water and preparing the tea, Small chatted with her. Her replies were always grave, her voice hushed but pleasantly modulated. It seemed to Port that she was much more like a young nun than a café dancer. At the same time he did not in the least trust her, being content to sit and marvel at the delicate movements of her nimble, henna-stained fingers as she tore the stalks of mint apart and stuffed them into the little teapot.

When she had sampled the tea several times and eventually had found it to her liking, she handed them each a glass, and with a solemn air sat back on her haunches and began to drink hers. "Sit here," said Port, patting the couch beside him. She indicated that she was quite happy where she was, and thanked him politely. Turning her attention to Smaïl, she proceeded to engage him in a lengthy conversation during which Port sipped his tea and tried to relax. He had an oppressive sensation that daybreak was near at hand—surely not more than an hour or so away, and he felt that all this time was being wasted. He looked anxiously at his watch; it had stopped at five minutes of two. But it was still going. Surely it must be later than that. Marhnia addressed a question to Smaïl which seemed to include Port. "She wants to know if you have heard the story about Outka, Mimouna and Aïcha," said Smaïl. "No," said Port. "*Goul lou, goul lou,*" said Marhnia to Smaïl, urging him.

"There are three girls from the mountains, from a place near Marhnia's bled, and they are called Outka, Mimouna and Aïcha." Marhnia was nodding her head slowly in affirmation, her large soft eyes fixed on Port. "They go to seek their fortune in the M'Zab. Most girls from the mountains go to Alger, Tunis, here, to earn money, but these girls want one thing more than everything else. They want to drink tea in the Sahara." Marhnia continued to nod her head; she was keeping up with the story solely by means of the place-names as Smaïl pronounced them.

"I see," said Port, who had no idea whether the story was a humorous one or a tragic one; he was determined to be careful, so that he could pretend to savor it as much as she clearly hoped he would. He only wished it might be short.

"In the M'Zab the men are all ugly. The girls dance in the cafés of Ghardaia, but they are always sad; they still want to have tea in the Sahara." Port glanced again at Marhnia. Her expression was completely serious. He nodded his head again. "So, many months pass, and they are still in the M'Zab, and they are very, very sad, because the men are all so ugly. They are very ugly there, like pigs. And they don't pay enough money to the poor girls so they can go and have tea in the Sahara." Each time he said "Sahara," which he pronounced in the Arabic fashion, with a vehement accent on the first syllable, he stopped for a moment. "One day a Targui comes, he is tall and handsome, on a beautiful mehari; he talks to Outka, Mimouna and Aïcha, he tells them about the desert, down there where he lives, his bled, and they listen, and their eyes are big. Then he says: 'Dance for me,' and they dance. Then he makes love with all three, he gives a silver piece to Outka, a silver piece to Mimouna, and a silver piece to Aïcha. At daybreak he gets on his mehari and goes away to the south. After that they are very sad, and the M'Zabi look uglier than ever to them, and they only are thinking of the tall Targui who lives in the Sahara." Port lit a cigarette; then he noticed Marhnia looking expectantly at him, and he passed her the pack. She took one, and with a crude pair of tongs elegantly lifted a live coal to the end of it. It ignited immediately, whereupon she passed it to Port, taking his in exchange. He smiled at her. She bowed almost imperceptibly.

"Many months go by, and still they can't earn enough money to go to the Sahara. They have kept the silver pieces, because all three are in love with the Targui. And they are always sad. One day they say: 'We are going to finish like this—always sad, without ever having tea in the Sahara—so now we must go anyway, even without money.' And they put all their money together, even the three silver pieces, and they buy a teapot and a tray and three glasses, and they buy bus tickets to El Goléa. And there they have only a little money left, and they give it all to a bachhamar who is taking his caravan south to the Sahara. So he lets them ride with his caravan. And one night, when the sun is going to go down, they come to the great dunes of sand, and they think: 'Ah, now we are in the Sahara; we are going to make tea.' The moon comes up, all the men are asleep except the guard. He is sitting with the camels playing his flute." Smaïl wriggled his fingers in front of his mouth. "Outka, Mimouna and Aïcha go away from the caravan quietly with their tray and their teapot and their glasses. They are going to look for the highest dune so they can see all the Sahara. Then they are going to make tea. They walk a long time. Outka says: 'I see a high dune,' and they go to it and climb up to the top. Then Mimouna says: I see a dune over there. It's much higher and we can see all the way to In Salah from it.' So they go to it, and it is much higher. But when they get to the top, Aïcha says: 'Look! There's the highest dune of all. We can see to Tamanrasset. That's where the Targui lives.' The sun came up and they kept walking. At noon they were very hot. But they

American Renegades

came to the dune and they climbed and climbed. When they got to the top they were very tired and they said: 'We'll rest a little and then make tea.' But first they set out the tray and the teapot and the glasses. Then they lay down and slept. And then"— Smaïl paused and looked at Port—"Many days later another caravan was passing and a man saw something on top of the highest dune there. And when they went up to see, they found Outka, Mimouna and Aïcha; they were still there, lying the same way as when they had gone to sleep. And all three of the glasses," he held up his own little tea glass, "were full of sand. That was how they had their tea in the Sahara."

Eileen Myles

Cool for You

I BET YOU NEVER heard of Vulcan. That was my favorite thing. An early Polish astronomer, Pierscienewicz, cited a tiny tiny planet, not an asteroid, but a planet, a sphere fulfilling all the elliptical characteristics of planetary solar revolutions, and it was even closer than Mercury to the sun. I never cared much about Mercury. But Vulcan was of particular interest to me because this one scientist had spotted it, and then there were a smattering of other reports during the mid-seventeenth century, of a teeny orange planet going around and around. There are no twentieth century sightings of Vulcan, none at all. Mainly it's the seventeenth century that harbored the Baroque notion that if you think Mercury's hot, we've got something even smaller faster and hotter for you, this clanging fierce-armed god of liquid fire. For me this planet practically had ears, it was the devil, or something really wild.

Because I suspected I was the only 20th century enthusiast of this planet, I treasured this spot in the solar system, even if it was now blank. What could have happened to my little planet. Tumbled into the inferno of our solar system, just fell off its axis or something, cracked down the middle from the heat of the sun, and maybe two pieces of Vulcan broke into four then sixteen. Perhaps a huge lick of the sun's tongue picked up poor Vulcan and flung him into the orbit of another planet, not exactly, but maybe in the neighborhood of Jupiter and Mars, becoming those not very interesting pieces of space dust, the asteroids.

I pulled a number two pencil off my night table and I did something I never do. See I have a total reverence for books. Maybe once on a library book I got really nervous. I think I went crazy. You're not supposed to get a library book dirty in any way, so I took a ballpoint pen and scribbled like crazy, then closed it instantly, feeling sick. Then I repaired it thoughtfully. Got a very soft eraser and gently went over the spot, rubbing. I got most of it out, and then it was due. I slid it onto the librarian's desk with a sense that this could be the end of my membership to my favorite place in the world, the best smelling, the most private, the most exciting. I have to tell you there's something about the library that always made me so happy I had to take a tremendous dump. Sometimes I had to run home, if some other kid was in there. I looked around and everywhere I could see there were more books, they would never run out, and it was free and it was quiet and I belonged. Smash. I threw my book down and ran to the toilet.

The children's library smelled different. I remember that.

But let me tell you about the book I owned. My special secret about Vulcan. It was a Collier's Junior Classic, no. 6, Greek & Roman Myths. I took a yellow pencil and I wrote carefully on the page that's glued to the inside of the book, before the book starts, and there was some uniform design there that was on the inside of all the volumes of this beautiful set of books that I owned. I wrote the secret of Vulcan, my loyalty to this planet, and the manner in which my tiny orange planet came to its end. I knew that someday I would be a famous scientist and they would find my books from my childhood and it would be incredible that even as a child she was thinking so much about science and had discovered something, the death of a planet. Later on I grew ashamed. That very same year, and I erased my theory, but it's there in the book, you can see the smudge and faintly make out the word "Vulcan."

Let me rip through the rest of the solar system while we're there. My grandmother died when I was seven. I imagine my little body sitting in school in the classroom that had its own special effects. Some days the sounds of the rulers and the chalk and the nun's voice would go all funny, like a rumbling beneath it. It was like I was going deaf. It became a dream, school, the regularity of our uniforms, the nun's habit, everything conspired to be regular, but in fact it wasn't. It was simply untrue, a momentary dream world, and I knew this sitting some days in school when everything echoed and wiggled and I was alone.

The Solar System, by Eileen Myles. Mercury, as we've mentioned, is a bore. Tiny, yellowish green. No characteristics, too hot for plant life. Maybe in about a million years when the sun cools down it will become fertile. Today, zilch.

Earth, blue. Blue and brown which are good colors to wear on this planet. Standing on Earth you think the color of the universe is blue, but it is not. It doesn't have a color. Color is a toy for people on this planet. They see everything in terms of it. Their heart would be broken if they knew it didn't exist. For instance it's not so odd that the greatest astronomers in history are from Poland and Italy. Especially Italy. Have you been there? There's a richness of landscape, and the beautiful red food (pasta) and of course the people are better looking than people anywhere in the world, and if you enjoy the Italian painting which I do, then it's clear you're kind of standing at the butthole of the illusion of beauty on the human planet, Earth, and from Italy they're so happy they even look at the sky, and enjoy the stars and eventually they aimed and focused their telescopes and discovered the planets. There's something loungey about the Poles as well. They have great legs. They love art, that's just a fact, and somehow art and astronomy are right next to each other, not just in the alphabet, but if your eye is hungry for God, for seeing him and you know you never will, there's this longing you live with in the light of the day and at night you find it in the stars, this sadness you know and you want to go home. They say when you die you move towards the light, and I say what else is new. I mean, are we on the same planet? I'll do a few more.

I think I did Earth. The waves splash. The nicest thing about the Earth is the sea. It's kind of like the sun, but it's wet. Gulls fly above the ocean. It recedes and everything that was covered, rocks and sticks and thousands of pebbles, sits there in the drool of the Earth's mouth, is momentarily exposed, it's like it's drawing its breath. It has moods, it has emotions, the Earth . . . I mean the sea does. It's kind of like a mirror. Echoes the heavens, absolutely the Moon, so if you want to know what's going on on the Moon, look at the Earth. The Earth is like New York. If you watch too closely, you'll forget everything you ever learned. Everything you know. It's busy, but there's nothing. So if you want to see nothing, look at the Moon. It is nothing. Which I like a lot. People are always comparing things to the Moon. I do it too. Like the back of my house. People compare asses to moons. Every big white face. But the Moon is emptier than that. It's reflective stone. It's like an altar flying through space, one without ritual, just going around and around. I keep changing my mind about whether the men who went there disturbed the Moon's privacy. Nobody cares about that. I do.

WILLIAM S. BURROUGHS

Junky

I WAS IN A cheap cantina off Dolores Street, Mexico City. I had been drinking for about two weeks. I was sitting in a booth with three Mexicans, drinking tequila. The Mexicans were fairly well dressed. One of them spoke English. A middle-aged, heavy-set Mexican with a sad, sweet face sang songs and played the guitar. He was sitting at the end of a booth in a chair. I was glad the singing made conversation impossible.

Five cops came in. I figured I might get a shake, so I slipped the gun and holster out of my belt and dropped them under the table with a piece of hop I had stashed in a cigarette package. The cops had a quick beer and took off.

When I reached under the table, my gun was gone but the holster was there.

I was sitting in another bar with the Mexican who spoke English. The singer and the other two Mexicans were gone. The place was suffused with a dim yellow light. A moldy-looking bullhead mounted on a plaque hung over the mahogany bar. Pictures of bullfighters, some autographed, decorated the walls. The word "saloon" was etched in the frosted-glass swinging door. I found myself reading the word "saloon" over and over. I had the feeling of coming into the middle of a conversation.

I inferred from the expression of the other man that I was in mid-sentence, but did not know what I had said or what I was going to say or what the discussion was about. I thought we must be talking about the gun. "I am probably trying to buy it back." I noticed the man had the piece of hop in his hand, and was turning it over.

"So you think I look like a junkie?" he said.

I looked at him. The man had a thin face with high cheekbones. The eyes were a gray-brown color often seen in mixed Indian and European stock. He was wearing a light gray suit and a tie. His mouth was thin, twisted down at the corners. A junkie mouth, for sure. There are people who look like junkies and aren't, just as some people look queer and aren't. It's a type that causes trouble.

"I'm going to call a cop," he said, starting for a phone attached to a support pillar.

I jerked the telephone out of the man's hand and pushed him against the bar so hard he bounced off it. The man smiled at me. His teeth were covered by a brown film. He turned his back and called the bartender over and showed him the piece of hop. I walked out and got a cab.

I remember going back to my apartment to get another gun—a heavy-caliber revolver. I was in a hysterical rage, though exactly why I cannot, in retrospect, understand.

I got out of a taxi and walked down the street and into the bar. The man was leaning against the bar, his gray coat pulled tight over his thin back and shoulders. He turned an expressionless face to me.

I said, "Walk outside ahead of me."

"Why, Bill?" he asked.

"Go on, walk."

I flipped the heavy revolver out of my waistband, cocking it as I drew, and stuck the muzzle in the man's stomach. With my left hand, I took hold of the man's coat lapel and shoved him back against the bar. It did not occur to me until later that the man had used my correct first name and that the bartender probably knew it too.

The man was perfectly relaxed, his face blank with controlled fear. I saw someone approaching from behind on my right side, and half turned my head. The bartender was closing in with a cop. I turned around, irritated at the interruption. I shoved the gun in the cop's stomach.

"Who asked you to put in your two cents?" I asked in English. I was not talking to a solid three-dimensional cop. I was talking to the recurrent cop of my dreams—an irritating, nondescript, darkish man who would rush in when I was about to take a shot or go to bed with a boy.

The bartender grabbed my arm, twisting it to one side out of the cop's stomach. The cop stolidly hauled out his battered .45 automatic, placing it firmly against my body. I could feel the coldness of the muzzle through my thin cotton shirt. The cop's stomach stuck out. He had not sucked it in or leaned forward. I relaxed my hold on the gun and felt it leave my hand. I half-raised my hands, palm out in a gesture of surrender.

"All right, all right," I said, and then added, "*bueno*."

The cop put away his .45. The bartender was leaning against the bar examining the gun. The man in the gray suit stood there without any expression at all.

"*Esta cargado*,"—("It's loaded")—said the bartender, without looking up from the gun.

I intended to say, "Of course—what good is an unloaded gun?" but I did not say anything. The scene was unreal and flat and pointless, as though I had forced my way into someone else's dream, the drunk wandering out on to the stage.

And I was unreal to the others, the stranger from another country. The bartender looked at me with curiosity. He gave a little shrug of puzzled disgust and slipped the gun into his waistband. There was no hate in the room. Perhaps they would have hated me if I had been closer to them.

The cop took me firmly by the arm. "*Vámanos gringo*," he said.

I walked out with the cop. I felt limp and had difficulty controlling my legs. Once I stumbled, and the cop steadied me. I was trying to convey the idea that, while I had no money on my person, I could borrow some "*de amigos*." My brain was numb. I mixed Spanish and English and the word for borrow was hidden in some filing cabinet of the mind cut off from my use by the mechanical barrier of alcohol-numbed connections. The cop shook his head. I was making an effort to reform the concept. Suddenly the cop stopped walking.

"*Ándale, gringo*," he said, giving me a slight push on the shoulder. The cop stood there for a minute, watching as I walked on down the street. I waved. The cop did not respond. He turned and walked back the way he had come.

I had one peso left. I walked into a cantina and ordered a beer. There was no draft beer and bottle beer cost a peso. There was a group of young Mexicans at the end of the bar, and I got talking to them. One of them showed me a Secret Service badge. Probably a phony, I decided. There's a phony cop in every Mexican bar. I found myself drinking a tequila. The last thing I remembered was the sharp taste of the lemon I sucked with the glass of tequila.

I woke up next morning in a strange room. I looked around. Cheap joint. Five pesos. A wardrobe, a chair, a table. I could see people passing outside, through the drawn curtains. Ground floor. Some of my clothes were heaped on the chair. My coat and shirt lay on the table.

I swung my legs out of the bed, and sat there trying to remember what happened after that last glass of tequila. I drew a blank. I got out of bed and took inventory of my effects. "Fountain pen gone. It leaked anyway . . . never had one that didn't . . . pocket-knife gone . . . no loss either . . ." I began putting on my clothes. I had the shakes bad. "Need a few quick beers . . . maybe I can catch Rollins home now."

It was a long walk. Rollins was in front of his apartment, walking his Norwegian elk-hound. He was a solidly built man of my age, with strong, handsome features and wiry, black hair a little gray at the temples. He was wearing an expensive sports shirt, whipcord slacks, and a suede leather jacket. We had known each other for thirty years.

Rollins listened to my account of the previous evening. "You're going to get your head blown off carrying that gun," he said. "What do you carry it for? You wouldn't know what you were shooting at. You bumped into trees twice there on Insurgentes. You walked right in front of a car. I pulled you back and you threatened me. I left you there to find your own way home, and I don't know how you ever made it. Everyone is fed up with the way you've been acting lately. If there's one thing I don't want to be around, and I think no one else particularly wants to be around, it's a drunk with a gun."

"You're right, of course," I said.

"Well, I want to help you in any way I can. But the first thing you have to do is cut down on the sauce and build up your health. You look terrible. Then you'd better think about making some money. Speaking of money, I guess you're broke, as usual." Rollins took out his wallet. "Here's fifty pesos. That's the best I can do for you."

I got drunk on the fifty pesos. About nine that night, I ran out of money and went back to my apartment. I lay down and tried to sleep. When I closed my eyes I saw an Oriental face, the lips and nose eaten away by disease. The disease spread, melting the face into an amoeboid mass in which the eyes floated, dull crustacean eyes. Slowly, a new face formed around the eyes. A series of faces, hieroglyphs, distorted and leading to the final place where the human road ends, where the human form can no longer contain the crustacean horror that has grown inside it.

I watched curiously. "I got the horrors," I thought matter of factly.

I woke up with a start of fear. I lay there, my heart beating fast, trying to find out what had scared me. I thought I heard a slight noise downstairs. "There is someone in the apartment," I said aloud, and immediately I knew that there was.

I took my 30-30 carbine out of the closet. My hands were shaking; I could barely load the rifle. I dropped several cartridges on the floor before I got two in the loading slot. My legs kept folding under me. I went downstairs and turned on all the lights. Nobody. Nothing.

I had the shakes bad, and on top of that I was junk sick! "How long since I've had a shot?" I asked myself. I couldn't remember. I began ransacking the apartment for junk. Some time before, I had stashed a piece of hop in a hole in one corner of the room. The hop had slid under the floorboards, out of reach. I had made several abortive attempts to recover it.

"I'll get it this time," I said grimly. With shaking hands, I made a hook out of a coat-hanger and began fishing for the hop. The sweat ran down my nose. I skinned my hands on the jagged wood edges of the hole. "If I can't get to it one way, I will another," I said grimly, and began looking for the saw.

I couldn't find it. I rushed from one room to the other, throwing things around and emptying drawers on the floor in a mounting frenzy. Sobbing with rage, I tried to rip the boards up with my hands. Finally, I gave up and lay on the floor panting and whimpering.

I remembered there was some dionin in the medicine chest. I got up to look. Only one tablet left. The tablet cooked up milky and I was afraid to shoot it in the vein. A sudden involuntary jerk of my hand pulled the needle out of my arm and the shot sprayed over my skin. I sat there looking at my arm.

I finally slept a little and woke up next morning with a terrific alcohol depression. Junk sickness, suspended by codeine and hop, numbed by weeks of constant drinking, came back on me full force. "I have to have some codeine," I thought.

I looked through my clothes. Nothing, not a cigarette, not a centavo. I went into the living room and reached into the sofa, where the sofa back joined the seat. I ran my hand along it. A comb, a piece of chalk, a broken pencil, one ten-centavo piece, one five. I felt a sickening shock of pain and pulled my hand out. I was bleeding from a deep cut in my finger. A razor blade, evidently. I tore off a piece of towel and wrapped it around my finger. The blood soaked through and dripped on the floor. I sent my wife out to try and borrow some money. She said, "We have about burned everybody down. But I will try." I went back to bed. I couldn't sleep. I couldn't read. I lay there looking at the ceiling, with the cellular stoicism that junk bestows on the user.

A matchbox sailed past the door into the bathroom. I sat up, my heart pounding. "Old Ike, the pusher!" Ike often sneaked into the house and manifested his presence like a poltergeist, throwing something or knocking on the walls. Old Ike appeared in the doorway.

"How you getting along?" he asked.

"Not so good. I got the shakes. I need a shot."

Ike nodded. "Yeah," he began, "M is the thing for the shakes. I remember once in Minneapolis—"

"Never mind Minneapolis. Have you got any?"

"I got it, but not with me. Take me about twenty minutes to get it." Old Ike was sitting down, leafing through a magazine. He looked up. "Why? You want some?"

"Yes."

"I'll get it right away." Ike was gone two hours.

"I had to wait for the guy to get back from lunch to open the safe in the hotel. I keep my stuff in the safe so nobody makes me for it. I tell 'em at the hotel it's gold dust I use—"

"But you got it?"

"Yes, I got it. Where is your works?"

"In the bathroom."

Ike came back from the bathroom with the works and began cooking up a shot. He kept talking. "You're drinking and you're getting crazy. I hate to see you get off this stuff and on something worse. I know so many that quit the junk. A lot of them can't make it with Lupita. Fifteen pesos for a paper and it takes three to fix you. Right away they start in drinking and they don't last more than two or three years."

"Let's have that shot," I said.

"Yes. Just a minute. The needle is stopped." Ike began feeling along the edge of his coat lapel, looking for a horsehair to clean out the needle. He went on talking: "I remember once out by Mary Island. We was on the boat and the Colonel got drunk and fell in the water and come near drowning with his two pistolas. We had a hell of a time to get him out." Ike blew through the needle. "Clear now. I see a guy used to be a hip down by Lupita's. They called him *El Sombrero* because he makes it grabbing people's hats and running. Comes up by a streetcar just when it starts. Reaches in and grabs a hat and *pfut*—he's gone. You should see him now. His legs all swelled up and covered with sores and dirty, oh my God! The people walk around him like this." Ike was standing with the dropper in one hand and the needle in the other.

I said, "How about that shot?"

"O.K. How much you want? About five centogramos? Better make it five."

The shot was a long time taking effect. It hit slowly at first, then with mounting force. I lay back on the bed like I was in a warm bath.

JOHN O'BRIEN

Leaving Las Vegas

TIME HAS BECOME VERY important to him, much more important than it was when he had a job. Too many times he has awakened at three a.m., having passed out the previous evening, only to find nothing alcoholic in the house. He has felt the panic increase exponentially as the minutes click off the eternity between him and the legally wet world of six a.m. His carefully laid stockpiles, meant to carry him over the tundra of two to six, were often consumed blindly from the abyss, after the line of careful laying had been crossed. Once he gave up and rushed to the all night convenience store, where he was grateful for the privilege of overpaying for a family size bottle of Listerine. Eight minutes later, parked in front of his apartment, the bottle was half empty and he had begun to calm down. He shut off the car, stopped the internal combustion.

So his life is punctuated by legislative break points and red flags of custom. At six a.m. the hardcore bars open and the stores can sell, though they sometimes choose to withhold, imposing their morality on some poor, sweating, shaking mess looking for his fix. Nine a.m. is considered a safe opening time for the bars that don't like to admit that people drink that early but can't let the business slip completely away; bartenders in these places tend to pause disapprovingly for an imperceptible moment before handing over a drink. The next milestone is eleven-thirty. At eleven-thirty everyone is willing to admit that the drinking day has begun and they proudly open their doors and pour their drinks. It's smooth sailing until midnight, when, if they haven't already, the more reputable bars bail out. Any place that stays open past midnight is probably good until two—actually one-forty-five—the most important time of all. Never let two o'clock happen unless there is more liquor in the house than you could possibly drink in four hours—no small quantity.

It takes about five hours to drive from Los Angeles to Nevada, land of anytime alcohol, and there are no commercial flights at that hour. Teasing, gnawing, when you're out of liquor at two-thirty in the morning it looms, conceptually bad, in the back of your head. Ben has often thought it through, but it's just not a solution; by the time he would get there the bars would be open in LA.

It's ten-thirty-one. Ben drains his glass and stands up. He mutters, "thank you," and turns toward the door without waiting for an acknowledgment. Outside it's still overcast—spring in Los Angeles. He walks straight and sure to his car. He feels okay, swinging up.

On his way home, having stopped off at a liquor store for a can of beer to drive by, Ben feels elated. His day is in gear and he has everything to look forward to; he has a plan. Things will tick along fine now. He turns up the radio and thinks about what album to listen to while he gets dressed. Checking his pocket, though he already knows its contents, he confirms that he'll need to stop at the automated teller machine.

Money, money. He's going through a ton of money these days. When he lost his job last week he gained a sizable final check; his former employer really liked him and felt terribly guilty about having to fire him. Never mind that he unwittingly delayed the dismissal meeting by staying all morning at the bar and, after checking in with the receptionist, was on his way out for an early lunch when his boss caught up with him. Ironically, had he known what was in store for him that morning, he would have made it a point to be on time; he is very conscientious in that way. So they called him in—by then he did know what for—and asked him to leave. He felt so bad, not that he was being fired, but because his boss was on the verge of tears. How could he blame them? For the last year and a half his daily routine had been: Come in late, say eleven; flirt with the receptionist; go to lunch early, eleven-thirty; return from lunch late, about three; copy must-do list from today's calendar page to tomorrow's; walk fast around the office; leave early, no later than four-thirty. Everyone knew it for almost as long as he did, and he knew that they knew. It all just flowed so nicely that no one wanted to fuck with it. Not that he didn't have his value, he did. He could be counted on to, at least, not let anything become a crisis, and he fixed everything that broke. The latter was not even required of him, but he could, so he did. He knew that being *handy* is the kind of conspicuous skill that makes it easier for others to tolerate you. They tolerated, and even liked him, for as long as they could. They eased their guilt by cutting him a padded check. Chockful of make believe vacation pay and sick leave, and iced with severance play pay, it was intended to help him get back on his feet while he looked for another job. But they knew and he knew that what it really represented was a whole fucking lot of booze.

Money, money. His final paycheck, added to what was left of his once substantial savings, gives him a net worth of around five thousand dollars. On top of that, he can wring at least that much again out of his credit cards; he's always been a good boy, and it will be sixty to ninety days before little flags start appearing next to his name on monitors and printouts from here to Arizona.

Money, money. That gives him ten thousand dollars in drinking money. If he stops paying his bills, and only pays, say, one month's rent, and keeps up his virtually non-existent social life and eating habits, then it can pretty much all stay drinking money. If he drinks one hundred dollars a day—and he can—he's got one hundred days to drink. It's just an arithmetic operation, simple logic.

In his kitchen he picks up the bottle of vodka. Center stage on the white tile counter and always threatening depletion, this is his home bottle. This is his sick bottle, his too-late bottle, his one for the road bottle. This is his utility bottle; it keeps him at his default setting. He pours a tall glass and cuts it with a splash of tonic. It's quite a lot of vodka, and it represents his last hurdle of the morning. He feels all right now, but if he can get this down he knows that he won't embarrass himself in public. Throwing up at your barstool is frowned upon in Beverly Hills. He carries the full glass into the shower with him, just to be on the safe side.

All goes well, and by the end of the shower he's feeling great. Craving music now, he drips over to the stereo without waiting to dry and plays one of the twenty-some cuts that he tends to play over and over again when he's been drinking, that he tends to play over and over again. He pours another drink and dances back into the bathroom for an ambitious morning shave.

To Ben, shaving is evidence that everything's fine. These few minutes of socially suggested practicality tend to convince him that he, like the rest of the normal world, is just living his life. He's just another guy that gets up and goes through a regular routine, wades through a non-spectacular day, and comes home and goes to sleep. He's a cog in the machine. He's a soma-driven epsilon who happens to be plagued with imagination. For instance, his habit is to shave around his mouth first; that way, he can sip his drink even if he's not finished shaving—his mind never rests.

He looks in the mirror and doesn't care that he is an alcoholic. The issue is entirely irrelevant to him. He does all this deliberately, with purpose. Yes, of course I'm an *alc*, he thinks. What about it? It's not what the story is about. There are a million ways to croak; he's only plucking a piece of life. Let go and fuck God. There are a thousand mind manipulations. As he and his friend used to joke about: It's time to cut your hair, get a job, and just give up. Ha Ha. The crime is not that he's an alcoholic; big deal! The crime is that he's disoriented, big time.

He gets dressed to the music, sometimes dancing with himself in the mirror: will you go out with me? He puts on too much too expensive cologne so he can stink of a different kind of alcohol. Tie done up right and suit looking sharp, he spins on his heel and walks into the living room, where he trips over the low coffee table and crashes through its glass top. He groans once and then starts snoring.

The always depressing experience of leaving a bar creates a sense of loss in him that gives his mind a little jolt. He should immediately proceed with the evening; it is getting late. His watch is accelerating as it nears two, and why not? he thinks. It always takes a long rest from two to six. There is time for only one stop at a bar near his home, but first he will stock up at the store. He has just enough cash left. The trip to the ATM, cleaning up the broken glass at home, that sort of stuff can wait for the wee hours, when he has nothing better to do.

Walking to his car he feels odd. Things could start crumbling fast now. He stands on the ledge, about to lose control of his handle on the world: alcohol. He's ready for this, ready to sit back and watch. Time is now the biggest irritation in his life. Las Vegas looms in the back of his head. Free from closing hours, lots of liquor always everywhere, it is inevitable that he will end up there. All he has to do is remember not to gamble drunk, which means not to gamble at all, and he can make his money last long enough to comfortably wrap things up and have fun doing it. Part of him is afraid to go, aware that this crystal-clear thinking is bound to elude him in Never Enough City. In any case he must go to the bank soon, during real hours, and withdraw most of his cash, leaving a token amount that he can pull out anytime from an ATM in Vegas, or wherever. He should have all his cash at hand; who knows what could happen? The bottom line is, now more than ever, always have access to a drink. Always have access to a drink.

At the store he can't bring himself to buy a half-gallon of cheap generic vodka. Remembering that there is still some at home, he settles for a fifth of Polish Vodka instead. Why fuck up at this late date? Purity of execution will only add to the artistic aspects of the whole wretched mess. So with the finality of this resolution keeping his chin up, he waits impatiently in the twelve items or less line. It's okay, he thinks, I have less than twelve items.

To him a daily benchmark is his final seat at the last bar of the night. It is his regular stop near his home. He doesn't like the place much and wouldn't normally go there, but the location is too good, too convenient. Suited well to the public safety, this place oozes its smoke laden atmosphere of tough fuck biker talk and dirty women out onto a sidewalk that travels less than two blocks to Ben's front door. This allows him to drink lethal quantities with no worry of dropping off at the wheel, for there have been occasions when even he knew that he couldn't possibly operate a motor vehicle with any degree of intelligence, much less safety. So if he should wake in the morning and find himself with neither his automobile nor the recollection of where it might be, he has only to stumble down the street and around a corner, and there it will stand, secure where he must have left it the previous evening, more or less in a parking space.

He sits at the filthy bar, amidst the leather vested fat guys, the worn and weary pool tables, the smelly sluts who are much harder and drunker than he'll ever be, the puke-piss-spit-blood encrusted carpeting, the brain-damaged human carcasses who have held their heads below their shoulders for longer than he's been alive, the slimy sidewalk penny-loafers who wanna be his pal, and the rest of the supporting cast with heads vacuous and pant seats full. He sits with his glasses and bottles in front of him. He sits as the last remnants of today and all that came before it slip into the void of blackout. He sits at the filthy bar and silently witnesses the change of watch from his will to his independently operating motor skills. His heart provides the musical accompaniment as the drinks are finished and he walks his crooked line home, as he clutches his bag of vodka and makes the distance to his door, as he puts his parcel on the floor carefully—even his body knows how important it is—and stumbles to his bed, where he turns off. His heart is beating him to sleep; there is no more required of him for now.

Holy Goofs

NEIL ORTENBERG

Jan and Jack

IN THE SUMMER OF 1975 I drove up to Lowell, Massachusetts, in my VW van with a group of then-youthful literary enthusiasts. Our destination: Jack Kerouac's gravesite, nestled in the sleepy New England town he grew up in. I had driven that VW cross-country many times the year before, always having to park the bus on an incline so that I could start it by releasing the brake, letting it roll, and then at the appropriate moment of speed, popping the clutch to wait for the old engine to come to life. In Lowell, I drove the loose posse of eager comrades I had assembled to the cemetery for a makeshift party to pay homage to the man who inspired many in my generation, and others, to write and celebrate the art of writing. We sat in a small circle around Kerouac's headstone, pouring beer and pot on the modest hard surface. We played guitars, recited poetry, got stoned, shared road stories, made a short film, and left Lowell with a few keepsakes of grass and dirt. Two weeks later, we read a cover story in *Rolling Stone* about a traveling group of artists and musicians called the Rolling Thunder Review. Made up of Bob Dylan, Allen Ginsberg, Sam Shepard, and other rogues of my generation, they had just visited the cemetery in Lowell, making a film, reciting poetry, . . .

I remember feeling some small connection to a greater cultural force, one with which I was an innocent bystander for sure, but nevertheless, the twinge of adrenaline I felt when I read the article was similar to the more hardened rush I had felt years later in my publishing office, where I met with John Sampas and Sterling Lord, Kerouac's brother-in-law and agent, to talk about a never-published collection of art that had been sitting dormant up in Lowell, waiting for just this publishing opportunity. The art book would be called *Departed Angels*, a modest addition to the Kerouac canon. I had published thousands of books in my publishing career by then, but sitting in that room with John and Sterling and my acquiring editor, Dan O'Connor, listening to stories about Jack (Sampas talked about a forthcoming facsimile book of the legendary scroll as well as the ongoing challenge of making *On the Road* into a film; Sterling told a story about calling Barney Rosset, the publisher of Grove at the time, to scream about the editing of Kerouac's *Subterraneans*), made me feel like things travel in fine arcs of light, circles of casual but significant destination.

I had one other experience, earlier in my career, with John Sampas, when I reissued two novels by Jack's only daughter, Jan. Sampas, the executor of the Kerouac estate, had been assailed by Jan and others before her death for a variety of reasons, and I had acquired her two previously published novels, as well as an unfinished literary work called *Parrot Fever*, a few years after her death from kidney failure. As I reissued *Baby Driver* and *Trainsong*, legal proceedings challenging Sampas's executorship were still unfolding, ultimately decided in his favor, but emotions were still running thick. The editions I published included material that was highly partisan, challenging Sampas's legitimacy as executor and showcasing ideas that Jan had embraced before her death. She felt that she had been mistreated emotionally and financially, not only by the Kerouac estate but also by other Sampas supporters, including her godfather, Allen Ginsberg, who believed her crusade to save her father's estate from illegitimate and corrupt hands was misguided. She wanted to preserve her dad's entire literary archive for a university, fearing that Sampas would sell it off piecemeal. The question of a forged will also arose. Of course, Sampas was offended that I had allowed the reissuing of her work to include attacks on his character and intentions, and phoned my assistant to let us know he was unhappy. Years later, sitting in my office to discuss the acquisition of Kerouac's art book, I couldn't help being moved by John's graceful forgiveness, even though he and I had never actually discussed his grievance. He was charming and sincere, and I was thrilled to have the opportunity to publish a book by Kerouac.

Jan Kerouac met her father only twice. On one of the two visits, as a nine-year-old child, her dad took her to a liquor store near her apartment, to buy a bottle of Harvey's Bristol Cream. As she wrote in *Baby Driver*, years later, as she was reading *On the Road* as an adult, "I had a picture of what he had been doing all this time, all over the country," why he hadn't had the time to be "fatherly." The other meeting was in Lowell. Jan was on her way to Mexico, still in adolescence, and she found her father drinking a fifth of whiskey, watching *The Beverly Hillbillies*. The meeting was brief and awkward, although he wished her well on her trip and encouraged her to write. Jan had grown up nearly impoverished, on the Lower East Side of New York, and by the age of fifteen had already been in and out of various detention facilities. She was a beautiful, sensual woman, the spitting image of the father, and spent much of her life emulating the dad who lived in everyone's imagination but who was never present for her.

She traveled throughout Mexico and South America, had affairs with numerous men, abused drugs and alcohol, sold her body, and generally lived hard. She died young, but unlike her father, she assumed a level of grace and maturity before her death—in, among other things, her crusade to save her dad's estate. I came to believe that this crusade was not necessarily based in fact but was rooted in healthy emotion. After years of excess, Jan was focused and sober, determined to do the right thing for the Kerouac legacy. I remember Gregory Corso telling me just before he died, "Jack should have spent more time with her; he was self-centered, and like a lot of us, he couldn't bring himself to take the parent shot." What interested me much more than the veracity of the charges she made against John Sampas was that Jan took a stand at the end of her life to try to protect the father who never protected her, an act of love and forgiveness. Forgiveness for the child who was not loved, and for the father, a generation's lost daddy. In 1993, a few years before her death, she wrote of a dream she had: "I was ice skating along a snowy icy road up in Canada . . . actually it was like Route 66, except it went North-South and I was going South. At first I was awkward on the skates and some people were laughing at me. But soon I learned to be graceful on them. In one of the houses along the snow-covered road, I found my father. He had been waiting for me all this time."

Jan Kerouac

Baby Driver

IN THE EMERGENCY ROOM was a regiment of enormous wood and wicker wheelchairs with hinged legs, but I had no time to admire them. They whisked me away, and after hours and hours and droves of doctors, the

Holy Goofs

diagnosis was hepatitis—a mild case. It wasn't the serum type though, so I must have caught it from seedy Bill at the hotel, and not from a needle.

A hospital madness began to rumble inside me. Everything fascinated me and I wanted to do everything and go everywhere—talking to doctors and janitors alike. I was wheeled into ward 3-C, which looked exactly like hospital wards I'd seen in old war movies—rows of iron-runged beds facing each other foot to foot with a path down the middle, and towering ceilings with big black subway fans whirring lazily. Poor Mommy, what would she do when she found I was *here?*

The first night there, everything impressed me with strange keenness, so much so that I couldn't sleep. I called for the nurse and told her, figuring I deserved a little tranquilizing goodie after my ordeal in Detentionville. To my surprise, she handed me a fat red Seconal just like nothing, which I swallowed as she watched. I plotted to get more and save some as I plummeted into a lead slumber.

The next day, my doctor, noticing the spelling of my last name, asked if I was any relation to Jack Kerouac.

"Yes, of course," I answered. "He's my son."

"No, really—" he protested, stars in his eyes, and I admitted the truth. Had I read all his books? No. In fact, I hadn't read any, just passages from *Visions of Cody*, and some haikus. He thought it was of utmost importance that I read *On the Road*, and next day he brought it to me.

I read it all in one night instead of ringing for a Seconal. And I was happy to know that my father's thought patterns were so similar to mine. Also, now that I had a picture of what he'd been doing all this time, all over the country, it made more sense that he hadn't had the time to be fatherly.

The first snowfall of the year descended, and I watched it from my hospital fortress. It made me feel all the more secure, and I basked in a certain joyful irresponsibility. Lincoln Hospital was a privileged vacation from my original lock-up, a softer pen to loll in, and with the snow blanketing rooftops and streets, it seemed softer still.

I contemplated escape: it would be so easy. The stairway on the side of the building was always open, and I went down several times in my snug-fitting flimsy robe and just opened the door to breathe gusts of icy freedom. But it was totally impractical to think of running through the snowy Bronx in slippers and a hospital gown. I'd just be caught and returned to Spofford where I'd have to start all over again in D-5. No, no . . . escape was out of the question.

Daily, I watched tubes and tubes of crimson fluid being extracted from my pale arms—a string of never-ending tests for the lab. I asked if I could keep one to observe the clotting action, saying I was interested in biology, and liked to see the plasma separate. They let me keep it, and after a few days I put a hole in the rubber stopper and began squirting it on a piece of drawing paper, making nice little splats and drips. After they dried and turned rust-colored, I outlined each shape, even the really tiny ones, in turquoise Pentel. It turned out quite striking and I hung it by my bed.

JACK KEROUAC

On the Road

I FIRST MET DEAN not long after my wife and I split up. I had just gotten over a serious illness that I won't bother to talk about, except that it had something to do with the miserably weary split-up and my feeling that everything was dead. With the coming of Dean Moriarty began the part of my life you could call my life on the road. Before that I'd often dreamed of going West to see the country, always vaguely planning and never taking off. Dean is the perfect guy for the road because he actually was born on the road, when his parents were passing through Salt Lake City in 1926, in a jalopy, on their way to Los Angeles. First reports of him came to me through Chad King, who'd shown me a few letters from him written in a New Mexico reform school. I was tremendously interested in the letters because they so naively and sweetly asked Chad to teach him all about Nietzsche and all the wonderful intellectual things that Chad knew. At one point Carlo and I talked about the letters and wondered if we would ever meet the strange Dean Moriarty. This is all far back, when Dean was not the way he is today, when he was a young jailkid shrouded in mystery. Then news came that Dean was out of reform school and was coming to New York for the first time; also there was talk that he had just married a girl called Marylou.

One day I was hanging around the campus and Chad and Tim Gray told me Dean was staying in a cold-water pad in East Harlem, the Spanish Harlem. Dean had arrived the night before, the first time in New York, with his beautiful little sharp chick Marylou; they got off the Greyhound bus at 50th Street and cut around the corner looking for a place to eat and went right in Hector's, and since then Hector's cafeteria has always been a big symbol of New York for Dean. They spent money on beautiful big glazed cakes and creampuffs.

All this time Dean was telling Marylou things like this: "Now, darling, here we are in New York and although I haven't quite told you everything that I was thinking about when we crossed Missouri and especially at the point when we passed the Boonville reformatory which reminded me of my jail problem, it is absolutely necessary now to postpone all those leftover things concerning our personal lovethings and at once begin thinking of specific worklife plans . . ." and so on in the way that he had in those early days.

I went to the cold-water flat with the boys, and Dean came to the door in his shorts. Marylou was jumping off the couch; Dean had dispatched the occupant of the apartment to the kitchen, probably to make coffee, while he proceeded with his love-problems, for to him sex was the one and only holy and important thing in life, although he had to sweat and curse to make a living and so on. You saw that in the way he stood bobbing his head, always looking down, nodding, like a young boxer to instructions, to make you think he was listening to every word, throwing in a thousand "Yeses" and "That's rights." My first impression of Dean was of a young Gene Autry—trim, thin-hipped, blue-eyed, with a real Oklahoma accent—a sideburned hero of the snowy West. In fact he'd just been working on a ranch, Ed Wall's in Colorado, before marrying Marylou and coming East. Marylou was a pretty blonde with immense ringlets of hair like a sea of golden tresses; she sat there on the edge of the couch with her hands hanging in her lap and her smoky blue country eyes fixed in a wide stare because she was in an evil gray New York pad that she'd heard about back West, and waiting like a longbodied emaciated Modigliani surrealist woman in a serious room. But, outside of being a sweet little girl, she was awfully dumb and capable of doing horrible things. That night we all drank beer and pulled wrists and talked till dawn, and in the morning, while we sat around dumbly smoking butts from ashtrays in the gray light of a gloomy day, Dean got up nervously, paced around, thinking, and decided the thing to do was to have Marylou make breakfast and sweep the floor. "In other words we've got to get on the ball, darling, what I'm saying, otherwise it'll be fluctuating and lack of true knowledge or crystallization of our plans." Then I went away.

During the following week he confided in Chad King that he absolutely had to learn how to write from him; Chad said I was a writer and he should come to me for advice. Meanwhile Dean had gotten a job in a parking lot, had a fight with Marylou in their Hoboken apartment—God knows why they went there—and she was so mad and so down deep vindictive that she reported to the police some false trumped-up hysterical crazy charge, and

Dean had to lam from Hoboken. So he had no place to live. He came right out to Paterson, New Jersey, where I was living with my aunt, and one night while I was studying there was a knock on the door, and there was Dean, bowing, shuffling obsequiously in the dark of the hall, and saying, "Hel-lo, you remember me—Dean Moriarty? I've come to ask you to show me how to write."

"And where's Marylou?" I asked, and Dean said she'd apparently whored a few dollars together and gone back to Denver—"the whore!" So we went out to have a few beers because we couldn't talk like we wanted to talk in front of my aunt, who sat in the living room reading her paper. She took one look at Dean and decided that he was a madman.

In the bar I told Dean, "Hell, man, I know very well you didn't come to me only to want to become a writer, and after all what do I really know about it except you've got to stick to it with the energy of a benny addict." And he said, "Yes, of course, I know exactly what you mean and in fact all those problems have occurred to me, but the thing that I want is the realization of those factors that should one depend on Schopenhauer's dichotomy for any inwardly realized . . ." and so on in that way, things I understood not a bit and he himself didn't. In those days he really didn't know what he was talking about; that is to say, he was a young jailkid all hung-up on the wonderful possibilities of becoming a real intellectual, and he liked to talk in the tone and using the words, but in a jumbled way, that he had heard from "real intellectuals"—although, mind you, he wasn't so naive as that in all other things, and it took him just a few months with Carlo Marx to become completely *in there* with all the terms and jargon. Nonetheless we understood each other on other levels of madness, and I agreed that he could stay at my house till he found a job and furthermore we agreed to go out West sometime. That was the winter of 1947.

One night when Dean ate supper at my house—he already had the parking-lot job in New York—he leaned over my shoulder as I typed rapidly away and said, "Come on man, those girls won't wait, make it fast."

I said, "Hold on just a minute, I'll be right with you soon as I finish this chapter," and it was one of the best chapters in the book. Then I dressed and off we flew to New York to meet some girls. As we rode in the bus in the weird phosphorescent void of the Lincoln Tunnel we leaned on each other with fingers waving and yelled and talked excitedly, and I was beginning to get the bug like Dean. He was simply a youth tremendously excited with life, and though he was a con-man, he was only conning because he wanted so much to live and to get involved with people who would otherwise pay no attention to him. He was conning me and I knew it (for room and board and

Holy Goofs

"how-to-write," etc.), and he knew I knew (this has been the basis of our relationship), but I didn't care and we got along fine—no pestering, no catering; we tiptoed around each other like heartbreaking new friends. I began to learn from him as much as he probably learned from me. As far as my work was concerned he said, "Go ahead, everything you do is great." He watched over my shoulder as I wrote stories, yelling, "Yes! That's right! Wow! Man!" and "Phew!" and wiped his face with his handkerchief. "Man, wow, there's so many things to do, so many things to write! How to even *begin* to get it all down and without modified restraints and all hung-up on like literary inhibitions and grammatical fears . . ."

"That's right, man, now you're talking." And a kind of holy lightning I saw flashing from his excitement and his visions, which he described so torrentially that people in buses looked around to see the "overexcited nut." In the West he'd spent a third of his time in the poolhall, a third in jail, and a third in the public library. They'd seen him rushing eagerly down the winter streets, bareheaded, carrying books to the poolhall, or climbing trees to get into the attics of buddies where he spent days reading or hiding from the law.

We went to New York—I forget what the situation was, two colored girls— there were no girls there; they were supposed to meet him in a diner and didn't show up. We went to his parking lot where he had a few things to do— change his clothes in the shack in back and spruce up a bit in front of a cracked mirror and so on, and then we took off. And that was the night Dean met Carlo Marx. A tremendous thing happened when Dean met Carlo Marx. Two keen minds that they are, they took to each other at the drop of a hat. Two piercing eyes glanced into two piercing eyes—the holy con-man with the shining mind, and the sorrowful poetic con-man with the dark mind that is Carlo Marx. From that moment on I saw very little of Dean, and I was a little sorry too. Their energies met head-on, I was a lout compared, I couldn't keep up with them. The whole mad swirl of everything that was to come began then; it would mix up all my friends and all I had left of my family in a big dust cloud over the American Night. Carlo told him of Old Bull Lee, Elmer Hassel, Jane: Lee in Texas growing weed, Hassel on Riker's Island, Jane wandering on Times Square in a benzedrine hallucination, with her baby girl in her arms and ending up in Bellevue. And Dean told Carlo of unknown people in the West like Tommy Snark, the clubfooted poolhall rotation shark and cardplayer and queer saint. He told him of Roy Johnson, Big Ed Dunkel, his boyhood buddies, his street buddies, his innumerable girls and sex-parties and pornographic pictures, his heroes, heroines, adventures. They rushed down the street together, digging everything in the early way they had, which later became so much sadder and perceptive and blank.

Holy Goofs

But then they danced down the streets like dingledodies, and I shambled after as I've been doing all my life after people who interest me, because the only people for me are the mad ones, the ones who are mad to live, mad to talk, mad to be saved, desirous of everything at the same time, the ones who never yawn or say a commonplace thing, but burn, burn, burn like fabulous yellow roman candles exploding like spiders across the stars and in the middle you see the blue centerlight pop and everybody goes "Awww!" What did they call such young people in Goethe's Germany? Wanting dearly to learn how to write like Carlo, the first thing you know, Dean was attacking him with a great amorous soul such as only a con-man can have. "Now, Carlo, let *me* speak—here's what *I'm* saying . . ." I didn't see them for about two weeks, during which time they cemented their relationship to fiendish allday-allnight-talk proportions.

Then came spring, the great time of traveling, and everybody in the scattered gang was getting ready to take one trip or another. I was busily at work on my novel and when I came to the halfway mark, after a trip down South with my aunt to visit my brother Rocco, I got ready to travel West for the very first time.

Dean had already left. Carlo and I saw him off at the 34th Street Greyhound station. Upstairs they had a place where you could make pictures for a quarter. Carlo took off his glasses and looked sinister. Dean made a profile shot and looked coyly around. I took a straight picture that made me look like a thirty-year-old Italian who'd kill anybody who said anything against his mother. This picture Carlo and Dean neatly cut down the middle with a razor and saved a half each in their wallets. Dean was wearing a real Western business suit for his big trip back to Denver; he'd finished his first fling in New York. I say fling, but he only worked like a dog in parking lots. The most fantastic parking-lot attendant in the world, he can back a car forty miles an hour into a tight squeeze and stop at the wall, jump out, race among fenders, leap into another car, circle it fifty miles an hour in a narrow space, back swiftly into tight spot, *hump*, snap the car with the emergency so that you see it bounce as he flies out; then clear to the ticket shack, sprinting like a track star, hand a ticket, leap into a newly arrived car before the owner's half out, leap literally under him as he steps out, start the car with the door flapping, and roar off to the next available spot, arc, pop in, brake, out, run; working like that without pause eight hours a night, evening rush hours and after-theater rush hours, in greasy wino pants with a frayed fur-lined jacket and beat shoes that flap. Now he'd bought a new suit to go back in; blue with pencil stripes, vest and all—eleven dollars on Third Avenue, with a watch and watch chain, and a portable typewriter with which he was going to start writing in a

Holy Goofs

Denver rooming house as soon as he got a job there. We had a farewell meal of franks and beans in a Seventh Avenue Riker's, and then Dean got on the bus that said Chicago and roared off into the night. There went our wrangler. I promised myself to go the same way when spring really bloomed and opened up the land. And this was really the way that my whole road experience began, and the things that were to come are too fantastic not to tell.

Yes, and it wasn't only because I was a writer and needed new experiences that I wanted to know Dean more, and because my life hanging around the campus had reached the completion of its cycle and was stultified, but because, somehow in spite of our difference in character, he reminded me of some long-lost brother; the sight of his suffering bony face with the long sideburns and his straining muscular sweating neck made me remember my boyhood in those dye-dumps and swim-holes and riversides of Paterson and the Passaic. His dirty workclothes clung to him so gracefully, as though you couldn't buy a better fit from a custom tailor but only earn it from the Natural Tailor of Natural Joy, as Dean had, in his stresses. And in his excited way of speaking I heard again the voices of old companions and brothers under the bridge, among the motorcycles, along the wash-lined neighborhood and drowsy doorsteps of afternoon where boys played guitars while their older brothers worked in the mills. All my other current friends were "intellectuals"—Chad the Nietzschean anthropologist, Carlo Marx and his nutty surrealist low-voiced serious staring talk, Old Bull Lee and his critical anti-everything drawl—or else they were slinking criminals like Elmer Hassel, with that hip sneer; Jane Lee the same, sprawled on the Oriental cover of her couch, sniffing at the *New Yorker*. But Dean's intelligence was every bit as formal and shining and complete, without the tedious intellectualness. And his "criminality" was not something that sulked and sneered; it was a wild yea-saying overburst of American joy; it was Western, the west wind, an ode from the Plains, something new, long prophesied, long a-coming (he only stole cars for joy rides). Besides, all my New York friends were in the negative, nightmare position of putting down society and giving their tired bookish or political or psychoanalytical reasons, but Dean just raced in society, eager for bread and love; he didn't care one way or the other, "so long's I can get that lil ole gal with that lil sumpin down there tween her legs, boy," and "so long's we can *eat*, son, y'ear me? I'm *hungry*, I'm *starving*, let's *eat right now!*"—and off we'd rush to *eat*, whereof, as saith Ecclesiastes, "It is your portion under the sun."

A western kinsman of the sun, Dean. Although my aunt warned me that he would get me in trouble, I could hear a new call and see a new horizon, and believe it at my young age; and a little bit of trouble or even Dean's eventual rejection of me as a buddy, putting me down, as he would later, on starving sidewalks and sickbeds—what did it matter? I was a young writer and I wanted to take off.

Somewhere along the line I knew there'd be girls, visions, everything; somewhere along the line the pearl would be handed to me.

JOYCE JOHNSON

Minor Characters

AS OF 1982, THERE is the Jack Kerouac Society for Disembodied Poetics, founded in Boulder, Colorado, in 1976. There is *Jack's Book*, as well as *Desolation Angel: Jack Kerouac, the Beat Generation and America* and *Kerouac: A Biography* and—the one I like best—*Kerouac: a Chicken Essay*, by a French-Canadian surrealist poet; as well as proliferating pamphlets, theses, articles, chapters in books. A journal published annually celebrates the Beats and the "Unspeakable Visions of the Individual." It's hagiography in the making. Jack, now delivered into the Void, would be amazed to know there's even a literary fan magazine devoted entirely to him, called *Moody Street Irregulars* (after the street in Lowell where he lived as a child). For a back issue, a graduate student somewhere put together a rather randomly chosen chronology of Jack Kerouac's life. In a column labeled 1957, there's a cryptic entry: *Meets Joyce Glassman*.

"Hello. I'm Jack. Allen tells me you're very nice. Would you like to come down to Howard Johnson's on Eighth Street? I'll be sitting at the counter. I have black hair and I'll be wearing a red and black checked shirt."

I'm standing in Elise's kitchen, holding the phone Allen has just handed me. It's a Saturday night shortly after New Year's.

"Sure," I say.

I put on a lot of eye shadow and my coat and take the subway down to Astor Place and begin walking westward, cross-town, passing under the bridge between the two buildings of Wanamaker's Department Store and the eye of the giant illuminated clock. It's a dark, bitter January night with ice all over the pavements, so you have to be careful, but I'm flying along, it's an adventure as opposed to a misadventure—under which category so far I've had to put most of the risky occurrences in my life.

The windows of Howard Johnson's are running with steam so you can't see in. I push open the heavy glass door, and there is, sure enough, a black-haired man at the counter in a flannel lumberjack shirt slightly the worse for wear. He looks up and stares at me hard with blue eyes, amazingly blue. He's the only person in Howard Johnson's in color. I feel a little scared as I walk up to him. "Jack?" I say.

There's an empty stool next to his. I sit down on it and he asks me whether I want anything. "Just coffee." He's awfully quiet. We both lack conversation, but then we don't know each other, so what can we say? He asks after Allen, Lafcadio, that kind of thing. I'd like to tell him I've read his book, if that wouldn't sound gauche, obvious and uncool.

When the coffee arrives, Jack looks glum. He can't pay for it. He has no money, none at all. That morning he'd handed his last ten dollars to a cashier in a grocery store and received change for a five. He's waiting for a check from a publisher, he says angrily.

I say, "Look, that's all right. I have money. Do you want me to buy you something to eat?"

"Yeah," he says. "Frankfurters. I'll pay you back. I always pay people back, you know."

I've never bought a man dinner before. It makes me feel very competent and womanly.

He has frankfurters, home fries, and baked beans with Heinz ketchup on them. I keep stealing looks at him because he's beautiful. You're not supposed to say a man is beautiful, but he is. He catches me at it and grins, then mugs it up, putting on one goofy face after another; a whole succession of old-time ridiculous movie-comedian faces flashes before me until I'm laughing too at the absurdity of this blind date Allen has arranged. (The notion of Allen Ginsberg arranging blind dates will crack people up years later when they ask me how on earth I met Kerouac.)

As for what he saw in me that night, I'm not sure at all. A very young woman in a red coat, round-faced and blonde. "An interesting young person," he wrote in *Desolation Angels*. "A Jewess, elegant middleclass sad and looking for something —she looked Polish as hell . . ." Where am I in all those funny categories?

As our paths converge in Howard Johnson's, we're looking for different things. At thirty-four, Jack's worn down, the energy that had moved him to so many different places gone. He's suddenly waited too long. The check for *The Subterraneans* will never arrive; *On the Road* will never be published. Why not let Allen rescue him? He can't go back to the two Virginias.

I see the blue, bruised eye of Kerouac and construe his melancholy as the look of a man needing love because I'm, among other things, twenty-one years old. I believe in the curative powers of love as the English believe in tea or Catholics believe in the Miracle of Lourdes.

He tells me he's spent sixty-three days on a mountaintop without anyone. He made pea soup and wrote in his journal and sang Sinatra songs to keep himself company.

Some warning to me in all this. "You really like being alone like that?" I ask.

"I wish I was there now. I should have stayed up there."

He could somehow cancel you out and make you feel sad for him at the same time. But I'm sure any mountaintop would be preferable to where he's staying—the Marlton Hotel on Eighth Street, with the dirty shades over the windows and the winos lounging on the steps.

"And where do you live?" Jack asks. He likes it that it's up near Columbia and the West End Bar where he used to hang out. Was Johnny the bartender still there? Johnny the bartender would remember him from the days when he was a football hero at Columbia but he broke his leg in his sophomore year and stayed in his room reading Celine and Shakespeare and never went back to football again—thus losing his scholarship at Columbia, but he's always had affection for the neighborhood. "Why don't you let me stay at your place?" he says.

"If you wish," I say in *Desolation Angels*, deciding fast. And I know how I said it too. As if it was of no great moment, as if I had no wishes of my own—in keeping with my current philosophy of nothing-to-lose, try anything.

We stood up and put on our coats, we went down into the subway. And there on the IRT, on a signboard I'd never seen before that night, was an ad for an airline with a brand-new slogan: FLY NOW PAY LATER.

"That's a good title for a novel," I said, and finally told Jack I was writing one, I wasn't just a secretary. He said *Pay Me the Penny After* would be a better title. "You should call your novel that." He asked me who my favorite writer was. I said Henry James, and he made a face, and said he figured I had all the wrong models, but maybe I could be a great writer anyway. He asked me if I rewrote a lot, and said you should never revise, never change any-thing, not even a word. He regretted all the rewriting he'd done on *The Town and the City*. No one could make him do that again, which was why he always got nowhere with publishers. He was going to look at my work and show me that what you wrote first was always best. I said okay, feeling guilty for all that I'd rewritten, but I still loved Henry James.

All through this literary conversation, Jack stood swaying above me on the subway, hanging on to the strap. Just before we got off, he leaned down. Our foreheads scraped, our eyeballs loomed up on each other—a funny game where I knew you weren't supposed to blink, no matter what.

That was the start of *Meets Joyce Glassman.*

The apartment I lived in at the time was dark and cavernous, on the first floor of a brownstone halfway down the block from the Yorkshire Hotel. Two furnished rooms—the furnishings being the uselessly massive, weak-jointed kind found in the lobbies of antediluvian apartment buildings. A small refrigerator and a two-burner stove stood behind a screen in one corner of the living room, but you had to wash your dishes in the bathroom sink. The windows looked out on a rank back yard where a large tree of heaven battened on bedsprings and broken bottles. I always felt very small in that apartment. One night outside the house a huge grey tomcat with a chewed ear had rubbed against my legs. I hauled him inside under the impression I was rescuing him, but he spent his days on the windowsill longing for the street, trying to pry the window open with his paw, or he lurked in the closet vengefully spraying shoes. Jack was the only person I'd brought home so far who saw the beauty of this animal, whom I'd unimaginatively named Smoke. He said he was going to call it Ti Gris, after a cat he once had in Lowell. He seemed to like to rename things. On the walk from the subway I'd become Joycey, which no one had called me since I was little, and he'd put his arm around me, leaning on me playfully and letting his hand dangle down over my breast—that was how men walked with their women in Mexico, he said. "Someday when you go there, you'll see that for yourself."

When we got in the door, he didn't ask to see my manuscript. He pulled me against him and kissed me before I even turned on the light. I kissed him back, and he acted surprised. He said I was even quieter than he was, he had no idea quiet girls liked kissing so much, and he undid the buttons of my coat and put both his hands up my back under my sweater. "The trouble is," Jack said with his voice against my ear, "I don't . . . like . . . blondes."

I remember laughing and saying, "Well, well in that case I'll just dye my hair"—wondering all the time if it was true.

In the morning Jack left to get his stuff out of the Marlton. He returned with a sleeping bag and a knapsack in which there were jeans and a few old shirts like the one he was already wearing and some notebooks he bought in Mexico City. That was all he owned. Not even a typewriter—he'd been borrowing other people's typewriters, he said. I'd never seen such foreign-looking notebooks, long and narrow with shiny black covers and thin, bluish paper on which Jack's slanted penciled printing sped across page after page interrupted here and there by little sketches. One notebook was just for dreams. He wrote in it every morning.

There was something heartbreakingly attractive in these few essentials to which Jack had reduced his needs. He reminded me of a sailor—not that I knew any sailors—something too about the way he looked coming out of the shower, gleaming and vigorous and ruddy with a white towel around his neck.

Very quickly it didn't seem strange to have him with me, we were somehow like very old friends—"buddies," Jack said, squeezing me affectionately, making me feel both proud and a little disappointed. Crazy as it was, I sometimes really wished I was dark—like this Virginia I felt jealous of for making him so wild. Or the girl named Esmeralda who lived in Mexico City and whom he'd loved tragically for a long time and written an entire novel about in one of his notebooks, calling her Tristessa. But he'd slept with her only once. She was a whore and a saint, so beautiful and lost—one of his mysterious *fellaheen* women, primeval and of the earth.

I was unprimeval and distinctly of the city. I was everydayness, bacon and eggs in the morning or the middle of the night, which I learned to cook just the way he liked—sunny-side up in the black iron frying pan. I'd buy slab bacon in the grocery store, like he'd always had in Lowell—not the skinny kind in packages—and add canned applesauce (a refinement I'd learned from Bickford's Cafeteria), which Jack had never thought of as anything that might enhance eggs. He took extraordinary pleasure in small things like that.

As a lover he wasn't fierce but oddly brotherly and somewhat reticent. I'd listen in amazement to his stories of Berkeley parties where everyone was naked and men and women engaged in some exotic Japanese practice called *yabyum* (but Jack, fully clothed, had sat apart brooding over his bottle of port, something he didn't tell me). In my memories of Jack in the good times we had together, I'm lying with my head on his chest, his heart pulsing against my ear. His smooth hard powerful arms are around me and I'm burying my face into them because I like them so much, making him laugh, "What are you doing there, Joycey?" And there's always music on the radio. Symphony Sid, whom he taught me to find on the dial, who always comes on at the stroke of midnight, bringing you the sounds of Charlie Parker, Lester Young, Miles Davis, and Stan Getz, and who, according to Jack, is a subterranean himself—you can hear it in his gravel voice smoked down to a rasp by innumerable weird cigarettes. "And now—after a few words about that fan-tastic Mo-gen David wine—the great Lady Day . . ." In the darkness of the room we drift together as Billie holiday bewails lost loves . . .

But then Jack leaves me. He goes into the small back bedroom where I never sleep because there's no radiator back there. He pulls the window all the way up, closes the door, and lies down on the floor in his sleeping bag alone. This is the cure for the cough he brought with him from Mexico City. In the morning he'll do headstands with his feet against the wall, to reverse the flow of blood in his body. He tells me a frightening thing about himself. He's known for eight years that a blood clot could finish him off at any minute.

How can you bear living, I wonder, knowing death could be so close? Little by little I'm letting go of what I learned on the abortionist's table in the white upstairs room in Canarsie.

I'm good for him, Jack tells me. I don't mind anything he does. I don't mind about the sleeping bag, do I?

I didn't really mind, that was the strange part. Everything seemed so odd, so charmed, so transformed. At night when the cold air came with a rush into the little room where Jack was sleeping, and seeped under the edges of the closed door, I could imagine myself in a place without walls, an immense campground where, lying wrapped in blankets, I could feel in my own warmth absolute proof of my existence.

> I'm a regular fool in pale houses enslaved to lust for women who hate me, they lay their bartering flesh all over the divans, it's one fleshpot—insanity all of it, I should forswear and chew em all out and go hit the clean rail—I wake up glad to find myself saved in the wilderness mountains—For that lumpy roll flesh with the juicy hole I'd sit through eternities of horror in gray rooms illuminated by a gray sun, with cops and alimoners at the door and the jail beyond?—It's a bleeding comedy—The Great Wise Stages of pathetic understanding elude me when it comes to harems—Harem-scarem, it's all in heaven now—bless their all their bleating-hearts—Some lambs are female, some angels have womanwings, it's all mothers in the end and forgive me for my sardony—excuse me for my rut.
>
> (Hor hor hor)

Not for Joyce Glassman to read, this bleak passage later written in *Desolation Angels*, this awful metaphysical linking of sex, birth, the grave. I hate Jack's woman-hatred, hate it, mourn it, understand, and finally forgive.

NEAL CASSADY

The First Third

Letter to Jack Kerouac, March 7, 1947 (Kansas City, Mo.)

Dear Jack:

I am sitting in a bar on Market St. I'm drunk, well, not quite, but I soon will be. I am here for 2 reasons; I must wait 5 hours for the bus to Denver & lastly but, most importantly, I'm here (drinking) because, of course, because of a woman & *what* a *woman!* To be chronological about it:

I was sitting on the bus when it took on more passengers at Indianapolis, Indiana—a perfectly proportioned beautiful, intellectual, passionate, person-ification of Venus De Milo asked me if the seat beside me was taken!!! I gulped, (I'm drunk) gargled & stammered NO! (Paradox of expression, after all, how can one stammer No!!?) She sat—I sweated—She started to speak, I knew it would be generalities, so to tempt her I remained silent.

She (her name Patricia) got on the bus at 8 PM (Dark!) I didn't speak until 10 PM—in the intervening 2 hours I not only of course, determined to make her, but, how to *DO IT*.

I naturally can't quote the conversation verbally, however, I shall attempt to give you the gist of it from 10 PM to 2 AM.

Without the slightest preliminaries of objective remarks (what's your name? where are you going? etc.) I plunged into a completely knowing, com-pletely subjective, personal & so to speak "penetrating her core" way of speech; to be shorter, (since I'm getting unable to write) by 2 AM I had her swearing eternal love, complete subjectivity to me & immediate satisfaction. I, anticipating even more pleasure, wouldn't allow her to blow me on the bus, instead we played, as they say, with each other.

Knowing her supremely perfect being was completely mine (when I'm more coherent, I'll tell you her complete history & psychological reason for loving me) I could conceive of no obstacle to my satisfaction, well, "the best laid plans of mice & men go astray" and my nemesis was her sister, the bitch.

Pat had told me her reason for going to St. Louis was to see her sister; she had wired her to meet her at the depot. So, to get rid of the sister, we peeked around the depot when we arrived at St. Louis at 4 AM to see if she (her sister) was present. If not, Pat would claim her suitcase, change clothes in the rest room & she and I proceed to a hotel room for a night (years?) of perfect

Holy Goofs

bliss. The sister was not in sight, so She (note the capital) claimed her bag & retired to the toilet to change ———————

This next paragraph must, of necessity, be written completely objectively ———————

Edith (her sister) & Patricia (my love) walked out of the pisshouse hand in hand (I shan't describe my emotions). It seems Edith (bah) arrived at the bus depot early & while waiting for Patricia, feeling sleepy, retired to the head to sleep on a sofa. That's why Pat & I didn't see her.

My desperate efforts to free Pat from Edith failed, even Pat's terror & slave-like feeling toward her rebelled enough to state she must see "someone" & would meet Edith later, *all* failed. Edith was wise; she saw what was happening between Pat & I.

Well, to summarize: Pat & I stood in the depot (in plain sight of the sister) & pushing up to one another, vowed to never love again & then I took the bus for Kansas City & Pat went home, meekly, with her dominating sister. Alas, alas ———————

In complete (try & share my feeling) dejection, I sat, as the bus progressed toward Kansas City. At Columbia, Mo. a young (19) completely passive (my meat) *virgin* got on & shared my seat . . . In my dejection over losing Pat, the perfect, I decided to sit on the bus (behind the driver) in broad daylight & seduce her, from 10:30 AM to 2:30 PM I talked. When I was done, she (confused, her entire life upset, metaphysically amazed at me, passionate in her immaturity) called her folks in Kansas City, & went with me to a park (it was just getting dark) & I banged her; I screwed as never before; all my pent up emotion finding release in this young virgin (& she was) who is, by the by, a *school teacher!* Imagine, she's had 2 years of Mo. St. Teacher's College & now teaches Jr. High School. (I'm beyond thinking straightly).

I'm going to stop writing. Oh, yes, to free myself for a moment from my emotions, you must read "Dead Souls" parts of it (in which Gogol shows his insight) are quite like you.

I'll elaborate further later (probably?) but at the moment I'm drunk & happy (after all, I'm free of Patricia already, due to the young virgin. I have no name for her. At the happy note of Les Young's "jumping at Mesners" (which I'm hearing) I close till later.

> To my Brother
>> Carry On!
>>> N. L. Cassady

CAROLYN CASSADY

Off the Road

HERE WITH US, JACK was trying to finish *On the Road*. I had only read random passages of the manuscript; I was too close to the pain of the events he described, and the more Neal chortled over it, the more fearful I became that I'd feel a necessity to start something again. The only details I'd heard of their trips were those Helen had revealed, and I was blissful in my ignorance. Jack was still writing additional scenes, and he became excited with the possibilities offered by the tape recorder to capture spontaneous discussions or stories. I was beginning to think the *Road* might become an interminable highway. Jack had found that he had an audience that believed he could do no wrong, and he was happy to share his daily efforts with us. He still carried a little five-cent notebook in his shirt pocket wherever he went to note impressions or new ideas which he would type up within a few days. One notebook he inscribed to me.

The liquor store was just around the corner on Hyde Street, and Jack sometimes bought a small bottle, or "poor-boy," of Tokay or Muscatel to sip late in the afternoon or after dinner, when he would share it with me. Sometimes I'd go with him to the liquor store to buy beer for Neal. One time when I stopped for beer alone, the proprietor said something about my "husband's" preference for sweet wine. It wasn't until I was outside that I realized he meant Jack, and I had to laugh. If only he knew how much trouble I had keeping one husband, let alone two.

One afternoon I was feeding John in his highchair when I heard the front door open and slam shut, and Neal came clumping down the stairs dragging his jacket behind him. He threw it down hard on the couch and said, "Shit." He hardly ever swore in front of me, so I knew he must be really angry.

"I've got to pack," he said. "I've drawn a two-week hold-down in San Luis." He stood looking out the window, clenching his jaw.

This kind of assignment was the only kind he didn't like. On hold-downs he had to go to a neighboring branch, and it meant staying in either a barren dorm, the "crummy" (caboose) or a sleazy hotel. He had to work the same local freight early every morning for at least two weeks, sometimes longer.

Neal blew off some steam and then accepted his lot, settling down to his own cheerful self again. He would never expand on his disappointments if it meant bringing someone else down.

Holy Goofs

He hadn't much time. While he went upstairs to pack, I hurried with the dinner, and he called up to Jack to explain why dinner would be earlier tonight. I was even more sorry than Neal at this sudden development, and I guessed maybe Jack would be, too. When alone together, Jack and I had still not found a firm footing in our relationship, and we needed Neal nearby as a buffer. Consequently, during this dinner we were both nervous, eyeing each other in a new and uncharted way.

Neal stood up from the table and planted his hands on either side of his chest in his Oliver Hardy stance, looking down at Jack and then at me.

"Well, kiddies I must be off. Just everyone pray I get back in fourteen days and no more."

He retrieved his jacket, kissed me and the children and strode to the stairs. At the landing he turned back as though he'd forgotten something, then said with a grin, "I don't know about leaving you two—you know what they say, 'My best pal and my best gal . . .' Ha, ha—just don't do anything *I* wouldn't do—okay kids?" He bounded up the stairs laughing, knowing, just as we did, that there was nothing he wouldn't do in a similar situation. I wanted to crawl under the table and disappear, I was so embarrassed, and I couldn't look at Jack. Instead, I jumped up and began grabbing dishes off the table and putting them in the sink. Jack bolted for the attic.

Jack had been taught that marriage was a sacrament, whereas my thinking was that if a person agreed to a set of rules and went so far as to choose to take vows, then he should play the game and keep the promises. Otherwise, don't do it—nobody *has* to get married nowadays. Neal, on the other hand, was torn between his beliefs and overpowering desires. Jack's courtesy and gentleness toward me resulted from my being the wife of his best friend, nothing more—at least that was all either of us could admit to, even to ourselves.

The more I thought about Neal's remark, the angrier I got and the more it hurt. Well, maybe I was jumping to conclusions again—maybe he really did mean it only as a joke. But it was no joke to me. During the next two weeks, Jack was out most of the time and rarely sat and talked to me. When he did agree to share a meal, however, it was so pleasant we'd soon forget the circumstances in the joys of conversation. But the silences brought back our discomfort at being alone together, Neal's remark hanging in the air around us.

When he returned we welcomed him with great relief. He seemed a little reserved the first evening at dinner, and I wondered if he supposed we had behaved as he would have done. When Jack hurriedly left us alone, I asked, "Remember what you said when you left, Neal? How could you say a thing like that? Do you know how that hurt? You made me feel I was no more precious to you than—a towel or something. Can you understand that? Don't you know I'm proud to show you I deserve your trust, that I like chances to prove my loyalty? Tell me, did you sincerely feel we should have made love, Jack and I—or were you just saying that to protect yourself in case we did?"

I was peering at Neal intently, waiting for his answer. He got up from the table looking uncomfortable and started toward the stairs. Then he paused and shrugged.

"A little of both, I suppose . . . yeah, actually . . . why not? I thought it would be fine." And up the stairs he went.

Goddamn the man! Well, I had asked for this second blow, but how could he be so unfeeling? I should know by now, I thought dejectedly. Hadn't he "shared" LuAnne—even though they were no longer married—and how many others? Again, I kept supposing I was different, meant more to him. This seemed a greater rejection even than desertion.

Dolefully, I did the dishes, mulling it over, finding no solace. When Neal came down to tell me he and Jack were going out, I got a vision once more of the future as an incessant repetition of the past, and I knew I must do something to change it. None of the old ways had worked, so defiantly, I said half-aloud, 'All right, Neal dear, let's try it your way.' And the anger drained out of me while I felt another conviction torn away as though I'd shed another skin. Suddenly I felt exposed, but with that came a coolness and a spurt of excitement mingled with fear. Never had I known how to play female games of deliberately setting out to trap a man. At least in this case it shouldn't require much aggression, just a few calculated moves. After all, Jack knew better than I how Neal would react. It was worth a try; anything was better than this.

An evening or two later, I made a few plans—nothing elaborate or unusual, but admittedly I manipulated circumstances as best I could. I'd asked Neal about the train he was called for and its schedule. He'd be gone until the following afternoon. When the children were settled for the night, I called softly up the attic stairs. "Jack?"

He came to the top of the steps. "Yeah?"

"I wondered if you'd like to join me for dinner. I've made an experimental sort of pizza, and there's way too much for me. It doesn't keep too well, so—how about it?"

"Okay, sure . . ." He looked hesitant. "Just give me a minute?"

"Oh, no hurry; it'll be another thirty minutes anyway, but there's some wine, too. So whenever you're ready." Pausing for a minute at my dressing table, I checked my appearance—mustn't be too obvious. I was already feeling like a wanton woman and had butterflies in my stomach. Too bad I

Holy Goofs

could only get away with jeans and a white shirt without arousing his suspicions; but I had been careful with my hair and makeup, and thought just a dab of cologne would be fair.

Downstairs I checked my ammunition there: new candle in the bottle, table set as usual, radio set at KJAZ, the station both Neal and Jack approved of for its ballads and progressive jazz. The oven was ready, so I popped in the pizza. I thought I'd better sample the wine to calm my nerves, and I fancy I appeared quite nonchalant when Jack descended from the attic to join me.

"Pour us some wine. Dinner will be ready in a jiffy."

I sat down opposite him at the table, raised my glass to my private scheme and smiled.

The wine helped put us both at ease and made us garrulous. Jack praised my cooking long and loud and plunged into stories, all self-consciousness gone. For my part, I forgot my preconceived plot and was lost in genuine enjoyment. He regaled me with the impressions of Bill Burroughs he'd gained in New York, what he knew of that strange individual's childhood, education and brilliant mind. Neither of us could guess why such a man had become so attracted to drugs and firearms. He told me the story of his own first wife, Edie Parker, and the hectic times in New York when he'd met them both. He was planning to visit Bill in Mexico in the summer and eagerly looked forward to another sojourn in that magic country. He loved the music and the slow, easy-going lifestyle. To him it seemed to represent a Utopian existence without hassles, a timeless peace. He and Neal favored Spengler's word *'fallaheen'* to describe the culture, but since to them the term meant a people who weren't going anywhere but had already been and were resting before the next creative cycle occurred, it sounded to me like the impossible dream for these two men who loved dashing about looking for 'kicks.'

When we had finished eating, I knew I had to keep Jack downstairs until I'd finished what I'd started; I'd never be able to repeat it. I poured more wine and walked to the couch we kept opened out to double-bed size. As I sat down on its edge, I held out Jack's glass to him. He followed me, accepted the wine and lay back upon the couch, balancing the glass on his chest. With his eyes closed, he hummed along to "My Funny Valentine" as it wafted from the radio.

I looked down at him but said nothing until the silence became thick and warm, then I asked, "Do you remember when we danced together in Denver?"

He turned his head, opened his eyes and looked at me tenderly. Then, smiling, he sat up and said softly, "Yeah . . . I wanted to take you away from Neal." He kept looking into my eyes but he had stopped smiling.

Barely audibly, I asked, "And do you remember the song we danced to?"
He leaned toward me: " 'Too Close for Comfort.' "

At that moment I knew plots and plans were foolish; my mind and will floated away and, just as in the movies, we both put down our glasses at the same time, not unlocking our eyes or looking at the table but making perfect contact. When his arms went around me, glints of light sparked in my head as if from a knife sharpening on a wheel, and my veins felt filled with warm, carbonated water.

The first morning light awakened me, and for a second I didn't know where I was. Then it came back, and seeing his form beside me a wave of remorse passed through me. What had I done? I was married to Neal, and now I felt sorry for him as well as afraid of what would happen next. The leather of the old couch was cold under me, and my muscles felt cramped. As quickly and silently as I could, I slid out from under the blanket and ran upstairs to my own bed, hoping for a few more hours of oblivion. It was no use. My mind kept frying the situation on all sides. I felt more shy of Jack than ever, and I didn't see how I could look him in the face. Would he be sorry?

I heard him getting up and come up the stairs, so I pretended to be asleep. All at once I felt his lips on my forehead, lingering, and a flood of soothing warmth poured over me as he climbed the stairs to his attic, and I drifted into sleep.

He accepted our new relationship more enthusiastically than I had expected, but I was pleased my guilt was thus diminished. Jack was a tender and considerate lover, though somewhat inhibited, and I suspected he wished I was more aggressive, but that I could never be. So our temperaments and our guilty feelings about Neal made actual love-making infrequent but more passionate. Although I could be wholly romantically in love with him, my heart still ached for Neal to be enough. Also, my compassion for anyone in Neal's position made me feel even more loving toward him, and I wavered in my resolve to teach him a lesson. I'd have sworn allegiance again in an instant, but I prodded my mind to remember his flippant words of indifference. I hoped sincerely that some lasting good would come from this, but for now there was nothing to do but relax and enjoy it.

Whenever Neal was home, Jack and I were extremely discreet, but there was no concealing the change in us. Neal couldn't help but notice, though the only evidence we had that he cared was his increased attentiveness to me.

The hope that my gamble would change the pattern of our lives was well founded. Like night changing into day, everything was showered with new light. Butterflies bursting from cocoons had nothing on me. Now, I was a part of all they did; I felt like the sun of their solar system, all revolved around me. Besides, I was now a real contributor for once; my housework and child-care had a purpose that was needed and appreciated. I was functioning as a female and my men were supportive. It may have taken two of them to complete the role usually filled by one, but the variety was an extra added attraction. They were such different types. How lucky could a girl get?

I provided for whichever of them was in residence according to his individual preferences. If they were both home during the day, Neal usually slept and Jack wrote, or Jack would go out and leave the husband and wife alone. On occasion, Jack and I would make love in his attic if the children were asleep. He'd produce a poor-boy of wine and play host. I think of him now whenever I smell unfinished wood, and remember how the sun sometimes lay across us like a blanket; or how, huddled under covers, we'd listen to the soft patter of the rain close above our heads.

When both men became accustomed to the idea, they dropped their defenses and joined me downstairs in the kitchen. While I performed my chores, they'd read each other excerpts from their writings-in-progress or bring out Spengler, Proust, Céline or Shakespeare to read aloud, interrupted by energetic discussions and analyses. Frequently they would digress and discuss a musician, or a riff or an interesting arrangement emanating from the radio. I was happy listening to them and filling their cups. Yet, I never felt left out any more. They'd address remarks to me and include me with smiles and pats, or request my view.

They still made forays together in search of tea or to buy necessities, but they were never gone long, and if Neal was at home, Jack and I sometimes took walks in the neighborhoods nearby. In Chinatown we marveled at the weird food displayed in the markets, the gorgeous embroidered clothing and the endless bric-a-brac in the tourist shops. Jack found an old-time Chinese restaurant with a white-tiled entrance on a little street adjacent to St. Francis Park. We'd buy steaming bowls of wonton soup for 35¢ or fried rice for 25¢. Often we warmed ourselves thus and then sat on a bench in the park beneath the magnificent Benny Bufano steel and marble statue of Sun Yat Sen. Other times we walked down the hill to Aquatic Park and drank Irish coffee in the Buena Vista or down the Union Street hill to Washington Square, taking French bread, cheese and wine purchased at the Buon Gusto market to nibble beneath the glittering gold spire of the cathedral. This reminded Jack of his childhood church in Lowell where he'd been baptized, St. Louis en l'Ile, and of his desire to see the original in Paris. On bright days we might hike up Telegraph Hill to Coit Tower and gaze out over the Bay, watching the ships, and that would be his cue to tell me of his seafaring adventures.

The times when Neal and I were alone were happier, too. We had the children's progress, illnesses and antics to discuss, as well as household economics. I felt especially affectionate toward him now, and he accepted and returned these expressions in better grace. I wondered if it was because he tended to appreciate his women more when the relationship was threatened, or whether a rival made him feel less trapped. At the moment I didn't care. Meals together amused me and gratified my ego. Here the two men were like small boys, vying for the most attention, for the best story, and felt slighted if one was allowed to hold the floor too long. Jack was the more sensitive, sometimes taking offense or sulking if Neal talked exclusively to me and behaved as though he weren't there. At times like these, Jack might stalk upstairs, and Neal would have to go and coax him back and make it up to him. Neal still had to prove he was the best man around. By and large, my cup was running over.

John Clellon Holmes

Go

"LOVE THAT IS DOOMED possesses me for some reason," Hobbes wrote to Liza a week later, the first week in August, in a fit of lonesome self pity. "I think of you and me as the doomed lovers we never were. We walk in some autumn's continual rain in my dream, and grasp at one another, as though each moment was the moment of parting, drinking in every feature, every change of expression. Each thing then becomes the last, and we wander down deserted streets, without touching, and are aliens wherever we go. Life is a perpetual defeat for us. We found each other reluctantly, allowed ourselves passion at the expense of sadness, opened to each other only out of irony. We said goodbye when we met the first secret time. We have no eagerness, no ecstasy, only the likeness of this sense of defeat. We come together rarely and then like two infected lovers in some contagious ruin, we lie down together only so that we might die warm. Each stolen moment is like a withering rose caught at the superb beauty of its decline, death already dreadfully kissing it. This is what I am thinking these days: of doomed lovers (you so rare and dark beside me), living a trapped life in a city set for destruction. How many beds we will get into tonight, apart, how many silences endure and how much longing will remain sweet and prisoned in our limbs without escape! Doomed lovers in buildings that will be ruins! Just part of my dream of you these days . . ."

But he did not send the letter, knowing it would only anger her, and put it in the growing sheaf of those which he had not sent, but saved as private documents of something. It was a rainy Friday, Kathryn would go from work to take a train to Westchester and her mother for the weekend. He faced two days dedicated to lonely, monkish idling, but walking up and down the apartment, snarled in a spiteful purposelessness, he had suddenly felt the uprush of self pity, like the maudlin but secretly cherished tears that one allows oneself while listening to that lovely, shallow music that dignifies adolescent memories, and he sat down and poured out all this in the letter, which, when it was finished, he could not even send. He was torn with a sense of his own lovelessness, like the suspicion of a hidden disease which has no symptoms, and he thought enviously of Kathryn and Pasternak.

Finally he called Estelle at her office, with the reckless audacity of a man who has resolutely decided to make a fool of himself. She seemed glad that he had called, and her voice was purring and confident at the other end. As though she was tuned in on his thoughts, she gently goaded him into asking if he might see her, and then told him (for which he was grateful) to meet her at six-thirty when she got out from work.

He walked across town in the rain, starting too early and having to dawdle. He realized that he did not know her, and had no idea of what the evening might hold; and among the scurrying summer crowds and the splashing taxis, he moved listlessly toward her, trying to expect nothing, and yet full of foolish, eager hopes.

When he saw her at the entrance of her building, unworried, calm, watching people that passed her with a strange, blank consideration of their existence, he realized that he must look like some dripping spaniel, his hair straggling wetly across his forehead, his selfconscious swagger giving away the awkwardness he actually felt.

She knew a restaurant on Fiftieth Street and took his arm firmly. He tried to get a cab, standing in a puddle waving his arms, cursing himself as inept for not being able to flag one down, although all of them were taken. Finally they walked, scampering from one awning to the next.

Over drinks and the eventual sauced scallops, it was better. He sat, feeling a vague sense of isolation that he could not describe even to himself, while she talked easily and at some length about her job. He carefully noticed the abstracted way she lit a cigarette in the middle of a word, and the direct gaze with which she listened to the few polite comments that he made, as though she could not hear them. When she said nothing for minutes on end, and seemed content to merely look at him without any particular meaning in her looks, he made sporadic attempts at amusing chatter, in which she would helpfully participate with everything but her eyes, which were intent elsewhere.

After more drinks, he experienced panic again when he realized that they must go somewhere else. He could think of no place to take her and would have been abjectly grateful if she had insisted on a movie in which he had no interest, but her very willingness to do anything he wanted terrified him. After a few aimless suggestions, he mentioned The Go Hole with a flippancy that was calculated to keep from her his own preference. She assented immediately and, as it was only a few blocks west, they walked. The rain was letting up, and Times Square was a huge, damp room with a red ceiling, and warm showers falling through great arcades of light.

They sat at a table at the back of the club in a half darkness. The place was nearly empty and the musicians played forlornly to the cluster of chairs in the bleacher section. Estelle observed everything silently, and even her enjoyment was indestructibly placid. She would nod her head when Hobbes explained the music and its devotees to her, giving him her attention as if it were a rare thing and reserved for him alone. But once, when he was quite unaware that he was staring at her profile as it was clearly cut against smoky light, looking at her face and memorizing it impersonally, she turned to him with her large, somehow intimate eyes showing no surprise, and putting a cool palm on his cheek, turned his face back to the music with a small laugh of playful remonstrance.

While they were there only one thing aroused his curiosity enough to distract him from her. It was a party of three that took a table nearby during one of the intermissions. He had been half-heartedly trying to explain to her what was suggested by the term "cool," as hipsters used it.

"When the music is cool, it's pleasant, somewhat meditative and without tension. Everything before, you see, just last year, was 'crazy,' 'frantic,' 'gone.' Now, everybody is acting cool, unemotional, withdrawn . . . What can one designate the moment that comes after 'the end,' after all? I suppose it's complete passivity, oblivion . . . But, look there, the guy coming to that table is 'cool'!"

And it was true. The man he indicated so perfectly epitomized everything that might conceivably be meant by the term that for ten minutes Hobbes could not take his eyes off him.

Wraithlike, this person glided among the tables wearily, followed by a six-foot, supple redhead in a green print dress, and a sallow, wrinkled little hustler, hatless and occupying a crumpled sport shirt as though crouched in it to

Holy Goofs

hide his withered body. The "cool" man wore a wide flat brimmed slouch hat that he would not remove, and a tan drape suit that seemed to wilt at his thighs. The stringy hair on his neck protruded over a soft collar, and his dark, oily face was an expressionless mask. He moved with a huge exhaustion, as though sleep walking, and his lethargy was so consummate that it seemed to accelerate the universe around him. He sprawled at the table between the redhead and the other fellow, his head sunk into his palms, the brim of his zoot hat lowered just far enough so that no light from the bandstand could reach him. He became particularly immobile during the hottest music, as though it was a personal challenge to his somnambulism on the part of the musicians. His passionless trance denied their very existence, and every now and again his head would literally drop to the table, and he would sit, snoozing like a peon in a cowboy film, his body folded down upon itself as though woven in an invisible cocoon in the air.

The tall girl paid absolutely no attention to him, watching the musicians, tapping long fingers and idly lighting cigarettes. She swung her broad shoulders languorously, letting her eyelids flutter closed when the tenor played a throaty ride, her teeth inside the full lips grinding together deliciously. The hustler, on the contrary, kept turning toward the "cool" man, with a slight, sardonic twist on his mouth, hunching forward. Every once in a while, eyes glowing over the unhealthy cheeks, he would whisper something, receiving no answer, and then he would run a swizzle stick inside the "cool" man's ear, tracing its contours; or devil it, under the hat, along the ridge of his nose, but he could raise no glimmer of life.

In the absurdly soft hat and the extreme drape, the "cool" man looked like a caricature of a petty hood, but if there was viciousness or depravity in his heart it could not penetrate through the thick torpor. Everything had dragged him so much that he no longer dug anything at all. One imagined that if a waiter had come up and requested him to remove the hat, he might have slowly, with weary irritation, reached to the holster under his arm and fingered a chilly automatic. Some night, in this very spot, when he had sunken to the abysses of his droopy lassitude, he might have pulled out his rod and sullenly shot up the place out of sheer ennui.

Estelle was intrigued by Hobbes' fascination with these three, but when he said, "You see, it's really the end of feeling, through feeling too much. Look, he's not even interested in the girl . . . or in anything! Even sex is a drag because he's gone to the end of it. He's gone to the end of everything!", she replied:

"Then let's get out of here, all right? He's so cool he's not even there, and that's too cool for me tonight. It might be catching!"

Holy Goofs

They went to an empty, paneled barroom on a nearby side street. It was almost three, and they sat among the deserted booths, with a soft juke box humming somewhere, and every once in a while the affable bartender would put down his newspaper and bring them more martinis. Hobbes suddenly had the feeling that the rain and the night had rejected them, driven both of them to a corner out of the turmoil and noise of the city, and their presence in that night was forgotten, unknown to anyone. It made him warm to think that, and he turned to Estelle, certain that everything she would do from then on would have a mysterious significance to him.

Without hesitation, peering into the large brown eyes with the clear flashes in them, he began to tell her about the "beat generation," tell her that though he did not know that it existed, somehow he sensed that it was there, tell her things which he had never thought out clearly himself, things the "cool" man and his own heightened concern about the evening had thrown into relief in his mind. He talked steadily, gravely, about the war and how it had wounded everyone emotionally, using the "cool" man as an example. He spoke of Hart and Stofsky and Pasternak and Agatson, of their faithlessness and his recognition of a similar discontent inside himself. For the first time in many months, he allowed himself the luxury of voicing insoluble questions, allowed himself to feel that desperation of disbelief, that bewilderment in the face of experience that he seemed cruelly incapable of comprehending, that had always soured the conclusions he had sought so terribly to believe.

Finally he ran down, and her presence across from him became evident again, their difference, their separation from each other became clear once more, and he was suddenly overwhelmed with embarrassment. They sat for an instant and he dared not look at her but could only mutter wildly: "Say something to me!"

But she would say nothing, and only leaned across the table, like a wise little girl listening, for the first time, to some female voice that a man can never hear, and bringing his face close to hers, put her moist lips against his with that intent preoccupation in the act itself that always amazed him.

GREGORY CORSO

An Accidental Autobiography

To James Laughlin   Paris
                                                          [ca. Dec. 25] 1959

Dear JL,

Arrived in Paris. Paris is lovely. I love it more than any city now, I really do. Felt so great walking in and out and around the gray little streets again. I immediately went to see Burroughs. After awhile he showed me the *Life* article. I read it quickly and thought "another down article." Then Burroughs asked me "Did you read it?" I said yes. Sensing my indifferent reaction he said "Read it again." I read it again, and what I read frightened me. How sinister and real! Did you read it? I asked myself "Is this the Beat Generation?" And I couldn't find a no in me. I read the article and asked myself what has night-horns sun-flies tons of dried fire to do with this big dark article? Here is no poetry, here is Stalin Trotsky politics, a no-politics politics; I read the article and I didn't know the Ginsberg the Kerouac he was writing about, mostly the Ginsberg who he set up as a raving intentional system breaker, how he must despise Allen! And Allen is all good, (doth the cause of such despite stem from that?) Then I began to wonder about myself. These last three months in Greece affected me very much, my last shakings of Death-probe, with the result of a ordinary stage prop illumination on Hydra; I was broken up after that because I went into Death and came out of it with a creation of invisibility, with a Hollywood powder-puff vision, if it were any vision at all. All right. I immediately dashed off that poem *Birthday's End,* it was a nowhere poem and it rated the "vision"; I, of course, being myself wanted better, so I "created" by use of poetry, an even worse poem, *Greece,* I "covered up" *Death* with *Greece.* Well I am very true to myself and I knew it wouldn't do. The best thing was to forget it, read mother goose, and I did.

I read the article as lightly as I have always taken the Beat Generation, I always made jokes or fantasies about it; I did not see what Kerouac or Ginsberg saw, or what the interviewers from *Arts,* French art paper here, saw. They interviewed Burroughs and myself last night, and asked such questions as: "Do you hate police?" "What do you think of surrealism?" They were probing for surrealism, that was the big thing, they were very good friends of Breton, and they wanted to get me to say the Beat Generation is founded on surrealism, because where surrealism left off, the Beats executed. It was strange, because all he wanted me to say was "hate" "against", and I told him no, I think cops are a necessary evil; I don't think surrealism has anything to do with Beat, surrealism was a social clique, keeping its surreal for themselves, not for the man who sells *poisson*, whereas the Beat claim that it is possible for any man to write a poem, even a great one at that, if he only "free" himself. "Beat is surely a movement and dangerously politic, such that it can annoy both existing powerful systems." After that I went upstairs with Burroughs and he showed me the *Life* article, and it all came clear to me, and I have written that poem I tried so foolishly to write under the dupe of death.

(I must clear time element) I came to Paris last night, Burroughs showed me *Life* article, I read it casually, went to sleep, next day word got round I was back, the photographers of *Arts* and the interviewers came to the hotel; Burroughs introduced me to them, we spoke, then went to Burroughs' room where he showed me article again. This is main idea that came to me and allowed following poem, if there is a *Bomb* then it eliminates war, if war is eliminated, then history is eliminated, if history is eliminated then Time is eliminated if Time is eliminated then we are immortal. I have never been more happy in my whole life. Here is poem:

> The Bomb prevents war / History ends / In the Beginning the
> desire to go <u>back</u> / has been fulfilled / We now begin / The
> height of elevation is Heaven / Heaven is the end of history /
> The history of Life and Time is done / We are in Heaven /
> And / Heaven is a <u>familiar</u> place / The night-horn blow / The
> sun-fly bless / Prince and princess / The universe's property /
> now disproportioned / Gone the winged children / The rabbit
> / The afterglow.

And so good tall kind sir who saw me in natural poesy, my last poem. I will continue to write, but what I'll write will be useless to what has already been done; I should feel very proud and happy of being a part of what has been done, nay not a part, but a cause. And I am happy. The thing now is, go beyond poetry. And so now that history is ended, now that immortality is before us, gather ye your rosebuds with eternal delay.

James is it not true that WITHOUT war all existing governments will fall? Please write to me about this, for if it is so, then I shall look upon the Beat Generation with new eyes; yet will I ever get over this antipathy I have for sandals and beards and beat pad life? One last thing, out of that *Life* article I also got this: Luce is God. He owns LIFE TIME <u>and</u> CHANCE (Fortune). In *Life* he is all strong, in *Time* he can write about something before it even happens! He made the Beat Generation! In the article O'Niel asks "How did this all come about?" And why did Luce make the Beat Generation? Because he is God and he knew that Beat would find that out and DID, so he choose Beat for his chess mate, thus CHANCE, here he was not all powerful, here he could LOSE, and did. That is why I say history is ended. There is no stopping this Beat thing, we simply do not verge or fall into a new era, eras are ended, done. Also consider this, in article Kerouac is "raised" so to speak to the "granddaddy" of the Beats, a genteel level, a quiet harmless level; Kerouac has made much money and has never really been Beat and has done his duty as informing the public of Beat—whereas the real sinisterism is the replica of Ginsberg; I know Ginsberg very well, that bearded picture in *Life* is NOT Ginsberg; I have received his last letters KNOWING it is not Ginsberg; Luce has made a replica of him. Remember Lorca: "I am no longer what I am, the house I own is not <u>mine</u> to sell"—I may be going a little too far, yet you can't deny I am close as to be burned of the Truth.

Well. And now what do all this mean to poetry, let's say my poetry; if all is done as I see it, what use the publication of *Happy Birthday*; what can it mean or say or do? Surely now I see that that poetry was not meant to entertain, but to mean and do; how do when do is done? In practical sense the book will sell, if anything, let's say as you publisher and I author, we have a book that will sell; and that's as far as it goes. I would like to see book published, my best poems are in that book, but it is too late; I think you can understand what I mean by this. I have been very straight with you; I await your reply; I never felt so clear of mind and body; even my face looks younger. I have achieved certainty.

Noel, Gregory

I dare not re-read this letter for fear of not sending it. So where is that achievement of certainty after all? O Gregory!

I did re-read it and damn it I am certain, and one thing I forgot in that article notice how they say of me GUNS—*Don't Shoot The Warthog, Bomb*, in photo: Corso aims as if to SHOOT—also notice, photo of Ginsberg lying in bed, the Sitwell "bad smell" comment, next to Ginsberg photo is an ad "how to get rid of bad smell from the house." I was with Allen when we saw Sitwell and she mentioned nothing of odor and had a fine lunch and spoke only of poetry. But that's minor. Of the article—it was more than an article, it was a great declaration of defeat,—Luce may be God but he is a failure God—and end result, in Heaven there is no God. I could go on for hours. I'd best go back to Mother Goose.

SAM SHEPARD

Rolling Thunder Logbook

OCTOBER—LOWELL

ALLEN QUOTES FROM KEROUAC'S favorite Shakespeare: "How like a winter hath my absence been. . . . What freezings have I felt, what dark days seen!/What old December's bareness everywhere!" It's right close to the time of year he died in. Trees sticking up naked, blankets of blowing leaves. Dylan and Ginsberg perched close to the ground, cross-legged, facing this tiny marble plaque, half buried in the grass: " 'TI-JEAN' [little Jack], JOHN L. KER-OUAC, Mar. 12, 1922–Oct. 21, 1969—HE HONORED LIFE—STELLA HIS WIFE, Nov. 11, 1918—." Dylan's tuning up his Martin while Ginsberg causes his little shoe-box harmonium to breathe out notes across the lawn. Soon a slow blues takes shape with each of them exchanging verses, then Allen moving into an improvised poem to the ground, to the sky, to the day, to Jack, to life, to music, to the worms, to bones, to travel, to the States. I try to look at both of them head-on, with no special ideas of who or what they are but just to try to see them there in front of me. They emerge as simple men with a secret aim in mind. Each of them opposite but still in harmony. Alive and singing to the dead and living. Sitting flat on the earth, above bones, beneath trees and hearing what they hear.

Road Dogs and Queens of Heart

Dee Dee Ramone Paintings

NEIL ORTENBERG

On Dee Dee Ramone

WHEN I FIRST MET Dee Dee at the Chelsea Hotel, he reminded me of another author who became my friend, Gregory Corso. The term "marching to your own drummer" doesn't even scratch the surface. Both of these guys defined cool, and had a cultural impact that few of us are lucky to even get near. Neither of them hung out at Elaine's, or mingled with Tina Brown.

They were real New Yorkers, the kind you remember. Once, I was telling Corso of my admiration and gratitude for how he and Kerouac, Burroughs, Ginsberg, and others had impacted on the bland culture of the fifties, and Gregory's response was "Hey, get out of the bongo days." Always unexpected, like a jazz solo, always on the money. These two guys, in a different era, could have done one-man shows like Leguizamo. All you had to do was get them going, and a rainbow of spontaneous, original, and unpretentious wisdom and poetry would arise and it was usually funny as hell. And yes, Dee Dee was a poet. He was the poet of the Ramones, the guy who lived the life and walked the walk. He was a poet after he left the Ramones and lived his life making music, painting, writing, and talking the words in the everyday language of a poet.

I remember driving around near Venice Beach with Dee Dee and his wife Barbara. Dee Dee had just finished talking about the death of his father, and how he had gone to the grave to talk to his father "privately," to put things right. A dutiful son, Dee Dee was always trying to make things better, if sometimes a bit late on the execution. The description was childlike and from a place that was entirely pure, and there was much of that pureness in Dee Dee. And like many people blessed and burdened with the talent of purity, Dee Dee found many ways throughout his life to cast away this inherent quality.

His death may have been the ultimate middle finger to the oppression of his pure side, to the challenges of middle age, to the expectations that come from being famous. The last time I saw Dee Dee was at Roseland, where he did one of his last gigs as a favor to me. He was playing with his band as well as Marky and C.J. Ramone, and Paul Kostabi. It was classic Ramones—full throttle, adrenaline fueled, burning down the house. There was a big sign that Arturo Vega made that read, "Happy Birthday Joey." Dee Dee wanted to honor Joey in public, since Joey's birthday was a few days away. Print articles had been covering the conflict between the various Ramones as Joey's posthumous birthday closed in. Dee Dee wanted to clear the air, make sure fans knew he really loved Joey, no matter how bad things may have gotten from time to time. When Jerry from the Misfits first raised the sign on the old stage at Roseland, the packed house responded with a volcanic wave of cheers. I raised the sign a few seconds later, and again, the crowd screamed in unison. An hour earlier, Dee Dee, C.J., and Marky played a spontaneous acoustic set of Ramones hits, down in the dressing room. It was a magical moment, unchoreographed, pared down, and straightforward. No bullshit, just the music. "Lobotomy," "Sheena Is a Punk Rocker," "Chinese Rock," the small group listened quietly as Dee Dee sang, C.J. played guitar, and Marky used his boot soles as percussion.

A week earlier, Dee Dee and I were hanging out at the Knitting Factory in L.A. for a literary reading. We were listening to Harry Dean Stanton, but Dee Dee had been upset with me for twisting his arm a few weeks back, the night before he accepted his Rock and Roll Hall of Fame award. That night I asked him to do the Roseland gig, an event for booksellers, publishers, agents, and book types. We would have Dee Dee come with his band, and share the stage with Tom Tom Club—his old pals Tina Weymouth and Chris Frantz from Talking Heads. As it turned out, the addition of Marky and C.J. created a mini Ramones reunion, but that night at the Knitting Factory Dee Dee was still angry that I had talked him into yet another gig. I had also made Dee Dee attend two book signings that weekend, one at Borders and the other at the L.A. Bookfair for *Lobotomy* and *Chelsea Horror Hotel*, his two books. Dee Dee had called me after the second signing and told me he really just wanted to be a painter and a writer, and do his art in peace and quiet. He was pissed off that I had taken advantage of his good will, the night before his Rock and Roll Hall of Fame award, and had gotten him to agree to another gig. He had been doing gigs most of his adult life and at this point all they brought were heartache and bad hotels. He was struggling to find a center in his life that would be appropriate for a fifty-year-old aging rock star, and life on the road was not, in his mind, going to be part of his next act. After Dee Dee finished screaming at me, he grew quiet and as Dee Dee would, after an explosion, he became apologetic. I told him we would meet at the Knitting Factory and discuss the whole thing, and if he didn't want to do the Roseland gig, I'd understand.

As Harry Dean Stanton continued his reading, Dee Dee and I were huddled at the bar, and I listened to Dee Dee talk about the early days of the Ramones with affectionate remembrances of Johnny Thunders, Sid Vicious, Stiv Bators, people now departed. It had been an electric time for Dee Dee, and there were certain moments when he would draw that time back from his memory, and it was like a big movie screen with all his friends as stars, young and unstoppable. He forgave me for the Roseland gig, and agreed to come. Maybe it would be good to be on stage at Roseland, with all its history, and ghosts of the past. I was grateful, and put my arm around Dee Dee to thank him. He was enjoying his generosity, and had that childlike Dee Dee look, even behind his sunglasses in that dark room.

All of a sudden Dee Dee jumped up and said it was time to go. We hugged and he left. Fifteen seconds later he came back and presented me with a dragon ring, which I wear now. He said it was a present for me, and then he rushed out of the room, spontaneous, unpredictable, guileless, just like that.

The day I heard Dee Dee was dead, it didn't seem possible, and yet it was, if you read his books, always just beneath the surface. I have a painting that Dee Dee gave me near my bed. It's a portrait of Sid Vicious with the words: "You can't trust no fuck'en body." It stands as the alter ego to the dragon ring I sport on my right index finger.

Dee Dee Ramone

Legend of a Rock Star

THE WAY I FEEL now is that I don't give a damn if I ever come back to Europe or Germany, and especially East Germany, ever again. I have no doubts in my mind where my loyalties are. They're with myself. I'm all I've got.

I used to feel sentimental about Germany. I grew up here. My mother is German. Maybe I don't fit in, in Germany. That's not my fault. What *auss-lander* does?

When we got to the town of Jenna, where I'm playing tonight, I was hoping I wouldn't take everything so personally. That it would be just another stop on the tour. It's a college town, sort of like Leeds, in England, except these krauts seem to be a lot better off. It's a bunch of self-absorbed, know-it-all students here, running to and fro from their classes like robots, and mommy and daddy or the state are paying the bills. I tried but there's no way I couldn't end up hating it here. I have always felt the sting of the upper-white-middle class. My only degree is in streetology. I'm uneducated. I had to leave school at sixteen and go to work in a supermarket to support myself. That's because I'm an honest person. I wouldn't know how to lean on society, or another person if I tried.

I had a feeling that, when I was playing the show at the college in Jenna, that the mostly student audience could tell how I felt. I could also tell how they felt. So I gave them a couple of Johnny Mathis-type versions of some Ramones songs to mimic their attitude. Oh, but careful, I'm in Germany, so I must be extra respectful. Ha. Ha.

When the East German government was in power they told these people every move they could make. Rock and roll music was forbidden. But I don't feel sorry for them. It's what they want. Now they might have a freedom of choice, but German peer pressure takes that away. Always. They have become so used to being American-haters that they hate rock and roll music. Okay! *Tuchuss*, you deserve the isolation that you have imposed upon yourselves. The audience in Jenna knows all this already. They knew that my concert there was a last-time kind of a thing. They tried to *macht show* but it wasn't good enough for me.

I'm not a punk, skin, Nazi, or snob. I'm defiant. I'm angry. You made me that way. So fuck you all. Yes, I'll want my turn in line. But if you want to give me dirty, impatient looks, to make tension or push your way in front of me because you don't think that trash like me belongs in the line, then you have got to expect trouble from me. What I had to end up becoming is an American fucking outlaw. So burn, Germany, burn. I'll light the fire.

Dragons . . . Imagine one flying over one of the meadows, high above New York City's Central Park, one crowed Sunday afternoon. Maybe this dragon could be Joey Ramone. I don't see why not. He could be a beautiful, golden-amber colored one with a silver lightning ambience radiating from his body and wings. He'd have two flashing and loving eyes and would wink down at everybody staring up at him in amazement. Then he would spread his fiery wings and fly towards the sun to California to go surfing and to have some fun.

I like dragons so much that I tried to look for one outside the window of the plane that I'm in now. I imagine that a dragon would love this part of the world that I'm flying through now. Dragons love to make it rain. I looked out the plane's window and scanned the clouds that are hanging so low in the sky because they're pregnant with rain water and sinking towards the ocean.

I spotted a dragon immediately. It was a sea dragon, disguised as the tip of a cloud framing itself in a beautiful gray sky. Then, when all I was seeing revealed itself to be an illusion, *what a beautiful sense of humor these creatures have,* I thought silently to myself.

Some of what I heard about how courageously Joey faced death and a horrible illness is truly amazing. He had faith until the end. Till they turned off his life support. All he wanted was to get better. He thought that he would only have to go through the cancer treatments that one last time.

He wanted to get out of the hospital and rock and roll some more. Whenever people used to ask me about him I would always say that Joey was a very tough guy. He had amazing courage to be so sickly and be in the Ramones. It was harder for him than the rest of us.

A couple of years ago I told him that this was going to kill him if he kept it up. I suggested to him that we both take off and go to Miami, and hide out, like when the Ramones first played California and we went to Huntington Beach. Joey just smiled when I said this. He didn't answer me, but I think he appreciated that I cared about him so much. The problem was that he was desperate for fame and success that he didn't think he'd achieved with the Ramones, and felt that the Ramones had held him back. He stayed in New York and I went to California. We never went to Miami.

I'm such a sentimental old bastard that I really don't want to stop playing music either. That's no good for me and I know that to do so would be seriously risking it. I know that I'm very lucky to be alive. That God blessed me. That I was very lucky to have started the Ramones and have been in the group.

My neighbor Chris, downstairs, is a guitar tech for a lot of big bands and is very much in demand. He also works part time for Schecter Guitars. I think he felt bad for me when I came home from the European tour. Joey died and that left me numb. I was freaked out by what happened to Jimmy Vapid. I wouldn't come out of the apartment or answer my door. After a week Chris finally just about broke the door to my apartment down and forced me to come out in the sunshine and go for a walk.

"Let's go over to Schecter and look around at the guitars," Chris suggested when we were at La Brea and Hollywood Boulevard.

"Sounds good," I answered.

They really like Chris over at Schecter. It's hard to believe how generous they are. I walked out of there later with a beautiful black Diamond series acoustic guitar and a black Telecaster. As beautiful as these two guitars are, when I got home with them and looked them over I started to worry. These two look dangerous, I thought to myself. They're just too nice. I'm going to have to play these guys, I realized.

Chris, Chase, and I got in a van on May sixteenth and drove up to somewhere on the outskirts of San Francisco. We're going to play six or seven more shows. Then we're going to stop for a while. My producer, Chris Spedding, who's even older than me and an even meaner old man than I am, will be available to do a new album in October. He's going to London this week for rehearsals with his old band Roxy Music, with Brian Ferry. He's doing fifty-five shows with them.

On June eighth I'm going back to New York. I'm having a private party for my new book the *Chelsea Horror Hotel*, which is just now being released and I'm also having an art exhibition with Paul Kostabi.

I won't be seeing Joey. That's hard. I also wish I could have played the Continental Divide one more time with my own band or the Remains, but that's never going to happen. I'm positive that everything will go well for me when I go back to New York again. It might even be the start of something new. I hope so and I don't hope so.

Today I was wondering what God was going to do with me now. Well, I know he's not going to refuse me into heaven, I'm not worried about that; more than anything, I just want to keep living. Please don't kill me now, God. I would love to be the last Ramone to die.

I guess I'm still the same old Dee Dee. In a lot of ways, I'm still like a street kid and always will be. All I need is a city to roam around in and I'm okay.

I like how things are for me now. Getting to walk around Hollywood Boulevard with nothing to do. It's fun just being myself. I was in one of the world's best rock and roll bands. And one of the toughest ones. It took me, Joey, John, Tommy, and Marky to do it. We all paid a price for it. It was a lot. The Ramones accomplished a lot. No one can deny that. We did what we did together. It couldn't have happened if any of these people had not been in their predestined roles.

I just never thought it would mean so much.

It's not too bad being an old rock and roll star. It's like having a tear in your eye and a smile on your face at the same time.

DMX

E.A.R.L.

NINETEEN-EIGHTY-FIVE WAS the best year of my life. I had survived my time in group home. I was back in Yonkers. I had a dog I called my own. Nineteen-eighty-five was the year I started robbing, running, fucking, the year I first heard "Silver Shadow," and the year that I bought my first pair of Timberlands.

But in 1986, well, that was something else . . .

It was Peanut's fault. He lived in building 10. He had been talking shit to me all morning so me and Blacky chased him right upstairs into his hallway. His mother heard us arguing and came out with a frying pan in her hand, so I went back downstairs to catch him later. Ten minutes later though, the police rolled up. When they saw me and Blacky posted in the front, they drew their guns and opened their car door halfway to shield themselves.

"Put the dog up against the fence!"

My first instinct was to run, but I didn't know if Blacky could keep up with me and I didn't want them to start shooting at my dog.

"Tie your dog against the fence and step this way."

I did what they said.

They put me in the back of the police car and when I asked them what was going on they said that the pound was on the way. Someone had called in a complaint about my dog.

When the handlers arrived, they put a loop around Blacky's neck to try to catch him but he was big and strong and when my dog saw that I wasn't getting out of the police car, he started going wild. They couldn't pull him in the paddy wagon. Blacky just kept barking.

"Yeah, boy. Get him, boy!" I yelled at him from behind the window. I wasn't going to let them take my dog.

The handlers wrestled with Blacky for ten more minutes, then I saw one of them nod to a police officer.

"Everybody please stand back . . ."

They hooked Blacky to the fence again and when I saw one of the police officers move directly in front of him I started screaming.

"NO! DON'T KILL MY DOG! NOOOO!"

Two shots later, Blacky was dead. They shot him right in front of the building. That's why I hate Peanut to this day because he got my dog killed. *Fucking bitch.*

In 1986, though, being broke wasn't my only problem.

A few years before, Ready Ron introduced me to something that was far more damaging to my life and my spirit then not having money. Until then, I drank forties with cats on corners, smoked whatever weed I came across, and experimented with bullshit drugs like mescaline when the mood arose, like the day me, Nick, and Reg went on that robbing spree. But that didn't make me much more than your average project nigga. There were no lingering effects of getting drunk one night off a bottle of malt liquor or passing a blunt with my niggas from School Street.

But when Ready Ron spoke of the great high I could get from a "woolie," the "new thing on the block," he didn't tell me how differently it would affect my life. He didn't tell me of the war that I would have to fight to kill my desire for one of the most addictive drugs on the street. He didn't tell me how quickly it would ruin what little was left of my relationship with my mother, my sisters, and even my uncles.

When I smoked a blunt laced with crack cocaine, he didn't tell me how much I would suffer. How wrong that was.

"I fucked up."

Collie found out about my problem the day I went into the shoebox he kept in his closet and took some of his stash. My uncle occasionally hustled to put some money in his pocket, mostly nickel or dime bags of weed, but every now and then he would flip the harder stuff.

"What do you mean you 'fucked up'?" he answered me back.

Then he saw what I had taken. Collie and me had never had a fight. We would disagree and argue like brothers, but we would never come to blows. That day I could feel his anger and disappointment fire at me like a shotgun blast.

He said he knew it wasn't me. I told him it wasn't a big deal.

But it got worse.

Now I had another reason to rob. Not only was I trying to eat, trying to keep some money in my pocket, but now I also had a habit to feed.

It didn't help that my aunts were also struggling, or that I bumped heads with my uncle Pinky in the same apartments on Ravine where I was getting high. At one point, Pinky lived next door to one of the buildings that served as my main stomping ground. Sometimes he would come and try to take me out of the hallways I was in, tried to pull me out of hell.

It was never easy.

I never talked to anyone about my problem. But I couldn't hide it. One day I saw my little sister Shayla walking home from school. She must have been no more than nine or ten years old. I didn't think she saw me.

"Earl."

I couldn't let her see me like this.

"Earl. I know that's you."

I had to hide my eyes. I wasn't the older brother she thought I was.

"Go home, Shayla."

"Earl, please come upstairs. Please come upstairs and I'll give you something to eat. Talk to me for a minute."

"No, not right now, girl. I'm not coming upstairs right now."

But at my darkest moments, I did go upstairs. These were the times I ran out of money, the times someone's wallet wasn't enough to pay my bill. The problem was that I knew whomever I needed to pay would accept anything that I could give them: VHS tapes, shoes, sneakers, even giant-size bottles of bleach or laundry detergent. I took them. I would lift coats out of my mother's closet, sweaters from my sisters, or swipe old clothes of my own that were still in my room—anything that would get me closer to that next high.

It didn't matter to me. There was a voice in my head louder and more powerful than anything I had ever heard before, and it wouldn't stop yelling.

A week after Blacky's murder, I walked into the lunchroom of Yonkers High School with a sawed-off shotgun taped to my leg. The gun came from the floor up to my knee, so it made me walk stiff, like I was crippled. I didn't give a fuck about nothing or nobody. I was ready to rob anybody I could.

Niggas thought I was bluffing.

"What, man, what? It can happen . . . Run your fucking pockets!"

I came home with about four dollars. A few days later, I was behind bars. It was dark and hell is hot.

LARRY HESTER FOR *VIBE* ONLINE

Interview with Tupac Shakur

JUNE 1996

WHAT MOTIVATES YOU?

Poverty, needs, wants, pain. Now I'm dealing with a more military type of philosophy—to mix the street life with respected, known, and proven military philosophy. So when I'm rapping and talking that hardcore shit, at least it'll be from a military mind-set.

What about your father—do you have any relationship with him?

I thought my father was dead all my life. After I got shot, I looked up and there was this nigga that looked just like me. And he was my father; that's when I found out. We still didn't take no blood test but the nigga looked just like me and the other nigga's dead, so now I feel that I'm past the father stage. I do want to know him and I do know him.

We did talk and he did visit and help me when I was locked down, but I'm past that. What I want to do is form a society in which we can raise ourselves; so we can become our own father figures and the big homies can become their father figures, and then you grow up, then it's your turn to be a father figure to another young brother. That's where I want to start. Nine times out of ten, though, we would want them to be there, they can't be depended on to be there. Now, some of the mothers can't be there because they doing their thing [working]. I can't blame them, they gotta do what they gotta do. So I think the youth should raise themselves since they got lofty ideas about what's theirs and their rights, what they should deserve. Since you can't whup their asses, these motherfuckers should get out and work at fifteen. I want to be a part of the generation that builds the groundwork for us to raise each other.

In one of your VIBE interviews, you mentioned an organization that you were starting with Mike Tyson. What happened with that?

Now I'm doing it with Death Row. I was going to do it myself and I found out when I was about to be sentenced to jail that there was a spot called "A Place Called Home." I was about to be sent to jail for an old gun case that I had. The judge was like "You can tell your side of who you are" and the prosecutor gave this big fat envelope of every time I got arrested and all this stuff that made me look like a crazed animal.

We got someone who didn't work for us to write my life's story, talking about everybody in my family and the people that I helped. This lady from the community center wrote as well. We were planning already to do this big concert with me and my homeboys to raise money to have a center in North Central where we can have the "at risk" kids come to a spot that they can call home—where they can get guidance, tutoring, love, nurturing. We're going to do a spot like that.

So instead of it just being a program with me and Tyson like I planned it, 'cause it's me sitting in the penitentiary thinking, is now moved into this program called "A Place Called Home" that I'm working closely with. There's also a program called "Celebrity Youth League," with me, Hammer, Suge, and all of these sports figures each going to sponsor a youth group all year in football, baseball, and basketball. We sponsor the team, buy the uniforms, hire the coach, and start our own Little League.

How do you relax from all this that you're doing?

There's three ways: shopping, driving down Sunset with the top down on any car, and being with my homeboys. Not necessarily the older homies but the younger ones. Vibing off of what they're talking about and what's going on, and dropping whatever I have to drop to them. Then it's not like I'm doing this shit in vain.

Do you still keep in touch with old friends?

On the whole, I don't have any friends. Friends come and go; I've lost my trust factor. I believe I have people who *think* they're my friends. And I believe that there are people probably in their heart who are friendly toward me or are friends to me. But they're not my friends, because what I learned is that fear is stronger than love. So soon as somebody scarier comes along, they won't be my friend anymore. I learned that on the floor at Times Square—so I don't have friends, I have family. You're either my all-the-way family or just somebody on the outside.

Are you tight with your family?

Yeah, we took it back to the old school. We got the head of the family, we listen to the rules and regulations, order and organization. Now we're a living, breathing family, when before we were a dying, dysfunctional family. We still got problems but now we're learning how to deal with it.

What religion are you?

I'm the religion that to me is the realest religion there is. I try to pray to God every night unless I pass out. I learned this in jail. I talked to every God [member of the Five Percent Nation] there was in jail. I think that if you take one of the "O's" out of "Good" it's "God," if you add a "D" to "Evil," it's the "Devil." I think some cool motherfucker sat down a long time ago and said, Let's figure out a way to control motherfuckers. That's what they came up with—the Bible. 'Cause if God wrote the Bible, I'm sure there would have been a revised copy by now. 'Cause a lot of shit has changed. I've been looking for this revised copy—I still see that same old copy that we had from then. I'm not disrespecting anyone's religion, please forgive me if it comes off that way, I'm just stating my opinion.

The Bible tells us that all these people did this because they suffered so much, that's what makes them special people. I got shot five times and I got crucified in the media. And I walked through with the thorns on, and I had shit thrown on me, and I had the word thief at the top; I told that nigga, "I'll be back for you. Trust me, it's not supposed to be going down, I'll be back." I'm not saying I'm Jesus, but I'm saying we go through that type of thing every day. We don't part the Red Sea, but we walk through the 'hood without getting shot. We don't turn water to wine, but we turn dope fiends and dope heads into productive citizens of society. We turn words into money—what greater gift can there be? So I believe God blesses us, I believe God blesses those that hustle. Those that use their minds and those that overall are righteous. I believe that everything you do bad comes back to you. So everything that I do that's bad, I'm going to suffer for it. But in my heart, I believe what I'm doing in my heart is right. So I feel like I'm going to heaven.

I think heaven is just when you sleep, you sleep with a good conscience— you don't have nightmares. Hell is when you sleep, the last thing you see is all the fucked-up things you did in your life and you just see it over and over again, 'cause you don't burn. If that's the case, it's hell on earth, 'cause bullets burn. There's people that got burned in fires, does that mean they went to hell already? All that is here. What do you got there that we ain't seen here? What, we're gonna walk around aimlessly like zombies? That's here! You ain't been on the streets lately? Heaven now, look! [He gestures to his plush apartment.] We're sitting up here in the living room, big-screen TV—this is heaven, for the moment. Hell is jail—I seen that one. Trust me, this is what's real. And all that other shit is to control you.

If the churches took half the money that they was making and gave it back to the community, we'd be all right. If they took half the buildings that they use to "praise God" and gave it to motherfuckers who need God, we'd be all right. Have you seen some of these got-damn churches lately? There's one's that take up the whole block in New York. There's homeless people out here. Why ain't God lettin' them stay there? Why these niggas got gold ceilings and shit? Why God need gold ceilings to talk to me? Why does God need colored windows to talk to me? Why God can't come where I'm at where he sent me? If God wanted to talk to me in a pretty spot like that, why the hell he send me here then? That makes ghetto kids not believe in God. Why?

Road Dogs and Queens of Heart

So that's wrong religion—I believe in God, I believe God puts us wherever we want to be at. That didn't make sense that God would put us in the ghetto. That means he wants us to work hard to get up out of here. That means he's testing us even more. That makes sense that if you're good in your heart, you're closer to God, but if you're evil, then you're closer to the devil; that makes sense! I see that everyday all that other spooky shit, don't make sense. I don't even believe, I'm not dissin' them, but I don't believe in the brothers, I've been in jail with 'em and having conversations with brothers; "I'm God, I'm God." You God, open the gate for me. You know how far the sun is and how far the moon is, how the hell do I pop this fuckin' gate? And get me free and up outta here. Then I'll be a Five Percenter for life.

Bob Dylan

Tarantula

LET ME SAY THIS about Justine—she was 5 ft.2 & had Hungarian eyes—her belief was that if she could make it with Bo Diddley—she could get herself straight—now Ruthy—she was different—she always wanted to see a cock fight & went to Mexico City when she was 17 & a runaway cast-off—she met Zonk when she was 18—Zonk came from her home town—at least that's what he said when he met her—when they busted up, he said he never heard of the place but that's beside the point—anyway these three—they make up the Realm Crew . . . i met them exactly at their table & they took 2 years of sanction from me but i never talk much about it myself—Justine was always trying to prove she existed as if she really needed proof—Ruthy—she was always trying to prove that Bo Diddley existed & Zonk he was trying to prove that he existed just for Ruthy but later on said that he was just trying to prove he existed to himself—me? i started wondering about whether anybody existed but i never pushed it too much—especially when Zonk was around— Zonk hated himself & when he got too high he thought everybody was a mirror

one day i discovered that my secrets were puny—i tried to build them up but Justine said "this is the Twentieth Century baby—i mean you know—like they dont do that anymore—why dont you go walk on the street—that'll build up your secrets—it's no use to spend all these hours a day doing it in a room—youre losing living—i mean like if you wanna be some kinda charles atlas, go right ahead . . . but you better head off for muscle beach—i mean you just might as well snatch jayne mansfield—become king of your kind & start some kind of secret gymnasium" . . . after being ridiculed to such a degree—i decided to leave my secrets alone & Justine—Justine was right—my secrets got bigger—in fact they grew so big that they outweighed my body . . . i hitchhiked alot in those days & you had to be ready—you never knew what kind of people you were gonna meet on the road

i sang in a forest one day & someone said it was three o'clock—that nite when i read the newspaper, i saw that a tenement had been set aflame & that three firemen & nineteen people had lost their lives—the fire was at three o'clock too . . . that nite in a dream i was singing again—i was singing the same song in the same forest & at the same time—in the dream there was also a tenement blazing . . . there was no fog & the dream was clear—it was not worth ana-lyzing as nothing is worth analyzing—you learn from a conglomeration of the incredible past—whatever experience gotten in any way whatsoever—controlling at once the present tense of the problem—more or less like a roy rogers & trigger relationship of which under present western standards is an impossibility—me singing—i moved from the forest—frozen in a moment & picked up & moved above land—the tenement blazing too at the same moment being picked up & moved towards me—i, still singing & this building still burning . . . needless to say—i & the building met & as instantly as it stopped, the motion started again—me, singing & the building burning—there i was—in all truth—singing in front of a raging fire—i was unable to do anything about this fire—you see—not because i was lazy or loved to watch good fires—but rather because both myself & the fire were in the same Time all right but we were not in the same Space—the only thing we had in common was that we existed in the same moment . . . i could not feel any guilt about just standing there singing for as i said i was picked up & moved there not by my own free will but rather by some unbelievable force—i told Justine about this dream & she said "that's right—lot of people would feel guilty & close their eyes to such a happening—these are people that interrupt & inter-fere in other people's lives—only God can be everywhere at the same Time & Space—you are human—sad & silly as it might seem" . . . i got very drunk that afternoon & a mysterious confusion entered into my body—"when i hear of the bombings, i see red & mad hatred" said Zonk—"when i hear of the bomb-ings, i see the head of a dead nun" said i—Zonk said "what?" . . . i have never taken my singing—let alone my other habits—very seriously—ever since then—i have just accepted it—exactly as i would any other crime

the soldier with the long beard says go ask questions my son but the shaggy orphan says that it's all a hype—the bearded soldier says what's a hype? & the shaggy orphan says what's a son? the taste of bread is common yet who can & who cares to tell someone else what it tastes like—it tastes like bread that's what it tastes like . . . to find out why Bertha shouldnt push the man off the flying trapeze you dont find out by thinking about it—you find out by being Bertha—that's how you find out

let me say this about Justine—Ruthy & Zonk—none of them understood each other at all—Justine—she went off to join a rock n roll band & Ruthy— she decided to fight cocks professionally & when last heard from, Zonk was working in the garment district . . . they all lived happily ever after

> where i live now, the only thing that keeps
> the area going is tradition—as you can figure
> out—it doesnt count very much—everything
> around me rots . . i dont know how long it has
> been this way, but if it keeps up, soon
> i will be an old man—& i am only 15—the only
> job around here is mining—but jesus, who wants
> to be a miner . . . i refuse to be part of such
> a shallow death—everybody talks about the middle
> ages as if it was actually in the middle ages—
> i'll do anything to leave here—my mind
> is running down the river—i'd sell my
> soul to the elephant—i'd cheat the sphinx—
> i'd lie to the conqueror . . . tho you might
> not take this the right way, i would even
> sign a chain with the devil . . . please dont
> send me anymore grandfather clocks—no more
> books or care packages . . . if youre going to
> send me something, send me a key—i shall
> find the door to where it fits, if it takes
> me the rest of my life

> your friend,
> Friend

Road Dogs and Queens of Heart

Miles Davis

Miles

ONE TIME I LEFT him in my apartment when I went to school and when I got back home the motherfucker had pawned my suitcase and was sitting on the floor nodding after shooting up. Another time, he pawned his suit to get some heroin and borrowed one of mine to wear down to the Three Deuces. But I was smaller than he was so Bird was up there on the bandstand with suit sleeves ending about four inches above his wrist and suit pants ending about four inches above his ankles. That was the only suit I had at the time, so I had to stay in my apartment until he got his suit out of the pawnshop and brought mine back. But man, the motherfucker walked around for a day looking like that, just for some heroin. But they said Bird played that night like he had on a tuxedo. That's why everybody loved Bird and would put up with his bull-shit. He was the greatest alto saxophone player who ever lived. Anyway, that's the way Bird was; he was a great and a genius musician, man, but he was also one of the slimiest and greediest motherfuckers who ever lived in this world, at least that I ever met. He was something.

I remember one time we was coming down to The Street to play from uptown and Bird had this white bitch in the back of the taxi with us. He done already shot up a lot of heroin and now the motherfucker's eating chicken—his favorite food—and drinking whiskey and telling the bitch to get down and suck his dick. Now, I wasn't used to that kind of shit back then—I was hardly even drinking, I think I had just started smoking—and I definitely wasn't into drugs yet because I was only nineteen years old and hadn't seen no shit like that before. Anyway, Bird noticed that I was getting kind of uptight with the woman sucking all over his dick and everything, and him sucking on her pussy. So he asked if something was wrong with me, and if his doing this was bothering me. When I told him that I felt uncomfortable with them doing what they was doing in front of me, with her licking and slapping her tongue like a dog all over his dick and him making all that moaning noise in between taking bites of chicken, I told him, "Yeah, it's bothering me." So you know what that motherfucker said? He told me that if it was bothering me, then I should turn my head and not pay attention. I couldn't believe that shit, that he actually said that to me. The cab was real small and we all three were in the backseat, so where was I supposed to turn my head? What I did was to stick my head outside the taxi window, but I could still hear them motherfuckers getting down and in between, Bird smacking his lips all over that fried chicken.

I liked Ornette and Don as people, and I thought Ornette was playing more than Don was. But I didn't see or hear anything in their playing that was all that revolutionary, and I said so. Trane was there a lot more than I was, watching and listening, but he didn't say nothing like I did. A whole lot of the younger players and critics jumped down my throat after I put down Ornette, called me "old-fashioned" and shit. But I didn't like what they were playing, especially Don Cherry on that little horn he had. It just looked to me like he was playing a lot of notes and looking real serious, and people went for that because people will go for anything they don't understand if it's got enough hype. They want to be hip, want always to be in on the new thing so they don't look unhip. White people are especially like that, particularly when a black person is doing something they don't understand. They don't want to have to admit that a black person could be doing something that they don't know about. Or that he could be maybe a little more—or a whole lot more—intelligent than them. They can't stand to admit that kind of shit to themselves, so they run around talking about how great it is until the next "new thing" comes along, and then the next and then the next and then the next. That's what I thought was happening when Ornette hit town.

Outside of a few places, hardly anybody had heard of Charlie Parker. But a lot of black people—the hip ones—knew. Then when white people finally found out about Bird and Diz it was too late. Duke Ellington and Count Basie and Fletcher Henderson never got their due. Louis Armstrong had to start grinning like a motherfucker to finally get his. White people used to talk about how John Hammond discovered Bessie Smith. Shit, how did he discover her when she was there already? And if he had really "discovered" her and did what he was supposed to, what he did for other white singers, she wouldn't have died the way she did on that Mississippi back road. She had an accident and bled to death because no white hospital would take her in. It's like, how did Columbus discover America when the Indians were already here? What kind of shit is that, but white people's shit?

The police fuck with me by stopping me all the time. This kind of shit happens to black people every day in this country. It's like what Richard Pryor said, " When you're black and you hear a white man go 'Yahhoo,' you better know it's time to get on up and get outta there, because you know something stupid is next."

I remember one time when Milton Berle, the comedian, came down to see me when I was playing at the Three Deuces. I was in Bird's band at the time. I think this was in 1948. Anyway, Berle was sitting at a table listening to us and somebody asked him what he thought of the band and the music. He laughed and turned to this group of white people he was with and said that we were "headhunters," meaning we were fucking savages. He thought it was funny, and I remember all those white people laughing at us. Well, I never forgot that. Then I saw him on an airplane about twenty-five years after that and we were both riding in first class. I went up and introduced myself to him. I said, "Milton, my name is Miles Davis and I'm a musician."

He started smiling and said, "Oh, yeah, I know who you are. I really love your music." He seemed happy that I had come up to him."

Then I said, "Milton, you did something to me and some people in the band I was playing with some years ago that I've always remembered, and I always told myself that if I ever got close enough to breathe on you that I was gonna tell you the way I felt when you said what you said that night." He was looking at me kind of funny now because he didn't know what he had said. And I could feel some of the anger of that night coming back so it must have been showing in my face. I told him what he said and I told him how they had all laughed at us. Now his face was turning red because he was embarrassed, and he had probably forgotten all about it. So then I told him, "I don't like what you called us that night, Milton, and none of the band liked it either after I told them what you said. Some of them also heard what you said."

He looked all pitiful and everything and then he said, "I'm very, very sorry."

And I said, "I know you are. But you're only sorry now, sorry after I told you, because you weren't sorry then." And then I turned around and went back to my seat and sat down and didn't say another word to him.

Snoop Dogg

Tha Doggfather

You might say that job I had selling candy on the street was like a training program to get me ready for the next step up the ladder of financial success. Only this time the candy I was selling was bad for a whole lot more than your grille and I didn't have to go out looking for the customers—they come to me, twenty-four seven, three hundred and sixty fucking five, with those big bills clenched in their sweaty hands and their eyes all beady and bright and that rasp in their voice that's about halfway between a whisper and a scream when they're asking you extra nice if you can please hook them up.

Experts are always talking about the economics of selling drugs as if any nigger with a third-grade education couldn't figure out from jump the simplest law of supply and demand: if you got a supply of what everyone demands, that's all the economics you're ever going to need. Naturally, peddling crack or chronic or crank or shine or whatever else is getting folks where they want to get is going to pay you more than flipping fishwiches at McD's or sitting on your ass in a bullet-proof booth at a gas station, taking money through a slot.

And when you got a whole generation up ahead of you trying to support themselves and their families with low-paying and menial jobs, you learn firsthand what it means to be stuck at the bottom of the ladder. And youngbloods aren't stupid, regardless of what their elders are always trying to tell them. They can see straight enough what twelve hours pushing a mop on the night shift will get you up against twelve hours standing on the corner selling dubs to the regulars.

That's where I learned the true nature of black and white, rich and poor, self-esteem and self-destruction. Selling rock is the best way I know to get a good look at human nature on the flip side, down and desperate, with none of the fake bullshit that's supposed to make us civilized. A white man in a Mercedes and a two-thousand-dollar suit is no different than a nigger in a Hyundai and three-day-old sweats when it comes to getting high. They're both ready to do what it takes, pay what it costs, and take any risk just to draw down on that rock one more time.

I've seen them all—five-hundred-dollar-an-hour attorneys and five-dollar-a-night whores; off-duty cops and schoolteachers on their lunch hour; housewives with their kids in the backseat and rock stars in the back of limos;

whites and blacks, young and old, rich and poor—nobody is immune from degrading themselves with drugs. And as long as the customers keep coming, the nigger on the corner is going to keep supplying. That's more than supply and demand. That's a pure fact of life.

Experts will tell you that the war on drugs can only be won when we lock up all the dealers, or get tough with all the users, or build a twelve-foot wall between us and the motherfuckers on the side of the border. I don't know about any of that shit, but I can tell you this, from firsthand experience: this war everyone's supposed to be fighting won't be over until someone invents a cure for getting high. You take away all the cocaine, fools will still be smoking indo; you take away the indo they'll be drinking; you bring back prohibition, they'll start sniffing glue. Let's face it—getting faded is a basic human drive, like food and water and sex and sleep. It's never been about some kind of so-called socioeconomic disadvantage. You can't educate people into staying straight; there's no percentage in trying to scare people away from whatever it is that scratches that particular itch. All you can do is admit that most all of us have got it, that addictive pull, then leave the choice up to each one of us. And whatever each one of us decides is worth living for, that's what we're going to give ourselves over to, heart and soul, mind and body. You can't explain that away, or pass a law against it, or try to convince everybody to *just say no.* For most mother-fuckers that's like saying no to air. And there's no one alive that can hold their breath for that long.

JAMES BROWN

James Brown: The Godfather of Soul

BY THE TIME I got back from Vietnam people were on my case about "America Is My Home," calling me an Uncle Tom, saying the song was a sellout, things like that. Some of the more militant organizations sent representatives backstage after shows to talk about it. "How can you do a song like that after what happened to Dr. King?" they'd say. I talked to them and tried to explain that when I said "America is my home," I didn't mean the government was my home, I meant the land and the people. They didn't want to hear that. I told them I was all for self-defense, but it made no sense for us to burn down our own communities. They didn't like that, either.

I was taking flak about having a white bass player, too. Over the years I have had several white cats in my bands, but Tim Drummond was the first and it upset a lot of people. When he first joined, we were playing the Regal. There were certain people I thought would get very heavy with him if they saw him on stage, so I told him to set up offstage and watch me for cues during the show. Right before the show, though, I said, "No, let's get it over with. You go on out there."

During the band's set, before I came on, there was a big, mean looking cat in the wings motioning to Tim to get off the stage. Tim ignored him for a while. Finally, during one of Maceo's solos, he laid down his bass and came off. The fella told him, "You're not supposed to be on this stage." Tim asked him who he was. He let on that he was with the union and with the Regal, so Tim came to my dressing room while the band was still on and told me about it. I cornered the cat and said, "You don't want him to play because he's white. Well, he's going to play, and if he doesn't, I'll pull my show out of here right now. I don't care if you're with the union or the theater or who. Now get out of my sight."

Another time, in Washington, I received an unsigned telegram that said, "You have a white man working for you and a black man needs a job." A lot of people didn't like the rap I gave in the show, either. I talked about my background—going from shining shoes to running radio stations and owning a jet. I talked about the importance of education. "Learn," I said, "don't burn. Get an education, work hard, and try to get in a position of owning things. That's Black Power." I said we had a lot of problems in the black community that we had to solve ourselves—wasn't anybody could do it for us.

A lot of people didn't want to hear that and didn't understand it. There were bomb threats, death threats. Once we were ordered by the police to evacuate a hotel in Atlanta. Sometimes there were threats about disrupting concerts with stink bombs, things like that. Some of the threats came to Mr. Neely and King Records. I didn't pay any attention to them. You couldn't. Entertainers get threats like that all the time. You can never really be sure where they're coming from anyway—it could be political or somebody with a personal grudge or people trying to muscle in on the business. It's hard to tell.

Pop wanted me to back off doing political things, too. From the time I first got into integrating concerts, we got into long discussions about it. They got a little more heated now.

"Why jump off into that?" he said. "Wait until your real hot run is over, then if you want to dabble in politics, do it as a kind of elder statesman, but not now. You can't do anything for anybody else if *you* don't have anything."

"If anybody's going to listen to me, it's going to be now. It would be a shame to have this big audience, with all that's going on, and not try to do some good."

He was afraid it would hurt my popularity. He turned out to be right, but he didn't understand that I didn't care. I had to say what I thought either way—whether it upset Afro-Americans or Caucasian Americans.

Meantime, my music was getting funkier and funkier. What I'd started on "Get It Together" and "I Can't Stand Myself," I took even further with "Licking Stick—Licking Stick." Pee Wee Ellis, Byrd, and I put it together, and I released it at the same time as "America Is My Home." It was another one-chord song like "I Can't Stand Myself," but it had even more of a funk groove. It was a rhythm section tune and exactly what the title said, a licking stick. If the people who were on me about "America Is My Home" wanted to know who James Brown was, all they had to do was listen to "Licking Stick." My *music* said where I stood.

There were some changes in the band, too. When Tim Drummond came down with hepatitis from Vietnam, Charles Sherrell replaced him on bass. "Sweet" Charles we called him. He hasn't gotten the credit as a bass player that he should have. A lot of the stuff that Bootsy Collins and some other bass players did later—like thumping the strings—Sweets did first. Fred Wesley replaced Levi Raspbury on trombone and turned out to be a real innovator and a real creator as an arranger. Around the same time trumpeter Richard "Kush" Griffith and a third drummer, Nate Jones, also joined.

I got back from Vietnam on June 17 and five days later played Yankee Stadium. Pop and I had a discussion about that, too. He wanted me to add a whole lot of extra acts to the show so I wouldn't embarrass myself with an empty stadium. I told him I wanted to prove a soul act could fill a place like that. I believe I had forty-eight thousand people there. I dreamed a lot of dreams in my life, but I could never have imagined playing Yankee Stadium. I called the show the National Soul Festival and took it around to huge places that summer like Soldier Field to show that somebody besides the Beatles could fill venues like that. I thought it would give a sense of pride to little black kids like the one I overheard at Yankee Stadium who said, "The Yankees can't even fill Yankee Stadium."

At the end of July I campaigned for Mr. Humphrey in Watts. That wasn't too popular, either. Mr. Humphrey didn't even have the nomination yet, and a lot of people blamed him for the way the war in Vietnam was going. And a lot of Afro-Americans, including me, had really been behind Senator

Kennedy, and it was hard to get over his death, coming so soon after Dr. King's. Some couldn't forgive Mr. Humphrey for being against Senator Kennedy. It's funny, though. When the election rolled around, Mr. Humphrey almost won. It took all that time for people to see he was his own man and that he was a good man.

He campaigned in Watts for several days. It was very difficult. The Saturday before I joined him, some militants booed him off the stage there. His security people didn't want him in Watts at all. When I joined him the following Monday, the security was unbelievable. Police were on all the rooftops looking over the crowd with binoculars. There were dozens of other policemen and Secret Service men all up and down the street and mingling with the crowd. I'm not sure, but I think maybe they had to know from their own informers about the threats I'd been getting.

I didn't just get up and endorse Mr. Humphrey flatly. I tried to get him into a discussion right there on the platform. I wanted him to make some promises not just to me but to the people. I said to the crowd, "I won't endorse Mr. Humphrey unless he promises to give the black man what he wants—ownership. He wants his own things: houses, banks, hotels. He wants to be able to walk into a bank and see people of all origins working there so he'll feel comfortable asking for a loan. When he goes to a hospital emergency room, he wants to see priority given to the people with the worst ailments, not the lightest skin."

Mr. Humphrey stepped up to the mike and said he had been for those things for years. "If you elect me president," he said, "you'll get them. I promise you that."

"I got the feeling," I said. "I endorse him." The band they had there struck up, and I even got the vice president to do a little dance. "You can do the boogaloo, man, if you have soul."

While I was in Los Angeles I planned to cut something that had been on my mind a long time—"Say It Loud, I'm Black and I'm Proud." There was a vamp we'd been playing on the show for quite a while, and during my last tour I wrote some words for it while we were flying from Canada to Seattle. I was ready to go into the studio with it, but I needed some kids to be a chorus. I got all the fellas in the band and people traveling with the show to invite their friends and relatives with kids to come to the studio in Hollywood that night.

People were still getting very heavy with me about "America Is My Home" and the Humphrey thing, and the night we were supposed to cut, a strange thing happened. I was in my hotel room fixing to go to the studio when I heard a loud knock on the door. When I went to answer it, nobody was there, but sitting on the carpet was a grenade with "James Brown" painted on it. I'd seen enough grenades in prison and in Vietnam to know it wasn't live, but it was the thought that counted. We were late getting started and most of those who were supposed to bring kids didn't show up. That was okay because I knew the thing needed a lot of work, and it was going to be way past bedtime for most kids anyway. We worked on the arrangement and I kept changing the lyrics, stopping the rehearsal and working on them. Somebody suggested we just put down the instrumental track and come back later for the vocal. I said no because I thought it ought to have a live feel to it to be inspiring, the way I intended it. We worked all night until I was satisfied. Then I was ready to cut, and when I'm ready, I'm *ready*. But we didn't have any kids. I told everybody to scatter outside the studio and just get kids off the street. Byrd got a bunch from a Denny's restaurant nearby. Other people brought them in from here and there. After a while we had about a dozen. We rehearsed them and explained about being quiet when they weren't singing. Each time I sang "Say it loud" all they had to do was answer with "I'm black and I'm proud!" The funny thing about it is that most of 'em weren't black. Most of 'em were white or Asian.

The song is obsolete now. Really, it was obsolete when I cut it, but it was needed. You shouldn't have to tell people what race you are, and you shouldn't have to teach people they should be proud. They should feel it just from living where they do. But it was necessary to teach pride then, and I think the song did a lot of good for a lot of people. That song scared people, too. Many white people didn't understand it any better than many Afro-Americans understood "America Is My Home." People called "Black and Proud" militant and angry—maybe because of the line about dying on your feet instead of living on your knees. But really, if you listen to it, it sounds like a children's song. That's why I had children in it, so children who heard it could grow up feeling pride. It's a rap song, too.

The song cost me a lot of my crossover audience. The racial makeup at my concerts was mostly black after that. I don't regret recording it, though, even if it was misunderstood. It was badly needed at the time. It helped Afro-Americans in general and the dark-skinned man in particular. I'm proud of that.

LOU REED

To Do the Right Thing

I WAS BACKSTAGE AT Wembley Stadium. I was there for the Nelson Mandela concert. The weather was typically English. It was hailing and outside 72,000 people were sitting in the cold. I didn't think I would meet Mr. Mandela but I was hoping to at least see him. I had been reading in the press about how the lineup for this Mandela concert was inferior to the previous one—no megastars. That we musicians were politically naive and stupid—didn't we know he was a Communist—he hasn't rejected violence, etc. Plus an interviewer from the BBC with incredibly bad breath had informed me that WEA—my record company—had taken out an ad to retailers saying, "Make Mandela work for you," and what did I have to say about that. Well, they're obviously capitalist dogs, I said, and we should cancel the concert right now, don't you agree. So what if Nelson Mandela went to jail unable to vote and emerged 27 years later still unable to vote—so what that he was being given the opportunity to speak to one billion people this night (except in America—America where it was deemed too political and people are tired of these benefits anyway).

And no, I didn't get to see Mr. Mandela, not in person anyway. I viewed him on a big video monitor and then on a TV just as you may have. And he was incredible at age 71, at any age, and I hoped I could be that way at that age, and I wondered another thought—how does anyone go to jail for 27 years over an idea. I couldn't comprehend 27 years. Three months, okay. A year. But 27 years. It reminded me of the old Lenny Bruce routine when he's playing a captured soldier and they threaten him—hey, this isn't necessary, here's their time, dates, do you want his home phone number.

This question stayed in my mind because I was leaving the next day to fly to Prague and interview Václav Havel, the new president of Czechoslovakia and a personal hero of mine—a man who like Mandela could have left. They wanted him to leave, he was a successful playwright—why didn't he leave. They'd told him—if you put a wreath on that dead dissident's grave you go to jail. He did it anyway, and went to jail. And now he was president of the country, his cabinet made of various other dissidents, the Communists removed from power, the Czech people rising up to demonstrate 300,000 strong in Wensislav Square for days, finally clashing with the soldiers over the senseless death of a 10-year-old boy. And Václav Havel was no longer in jail but president. A poet, a playwright, a great man.

Before leaving we had had some strange conversations with our Czechoslovakian contacts, exacerbated, no doubt, by the language problem. It was Kafkaesque. Phones dropped off hooks—footsteps clicking down long corridors, it was hard to get clear answers to the most basic requests. The line that made me nervous was when we were told with exasperation—the government will take care of you. I'm from New York. I wouldn't want the government to take care of me. Plus they wanted me to play. At a club. For the local promoter. Visions of various people I knew raced through my mind making me nervous—scalpers, bootlegs, ticket prices. I said no, I didn't want to play for the local promoter. Maybe later when I do a real tour, and no photos or press conference at the airport. After all I said I'm here as a journalist.

Prague is so clean, so elegant, so old. We were in the International Hotel, which at a distance looked to me like a project. Close up it was actually okay, just very boxlike and brown. It had actually been hard to get a room because there were so many journalists and tourists in town. The Pope was coming to Czechoslovakia in two days. We were taken around Prague by Paul, a German photographer, and later by a man who I think became a new old friend, Kočař. Kočař's real name was Kosarek It's a 400-year old name and means small carnage. When he grew up his name became Kočař or big carriage. Kočař was a very streetwise person who spoke what he called street English and had resisted all attempts to enroll him in a school to teach him correct grammar. But he spoke just fine. He told us that only a while ago Havel was hiding in his house trying to get the dissidents of Charter 77 together yet again for more protests against the government. And now he was president.

Kočař apologized for the very large, clumsy man following us, another bodyguard. Havel has many enemies. The Communists hate him. And he said, making a gun with his hand and pointing to me, they'd like to hurt his friends. Havel, Kočař said, gets 20 death threats a day. Of course 99 percent of these are not serious. But one might be.

And so we went through Prague waiting for the interview. We saw where the 30-meter bust of Stalin was destroyed. Kočař pointed to the spot with particular revulsion. He'd been 14 in 1968 when the Russian tanks came and had blown up two tanks himself. The Russians are stupid, he said. Their gas tanks are on the rear of the tank quickly available to a hammer and a match and then you run quick. In the demonstration that overturned the Communists he said if you were in the front lines, and he was, the secret was hit and run quick. He had seen an 80-year old woman beaten by a soldier after she'd told him he was worse than a Nazi. Kočař attacked him and I supposed that was how he lost his front teeth.

We went to the Jewish ghetto and the Jewish cemetery, which was very sad. There was so little land the bodies could not have individual graves—the tombstones were piled atop and next to one another. Isn't that sad, I said. Isn't that beautiful, said our translator Yana, I hope misunderstanding.

We went to the old square. There was a large crowd gathered in front of the astrological clock. On the hour saints popped out of the windows and at the end a brass rooster crowed. We went across the Charles Bridge, named for Charles IV, their greatest king from the thirteenth century, a king of their people. The bridge had 30 statues of various Catholic icons placed 10 feet from one another on both sides of the bridge. Young kids were playing Beatles songs and Czech country songs. Prior to Havel no music could be played or sung on the bridge. No young people could gather there. You never knew what they might come up with. We passed a Czech-French film crew. We passed a bust of Kafka on a street but were told not to bother to see his apartment—everything had been ripped out. We ate some dumplings in the oldest restaurant in Prague and then gathered ourselves to go to the castle to meet Václav Havel.

The castle is just that, a large castle in yet another square directly opposite a very beautiful church with a gold-plated clock. We were met outside by Sacha Vandros, the young bespectacled secretary of state. He led us up the red-carpeted stairway to the president's office. We went inside the office and sat at a medium-sized table. The press secretary was to act as our translator. President Havel's English, he said, was not so good. I set up my tape recorder, and suddenly there he was, President Václav Havel.

He's the kind of person you like on sight and things only get better when he talks. He searched for a cigarette and chain-smoked the whole hour. I'd been told he put in 18-hour days, which was a little rough on him since only three weeks ago he'd had a hernia operation. He's one of the nicest men I've ever met. I asked him if it was okay to turn on the tape.

LEGS MCNEIL AND GILLIAN MCCAIN

Please Kill Me

Iggy Pop: Once I heard the Paul Butterfield Blues Band and John Lee Hooker and Muddy Waters, and even Chuck Berry playing his own tune, I couldn't go back and listen to the British Invasion, you know, a band like the Kinks. I'm sorry, the Kinks are great, but when you're a young guy and you're trying to find out where your balls are, you go, "Those guys sound like pussies!"

I had tried to go to college, but I couldn't do it. I had met Paul Butterfield's guitarist, Mike Bloomfield, who said, "If you really want to play, you've got to go to Chicago." So I went to Chicago with nineteen cents.

I got a ride with some girls that worked at Discount Records. They dumped me off at a guy named Bob Kester's house. Bob was white and ran the jazz record mart there. I crashed with him and then I went out to Sam's neighborhood. I really was the only white guy there. It was scary, but it was also a travel adventure—all these little record stores, and Mojos hanging, and people wearing colorful clothes. I went to Sam's place and his wife was very surprised that I was looking for him. She said, "Well, he's not here, but would you like some fried chicken?"

So I hooked up with Sam Lay. He was playing with Jimmy Cotton and I'd go see them play and learned what I could. And very occasionally, I would get to sit in, I'd get a cheap gig for five or ten bucks. I played for Johnny Young once—he was hired to play for a white church group, and I could play cheap, so he let me play.

It was a thrill, you know? It was a thrill to be really close to some of those guys—they all had an attitude, like jive motherfuckers, you know? What I noticed about these black guys was that their music was like honey off their fingers. Real childlike and charming in its simplicity. It was just a very natural mode of expression and life-style. They were drunk all the time and it was all sexy-sexy and dudey-dudey, and it was just a bunch of guys that didn't want to work and who played good.

I realized that these guys were way over my head, and that what they were doing was so natural to them that it was ridiculous for me to make a studious copy of it, which is what most white blues bands did.

Then one night, I smoked a joint. I'd always wanted to take drugs, but I'd never been able to because the only drug I knew about was marijuana and I was a really bad asthmatic. Before that, I wasn't interested in drugs, or getting drunk, either. I just wanted to play and get something going, that was all I cared about. But this girl, Vivienne, who had given me the ride to Chicago, left me with a little grass.

So one night I went down by the sewage treatment plant by the Loop, where the river is entirely industrialized. It's all concrete banks and effluvia by the Marina Towers. So I smoked this joint and then it hit me.

I thought, What you gotta do is play your own simple blues. I could describe my experience based on the way those guys are describing theirs . . .

So that's what I did. I appropriated a lot of their vocal forms, and also their turns of phrase — either heard or misheard or twisted from blues songs. So "I Wanna Be Your Dog" is probably my mishearing of "Baby Please Don't Go."

Danny Fields: The night the MC5 played at the Fillmore East was a historic night in the history of rock & roll and alternative culture. It was just after *Kick Out the Jams* was released.

The background is that the Motherfuckers were a radical East Village group who had been demanding that Bill Graham turn the Fillmore East over to them one night a week because it was in the "Community." My favorite word, the "Community." They wanted to cook meals in there and have their babies make doody on the seats. These were really disgusting people. They were bearded and fat and Earth motherish and angry and belligerent and old and ugly and losers. And they were hard.

So Bill Graham and the Fillmore were under pressure from the Community and the radical elements of the Lower East Side to turn the theater over to them. Meanwhile, the MC5 album came out and Jac Holzman thought, Wouldn't it be a great idea if we present the band at the Fillmore and give all the tickets away free! The "people's band"! This way the Fillmore gets a lot of publicity and we can promote the show on the radio and everyone will be happy!

So they booked a Thursday night, and to placate the Community five hundred tickets were given to the Motherfuckers to distribute to their fat, smelly, ugly people. Then we found out later the tickets were locked in Kit Cohen's desk. The tickets never left his desk! The time for the show approached and the Community was getting more and more angry about what happened to their entrée into the show. And since the MC5 were legendary as the band of the Movement, the only band to have played Chicago in 1968, the audience was composed of the leaders of the antiwar movement in America, people like Abbie Hoffman and Jerry Rubin. This was very high level underground stuff.

And then I did perhaps the stupidest thing in my life. There I was, sitting up at the Elektra offices, smoking cigarettes, sucking acid, smoking pot, saying, "Aaww, I have to get this band downtown? What do I do?"

So I called ABC Limo Company. We arrived downtown in the midst of the Motherfuckers banging on the doors of the Fillmore to be let in free. And right at that moment comes this big symbol of capitalist pigism, a huge stretch limo, and the MC5 get out. The Motherfuckers start screaming, "TRAITORS! BETRAYAL! YOU'RE ONE OF THEM, NOT ONE OF US!"

And the MC5 are going, "What did we do wrong?" Maybe I should have sent them in a jeep or a psychedelic van. It didn't occur to me. I didn't anticipate how the image of a limo was going to affect these loathsome people. You can imagine, a bunch of people that would call themselves the "Motherfuckers," what they would be like.

Wayne Kramer: Rob Tyner sometimes had the uncanny ability to put his foot in his mouth. He'd get nervous and make a stand on something—but he'd say the wrong thing.

So he gets up onstage at the Fillmore and tells the audience, "We didn't come to New York for politics, we came to New York for rock & roll!"

Of course all the Motherfuckers go, "GRRRRRR!"

The place erupted in a riot. They started trashing our gear. I was standing behind a curtain, and I saw knives cutting the curtain down.

Dennis Thompson: We were warned that there were true revolutionaries out there—and here they were, smashing our equipment, setting the seats on fire, and coming through the curtain after us. So they grabbed us and escorted us out into the middle of the theater. We were surrounded by about five hundred Motherfuckers, ha ha ha. Then all this revolutionary banter starts going back and forth. One guy would get up and say, "You guys preach revolution, so why don't you put up or shut up? Time to get started right now, don't you think?"

Then we'd go, "But uh, but uh, we don't mean to blah, blah, blah, we just want to blah, blah, blah."

Another one would pop up, "You guys are a bunch of fucking pussies. You're pussy motherfuckers. This is the time for revolution. You guys are either gonna be the real thing or if not, we're gonna kill you."

It was getting more and more intense—they weren't giving us much time to say anything—and then this knife comes out and goes right for Wayne Kramer's back.

Jesse Crawford grabs this guy's hand with the knife in it, wrestles it away, and we're all being spun around, and it's getting very violent. I grab Wayne, we just sorta plow our way through these people, and I said, "RUN!"

Wayne Kramer: We ran outside, and there's this limousine waiting and there's all the Motherfuckers and their women, crying and screaming. We gave away a bunch of free records and they started smashing the records on the limousine screaming, "YOU SOLD US OUT! YOU SOLD US OUT!"

Dennis Thompson: They're all over the car, jumping on it, hitting it, throwing rocks and bottles. It's just like we're down in one of those domino countries, where the politico shows up and everyone jumps the car, and we're driving away with these monkeys falling off.

So we finally escape and we're all going like, "OOHHH! What are we doing? Fuck this revolution shit. We should have just stayed in Detroit."

• • •

Scott Kempner: I was terrified watching the Stooges at Ungano's. I was going down there to see this amazing band and be ready for anything, but it was ten times more than I bargained for.

I mean, I was scared, actually nervous, but so exhilarated, and so involved in the sound of this band and this unbelievable guy Iggy—this wiry little thing—who could cause more damage than all the tough guys I knew in my neighborhood.

Other guys would punch you in the mouth, that would heal, but Iggy was wounding me psychically, forever. I was never gonna be able to be the same after the first twenty seconds of that night—and I haven't been.

We went back the next night, and it was the exact same songs, but it was totally brand-new. This had nothing to do with last night, this had nothing to do with rehearsal, this had nothing to do with sound check—this was living and being born and coming for your fucking children in the middle of the night right in front of you . . .

And every time I saw that band it was the same thing—there was never a yesterday, there was never a set they'd played before, there was never a set they were ever gonna play again. Iggy put life and limb into every show. I saw him bloody every single show. Every single show involved actual fucking blood.

From then on, rock & roll could never be anything less to me. Whatever I did—whether I was writing, or playing—there was blood on the pages, there was blood on the strings, because anything less than that was just bullshit, and a waste of fucking time.

• • •

Jim Marshall: I was still in high school in Florida, and I was trying to get a Xeroxed fanzine together. I knew a lot of drug dealers and people who had money, so I knew I could get somebody to publish this thing. So when I heard Patti was coming to play Tampa, I just called up her management company in New York and they set up an interview for me. You know, I was just a sixteen-year-old kid with a tape recorder who showed up thinking, I'm gonna get thrown outta their hotel room.

But Patti and Lenny and the band were really, really nice. I ended up interviewing her for four ninety-minute cassettes and hanging out with them for two days. They weren't big drinkers so they gave me almost all their beer. They were all smoking pot and I brought them a bunch of pot, so of course they liked that. Patti was absolutely like the nicest, most inspiring person. She was the first person who put the idea in my head of moving to New York City. She said, "Oh, you should move to New York. There's more people up there that like that kind of music. You might be able to like figure out what to do with your life if you got outta where you are."

The Patti Smith Group was playing at this sports arena in Tampa, Florida. The place was like something out of *Spinal Tap*. It was this horrible arena where Ted Nugent, Aerosmith, and Kiss used to play.

Patti was opening for Bob Seger, and they went over like a lead balloon. It was classic: Patti and the band did their first song, and there was, like, no applause. The audience just stared at them. So they started playing their second song, "Ain't It Strange," and Patti was twirling around. The stage there was really high, like ten or twelve feet off the ground, and below it was this pit filled with these two by fours that were all nailed together to make a barrier.

Jay Dee Daugherty: We were opening for Bob Seger and they wouldn't let us use all their lights. Patti had ventured over to the edge of the stage during "Ain't It Strange," which is a confrontation with God. It's like, "Come on, gimme your best shot, I can take it, motherfucker," sort of very defiant—like, "I'll meet you on your terms."

James Grauerholz: Patti told me that she considered every performance to be a life and death encounter with ecstasy. She had a "whirling dervish" philosophy about her performance, and felt that her obligation to the audience was to put herself into a trance. So she told me that she used to masturbate onstage.

Lenny Kaye: Patti and I would always do a little ballet in the middle of "Ain't It Strange." Then she would sing the part in the song where she'd challenge God—"C'mon, God, make a move"—and she would start spinning.

We're playing it, and we're really locked at this point, we're riding this thing, we start wobbling the beat, so Patti's twirling and she twirls and she reaches for the microphone—and misses.

Jay Dee Daugherty: It was dark, and there was a monitor on the floor, which she didn't see because it was painted black. She fell over backwards. I saw her go over, and my first thought was, Oh my god, she's either dead or she's gonna jump back up onstage, and then my second thought was, Oh fuck, I'm out of a gig. You know, it was a very human thing, but I always felt extremely guilty about that.

Jim Marshall: Patti literally twirled right off the stage—backwards. I was standing three feet away, literally, when she was going down. I tried to catch her, like put my arms up. Her brother, Todd, was a roadie—he was on the other side, and he tried to catch her too.

Patti hit the base of her neck on these two by fours in the pit—BANG. Then flopped up and hit the back of her head—a second shot on the floor. There was blood everywhere. I don't know if I imagined it or not, but it sounded like a very loud crack, like on the level of Joe Theismann's leg breaking—CRACK!

It was obvious she's really fucked-up. She was twitching and there was blood everywhere, and it looked like she had broken her neck. They had to strap her into one of those big stretchers with the wheels on it and took her to the hospital. No visitors. I think they thought she'd broke her neck, and then they flew her back to New York the next day or so.

Lenny Kaye: The stage shows had been getting crazier and crazier. It seemed like there was no place for them to go but total chaos. When Patti spun off the stage in Tampa and cracked a vertebra in her neck, it seemed like *there* was the moment.

At that point, the universe began contracting. We'd ridden our challenge as far as it could go. It was "Jesus died for somebody's sins, but not mine" up to that point.

After the fall, "reconciliation" is what we were about. We got off the read. We had to cancel the European tour. We stayed home for a year, the year punk rock took over the world. And we were there on the sidelines, really frustrated.

Jay Dee Daugherty: We never performed "Gloria" again after that. I think Patti changed and came to grips with her own spirituality and some sort of a spiritual system. I think she didn't feel that way anymore. This is something

I've not talked to her about, this is my own observation. She was working out some theme of resurrection and coming to a different place, but I was working on the crucifixion at that point, my own personal Golgotha. We went back to New York and all went on unemployment. That's when I thought maybe this drinking during the day wasn't such a bad concept.

Legs McNeil: Patti sent me a note thanking me for the interview and said to call her. So I did. I had heard that she had fallen off the stage in Florida, but I didn't know how bad she was hurt. It didn't seem like a big deal, because you'd heard stories of Iggy falling off the stage for years and never thought about him getting hurt.

At that time, people still seemed indestructible. There was a cartoon quality to everyone's life. For all the sex and drugs and falling down everyone did, people didn't seem to get hurt. But Patti was hurt, she was really in pain. She told me not to make her laugh because it hurt too much.

Jim Carroll: I always found Patti to be very Christian; very, very Christian. I mean, we didn't go to church or anything, but she would read stuff from the Bible. People talk about "Jesus died for somebody's sins but not mine," but to me she was always Christian.

I don't know, maybe she knew I was this Catholic kid and I never really lost that. I mean, I love the rituals of Catholicism. I hate the fucking politics, and the pope and shit, but the rituals of it are magic. I mean, the mass is a magic ritual for God's sake, it's a transubstantiation, and the stations of the cross—I mean a crown of thorns? Getting whipped? It's punk rock!

● ● ●

Cheetah Chrome: Dee Dee Ramone had given Stiv Bators a 007 knife at one of our first gigs. Stiv carried it all the time, and one time, we were up at the Chelsea Hotel and the 007 was just lying there on a nightstand or something. Stiv just picked it up and mentioned that Dee Dee had given it to him.

Sid Vicious was infatuated with Dee Dee Ramone. Dee Dee was Sid's hero and as soon as Sid found out Dee Dee had given the knife to Stiv, Sid wanted one too. So a couple days later we all went up to Times Square so that Sid could buy one.

It was really funny because Nancy had all this cash, and they were so out of it—they had taken a bunch of Tuinals—so she was dropping hundred-dollar bills on the ground. We had all of Times Square following us, a crowd following us waiting for the next bundle to fall out.

Nancy liked the knife. She was into it. I think she even bought one for herself. She wanted to have a knife because she was getting hassled by people and wanted to have some protection.

You see, they didn't know how to cop dope. Sid got beat a lot. He got sold a lot of crap because he was a born victim.

Sid was a mess. He'd draw attention, he'd draw heat. And that's not something you wanna do when you're copping dope. It's a serious thing. You wanna get in and get out quick.

But fucking Sid and Nancy were a pain in the ass—you know, everybody would be laughing at Sid, he would be bumping into telephone poles, Nancy would be bitching at him, and then she never wanted to pay full price for the stuff. I mean, these were not people you fucking bicker and bargain with.

And fucking Sid would be asking all these dumb questions: "Can you give me a deal?"

You know, buying heroin is not negotiable. You don't bargain with dope dealers. It's a fixed price. Like William Burroughs said, "It's the ultimate merchandise, and a customer will crawl through a sewer and beg to buy it."

And fucking Nancy, if someone you knew was selling dope, she'd sneak off and try and buy up all the dope, before you got there. So I'd just as soon go cop by myself.

Fucking Nancy. If Sid hadn't killed her, I woulda.

GIL SCOTT-HERON

The Vulture

AUGUST 29, 1968

THE SUMMER JUST SEEMED to fade away. It always seems as though the things you enjoy last no time at all. I widened the gap between myself and the gang. I still went around to get high every now and then, but there was no more to it than that. I didn't feel up to the lies or the highs anymore. Once we had all sat out in the park and told tales about fantastically built chicks that wanted no more from life than to get screwed over and over by us live and in living color. I was no longer able to put myself in those lies, because I had been blown away. I had had a chance with Debbie Clark, one of the finest little asses in the neighborhood, and just because she was high, I pushed her away. I couldn't understand why people got girls high on purpose to screw them, and when my opportunity came, Debbie disgusted me. None of the people at the party had paid any attention to Debbie, because she was drunk, and none of the gang knew about it, because they hadn't been there, but I had been there and I still had my memory.

"Junior, is that you?"

"Yeah. It's me. What'choo doin' up?"

"Just having some coffee. Come in here."

I walked into the kitchen. My mother sat in her bathrobe at the dinner table. Her hair was in rollers, and there was cream on her face and forehead.

"It's almost two o'clock. Now I told you to come in earlier this evening because you have to start getting back into that routine. There will be school next week, as far as we know. There's no use in you counting on this teacher-strike thing for keeping you up until all hours of the night. Remember, Bobby will be going to school this time."

I sat down opposite her and lit a cigarette.

"I guess you jus' ain't gonna listen to nothing that I say, is that it?" She got up and went over to the cupboard and found two cups. She placed one in front of me and then poured both cups full.

"How come you can't say anything?" she asked.

"I'm tired."

"I guess so. Runnin' the streets until all hours of the night like I don't tell you different. Don't half eat the food that's fixed for you. Livin' off beer, and cigarette-smokin' like you grown. Wouldn't do no good for me to tell you to do this or that. You so grown. I done tol' you, though. Don't have the Man knockin' on my door when you get picked up, 'cause I will swear that I never heard of you, you hear?"

"I hear you." I sipped the steaming coffee. I heard her, and the people in the next block probably heard her. I had heard her before, too. She had no real time or energy to worry about where I was or what I was doing. She didn't know what she would have me do if I told her I would do anything that she wanted.

All she really knew was what she didn't want. She didn't want me in the Navy like Matt. Each day she secretly expected a letter from Uncle Sam so that she could cry some more. The letter would be headed "We regret to inform you . . ." and she would burst into tears and run across the hall for consolation. I knew that Mrs. Boone, our neighbor, must hate to see her coming. Always another tale of woe. My mother was a one-woman soap opera. She cried and cried, always on the brink of tears, but no matter what happened, she would always fall back on that same weak story about God testing her.

She couldn't tell me what to do, because she wasn't doing anything for her own peace of mind. She didn't want me to be like my father, who died when his kidneys and liver rejected his style of life. His heavy drinking had been the cause of his death and had led to a nervous breakdown for my mother. At sixteen, I had been fatherless for almost eight years. The sign on the tombstone said that my father had been forty-three when he died. I remembered a man of sixty, complete with wrinkles and white hair. Alcohol had turned big patches of his skin to a bluish-purple. What the sign in the graveyard did not say was that when my father died he left behind a woman with a third son in her belly, and two older sons who had no reason to respect anything at all. It did not say that my father had been driven to his death by my mother. Matt realized all this and ran away to the Navy. Her whining and complaining had become as much a part of my life as breakfast. I inherited the position of whipping boy. From the day that my brother left, anything that went wrong with her world was my fault. I started to ask to go out more often, and whereas I hadn't cared for the neighborhood when we first moved from Brooklyn, I really started to enjoy leading my own group. I began to return later than I said I would, and instead of correcting me, she seemed to get more and more into her "Patience of Job" thing. By the time I was fourteen, Matt had been gone for almost a year. I was riding the corner horses every night of the week. By then I didn't even bother to ask to go out; I just went. That was another source of screaming. She had raised me and loved me and given me all that I had in the world, and I had no respect for her. That was her side of the story, and it was always consistent.

"I'm goin' t'bed," I told her.

"Goodnight," she said tolerantly.

I wanted to leave and get out of the way of her latest kick. She complained now that I was trying to embarrass her in front of all the parents in the neighborhood. My behavior was not an indication of the way I had been raised. I was turning out to be my father's son.

I passed my little brother's bed and looked down on him. There was no question about whose son she wanted him to be. Draped over the back of the bed was the baseball shirt with the number seven. I could never tell him enough about baseball, and particularly Mickey Mantle. Once or twice he had talked me into going with him to see the Yankees. But his interest was more the thrill of going somewhere with a million people than the game. He was only seven. He had had pneumonia the year before, when it was time to start school, and missed a year. Now all I could hear about lately was starting school. No more Mickey Mantle. I was a Mets fan anyway, if I was anything. The Mets were losers from the word "go." The only kinds of records they set were for the most games lost and most people coming to the game. Shea Stadium was a madhouse. The people got more hits than the team did. Somebody would get high and start cursing, and the next thing you knew, whole sections were being kicked out. The Man was ruthless. The Mets were the team that the Negro and Puerto Rican people could identify with. They were the ones with the whipped heads and the kicked asses. They were the underdog on the streets of New York, like the Mets were on the baseball diamond. The fans who got drunk and swung on the Man when he tried to quiet them down were heroes, because they were striking a blow for under-dogs everywhere. When they were finally subdued and beat into uncon-sciousness, it was a sad, proud moment. They had not given up.

Eric Burdon

Please Don't Let Me Be Misunderstood

WHEN I WAS ON the West Coast and had some time off, I'd flee L.A. for the mighty desert surrounding Palm Springs. Back then, the clean air and the big white sand dunes were straight out of *Beau Geste*. The great dunes are gone now, blitzkreiged by the mighty yellow Caterpillars for housing and golf courses, but the area is still spectacular: the mountains are magenta, black and blue, and the hot sun keeps the skies open even when it's raining in L.A.

Back in the late '60s, a girlfriend of original Animals guitarist Hilton Valen-tine settled in the fledgeling community of Palm Desert. An accomplished artist who continues to live and work in the area, Ming Lowe at that time had a little house and studio which became a refuge from the madness of Hollywood. It was a great meeting place for artists and travellers attracted to the desert.

I'd arrive in my old El Camino, rifle in the rack, my collie dog Geordie and my dirt bike in the back. Riding the open desert at twilight in the winter, seeing the landscape blur by, was as seductive as anything I've known. Two hours east of L.A., it could have been North Africa . . . it could have been any one of the exotic deserts. It was California at its best, and it's where I became a running mate of one of my screen heroes, Steve McQueen.

Road Dogs and Queens of Heart

The first time I ran into Steve—and I mean just about literally ran into him—was when I was on a borrowed Harley from one of Frank Zappa's boys, headed down Sunset toward the beach. I was flying along in Brentwood when a traffic light turned yellow. I didn't want to run the light and started to brake hard, only to encounter a wet patch of pavement under one of the giant trees. In the left lane there was a green Porsche, and the driver saw what was about to happen. He was paying attention to what was going on around him and really knew what he was doing as he spun the Porsche out of the left lane, leaving me room to skid by. When I made the corner, the pavement was dry and I came to a stop safely. When I looked back, there was McQueen, a quick flash of white teeth before the Porsche sped away.

When I rented a house at the north end of Palm Springs in 1969, I was thrilled to find out McQueen lived nearby. My secretary had been out for a wild ride with him on the back of a Triumph motorcycle that he'd had specially doctored for the sand. She had been so impressed that she convinced me to connect with McQueen the following weekend.

There was something really strange about seeing him just mucking around in the sandbox. This guy had a smell of gasoline, black powder and pot that seemed to drift behind him everywhere he went. I told him it made me imagine him as a young Erwin Rommel and at times he'd adopt a mock German tone to his American accent.

We always had girlfriends around, fresh from out of town, making their first trip to the desert. We'd run them out into the dunes toward the east end of the valley, me on my 350 Yamaha and Steve on his desert Triumph.

All along the valley, tamarisk trees had been planted as windbreaks. They were a clear mark of where civilization ended and the desert began.

"Step this way," I'd say, pushing the branches aside for the girls, their bare feet landing in warm, silky sand, the black sky above with a billion stars and a thumbnail moon. There must have been a hundred nights like this.

There were two things you didn't ask Steve about. One was Charles Manson. McQueen was friends with Sharon Tate and Roman Polanski and was supposed to visit her on the night the Manson gang entered and slaughtered the home's occupants. Later on, Steve's name was found on the list of celebrities that Manson wanted to kill.

The other thing you didn't ask Steve about was the big motorcycle jump stunt in his great war film *The Great Escape*. Due to insurance restrictions, he'd not been allowed to film the scene himself and it was always a sore point with him. Instead, his riding buddy and stunt double Bud Egans had done the jump. I had no doubt that Steve could have done it, however. One time we went out riding together he took me to an area where there was a large sandy berm at the edge of a long wooden fence. Without prompting, he told me it was roughly the same kind of jump as in *The Great Escape*. He didn't offer any more information and I didn't ask. As I rode my bike around the berm, Steve didn't think twice about it and hit the thing throttle open, piloting his Triumph into the air.

It was skill. And it was balls. As Bette Davis once asked him, "Why do you ride those motorcycles like that and maybe kill yourself?"

Steve's answer: "So I won't forget that I'm a man and not just an actor."

On one of our many trips out to the dunes—the day of Ike's funeral in April 1969, in fact—we stood looking at Mount Eisenhower off in the distance. Steve pulled a joint out of his pocket and fired it up. As he exhaled, he said, "You know, there's a rumor that Ike had secret meetings with space aliens. Some people even think he was a space creature himself."

I laughed and McQueen said, "No, I'm not joking. Who else could have won the war? Who else could have beat the Germans?"

Tough, gruff . . . and he had a great sense of humor. Though Steve wasn't given to deep, introspective conversation, he was also a little self-conscious about his image at this time. Despite great reviews and box office, his film, *Bullitt*, was concerning him. He said he was uneasy about having taken on the role of a cop, thinking it might jeopardize his image as a rebel.

"You got nothing to worry about," I told him. "Bullitt IS a rebel—he's a hip cop."

A few years later, after he'd married Ali MacGraw, the two of them were out cruising Palm Springs. He told me they'd dropped in at the grand opening of a new restaurant in town, Melvyn's (now a legendary celebrity hangout), and were turned away by the owner without a second glance.

"You really are judged by what you look like," Steve said, somewhat surprised at the time, since at that time he was the biggest and highest-paid movie star in the world.

The restaurant's owner, Mel Haber, is truly a gentleman, one of the most charming businessmen in the Palm Springs area, and remembers feeling bad after turning them away, not knowing who they were.

"It was our opening night, and everybody was beautifully dressed and they came right up on the motorcycle," he remembers these days. "Later on my parking attendant asked about Steve McQueen and Ali MacGraw and I said they never showed up. That's when I realized!"

Of course, Steve and Ali seemed to take it in stride and later did dine at Melvyn's, sans motorcycle.

Before I'd met McQueen, we each had been big fans of the legendary Von Dutch, and had frequented his San Fernando Valley shop. Von Dutch was a top automotive artist, gunsmith, engineer, innovator and great friend of McQueen. His design ideas would become an influence on great artists such as Robert Williams and be the basis of the California Kustom Kar Kulture that's still going strong today. His most popular single piece of art, the Flying Eyeball concept based on an ancient Middle Eastern cultural icon, would become the working title for my 1994 band.

If you're a real cult film fan, you might know that Von Dutch painted all the houses in the way-out film *Angels from Hell*, which starred my long-time buddy Ted Markland—who played the guy in the wheelchair in *One Flew Over the Cuckoo's Nest*. Von Dutch did a great paint job on Ted's personal bike, as well. All gold with Egyptian symbols all over it. Back before I met Steve, he and Ted used to run in the hills off Mulholland Drive in Hollywood.

After I met Steve, the more we saw of each other the more I liked him. I was amazed to see that such an action hero in the cinema would be, in the 1960s, accepted by people of the hip persuasion as well as the straights. But we never talked about the war—and since he didn't volunteer, I didn't ask.

Through his corporation Solar, he'd developed a plastic for gas tanks, and he wanted to show me his new design one morning. So I rode my dirt bike out over the giant dunes and met him with a couple of members of his crew, who were helping with his specially designed dune buggy—powered by a Porsche 911 engine.

I climbed into the bucket seat, a special design that Steve received a patent for. He showed me how to strap down the racing safety harness. As the massive rear tires dug into the white sand I was pinned backward. It was all I could do to clench my teeth and hang onto the roll bars, screaming, as we headed east toward Indio. Then, a quick turnaround to the left and we headed back toward the San Jacinto mountains at the west end of the valley and soon were tearing up the walls of one of the big dunes.

"See," he yelled over the racket of the engine, "we don't need no gas gauge, all I've got to do is look over my shoulder and I can see how much gas there is in the tank."

"Yeah," I agreed, "it's fantastic."

"So simple. I can adapt these tanks for dirt bikes as well. All you gotta do is glance down and you know where you're at."

"Cool," I yelled over the din of the engine, hanging on for dear life.

As we reached the crest of the dune, my tongue was stuck on the roof of my mouth. We came off the top of the dune and he gunned the engine. I held on for dear life as we flipped. The roll bar connected with the sand. He cut the engine and we came to a screeching halt. I was laughing hysterically.

Steve turned to me and through his yellow-tinted glasses, he squinted at me, his mouth open, "Sshhh . . . quiet."

We both listened—to what, I'm not quite sure. One of the rear wheels was still spinning. He turned to look at the gas tank, the gasoline still slopping around inside. "Hey," he said, "it works."

With that, he unhooked one of the button-down clasps on his blue jean shirt pocket, pulled out a joint, stuck it in his mouth and lit up, taking a huge hit before passing it to me. "Now you can laugh," he said.

"What are we going to do now?"

"C'mon. Help me roll it over. It shouldn't be a problem."

McQueen was fearless. His old buddy Bud Egans once told me a great story about Steve getting busted by Hollywood cops. They'd been trying for ages to trap Steve as he screamed up and down Mulholland in the Hollywood Hills. It's a crowded residential area now, but back in the '60s it was still the wilds, and a lot of us used to tear up and down the winding street from the coast on up high into the hills. I had an old Jensen, and McQueen proudly raced his rare D-Model Jaguar—basically a Le Mans racer that was technically not street legal, something he got around with a bit of fame and intimidation at the DMV, I'd imagine.

For most of us speeding along the same route, the cops just let us go—one told me once that they'd wait until we crash . . . no sense in risking their own lives chasing us. With McQueen, though, the stakes were higher. It was a game. They'd set speed traps and do everything they could to nab him on his midnight runs, but his Jag ran circles around the cops' old clunky Fords.

Until one night: trapped by a line of cruisers, McQueen finally got nabbed. It was all fun and games until the cops hauled him away to a Hollywood police station and threw him in a cell. At first, he kept laughing that it was all a game of cat and mouse, and that they weren't really going to throw the book at him . . . they were just pissed since it took so long to catch him. The longer he sat in the cell, though, the more worried he got that maybe he really was facing some charges. The one thing that meant everything to him was his driver's licence.

Then one of the cops came in and opened his cell door.

"You're right, we are just fucking with you. You're free to go."

It did get McQueen to stop doing his midnight runs up and down Mulholland in the Jag, however.

Probably the best story I ever heard about McQueen was also from Egans. By the time Steve had terminal cancer, he'd amassed a great collection of nearly 200 motorcycles, 50-some cars and 5 planes stored at the Santa Paula airport north of L.A.

One day, near the end of his life, Steve showed up at Von Dutch's workshop. He picked up a .45 automatic, checked to see that it was loaded, stuffed it into his belt and walked out. He got into the cockpit of his PT-17 Stearman biplane, taxied down the runway and took off out over the Pacific.

Von Dutch figured that was the last he'd ever see of McQueen . . . or the plane. Not a bad way for a living legend to take his leave of the world.

Hours passed, Von Dutch recalled, when finally out of the dusk came the sound of a sputtering plane engine running on empty. McQueen dropped down out of the sky and landed the biplane, taxiing back to its parking space in front of the hangar.

As McQueen got out of the plane, Von Dutch said, "Chicken shit."

"Fuck you," McQueen replied. "I just didn't want to scratch it."

In the years since running with Steve in the desert, I've been through my share of Harleys. I gave up riding for a few years in the 1990s because of chronic neck pain—and in protest of California's 1992 mandatory helmet law. But by the year 2000, I couldn't resist temptation and got back in the saddle with a new Harley.

The dunes of the desert are a distant memory, but on still evenings, as the sun sets over the west end of the valley and I cruise quiet back roads, the thought of Steve McQueen is never far away.

GREIL MARCUS

The Old, Weird America

ONE NIGHT, IN CARDIFF, Wales, Dylan greeted Johnny Cash backstage. As caught by D. A. Pennebaker's camera, Cash is thin, his face scarred. At thirty-three he looks like cancer.

The two men sit down at a piano and begin searching for the melody in Cash's "I Still Miss Someone," a lovely, seemingly traditional ballad. Dylan bangs the keys with leaden fingers, and together he and Cash reach for the first line: "At my door—" They miss. "At my dooooooor . . ." They stop. They're too tired, or too wasted, to find the song they're looking for. It's the simplest song in the world and they can't touch it. Cash punches Dylan in the chest. "Oh my God!" Dylan says, trying not to laugh. "You wouldn't do that to your best friend!" They turn back to the piano and stumble to the end of the chorus: "And I still miss someone." "You sing it," Dylan says, "I'll sing harmony." "At my *door*," Cash groans, then, "at my *dooooooor*," lifting the last word. The piano begins to ring. Something begins to come into focus, then it's gone.

With everything coming out of their mouths a drunken slurring, the notes on the piano now begin to gong. Each note is separate, standing alone. You can hear one note fade completely into the air before the next note begins; the theme is all in pieces. Cash follows the broken line Dylan is drawing like a man trying to negotiate a DUI test on the side of a highway, but Dylan is on another road. His piano is stately now, full of silences and room for visions; the gonging has turned to chiming, and the chiming makes the ratty backstage into a church. As Cash begins to ride the melody, Dylan presses for a rhythm the country song won't give up. The notes come faster, hitting each other as they rise and fall, and the song itself begins to play. Its door opens, its leaves fall, its singer stands gazing out over his garden, or a prairie, or a river. He looks out across the landscape of his life, and all he sees are those blue eyes: "I see them everywhere." But the piano stops: ". . . the melody," Dylan says thickly, "I can't remember this." Cash mutters through a fog too deep to penetrate, as if from the far side of sixty. "That's the greatest song I ever heard," says Dylan, suddenly bright and eager, sounding at least seventeen.

They try again; Dylan picks up the pace slightly, takes the song, his voice raw and high, with Cash just a burr, the rhythm of his fatigue countering the rhythm of Dylan's reach for notes he can't hit, notes that seem to be straining as hard toward him as he is toward them. They go on; they fall short again.

"At my dooooooor," Cash tries once more, then stops. "No, no," he says to Dylan, "let's do it your way." "Oh, my way," Dylan says, as if this is the best joke of the night, "my way *sucks*." "If I do it too," Cash says, unsteadily but warmly, like an older brother, "it'll make you look good." The best joke of the night is now a better one. "Well," Dylan says, "I'm not known for looking good—Don't you dare! I've—" (there are words that can't be made out), "I—" (or that never quite got made), "Why, I'll mystify this whole *room*!"

They banter for a moment more, Cash leans back, and then without a pause Dylan hits the keys hard. Coming directly off the last words of the conversation ("You didn't know I was a piano player, did you?" "Yeah, I did too"), a theme far more suggestive than any found in their earlier palavers comes up. Dylan opens his mouth, and wind and rain come out. The lights in the room seem to dim. Even if he is making it up out of the air, the song he's now singing feels older than the grandparents of anyone in the room and more familiar than anyone's own face. There are a few words, and a scattered

Road Dogs and Queens of Heart

blues melody—"I bought me a ticket, for a one-way train," Dylan sings, completely and happily lost, utterly alone even as Johnny Cash comes in for the next line, "I bought me a ticket, for a one-way track"—and as the film runs out in the camera Dylan disappears into the tunnel of the song. When he finally comes out on the other side he is in another country: the U.S.A., to be sure, though for the moment this is an America that exists only in the basement of a big pink house, a country that no one has exactly inhabited before. "Lo and behold!" he exclaims. "Lo and behold!"

Fists in the Air

MERIDEL LE SUEUR

Ripening

MINNEAPOLIS, 1934

I HAVE NEVER BEEN in a strike before. It is like looking at something that is happening for the first time and there are no thoughts and no words yet accrued to it. If you come from the middle class, words are likely to mean more than an event. You are likely to think about a thing, and the happening will be the size of a pin point and the words around the happening very large, distorting it queerly. It's a case of "Remembrance of Things Past." When you are in the event, you are likely to have a distinctly individualistic attitude, to be only partly there, and to care more for the happening afterwards than when it is happening. That is why it is hard for a person like myself and others to be in a strike.

Besides, in American life, you hear things happening in a far and muffled way. One thing is said and another happens. Our merchant society has been built upon a huge hypocrisy, a cut-throat competition which sets one man against another and at the same time an ideology mouthing such words as "Humanity," "Truth," the "Golden Rule," and such. Now in a crisis the word falls away and the skeleton of that action shows in terrific movement.

For two days I heard of the strike. I went by their headquarters, I walked by on the opposite side of the street and saw the dark old building that had been a garage and lean, dark young faces leaning from the upstairs windows. I had to go down there often. I looked in. I saw the huge black interior and

181

live coals of living men moving restlessly and orderly, their eyes gleaming from their sweaty faces.

I saw cars leaving filled with grimy men, pickets going to the line, engines roaring out. I stayed close to the door, watching. I didn't go in. I was afraid they would put me out. After all, I could remain a spectator. A man wearing a polo hat kept going around with a large camera taking pictures.

I am putting down exactly how I felt, because I believe others of my class feel the same as I did. I believe it stands for an important psychic change that must take place in all. I saw many artists, writers, professionals, even business men and women standing across the street, too, and I saw in their faces the same longings, the same fears.

The truth is I was afraid. Not of the physical danger at all, but an awful fright of mixing, of losing myself, of being unknown and lost. I felt inferior. I felt no one would know me there, that all I had been trained to excel in would go unnoticed. I can't describe what I felt, but perhaps it will come near it to say that I felt I excelled in competing with others and I knew instantly that these people were NOT competing at all, that they were acting in a strange, powerful trance of movement *together*. And I was filled with longing to act with them and with fear that I could not. I felt I was born out of every kind of life, thrown up alone, looking at other lonely people, a condition I had been in the habit of defending with various attitudes of cynicism, preciosity, defiance, and hatred.

Looking at that dark and lively building, massed with men, I knew my feelings to be those belonging to disruption, chaos, and disintegration and I felt their direct and awful movement, mute and powerful, drawing them into a close and glowing cohesion like a powerful conflagration in the midst of the city. And it filled me with fear and awe and at the same time hope. I knew this action to be prophetic and indicative of future actions and I wanted to be part of it.

Our life seems to be marked with a curious and muffled violence over America, but this action has always been in the dark, men and women dying obscurely, poor and poverty-marked lives, but now from city to city runs this violence, into the open, and colossal happenings stand bare before our eyes, the street churning suddenly upon the pivot of mad violence, whole men suddenly spouting blood and running like living sieves, another holding a dangling arm shot squarely off, a tall youngster, running, tripping over his intestines, and one block away, in the burning sun, gay women shopping and a window dresser trying to decide whether to put green or red voile on a manikin.

In these terrible happenings you cannot be neutral now. No one can be neutral in the face of bullets.

The next day, with sweat breaking out on my body, I walked past the three guards at the door. They said, "Let the women in. We need women." And I knew it was no joke.

At first I could not see into the dark building. I felt many men coming and going, cars driving through. I had an awful impulse to go into the office which I passed, and offer to do some special work. I saw a sign which said "Get your button." I saw they all had buttons with the date and the number of the union local. I didn't get a button. I wanted to be anonymous.

There seemed to be a current, running down the wooden stairs, toward the front of the building, into the street, that was massed with people, and back again. I followed the current up the old stairs packed closely with hot men and women. As I was going up I could look down and see the lower floor, the cars drawing up to await picket call, the hospital roped off on one side.

Upstairs men sat bolt upright in chairs asleep, their bodies flung in attitudes of peculiar violence of fatigue. A woman nursed her baby. Two young girls slept together on a cot, dressed in overalls. The voice of the loudspeaker filled the room. The immense heat pressed down from the flat ceiling. I stood up against the wall for an hour. No one paid any attention to me. The commissary was in back and the women came out sometimes and sat down, fanning themselves with their aprons and listening to the news over the loudspeaker. A huge man seemed hung on a tiny folding chair. Occasionally someone tiptoed over and brushed the flies off his face. His great head fell over and the sweat poured regularly from his forehead like a spring. I wondered why they took such care of him. They all looked at him tenderly as he slept. I learned later he was a leader on the picket line and had the scalps of more cops to his name than any other.

Three windows flanked the front. I walked over to the windows. A red-headed woman with a button saying "Unemployed Council" was looking out. I looked out with her. A thick crowd stood in the heat below listening to the strike bulletin. We could look right into the windows of the smart club across the street. We could see people peering out of the windows half hidden.

I kept feeling they would put me out. No one paid any attention. The woman said without looking at me, nodding to the palatial house, "It sure is good to see the enemy plain like that." "Yes," I said. I saw that the club was surrounded by a steel picket fence higher than a man. "They know what they put that there fence there for," she said. "Yes," I said. "Well," she said, "I've got to get back to the kitchen. Is it ever hot!" The thermometer said ninety-nine. The sweat ran off us, burning our skins. "The boys'll be coming in," she said, "for their noon feed." She had a scarred face. "Boy, will it be a mad house!" "Do you need any help?" I said eagerly. "Boy," she said, "some of us have been pouring coffee since two o'clock this morning, steady without no let-up." She started to go. She didn't pay any special attention to me as an individual. She didn't seem to be thinking of me, she didn't seem to see me. I watched her go. I felt rebuffed, hurt. Then I saw instantly she didn't see me because she saw only what she was doing. I ran after her. I found the kitchen organized like a factory. Nobody asks my name. I am given a large butcher's apron. I realize I have never before worked anonymously. At first I feel strange and then I feel good. The forewoman sets me to washing tin cups. There are not enough cups. We have to wash fast and rinse them and set them up quickly for buttermilk and coffee as the line thickens and the men wait. A little shortish man who is a professional dishwasher is supervising. I feel I won't be able to wash tin cups, but when no one pays any attention except to see that there are enough cups I feel better.

The line grows heavy. The men are coming in from the picket line. Each woman has one thing to do. There is no confusion. I soon learn I am not supposed to help pour the buttermilk. I am not supposed to serve sandwiches. I am supposed to wash tin cups. I suddenly look around and realize all these women are from factories. I know they have learned this organization and specialization in the factory. I look at the round shoulders of the woman cutting bread next to me and I feel I know her. The cups are brought back, washed and put on the counter again. The sweat pours down our faces, but you forget about it.

Then I am changed and put to pouring coffee. At first I look at the men's faces and then I don't look any more. It seems I am pouring coffee for the same tense dirty sweating face, the same body, the same blue shirt and overalls. Hours go by, the heat is terrific. I am not tired. I am not hot. I am pouring coffee. I am swung into the most intense and natural organization I have ever felt. I know everything that is going on. These things become of great matter to me.

Eyes looking, hands raising a thousand cups, throats burning, eyes bloodshot from lack of sleep, the body dilated to catch every sound over the whole city. Buttermilk? Coffee?

"Is your man here?" the woman cutting sandwiches asks me.

"No," I say, then I lie for some reason, peering around as if looking eagerly for someone, "I don't see him now."

But I was pouring coffee for living men.

For a long time, about one o'clock, it seemed like something was about to happen. Women seemed to be pouring into headquarters to be near their men. You could hear only lies over the radio. And lies in the papers. Nobody knew precisely what was happening, but everyone thought something would happen in a few hours. You could feel the men being poured out of the hall onto the picket line. Every few minutes cars left and more drew up and were filled. The voice of the loudspeaker was accelerated, calling for men, calling for picket cars.

I could hear the men talking about the arbitration board, the truce that was supposed to be maintained while the board sat with the Governor. They listened to every word over the loudspeaker. A terrible communal excitement ran through the hall like a fire through a forest. I could hardly breathe. I seemed to have no body at all except the body of this excitement. I felt that what had happened before had not been a real movement, these false words and actions had taken place on the periphery. The real action was about to show, the real intention.

We kept on pouring thousands of cups of coffee, feeding thousands of men.

The chef with a woman tattooed on his arm was just dishing the last of the stew. It was about two o'clock. The commissary was about empty. We went into the front hall. It was drained of men. The chairs were empty. The voice of the announcer was excited. "The men are massed at the market," he said. "Something is going to happen." I sat down beside a woman who was holding her hands tightly together, leaning forward listening, her eyes bright and dilated. I had never seen her before. She took my hands. She pulled me toward her. She was crying. "It's awful," she said. "Something awful is going to happen. They've taken both my children away from me and now something is going to happen to all those men." I held her hands. She had a green ribbon around her hair.

The action seemed reversed. The cars were coming back. The announcer cried, "This is murder." Cars were coming in. I don't know how we got to the stairs. Everyone seemed to be converging at a menaced point. I saw below the crowd stirring, uncoiling. I saw them taking men out of cars and putting them on the hospital cots, on the floor. At first I felt frightened, the close black area of the barn, the blood, the heavy moment, the sense of myself lost, gone. But I couldn't have turned away now. A woman clung to my hand. I was pressed against the body of another. If you are to understand anything you must understand it in the muscular event, in actions we have not been trained for. Something broke all my surfaces in something that was beyond horror and I was dabbing alcohol on the gaping wounds that buckshot makes, hanging open like crying mouths. Buckshot wounds splay in the body and then swell like a blow. Ness, who died, had thirty-eight slugs in his body, in the chest and in the back.

The picket cars kept coming in. Some men have walked back from the market, holding their own blood in. They move in a great explosion, and the newness of the movement makes it seem like something under ether, moving terrifically toward a culmination.

From all over the city workers are coming. They gather outside in two great half-circles, cut in two to let the ambulances in. A traffic cop is still directing traffic at the corner and the crowd cannot stand to see him. "We'll give you just two seconds to beat it," they tell him. He goes away quickly. A striker takes over the street.

Men, women, and children are massing outside, a living circle close packed for protection. From the tall office building business men are looking down on the black swarm thickening, coagulating into what action they cannot tell.

We have living blood on our skirts.

That night at eight o'clock a mass-meeting was called of all labor. It was to be in a parking lot two blocks from headquarters. All the women gather at the front of the building with collection cans, ready to march to the meeting. I have not been home. It never occurs to me to leave. The twilight is eerie and the men are saying that the chief of police is going to attack the meeting and raid headquarters. The smell of blood hangs in the hot, still air. Rumors strike at the taut nerves. The dusk looks ghastly with what might be in the next half hour.

"If you have any children," a woman said to me, "you better not go." I looked at the desperate women's faces, the broken feet, the torn and hanging pelvis, the worn and lovely bodies of women who persist under such desperate labors. I shivered, though it was 96° and the sun had been down a good hour.

The parking lot was already full of people when we got there and men swarmed the adjoining roofs. An elegant café stood across the street with water sprinkling from its roof and splendidly dressed men and women stood on the steps as if looking at a show.

The platform was the bullet-riddled truck of the afternoon's fray. We had been told to stand close to this platform, so we did, making the center of a wide massed circle that stretched as far as we could see. We seemed buried like minerals in a mass, packed body to body. I felt again that peculiar heavy silence in which there is the real form of the happening. My eyes burn. I can hardly see. I seem to be standing like an animal in ambush. I have the brightest, most physical feeling with every sense sharpened peculiarly. The movements, the masses that I see and feel I have never known before. I only partly know what I am seeing, feeling, but I feel it is the real body and gesture of a future vitality. I see that there is a bright clot of women drawn close to a bullet-riddled truck. I am one of them, yet I don't feel myself at all. It is curious, I feel most alive and yet for the first time in my life I do not feel myself as separate. I realize then that all my previous feelings have been based on feeling myself separate and distinct from others and now I sense sharply faces, bodies, closeness, and my own fear is not my own alone, nor my hope.

The strikers keep moving up cars. We keep moving back together to let cars pass and form between us and a brick building that flanks the parking lot. They are connecting the loudspeaker, testing it. Yes, they are moving up lots of cars, through the crowd and lining them closely side by side. There must be ten thousand people now, heat rising from them. They are standing silent, watching the platform, watching the cars being brought up. The silence seems terrific like a great form moving of itself. This is real movement issuing from the close reality of mass feeling. This is the first real rhythmic movement I have ever seen. My heart hammers terrifically. My hands are swollen and hot. No one is producing this movement. It is a movement upon which all are moving softly, rhythmically, terribly.

No matter how many times I looked at what was happening I hardly knew what I saw. I looked and I saw time and time again that there were men standing close to us, around us, and then suddenly I knew that there was a living chain of men standing shoulder to shoulder, forming a circle around the group of women. They stood shoulder to shoulder slightly moving like a thick vine from the pressure behind, but standing tightly woven like a living wall, moving gently.

I saw that the cars were now lined one close fitted to the other with strikers sitting on the roofs and closely packed on the running boards. They could see far over the crowd. "What are they doing that for?" I said. No one answered. The wide dilated eyes of the women were like my own. No one seemed to be answering questions now. They simply spoke, cried out, moved together now.

The last car drove in slowly, the crowd letting them through without command or instruction. "A little closer," someone said. "Be sure they are close." Men sprang up to direct whatever action was needed and then subsided again and no one had noticed who it was. They stepped forward to direct a needed action and then fell anonymously back again.

We all watched carefully the placing of the cars. Sometimes we looked at each other. I didn't understand that look. I felt uneasy. It was as if something escaped me. And then suddenly, on my very body, I knew what they were doing, as if it had been communicated to me from a thousand eyes, a thousand silent throats, as if it had been shouted in the loudest voice.

THEY WERE BUILDING A BARRICADE.

Two men died from that day's shooting. Men lined up to give one of them a blood transfusion, but he died. Black Friday men called the murderous day. Night and day workers held their children up to see the body of Ness who died. Tuesday, the day of the funeral, one thousand more militia were massed downtown.

It was still over ninety in the shade. I went to the funeral parlors and thousands of men and women were massed there waiting in the terrific sun. One block of women and children were standing two hours waiting. I went over and stood near them. I didn't know whether I could march. I didn't like marching in parades. Besides, I felt they might not want me.

I stood aside not knowing if I could march. I couldn't see how they would ever organize it anyway. No one seemed to be doing much.

At three-forty some command went down the ranks. I said foolishly at the last minute, "I don't belong to the auxiliary—could I march?" Three women drew me in. "We want all to march," they said gently. "Come with us."

The giant mass uncoiled like a serpent and straightened out ahead and to my amazement on a lift of road I could see six blocks of massed men, four abreast, with bare heads, moving straight on and as they moved, uncoiled the mass behind and pulled it after them. I felt myself walking, accelerating my speed with the others as the line stretched, pulled taut, then held its rhythm.

Not a cop was in sight. The cortege moved through the stop-and-go signs, it seemed to lift of its own dramatic rhythm, coming from the intention of every person there. We were moving spontaneously in a movement, natural, hardy, and miraculous.

We passed through six blocks of tenements, through a sea of grim faces, and there was not a sound. There was the curious shuffle of thousands of feet, without drum or bugle, in ominous silence, a march not heavy as the military, but very light, exactly with the heart beat.

I was marching with a million hands, movements, faces, and my own movement was repeating again and again, making a new movement from these many gestures, the walking, falling back, the open mouth crying, the nostrils stretched apart, the raised hand, the blow falling, and the outstretched hand drawing me in.

I felt my legs straighten. I felt my feet join in that strange shuffle of thousands of bodies moving with direction, of thousands of feet, and my own breath with the gigantic breath. As if an electric charge had passed through me, my hair stood on end. I was marching.

Fists in the Air

MARGARET SANGER

The Woman Rebel

TO COMRADES AND FRIENDS

Sanger's trial was rescheduled to begin on October 13, 1914. In her Autobiography, she indicated that she appeared in court that morning and asked for a postponement but that Harold Content, the assistant U.S. attorney, objected, saying, "Every day's delay means that her violations are increased." Judge Hazel agreed and told her to return after lunch with a lawyer. Sanger returned with the attorney Simon Pollack, whose request for a postponement was also denied. The trial was on the calendar to begin October 20, but Sanger did not appear. She later claimed to have sent both Hazel and Content copies of Family Limitation *along with letters announcing her intention to leave the country "until I made ready my case," but the letters were not found. (H. Snowden Marshall to MS, Oct. 7, 1914, herein; MS, Autobiography, 118–20; New York Call, Oct. 20, 1914.)*

New York [N.Y.]
Oct. 28th 1914

COMRADES AND FRIENDS

Every paper published should have a message for its readers. It should deliver it and be done. *The Woman Rebel* had for its aim the imparting of information of the prevention of conception. It was not the intention to labor on for years advocating the idea, but to give the information directly to those desired it. The March, May, July, August, September and October issues have been suppressed and confiscated by the Post Office. They have been mailed regularly to all subscribers. If you have not received your copies, it has been because the U.S. Post Office has refused to carry them to you.

My work on the nursing field for the past fourteen years has convinced me that the workers desire the knowledge of prevention of conception. My work among women of the working class proved to me sufficiently that it is they who are suffering because of the law which forbids the imparting of this information. To wait for this law to be repealed would be years and years hense.

Thousands of un-wanted children may be born into the world in the meantime. Thousands of women made miserable and unhappy.

Why should we wait?

Shall we who have heard the cries and seen the agony of dying Women respect the law which has caused their death?

Shall we watch in patience the murdering of 25000 women, who die each year in U.S. from criminal abortion?

Shall we fold our hands and wait until a body of sleek and well fed politicians get ready to abolish the cause of such slaughter?

Shall we look upon a piece of parchment as greater than human happiness greater than human life?

Shall we let it destroy our womanhood, and hold millions of workers in bondage and slavery? Shall we who respond to the throbbing pulse of human needs concern ourselves with indictments, courts and judges, or shall we do our work first and settle with these evils later?

This law has caused the perpetuation of quackery. It has created the fake and quack who benefits by its existence.

Jail has not been my goal. There is special work to be done and I shall do it first. If jail comes after I shall call upon all to assist me. In the meantime I shall attempt to nullify the law by direct action and attend to the consecquences later.[1]

Over 100000 working men and women in U.S. shall hear from me.

The Boston Tea Party was a defiant and revolutionary act in the eyes of the English Government, but to the American Revolutionist it was but an act of courage and justice. Yours Fraternally

Margaret H. Sanger

"WHY THE WOMAN REBEL?"

> *This article was published on the last page of the first issue of* The Woman Rebel.

[*March 1914*]

Because I believe that deep down in woman's nature lies slumbering the spirit of revolt.

Because I believe that woman is enslaved by the world machine, by sex

---

[1] MS took a train to Montreal the next day, October 29, to avoid prosecution. She arranged to have *Family Limitation* distributed once on board the England-bound RMS *Virginian* in early November.

conventions, by motherhood and its present necessary child-rearing, by wage-slavery, by middle-class morality, by customs, laws and superstitions.

Because I believe that woman's freedom depends upon awakening that spirit of revolt within her against these things which enslave her.

Because I believe that these things which enslave woman must be fought openly, fearlessly, consciously.

Because I believe she must consciously disturb and destroy and be fearless in its accomplishment.

Because I believe in freedom, created through individual action.

Because I believe in the offspring of the immigrant, the great majority of whom make up the unorganized working class to-day.

Because I believe that this immigrant with a vision, an ideal of a new world where liberty, freedom, kindness, plenty hold sway, who had courage to leave the certain old for the uncertain new to face a strange new people, new habits, a strange language, for this vision, this ideal, certainly has brought to this country a wholesome spirit of unrest which this generation of Americans has lost through a few generations of prosperity and respectability.

Because I believe that on the courage, vision and idealism of the immigrant and the offspring does the industrial revolution depend.

Because I believe that through the efforts of the industrial revolution will woman's freedom emerge.

Because I believe that not until wage slavery is abolished can either woman's or man's freedom be fully attained.

Because I have six months' time to devote to arousing this slumbered spirit in the working woman, and if within this time I shall have succeeded in arousing my own laggard self I shall have succeeded sufficiently to continue this paper until all the slumbered spirits have awakened to its assistance or its destruction.

CALLIE KHOURI

Thelma & Louise

EXT. DESERT—DAY

Behind them is a huge wall of dust created by all the police cars following them. In front of them, looking larger every moment, is the awesome splendor of the Grand Canyon.

INT. CAR—DAY

> THELMA
> (*elated*)

Isn't it beautiful?!!

LOUISE has tears streaming down her face as she realizes there is absolutely no escape. She continues barreling toward it without slowing down. All the police cars are still following about half a mile behind. The car is bouncing and flying across the desert. Finally, they get about two hundred yards from the edge and LOUISE slams on the brakes.

> THELMA

It's amazing, isn't it?

> LOUISE

What is?

> THELMA

How one thing . . . one little . . .

She can't think of the words.

> LOUISE

. . . moment of weakness . . .

> THELMA

. . . yeah . . . just one little slip . . . can just change everything.

Fists in the Air

LOUISE

We're never gonna get out of this. You know that, right? This is never gonna be over.

THELMA and LOUISE are just waiting for the cars to catch up. The police cars stop in a line about two hundred yards behind them. The dust from the cars is blowing across them. They just sit looking at the Grand Canyon. From the canyon the FBI helicopter rises up in front of the car.

INT. FBI HELICOPTER—DAY

HAL *sees* THELMA *and* LOUISE *for the first time. They are sitting in the car, oblivious, in a way, to all the activity around them. He takes his eyes off them only long enough to look at* MAX. *His eyes say, "I didn't expect them to look so human!"*

INT. CAR—DAY

THELMA

You're a good friend.

LOUISE

You too, sweetie, the best.

THELMA

I guess I went a little crazy, huh?

LOUISE

No . . . You've always been crazy. This is just the first chance you've had to really express yourself.

THELMA
(serious)
I guess everything from here on in is gonna be pretty shitty.

LOUISE

Unbearable, I'd imagine.

THELMA

I guess everything we've got to lose is already gone anyway.

                              LOUISE

How do you stay so positive?

They smile.

INT. FBI HELICOPTER—DAY

Hal's POINT OF VIEW: *He sees* THELMA *and* LOUISE *facing each other. They look so nice. He can't stop looking. He borrows the binoculars from* MAX. *As they fly above the scene* HAL *sees the row of police officers surrounding* THELMA *and* LOUISE *on the ground. Some of the police sharpshooters are sporting sniper rifles.* HAL *looks to* MAX.

                              HAL

Hey! Don't let them shoot those girls. This is too much. They got guns pointed at 'em!

                              MAX

The women are armed, Hal. This is standard. Now, you stay calm here. These boys know what they're doin'.

INT. CAR—DAY

                            THELMA

God, I don't know if I've got the strength for this one.

                            LOUISE
                      (*shaking her head*)

I know I don't.

                            THELMA
                           (*tired*)

Then let's not.

                            LOUISE

What?

                            THELMA

Let's not get caught.

Fists in the Air

LOUISE

What are you talkin' about?

THELMA
(indicating the Grand Canyon)

Go.

LOUISE

What?

THELMA is smiling at her.

THELMA

Go.

They look at each other, look back at the wall of police cars, and then look back at each other.

POLICE
(over loudspeaker)

THIS IS THE ARIZONA HIGHWAY PATROL. YOU ARE UNDER ARREST. YOU ARE CONSIDERED ARMED AND DANGEROUS. ANY FAILURE TO OBEY ANY COMMAND WILL BE CONSIDERED AN ACT OF AGGRESSION AGAINST US.

TIGHT SHOT of cartridges being loaded into automatic rifle.

SHOT of THELMA and LOUISE through the cross hairs of a gun sight. LOUISE and THELMA are looking at each other. They are trying to smile, but their mouths are twisted with fear.

POLICE
(over loudspeaker)

TURN OFF THE ENGINE AND PUT YOUR HANDS IN THE AIR!

INT. FBI HELICOPTER—DAY

HAL *is about to crawl out of his skin! He can't believe this thing is getting out of control.*

HAL
(*to* MAX)
Let me talk to 'em! I can't believe this!

MAX goes around HAL and continues walking. HAL jumps in front of MAX again and blocks his way.

MAX
(*sternly*)
We are way out of your jurisdiction, now come on! Calm down!

HAL
(*under his breath*)
Shit! I can't fucking believe this!

HAL walks along with a look of total disbelief on his face. He's shaking his head. Slowly he breaks into a trot and starts heading toward the front line.

MAX
(*shouting*)
Hey. Hey!

HAL is running now and clears the front line of cars. There is a lot of confusion among the officers on the front row. Some shout, some lower their guns to look.

INT. CAR—DAY

They are still looking at each other really hard. They smile, they embrace and kiss, best friends. A B. B. King song entitled "Better Not Look Down" begins. It is very upbeat.

LOUISE
Are you sure?

THELMA nods.

THELMA
Hit it.

Fists in the Air

LOUISE puts the car in gear and floors it. Cut to:

INT. FBI HELICOPTER—DAY

HAL's *eyes widen for a moment at what he sees and then a sense of calm over-takes him and he mouths the words "all right."*

> B. B. KING SONG: *I've been around and I've seen some things*
> *People movin' faster than the speed of sound*
> *Faster than a speedin' bullet.*
> *People livin' like Superman, all day and all night*
> *And I won't say if it's wrong or I won't say if it's right*
> *I'm pretty fast myself. But I do have some advice to pass along*
> *Right here in the words to this song . . .*

EXT. DESERT—DAY

The cops all lower their weapons as looks of shock and disbelief cover their faces. A cloud of dust blows through the frame as the speeding car sails over the edge of the cliff.

> B.B. KING SONG: *Better not look down, if you wanna keep on*
>   *flyin'*
> *Put the hammer down, keep it full speed ahead*
> *Better not look back or you might just wind up cryin'.*
> *You can keep it movin' if you don't look down . . .*

FADE TO WHITE . . .

Valerie Solanas

SCUM Manifesto

LIFE IN THIS SOCIETY being, at best, an utter bore and no aspect of society being at all relevant to women, there remains to civic-minded, responsible, thrill-seeking females only to overthrow the government, eliminate the money system, institute complete automation, and destroy the male sex.

It is now technically possible to reproduce without the aid of males (or, for that matter, females) and to produce only females. We must begin immediately to do so. Retaining the male has not even the dubious purpose of reproduction. The male is a biological accident: the Y (male) gene is an incomplete X (female) gene, that is, has an incomplete set of chromosomes. In other words, the male is an incomplete female, a walking abortion, aborted at the gene stage. To be male is to be deficient, emotionally limited; maleness is a deficiency disease and males are emotional cripples.

The male is completely egocentric, trapped inside himself, incapable of empathizing or identifying with others, of love, friendship, affection, or tenderness. He is a completely isolated unit, incapable of rapport with anyone. His responses are entirely visceral, not cerebral; his intelligence is a mere tool in the service of his drives and needs; he is incapable of mental passion, mental interaction; he can't relate to anything other than his own physical sensations. He is a half-dead, unresponsive lump, incapable of giving or receiving pleasure or happiness; consequently, he is at best an utter bore, an inoffensive blob, since only those capable of absorption in others can be charming. He is trapped in a twilight zone halfway between humans and apes, and is far worse off than the apes because, unlike the apes, he is capable of a large array of negative feelings—hate, jealousy, contempt, disgust, guilt, shame, doubt—and moreover he *is aware* of what he is and isn't.

Although completely physical, the male is unfit even for stud service. Even assuming mechanical proficiency, which few men have, he is, first of all, incapable of zestfully, lustfully, tearing off a piece, but is instead eaten up with guilt, shame, fear, and insecurity, feelings rooted in male nature, which the most enlightened training can only minimize; second, the physical feeling he attains is next to nothing; and, third, he is not empathizing with his partner, but is obsessed with how he's doing, turning in an A performance, doing a good plumbing job. To call a man an animal is to flatter him; he's a machine, a walking dildo. It's often said that men use women. Use them for what? Surely not pleasure.

Eaten up with guilt, shame, fears, and insecurities and obtaining, if he's lucky, a barely perceptible physical feeling, the male is, nonetheless, obsessed with screwing; he'll swim a river of snot, wade nostril-deep through a mile of vomit, if he thinks there'll be a friendly pussy awaiting him. He'll screw a woman he despises, any snaggletoothed hag, and, furthermore, pay for the opportunity. Why? Relieving physical tension isn't the answer, as masturbation suffices for that. It's not ego satisfaction; that doesn't explain screwing corpses and babies.

Completely egocentric, unable to relate, empathize, or identify, and filled with a vast, pervasive, diffuse sexuality, the male is psychically passive. He hates his passivity, so he projects it onto women, defines the male as active, then sets out to prove that he is ("prove he's a Man"). His main means of attempting to prove it is screwing (Big Man with a Big Dick tearing off a Big Piece). Since he's attempting to prove an error, he must "prove" it again and again. Screwing, then, is a desperate, compulsive attempt to prove he's not passive, not a woman; but he is passive and does want to be a woman.

Being an incomplete female, the male spends his life attempting to complete himself, to become female. He attempts to do this by constantly seeking out, fraternizing with, and trying to live through and fuse with the female, and by claiming as his own all female characteristics—emotional strength and independence, forcefulness, dynamism, decisiveness, coolness, objectivity, assertiveness, courage, integrity, vitality, intensity, depth of character, grooviness, etc.—and projecting onto women all male traits—vanity, frivolity, triviality, weakness, etc. It should be said, though, that the male has one glaring area of superiority over the female—public relations. (He has done a brilliant job of convincing millions of women that men are women and women are men.) The male claim that females find fulfillment through motherhood and sexuality reflects what males think they'd find fulfilling if they were female.

Women, in other words, don't have penis envy; men have pussy envy. When the male accepts his passivity, defines himself as a woman (males as well as females think men are women and women are men), and becomes a transvestite he loses his desire to screw (or to do anything else, for that matter; he fulfills himself as a drag queen) and gets his cock chopped off. He then achieves a continuous diffuse sexual feeling from "being a woman." Screwing is, for a man, a defense against his desire to be female. Sex is itself a sublimation.

The male, because of his obsession to compensate for not being female combined with his inability to relate and to feel compassion, has made of the world a shitpile.

After the elimination of money there will be no further need to kill men; they will be stripped of the only power they have over psychologically-independent females. They will be able to impose themselves only on the doormats, who like to be imposed on. The rest of the women will be busy solving the few remaining unsolved problems before planning their agenda for eternity and Utopia—completely revamping educational programs so that millions of women can be trained within a few months for high-level intellectual work that now requires years of training (this can be done very easily once our educational goal is to educate and not to perpetuate an academic and intellectual elite); solving the problems of disease and old age and death and completely redesigning our cities and living quarters. Many women will for awhile continue to think they dig men, but as they become accustomed to female society and as they become absorbed in their projects, they will eventually come to see the utter uselessness and banality of the male.

The few remaining men can exist out their puny days dropped out on drugs or strutting around in drag or passively watching the high-powered female in action, fulfilling themselves as spectators, vicarious livers,* or breeding in the cow pasture with the toadies, or they can go off to the nearest friendly suicide center where they will be quietly, quickly, and painlessly gassed to death.

Prior to the institution of automation, to the replacement of males by machines, the male should be of use to the female, wait on her, cater to her slightest whim, obey her every command, be totally subservient to her, exist in perfect obedience to her will, as opposed to the completely warped, degenerate situation we have now of men not only not existing at all, cluttering up the world with their ignominious presence, but being pandered to and groveled before by the mass of females, millions of women piously worshipping before the Golden Calf, the dog leading the master on the leash, when in fact the male, short of being a drag queen, is least miserable when his dogginess is recognized—no unrealistic emotional demands are made of him and the completely together female is calling the shots. Rational men want to be squashed, stepped on, crushed, and crunched, treated as the curs, the filth that they are, have their repulsiveness confirmed.

---

* It will be electronically possible for him to tune in to any specific female he wants to and follow in detail her every movement. The females will kindly, obligingly consent to this, as it won't hurt them in the slightest and it is a marvelously kind and humane way to treat their unfortunate handicapped fellow beings.

Fists in the Air

The sick, irrational men, those who attempt to defend themselves against their disgustingness, when they see SCUM barreling down on them, will cling in terror to Big Mama with her Big Bouncy Boobies, but Boobies won't protect them against SCUM; Big Mama will be clinging to Big Daddy, who will be in the corner shitting in his forceful, dynamic pants. Men who are rational, however, won't kick or struggle or raise a distressing fuss, but will just sit back, relax, enjoy the show, and ride the waves to their demise.

● ● ●

Early in 1967 Solanas approached Andy Warhol at his studio, the Factory, about producing *Up Your Ass* as a play and gave him her copy of the script. At the time Warhol told the journalist Gretchen Berg: "I thought the title was so wonderful and I'm so friendly that I invited her to come up with it, but it was so dirty that I think she must have been a lady cop. . . . We haven't seen her since and I'm not surprised. I guess she thought that was the perfect thing for Andy Warhol."

Also in early 1967 Solanas wrote and self-published the *SCUM Manifesto*. While selling mimeographed copies on the streets, she met Maurice Girodias of Olympia Press (French publisher of *Lolita, Candy* and *Tropic of Cancer*) who gave her an advance for a novel based on the manifesto. (With this $600 cash she visited San Francisco.)

During this time Ultra Violet read the Manifesto to Warhol who commented, "She's a hot-water bottle with tits. You know, she's writing a script for us. She has a lot of ideas."

Later, in May 1967, after Warhol had returned from a trip to France and England, Solanas demanded her script back; Warhol informed her he had lost it. Apparently, Warhol had never any intention to produce *Up Your Ass* as either a play or a movie; the script was simply lost in the shuffle, thrown into one of the Factory's many stacks of unsolicited manuscripts and papers. Solanas began telephoning insistently, ordering Warhol to give her money for the play.

In July 1967 Warhol paid Solanas twenty-five dollars for performing in *I, a Man*, a feature-length film he was making with Paul Morrissey. Valerie appeared as herself, a tough lesbian who rejects the advances of a male stud with the line that she has instincts that "tell me to dig chicks—why should my standards be lower than yours?" Solanas also appeared in a nonspeaking role in *Bikeboy*, another 1967 Warhol film.

Warhol was pleased with her frank and funny performance; Solanas also was satisfied enough that she brought Girodias to the studio to see a rough cut of the film. Girodias noted that Solanas "seemed very relaxed and friendly with Warhol, whose conversation consisted of protracted silences."

In the fall of 1967 at the New York cafe, Max's Kansas City, Warhol spotted Solanas sitting at a nearby table. He instigated Viva's insult of Solanas: "You dyke! You're disgusting!" Valerie answered with the story of her sexual abuse at the hands of her father. "No wonder you're a lesbian," Viva callously replied.

Over the winter of 1967–68, Solanas was interviewed by Robert Mamorstein of the *Village Voice*. The article, "SCUM Goddess: a Winter Memory of Valerie Solanas" was not published until June 13, 1968, after the shooting. Solanas commented on the men interested in SCUM: ". . . creeps. Masochists. Probably would love for me to spit on them. I wouldn't give them the pleasure. . . . The men want to kiss my feet and all that crap." Her comments on women and sex: "The girls are okay. They're willing to help anyway they can. Some of them are interested in nothing but sex though. Sex with me, I mean. I can't be bothered . . . I'm no lesbian. I haven't got time for sex of any kind. That's a hang-up." She told Mamorstein that Warhol was a son of a bitch: "A snake couldn't eat a meal off what he paid out."

Solanas also talked about her life; she had surfed as a young girl. She panhandled and even sold an article on panhandling to a magazine. "I've had some funny experiences with strange guys in cars." According to the interview, she wrote a few pulp sex novels and was paid $500 for one. (Could this have been the novel that was to have been based on the *SCUM Manifesto?*) She was interviewed on Alan Burke's TV talk show; when she refused to censor herself, he walked off the set. The interview was never aired.

According to Paul Morrissey in a 1996 interview with Taylor Meade, the contract that Solanas signed with Olympia Press was "this stupid piece of paper, two sentences, tiny little letter. On it Maurice Girodias said: 'I will give you five hundred dollars, and you will give me your next writing, and other writings.'" Solanas had interpreted it to mean that Girodias would own everything she ever wrote. She told Morrissey: "Oh, no—everything I write will be his. He's done this to me, He's screwed me!"

Morrissey believed Solanas couldn't write the novel based on the *SCUM Manifesto* she had promised to Girodias and used this idea that Girodias owned all that she wrote as an excuse. In Solanas' mind, Warhol, having appropriated *Up Your Ass*, wanted Girodias to steal her work for Warhol's use and never pay her so he got Girodias to sign this contract with her.

In the spring of 1968, Solanas approached underground newspaper publisher *(The Realist)* Paul Krassner for money, saying "I want to shoot Maurice Girodias." He gave her $50, enough for a .32 automatic pistol.

On June 3, 1968 at 9 a.m. Solanas went to the Chelsea Hotel where Maurice Girodias lived; she asked at the desk for him and was told that he was gone for the weekend. Still, she remained there for three hours. She also visited the office of Grove Press and asked for Barney Rosset who was also not in. Around noon she went to the newly relocated Factory and waited outside for Warhol. Paul Morrissey met her in front and asked her what she was doing there. "I'm waiting for Andy to get money," she replied. To get rid of her, Morrissey told her that Warhol wasn't coming in that day. "Well, that's alright. I'll wait," she said.

About 2:00 she came up to the studio in the elevator. Once again Morrissey told her that Warhol wasn't coming and that she couldn't hang around so she left. She came up the elevator another seven times before she finally came up with Warhol at 4:15. She was dressed in a black turtleneck sweater and a raincoat, with her hair styled and wearing lipstick and make-up; she carried a brown paper bag. Warhol even commented "Look—doesn't Valerie look good!" Morrissey told her to get out ". . . We got business, and if you don't go I'm gonna beat the hell out of you and throw you out, and I don't want . . ." Then the phone rang; Morrissey answered—it was Viva, for Warhol. Morrissey then excused himself to go to the bathroom. As Warhol spoke on the phone, Solanas shot him three times. Between the first and second shot, both of which missed, Warhol screamed, "No! No! Valerie, don't do it." Her third shot sent a bullet through Warhol's left lung, spleen, stomach, liver, esophagus, and right lung.

As Warhol lay bleeding, Solanas then fired twice upon Mario Amaya, an art critic and curator who had been waiting to meet with Warhol. She hit him above the right hip with her fifth shot; he ran from the room to the back studio and leaned against the door. Solanas then turned to Fred Hughes, Warhol's manager, put her gun to his head and fired; the gun jammed. At that point the elevator door opened; there was no one in it. Hughes said to Solanas, "Oh, there's the elevator. Why don't you get on, Valerie?" She replied: "That's a good idea" and left.

Warhol was taken, clinically dead, to the Columbus–Mother Cabrini Hospital where five doctors operated for five hours to save his life.

That evening at 8 p.m. Solanas turned herself in to a rookie traffic police officer in Times Square; she said, "The police are looking for me and want me." She then took the .32 automatic and a .22 pistol from the pockets of her raincoat, handing them to the cop. As she did so, she stated that she had shot Andy Warhol and in way of explanation offered, "He had too much control of my life."

A mob of journalists and photographers shouting questions greeted Solanas as she was brought to the 13th Precinct booking room. When asked why she did it, her response was, "I have a lot of reasons. Read my manifesto and it will tell you what I am." Solanas was fingerprinted and charged with felonious assault and possession of a deadly weapon.

Later that night Valerie Solanas was brought before Manhattan Criminal Court Judge David Getzoff. She told the judge: "It's not often that I shoot somebody. I didn't do it for nothing. Warhol had me tied up, lock, stock, and barrel. He was going to do something to me which would have ruined me."

When the judge asked if she could afford an attorney, she replied: "No, I can't. I want to defend myself. This is going to stay in my own competent hands. I was right in what I did! I have nothing to regret!" The judge struck her comments from the court record, and Solanas was taken to the Bellevue Hospital psychiatric ward for observation.

On June 13, 1968 Valerie Solanas appeared in front of State Supreme Court Justice Thomas Dickens; she was then represented by radical feminist lawyer Florynce Kennedy who called Solanas "one of the most important spokeswomen of the feminist movement." Kennedy asked for a writ of habeas corpus because Solanas was inappropriately held in a psychiatric ward, but the judge denied the motion and sent Solanas back to Bellevue. Ti-Grace Atkinson, the New York chapter president of NOW, attended Solanas' court appearance and said she was "the first outstanding champion of women's rights."

On June 28 Solanas was indicted on charges of attempted murder, assault, and illegal possession of a gun. In August, Solanas was declared incompetent and was sent to Ward Island Hospital.

August 1968, Olympia Press published the *SCUM Manifesto* with essays by Maurice Girodias and Paul Krassner.

● ● ●

Solanas: "I consider that a moral act. And I consider it immoral that I missed. I should have done target practice."

—Freddie Baer

GRACE PALEY

The Illegal Days

IT WAS THE LATE thirties, and we all knew that birth control existed, but we also knew it was impossible to get. You had to be older and married. You couldn't get anything in drugstores, unless you were terribly sick and had to buy a diaphragm because your womb was falling out. The general embarrassment and misery around getting birth control were real.

There was Margaret Sanger at that time, and she had a clinic right here in Manhattan in a beautiful house on Sixteenth Street; I still walk past and look at it. As brave as the Margaret Sanger people were, they were under very tough strictures. It was scary to go there. I was eighteen, and it was 1940 when I tiptoed in to get a diaphragm. I said I was married.

When I was young, it really angered me that birth control was so hard to get. Kids who were not as sophisticated as we Bronx kids just didn't know what to do. But I never felt that this was happening just to me. I had a very good social sense then from my own political family. I also had a lot of good girl friends, and we used to talk about it together. We had in common this considerable disgust and anger at the whole situation.

I grew up in the Bronx in a puritanical, socialist, Jewish family. My mother was particularly puritanical, and all that sex stuff was very hard for her to talk about—so she didn't. My father was a doctor, but we still didn't talk about such things. I really never felt terribly injured by all that. It just seemed to be the way it was with all of my friends. We considered ourselves freethinkers—in advance of our parents.

Most of my friends married early. I married when I was nineteen; then my husband went overseas during the Second World War. I would have loved it if I had had a child when he went overseas, but we had decided against it.

When he came back, I was in my late twenties, and in the next couple of years, I had two children. When the children were one and a half and three, I got pregnant again. I don't remember if my birth control failed . . . I wasn't the most careful person in the world. Something in me did want to have more children, but since I had never gotten pregnant until I really wanted to—I was twenty-six and a half when I had my first child—I had assumed that that general mode would continue.

I knew I couldn't have another child. I was exhausted with these two tiny little kids; it was just about all I could do to take care of them. As a child, I had been sick a lot, and people were always thinking I was anemic . . . I was having bouts of that kind. I just was very tired, all the time. I knew something was wrong because my whole idea in my heart had always been to have five, six children—I *loved* the idea of having children—but I knew I couldn't have this kid.

Seeing the state I was in, even my father said, "You must not have another child." That gives you an idea of my parents' view. They didn't feel you had to just keep having babies if you had a lot to do, small children, and not a lot of money.

And my husband and I were having hard times. It was really rough. My husband was not that crazy about having children anyway; it was very low on his list of priorities. We lived where the school is now, right next door, and were supers of the rooming house. He was just beginning his career. He eventually made documentary films, but he'd come back from the Army and was getting it all together, like a lot of those guys. So anyway, it was financially hard. But it was mostly the psychological aspect of it that would have been hard for him.

In the 1930s, my late teens, I really didn't know a lot of people who had had abortions, but then later on—not much later, when I was a young married woman in the 1940s—I heard much more. People would talk about it. By then, women were traveling everywhere—to this famous guy in Pennsylvania, to Puerto Rico. And you were always hearing about somebody who once did abortions but wasn't there doing them anymore.

I didn't ask my father for help. I wasn't really a kid, stuck and pregnant and afraid that the world would fall down on me. I was a woman with two small children, trying to be independent. I didn't want to distress him. He already wasn't feeling very well; he had a very bad heart. And he really couldn't travel; he lived in the North Bronx, and I was living on Eleventh Street—it would have been a terrible subway trip. I just didn't want to bother him.

I talked the situation over with the women in the park where I used to hang out with the kids. None of them thought having an abortion was a terrible thing to do. You would say, "I can't have a kid now . . . I can't do it," and everybody was perfectly sympathetic. They said to me, "Ask So-and-so. She had one recently." I did, and I got a name. The woman didn't say anything about the guy; she just said, "Call." I assumed he was a real doctor, and he was. That may have been luck.

My abortion was a very clean and decent affair, but I didn't know until I got there that it would be all right. The doctor's office was in Manhattan, on West End Avenue. I went during the day, and I went with my husband. The doctor had two or three rooms. My husband sat and waited in one of them.

There were other people waiting for other kinds of care, which is how this doctor did it; he did a whole bunch of things. He saw someone ahead of me, and when he put me in another room to rest for a few minutes afterward, I heard him talking to other patients.

The nurse was there during the procedure. He didn't give me an anesthetic; he said, "If you want it, I'll give it to you, but it will be much safer and better if I don't." It hurt, but it wasn't that painful. So I don't have anything traumatic to say about it. I was angry that I had to become a surreptitious person and that I was in danger, but the guy was very clean, and he was very good, and he was arrested within the next year. He went to jail.

I didn't feel bad about the abortion. I didn't have the feelings that people are always describing. I may have hidden some of the feelings, but having had a child at that time would have been so much worse for me. I was certainly scared, and it's not something you want necessarily to do, but I don't see it in that whole ethical or moral framework. I guess I really didn't think of the fetus as a child until it was really a child.

But you'll hear plenty of abortion stories. I will tell you what happened next after that was over, which is what I really want to talk about. I became pregnant again a couple of years later. I wanted to have the child, but my husband didn't. It was very hard; I didn't know what to do. I was kind of in despair.

I got three or four addresses, again from women in the park. My husband wasn't going to come with me. Partly I didn't want him to come; I probably was mad at him. I had this good friend, and she said, "You're not going alone." I was very grateful to her. She said, "I'll go with you," and she did.

I remember very clearly traveling to those places—to the end of Long Island and the end of Queens and the end of Brooklyn. I went to each one of these guys, but they wouldn't do it. One guy said, "Look, if you weren't married, I would risk it, but you're married and maybe you just have to make do." He felt I didn't need an abortion that much. I'll never forget. The only person we could find was some distance away and didn't sound very good to me at all. I was frightened . . . terribly frightened.

A week or two later, I remember, it was a freezing night; I was visiting people, and I ran home very fast. I was distraught and terrified because I was going to have to go either to Puerto Rico or someplace else. It was late in the pregnancy; it might have been the second trimester. That night I ran home at top speed—I can't tell you—in the cold, crying, from about eight blocks away. I ran all the way home and just fell into bed. I remember I had a terrible bellyache from the running.

When I woke up the next morning, I was bleeding fiercely. It seemed to me I was having a miscarriage. I'd had another miscarriage, and both my children were born early, so it was not a weird thing that this would happen to me.

So I called this doctor I'd been to several times before, and he said to me, "Did you do something?" I said, "No! It's just like the last time I had a miscarriage. I'm bleeding." And he said, "Call somebody in your family. Get some ergot [a drug that stops uterine contractions]." I said, "Don't you want me to come over?" and he said, "No! *Don't come.*"

By this time my father had had a serious heart attack, so I didn't tell him anything about it. I continued to bleed. I bled and bled, for three, four days. I was really in terrible shape, and I couldn't get anyone to take care of me. On about the third or fourth day, my doctor finally said, "Come over." He had to do a D&C.

Sometime after that, when I spoke to my father about it, he said, "That doctor was being watched. There's no other explanation. He was a kind guy. He knew you. He must have recently done something, and he was scared."

These things are not talked about a lot, this kind of criminalization of the medical profession, the danger these doctors were in. It meant that they could not take care of you. It's not even about abortion.

A good friend had an even clearer experience with this. She also was bleeding at the wrong time, and it didn't stop. She went to the emergency room here at a Catholic hospital, and they refused to take care of her. They just flatly refused. They said she had to have a rabbit test to see if she was pregnant and the results would take a couple of days. They would not touch her because she *might* be pregnant, and they *might* disturb the child. She continued to bleed, and they would not take care of her. She was a little skinny woman; she didn't have that much blood. Well, she wasn't pregnant. It turned out she had a tumor. It was an emergency—she had to be operated on immediately.

Your life, a woman's life, was simply not the first thing that hospital had on its mind at all. Not only that: Even if the doctor had compassion—and in my friend's case, one of the doctors was very anxious about her—they couldn't do anything unless they were willing to risk a great deal.

I think women died all the time when abortions were illegal. The horrible abortions were one way; the other way was the refusal of institutions—medical, church, and state—to care for you, their willingness to let you die.

It's important to be public about the issue, and I have been for years. I helped organize one of the first abortion speak-outs in the country, which was held at the Washington Square Methodist Church in New York City back in the late sixties.

But I'll be very truthful. I never liked the slogan "Abortion on demand," and most of my friends hated it. We'd go on marches, and we could never say it. It's such a trivialization of the experience. It's like "Toothpaste on demand." If somebody said there should be birth control on demand, I would say yes. That would make a lot of sense. If I ask for a diaphragm, if I ask for a condom, I should just get it right off the bat.

But an abortion . . . After all, it's a surgical procedure and really a very serious thing to undertake. It's not a small matter. Just because I didn't suffer a lot around my abortion, suffering is not the only thing that makes something important. I didn't suffer, but it was important. And when you say "on demand," it ignores the real question, which is: Where are you in your pregnancy? If you're in the sixth month, it's probably not wise, not good for you, even dangerous. Not that I think if a woman goes to a clinic and wants to have an abortion, she shouldn't have it when she needs it. It's just that there's a lot to think about.

The last demonstration I went to was in Montpelier, Vermont (Mobilization for Women's Lives, November 12, 1989). There were about twenty-five hundred women and men. The governor spoke, a woman governor, Madeleine Kunin; and, one of the great highlights, an older woman—older than me, even (I'm sixty-seven)—from Catholics for a Free Choice spoke; and I spoke.

I said that abortion is only the tip of the iceberg. These guys who run at the clinics—and by the way, our Burlington clinic was really raided, with people knocked down—are point men who make the noise and false, hypocritical statements about human life, which they don't much care about, really. What they really want to do is take back ownership of women's bodies. They want to return us to a time when even our children weren't our own; we were simply the receptacles to have these children. The great novels of the nineteenth and early-twentieth centuries were often about women who knew that if they took one wrong step, their children would be taken from them.

And another point I made is that abortion isn't what they're thinking about; they're really thinking about sex. They're really thinking about love and reducing it to its most mechanical aspects—that is to say, the mechanical fact of intercourse as a specific act to make children in this world, and thinking of its use in any other way as wrong and wicked. They are determined to reduce women's normal sexual responses, to end them, really, when we've just had a couple of decades of admitting them.

My generation—and only in our later years—and the one right after mine have been the only ones to really enjoy any sexual freedom. The kids have to know that it's not just the right to abortion which is essential; it's their right to a sexual life.

—1991

Obviously, the AIDS epidemic had not yet assaulted that next generation when I spoke/wrote this piece.

Emma Goldman

Living My Life

THE MEETING AT UNION SQUARE was preceded by a demonstration, the marching columns counting many thousands. The girls and women were in front, I at their head carrying a red banner. Its crimson waved proudly in the air and could be seen for blocks. My soul, too, vibrated with the intensity of the moment.

The atmosphere in the ranks had become very tense, owing to the events of that week. Labour politicians had appealed to the New York legislature for relief of the great distress, but their pleas met with evasions. Meanwhile the unemployed went on starving. The people were outraged by this callous indifference to the suffering of men, women, and children. As a result the air at Union Square was charged with bitterness and indignation, its spirit quickly communicating itself to me. I was scheduled as the last speaker and I could barely endure the long wait. Finally the apologetic oratory was over and my turn came. I heard my name shouted from a thousand throats as I stepped forward. I saw a dense mass before me, their pale, pinched faces upturned to me. My heart beat, my temples throbbed, and my knees shook.

"Men and women," I began amidst sudden silence, "do you not realize that the State is the worst enemy you have? It is a machine that crushes you in order to sustain the ruling class, your masters. Like naïve children you put your trust in your political leaders. You make it possible for them to creep into your confidence, only to have them betray you to the first bidder. But even where there is no direct betrayal, the labor politicians make common cause with your enemies to keep you in leash, to prevent your direct action.

The State is the pillar of capitalism, and it is ridiculous to expect any redress from it. Do you not see the stupidity of asking relief from Albany with immense wealth within a stone's throw from here? Fifth Avenue is laid in gold, every mansion is a citadel of money and power. Yet there you stand, a giant, starved and fettered, shorn of his strength. Cardinal Manning long ago proclaimed that 'necessity knows no law' and that 'the starving man has a right to a share of his neighbour's bread.' Cardinal Manning was an ecclesiastic steeped in the traditions of the Church, which has always been on the side of the rich against the poor. But he had some humanity, and he knew that hunger is a compelling force. You, too, will have to learn that you have a right to share your neighbor's bread. Your neighbors—they have not only stolen your bread, but they are sapping your blood. They will go on robbing you, your children, and your children's children, unless you wake up, unless you become daring enough to demand your rights. Well, then, demonstrate before the palaces of the rich; demand work. If they do not give you work, demand bread. If they deny you both, take bread. It is your sacred right!"

Uproarious applause, wild and deafening, broke from the stillness like a sudden storm. The sea of hands eagerly stretching out towards me seemed like the wings of white birds fluttering.

The following morning I went to Philadelphia to secure relief and help organize the unemployed there. The afternoon papers carried a garbled account of my speech. I had urged the crowd to revolution, they claimed. "Red Emma has great swaying power; her vitriolic tongue was just what the ignorant mob needed to tear down New York." They also stated that I had been spirited away by some husky friends, but that the police were on my track.

On that morning the papers brought the news that my whereabouts had been discovered, that detectives were on their way to Philadelphia with a warrant for my arrest. I felt that the important thing for me was to manage to get into the hall and address the meeting before my arrest could take place. It was my first visit to Philadelphia, where I was unknown to the authorities. The New York detectives would hardly be able to identify me by the pictures that had so far appeared in the press. I decided to go to the hall unaccompanied and slip in unnoticed.

The streets near by were blocked with people. No one recognized me as I walked up the flight of steps leading to the meeting-place. Then one of the anarchists greeted me: "Here's Emma!" I waved him aside, but a heavy hand was immediately on my shoulder, and a voice said: "You're under arrest, Miss

Goldman." There was a commotion, people ran towards me, but the officers drew their guns and held back the crowd.

The second morning after my arrest I was transferred to Moyamensing Prison to await extradition. I was put into a fairly large cell, its door of solid sheet iron, with a small square in the center opening from the outside. The window was high and heavily barred. The cell contained a sanitary toilet, running water, a tin cup, a wooden table, a bench, and an iron cot. A small electric lamp hung from the ceiling. From time to time the square in the door would open and a pair of eyes would look in, or a voice would call for the cup and it would be passed back to me filled with tepid water or soup and a slice of bread. Except for such interruptions silence prevailed.

After the second day the stillness became oppressive and the hours crept on endlessly. I grew weary from constant pacing between the window and the door. My nerves were tense with the strain for some human sound. I called for the matron, but no one answered. I banged my tin cup against the door. Finally it brought response. My door was unlocked and a large woman with a hard face came into the cell. It was against the rules to make so much noise, she warned me. If I did it again, she would have to punish me. What did I want? I wanted my mail, I told her. I was sure there was some from my friends, and I also wanted books to read. She would bring a book, but there was no mail, the matron said. I knew she was lying, for I was certain Ed had written, even if no one else. She went out, locking the door after her. Presently she returned with a book. It was the Bible and it recalled to my mind the cruel face of my religious instructor in school. Indignantly I flung the volume at the matron's feet. I had no need of religious lies; I wanted some human book, I told her. For a moment she stood horror-stricken; then she began raging at me. I had desecrated God's word; I would be put in the dungeon; later on I would burn in hell. I replied heatedly that she did not dare punish me, because I was a prisoner of the State of New York, that I had not yet been tried and therefore still had some civil rights. She flung out, slamming the door after her.

One day the matron came to announce that extradition had been granted and that I was to be taken to New York. I followed her into the office, where I was handed a large package of letters, telegrams, and papers. I was informed that several boxes of fruit and flowers had come for me, but that it was against the rules for prisoners to have such things. Then I was handed over to a heavy-set man. A cab waited outside the prison and we were driven to the station.

We travelled in a Pullman car, and the man introduced himself as

Detective-Sergeant—. He excused himself, saying he was only doing his duty; he had six children to support. I asked him why he had not chosen a more honorable occupation and why he had to bring more spies into the world. If *he* did not do it, someone else would, he replied. The police force was necessary; it protected society. Would I have dinner? He would have it brought to the car to save my going to the diner. I consented. I had not eaten anything decent for a week; besides, the City of New York was paying for the unsolicited luxury of my journey.

Over the dinner the detective referred to my youth and the life "such a brilliant girl, with such abilities" had before her. He went on to say that I never would earn anything by the work I was doing, not even my salt. Why shouldn't I be sensible and "look out for number one" first? He felt for me because he was a *Yehude* himself. He was sorry to see me go to prison. He could tell me how to get free, even to receive a large sum of money, if I would only be sensible.

"Out with it," I said; "what's on your mind?"

His chief had instructed him to tell me that my case would be quashed and a substantial sum of money presented to me if I would give way a little. Nothing much, just a short periodic report of what was going on in radical circles and among the workers on the East Side.

A horrible feeling came over me. The food nauseated me. I gulped down some ice-water from my glass and threw what was left into the detective's face. "You miserable cur!" I shouted; "not enough that you act as a Judas, you try even to turn me into one—you and your rotten chief! I'll take prison for life, but no one will ever buy me!"

"All right, all right," he said soothingly; "have it your own way."

On the way from the Tombs to the court New York looked as if it were under martial law. The streets were lined with police, the buildings surrounded by heavily armed cordons, the corridors of the courthouse filled with officers. I was called to the bar and asked if I had "anything to say why sentence should not be passed." I had considerable to say; should I be given the chance? No, that was impossible; I could only make a very brief statement. Then I would say only that I had expected no justice from a capitalist court. The court might do its worst, but it was powerless to change my views, I said.

Judge Martin sentenced me to one year in Blackwell's Island Penitentiary. On my way to the Tombs I heard the news-boys shout: "Extra! Extra! Emma Goldman's speech in court!" and I felt glad that the *World* had kept its promise. I was at once placed in the Black Maria and taken to the boat that delivers prisoners to Blackwell's Island.

• • •

I was called before the head matron, a tall woman with a stolid face. She began taking my pedigree. "What religion?" was her first question. "None, I am an atheist." "Atheism is prohibited here. You will have to go to church." I replied that I would do nothing of the kind. I did not believe in anything the Church stood for and, not being a hypocrite, I would not attend. Besides, I came from Jewish people. Was there a synagogue?

She said curtly that there were services for the Jewish convicts on Saturday afternoon, but as I was the only Jewish female prisoner, she could not permit me to go among so many men.

After a bath and a change into the prison uniform I was sent to my cell and locked in.

I knew from what most had related to me about Blackwell's Island that the prison was old and damp, the cells small, without light or water. I was therefore prepared for what was awaiting me. But the moment the door was locked on me, I began to experience a feeling of suffocation. In the dark I groped for something to sit on and found a narrow iron cot. Sudden exhaustion overpowered me and I fell asleep.

I became aware of a sharp burning in my eyes, and I jumped up in fright. A lamp was being held close to the bars. "What is it?" I cried, forgetting where I was. The lamp was lowered and I saw a thin, ascetic face gazing at me. A soft voice congratulated me on my sound sleep. It was the evening matron on her regular rounds. She told me to undress and left me.

But there was no more sleep for me that night. The irritating feel of the coarse blanket, the shadows creeping past the bars, kept me awake until the sound of a gong again brought me to my feet. The cells were being unlocked, the doors heavily thrown open. Blue and white striped figures slouched by, automatically forming into a line, myself a part of it. "March!" and the line began to move along the corridor down the steps towards a corner containing wash-stands and towels. Again the command: "Wash!" and everybody began clamoring for a towel, already soiled and wet. Before I had time to splash some water on my hands and face and wipe myself half-dry, the order was given to march back.

Then breakfast: a slice of bread and a tin cup of warm brownish water. Again the line formed, and the striped humanity was broken up in sections and sent to its daily tasks. With a group of other women I was taken to the sewing-room.

I was put in charge of the sewing-shop. My task consisted in cutting the cloth and preparing work for the two dozen women employed. In addition I had to keep account of the incoming material and the outgoing bundles. I welcomed the work. It helped me to forget the dreary existence within the prison. But the evenings were torturous. The first few weeks I would fall asleep as soon as I touched the pillow. Soon, however, the nights found me restlessly tossing about, seeking sleep in vain. The appalling nights—even if I should get the customary two months' commutation time, I still had nearly two hundred and ninety of them. Two hundred and ninety—and Sasha? I used to lie awake and mentally figure in the dark the number of days and nights before him. Even if he could come out after his first sentence of seven years, he would still have more than twenty-five hundred nights! Dread overcame me that Sasha could not survive them. Nothing was so likely to drive people to madness, I felt, as sleepless nights in prison. Better dead, I thought. Dead? Frick was not dead, and Sasha's glorious youth, his life, the things he might have accomplished—all were being sacrificed—perhaps for nothing. But—was Sasha's *Attentat* in vain? Was my revolutionary faith a mere echo of what others had said or taught me? "No, not in vain!" something within me insisted. "No sacrifice is lost for a great ideal."

One day I was told by the head matron that I would have to get better results from the women. They were not doing so much work, she said, as under the prisoner who had had charge of the sewing-shop before me. I resented the suggestion that I become a slave-driver. It was because I hated slaves as well as their drivers, I informed the matron, that I had been sent to prison. I considered myself one of the inmates, not above them. I was determined not to do anything that would involve a denial of my ideals. I preferred punishment. One of the methods of treating offenders consisted in placing them in a corner facing a blackboard and compelling them to stay for hours in that position, constantly before the matron's vigilant eyes. This seemed to me petty and insulting. I decided that if I was offered such an indignity, I would increase my offence and take the dungeon. But the days passed and I was not punished.

News in prison travels with amazing rapidity. Within twenty-four hours all the women knew that I had refused to act as a slave-driver. They had not been unkind to me, but they had kept aloof. They had been told that I was a terrible "anarchist" and that I didn't believe in God. They had never seen me in church and I did not participate in their ten-minute gush of talk. I was a freak in their eyes. But when they learned that I had refused to play the boss over them, their reserve broke down. Sundays after church the cells would be opened to permit the women an hour's visit with one another. The next Sunday I received visits from every inmate on my tier. They felt I was their friend, they assured me, and they would do anything for me. Girls working in the laundry offered to wash my clothes, others to darn my stockings. Everyone was anxious to do some service. I was deeply moved. These poor creatures so hungered for kindness that the least sign of it loomed high on their limited horizons. After that they would often come to me with their troubles, their hatred of the head matron, their confidences about their infatuations with the male convicts. Their ingenuity in carrying on flirtations under the very eyes of the officials was amazing.

My three weeks in the Tombs had given me ample proof that the revolutionary contention that crime is the result of poverty is based on fact. Most of the defendants who were awaiting trial came from the lowest strata of society, men and women without friends, often even without a home. Unfortunate, ignorant creatures they were, but still with hope in their hearts, because they had not yet been convicted. In the penitentiary despair possessed almost all of the prisoners. It served to unveil the mental darkness, fear, and superstition which held them in bondage. Among the seventy inmates, there were no more than half a dozen who showed any intelligence whatever. The rest were outcasts without the least social consciousness. Their personal misfortunes filled their thoughts; they could not understand that they were victims, links in an endless chain of injustice and inequality. From early childhood they had known nothing but poverty, squalor, and want, and the same conditions were awaiting them on their release. Yet they were capable of sympathy and devotion, of generous impulses.

I was gradually given entire charge of the hospital ward, part of my duties being to divide the special rations allowed the sick prisoners. They consisted of a quart of milk, a cup of beef tea, two eggs, two crackers, and two lumps of sugar for each invalid. On several occasions milk and eggs were missing and I reported the matter to a day matron. Later she informed me that a head matron had said that it did not matter and that certain patients were strong enough to do without their extra rations. I had had considerable opportunity to study this head matron, who felt a violent dislike of everyone not Anglo-Saxon. Her special targets were the Irish and the Jews, against whom she discriminated habitually. I was therefore not surprised to get such a message from her.

A few days later I was told by the prisoner who brought the hospital rations that the missing portions had been given by this head matron to two husky Negro prisoners. That also did not surprise me. I knew she had a special fondness for the colored inmates. She rarely punished them and often gave them unusual privileges. In return her favorites would spy on the other prisoners, even on those of their own color who were too decent to be bribed. I myself never had any prejudice against colored people; in fact, I felt deeply for them because they were being treated like slaves in America. But I hated discrimination. The idea that sick people, white or colored, should be robbed of their rations to feed healthy persons outraged my sense of justice, but I was powerless to do anything in the matter.

After my first clashes with this woman she left me severely alone. Once she became enraged because I refused to translate a Russian letter that had arrived for one of the prisoners. She had called me into her office to read the letter and tell her its contents. When I saw that the letter was not for me, I informed her that I was not employed by the prison as a translator. It was bad enough for the officials to pry into the personal mail of helpless human beings, but I would not do it. She said that it was stupid of me not to take advantage of her goodwill. She could put me back in my cell, deprive me of my commutation time for good behavior, and make the rest of my stay very hard. She could do as she pleased, I told her, but I would not read the private letters of my unfortunate sisters, much less translate them to her.

Then came the matter of the missing rations. The sick women began to suspect that they were not getting their full share and complained to the doctor. Confronted with a direct question from him, I had to tell the truth. I did not know what he said to the offending matron, but the full rations began to arrive again. Two days later I was called downstairs and locked up in the dungeon.

I had repeatedly seen the effect of a dungeon experience on other women prisoners. One inmate had been kept there for twenty-eight days on bread and water, although the regulations prohibited a longer stay than forty-eight hours. She had to be carried out on a stretcher; her hands and legs were swollen, her body covered with a rash. The descriptions the poor creature and others had given me used to make me ill. But nothing I had heard compared with the reality. The cell was barren; one had to sit or lie down on the cold stone floor. The dampness of the walls made the dungeon a ghastly place. Worse yet was the complete shutting out of light and air, the impenetrable blackness, so thick that one could not see the hand before one's face. It gave me the sensation of sinking into a devouring pit. "The Spanish Inquisition come to life in America"—I thought of Most's description. He had not exaggerated.

After the door shut behind me, I stood still, afraid to sit down or to lean against the wall. Then I groped for the door. Gradually the blackness paled. I caught a faint sound slowly approaching; I heard a key turn in the lock. A matron appeared. I recognized Miss Johnson, the one who had frightened me out of my sleep on my first night in the penitentiary. I had come to know and appreciate her as a beautiful personality. Her kindness to the prisoners was the one ray of light in their dreary existence. She had taken me to her bosom almost from the first, and in many indirect ways she had shown me her affection. Often at night, when all were asleep, and quiet had fallen on the prison, Miss Johnson would enter the hospital ward, put my head in her lap, and tenderly stroke my hair. She would tell me the news in the papers to distract me and try to cheer my depressed mood. I knew I had found a friend in the woman, who herself was a lonely soul, never having known the love of man or child.

She came into the dungeon carrying a camp-chair and a blanket. "You can sit on that," she said, "and wrap yourself up. I'll leave the door open a bit to let in some air. I'll bring you hot coffee later. It will help to pass the night." She told me how painful it was for her to see the prisoners locked up in the dreadful hole, but she could do nothing for them because most of them could not be trusted. It was different with me, she was sure.

At five in the morning my friend had to take back the chair and blanket and lock me in. I no longer was oppressed by the dungeon. The humanity of Miss Johnson had dissolved the blackness.

When I was taken out of the dungeon and sent back to the hospital, I saw that it was almost noon. I resumed my duties. Later I learned that Dr. White had asked for me, and upon being informed that I was in punishment he had categorically demanded my release.

In March 1894 we received a large influx of women prisoners. They were nearly all prostitutes rounded up during recent raids. The city had been blessed by a new vice crusade. The Lexow Committee, with the Reverend Dr. Parkhurst at its head, wielded the broom which was to sweep New York clean of the fearful scourge. The men found in the public houses were allowed to go free, but the women were arrested and sentenced to Blackwell's Island.

Most of the unfortunates came in a deplorable condition. They were suddenly cut off from the narcotics which almost all of them had been habitually using. The sight of their suffering was heart-breaking. With the strength of giants the frail creatures would shake the iron bars, curse, and scream for dope and cigarettes. Then they would fall exhausted to the ground, pitifully moaning through the night.

One day a young Irish girl was brought to the hospital for an operation. All night I watched her struggle for life. In the morning I sent for the priest. Everyone was surprised at my action, particularly the head matron. How could I, an atheist, do such a thing, she wondered, and choose a priest, at that! I had declined to see the missionaries as well as the rabbi. She had noticed how friendly I had become with the two Catholic sisters who often visited us on Sunday. I had even made coffee for them. Didn't I think that the Catholic Church had always been the enemy of progress and that it had persecuted and tortured the Jews? How could I be so inconsistent? Of course, I thought so, I assured her. I was just as opposed to the Catholic as to the other Churches. I considered them all alike, enemies of the people. They preached submission, and their God was the God of the rich and the mighty. I hated their God and would never make peace with him. But if I could believe in any religion at all, I should prefer the Catholic Church. "It is less hypocritical," I said to her; "it makes allowance for human frailties and it has a sense of beauty." The Catholic sisters and the priest had not tried to preach to me like the missionaries, the minister, and the vulgar rabbi. They left my soul to its own fate; they talked to me about human things, especially the priest, who was a cultured man. My poor patient had reached the end of a life that had been too hard for her. The priest might give her a few moments of peace and kindness; why should I not have sent for him? But the matron was too dull to follow my argument or understand my motives. I remained a "queer one," in her estimation.

Of the friends I made on Blackwell's Island the priest was the most interesting. At first I felt antagonistic to him. I thought he was like the rest of the religious busybodies, but I soon found that he wanted to talk only about books. He had studied in Cologne and had read much. He knew I had many books and he asked me to exchange some of them with him. I was amazed and wondered what kind of books he would bring me, expecting the New Testament or the Catechism. But he came with works of poetry and music. He had free access to the prison at any time, and often he would come to the ward at nine in the evening and remain till after midnight. We would discuss his favorite composers—Bach, Beethoven, and Brahms—and compare our views on poetry and social ideas. He presented me with an English-Latin dictionary as a gift, inscribed: "With the highest respect, to Emma Goldman."

On one occasion I asked him why he never gave me the Bible. "Because no one can understand or love it if he is forced to read it," he replied. That appealed to me and I asked him for it. Its simplicity of language and legendry fascinated me. There was no make-believe about my young friend. He was devout, entirely consecrated. He observed every fast and he would lose himself in prayer for hours. Once he asked me to help him decorate the chapel. When I came down, I found the frail, emaciated figure in silent prayer, oblivious of his surroundings. My own ideal, my faith, was at the opposite pole from his, but I knew he was as ardently sincere as I. Our fervor was our meeting-ground.

Warden Pillsbury often came to the hospital. He was an unusual man for his surroundings. His grandfather had been a jailer, and both his father and himself had been born in the prison. He understood his wards and the social forces that had created them. Once he remarked to me that he could not bear "stool-pigeons"; he preferred the prisoner who had pride and who would not stoop to mean acts against his fellow convicts in order to gain privileges for himself. If an inmate asseverated that he would reform and never again commit a crime, the Warden felt sure he was lying. He knew that no one could start a new life after years of prison and with the whole world against him unless he had outside friends to help him. He used to say that the State did not even supply a released man with enough money for his first week's meals. How, then, could he be expected to "make good?" He would relate the story of the man who on the morning of his release told him: "Pillsbury, the next watch and chain I steal I'll send to you as a present." "That's my man," the Warden would laugh.

Pillsbury was in a position to do much good for the unfortunates in his charge, but he was constantly hampered. He had to allow prisoners to do cooking, washing, and cleaning for others than themselves. If the table damask was not properly rolled before ironing, the laundress stood in danger of confinement to the dungeon. The whole prison was demoralized by favoritism. Convicts were deprived of food for the slightest infraction, but Pillsbury, who was an old man, was powerless to do much about it. Besides, he was eager to avoid a scandal.

The nearer the day of my liberation approached, the more unbearable life in prison became. The days dragged and I grew restless and irritable with impatience. Even reading became impossible. I would sit for hours lost in reminiscences. I thought of the comrades in the Illinois penitentiary brought back to life by the pardon of Governor Altgeld. Since I had come to prison, I realized how much the release of the three men, Neebe, Fielden, and Schwab, had done for the cause for which their comrades in Chicago had been hanged. The venom of the press against Altgeld for his gesture of justice proved how deeply he had struck the vested interests, particularly by his analysis of the trial and his clear demonstration that the executed anarchists had been judicially killed in spite of their proved innocence of the crime charged against them. Every detail of the momentous days of 1887 stood out in strong relief before me. Then Sasha, our life together, his act, his martyrdom—every moment of the five years since I had first met him I now relived with poignant reality. Why was it, I mused, that

Sasha was still so deeply rooted in my being? Was not my love for Ed more ecstatic, more enriching? Perhaps it was his act that had bound me to him with such powerful cords. How insignificant was my own prison experience compared with what Sasha was suffering in the Allegheny purgatory! I now felt ashamed that, even for a moment, I could have found my incarceration hard. Not one friendly face in the court-room to be near Sasha and comfort him—solitary confinement and complete isolation, for no more visits had been allowed him. The Inspector had kept his promise; since my visit in November 1892, Sasha had not again been permitted to see anyone. How he must have craved the sight and touch of a kindred spirit, how he must be yearning for it!

My thoughts rushed on. Fedya, the lover of beauty, so fine and sensitive! And Ed. Ed—he had kissed to life so many mysterious longings, had opened such spiritual sources of wealth to me! I owed my development to Ed, and to the others, too, who had been in my life. And yet, more than all else, it was the prison that had proved the best school. A more painful, but a more vital, school. Here I had been brought close to the depths and complexities of the human soul; here I had found ugliness and beauty, meanness and generosity. Here, too, I had learned to see life through my own eyes and not through those of Sasha, Most, or Ed. The prison had been the crucible that tested my faith. It had helped me to discover strength in my own being, the strength to stand alone, the strength to live my life and fight for my ideals, against the whole world if need be. The State of New York could have rendered me no greater service than by sending me to Blackwell's Island Penitentiary!

ANDREA DWORKIN

Intercourse

JOAN OF ARC, SOLDIER, MILITARY strategist, virgin, was born in Domremy, a parish in the province of Lorraine, circa 1412 (perhaps on January 6). She was female, illiterate, a peasant. In Rouen in 1431, at the age of nineteen, she was tried and burned as a witch. By the time of her arrest (taken prisoner in a military action) and imprisonment in 1430, she had routed the English from much French territory and established the military and nationalistic momentum for their eventual expulsion from French soil; and she had gotten Charles VII crowned King of France, creating a head-of-state so that a nation might emerge around him. Her will, her vision, and her military acumen provided the impetus and groundwork for the emergence of a French nation-state, heretofore nonexistent; and she was, for better or worse, the first French nationalist, a military liberator of an occupied country that did not yet see itself as she clearly, militantly, saw it—as a political and cultural unity that must repel foreign domination. The English, using the machinery of the Inquisition, got her convicted and killed; the Catholic Church did the actual dirty work. But no invader yet, including the Nazis, has killed what she created: France. At her trial,

> Asked why she, sooner than another,
> She answered: It pleased God so to do, by means of a simple
> maid to drive back the king's enemies.

The Church, in ongoing if not particularly credible remorse, issued a series of apologies for burning her. In 1456, she was "rehabilitated" by papal decree—essentially the Church conceded that she had not been a witch. Charles needed her name cleared once he won, because of her prominence at his coronation[*]; the Church cooperated with him as it had with the English when it burned her. In 1869, the case for canonizing Joan was placed before the Vatican: a hiatus in reparation of over four hundred years. In 1903, Joan was designated as Venerable. In 1909 she was beatified. In 1920 she became Saint Joan. The Church that killed her may now identify her as a martyr; but for women inspired by her legend, she is a martial hero luminous with genius and courage, an emblem of possibility and potentiality consistently forbidden, obliterated, or denied by the rigid tyranny of sex-role imperatives or the outright humiliation of second-class citizenship. Women have many martyrs, many valiant pacifists, sung and unsung; few heroes who made war. We know how to die, also how not to kill; Joan inexplicably knew how to make war. At her trial, Joan insisted that she had never killed on the battlefield, improbable since the combat was hand-to-hand; but she was known among her own men for standing against the commonplace practices of sadism on the battlefield. It is hard to believe that she did not kill; but whether she did or did not, she was an exemplary martial liberator—nearly

---

[*] Carrying her combat banner, Joan stood next to Charles at his coronation. Asked at her trial why her banner was given such prominence, she answered: "It had borne the pain, it was reason enough it should have the honor." Warner, *Joan of Arc,* p. 166.

unique in the iconography and history of the European female, that tamed and incomprehensibly peaceful creature. Joan's story is not female until the end, when she died, like nine million other women, in flames, condemned by the Inquisition for witchcraft, heresy, and sorcery. Precisely because she was a hero whose biography brazenly and without precedent violates the constraints of being female until the terrible suffering of her death, her story, valorous and tragic, is political, not magical; mythic because she existed, was real, not because her persona has been enlarged over the centuries. Her virginity was not an expression of some aspect of her femininity or her preciousness as a woman, despite the existence of a cultish worship of virginity as a feminine ideal. She was known as Joan the Maid or, simply, The Maid (*"La Pucelle"*). Her reputation, her declaration, preceded her, established her intention and her terms; not in the context of being a holy or ideal female but in the context of waging war. Her virginity was a self-conscious and militant repudiation of the common lot of the female with its intrinsic low status, which, then as now, appeared to have something to do with being fucked. Joan wanted to be virtuous in the old sense, before the Christians got hold of it: *virtuous* meant *brave, valiant.* She incarnated virtue in its original meaning: strength or manliness. Her virginity was an essential element of her virility, her autonomy, her rebellious and intransigent self-definition. Virginity was freedom from the real meaning of being female; it was not just another style of being female. Being female meant tiny boundaries and degraded possibilities; social inferiority and sexual subordination; obedience to men; surrender to male force or violence; sexual accessibility to men or withdrawal from the world; and civil insignificance. Unlike the feminine virgins who accepted the social subordination while exempting themselves from the sex on which it was premised, Joan rejected the status and the sex as one thing—empirical synonyms: low civil status and being fucked as indistinguishable one from the other.

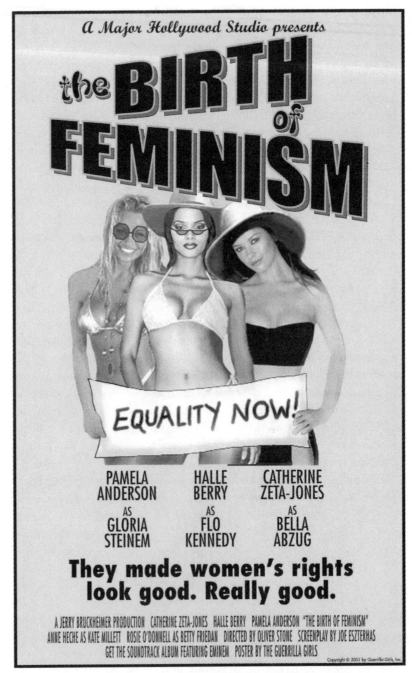

Guerilla Girls *The Birth of Feminism*

Chainwhipped

RALPH "SONNY" BARGER

Hell's Angel

TOWARD THE END OF November in 1969, the Rolling Stones got it into their heads that they wanted to play in the San Francisco area. The story goes that they wanted to have their own Woodstock, but Mick Jagger–style. What they had in mind was a large-scale free concert that would signal the end of their American *Let It Bleed* tour.

Rolling Stones representative Sam Cutler, a San Francisco hipster named Emmett Grogan, and a Grateful Dead guy named Rock Scully contacted the San Francisco parks and recreation department about staging a free concert in Golden Gate Park. When reporters from the *Los Angeles Free Press* and the *San Francisco Chronicle* found out about it and leaked the story, the public started going wild. Another idea was an impromptu set at the Fillmore, but that was killed because the place was too small and the Golden Gate Park idea was gaining steam anyway. The problem with Golden Gate was security. It was Grogan who first thought of using the Hell's Angels.

"We'll have one hundred Hell's Angels on their hogs escort the Stones into Golden Gate Park," Grogan was quoted as saying. "Nobody'll come near the Angels, man. They wouldn't dare."

A deal was apparently struck between the Stones' people and the Frisco Angels. For $500 worth of beer, Pete Knell, president of the Frisco Angels, gave his word that they would provide security. Pete was a Frisco Hell's Angel of high standing. We respected each other, even when Oakland and Frisco were at war. By the late sixties, the two charters had patched things up and everything was way cool.

I was at the monthly Hell's Angels OM (officers' meeting) when Knell came in with the news: there was going to be a free Rolling Stones concert and the surrounding chapters were invited to attend. The deal was simple: would we join Frisco and sit up on the stage, watch the crowd, and drink free beer? Soon enough, the Stones would find out that California Hell's Angels were a little bit different from their English counterparts of the day. As Stones guitarist Mick Taylor said, "These guys in California are the real thing. They're very violent."

The plan for the Stones playing Golden Gate fizzled. The park was nowhere near large enough to hold the crowds they expected, and the San Francisco parks and recreation department backed down on the permits.

The next place chosen was Sears Point Raceway, north of San Francisco in Sonoma County. It could handle the masses. When local officials put a stop to that, stage construction was halted and the negotiations between the Stones and the Sears Point Raceway owners—Filmways—was over. Filmways controlled Concert Associates, who promoted the Stones' Los Angeles appearance, and when the Stones refused to add an extra performance, the plan to use Sears Point Raceway unraveled. Filmways supposedly demanded a huge insurance liability policy, and a hundred grand just for rent, plus an interest in the distribution of a film that was going to be made of the concert. None of this sat well with anyone. The local radio stations, television news, and local papers that had heavily publicized the event suddenly had nothing.

A man named Dick Carter had been staging drag strip races at his Altamont Raceway, which was located in the Livermore Valley, between two small towns—Tracy and Livermore—thirty miles from Oakland. Carter had been getting advice from a Stanford University business administration student to expand his drag strip business to include outdoor rock events, so Carter stepped forward. Through San Francisco attorney Melvin Belli, he contacted Sam Cutler and the Stones to offer his site after Sears Point had been killed. In a matter of a couple of days, the deal was done. Altamont was going to be the place to see the Stones for free.

The Frisco members and a few other members from around the Bay Area left early on Saturday, December 5, making their way to Altamont in the yellow school bus owned by the Frisco chapter. Others rode their bikes earlier in the day. The bus ended up about a hundred yards from the stage that the Stones road crew had constructed the night before. In addition to the Hell's Angels, the Stones organization brought in six security guys from New York who were dressed in golf jackets and sported short haircuts. When Mick

Jagger came out the night before to see the stage built by Chip Monck (who had done the staging for Woodstock earlier that summer), his rented limousine ran out of gas.

As the crowds filled the cow pastures in Altamont, we were finishing up our OM in Oakland. I rode home to pick up Sharon before heading off to the speedway late in the afternoon. As we rode past Hayward and Livermore, tens of thousands of people were still making their way to the free concert site. Parking was nonexistent and the freeway was still under construction. A lot of people ditched their cars on the highway near the freeway exits. From there they hitchhiked or walked the remaining miles. VW buses full of lads picked up stragglers stumbling on the side of the uncompleted freeway.

To avoid the traffic, we took an even shorter route—our very own shortcut. I signaled for the rest of us to cut over on our bikes through the hills, past the frontage road, coming up off the top of the hill overlooking the Altamont stage. I was relatively clean, meaning I hadn't taken any major drug. Sharon and I had a nice ride out there. When we arrived, the concert had already been going on for a few hours, and when we pulled into the valley we saw two or three hillsides crammed with kids sitting on blankets and sleeping bags. I immediately thought about the problems of getting in and out of such a crowded place. As we rode down the hill toward the stage, the crowd parted for us. Somebody handed Sharon and me a jug of wine. We were lucky it wasn't laced with acid.

Before we got there, there had been a fight onstage between Marty Balin of Jefferson Airplane and a Hell's Angel named Animal. A bunch of Hell's Angels jumped on a black kid. When Balin got in Animal's face and told him, "Fuck you," Animal's response was to knock him out—during his set. Airplane manager Bill Thompson pulled Animal aside and asked him why he had cold-cocked his band's singer, and was told, "He spoke disrespectful to an Angel." Another band member, Paul Kantner, announced to the crowd that a Hell's Angel had just punched out their lead singer. There was no reaction.

When Sharon and I, with a few others on bikes, got to the bottom of the gorge where the stage was, we parked our motorcycles four feet from the front edge of the stage. It formed a sort of buffer zone. Right away I was surprised to see how low the stage was. It was barely three feet off the ground! As we parked, Gram Parsons and the Flying Burrito Brothers and then Crosby, Stills, Nash & Young played their sets. When some of the crowd took to yelling at us, Crosby stood up for us. We took on the task of trying to keep order amid organized confusion.

The night before, looking at a fence broken down by anxious fans arriving early, Keith Richards uttered ominously, "Ah, the first act of violence." Later,

Chainwhipped

the afternoon of the show, when a helicopter had delivered the Rolling Stones, someone approached Jagger yelling, "I'm gonna kill you, I hate you," and slugged him. Jagger's jaw and ego were bruised, and he quickly ran and hid in the offstage trailer.

Terry the Tramp, Sharon, some of the Hell's Angels officers, and I were escorted to a backstage area and introduced to the Rolling Stones. They came out of the trailer in their prissy clothes and makeup and we shook hands, then they disappeared back inside. It was like they were little kids as they ran back into the house to hide or something. They didn't say anything.

All the opening bands had finished playing, and it was time for the Stones to come out. The sun was still out and there was plenty of daylight left. The crowd had waited all day to see the Stones perform, and they were sitting in their trailers acting like prima donnas. The crowd was getting angry; there was a lot of drinking and drugging going on. It was starting to get dark.

After sundown the Stones still wouldn't come out to play. Mick and the band's egos seemed to want the crowd agitated and frenzied. They wanted them to beg, I guess. Then their instruments were set up. It took close to another hour before the band finally agreed to come out. A cold wind was blowing through the valley.

Nobody from the Stones organization told me anything. So we just sat and drank beer, watching the crowd getting more and more fucked up. When it was totally dark, the Rolling Stones ordered me and the Hell's Angels to escort the band out to the stage. I wouldn't do it. I didn't like the fact that they wouldn't come out earlier. I could no longer picture the Hell's Angels playing the part of bodyguards for a bunch of sissy, marble-mouthed prima donnas. When they finally got out, I didn't like the way they acted onstage either. They had accomplished what they'd set out to do. The crowd was plenty pissed off and the craziness began.

The Stones' ego trips had turned into our problem. The people who were the most fucked up on drugs were the ones who got to Altamont first—the so-called Friday-nighters—the ones who camped a day earlier to get a good seat. They'd been exposed to the open air and hot sun for hours on end. They'd staked their territory up front. When we came in on our bikes, they wouldn't give up their space. But . . . they moved. We made sure of that. We pushed them back about forty feet. When the Stones came out onstage, people moved back in toward the roped-in area where our bikes were parked, trying to jump up on the stage. In response, we began pushing them off the stage. Plus, they were messing with our bikes.

One Frisco Hell's Angel named Julio had parked his bike near mine. The battery on Julio's motorcycle was near the oil tank, with the springs of his seat right above the tank on each side of the battery posts. Some fan was kneeling on the seat, his weight causing contact between the springs and the battery, shorting out Julio's bike. I saw smoke coming out around the battery and yelled at the guy from the stage to get off Julio's bike. He wasn't paying any attention at all, so I jumped off the stage and pushed him off the bike. A number of Hell's Angels jumped down with me and pushed their way through the crowd. They didn't know what I was doing at the time, but they were getting everybody out of the way to give me room so I could snuff out the burning motorcycle. That single incident ignited even more tension between the Hell's Angels and the crowd. While we secured the stage, some of the people who had been hit and pushed got mad and started throwing bottles at us and really started messing with our bikes. Big mistake. That's when we entered the crowd and grabbed some of the assholes vandalizing our bikes and beat the fuck out of them.

Now that the situation had totally spun out of control, the Stones were talking a lot of "brothers and sisters" type of hippie shit. Everybody who tried to rush the stage was thrown off. A big fat girl was trying to get up on the stage. She was topless and probably very fucked up on drugs. Some of the Angels tried to stop her, and it looked to me like they were trying to get her off the stage without hurting her. Keith Richards of the Stones leaned over to me and said, "Man, I'm sure it doesn't take three or four great big Hell's Angels to get that bird off the stage." I just walked over to the edge of the stage and kicked her in the head. "How's that?"

Richards walked over to me after finishing "Love in Vain" and told me the band wasn't going to play anymore until we stopped the violence. "Either these cats cool it, man, or we don't play," he announced to the crowd. I stood next to him and stuck my pistol into his side and told him to start playing his guitar or he was dead.

He played like a motherfucker.

I didn't see the stabbing of Meredith Hunter but I remember him. Hunter had a loud green suit on and really stuck out from the crowd. When he rushed the stage and pulled out a huge black gun, the rest of what went down happened pretty fast. Jagger was singing "Under My Thumb" when the Hell's Angels bravely moved quickly toward the gunman. Once we jumped off the stage, that's when I heard the gun go off. All I know is that Hunter was up on the stage, got knocked off, a gun was flashed and fired. Then he was stabbed. He was close to the stage when we stopped him. By the time I got to Hunter he had already been stabbed. We picked him up and passed him over to the medics.

Meredith had shot a Hell's Angel. Since the guy he shot was a fugitive at

Chainwhipped

the time, we couldn't take him to a doctor or an emergency ward. It was just a flesh wound anyway.

Afterward, I didn't feel too bummed about what had happened at the concert. It was another day in the life of a Hell's Angel. I did feel it was lucky more people—including the Stones—hadn't been shot dead by this guy, Meredith Hunter. I felt as though the Hell's Angels had done their job.

The press said that Hunter experienced "shock and hemorrhage due to multiple wounds in the back, a wound in the left side of the forehead and right side of the neck." Even if he had been on the doorstep of a hospital or a doctor's office, after all of that he still would have died.

The Hell's Angels stayed at the site until it was over. We hung out in the audience for a while, drank some wine, and smoked a little bit of pot with the straggling crowd. The Stones' *Let It Bleed* tour ended with blood, all right.

Say what you want, but I blame the Stones for the whole fucking bad scene. They agitated the crowd, had the stage built too low, and then used us to keep the whole thing boiling. They got exactly what they originally wanted—a dark, scary environment to play "Sympathy for the Devil."

It's hard to say what we could have done to improve the situation had we been asked, but we were in a very bullshit position. Had I known how poor the arrangements were and how the Hell's Angels were actually being used, I wouldn't have agreed to do it. We would have planned things differently, with probably a much more informal role as security.

We rode the beef on Altamont for years.

As far as I'm concerned, the Stones are a good band and everybody likes them. But just because you sing well doesn't mean you can act like a bunch of assholes to your fans—and that's what they did that night in Altamont.

Just before midnight, we jumped on our bikes and cut over the fields for about five miles to Highway 5, around to Junction 680, and headed back to Oakland. It's funny, I've been back to that area since and have never been able to figure out how we did it.

When we got to the main highway, Terry the Tramp's motorcycle ran out of gas. We decided to "peg" Terry home—I stuck my leg out and put my foot on his foot peg, and pushed Terry home while he leaned his bike into mine, so as to keep them next to each other. Marcy was on the back of Terry's bike, and Sharon was on the back of mine. None of us thought about how dangerous it was with the terrain, the heavy traffic, and the high speeds we were going. I pegged Terry the twenty-something miles to our house, not even stopping for gas. When we got back, the girls confessed how scared they'd really been. We made a fire in the fireplace and there were all kinds of phone calls from friends who heard on the news about what had happened.

Chainwhipped

The next day there were comments that racial elements were involved in Meredith Hunter's death. He was at the concert with a white girl and apparently he had been a problem all day long. You can see it in the pictures in *Look* or *Life* magazine. He was there looking for trouble.

KSAN, the underground rock 'n' roll radio station, held a special phone-in show the next night trying to make sense of what had happened. People were calling in about the aftermath of Altamont. Sam Cutler from the Stones organization was on the air trying to explain the Stones' side of things. Bill Graham came down heavily against Mick Jagger on the air. I never really got along with Graham, and others in the club didn't either, but this time he agreed with us. Mick Jagger had been responsible for letting it get out of hand. It was his trip.

Somebody phoned me at home to tell me about the show, so I called KSAN to stand up for the Hell's Angels. I took all the cocaine we had in the front room with me into the bedroom and called the station. They gave me the runaround until I convinced them I was actually who I said I was. Then they put me on the air. I was loaded.

"Flower people ain't a bit better than the worst of us," I said. "It's about time everybody started realizing that. We were told if we showed up we could sit on the stage and drink some beer that the Stones' manager had bought us, you know. I didn't fucking like what happened there. We were told we were supposed to sit on the stage and keep people off and a little back. We parked where we were told we were supposed to park. . . . I didn't go there to fight. I went there to have a good time and sit on the fucking stage."

I didn't know anything about anybody getting beaten during the day with pool cues. As far as I was concerned, if you're going to beat somebody, you should use an ax handle or a baseball bat. A pool cue is a very bad weapon to use on somebody because they break too easily.

I spoke about how some of the people started knocking over our bikes. "Now I don't know if you think we pay fifty dollars for them things, or steal them, or pay a lot for them or what. But most of us that's got a good Harley chopper got a few grand invested in it. Ain't nobody gonna kick my motorcycle. And they might think because they're in a crowd of three hundred thousand people that they can do it and get away with it. But when you're standing there looking at something that's your life, and everything you got is invested in that thing, and you love that thing better than you love anything in the world, and you see some fuck kick it . . . if you got to go through fifty people to get to him, you're gonna get to him.

"That stuff made it personal to me. You know what? I'm a violent cat when I got to be. But there ain't nobody gonna take anything I got and try to

Chainwhipped

destroy it. And that Mick Jagger, he put it all on the Angels. He used us for dupes. As far as I'm concerned, we were the biggest suckers for that idiot that I could ever see."

All that shit about Altamont being the end of an era was a bunch of intellectual crap. The death of Aquarius. Bullshit, it was the end of nothing. One magazine article said that the sheriff's department was slow to investigate the Altamont death because the Hell's Angels had some kind of arrangement after our presence at the 1965 VDC peace rally. There was even rumor in the press that Altamont had taken a toll on the membership of the Hell's Angels.

Wrong on both counts.

Altamont might have been some big catastrophe to the hippies, but it was just another Hell's Angel event to me. It made a lot of citizens dislike us, but most of the hippies and journalists and liberals didn't like us anyway. When it comes to pleasing the right people at the right time, the Hell's Angels never came through. As for me, with the 1970s on hand, I was headed for some wilder times that would make Altamont look like a church picnic.

CHUCK ZITO

Street Justice

THIS IS THE WAY it is for me. When the lights go out and the doors slam shut and the tier finally falls silent—when grown men take themselves into their sticky palms and become lost in some adolescent fantasy or weep quietly for the lives they've lost and left behind—I drift away, carried to another place by sweet and merciful sleep.

I'm in the driveway of my home in New Rochelle right now, the home I renovated with my own hands and sweat and money. In the garage now I'm flat on my back, tinkering and tuning my Harley-Davidson, chatting and laughing with my beautiful daughter, Lisa, who assists me the way a nurse helps a surgeon, skillfully slapping tools into my hand with a knowing smile and a look of unconditional love.

There is a jump cut, in that odd way of dreams, and suddenly Lisa is gone and I'm on my own again, looking down at someone, a lone figure on a motorcycle, cruising along on a sun-bleached day, Hell's Angels jacket flapping in the breeze. The rider unstraps his helmet, one of those flimsy little sheaths we bikers refer to as "brain buckets," and tosses it over his shoulder. It hits the pavement, bounces high into the air, and shatters into a hundred tiny pieces. I can see the rider's face now, and I recognize it as my own. I can feel my hand lean into the throttle as the bike explodes forward, rushing off into the open road, which stretches before me now like a great black carpet—long, empty, forgiving.

"*Chuck?*"

There is a crackling in my ear as the picture fades and my mind goes dark, like a movie screen when the film breaks.

"*Chuck?*"

I open my eyes and through the haze of sleep see the steel ceiling above me, the bars in front of me, the slow-footed gait of inmates in the hallways, the tentative, wary movement of the corrections officers. I see someone outside my room, looking in through the thick glass door, the one that robs me of any privacy and humanity, the one that never lets me forget that I am a prisoner . . . a convict. That this is a prison and that escape comes only in dreams.

"*Hey, Chuck . . . you okay?*"

Wait a minute . . . He's in the doorway now, strolling in casually, as if the rules don't apply. He wears jeans and sneakers and carries a clipboard, and I recognize him, by face if not by name. I sit up on my bunk and rub my hands through my hair, try to shake the cobwebs loose.

"Sorry, I must have fallen asleep."

He smiles. "Yeah, well, that's understandable. There's a lot of downtime between scenes. Anyway, you're up in fifteen minutes."

"Thanks."

He walks out, leaving the door open in his wake, and I can see them out there now, the cast and crew of *Oz*, the HBO prison drama in which, starting today, I have a supporting role. I look around my cell, which is startlingly realistic, a fine approximation of the shit-holes in which I wasted six years of my life, and I can feel the sweat evaporating on my back. A sense of relief washes over me, and I laugh quietly under my breath.

My name is Chuck Zito, and I am a free man.

Life takes the strangest twists and turns. If my affiliation with the Hell's Angels has gotten me into trouble from time to time, it's also been responsible for countless opportunities. If not for my membership in the club, it's unlikely I would have been hired as a bouncer at Café Central, no small irony considering Peter Herrero's initial response on the night we met. Now, though, my reputation as a fighter, and a fighter with influential, potentially dangerous friends, was seen not as a liability but as an advantage.

Not that I advertised my ties to the club. A stipulation of my hiring at Café Central was that I agree to wear a suit and tie. I didn't have a problem with that. Once I was an employee, the rules changed. The club prohibits members from wearing their Hell's Angels patches when working. It's logical, really: a bouncer who wears a Hell's Angels jacket while on duty is either inviting confrontation or promoting the club, neither of which is acceptable. And, to be perfectly candid, I didn't really need the jacket. Word gets around, after all, and most of the regulars at Café Central knew of my membership in the Hell's Angels. My job was to be visible, but in a subtle, nonthreatening way. Intimidation was not the goal; security was the goal. Customers were supposed to understand that if they caused any problems at Café Central, there would be hell to pay (so to speak).

Although I did not promote the Hell's Angels while working at Café Central, I did occasionally take advantage of the opportunity to promote my own private endeavors. When I'd meet one of the many celebrities who called Café Central home, I'd make it a point to slip him or her a business card. Charlie's Angels Bodyguard Service was slow to develop, but eventually it worked.

My good fortune began one night at Café Central when Paul Herman introduced me to Liza Minnelli. Liza, of course, was one of the biggest stars in the world at the time. A few years earlier she'd won an Academy Award for *Cabaret*, and more recently she'd starred alongside Dudley Moore in *Arthur*, a huge box-office hit. Liza was a sensational singer, actress, and all-around performer at the peak of her career. It was a pleasure to meet her, and I told her as much. As often happens, though, she seemed more interested in meeting me. I could tell after just a few minutes that she had something serious on her mind.

"I have a job for you," she said. "If you're interested."

It turned out that Liza was recruiting me on behalf of her sister, Lorna Luft, who was also a talented (although less famous) actress. Lorna was performing in a play in New York at the time, and apparently she had been receiving threatening phone calls and letters from a deranged fan (or critic). In all likelihood, nothing would come of the threats, but Liza was taking no chances. She wanted to hire me as her sister's personal bodyguard for the duration of her performance in the show.

"Sounds good," I said. "Why don't I meet her, we'll talk, and if it seems like we'd get along, I'd be happy to do the job." (I was new at the job, but already I understood the importance of having a good relationship with a client; a bodyguard spends a lot of time in close proximity with the person he's paid to protect—it helps if they can at least have a cordial conversation.)

So I went to Lorna's play, and afterward I went backstage and we chatted for a while. Like Liza, she seemed to be a genuinely decent woman with a terrific attitude toward her work. I saw no reason to believe we'd have any problem getting along. And we didn't. I worked with Lorna for a couple months, without incident. Not more than a few days after Lorna finished the show, I got another call from Liza. She thanked me for keeping an eye on her sister and for behaving in a thoroughly professional manner.

"No problem," I said. "I'm available anytime."

"Well," Liza continued, "I'm glad you said that . . ."

"Oh?" I had a hunch about what was coming next, but I tried to play it cool.

"Yes," she continued. I'm rehearsing a play called *The Rink*, at the Martin Beck Theater, and when the show opens, in a couple weeks, I'm going to need a bodyguard."

There was a pause. Again, I played it very cool.

"And?"

"And . . . Lorna speaks very highly of you. So I'd like you to work for me, too—if you're available."

"Hold on," I said. "Let me check my calendar." (In any business, you want potential clients to think you're a hot commodity, right? Always in demand?) I stalled for a few seconds, then cleared my throat. "Should be okay."

"Great," Liza said. "I really appreciate it."

This assignment proved to be the break I'd been waiting for. I knew Liza was an A-list celebrity, a superstar in the truest sense of the word, but until I began working for her I didn't realize just what that meant. Not only did she sell out the Martin Beck, but she also attracted a seriously high-profile audience. The list of big-name actors and actresses and other celebrities who stopped backstage each night was endless: John Travolta, Robert De Niro, Andy Warhol, Al Pacino, Liberace, Elizabeth Taylor, Michael Jackson, Sylvester Stallone. These people, and many others, saw me with Liza, walking side by side with her, chatting with her, and they figured I knew what I was doing. From this single assignment word spread faster than I'd ever imagined possible.

It helped, obviously, that Liza gave me great recommendations. I found her to be a genuinely likable and decent woman with a great sense of humor, which made my job easier and more enjoyable. For instance: When Liza pulled up in front of the Martin Beck each day she was accustomed to seeing me waiting outside. One day, though, Chuck Zito wasn't there. Instead, Liza was greeted by a scraggly-looking bum who approached the car and began aggressively begging for money. The driver tried to chase the bum away, but the bum was persistent—and more than a little disgusting. When no money was forthcoming, he turned to the time-honored New York tradition of washing windows in exchange for a few bucks. Lacking any of the proper equipment—a squeegee or squirt bottle—the bum simply spit on the windshield and wiped the glass clean with his shirtsleeve.

"Get out of here!" the driver yelled.

In the backseat, Liza squirmed and wondered, *Where is Chuck?*

Finally, two doormen ran to the limo and grabbed the bum.

"Gimme some money!" the bum yelled, flailing his arms like a madman, tossing the doormen aside with ease. "I need money!"

"Wait a minute," one of the doorman said, no doubt wondering how a panhandler developed such tremendous upper-body strength. "This ain't no ordinary bum."

"You're right!" the bum yelled. "It ain't!" And with that I removed my mask and beard—the most vital parts of a disguise that had required me to sit still in a makeup chair for more than an hour. "It's me—Chuck!"

Liza jumped out of the car, laughing uncontrollably. "Are you nuts?!" she screamed.

"Nope . . . just having a little fun."

I liked Liza a lot, and I know she liked me, too. She even invited me to a party celebrating her fourth wedding anniversary.

"I'm just having a few friends over," she said. "I'd really like you to be there."

A *few friends* . . . I didn't realize what that meant until I arrived at Liza's apartment on the Upper East Side. I pulled up on my motorcycle, and it was obvious right away that the doorman wasn't accustomed to guests like me. I was dressed in an outfit that looked like something out of Elvis Presley's closet: white leather pants, white leather boots, a jacket with long, flowing red, white, and blue fringe (and a matching red, white, and blue headband); the whole outfit was studded with rhinestones. And, of course, I was wearing my signature Hell's Angels vest.

"I'm here to see Liza," I told the doorman, who looked at me like I'd come from another planet.

"Who are you?" he asked.

"Just tell her Chuck Zito is here."

He picked up the phone, talked for less than ten seconds, then invited me in.

"Twelfth floor," he said.

"What apartment?"

"Twelfth floor," he repeated.

"Yeah, but what's the apartment number?"

He smiled. "The apartment is the whole floor, sir."

"You've gotta be shittin' me."

"No, sir."

Liza's place was the biggest apartment I'd ever seen, with an incredible view of the city and a living room bigger than my entire house. There were more than a hundred people there, including some of the biggest stars in show business: Liberace, Steve Rubell, Halston, Andy Warhol, and Truman Capote in one corner; Gregory Peck, Lucille Ball, James Mason, and Diana Ross in another corner; Robert De Niro, Al Pacino, Joe Pesci, Christopher Walken, and Danny Aiello in another. And me, the kid from New Rochelle . . . the Hell's Angel dressed like Elvis . . . in the middle of them all.

BONNIE BREMSER

Troia

DISTRACTION—I CAN'T FIGURE where to start—a chick on the make to get her husband out of jail—not just that—brought back to a country I had hoped never to see again. I am violently afraid of the United States and Texas, but I am coming to you fast, Ray, like a tornado, fast as every irregular bag of tricks I can muster will get me there. Gotta get there fast, Ray might not last. I fuck a border Mexican cop and make it across the border illegally on a bus full of Mexican shoppers—I don't care. That was the first time I ever fucked someone for something other than money or love. I had been informed at the ten mile checking point that I could not cross the border, for my papers had expired and I didn't have the baby with me, and the immigration officials were waiting for me at the New Laredo bus stop. I had tried to con the bus driver to let me off early but he wouldn't have anything to do with it though sympathetic and I was taken immediately to the chief of the immigration who tells me that I will have to go back to get the baby in Veracruz before I can even talk to him about crossing the border—meanwhile Ray is waiting desperate and I am wild to get to him, there must be some solution to this and I must somehow get to see him immediately, tonight. It is growing dark and I am in a complete panic, everything is so much already thoroughly out of whack; the end of the world has come. I tell him I have no money to return to Veracruz and I will have to wire my mother for it, so I am put in a hotel right next to the customs station. I wonder about chances of turning a trick in this forsaken atmosphere, am admitted to the hotel and call my mother, who refuses to go to get the baby for me but sees that she has to send me the fare to go myself. I drink a Coca-Cola, take a shower, send the hotel owner's son to pick up my letter from Ray in Laredo, which cools me a little, decide that I will go out to look around, nothing to lose. The sun has set, my dress is wool and I am immediately sweating. I have in mind to go again to see the chief of immigration and beg him to let me cross to see my husband in jail; he is not there, but the officer I talk to, in a very confidential sort of way, says that it can be fixed up. I lay it on the line, I am desperately in love and will do anything I can to see my husband, he asks me to walk across the street to the back of a parking lot where he will pick me up in his truck; we don't want to be seen. B the cop, became our friend, for this was the biggest favor I ever fucked for. B took me to dinner somewhere out of the city where I was introduced to the local music and deliciousness of roast goat with good tortillas. He says to me that I will not be able to stay in my hotel room that night for "they will be looking for me." I am afraid he is going to pull an inhuman burn, but the risk must be taken at this point, so as he gets drunk, we dance, then drive through the flat and dry night, sounds of dogs and the city gaiety, always something happening there to amuse the passers-through, into the cricket cool of a deserted motel where two story high up room awaits my baggage of green dress and sun tan and somehow hardship savored flesh grows not to mind his sympathies though he was one of the hardest lays to cope with I have ever come across, a definite streak of what I immediately term as fag, insisting on my meticulous administrations to his ass-hole. Although he is attentive and even reverent of my body, I somehow connect his demands with the most masculine of attitudes, even reminding me of Ray's, although that might have been due to the circumstances.

B falls asleep finally, satisfied and drunken. He has come on very affectionately through the whole thing, and I am inclined to accept it with as much good grace as I can muster, for I am putting all my money on getting across the border in the morning, but I am left the rest of the night with my doubts, so separate from everything, Ray across the border, Rachel in Veracruz, the shock only one day old, a letter in my bosom, portends prisons and death. Morning dawns brilliantly hot with no sea breeze or hope of escape from the heat, it suits my mood, this hole is a perfect place for Hell. B wants me to have breakfast. I object, but he insists, and he is no person to argue with, so I do, the doubts growing in my head, but finally he tells me "I am going to stop the jeep along this road here, this is where the bus to Laredo starts, all you have to do is get on and sit low down in the seat so you won't be recognized when it stops this side of the bridge—I am going to drive along behind so I will know if you make it or not, good luck." I thank him with all my heart, thank him, though I had done my part of the deal and the bus is off, my heart is in my throat, we are through the dusty streets of Nuevo Laredo, I feel the eyes of Mexicans on me, I am paranoid that everyone knows what is happening, through the checking points of customs, this is a regular shopping bus trip, Mexicans can go over for a day with no problem . . .

And they treated me so badly on the other side that I saw the "help" I had received from B in an even more romantic light and decided, when I got back to Veracruz that I would prefer to stay in Nuevo Laredo than even put myself at the mercy of American ways of life again.

The street in the night in Laredo, after seeing Ray, after walking beneath his window in hopeful ritual circles, a prowl car circling me, it is white and scary, it thinks that I am going to stay around to jive with it, but I am on the alert, predict its movements and run when it is not in sight and make it into my hotel room just before it rounds the corner to see where I have gone. I cannot go back across the border yet so I stay one night in Laredo, and watch the police search the empty lot beside my hotel with flashlights. Border town ballyhoo-sounds of the Rio Grande night, slap of water against the wetback thigh, two nations are at war, the border patrol has antennas and cruises the river marsh bank for the smell of marijuana plants grown from seeds lost from an immigrant pocket. The cop atmosphere here is unbearable. I see persecution as I never knew it existed. My citizenship is questioned every time I cross the bridge, though they are well trained to recognize the difference between flavor and true nationality, they are better trained to offend and I put them on at every turning.

Laredo is a vision of small town horror with cheap department stores and several varieties of five and dime lining the streets. The streets are hot and bare and sterile, the Texans have no conception of being a part of the land: all spaces of earth or trees have signs saying keep off, and the remainder is a continuous vista of paved concrete, starting with the "international bridge" which has a dividing marker in the middle of the Rio Grande which is supposed to suggest some mutual amity but it is all a farce signed by Roosevelt, the whole thing, the Mexican half included has been built and monsterized by capitalism, the dream ends on the south side where Mexican immigration facilities have not kept up with the times of the new bridge and still look like a sleepy bus depot as opposed to the forsaken Laredo customs which resembles F. B. I. headquarters. . . . I file through from the shopping bus crowd and look an American policewoman with florid mouth in the eye, saying I have just been across for a couple of hours. I breeze through, while an honest Mexican behind me is questioned vulgarly about his life.

The post office building and courthouse areas are meccas of American stature—the post office is the more impressive of the two for it is the FEDERAL ideal, housing the Federal Courthouse as well, as opposed to Webb County Spittoon Jail and Courthouse properties of trees. The Federal agent who arrested Ray (get out of Mexican deportation truck on the other side of the bridge still in Mexico: "What's happening?" "Just walk, across the bridge." Ray walks across the bridge, internationally free all the concrete of the bridge between him, the world and the sky, concrete creaks in border nightmares of plank bridge lost and floated away floodwise down the river. So Ray walks across the bridge, a free man, and on the other side a Federal agent, a youth, taps him on the shoulder saying "Ray Bremser?" and flips his credentials eye-high from out of his certified rump equipage, Ray jumps with surprise "O Lord don't shoot!" oh wail baby, put alla them gringos on)—this same agent receives me in his brick office of no interest, brick front professional one purpose building, flat on the street and midway sterile between Webb County plaza of processless law and the Federal beehive building of enormous post office flag so high you can see it from the other side of the river.—His building is graceless of trees, the front door is inscrutable glass like the shithouse window on a train—I find Ray's case documented with no more than a paper signed by himself, not even original, which makes no official charge, no warrant from New Jersey or Webb County, just a little memo, which, signed by his federal hand, has already doomed us.—He tells me pleasantly that he recommended $10,000 bail, I point out that he is completely out of order and am appraised by his federal eye.

The señora from La Telepa had insisted that I go to the American Consul even before I found out how the baby was—kids ran down to fetch her from her house—the whole neighborhood down to the last scroungy dog is involved in the fall of our household. J appears but I leave her on the step unheeded because I am going to see the American Consul immediately. I didn't want to see him but then thought maybe he would have something pertinent to say so the señora, my creditor, and most jealous admirer of baby Rach (who tried to tell me in the taxicab bad things about J, and how the baby should not be with her) got a taxi and drove me to the American

Consulate, by the water, on the Maleçon, near the lighthouse and fancy apartments of the fresher and more presentable part of the city. The señora intends to go in with me but I send her home and ring on the "at home" section of the Consulate doorbells; a woman answers and speaks English. I am left standing on the doorstep while she goes to get her husband; having received my name, the Consul comes five minutes later, still getting himself together. His name is Black or Jeeves or something equivalently stupid, I note at the time. He greets me at the door, "oh yes Mrs. Bremser," leads me through the darkened secretarial room of the building, not bothering to turn on the lights (saving electricity?) as he goes ahead of me. "Come in here Mrs. Bremser"—the light is on in a very small room with a large desk and one straight chair opposite where I sit. I say I want to know about my husband immediately as I am in something of a rush. He has opened the conversation with questions about the robbery Ray is known to have committed and why he did it. I figure since he has nothing better to win me over with that the conversation was going to be a flop. I am looking for information. He starts to give me sympathy and I reject it saying my husband hasn't done anything and intimate that he is a better man than the Consul by far. Playing the game to the hilt, I ask him how I am going to get to Texas to find my husband. He says I will be sent by the American Consul by bus to Laredo. And suppose I don't want to go that way? "The Veracruz police are looking for you, Mrs. Bremser, you would be doing a very foolish thing if you try to get to Laredo by yourself, you will be arrested by the Veracruz police as soon as you go out this door and I won't lift a finger to help you then. We've been watching you for a long time. You and your husband (the way you dress!) have stuck out like sore thumbs; this is a small town." I interject my own private opinion of his public stature; rising from the chair he says "you'll be arrested." I find my own way out through the dark rooms with him pursuing and keeping up with the talk I no longer listen to. I pause at the door and tell him loudly that his wife is a whore and spit on his doorstep in passing and walk out into the Veracruz air, night thunderstorm breaking. I am free, my thoughts are my own, in the night air, I am alone and the rain soaks me as I walk to the telegraph office, crying, thinking, unheeding, planning for our escape out of this. Fuck the American Consul, I telegraph Ray I am on my way babe, hang on.

Frank Reynolds
as told to Michael McClure

Freewheelin Frank

It was the Fourth of July, 1966, run for the Hell's Angels Motorcycle Club newly brought together under the California rocker. We were heading towards Bass Lake. This is an annual run of the year, not always to the same place, but Bass Lake has been our scene on several Fourth of Julys. All seven chapters arrived at the lake in the early morning hours of the Fourth of July weekend.

There before our eyes was the special squadron of cops assigned to the Hell's Angels. Buckingham, the head of it, we got to know quite well in a very short time. This plain-clothes inspector is very clever and specially trained to keep track of us. He and his special little cops had made an agreement with us that we would not give this special squad any trouble about giving them our names and letting them check out our engine numbers. In the past there was always an all-out alert on the main runs of all chapters. This caused chaos and confusion among the cops for they would all head for the designated area.

In the early days we had been forced out of Reno. And the death of Lovely Larry, on the prior April run, is what really put the cap on getting this special little squadron of cops to take care of us. The place where Lovely Larry was killed was Assafocko Lake near San Luis Obispo. It was a specially called run in April because everybody wanted to get out on a spring run. As it turned out a large mob of cops of all kinds descended onto the area around the lake where we had camped. There were approximately three hundred of us, three-quarters on motorcycles. The cops had a field day with roadblocks. Many bikes were confiscated. The cops had planned this as one of their definite big steps in breaking up the Hell's Angels. With Armies of policemen in helicopters they just figured they'd walk right in and show us how it is, and show us that State Attorney General Lynch wasn't fooling when he said, "All-out war on the Hell's Angels . . . Statewide investigation . . ." As I said sometime before, as Lovely Larry went through the roadblocks, one after another, they blew his mind because he hated cops when they pushed a man. And then the report said that he was run over by an unidentified motorist. There was no car cited. I mean how could there be—there were so many squad cars on the highway! And they drug him away by the feet—first-aid treatment

California-Highway-Patrol style recommended by all . . . The whole country loves it . . . backs them up all the way. Well, so here we are. I've run it down so I don't have to go through it again. So we'll just jump right back to Bass Lake which is the next run after Larry's death.

And here we are with the special little squadron, like I say, checking out the motorcycles. This time they weren't so perked up and popping off at the mouth. I think all the cops and especially the assigned investigators well knew who carried the guilt of Lovely Larry's death. They sure made a definite change awful fast.

This time there was only one little roadblock leading into our special encampment area. If there were any cameras they were well hidden. Nobody saw any helicopters. The cops at the gate kept all outsiders away from us. The Gypsy Jokers were headed for Bass Lake too, along with scores of other motorcycle trip hangers-on. We had arrived first, naturally—it was our scene, as it will always be. But we told the cops to let all the other little outlaw clubs in. A lot of us had specially in mind the Gypsy Jokers, due to the fact that they had been branching out throughout the state. Whether it was a rumor started by one of our war-mongers or not doesn't matter, but it was said, "The Gypsy Jokers are going to come together and branch out, and after organizing enough they are going to kick the ass of the Hell's Angels." Everybody was heated up over this story but, as they rode in, we stood back and smiled and waved them on in. For a whole afternoon we let em sit around and drink and speak to us. And then it went into the first night of the weekend when a few of their women on the mama level were dragged off without a sound bein made, and a few of the tough-looking characters were accidently dropped into the lake from the overhanging cliff. They were big and strong and they made it back up. Accidents in the quiet night.

It was a warm night and a little fog rolled off the lake. There were a lot of weeping willow trees, a lot of sycamore, alder, oak and even more evergreens. In the night it was pitch black only a few feet from the bonfire—a huge bonfire of tree trunks—yet a few feet away it was very dark. We hadn't planned anything the first night as far as putting it on the Jokers and the rest of these loose-like cats—here today and gone tomorrow—as to what the trip is that they're smelling up, with their short sleeves and makeup frowns and sneers. Because we had two days to go, we left that night up to our individual sex deviates, for all the perverts were havin a trick or treat. While the rest of us stood about the fire and discussed the mind trip in the future, on the level of chess-game Angels. Though it wasn't spoken of and stressed as a chess game we all knew it was to be. Meanwhile out in the tules in pairs of two and three, the loose, outlawed women who came with these hotdog characters

Chainwhipped

were being tasted by all of our master deviates. These were their finest hours as they would gruel and grin going down to scarf their box and trying to make them wince and scream as much as possible. Every now and then you'd hear the slapping whapping sound of a long black bull-whip. On the other end of it always and forever—was Blind Bob. Blind Bob, the leading sexual insane Hell's Angel. Need I say what chapter he is from? The newspapers and the magazines all run him down but never will they ever get the point. If they knew they'd surely blow it. For I have never read or never heard of anything to likely compare to Blind Bobby.

He swings the black whip above his head cracking it in the faces of strangers or anyone he might want to see squirm, yet he never has ever cut the face of a person he knew had something going. But he'll cut the face of many a little girl who'll say, "*No, stop. I came to be here with you Hell's Angels of such colorful strength!* You men who make all the old ladies shudder and the children run out in the street. You're so brave! Don't hurt me!" And all the time most of them dig it. One out of a thousand, I should say, one out of a million is a rape case. Where they get on a bummer and think they want it this way—and in spite of it they will come back on us.

Blind Bob is mad at those pop bottle lenses of his glasses but he wears a constant grin. He always has two or three women with him all the time. They look like they're in a trance. They might even dig ripping off the clothes of another broad as he goes into his deep convulsions with his witchlike maids.

As Peter, our new president of the Frisco Chapter, says, "Every cat's got his part among us. We all cannot be the same." That's when I did tell him I agreed. He then applied chess-game terms to what he had said: Some wicked knights and rooks . . . Though there's many chapters they sure come out in a gleam.

As the sun sprang up the morning air burst in a still whiteness, the black smoky clouds had changed the trees to darkness in the daylight. It looked as though a spell had been cast upon this part of Bass Lake which was our land. We would have claimed it whether or not given the permission which we had been given. Only one time did the cops walk in: a couple of sheriff's deputies and three of Buckingham's goons. They didn't get all the way into the circle before we saw their backs turned stepping away, a little bit swaggery as they tried to hold that chest-out chin-up stance, as they departed going out the same way they came in, not saying a word, leaving nothing but wrappers of tums for the tummy.

About the area lay sleeping bags stained with wine and blood, though just a few showed bloodstains, as proof of Bobby's whip and the other deviates. Many of the girls were specially chosen Gypsy Joker women of beauty who knew damn well what the trip was when they entered our gates. The first night, only the lame men lost their women. If they would not stand up and defend their women then the deviates led them away. Though it was not still and quiet they kept it from becoming sharp and loud. Professional is not a good enough word for this Hell's Angel kind of play. It's putting it down the way it is and people had better damn well see it. Yet for eleven years or more they been coming back. The country thinks it's got some production lines; they ought to line it up with our production line of women! It would make all those suburb cats howl. They'd be lighting bonfires in the parks on election day if it were a bummer.

Meanwhile the second day grew into the hot sun. There was a stillness among all the outlawed, which is too good a word for the hotdog riders. They were getting a little worried. They were breaking the gates down trying to get out more than five at a time for breakfast, which was in the contract. We didn't want our gates broke down so we stopped them. By midafternoon of the second day all of the loose hotdog riders that were going to show up had shown up. There were so many different oddball clubs. I'd never be able to remember all of the odd names, such as Cross Men, Question Marks, etc. I could go on and on. All the strange clubs usually wear some kind of a skull on the back of their jackets. They try to get as near to copying us as possible, They're all the same as far as the way they dress, for they try to dress exactly as we do, but the trip is—they are only out to try to catch the eye of the public for a few days and then they go back to whatever trip they are really on. It is not a everyday trip for them, as it is for us, not for a lifetime.

On the lake many motorboats were wheeling around and capsizing as they veered from left to right. Many Hell's Angels were throwing their women into the water and holding them under, as if to baptize them Angel style—always naked. As the evening shadows started to move in the whole area was heavily clouded in marijuana smoke. Wood had been gathered for the night's fire. Cases of beer stood up in the air six feet high from the day's thievery and what money had been collected to buy wine and beer. This was the second night . . . it would be the most festive night of the three-day weekend. Many of the cherub-like Angels were already drunk and mad on wine. In their madness of not knowing why or giving a damn why they began to swing on strangers, occasionally slapping the face of a strange broad. Then, if her old man would not do anything about it, they would rip him completely to the ground. For instance, one broad who stood about as if she was anxious for something to happen was suddenly yanked by her long black hair and shoved. Her old man, who was nothing but a hot dog rider, of the Jokers, looked around and, instead of sticking up for her, screamed at her, saying, "GET OVER THERE AND SIT DOWN!"

Chainwhipped

One Angel says, "DONT TALK TO HER LIKE THAT," breaking a fifth of wine over his forehead. The Joker then slumped to his knees biting the dust—out of breath forever as he fell. His broad meanwhile was yanked and thrown upon the ground, one Angel saying to her, "You'd better get yourself a real old man!" Pulling her pants off her he poured wine all over. After he'd finished, he called out, "LET'S TURN HER OUT!" Many who liked the broad immediately got in line waiting their turn. In the background motorcycles roared like thunder as they raced down the dusty trails around and around the encampment. Occasionally one would hit a bare stump throwing rider and motorcycle into the air. No one received any broken bones during the whole weekend within the encampment. Everybody gets so loose and drunk and free on a run that they're so limber it is impossible to break a bone, I think. It was quite a usual thing to see an Angel walk over and steal the bike of a hot dog rider and go racing off into the woods, not caring if he wrecked it and himself both. Each chapter had at least one prospective member. Through the three-day meeting the prospectives of each chapter were put to the test to prove that their chapter was the best. And in turn each chapter tried to prove that its prospective was the stronger and could do the most out-of-sight things. For instance, they were all put in barrels and rolled off this long sloping cliff that runs down into the lake, as one trick in the Ceremony of Prospects. Bo from Oakland won when he didn't come up for five minutes. Bo is like a reincarnation of Houdini, but looks like a blond vicious Viking. There was so much activity going on that one could not observe all of it.

What looked like a barbarian sale of women began as the evening shadows closed in. Upon an orange crate women were being stood with their hands tied behind them and auctioned off. The sign read: CHICKS FOR SALE. WE ACCEPT ANYTHING. A tall lanky Angel by the name of Buzzard was the auctioneer. He would stand and describe the tall or shortlike broad, describing how she sucked and fucked. Quoting, "Here is a broad I have before me, who is not only a nympho, she is also a bisexual. She can take care of your old lady as well as you. What is my offer?" The beautiful broad with long brown hair and a large bust with slim hips was quickly yanked from the orange crate as the long black whip cracked around her neck and jerked her from it. This time it was someone else wielding Bobby's whip: it was one of Satan's Slaves, who are very good friends of the Hell's Angels. They are from the South—and are known for their sexual deviation, for yanking women right off the streets and taking them into their bars and raping them. The Satan's Slaves are number one when it comes to sexual diversion. They are of Satan himself.

As darkness crept in the trees seemed covered with black smoke. The moon was full and the howls of women as they were being raped rang out into the night. This was the biggest sex orgy we had ever had in our lifetime. Everyone by this time was covered with filth from falling in the lake and wallowing in the dust and sloshing wine over each other. The smell of sexual orgies reeked along with the honeywind of marijuana. In some jagged stump-like corners of the forest certain characters were rolling their sleeves up geezing their arms full of crystal and opiates, jacking themselves completely off the ground in their insane way. Everyone was completely mad! Stark raving crazy! The hotdog stand riders had had their bikes taken away, kicked up and revved over till the engines BLEW scattering metal all over the ground. Those who had remained clean were sloshed with wine and spit on! At times a turd would come slinging through the air—shit splattering upon each other's faces. No one was to remain without filth upon his body.

In order to leave our campsite one had to follow a long winding trail that led through the trees before coming to the roadblock and the road. As some of the riders tried to leave from time to time during the night, some of the wildest Angels who had hidden themselves up trees along the roadway would jump down off the branches right on top of the bike rider knocking him from his motorcycle, leaving him sprawled out unconscious along the side of the trail. Then they'd drag the motorcycle, the broad, and the rider off into the weeds. The Angels would climb back up into the trees to wait for the next Gypsy Jokers or hotdog riders trying to escape.

From the overhanging branch of one tree, a hotdog rider was hanging by his heel after being tied and strung into the air. For who knows what—it didn't really matter. Many caps of LSD had been brought. This was an insane forest with a now higher fire that was raging into the sky. The cops did not dare come in. If they had come in they would have been ripped clean of their flesh and probably eaten.

I was high on acid by this time myself, and I could not comprehend what was happening and it probably didn't matter. The sounds were like an African jungle during the great fire when all of the animals grow angry and mad on the rampage. Anyone who was not a Hell's Angel or a close friend was smashed and beaten. Graves were being dug. I don't know if anyone was buried or not.

All night long this insane wildness went on. A jazz band was brought in from a local nightclub and forced against their will to stand by the fire and play as loud as they could. Many harmonicas blew insanely into the night—music in wild distortion. Women who had been raped during the previous days now walked along as if in a deep trance, not caring if the world had ended or not. It was as though we all hoped someone would come in trying

Chainwhipped

to resist what we had started so we could rip them from bone to bone. But not once did we turn against one another. This was the closest the Hell's Angels had ever been, and we could not get any closer than we were. We loved one another and we could not hurt one another. We only wanted to hurt *anyone* who was not one of us.

The officers all talked of how people hated us—and wanted to see an end put to us. "We must stick together. We must become as one! We are the Gods!" We cried out in insane anger.

"We must strike out against those who attack us!"

"All men wish to put an end to us! And can not!"

"When we stick together we are an army!"

"When we stick together we are an ARMY!" George cried out. "No one can stop us!"

I had already had four or five women, maybe more—I had lost count. Now all I could do was to fool about. If I did not like the woman, I bit her. I was tired and wornout. Finally I fell into a bed of hot coals which seemed to be warm. Then I went to sleep. When I awoke I was covered with black soot. My clothes had been burned but not my skin. Why, I don't know. It didn't really matter. We had all undergone a spell which we had created ourselves. It was day and time to start breaking camp. No one was stirring. Clothing lay about the ground stained and ripped. Bodies hung out of trees—some half in the water and half out. One of my nearby brothers slept inside a garbage can, his feet dangling out.

It was so still not even birds were singing. It was cold before the sun had crept over the mountain. I kicked a can trying to make some noise and found out my ears were completely plugged. When I slapped the side of my head to make them open up I heard the sound of a horn blowing. I looked about to see who was blowing it but saw no one. Then I heard the rustle of branches breaking as someone fell from a tree right into the midst of a pile of sleeping bags. Someone stood up and screamed, "You god-damned sonofabitch bastard!!"

I noticed I had stepped on a hat, containing change and a couple of crumpled dollar bills, which had been passed around by Johnny Angel, collecting for booze—is what he had said—but really he was collecting for his own pocket. It is an old Angel tradition to collect money when you are broke. The idea comes from the church where they pass a collection plate around every Sunday. Always at the start of a run you will see somebody passing a hat around to the hotdog riders and people dropping change in it. —This is supposed to be for booze but it is to fill one's own pocket and to get some money to eat on. This is usually only collected from the hotdog riders, unless an Angel is fool enough to drop a coin into it, which I doubt.

Then we broke camp, leaving behind the rumble of rubbish. The two toilets were burnt to the ground and we had to pay seventy-five dollars to replace them. Many drunken bodies of hotdog riders were left behind to pick themselves up—if they ever did. The cops jumped back from the gates as we roared out—they, too, looked insane after the two days. We broke onto the road in a roar, and as our heads cleared in the morning summer air, we roared out of the valley back to our cities and towns in California, knowing that we had a lot ahead of us. Knowing that we had brought our minds close together over the three days, we were riding out like saints with many prophecies to be delivered. There was work to be done. We had to get on with it. The festival was over, the 1966 Fourth of July run for the Hell's Angels Motorcycle Club of California.

I don't know where the Satan's Slaves are from. They come out of the San Fernando Valley, in southern California, from San Gabriel or San Joaquin—who knows? We consider them friends because they're so loose. They go into things with no thought of fear or of being afraid or anything. On the runs they always come in a big group. They are feared by the law. So we have no reason to place them in the same category as the Gypsy Jokers and all of the other hotdog riders. They were offered a charter under the Hell's Angels, but did not want it because they had had the name of Satan's Slaves for so long that I guess they feel it would be bad luck to change names now. Pete says we have to watch out for them. Pete is a great man, a man that likes to see and has a great understanding of men. He likes to talk a lot. The Satan's Slaves have no feelings for the law, just as we have none. But they take more of a destructive attitude towards the law, one that will be their own destruction if they do not watch out and are not very careful. For instance, we heard on the radio once that the landlord had evicted one Satan's Slave from an apartment house in southern California. In turn the Satan's Slaves ran through the apartments, ripping them apart, throwing the furniture into the pool, completely demolishing the house. This is why the Hell's Angels respect them, because they don't take no shit like we don't. We take care of business and then let the people ask the questions. I think we leave a very good telltale essence behind us. Either have respect for a man or this is the way you'll end up. When one thinks about it it's true. Tell me this is not the way it is going to end up in the end *end*. Need I say more? Destruction is on the menu for everyone.

The Satan's Slaves have a top rocker and bottom rocker on the back of their jackets. The top rocker reads: SATAN'S SLAVES. The bottom rocker gives the name of the place they're from, and in the center, where our death's head is, they have a bike coming forward with high handlebars and in between the handlebars is the face of a devil. Their colors are black and white where ours are red and white. Nobody knows too much about them. All we know is that they're usually along on the runs. And they ride off together when the run is over. As we do.

We once went to San Bernardino for an incorporation meeting, the reason was to form a corporation of the Hell's Angels. There was a lawyer there by the name of Jeremiah Castelman, who had many ideas about making money, which would make him richer than everyone, naturally. We were ready for him at the Berdoo Ranch, for the officers of the chapters had brought along a tape recorder. When the lawyer saw the tape recorder he balked and stammered and stuttered with many words. For an hour or so he ran down the ifs and ands and buts of how we could make money. In the end the only chapters that were behind him were two out of seven chapters, and funny it was to note that it was the southern chapters that were behind him—the Berdoo Chapter and the Dago Chapter, both from the South.

The South is where the money is with all the movie producers, and all the production cats that want to go on the Batman trip for the Hell's Angels. We told him to take his Hell's Angels T-shirts, boots, purses, bands, and what not and shove them straight up his ass. Ralph Barger told him, over the tape recorder, "When I'm ready to use this death's head on my back to make money—that's the day I quit the Hell's Angels." And quote, "Before I see anyone use this death's head to make money, I'll kill the son of a bitch." And he meant it, just like we mean it, though it took only one of us to say it. We're not on no money trip. We hate money, and all that love it we hate.

The day will come when Blind Bob will be able to whip anyone who sells his soul for money. Right now he's just getting into practice. This earth is Hell, and when the fire comes Blind Bob is going to be ready to torture all those souls of destruction who fall for the Devil's Fortune and Fame. So you the people better rise up and off of it and start getting with the real thing. On the back of my courtesy cards I write six words: on the top it says LIFE SOUL DEATH, on the bottom it says LOVE FORTUNE FAME. I link up LIFE with an arrow. I link your SOUL with LOVE and I link your DEATH with FORTUNE, with arrows going from one word to the other. Write the six words down and line them up to see which direction your soul is headed towards. In other words, as you read your papers and books, all you'll see and hear of is FORTUNE and FAME. Have you ever asked yourself what happened to Love?

Do you know that God is Love? What happened to the creators? They're now shoved into the gutter . . . and the blasted production line has taken over. The true people on this earth are the creative people like the poets, the teachers, the painters—anyone who creates with his hands. These are people of Love, not of Fortune and Fame. Satan created Fortune and Fame. He came to the world with it. While God is Love. His people are creators as he is. In the end they will come together and Fortune and Fame will be left to burn as it is written.

TOM WOLFE

The Electric Kool-Aid Acid Test

KESEY MET THE HELL'S ANGELS one afternoon in San Francisco through Hunter Thompson, who was writing a book about them. It turned out to be a remarkable book, as a matter of fact, called *Hell's Angels, a Strange and Terrible Saga.* Anyway, Kesey and Thompson were having a few beers and Thompson said he had to go over to a garage called the Box Shop to see a few of the Angels, and Kesey went along. A Hell's Angel named Frenchy and four or five others were over there working on their motorcycles and they took to Kesey right away. Kesey was a stud who was just as tough as they were. He had just been busted for marijuana, which certified him as Good People in the Angels' eyes. They told him you can't trust a man who hasn't done time, and Kesey was on the way to doing time, in any case. Kesey said later that the marijuana bust impressed them but they couldn't have cared less that he was a novelist. But they knew about that, too, and here was a big name who was friendly and interested in them, even though he wasn't a queer or a reporter or any of those other creep suck-ups who were coming around that summer.

And a great many were coming around in the summer of 1965. The summer of 1965 had made the Hell's Angels infamous celebrities in California. Their reputation was at its absolutely most notorious all-time highest. A series of incidents—followed by an amazing series of newspaper and magazine articles, *Life* and the *Saturday Evening Post* among them—had the people of the Far West looking to each weekend in the Angels' life as an invasion by baby-raping Huns. Intellectuals around San Francisco, particularly at Berkeley, at the University of California, were beginning to romanticize about the Angels in terms of "alienation" and "a generation in revolt," that kind of thing. People were beginning to get in touch with Thompson to see if he couldn't arrange for them to meet the Angels—not the whole bunch,

Chainwhipped

Hunter, maybe one or two at a time. Well, Kesey didn't need any one or two at a time. He and the boys took a few tokes on a joint, and the Hell's Angels were on the bus.

The next thing the citizens of La Honda knew, there was a huge sign at the Kesey place—15 feet long, three feet high, in red white and blue.

THE MERRY PRANKSTERS
WELCOME THE HELL'S ANGELS

Saturday, August 7, 1965, was a bright clear radiant limelit summer day amid God's handiwork in La Honda, California. The citizens were getting ready for the day by nailing shut their doors. The cops were getting ready by revving up a squad of ten patrol cars with flashing lights and ammunition. The Pranksters were getting ready by getting bombed. They were down there in the greeny gorge, in the cabin and around it, under the redwoods, getting bombed out of their gourds. They had some good heavy surges of God-given adrenaline going for them, too. Nobody ever came right out front and said it, but this happened to be the real-life Hell's Angels coming, about forty of them, on a full-fledged Angels' "run," the sort of outing on which the Angels did their thing, their whole freaking thing, *en* mangy raunchy head-breaking fire-pissing rough-goddamn-housing *masse.* The Pranksters had a lot of company for the occasion. It was practically like an audience, all waiting for the stars to appear. A lot of the old Perry Lane crowd was there, Vic Lovell, Ed McClanahan, and the others. Allen Ginsberg was there and so was Richard Alpert and a lot of San Francisco and Berkeley intellectuals. *Tachycardia*, you all—but Kesey was calm and even laughing a little, looking strong as an ox in his buckskin shirt, the Mountain Man, and he made it all seem right and inevitable, an inevitable part of the flow and right now in this moment. Hell, if the straight world of San Mateo County, California, had decided to declare them all outlaws over an innocuous thing like marijuana, then they could freaking well go with the flow and show them what the saga called Outlaw was really like. The Angels brought a lot of things into synch. Outlaws, by definition, were people who had moved off of dead center and were out in some kind of Edge City. The beauty of it was, the Angels had done it like the Pranksters, by choice. They had become outlaws first—to *explore*, muvva—and then got busted for it. The Angels' trip was the motorcycle and the Pranksters' was LSD, but both were in an incredible entry into an orgasmic moment, *now*, and within forty-eight hours the Angels would be taking acid on board, too. The Pranksters would be taking on . . . Ahor, the ancient horror, the middle-class boy fear of Hell's Angels, *Hell's Angels*, in

Chainwhipped

the dirty flesh, and if they could bring that dark deep-down thing into their orbit—

Kesey! What in the freaking—tachycardia, you all . . .

Bob Dylan's voice is raunching and rheuming in the old jacklegged chants in huge volume from out the speakers up in the redwood tops up on the dirt cliff across the highway—*He-e-e-ey Mis-ter Tam-bou-rine Man*—as part of Sandy Lehmann-Haupt's Non-Station KLSD program, the indomitable disco-freak-jockey Lord Byron Styrofoam himself, Sandy, broadcasting over a microphone in a cabin and spinning them for you—Cassady revved up so tight it's like mechanical speed man sprocket—Mountain Girl ready—*Hey, Kesey!*—Hermit grin—Page ablaze—men, women, children, painted and in costume—ricochet around the limelit dell—*Arggggggghhhhh*—about 3 p.m. they started hearing it.

It was like a locomotive about ten miles away. It was the Hell's Angels in "running formation" coming over the mountain on Harley-Davidson 74s. The Angels were up there somewhere weaving down the curves on Route 84, gearing down—*thraggggggggh*—and winding up, and the locomotive sound got louder and louder until you couldn't hear yourself talk any more or Bob Dylan rheumy and—*thraaaaaaagggggghhh*—here they came around the last curve, the Hell's Angels, with the bikes, the beards, the long hair, the sleeveless denim jackets with the death's head insignia and all the rest, looking their most royal rotten, and then one by one they came barreling in over the wooden bridge up to the front of the house, skidding to a stop in explosions of dust, and it was like a movie or something—each one of the outlaws bouncing and gunning across the bridge with his arms spread out in a tough curve to the handlebars and then skidding to a stop, one after another after another.

The Angels, for their part, didn't know what to expect. Nobody had ever invited them anywhere before, at least not as a gang. They weren't on many people's invitation lists. They figured they would see what was there and what it was all about, and they would probably get in a hell of a fight before it was all over, and heads would break, but that was about par for the course anyway. The Angels always came into alien situations black and wary, sniffing out the adversary, but that didn't even register at this place. So many people were already so high, on something, it practically dissolved you on the spot. The Pranksters had what looked like about a million doses of the Angels' favorite drug—beer—and LSD for all who wanted to try it. The beer made the Angels very happy and the LSD made them strangely peaceful and sometimes catatonic, in contrast to the Pranksters and other intellectuals around, who soared on the stuff.

June the Goon gave a Hell's Angel named Freewheeling Frank some

LSD, which he thought was some kind of souped-up speed or something—and he had the most wondrous experience of his life. By nightfall he had climbed a redwood and was nestled up against a loudspeaker in a tree grooving off the sounds and vibrations of Bob Dylan singing "The Subterranean Homesick Blues."

Pete, the drag racer, from the San Francisco Hell's Angels, grinned and rummaged through a beer tub and said, "Man, this is nothing but a goddamn wonderful scene. We didn't know what to expect when we came, but it turned out just fine. This time it's all ha-ha, not thump-thump." Soon the gorge was booming with the Angels' distinctive good-time lots-a-beer belly laugh, which goes: Haw!—Haw!—Haw!—Haw!—Haw!—Haw!

Sandy Lehmann-Haupt, Lord Byron Styrofoam, had hold of the microphone and his disco-freak-jockey rapping blared out of the redwoods and back across the highway: "This is Non-Station KLSD, 800 micrograms in your head, the station designed to blow your mind and undo your bind, from up here atop the redwoods on Venus!" Then he went into a long talking blues song about the Hell's Angels, about fifty stanzas worth, some of it obscure acid talk, some of it wild legends, about squashing turtles on the highway, nutty stuff like that, and every stanza ending with the refrain:

> Oh, but it's great to be an Angel,
> And be dirty all the time!

What the hell—here was some wild-looking kid with the temerity to broadcast out over the highways of California that Angels were dirty all the time—but how the hell could you resist, it was too freaking madly manic—and pretty soon the Angels and everybody else were joining in the chorus:

> Oh, but its great to be an Angel,
> And be dirty all the time!

Then Allen Ginsberg was in front of the microphone with finger cymbals on each hand, dancing around with a beard down to his belly and chanting Hindu chants into the microphone booming out over California, U.S.A., *Hare krishna hare krishna hare krishna hare krishna*—what the mollyfock is hairy krishna—who is this hairy freak—but you can't help yourself, you got to groove with this cat in spite of yourself. Ginsberg really bowled the Angels over. He was a lot of things the Angels hated, a Jew, an intellectual, a New Yorker, but he was too much, the greatest straightest unstraight guy they ever met.

> And be dirty all the time!

Chainwhipped

The filthy kooks—by nightfall the cops were lined up along the highway, car after car, just across the creek, outside the gate, wondering what the fock. The scene was really getting weird. The Pranksters had everything in their electronic arsenal going, rock 'n' roll blazing through the treetops, light projections streaming through the gorge, Station KLSD blazing and screaming over the cops' heads, people in Day-Glo regalia blazing and lurching in the gloom, the Angels going *Haw—Haw—Haw—Haw,* Cassady down to just his hell of a build, nothing else, just his hell of a build, jerking his arms out and sprocketing around under a spotlight on the porch of the log manse, flailing a beer bottle around in one hand and shaking his other one at the cops:

"You sneaky motherfuckers! What the fuck's wrong with you! Come on over here and see what you get . . . goddamn your shit-filled souls anyway!"— laughing and jerking and sprocketing—"Don't fuck with me, you sons of shit-lovers. Come on over. You'll get every fucking thing you deserve."

The hell of it, men, is here is a huge obscene clot of degradation, depradation and derogation proceeding loose and crazed on the hoof before our very eyes, complete with the very Hell's Angels, and there is nothing we can do but contain it. Technically, they might have been able to move in on the grounds of Cassady's exposing himself or something of the sort, but no real laws were being broken, except every law of God and man—but sheer containment was looking like the best policy. Moving in on those crazies even with ten carloads of armed cops for a misdemeanor like lewd display—the explosion was too grotesque to think of. And the cops' turret lights revolved and splashed against the dirt cliff in a red strobe light effect and their car-to-headquarters radios were wide open and cracking out with sulphurous 220-volt electric thorn baritones and staticky sibilants—*He-e-e-ey Mis-ter Tam-bou-rine Man*—just to render the La Honda gorge totally delirious.

Meanwhile, the Angels were discovering the goddamnedest thing. Usually, most places they headed into on their runs, they tested people's cool. What are *you* looking at, mother. As soon as the shock or naked terror registered, they would be happy. Or if there was no shock and terror but instead somebody tried some brave little shove back, then it was time to break heads and tear everybody a new asshole. But these mollyfocking Pranksters were test-proof. The Angels didn't know what permissive was until they got to Kesey's. *Go with the flow!* The biggest baddest toughest most awfulest-looking Hell's Angel of them all was a big monster named Tiny. The second biggest baddest toughest most-awfulest-looking Hell's Angel was a big raw-boned guy named Buzzard, dark-looking, with all this dark hair and a beard, all shaggy and matted and his nose came out like a beak and his Adam's apple hung down about a foot, and he was just like an enormous buzzard. Tiny and

Chainwhipped

Buzzard had a thing of coming up to each other when they were around non-Angels and sticking out their tongues and then licking each other's tongues, a big sloppy lap it up, just to shake up the squares, it really jolted them—so they came up right in front of this tall broad of Kesey's, Mountain Girl, and la-a-a-a-ap—and they couldn't believe it. She just looked right at them and grinned and exploded sunballs out of her eyes and started laughing at them, *Haw—Haw—Haw*, as if to say in plain language: What a bullshit thing. It was freaking incredible. Then some of them passed a joint around and they passed it to Mountain Girl and she boomed out:

"Hell, no! What the hell you doing putting your dirty mouth on this clean joint for! This is a clean joint and you're putting your dirty mouths on it!" Nobody in living memory had ever refused a toke from a joint passed by Angels, at least not on grounds of sanitation, except this crazy girl who was just bullshitting them blind, and they loved it.

It even got to the point where Mountain Girl saw Tiny heading into the mad bathroom with a couple of beer cans like he is going to hole up in there and drink a couple of cans in peace, but this is the bathroom all the girls around here are using, and Mountain Girl yells out to Sonny Barger, the maximum leader of the Hell's Angels, "Hey, Sonny! Tell this big piece of trash to stay out of our clean bathroom!"—in a bullshit tone, of course—and Sonny picks it up, "Yeah, you big piece of trash! Stay out of the clean bathroom! They don't want you in there!"—and Tiny slinks out the door, outside, in a bullshit slink, but he does it—

And that's it! It's happening. The Hell's Angels are in our movie, we've got 'em in. Mountain Girl and a lot of the Pranksters had hit on the perfect combination with the Angels. They were friendly toward them, maybe friendlier than anybody had been in their lives, but they weren't craven about it, and they took no shit. It was the perfect combination, but the Pranksters didn't even have to think of it as a combination. They just did their thing and that was the way it worked out. All these principles they had been working on and talking about in the isolation of La Honda—they freaking well *worked.*

Go with the flow—and what a flow—these cats, these Pranksters—at big routs like this the Angels often had a second feature going entitled *Who Gets Fucked?*—and it hadn't even gotten to that before some blonde from out of town, one of the guests from way out there, just one nice soft honey hormone squash, she made it clear to three Angels that she was ready to go, so they all trooped out to the backhouse and they had a happy round out there. Pretty soon all the Angels knew about the "new mamma" out in the backhouse and a lot of them piled in there, hooking down beers, laughing, taking their turns, making various critiques. The girl had her red and white dress pushed up around her chest, and two or three would be on her at once, between her legs, sitting on her face in the sick ochre light of the shack with much lapping and leering and bubbling and gulping through furzes of pubic hair while sweat and semen glistened on the highlights of her belly and thighs and she twitched and moaned, not in protest, however, in a kind of drunken bout of God knew what and men with no pants on were standing around, cheering, chiding, waiting for their turn, or their second turn, or the third until she had been fenestrated in various places at least fifty times. Some of the Angels went out and got her ex-husband. He was weaving and veering around, bombed, they led him in there under glare and leer and lust musk suffocate the rut hut they told him to go to it. All silent—shit, this is going too far— but the girl rises up in a blear and asks him to kiss her, which he does, glistening secretions, then he lurches and mounts her and slides it in, and the Angels cheer Haw Haw—

—but that is her movie, it truly is, and we have gone with the flow.

So much beer—which is like an exotic binge for the Pranksters, beer. Mountain Girl and Kesey are up in the limelit bower and the full moon comes down through the treetop silhouettes. They are just rapping in the moonlight, and then Sandy wanders on up there and sits with them, high on acid, and he looks down and the floor of the forest is rippling with moonlight, the ground shimmers and rolls like a stream in the magic bower and they just sit there—a *buzzard!* Buzzard is wandering up the slope toward them and there in the moonlight in the dark in the magic bower he . . . *is* a buzzard, the biggest ever made, the beak, the deathly black, the dopply glottal neck, the shelled back and dangling wings, stringy nodule legs—Kaaawwwwwww!— and Kesey jumps up and starts throwing his arms up at him, like the way you would scare away a buzzard, and says,

"Aaaaagh! a buzzard! Hey! Get away, you're a buzzard! Get this buzzard out of here!"

It's a bullshit gesture, of course—and Buzzard laughs—*Haw! Haw! Haw!*—it is not real, but it is . . . *real*, real buzzard, you can see the whole thing with two minds—Kaw Kaw Kaaawwwww—and Buzzard jumps and flaps his arms—and the whole . . . connection, the *synch*, between the name, the man, the bird, flows together right there, and it doesn't matter whether he is buzzard or man because it has all come together, and they all see it . . .

They all see so much. Buzzard goes, and Sandy goes, and Kesey and Mountain Girl are in the moonlight ripply bower. By and by—where?— Kesey and Mountain Girl—and so much flows together from the lights and the delirium and the staticky sibilants down below, so much is clear, so much

flows in lightness, that night, under the full moon, up above the flails and bel-
lows down below—

The Hell's Angels party went on for two days and the cops never moved in.
Everybody, Angels and Pranksters, had a righteous time and no heads were
broken. There had been one gang-bang, but the girl was a volunteer. It was
her movie. In fact, for the next six or seven weeks, it was one long party with
the Angels. The news spread around intellectual-hip circles in the San Fran-
cisco-Berkeley area like a legend. In these circles, anyway, it once and for all
put Kesey and the Pranksters up above the category of just another weirdo
intellectual group. They had broken through the worst hangup that intellectuals know—the *real-life* hangup. Intellectuals were always hung up with
the feeling that they weren't coming to grips with real life. Real life belonged
to all those funky spades and prize fighters and bullfighters and dock workers
and grape pickers and wetbacks. *Nostalgie de la boue*. Well, the Hell's Angels
were real life. It didn't get any realer than that, and Kesey had pulled it off.
People from San Francisco and Berkeley started coming by La Honda more
than ever. It was practically like an intellectual tourist attraction. Kesey
would talk about the Angels.

"I asked Sonny Barger how he picks new members, new Angels, and he
told me, 'We don't pick 'em. We *recognize* 'em.'"

And everybody grokked over that.

Likely as not, people would find Hell's Angels on the place. The Angels
were adding LSD to the already elaborate list of highs and lows they liked, beer,
wine, marijuana, benzedrine, Seconal, Amytal, Nembutal, Tuinal. Some of
them had terrible bummers—bummer was the Angels' term for a bad trip on a
motorcycle and very quickly it became the hip world's term for a bad trip on
LSD. The only bad moment at Kesey's came one day when an Angel went
berserk during the first rush of the drug and tried to strangle his old lady on
Kesey's front steps. But he was too wasted at that point to really do much.

So it was wonderful and marvelous, an unholy alliance, the Merry
Pranksters and the Hell's Angels, and all hours of the day or night you could
hear the Hell's Angels gearing and winding down Route 84 to Kesey's, and the
people of La Honda felt like the plague had come, and wasn't there anything
that could be done. More than one of the Pranksters had his reservations, too.
The Angels were like a time bomb. So far, so good—one day the Angels even
swept and cleaned up the place—but they were capable of busting loose into
carnage at any moment. It brought the adrenaline into your throat. The
potential was there, too, because if the truth were known, there were just a
few of the Pranksters who could really talk to the Angels—chiefly Kesey and

Mountain Girl. Mainly it was Kesey. Kesey was the magnet and the strength, the man in both worlds. The Angels respected him and they weren't about to screw him around. He was one of the coolest guys they had ever come across. One day, finally, Kesey's cool came to the test with the Angels and it was a strange moment.

Kesey and the Pranksters and the Angels had taken to going out to the backhouse and sitting in a big circle and doing the Prankster thing, a lot of rapping back and forth and singing, high on grass, and you never knew where it was going to go. Usually it went great. The Angels took to the Prankster thing right away. They seemed to have an immediate intuitive grasp of where it was going, and one time Kesey started playing a regular guitar and Babbs started playing a four-string amplified guitar and Kesey got into a song, off the top of his head, about "the vibrations," a bluesy song, and the Angels joined in, and it got downright religious in there for a while, with everybody singing, "Oh, the vi-bra-tions . . . Oh, the vi-bra-tions . . ."

And then Kesey and a few of the Pranksters and a lot of the Angels, including Sonny Barger of the Oakland Chapter, the maximum leader of all the Angels, were sitting around in the backhouse passing around joints and rapping. The subject was "people who are bullshit."

There are certain people who are bullshit and you can always recognize them, Kesey was saying, and the Angels were nodding yeah, that certainly is right.

"Now you take ———," said Kesey, mentioning one of the Angels who was not present. "He's a bullshit person."

A *bullshit person* — and man —

"Listen, Kesey," says Barger, 100 percent Hell's Angel, "——— is an Angel, and nobody — *nobody* — calls an Angel a bullshit person."

— the freaking gauntlet is down. It's like forever and every eye in the place pins on Kesey's face and you can hear the blood squirt in your veins. But Kesey doesn't even blink and his voice doesn't even change one half tone, just the old Oregon drawl:

"But I *know* him, Sonny. If I didn't *know* him, I wouldn't call him a bullshit person."

Yeah — we-e-e-elll — everybody, Angels and Pranksters — well — Kesey *knows* him — there is nothing to do but grok over this statement, and everybody sits there, still, trying to grok over it, and after a second, the moment where heads get broken and fire gets pissed is over — *We-e-ell, ye-ah* —

Two or three days later it occurs to some of the Pranksters that they *still* don't know what the hell Kesey meant when he said that. He *knows* the guy. It doesn't make any sense. It's a concept with no bottom to it — but so what!

Chainwhipped

At the moment he said it, it was the one perfect thing he could have said. Kesey was so totally into the moment, he could come up with it, he could break up that old historic push me, shove you, yeah-sez-who sequence and in an instant the moment, that badass moment, was over.

The Pranksters got pretty close to several of the Angels as individuals. Particularly Gut and Freewheeling Frank and Terry the Tramp. Every now and then somebody would take one or another of the Angels up into the tree house and give them a real initiation into psychedelics. They had a huge supply of DMT. As somebody once put it, LSD is a long strange journey; DMT is like being shot out of a cannon. There in the tree house, amid the winking googaws, they would give the Angels DMT, and Mountain Girl saw some of them, like Freewheeling Frank, after they came down. They would walk around in no particular direction, listing slightly, the eyes bugged wide open, glazed.

"They were as naked as an Angel is ever gonna git," she told Kesey.

Roxanne Dunbar-Ortiz

Outlaw Woman

> FBI. 8/11/71. Roxanne Dunbar. Subject's current residence and employment are unknown. She moved from former residence, 1024 Jackson Avenue, New Orleans, La., during first week of June, 1971.

OVER MEMORIAL DAY, HOMER, Sheila, and I disappeared. Homer quit his cab job saying he was going to Mexico. We each called family members and friends with the same story. We hoped to divert the FBI so that their Mexican contacts would look for us there, or for them to believe we'd gone to Cuba. I sold the VW station wagon for cash with mixed feelings, because Abby had bought it. We turned the flat with all the office equipment over to a local women's liberation group who thought we were leaving the area. Laura and the other women from our group would continue the women's organizing and hint that we'd gone to Cuba. Hannah stayed in St. Bernard Parish under her own name but, like Laura, had access to all the safe houses, where they would meet us regularly.

Chainwhipped

We bleached Homer's straight, dark hair and gave him a permanent, and with the addition of some horn-rimmed glasses, he looked remarkably different. Because he would be seeking employment as an oil field roustabout, he would continue to wear jeans, but now with a snap-button Western shirt and scuffed cowboy boots and a hat. We cut the sleeves out of a jean jacket for him to wear over his shoulder holster.

Sheila also became a bleached blonde. She wore tight-fitting slacks with a matching top and gold sandals, and carried a purse large enough for her Browning. She looked older and brassy, quite unlike her sweet and modest self.

I knew my hair would not hold a curl, not even a wave, so we died it black. I parted it on the side and pinned back the bangs. With makeup and aluminum framed glasses I looked different enough. I wore Western clothes and cowboy boots and carried a shoulder bag for my Browning.

Our first month underground during June 1971 was one of the hottest months on record in southern Louisiana. The temperature was over 100 degrees with 100 percent humidity every day. Night brought no relief, and though the rain came often, it was hard to distinguish from the humidity.

Keeping our scattered weapons from rusting became a full-time job. The apartments were air-conditioned, but we had stashed the weapons and documents in locked closets where there were no air ducts. The closets became steam baths in the heat and humidity, and so we had to air the weapons and clean them daily. We feared leaving them out in the apartment lest a nosy manager or utilities worker discover them when we were not there.

While Homer waited to be hired as a roustabout, Sheila took a job in a rest home in St. Bernard Parish. We decided that I shouldn't take a job because I was too well known and easy to identify, so I made the rounds checking on the apartments and cleaning the guns. I also kept the apartments supplied with food. We were in for the long haul, figuring it would take years for us to merge ourselves with the industrial workers while carrying out sabotage on the pipelines and barges without being detected. So the tedious tasks that summer resonated with a larger meaning and didn't seem futile at all.

The best moments were when all of us gathered once a week at the Algiers apartment. Laura would arrive wearing a blonde wig that made her look like a man dressed up as a woman. She brought our mail, told us all the news, and made us laugh with her stories. One day, though, Laura brought news that changed the course of events.

"Roxanne, a man named Buddy has been to the Jackson Avenue house looking for you every evening. He says it's shrimp season and he wants to take you out shrimping with him," she told me.

"That's the guy I met three weeks ago, just before we went underground. When did he start coming by?" I asked.

"Right after I was last here. What do I tell him? I didn't want to say you'd gone to Cuba without asking. I said you were on vacation."

"I think I should tell him some of what we're up to," I told the group. "He could be useful to us—he knows the place, and even gets along with the Cajuns. He's experienced with explosives. We have to take some risks with people or we'll never get anywhere. Might as well start with him." After a short discussion, everyone agreed that I should go and see Buddy and confide in him.

My heart sped as I drove to the construction site Buddy had shown me. It was 10 a.m., a time it seemed he'd most likely be on the job. *Brown and Root, Houston, Texas,* was written on the side of a small trailer at the edge of the site. I knocked on the door and realized I didn't even know Buddy's name. A middle-aged cowboy opened the door and a waft of cold air hit me in the face. He said that Buddy had worked all night and had gone to his trailer to sleep—he gave me exact directions.

I drove north on the St. Bernard Highway and found the trailer park with Buddy's white van parked in front. I knocked on the flimsy aluminum door, making more of a rattle than a knock. The door opened. Buddy was buttoning the top metal button on his Levis. He was barefoot and shirtless.

"Yeah, whatcha want?" He squinted in the light.

"Hi, Buddy. Sorry to wake you."

"Who are you anyway?" he asked.

"Roxanne. You remember me? Your boss said you'd gone home."

"San Antonio rose? I'll be damned, but you've changed. I didn't hardly recognize you."

"Yes I've changed. I won't bother you now, just wanted to make contact so we can meet later. I don't live on Jackson Avenue anymore but the people there said you'd been around looking for me."

"Climb up and share a beer. I don't have no crawdaddies on hand for you." He winked and laughed, and I laughed with him.

I stepped up into the tiny kitchen. "Watch out, or you'll bump your head. You can see why my wife left me." I sat down at the built-in dining nook. Buddy popped two cans of Bud and sat down facing me.

"I wanted to invite you out shrimping. It's the season and I've been taking out a shrimp boat an old boy has for sale. Come out with me today."

"Do you always take women shrimping on the first date?"

"It'll be our second date, only on the second date."

"I need to tell you something." I felt absurd. How could I tell this stranger that I was an underground revolutionary?

Chainwhipped

"Well, first I've changed my name and appearance. If we're to see each other you have to call me by a different name, Lily, and not tell anyone my real name."

"Lily's a good name, my mama's favorite flower."

"I'm a member of an armed underground group. We're revolutionaries." I took the Browning out of my purse and placed it on the table.

"Whooee! A regular pistol-packing mama you be. You rob banks like Bonnie Parker?"

"Not yet. Right now we're planning to blow up some industrial installations."

"Great, more work for me to rebuild them. How about blowing up that new refinery we're putting up? The hours we're working, it'll be finished in two months and I'll have to move on."

"You don't disapprove?"

"Hell no. I got a brother-in-law in Huntsville for armed robbery. Come from a long line of jailbirds, mama says we're related to John Wesley Harding. Me, I never been locked up for nothing more than drunk driving, but I been beat to a pulp by cops more than once. I ain't got no love for the law."

"What about the political part? We're revolutionaries, and we want to overthrow the capitalist system. We like red China and Cuba and we support the communists against the Americans in Vietnam. And we oppose racism and believe in women's liberation."

"You got my vote. I'm not as dumb as I sound. I know about them things and think about them. No way, I'd go to no war to make the Rockefellers richer. Mexicans, Negroes, Cajuns, rednecks, we're all plain working folk."

I didn't know if he was telling the truth or just saying what he thought I wanted to hear. But it was enough to convince me that there was a rational basis for my attraction to him. We made love and I drove home like a teenager in love for the first time.

Two days later, Buddy and I moved in together to a larger trailer in another trailer park, not far from the construction site. Our group decided we would allow him to know about only one of the safe houses. While he worked, I made my usual rounds checking on the weapons and meeting with the others. At the same time, Homer was hired as a roustabout. He worked west of Baton Rouge near the interstate pipeline and came into New Orleans to meet with us every week.

It was Laura's idea for me to build an identity as a shrimper, to be accepted—and protected—by the local Cajuns. I bought a shrimp boat and trawl for $500 under my alias. Buddy was overjoyed to be my partner: "I got the time, honey, if you got the money." We shrimped on Sundays, and some of the days after he had worked all night. Buddy was well liked by his Cajun friends, who visited the trailer and went out shrimping with us. The conjunction of my need for an identity and Buddy's dream of being a shrimper was working well. Our group viewed the shrimp boat as a good cover and an eventual means for transporting weapons and explosives. I charted the barges coming downriver from the heartland, laden with wheat, corn, and soy, for export.

I savored my newfound anonymity. The banality of this new life was almost exotic for me after three years of living in the spotlight. Living with an ordinary workingman who spoke the language of my childhood made me feel more real than I had in years, ever since I left home. Yet it was a terrible illusion, self-deception on a grand scale. I was caught in a bundle of contradictions that would take me years to unravel, but I didn't realize it at the time. And for the first time in my life, I began to abuse alcohol and show all the signs of my inherited alcoholism. Worse, the relationship quickly morphed from benign-traditional—already a betrayal of my women's liberation ideals—to abusive.

On July 4, I stumbled out of bed at 6 a.m. to cook breakfast and fix Buddy's lunch as usual. When I finished, I woke him.

"What the hell, woman? I ain't going to work on no holiday. It's the damned Fourth of July. Even Brown and Root's closed down today. We're going shrimping with the Verots," Buddy bellowed.

"I didn't know you were off for the Fourth. I'm supposed to meet the others this morning." Actually, I hadn't even remembered that July 4 was a holiday.

"Well, you ain't going. We have plans."

"You didn't tell me."

"How dumb can you be not to know it's a holiday? I'm telling you now."

Anger made my skin burn. Buddy had never spoken that way to me, although he was often jealous when I spoke to men or was alone with Homer.

"I have to go there and at least tell them. We call each other only in emergencies," I said.

Buddy swung his legs to the floor, pulled on his jeans, and stood up. His mouth twisted in a snarl and his hands clenched into fists.

"You're gonna do what I say. You're my woman. I'm sick and tired of you and your little gang. From now on, I call the shots."

"What's gotten into you? Why are you talking this way?"

The blow came so swiftly and unexpectedly that I thought I'd been struck by a natural force. My face was pressed flat against the prickly green carpet. I instinctively rolled into a fetal position, just in time. He kicked me hard, aiming for my stomach.

Chainwhipped

"You got it straight now? Get dressed. We're supposed to meet them at the boat in ten minutes."

I put makeup on the bruise—a black eye—and wore sunglasses. We didn't speak as we drove down the highway. I suppressed the fury churning inside me by telling myself that I was underground, that I could not behave as I would normally. Buddy stopped for a case of beer and a sack of ice. The Verots, a Cajun couple, were loading the boat with bags of groceries to make our lunch.

"You best be friendly, hear. They already think you're stuck up. You be nice to my friends, you hear?" Buddy said before we got out of the van. I didn't answer him.

After eight seemingly endless hours on the boat, we docked and unloaded. The woman, Fran, was shy and quiet, and I couldn't think of anything to say to her. By the time we reached shore the two men were tottering drunk. Buddy invited the Verots over for a shrimp boil. At the trailer, I was relieved to have work to do, preparing the shrimp with Fran. The men sprawled in front of the TV watching a baseball game.

"Ain't it great to have slaves to do the cooking?" Buddy said.

Verot laughed, "Hell yes, beats a nigger any day."

Buddy rolled over on the floor laughing, "Sure thing. Can't fuck no nigger." I ran to the bathroom and locked the flimsy door. When I came out the Verots were gone and Buddy was passed out on the floor.

The next morning I left five minutes after Buddy did, and drove to the apartment where we'd been supposed to meet. Sheila was there alone.

"What happened to you? I came to the trailer looking for you and your car was there. Are you all right? What happened to your eye?"

The words stuck in my throat. I was too ashamed to tell Sheila what had happened, and I'd already convinced the group of Buddy's importance to our work.

"I slipped and fell on the boat. Yesterday was a big mix-up. Buddy had planned to shrimp with another couple and I couldn't get out of it." I was covering up for him and putting my own safety at risk, behaving like a battered woman who had never heard of women's liberation.

"Homer's going to call tonight to see if you're all right. Did you hear that Jim Morrison died of a drug overdose in Paris?" I hadn't heard.

That evening, Buddy came home from work apologetic and wanted to take me dancing. "That was dumb of me. I'm sorry I hit you. I just get so dammed jealous of you being with your friends all the time."

"Just don't ever do it again or I'll leave you," I said.

"I won't do it no more, but don't go threatening me. If anyone does any leaving around here it'll be me."

Chainwhipped

Bad Ass

Luis Rodriguez

Always Running

I worked as a bus boy in a Mexican restaurant in San Gabriel when I was 15 years old. My hours were in the evening until closing, which kept me up until 2 a.m. most nights. The father of a former Southside Boy managed the restaurant, which is how I got the job. It was kicking, hard work. Sometimes I'd be practically asleep while walking the dining areas—but we had to keep moving. We carried thick plastic trays heaped with dirty dishes, cleaned up tables, poured water into glasses, provided extra coffee—and took abuse from the well-to-do people who came there.

"Hey boy, clean up this mess,"

"Hey boy, how about some more water."

"Hey boy, this steak is too well done."

Hey Boy became my new name.

The clientele arrived in suits and evening dresses. They ordered the margaritas, considered the best in "aallll Caliiforniaaa." They ordered and ordered. Even before dinner arrived, they were already pushed back against the chairs, ties undone and stupefied.

Before the night finished, white-haired women tried to do Spanish fan dances on the dining floor as businessmen called everyone "pancho," holding dollar bills in our faces for more service.

We had our ways of getting back. The usual: putting snot and piss in their food before it got to their tables or "accidentally" spilling ice cold water on their laps or backs.

"So sorry, *señor*. How clumsy of me. A thousand pardons."

But there were some fringe benefits. These people would order the best steaks, lobsters, and Mexican specialties and leave almost everything when they left. We stuffed the food in and later had feasts. Every once in a while I took home cooked lobsters and two-inch thick prime ribs!

My best friends were the waitresses and waiters. One waiter, a gay dude from Mexico, actually protected us younger guys from the cooks who ordered us around. I always thought it was because he wanted to get to me, but even so I must say he never raised this issue. One time he let us borrow his X-rated 16-millimeter films. After work, the bus boys got together for a marathon viewing of his films while dropping pills and chasing them with tequila.

The waitresses were cool and understanding, considering they had to endure even more abuse since they were women—dressed in peasant blouses which had been plunged down to reveal their shoulders and short *poblana* skirts with ruffles. They helped make sure I didn't get cheated on the tips, something the waiters were less inclined to do.

But the most interesting part of the job involved the raids. Almost everyone who worked in the restaurant was an undocumented immigrant. Every so often, the immigration authorities assaulted the place. They would close doors and pull out badges.

"This is the United States Border Patrol," they'd yell. "Nobody move . . . *nadie se mueve.*"

Cooks flew out of kitchen windows.

They tried to pull me into their detention vans, but I carried a food-stained and slightly torn copy of my birth certificate in my pocket. It saved me from being deported, although there were times I thought it wouldn't matter and I'd have to call home from Tijuana.

After about a week, the ones they threw across the border were back at work.

Not going to school meant a lot of free time. Sniffing became my favorite way to waste it. I stole cans of anything that could give a buzz: carbono, clear plastic, paint or gasoline. Sometimes I'd mix it up in a concoction and pour it on a rag or in a paper bag we sniffed from.

Behind the school, on the fields, inside the tunnel, at Marrano Beach and alongside the concrete banks of the San Gabriel River: I sniffed. Once I even climbed on top of a back hoe at a construction site, removed the lid off the gas tank and inhaled until somebody checked out the noise and chased me away.

Spray was dangerous; it literally ate your brain. But it was also a great escape. The world became like jello, like clay, something which could be molded and shaped. Sounds became louder, clearer—pulsating. Bodies removed themselves from bodies, floating with the sun. I sought it so desperately. I didn't want to be this thing of bone and skin. With spray I became water.

Once I sniffed with Chicharrón and Yuk Yuk behind the "Boys" Market in San Gabriel. I don't remember the trip, but they told me I suddenly stood up and proceeded to repeatedly bang my head against a wall. Pieces of hair and skin scraped on the brick. Chicharrón walked me home; refused to give me any more spray.

While on spray I yelled. I laughed. I clawed at the evening sky. I felt like a cracked egg. But I wouldn't stop.

Then another time Baba, Wilo and I gathered in the makeshift hideout we had alongside the Alhambra Wash, next to the drive-in. We sat ourselves down on the dirt, some blankets and rags nearby to lie on. We covered the entrance with banana leaves and wood planks. There were several cans of clear plastic—what we called *la ce pe*—around us. We each had paper bags and sprayed into them—and I had already dropped some pills and downed a fifth of Wild Turkey. I then placed the bag over my mouth and nose, sealed it tightly with both hands, and breathed deeply.

A radio nearby played some Led Zeppelin or Cream or some other guitar-ripping licks. Soon the sounds rose in pitch. The thumping of bass felt like a heartbeat in the sky, followed by an echo of metal-grating tones. I became flesh with a dream. The infested walls of the wash turned to mud; the trickle of water a vast river. The homeboys and I looked like something out of Huckleberry Finn or Tom Sawyer. With stick fishing poles. The sparkle of water below us. Fish fidgeting below the sheen.

Dew fell off low branches as if it were breast milk. Birds shot out of the tropical trees which appeared across from us. Perhaps this trip had been the pages of a book, something I read as a child. Or saw on TV. Regardless, I was transported away from what was really there—yet it felt soothing. Not like the oil stains we sat in. Not like the factory air that surrounded us. Not this plastic death in a can.

I didn't want it to end. As the effect wore thin, I grabbed spray and bag, and resumed the ritual. Baba and Wilo weren't far behind me.

Then everything faded away—the dew, the water, the birds. I became a cartoon, twirling through a tunnel, womb-like and satiated with sounds and lines and darkness. I found myself drifting toward a glare of lights. My family called me over: Seni, Mama, Papa, Tía Chucha, Tío Kiko, Pancho—everybody. I wanted to be there, to know this perpetual dreaming, this din of exquisite screams—to have this mother comfort surging through me.

The world fell into dust piles around me. Images of the past pitched by:

my brother tossing me off rooftops, my mother's hearty laughter, my father's thin and tired face, the homeboys with scarred smiles and the women with exotic eyes and cunts which were the churches I worshipped in. Everything crashed. Everything throbbed. I only knew I had to get to the light, that wondrous beacon stuffed with sweet promise: Of peace. Untroubled. The end of fear. *Don't close the door, Mama. I'm scared. It's okay, m'ijo. There's no monsters. We'll be here. Don't be scared.*

No more monsters. Come to the light. I felt I would be safe there—finally. To the light. The light.

Suddenly everything around me exploded. An intense blackness enveloped me. A deep stillness. Nothing. Absolute. No thinking. No feeling. A hole.

Then an electrified hum sank its teeth into my brain. Hands surrounded me, pulled at me, back to the dust of our makeshift hideaway.

A face appeared above me. It leaned down and breathed into me. Images of leaves, crates, stained blankets came into view. Wilo pulled back and looked into my eyes. A haze covered everything. I felt dizzy. And pissed off.

"Give me the bag, man."

"No way," Baba said. "You died Chin—you stopped breathing and died."

I tried to get up, but fell back to the ground. A kind of grief overwhelmed me. I was no longer this dream. I was me again. I wished I did die.

"You don't understand," I yelled to the homeboys. "I have to go back."

I crept toward a paper bag but Baba kicked it out of my reach. Later I found myself stepping down a street. Baba and Wilo had pointed me in the direction of home and I kept going. I hated being there. I didn't know what to do. God, I wanted that light, this whore of a sun to blind me, to entice me to burn—to be sculptured marble in craftier hands.

Chester Himes

If He Hollers Let Him Go

That night I dreamed that a white boy and a coloured boy got to fighting on the sidewalk and the coloured boy pulled out a long-bladed knife and ran at the white boy and began slashing at him and the white boy broke and ran across the street digging into his pocket and at a grocery store on the other side the colored boy caught up with him and it looked as if he was going to cut him all to pieces but the white boy brought his hand out of his pocket and every time the colored boy slashed at him he hit at the back of the colored boy's hand. The white boy was crying and hitting at the back of the colored boy's hand with his fist and the colored boy was screaming and cursing and jumping in at the white boy to slash at him with the knife; but he couldn't cut the white boy because the white boy kept ducking and dodging and hitting at the back of his hand. Finally the white boy hit the back of the colored boy's hand that held the knife and made a slight cutting movement and the knife fell from the colored boy's hand. When I saw the blood start flowing from the back of the colored boy's hand I knew the white boy had a small-bladed knife gripped in his fist. The colored boy picked up the knife with his left hand and began slashing again and the white boy kept on ducking and dodging until he hit the back of the colored boy's left hand and cut the tendons in that one also. Then the white boy began chasing the colored boy down the street stabbing him all about the head and neck with the tip of the small-bladed knife. Everybody standing around looking at the white boy chasing the colored boy down the street thought he was beating him with his fist, but I knew he was digging a thousand tiny holes in the colored boy's head and neck and that it was only a matter of time before the colored boy fell to the street and bled to death; but the white boy wasn't crying any more and he wasn't in a hurry any more; he was just chasing the colored boy and stabbing him to death with a quarter-inch blade and laughing like it was funny as hell.

I woke up and I couldn't move, could hardly breathe. The alarm was ringing but I didn't have enough strength to reach out and turn it off. My hangover was already with me and my body trembled all over as if I had the ague.

Somewhere in the back of my mind a tiny insistent voice kept whispering, *Bob, there never was a nigger who could beat it.* I blinked open my eyes, closed them tight again. But it kept on saying it. And I knew it was a fact. If I hadn't had the hangover I might have gotten it out my mind. But the hangover gave me a strange indifference, a weird sort of honesty, like a man about to die. I could see the whole thing standing there, like a great conglomeration of all the peckerwoods in the world, taunting me, *Nigger, you haven't got a chance.*

I agreed with it. That was the hell of it. With a strange lucid clarity I knew it was no lie. I knew with the white folks sitting on my brain, controlling my every thought, action, and emotion, making life one crisis after another, day and night, asleep and awake, conscious and unconscious, I couldn't make it. I knew that unless I found my niche and crawled into it, unless I stopped hating white folks and learned to take them as they came, I couldn't live in America, much less expect to accomplish anything in it.

It wasn't anything to know. It was obvious. Negro people had always lived on sufferance, ever since Lincoln gave them their freedom without any bread. I thought of a line I'd read in one of Tolstoy's stories once—"There never had been enough bread and freedom to go around." When it came to us, we didn't get either one of them. Although Negro people such as Alice and her class had got enough bread—they'd prospered from it. No matter what had happened to them inside, they hadn't allowed it to destroy them outwardly; they had overcome their color the only way possible in America— as Alice had put it, by adjusting themselves to the limitations of their race. They hadn't stopped trying, I gave them that much; they'd kept on trying, always would; but they had recognized their limit—a nigger limit.

From the viewpoint of my hangover it didn't seem a hard thing to do. You simply had to accept being black as a condition over which you had no control, then go on from there. Glorify your black heritage, revere your black heroes, laud your black leaders, cheat your black brothers, worship your white fathers (be sure and do that), segregate yourself; then make yourself believe that you had made great progress, that you would continue to make great progress, that in time the white folks would appreciate all of this and pat you on the head and say, "You been a good nigger for a long time. Now we're going to let you in." Of course you'd have to believe that the white folks were generous, unselfish, and loved you so much they wanted to share their world with you, but if you could believe all the rest, you could believe that too. And it didn't seem like a hard thing for a nigger to believe, because he didn't have any other choice.

But my mind kept rebelling against it. Being black, it was a thing I ought to know, but I'd learned it differently. I'd learned the same jive that the white folks had learned. All that stuff about liberty and justice and equality. . . . All men are created equal. . . . Any person born in the United States is a citizen. . . . Learned it out the same books, in the same schools. Learned the song too: ". . . o'er the land of the free and the home of the brave. . . ." I thought Patrick Henry was a hero when he jumped up and said, "Give me liberty or give me death," just like the white kids who read about it. I was a Charles Lindbergh fan when I was a little boy, and thought George Washington was the father of my country—as long as I thought I had a country.

I agreed with the Hearst papers when they lauded the peoples of the conquered European countries for continuing their underground fight against "Nazi oppression"; I always bought the Los Angeles Sunday *Times* too, and the *Daily News*; read the *Saturday Evening Post* and *Reader's Digest* sometimes out at Alice's house while I was waiting for her to dress; I even got taken in by Pegler plenty times. Like the guys said out at the yard, "Ah believe it."

That was the hell of it: the white folks had drummed more into me than they'd been able to scare out.

I knew the average overpatriotic American would have said a leaderman was justified in cursing out a white woman worker for refusing to do a job of work in a war industry in time of war—so long as the leaderman was white. Might have even called her a traitor and wanted her tried for sabotage.

It was just that they didn't think I ought to have these feelings. They kept thinking about me in connection with Africa. But I wasn't born in Africa. I didn't know anyone who was. I learned in history that my ancestors were slaves brought over from Africa. But I'd forgotten that, just like the aristocratic blue bloods of America have forgotten what they learned in history—that most of their ancestors were the riffraff of Europe—thieves, jailbirds, beggars, and outcasts.

So even though the solid logic of my hangover told me that Alice's way was my only out, I didn't have anything for it but the same contempt a white person has for a collaborator's out in France. I just couldn't help it. That much of the white folks' teaching was still inside of me.

I knew I could marry Alice—the chick loved me. Could marry her, go back to college and get a degree in law, go on to become a big and important Negro. I knew that most people would consider me a lucky black boy.

I knew I would be lucky too. Lying there with the hangover beating in my head like John Henry driving steel, I could see it from every angle—I couldn't keep from seeing it. I didn't have the strength to keep it from my mind.

In the first place my old man had been a steel-mill worker at National Malleable in Cleveland, Ohio, when I was born, and my mother had died when I was three. I had two brothers older than I, and we'd been poor boys. My old man had married again and had three other children by our step-mother and I lived in a cold attic room for twelve long years. Shep, my oldest brother, went East when he finished Central High and the last I heard of him he was in the rackets in Washington, D.C. Dick wanted to be an artist and fooled around with the group at Karamu; he's still in Cleveland, some sort of politician. I was the ambitious one, I'd wanted to be a doctor. I'd gotten my two years at Ohio State by washing dishes in the white fraternity houses about the campus. But when my old man took sick in '38 I had to stay home and dig in with the rest; and I never got back. I puttered about with pottery at Karamu and worked with the theater group for a time—met some fine chicks, too, but none like Alice.

All I had when I came to the Coast was my height and weight and the fact

I believed that being born in America gave everybody a certain importance. I'd never had two suits of clothes at one time in my life until I got in this war boom.

In the three years in L.A. I'd worked up to a good job in a shipyard, bought a new Buick car, and cornered off the finest colored chick west of Chicago— to my way of thinking. All I had to do was marry her and my future was in the bag. If a black boy couldn't be satisfied with that he couldn't be satisfied with anything.

But what I knew about myself was that my desire for such a life was conditional. It only caught up with me on the crest of being black—when I could accept being black, when I could see no other out, such a life looked great.

But I knew I'd wake up someday and say to hell with it, I didn't want to be the biggest Negro who ever lived, neither Toussaint L'Ouverture nor Walter White. Because deep inside of me, where the white folks couldn't see, it didn't mean a thing. If you couldn't swing down Hollywood Boulevard and know that you belonged; if you couldn't make a polite pass at Lana Turner at Ciro's without having the gendarmes beat the black off you for getting out of your place; if you couldn't eat a thirty-dollar dinner at an hotel without choking on the insults, being a great big "Mister" nigger didn't mean a thing.

Anyone who wanted to could be nigger-rich, nigger-important, have their Jim Crow religion, and go to nigger heaven.

I'd settle for a leaderman job at Atlas Shipyard—if I could be a man, defined by Webster as a male human being. That's all I'd ever wanted—just to be accepted as a man—without ambition, without distinction, either of race, creed, or color; just a simple Joe walking down an American street, going my simple way, without any other identifying characteristics but weight, height, and gender.

I liked my job as leaderman more than I had ever admitted to myself before. More than any other job I could think of; more than being the first Negro congressman from California. But it was just the same as all the rest: if I couldn't have everything that went along with it, if I couldn't be in authority over white men and women just the same as any other leaderman, to hell with it too.

I knew that that was at the bottom of it all. If I couldn't live in America as an equal in the minds, hearts, and souls of all white people, if I couldn't know that I had a chance to do anything any other American could, to go as high as an American citizenship would carry anybody, there'd never be anything in this country for me anyway.

Push

WHEN I GET TO school early sometimes I just sit in front part on the black plastic couch that need tape where it cut and the yellow foam pads show through. School start at 9 o'clock. The secretary get here at 8:00 a.m. I don' get here before that 'cause the door locked and I would have to wait in the lobby downstairs. Which I don't like.

Our room is nice. Nicer since we have one day where we come in "raggedy" and bring our own cleaning stuff 'n posters, pictures, 'n plants from home 'n fix up our room. Ms Rain say bring something of YOU! I bring picture of Abdul and plant from Woolworth on 125th Street. It growed. Leaves big. Ms Rain done changed its pot three times.

Ms Rain get here 'bout 8:15 or so, usually right behind or in front of Rita or Rhonda. They bofe erly birds too. Ms Rain jus' give whoever here the keys from her purse to open up our classroom while she do whatever she do—fix coffee, git books from supply room—stuff like that. By 8:30 a.m. early birds good to go! Room quiet sunny. We just open our notebook, Ms Rain usually say something like, You got 10 or 15 minutes 'fore the "rabble" get here. Yeah, I don't know exactly what is the rabble. She jus' joking for Jermaine and them who hit the door roun' 9:05 a.m. Always a little late, always complaining 'bout something—the weather, train, what the newspaper say.

Me, I, just look at the sun coming in through the front window. Pretty soon it move around and come in through the side window. I like the routine of school, the dream of school. I wonder where I be if I had been learning all those years I sit at I.S. 146. Favorite book? Maybe it's our book, the big book with all our stories in it. Not mine yet. I'm just putting stuff in my journal now.

Telling time is *easy*. Fractions, percents, multiplying, dividing is EASY. Why no one never taught me these things before. Rita say, All people with HIV or AIDS is innocent victims; it's a disease, not a "good," a "bad." You know what she mean? Well, thas good 'cause I don't. I cannot see how I am the same as a white faggit or crack addict. Rita kiss my forehead, hold each my cheeks with her hands, look me in my eyes, "Negra," she say, her eyes big like babies', black black eyes. "You don't see now but will. You will."

I don't know how I will, I don't even know what she's talkin' about. She's talking about *Life*, Ms Rain say. Well, I don't know what life is all about either. I know I'm eighteen, magic number. And my reading score is 2.8. I ask

Ms Rain what that mean. She say it's a number! And can't no numbers measure how far I done come in jus' two years. She say forget about the numbers and just keep working. The author has a message and the reader's job is to decode that message as thoroughly as possible. A good reader is like a detective, she say, looking for clues in the text. A good reader is like you Precious, she say. Passionate! Passionately involved with whut they are reading. Don't worry about numbers and fill in the blank, just read and write!

I'm changing. Things I don't care about no more:

> if boyz love me
> extensions
> new clozes

> what I care about is:

> STAYING HEALTHY
> sex (_____)
> notebook, writing poems

Ms Rain say don't always rhyme, stretch for words to fall like drops of rain, snowflakes—did you know no two snowflakes is alike? Have you ever seen a snowflake? I haven't! All I seen is gobs of dirty gray shit. You mean to tell me that nasty stuff is made of snowy flakes. I don't believe it.

Each day is different. All the days is gobbed together to make a year, all the years gobbed together to make a life. I have a secret. Secret is, I mean I think Rita and Ms Rain halfway know but they too nice to get any further in my business than I want them in. I mean I have kids. But I never have a guy, you know like that. It never usta be on my mind. All I want before is Daddy get the fuck off me! But now I think about *that*, you know, that being fucking a cute boy. I think about that and I think about being a poet or rapper or an artist even. It's this guy on one-two-five, Franco, he done painted pictures on the steel gates that's over almos' all the store windows. At night you walk down and each one is painted different. I like that better than museum.

It's so many different ways to walk the few blocks home. Turn a corner and you see all different. Pass 116th 'n Lenox, more abandoned land, buildings falling down. How it git so ugly is people throw trash all in it. City don't pick it up; dogs doo doo. Peoples wif no bafroom piss 'n shit. Ugliness grow multiplied by ten. Keep walkin' down Lenox to one-twelve you pass projects. I never did live in projects. I live in 444 Lenox Avenue almost all my life. Where I live before that house I don't know, maybe wif my grandmother.

Wonder about Mama sometimes. Wonder about Carl more. Carl Kenwood Jones. I got session wif counselor today. Last week we try to figure out how long I been infected. People at retard place say Lil Mongo don't got it. She say that could mean Daddy get AIDS pretty fast from time he first infected to time he die? 'Cause if Lil Mongo don't got it maybe he didn't have it 1983 when she born. Then after she born he go away a long time. So maybe I get it eighty-six, eighty-seven? Counselor say, I'm on top now. I'm young, is got no disease and stuff, not no drug addict. I could live a long time, she say. I ask her what's a long time. She don't say.

I think some of the girls at Advancement House know I am . . . am *positive*. I mean wifout trying I know some of they bizness. They never was too friendly; since Mama come wif her news, they even less friendly. But who cares? I'm not tight wif these girls in the house. These bitches got problems, come in room and steal shit. I know I ain' the only one that got it, even though that's how it feels. But I'm probably the only one get it from they daddy. Counselor, Ms Weiss, say she try to find out as much about Daddy for me as she can.

How much I want to know? And for what? I tell counselor I can't talk about Daddy now. My clit swell up I think Daddy. Daddy sick me, *disgust* me, but still he sex me up. I nawshus in my stomach but hot tight in my twat and I think I want it back, the smell of the bedroom, the hurt—he slap my face till it sting and my ears sing separate songs from each other, call me names, pump my pussy in out in out in out awww I come. He bite me *hard*. A hump! He slam his hips into me HARD. I scream pain he come. He slap my thighs like cowboys do horses on TV. Shiver. Orgasm in me, his body shaking, grab me, call me Fat Mama, Big Hole! You LOVE it! Say you love it! I wanna say I DON'T. I wanna say I'm a chile. But my pussy popping like grease in frying pan. He slam in me again. His dick soft. He start sucking my tittie.

I wait for him get off me. Lay there stare at wall till wall is a movie, *Wizard of Oz*, I can make that one play anytime. Michael Jackson, scarecrow. Then my body take me over again, like shocks after earthquake, shiver me, I come again. My body not mine, I hate it coming.

Afterward I go bafroom. I smear shit on my face. Feel good. Don't know why but it do. I never tell nobody about that before. But I would do that. If I go to insect support group what will I hear from other girls. I bite my fingernails till they look like disease, pull strips of my skin away. Get Daddy's razor out cabinet. Cut cut cut arm wrist, not trying to die, trying to plug myself back in. I am a TV set wif no picture. I am broke wif no mind. No past or present time. Only the movies of being someone else. Someone not fat, dark skin, short hair, someone not fucked. A pink virgin girl. A girl like Janet

Jackson, a sexy girl don't no one get to fuck. A girl for value. A girl wif little titties whose self is luvlee just Luv-Vell-LEE!

I hate myself when I think Carl Kenwood Jones. Hate wif a capital letter. Counselor say, "Memories." How is something a memory if you never forgit? But I push it to the corner of my brain.

I exhausted, I mean wipe out! What kinda chile gotta think about a daddy like I do? But I'm not a chile. I'm a mother of a chile myself!

In school we had to memorize a poem like the rappers do. And say it in front the class. Everybody do real short poems except me and Jermaine. She do poem by lady name Pat Parker. I get up to do my poem, it's by Langston Hughes, I dedicate it to Abdul. Introduce myself to the class (even though everybody know me). I say my name is Precious Jones and this poem is for my baby son, Abdul Jamal Louis Jones. Then I let loose:

MOTHER TO SON
Well, son, I'll tell you:
Life for me ain't been no crystal stair.
It's had tacks in it,
And splinters,
And boards torn up,
And places with no carpet on the floor—
Bare.
But all the time
I'se been a-climbin' on,
And reachin' landin's,
And turnin' corners,
And sometimes goin' in the dark
Where there ain't been no light.
So boy, don't you turn back.
Don't you set down on the steps
'Cause you finds it's kinder hard.
Don't you fall now—
For I'se still goin', honey,
I'se still climbin',
And life for me ain't been no crystal stair.

And after I finish everyone goin', Yeah! Yeah! Shoutin', Go Precious! And clapping and clapping and clapping. I felt very good.

Ms Rain say write our fantasy of ourselves. How we would be if life was perfect. I tell you one thing right now, I would be light skinned, thereby treated right and loved by boyz. Light even more important than being skinny, you see them light-skinned girls that's big an' fat, they got boyfriends. Boyz overlook a lot to be wif a white girl or yellow girl, especially if it's a boy that's dark skin wif big lips or nose, he will go APE over yellow girl. So that's my first fantasy, is get light. Then I get hair. Swing job, you know like I do with my extensions, but this time it be my own hair, permanently.

Then, this part is hard to say, because so much of my heart is love for Abdul. But I be a girl or woman—yeah girl, 'cause I would still be a girl now if I hadn't had no kids. I would be a virgin like Michael Jackson, like Madonna. I would be a different Precious Jones. My bress not be big, my bra be little 'n pink like fashion girl. My body be like Whitney. I would be thighs not big etc etc. I would be tight pussy girl no stretch marks and torn pussy from babies's head bust me open. That HURT. Hours hours push push push! Then he out, beautiful. Jus' a beautiful baby. But I'm not. I'm eighteen years old. One time boy come to Advancement House to see girlfriend, he think I'm somebody's mother. That bother me.

So there if I have a fantasy it be how I look. Ms Rain say I am beautiful like I am. Where? How? To who? To not have no kids mean I woulda had a different life. Counselor ask me one time is it the kids or is it I get raped to have 'em. Bofe; 'cause even if I not raped, who want a baby at twelve! Thas how old I was when I had Little Mongo.

What is a normal life? A life where you not 'shamed of your mother. Where your friends come over after school and watch TV and do homework. Where your mother is normal looking and don't hit you over the head wif iron skillet. I would wish for in my fantasy a second chance. Since my first chance go to Mama and Daddy.

Ms Rain always saying write remember write remember. Counselor say talk about it, talk about it—the PAST. What about NOW! At least wif school I am getting' ready for my future (which to me is right now).

I don't know why I don't like counselor but Ms Rain say TALK, it gonna make things better whether I like her or not. But you know she jus' another social worker scratching on a pad. I know she writing reports on me. Reports go in file. File say what I could get, where I could go—if I could get cut off, kicked out Advancement House. Make me feel like Mama.

Donald Goines

Never Die Alone

PAUL PAWLOWSKI LEANED DOWN beside the well-dressed black man. Blood was seeping through the man's light dress shirt. As Paul's face drew near, the man gasped.

"Help me to my car, mister. Don't want to die layin' in no gutter." King David gripped Paul's arm firmly. "I'll pay you, mister. Don't mind payin', just don't want to die alone in the street."

Paul pulled back the shirt and examined the wounds. Instantly he knew the man at his feet had spoken the truth. He was going to die. The wound in his chest alone had been enough to kill him. Paul glanced down at the hand on his arm. It was bloody. When Paul pried the fingers loose, there was a ring of blood around his sleeve.

"My car's at the curb. Help me, friend." King could feel his strength leaving. "Please, mister?" he begged. He had seen too many black men bleed their life's blood out on the dirty floor of a poolroom, or inside some dimly lit nightclub.

Paul glanced over at the expensive car near the curb. What the hell, he told himself. If the guy wanted to die in his own car, at least he could help the poor bastard die where he chose. Slowly and with care, Paul lifted the man.

The man in his arms made a deep moan as Paul steadied himself with the load. He made his way slowly toward the car. He was careful as he placed the man down inside the automobile. Paul ran around the car and jumped in behind the steering wheel. He doubted whether his patient would hold up that long, but since they were in the car, they might as well rush over to the nearest hospital.

Paul didn't have to search for the keys; they were already in the car. He started the motor. The sound of the wounded man's voice came to him clearly.

"Ain't no use, man. I done cashed in the big ticket." King David's voice got weaker as he continued. "Life's a bitch, man. It just ain't no win. Here I thought I had Jesus in a jug, no lookin' back. Done stung for all the bread a nigger needs to get over with, now this shit come up out of nowhere. Can you dig it?" He tried to laugh, but blood rushing out of his mouth choked him.

"Just take it easy, fellow," Paul said as he expertly drove the big car in and out of the light evening traffic. "It won't be long before I have you at the hospital, then everything will be all right."

This time King David did manage to laugh. "Big fuckin' deal, man," he answered dryly. "It wouldn't make any difference if we were at two hospitals right now. Ain't nothing a doctor can do for me now, man. I done bought the big ticket; it ain't but one more step left for me." The wounded man fell silent; his last words seemed to linger in the air.

Paul tried to change the mood. "I don't know about that, buddy; you can never tell. I glanced at your wounds and I've seen guys live with worse ones." Paul knew that the wounded man knew that he was lying.

"Okay, brother," King David stated, "have it your way. I just don't want to die alone, that's all. Just picturing myself stretched out in that fuckin' street dying alone is damn near too much to bear."

"Don't think about it!" Paul cautioned sharply. "Think about gettin' patched up. Why don't you try to save some of your strength? Don't talk so much; you ain't doing nothing but wearing yourself out."

As the car went over a slight bump in the street, King David let out a grunt. His face twisted up hideously from the pain. "Talkin' helps to take my fuckin' mind off the pain, man. It's all I got left. Life is a motherfuckin' bitch," he stated again, this time more bitterly than before. "It's not fair. I mean, a guy busts his ass trying to reach up and pull himself out of the fuckin' gutters, then when he can finally see some kind of light, some shit like this happens. Oh no, baby, it just ain't right. It couldn't happen to nobody else but me." Tears rolled down the man's cheeks as he talked. "All I been through, everything I've done, I mean, ain't no way it should end like this."

"This ain't got to be the end," Paul stated feebly. He realized that he was just using words, saying anything to fill the void.

King David continued as if Paul hadn't spoken. "I've always tried to be honest with myself, but now, when I'm face to face with the final act, I can't accept it. Not this." He broke down and began to sob. Deep sobs, the kind that no one should ever witness of another.

Paul glanced at the man out of the corner of his eyes. Damn! he cursed. It looked like King David had taken a bath in blood. His suit coat was completely covered from where it had seeped through his shredded shirt. Even the upholstery in the car was covered with the dark reddish stain of blood. Where King David's arm rested on the front seat, a small pool of blood had formed.

Christ almighty, Paul swore, how much blood can this guy lose without passing out? If he doesn't die from the stab wounds, the poor bastard should bleed to death before we get to the hospital. As he took another quick look at the wounded man, Paul thought that the injured man had finally passed away.

King David's head had dropped onto his chest and it appeared as if he had stopped breathing. But it was not death that closed the man's mouth. The pain had finally reached unbearable stages. King David closed his eyes and gritted his teeth. He tried to slump back against the door padding. Maybe if he lay in another position it would ease some of the hurt. He tried to breathe lightly but every time he took any kind of deep breath, he could feel the pain all over his chest.

"This dying crap is one hell of a job," King David managed to say. Somehow talking seemed to relieve the pain.

Paul stared over at the man in astonishment. He was surprised that the man was still alive and noticed that the man's voice was growing much weaker. It wouldn't be long now, he reflected.

"Just hold on a little longer," Paul stated as he pressed down harder on the gas pedal. "The hospital's just a couple of blocks away." When they had first got in the car, he wouldn't have taken odds that the man would live to reach the hospital. He had just been going through the motions.

"You know, if it hadn't been for you, mister, I'd still be laying back there in the street."

"It wasn't nothin' anybody else wouldn't do. I just happened to be the one that came along at the time, that's all," Paul stated.

King David didn't waste his strength answering, but both men knew that the statement was a lie. He would have lain in the gutter until the police arrived, then they would have left him there while they called for an ambulance. No way in the world would they have put him in the police car bleeding the way he was bleeding. He would have lain there and died in the gutter, the thing he had always feared. Paul had been the one person in a hundred, a man who didn't mind getting involved. King David knew that a black man wouldn't have taken the chance. The average black man would have crossed the street and hurried on his way before he'd allow himself to get involved in a murder.

For one of the few times in his life King David felt gratitude. It was a strange feeling for him. He was a man used to playing on people who were unlucky enough to cross his path. He took kindness for weakness, friendship as an opportunity to take advantage of the person foolish enough to offer it. The pain in his body was everywhere. Never before had he hurt like he was hurting now. The sight of the hospital gave him a sense of relief. He tried to blank out the pain as they entered the lane that led to the emergency entrance.

The emergency ward was at the rear of the hospital. Paul drove the car down to the back doors and parked next to an ambulance. As he got out and ran around the car, he waved to an attendant standing on the back dock taking a smoke.

"Hey, buddy, how about giving me a hand here. I've got a man who's hurt real bad." Paul opened the door on the passenger side.

The short Negro on the dock came down the ramp pushing a wheelchair. The man let out a whistle when he saw all the blood on King David. "Looks like somebody been butcherin' steers inside that car," he said as he maneuvered the wheelchair in place.

Paul didn't bother to answer the man as he reached in and grabbed King David under the armpits. Both men tried to lift him as gently as possible, but a cry of pain escaped from the wounded man as they lifted him from the car. When they set him down in the wheelchair, his head dropped down over his chest. As Paul straightened up from placing King David's feet together on the wheelchair foot-rest, he looked at the head resting lifelessly on his chest. At once Paul believed the man had finally died.

"Looks like he didn't make it to the hospital after all," Paul said quietly.

"He ain't dead!" The orderly stated flatly as he began to push the chair toward the ramp. "You better park your car back out of the way, then come on in. I'll take him on ahead and get some doctors to start work on him as soon as possible." Without another word, the man rushed on up the ramp, pushing the wheelchair as fast as he could.

Paul glanced around quickly, trying to spot somewhere to park the car. He got in and drove slowly back around to the visitors' parking lot. For a minute he was undecided on what to do. It would be easier just to leave the car and go on about his business. That way, he wouldn't become any more involved than he was already. After all, he had done all that he could do. It didn't make sense to get any more involved. But someone should know where the man's car was, he reasoned. After parking, he walked slowly toward the entrance of the hospital.

As soon as he entered, the short black orderly rushed up to him. "What's your name, mate?" the man asked quickly.

Paul hesitated, then gave it to him. He watched the man hurry off toward the rear of the hospital. As he stood in the hallway, an officer walked up to him. "You're the guy who brought the Negro in who was all cut up, aren't you?" the white policeman inquired in a harsh voice.

For a minute Paul didn't want to answer, but finally he shook his head in agreement. "Yeah, I saw him in front of the building where I live and rushed him down here."

The policeman removed a pencil from his pocket. "Well, I'm going to have to make a report on it, so you might as well relax. You and I are going to be here together for a few minutes."

Paul let out a sigh. "I knew it was coming," he said quietly. "Before this shit stops, I'm going to wish that I had never gotten involved."

The tall, red-faced officer grinned, revealing yellow teeth. "Yeah, well, it's too late to cry over spilled milk now. If you didn't want to get involved, you should have left the nigger laying in the street."

Paul glanced up at the man. "Would you have left him lying in the street?" he asked and knew the answer at once.

"Well, I'll tell you this much," the officer began, "I wouldn't have gotten his blood all over my clothes." For the first time, Paul glanced down and saw the front of his only suit covered with dark spots of blood.

The sight of the blood on his clothes didn't anger him half as much as the officer's attitude. He tried to conceal his anger, but it was difficult to keep it out of his voice. "Okay, so I got a little blood on my clothes. You think that's more important than trying to save a guy's life?"

The white officer laughed. "If the shoe had been on the other foot, you think that guy back there would have gone through the trouble of gettin' his clothes bloody while rushing you to the hospital? You can bet your ass he wouldn't have bothered. If anything, he'd have been busy trying to beat you out of your wallet."

Before Paul could give his angry reply, the orderly rushed up. In his hands he was holding an envelope. "Hey mate, you done hit a gold mine."

Paul glanced around at him, not understanding what the man was saying. "How's the guy I brought in?"

The orderly shook his head. "He passed away, buddy. There was nothing the doctors could do for him. He had been cut too many times. I'm surprised he lived as long as he did."

The white officer and Paul stared at each other. The thought of the man dying left an empty feeling inside Paul. He hadn't known the man, but he had hoped, even though his common sense told him the man couldn't live, that by some luck he might pull through. It hadn't happened, and now it was all for nothing. But not really, Paul remembered. The man hadn't wanted to die in the gutter, so Paul had saved him from that fate.

The orderly held out the envelope. "Here, mate, the guy made you his beneficiary; that's why I needed your name. He had the doctors as witnesses and left you everything, even the problem of buryin' him."

At once, before the orderly could say any more, the policeman burst out laughing. Paul looked at him angrily. But the orderly was serious. His eyes were cold and angry. "It ain't no welfare case, mate; he left you enough money to bury him with." The orderly glared around at the officer. "Yeah, mate, from what I witnessed, I'd say you came out of the deal damn well. The poor guy knew he couldn't live, so he spent the last few minutes of his time tryin' to repay you for the trouble you went through. In this envelope is some cash money, plus the pink to his car. He signed it over to you. Seems as if it's paid for. He had the doctors witness everything he did. He also said to tell you that he had some notes he'd written down about himself, and that he hoped you wouldn't destroy them without reading some of it." The orderly handed Paul the envelope. "You'll find enough money inside to bury him properly if you should decide to follow his wishes."

"Hey, wait a minute there," the policeman said, "I don't know if this is right or not. You had better give that envelope to me. After I check it out with my office, then I'll let you know if it's all right or not."

Before the officer could reach out and take it, the orderly yanked it back. "Maybe you didn't hear what I said, officer. I said the man had the doctors sign as witnesses, so you don't have a damn thing to do with what's in this envelope. The man left it to this guy. It was his last request. He did it so that he wouldn't have to be buried by the city, and here you are trying to spoil it all. No way, I mean it. If I were to give this to you, it would be tied up downtown until after this man is buried, and his last wish would be spoiled. Now you haven't any right whatsoever to his belongings. They go to his nearest kin, or wife, or whatever, and since the man had three doctors sign a note to the effect that he was in his right mind, you are way out of line trying to take his last request from him."

The orderly turned to Paul. "Nobody can force you to spend the money he left you to bury him, but I do hope you will see to it that he doesn't have to be buried by the city. He asked me to tell you this."

Paul shook his head dumbfoundedly. Things were happening too damn fast for him to really know what was up or down. "If he left enough money to buy a casket, I'll get it for him, and if it's not enough, I'll sell the car and raise the money. I give you my word on it," Paul said and took the envelope from the orderly. As he walked toward the front entrance of the hospital the orderly relaxed. For some reason he believed the tall young white man would keep his word.

Melvin Van Peebles

Sweet Sweetback's Baadasssss Song

In 1971, Melvin Van Peebles's independently produced film Sweet Sweetback's Baadasssss Song *became the top-grossing independent film of that year, helped usher in the blaxploitation genre, and served as the flag-bearer for independent filmmakers.*

To get the Man's foot out of my ass means to me logically to get the Man's foot out of all our black asses. This seems to me an apparent truth, but many of the buszwazee brothers don't seem to realize it. They don't seem to understand that they are not free as long as their other brothers are still in slavery. (If they would get out of some of those limousines once in a while and even try and catch a cab or two, the truth would come home to them very rapidly.)

Anyway next step, how specifically to get the Man's foot out of our ass. The first beachhead, the very first thing that we must do is to reconquer our own minds. The biggest obstacle to the Black revolution in America is our conditioned susceptibility to the white man's program. In short, the fact is that the white man has colonized our minds. We've been violated, confused and drained by this colonization and from this brutal, calculated genocide, the most effective and vicious racism has grown, and it is with this starting point in mind and the intention to reverse the process that I went into cinema in the first fucking place.

"Where is Brer?" I asked me, he was digging TV, movies and the sounds. But TV was out; television at this stage of the game, as it is practiced in America at least, is not a feasible tool for carrying really relevant ideas to the minds of the disenfranchised. The umbilical cord from the TV program to its sponsor is short and very vital and can be cut abruptly, too abruptly for a program to get away with pushing any extra-uppity ideas. Each thing must be self-contained breadwise. Artistically, we must be guerilla units too. Each project must be a self-contained unit, otherwise it will be subject to the inevitable slings and arrows of outrageous racist economic pressures.

Anyway story-wise, I came up with an idea, why not the direct approach.

Bad Ass

Since what I want is the Man's foot out of our collective asses, why not make the film about a brother *getting* the Man's foot out of his ass. That was going to be the thing.

Now to avoid putting myself into a corner and writing something that I wouldn't be able to shoot, I made a list of the givens in the situation and tried to take those givens and juggle them into the final scenario.

Given:
1. NO COP OUT.

    A. I wanted a victorious film. A film where niggers could walk out standing tall instead of avoiding each other's eyes, looking once again like they'd had it.
2. MUST LOOK AS GOOD AS ANYTHING CHUCK EVER DID.

    Very delicate point. One of the problems faced by a black filmmaker (in fact any American independent filmmaker who wants to produce his own feature, just more so for a brother) is that Hollywood polishes its product with such a great deal of slickness and expensive perfection that it ups the ante. That is, if I made a film in black and white with poor sound, even if it had all the revolutionary and even story elements that anyone could hope it would have, brother would come out saying, well, shit, niggers can't do anything right. I saw such and such a film in color and 35 mm and so on and so on, how come we have to make such rinky-dink stuff. Not realizing of course that the price of freedom is often poverty of means. Well I felt that this problem was a little too involved to attack, so I was determined that the film was going to look as good as anything one of the major studios could turn out.)
3. ENTERTAINMENT-WISE, A MOTHER FUCKER. (I had no illusion about the attention level of people brain-washed to triviality.)

    A. The film simply couldn't be a didactic discourse which would end up playing (if I could find a distributor) to an empty theater except for ten or twenty aware brothers who would pat me on the back and say it tells it like it is.

    B. If Brer is bored, he's bored. One of the problems we must face squarely is that to attract the mass we have to produce work that not only instructs but entertains.

    C. It must be able to sustain itself as a viable commercial product or there is no power base. The Man has an Achilles pocket and he might go along with you if at least there is some bread in it for him. But he ain't about to go carrying no messages for you, especially a relevant one, for free.

4. A LIVING WORKSHOP.

A. I wanted 50% of my shooting crew to be third world people. (This could conflict with point 2 if a script was not developed extremely carefully.) So at best a staggering amount of my crew would be relatively inexperienced. Specifically, this meant that any type of film requiring an enormous technical sophistication at the shooting stage should not be attempted.

5. BREAD.

A. SHORT! SHORT! SHORT!

B. Normal financing channels probably closed.

6. MONKEY WRENCHING.

A. I would have to expect a great deal of animosity from the film media (white in the first place and right wing in the second) at all levels of filmmaking. (I would have to double check my flanks at all times and not expose myself to the possibility of racism, in everything from keeping tight security about the 'real' script to choosing locations to dealing with the labs and perhaps a portion of the cast and crew too. As costly as it would be, I felt I would have to leave myself a security margin.)

7. UNKNOWNS AND VARIABLES.

A. CALIBER OF ACTORS.

B. CALIBER OF CREW.

I would have to write a flexible script where emphasis could be shifted. In short, stay loose.

I suppose I could have made an infinite list of liabilities and assets, especially liabilities . . . but anyway.

(ASSET 1.) I kept asking myself what could I do that Hollywood major studios couldn't. The thing that kept occurring to me was that I could delve into the black community as they would never be able to do because of their cumbersome technology and their lack of empathy.

(POSSIBILITY 1.) Something begins to jell. Strange how you store things. Somewhere I read an interview with this big director where the interviewer asked how he managed to get away with such audacious shots. He replied something to the effect that as long as you kept the story moving, you can put the camera anywhere you want and cut anywhere you desire. WHAMMO. I decided I would pack the scenario with enough action for three goddamn films so I would be able to get away with anything. I would even use triple or quadruple screen effects like they do to prop up television detective stories if I had to.

(OPPORTUNITY 1.) Most filmmakers look at a feature in terms of image and story or vice versa. Effects and music (most directors can't carry a tune in a fucking bucket) are strictly secondary considerations. Very few look at film with sound considered as a creative third dimension. So I calculate the scenario in such a way that sound can be used as an integral part of the film.

I would have to choose a story line strong enough to provide continuity, but simple enough to give enough room for digression without losing its directness. I approached the film like you do the cupboard when you're broke and hungry: throw in everything eatable and hope to come out on top with the seasoning, i.e., by editing.

A couple of the unknowns still bothered me. To keep this strong story line going, I felt I would have to use one actor as the principal vehicle that I could hinge other things onto. Next, I had decided to use cameos but because of the looseness of their construction, I couldn't foresee the exact running time of the film, so I devised an accordion section for the film that could be lengthened or shortened according to the time consumed by the various other parts of the script.

All this shit swarmed around and around in my head. About this time I had a burden lifted, it dawned on me that I was in charge, and whereas I usually try to impart in my work the idea of getting the Man's foot out of our ass without letting it show to the Man too soon, I did not have to do that this time. So I thought, well, why don't I then, since this could be it, why don't I make a film directly about, accent the positive, what I'm all about, what we are all about. That is, it would be the story itself of a man getting the Man's foot out of his ass that on close examination would fit the necessity of the script for a strong, action-packed story line if it were told in that way. That's where it's at.

CLARENCE COOPER JR.

The Scene

AT THE SIXTH PRECINCT, Rudy Black was called out of his cell for interrogation at one-thirty. He was gaunt and unshaven, and his hair stood out wildly stiff from its marcelled contours. He was beginning to get extremely sick; his joints were stiffening and his eyes were beginning to water. He was ushered into a small bare room off the entrance to the single tier of cells. The room had one small window with bars, two chairs, a table, and a scorched wooden ashtray.

He sat down, pressing both his knees together to ease the ache in them. He held his head in his hands and watched the tears drip from his eyes and soil the creases of his green, wrinkle-proof gabardine slacks. Somewhere, muffled but vaguely audible, two men were laughing. The sound of a cell door closing came to him, followed by the loud shrill screaming of a man. Another man could be heard shouting, then the screaming stopped suddenly.

The voices of the two men came again, laughing.

Someone was whimpering.

Rudy lit a cigarette and felt the hot smoke rake his throat. He tried to sit up straight; the bones snapped. He bent over with his head between his hands and watched the teardrops again. He yawned, then shivered convulsively. A tickle shot through his groin and testicles with a gnawing that brought sweat to his forehead.

I ain't this far out! I know I ain't!

He heard the doorknob turn but didn't look around. He felt too miserable to look up.

"Black?" a voice said.

He didn't answer.

"Black," the voice said, a little more firmly. "I'm Detective Patterson. I want to talk to you."

"I ain't got nothin to talk about," Rudy said, but he looked up and saw the young face, remembering the name, remembering, from the latest communiques on the Scene, the news that Davis had taken on a new partner.

Patterson sat down in the chair across from him, putting a blank envelope on the table. "Are you sick?" he asked, and Rudy was tempted to laugh at his manner, his voice, the slim, dignified cut of suit, the thick-soled shoes—a square.

"I'm feelin great," he said, "just great!"

"Let's not have any jokes. I don't think you're in the position right now."

"I'm not jokin."

"Would you like a fix?"

Rudy looked at him and smiled sickly. "For what? For the moon? Talk about jokes! Listen, my man, you cut me loose and I'll get my own fix."

Patterson strained against the barrier, repelled by the sloppy speech, the baked head of hair. He opened the envelope and took out two white capsules. From his pocket he took a book of matches and tore off half the back, following Davis' instructions. He offered them to Rudy. "Go ahead, it's your stuff."

Rudy hesitated. 'Whadda you mean, *my stuff?* I never had no stuff. You tryin to make a joke?'

"I'm in no position to joke either," Patterson said, pushing the things into Rudy's hand. "Go ahead and snort it, get your sickness off. We'll both feel better if you do."

Rudy bent the match cover and emptied both capsules into it, then he placed it against one nostril and drew up loudly, choking as the drug bit into the tender tissues of his nose, tasting it warm and bitter in his throat. He took a draw on his cigarette and sat back, letting the taste of the drug fill his mouth and nose, relaxing. "Thanks, my man," he said. "That was real George."

Patterson nodded. "Don't worry; I know that fix doesn't buy you."

"It sure don't."

Patterson was stymied for a moment at the tone of the reply. 'You were arrested with ninety-seven capsules this morning, Black—over a hundred dollars retail. That's as much as I make in a week.'

"Wait a minute," Rudy said. "You didn't bust me with no drugs! Them drugs was outside my door, somebody else could've dropped 'em. For another thing, I don't give a damn how much you make in a week. I'm concerned about nobody but little Rudy, little Rudy Black."

Patterson frowned. "Just because the drugs weren't in your possession doesn't mean we can't go to court and prove they're yours—"

"Yeah, that's it," Rudy said. "You could take me to court and paint me on the wall, that's what you'd do. You cops like to send innocent guys to jail."

"We know for a fact that you've been pushing on the Scene," Patterson backed up his claim. "We know for a fact that you've been pushing for The Man."

'Well, you know a hell of a lot more than I know,' Rudy said, his belly warmed over by the drugs. "You cops like to *lie* on guys, you'd go to court and lie me into the joint, that's what you'd do!"

"Look here, Black, you're going to co-operate with us—or else."

Rudy's bloodshot eyes flickered. "Co-operate and send myself to the joint? Is that how you want me to co-operate?"

"You *will*, sooner or later."

"Oh," Rudy said, suddenly assuming the role of martyr. "So you're gonna beat me, huh? You're gonna wax me? You're gonna wax me and make me say I did somethin I didn't do?" He squared himself in his chair, the heroin adding a timbre to his voice. "Well, go ahead, copper, go ahead and beat me up!"

"I hoped this would be different," Patterson said between his teeth. "I thought a talking without beating would make you come to your senses. A beating is what you expected, and I'm almost tempted to do it."

"Why don't you?"

"Would you beat a drunk?" Then he felt silly after saying it, knowing full well that beating a drunk would mean less than nothing to Rudy Black.

Leaning forward, Rudy said, "Let me talk."

"Go ahead."

"You want me to co-operate, huh? Tell ya what, copper, I'm gonna co-operate, I'm gonna flip."

Patterson eyed him speculatively.

"You say them drugs you guys picked up is mine, huh?" Rudy said. "Okay, they're my drugs. You say I was pushin, huh? Okay, yeah, I was pushin 'em— right up my arm!"

"You listen, Black! You want a break, don't you?"

"What kinda break? I don't need no break!"

"You just admitted the narcotics were yours—"

"You just try to make me say that again in front of somebody besides you!"

Exasperated, Patterson got up and took a pair of cuffs off the clip at his side. "Hold out your hands."

Rudy looked at the cuffs suspiciously, his bravado deserting him for a moment. "What's this?"

"Shut up and put your hands in these."

Rudy obeyed. "So I get waxed now, huh?"

Patterson could visualize Davis' face when he brought Rudy out. He'd be smirking. He had practically begged Davis to give him a chance with Rudy, trying to make up for his fluff on the Bertha Travis thing, trying to show that he could come through with a little sensible police work—but even after a few minutes he knew that trying to get Rudy Black to incriminate himself was like trying to get an elephant to sit on a three-legged stool!

Picturing the wide, satisfied smile on Davis' face, Patterson tried again, this time feeling the fork in his tongue.

"I really don't want to see you go through all this for nothing, Black," he said. "I want to help you all I can, whether you believe that or not. The Man is the biggest dope man in town. As one of his pushers, you're in a position to kick the supports down and come out on top. Am I getting to you?"

"Listen—" Rudy said, eying Patterson slyly.

"I'm listening, Black."

"I've done time before," Rudy said.

"I know your record."

"So, dig," said Rudy, easing himself back in the chair, letting his hands fall to his lap, closing his eyes until they were small slits. "I'm bugged. Do you get bugged sometimes? Stuff gets you like that sometimes—it scares you."

Strangely, there seemed to be a note of truth in his words; Patterson was struck by the sudden change.

"Can I talk?" Rudy said, then continued after Patterson nodded. "You know my record? Dig . . . A long time ago I got hit by a car and wet my pants I was so scared. So I told myself I wasn't gonna ever get hit by no more cars, and I didn't. Then me and some more guys was raifieldin a radio shop and got caught, and I got sapped up and went to the Hill for eighteen months. I was so scared I never raifielded no more. I kept stealin but I never raifielded. But then I got hooked, after I got my woman, and I got scared again . . ."

It was coming out like an explosion of a dam, yet Rudy couldn't help himself. More than anything, it was important that he say this, even if the Roller didn't understand. It was more for Rudy, this review of his life; in the warm surge of heroin he felt almost clean looking back on what he used to be, exposing the dirt of himself. And then he saw the look of sympathy on Patterson's face and knew that it was serving a double purpose.

"But you couldn't stop this time," Patterson nudged.

"Do you know how it was?" Rudy said. "It's like nothin—" He stopped; something inside him made him stop.

"Go on, Black, it's no secret. You got hooked and you couldn't unhook yourself even though you were afraid, isn't that it?"

"Let *me* tell it!" Rudy shouted. "What do *you* know?"

"Only what you tell me."

"I'm hip! You can't even *think* how it was the first time I kicked in the County Jail; it's nothin you, a Roller, would know anything about. All you do is bust a junkie and lock him up for thirty days or thirty years! What the hell do you care?"

"But I do care!" Patterson said inadequately. "I'm listening to you. If I didn't care I wouldn't listen to you."

"That's right . . . if you weren't interested, you'd be slappin my cap off, right?"

Patterson could merely nod, brought face to face with a strangely capricious monster.

"What's the use," Rudy said, retreating into himself.

"You tell me, Black, I'm listening. I swear to you I'm listening!"

Rudy was quick to receive the feeling that was communicated. Without actually thinking, he responded in an effort to gain Patterson's confidence.

"So this is the way it was, Mr. Patterson," he began. "I've never told this, the way I feel, to nobody, and the only reason I'm telling you is because people like me get bugged and they have to tell somebody—even if it's a Roller."

"Go ahead," Patterson said, ready to grasp any guide to Rudy's twisted psychology.

"Dig," Rudy went on. "So when I got hooked, I was scared too. There wasn't no way for me to stop. When I went and kicked the first time, I was so sick I couldn't see. So listen, man, what do you think I did? When I got out I said, 'Nothin—not me again,' but it wasn't so easy. I come right out and copped again. I was all the time around stuff. There was plenty smack around the neighborhood. I started usin again, one thing at a time. I had Nina and she was makin nice money, and with all that bread comin in I started buyin more stuff. Pretty soon I was usin two things, then three, then four, then I was usin five twice a day." He stretched his hands apart in the handcuffs. "Nina was hooked, too. Now this is what I figured. Here's a jinx I can't get away from, so what will I do? I'm gonna keep so much stuff, I'll never be scared no more. I'll keep the sickness off all the time. But there's just one thing against this. The Rollers. But I'm more scared of bein sick than I am of the Rollers."

Patterson waited, then stared at him when Rudy didn't go on. "You've told me?"

Rudy grinned expectantly. "That's it. All of it. Now I did have those ninety-some caps, but you can't make me say that on paper. Me and my woman use ninety-some caps a week, sometimes more."

"Black—"

"That's the truth, Mr. Patterson."

"Black, you're lying," Patterson said.

Rudy said nothing. He sat back in the chair and closed his eyes completely.

"I thought it'd be easier, talking to you like this." Patterson was becoming angry now at the thought Rudy had made a fool of him. "You don't even know when you're lying; that's typical of you addicts."

"Don't shoot me none of them words," Rudy snapped. "Either cut me loose or beat my ass."

"We know you're dealing with The Man. You're going to make a buy for us, Black."

Rudy looked at him hard. "*No!* Double n-o, Roller!"

A fine spray of heat seemed to splatter Patterson's face, "We don't even have to beat you. All we have to do is lock you up for a couple of hours and you'll be begging to make a buy. Why do all you junkies react this way?"

Rudy leaned forward in his chair, twisting the loose bands of steel into his wrists. "*Because!*" he shouted. "Because you guys bug us to death!"

"Who?"

"YOU! People like you! Why don't you set up a country for junkies and leave us alone? Have you ever heard that sayin, 'Once a junkie always a junkie'? Well, it's true! You Rollers keep bustin us and bustin us and bustin us! Don't you know it ain't doin us no good? Don't you know the sonofabitch who said that sayin was *right*? Say, man, *dig*: a junkie don't want your help! A junkie don't want no help at all!"

"What *do* you want?" Patterson asked angrily.

"Smack," bubbled Rudy. "Nothin but boy and more boy, with a little girl on the side to make it worth livin. Listen, daddy, *you*, you don't know what you're missin! If you did, you'd give up that tin badge and lay up in a crib somewhere and use your gun to blow anybody in two who tried to mess with you while you was usin!"

"That doesn't answer my question, Black!" Patterson shouted. "We've got you now and you *do* need help! What do you want? You must want something! What is it?"

"Nothin," Rudy said calmly.

"*Nothing?*"

"I'm sayin this, Mr. Patterson, Mr. Roller, sir," Rudy sneered. "I say you can lock me up for two months or two years, and I still won't flip! I'm a thoroughbred! I came up in the street with nothin! I had a father and mother and I still had nothin! I dragged my butt in the mud until I was big enough to drag it out and start kickin people the way they been kickin me! I started livin and usin drugs and buyin clothes, strides and stomps that'd set you back a whole month's pay! And I *like* livin like this, man, 'cause it's pure, like grade-A boy! I got my wings and bought a Cadillac, and it's paid for—almost paid for—already, the kind of car you couldn't buy if you didn't eat all year!"

Patterson lost control of himself. "This is living? Being a thoroughbred with a habit and a whore—this is what you consider really living?"

"You sure know what to say, copper," Rudy laughed. "You took the words right out of my mouth! And you know why, Mr. Police? 'Cause they're the kind of things you want and ain't got the nerve to get!"

Patterson stopped himself before he struck Rudy. He sat back and waited, easing the tension in his body. He said after a while, "You know, I've got a lot to learn, Black."

Rudy smiled. "Sure you have, sure you have. You gotta crawl before you walk, they say."

Patterson excused himself piteously. "I sat here thinking, this is a boy who can be helped; I can do something for him, not just bust him and send him away."

Rudy was not fooled. "I know that's what you were thinkin, Mr. Patterson —yes, sir."

Patterson felt maddened by this one-sided conflict. "I know this, too, Black. I know you're going to come back here, and when you do it's going to be for keeps!"

Rudy stood up. "Let's go see Mr. Davis. He's waitin, ain't he?"

"Yes. He knew."

"And now you know," Rudy said again.

Patterson got up and took him by the arm. "Let's go."

In the hallway they met Davis.

"Let him go," he told Patterson sharply.

"Why?"

"Becker just called. Said he received a writ for Black's and the girl's release."

Rudy was smiling. When his hands were freed he smoothed back the daggers of hair at his scalp. He felt good now. He felt like there was a God. He felt the heroin Patterson had given him running through his body, every vein, making his whole system gurgitate with the desire for more.

He said, laughing deep in his chest so the officers could not hear, "Can I go? Am I free?"

"Go ahead," Patterson said ruefully. "You'll be back."

"If I didn't come back," Rudy said, starting off, "you guys'd be outta business and lookin for new haims."

Davis ran down the hall after Rudy and kicked him high on the leg. Rudy bent over in pain, smiling at Patterson, his mouth twisted, his body angled over like a broken piece of kindling wood.

"You see?" he said. "It's the same old crap all the time . . ."

PAUL BEATTY

The White Boy Shuffle

WITH THE CROWD ROUSED to a frenzy, Dexter held up my book. "I'd like you to take your copy of Gunnar Kaufman's phenomenal volume of verse, *Watermelanin*, and turn to page 133. Now read aloud with me from 'Dead Niggers Don't Hokum.' "

Every demonstrator from Boston local to university homesteader seemed to have a copy of the book. They read silently to themselves as Dexter read aloud.

> . . . I am the lifelessness of the party, the spade who won't put on
> the lampshade . . .

I couldn't hear the recitation very well because Nicholas was hugging me so tight my vertebrae popped like a string of firecrackers. When he released me, his wet cheek stuck to my face. "I'm proud of you, nigger." I heard my name crackle from the loudspeakers and made my way to the podium. "Now it is with great pride I introduce star athlete, accomplished poet, black man extraordinaire, voice of a nation, Gunnar Kaufman. Remember, America, Boston University, the world is watching."

A camera mounted on a crane swung down and bobbed in my face like a giant metal hummingbird. I looked directly into the lens. "Don't do that," the cameraperson whispered. I continued to look directly into the lens. When I was seven years old, my favorite television personality was Transient Tammy. Sporting patchwork overalls and a floppy hat, Transient Tammy welcomed me home after school with a hearty "Howdy, vagrants." Before introducing the last cartoon, she'd put on a pair of enormous sunglasses. These magic glasses gave Transient Tammy the power to see her bummy friends in television-land. She'd steal toward the camera, dirty knees bursting through her jeans. "I see Suzette in Arcadia, Ingrid in Alhambra, Anthony in Inglewood." I peered into the camera, looking for my mom and Psycho Loco in Hillside, my father, but I didn't see anyone, just my wall-eyed reflection in the lens.

The applause died down, leaving a hum in the air, and I nervously cleared my throat. I wanted to address the crowd like a seasoned revolutionary, open with a smooth activist adage, "There's an old Chinese saying . . . ," but I didn't know any Chinese sayings, old or new. My hesitancy grew embarrassing.

Yoshiko waddled over and ran my hand over the circumference of her bloated belly. I rubbed and smiled but still said nothing. I thought, *If I were down there down among the mob, what would I want to hear?*

Scoby broke the silence, shouting, "Thus do I ever make my fool my purse." I laughed. The gathering laughed because I laughed. I decided I'd want to hear candor.

In the middle of the throng stood a commemorative sculpture. A slightly abstract cast-iron flock of birds in memory of Martin Luther King, Jr., who received his doctorate in theology from Boston University. "Do you see that sculpture?" I asked, pointing to this commissioned piece of artwork, which did not dedicate a small piece of the earth and time to Reverend King so much as it took partial credit for his success. "Notice them steel birds are migrating south—that's BU's way of telling you they don't want you here." The black people began to elbow their way to the front. I was speaking to the Negroes, but the white folks were listening in, their ears pressed to my breast, listening to my heart. "Who knows what it says on the plaque at the base of the sculpture?" No one spoke. "You motherfuckers pass by that ugly-ass sculpture every day. You hang your coats on it, open beer bottles on it, meet your hot Friday night dates there, now here you are talking about freedom this and whitey putting-shit-in-the-game that and you don't even know what the plaque says? Shit could say '*Sieg Heil! Kill All Niggers! Auslander Raus!*' for all you know, stupid motherfuckers. African-Americans, my ass. Middle minorities caught between racial polarities, please. Caring, class-conscious progressive crackers, shit. Selfish apathetic humans like everybody else."

The crowd gave a resounding roar of approval. Here I was denigrating them and the people urged me forward. Candor, I reminded myself, candor.

"Now I'm not going to front, act like the first thing I did when I got to Boston University was proceed directly to the Martin Luther King Memorial and see what the goddamn plaque says. Only reason I know what it says is that I was coming out of Taco Bell on my way to basketball practice when I dropped my burrito deluxe at the base of the monument. When I bent down to wipe the three zesty cheeses, refried beans, and secret hot sauce off my sneakers, I saw what the plaque said. It says, 'If a man hasn't discovered something he will die for, he isn't fit to live. Martin Luther King, Jr.' How many of you motherfuckers are ready to die for black rule in South Africa—and I mean black rule, not black superintendence?"

Yells and whistles shot through the air.

"You lying motherfuckers. I talked to Harriet Velakazi, the ANC lieutenant you heard speak earlier, and *she's* willing to die for South Africa. She don't give a fuck about King's sexist language, she ready to kill her daddy and if need be kill her mama for South Africa. Now don't get me wrong, I want them niggers to get theirs, but I am not willing to die for South Africa, and you ain't either."

The audience hushed, their Good Samaritan opportunism checkmated. There was nothing they could say. "I'm willing to die for South Africa, where do I sign"?

I rubbed my tired eyes, licked my lips, and leaned into the microphone. "So I asked myself, what am I willing to die for? The day when white people treat me with respect and see my life as equally valuable to theirs? No, I ain't willing to die for that, because if they don't know that by now, then they ain't never going to know it. Matter of fact, I ain't ready to die for anything, so I guess I'm just not fit to live. In other words, I'm just ready to die. I'm just ready to die."

I realized I'd made a public suicide pact with myself and stole a glance toward Scoby and Yoshiko. Scoby was nodding his head in agreement, while Yoshiko was pointing to her stomach and yelling, "What the fuck are you talking about?"

I swallowed and continued, "That's why today's black leadership isn't worth shit, these telegenic niggers not willing to die. Back in the old days, if someone spoke up against the white man, he or she was willing to die. Today's housebroken niggers travel the country talking themselves hoarse about barbarous white devils, knowing that those devils aren't going to send them to a black hell. And if Uncle Sam even lights a fire under their asses, they backtrack in front of the media—'What I meant to say was . . . The quote was taken out of context . . .' What we need is some new leaders. Leaders who won't apostatize like cowards. Some niggers who are ready to die!"

The crowd's response startled me. "You! You! You!" they chanted, pointing their fingers in the air, proclaiming me king of the blacks.

Seizing the moment, Dexter Waverly snatched the microphone, put a warm arm around my shoulder. "Our new black leader, Gunnar Kaufman." All I could think was *What, no scepter? Don't I at least get a scepter?*

The next morning the annoyingly perky hosts of *Good Morning, America* and its sister shows around the globe—*Buenos Dias, Venezuela, Guten Morgen, Deutschland,* among others—took over my living room, asking questions from leather swivel chairs.

"*Buon giorno, Italia.* Signore Kaufman, did you know that during last night's reception for M'm'mofo Gottobelezi, Dexter Waverly killed himself in the college president's office?"

"No."

"*Si, si,* he held a knife to his throat and demanded that President Filbey

Bad Ass

rip up the hundred-million-dollar check and spit in Gottobelezi's champagne or he'd slash his throat."

"And what happened?"

"Filbey ripped up the check and spit in the Zulu's champagne. Signore Waverly apologized for the interruption, read a death poem dedicated to you, then plunged the knife into his throat."

"Wow."

"Don't you feel responsible, Signore Kaufman? After all, it was your speech that inspired Signore Waverly."

"I don't know. What did the poem say?"

Death Poem for Gunnar Kaufman

Abandoning all concern
my larynx bobs,
enlightenment is a bitch.

"That's not a bad poem. But I don't feel responsible for anything anyone else does. I have enough trouble being responsible for myself. Besides, it looks like Dexter's death prevented one hundred million dollars from being deposited in the National Party's coffers."

"*Bonjour, France.* Monsieur Kaufman, but what about your endorsement of freedom through suicide?"

"My suicide, no one else's."

"Yes, but people are following your example. There are reports of black people killing themselves indiscriminately across the United States. Don't you have anything to say?"

"Yes, send me your death poems."

"*Hyvää huomenta, Finland.* Mr. Kaufman, isn't suicide a way of saying that you've—that black people have given up? Surrendered unconditionally to the racial status quo?"

"That's the Western idea of suicide—the sense of the defeated self. 'Oh, the dysfunctional people couldn't adjust to our great system, so they killed themselves.' Now when a patriotic American—a soldier, for example—jumps on a grenade to save his buddies, that's the ultimate sacrifice. They drape a flag on your coffin, play taps, and your mama gets a Congressional Medal of Honor to put on the mantelpiece."

"So you see yourself as a hero?"

"No. It is as Mishima once said: 'Sometimes hara-kiri makes you win.' I just want to win one time."

"Last laugh?"

"I don't see anyone laughing."

"This is *Namasté, India.* And when do you plan to commit suicide, Mr. Kaufman?"

"When I'm good and goddamn ready."

PIRI THOMAS

Down These Mean Streets

WE PICKED UP BILLY and started driving back to Harlem. I almost liked the big gringo. He had a warm, easy way with him. I didn't trust him all the way, but I almost liked him. We talked and made plans, and when it was over, Danny looked at Louie and me and said, "You know, we're like a League of Nations. Billy's a Polack, I'm Irish, Louie is a white Porto Rican, and you"—Danny looked at me—"who the hell knows? But we're sure gonna—"

"I'm me, Mr. Charlie," I said, feeling hot in my chest.

"Whooo, smooth down, friend," Danny said. "I didn't mean no insult. I mean, like you're mixed with two or three races and—"

"Yeah, Piri," said Louie, "he didn't mean nothing. Practically all Puerto Ricans are mixed."

But in my mind, Danny's words, "and you, who the hell knows?"—were burning. *He's right,* I thought, *this bastard's right—who the hell knows?* That kept going through my mind. Then I heard voices breaking through my *pensamientos* and I dug Louie saying, "Well, if we gotta be proved . . ." And I said, "Proved in what?"

"Ain't you listening, Piri?" Louie said. "Danny and Billy feel on account they got *mucho* experience they know what they can do, but they haven't seen us work."

I said, "I ain't seen them work, either."

"Yeah, Piri, but they've been in jail."

"So, shit, what's that prove except maybe they ain't so good? But it's okay with me. What's the big *prueba?*"

"Well, you guys pull a job," Danny said, "and we'll watch from across the street and see how it goes, 'cause we don't want to take a chance with guys that may not have what it takes when the pressure is on."

I looked out of the car window and saw a cigar store on Third Avenue. I said, "You wanna see heart, eh, Mr. Charlies? Okay, park the car. Me and Louie is gonna pull a score right now."

"Man, Piri, we ain't ready yet," said Louie.

"You got that baby piece, Louie, that twenty-five cal?"

"Yeah, but it ain't loaded."

"Fuck it, we goin' shit for broke." I looked at the two paddies and winked at them. "This one's on us," I said. "Come on, Louie!"

Louie walked alongside me and he was talking a mile a minute. "*Caramba*, man, this is stupid, we ain't ready yet."

"When does one get ready for this kinda shit, man? You just jump into it with both feet. What do you expect, Louie, to go to school? You just start, *vente!*"

Danny and Billy were right across the street where they could watch the action. *Man*, I thought, *even if it was a bank, I'd pull it, just to shove it down them paddies' throats.*

Louie and me walked into the cigar store. There was only the owner there. "Walk to the back," I whispered to Louie. I stood near the candy counter, picking out candy bars.

"Can I help you?" said the owner.

"Yeah, *amigo*, you can give us your bread, money!"

He turned white. "Are you guys kidding?"

I said, "Listen, *maricón*, if you wanna die, then we're kidding; otherwise we're not. Just put the money in a paper bag. Your wallet, too. Louie, if the motherfucker makes a move, fuck him up good."

Louie just stood there, like he wished he was some place else, but for that matter, so did I.

"Show him the piece, Louie."

Louie pulled out the *pistolita* and it looked even smaller. "Look, mister, no more shit," he said.

"Don't shoot, please, don't shoot."

It was hard to say who was more scared, him or us.

He put the money in a bag and handed it to us. We locked him in a back room and made it. Just like that we had over $100 for a couple minutes' work. Woooie! We walked down toward the car and I felt Louie straining to start running.

"Cool it, man," I said. "If we run, them paddy boys are gonna think we ain't got heart."

Danny and Billy were sitting in the car with the motor running. Louie and me strolled over, smooth-like, opened the door, cool-like, and sat down. "Candy, anybody?" I softly asked, while that heart of mine was beating like crazy.

We were in. I could see it in the paddies' eyes. I counted the money as we drove. Danny was watching me through the rearview mirror. I said, "Pull over to the curb, man."

"What for?"

"Gotta see my *muchacha*," I said. Danny smiled and started to say something smart. "Don't say nothing," I added, "if it ain't nice, Mr. Charlie."

His smile washed off. "What's this 'Mr. Charlie' stuff you've been throwing around?" he asked.

"It's just a name, man, like one kinda people got for another kind of people. Ain't you down?"

He didn't answer. I got out of the car and handed Louie $75. "We split four ways, even."

As I walked down Madison Avenue, I thought, *Shit—splitting with paddies: Brew should see me now.*

F. X. Toole

Rope Burns

THE PLACE WASN'T CROWDED, and I noticed for the first time that the tables were arranged in little booths made up of dividers, with screens between the tables, for privacy. On my way back to my table from the buffet, I saw that Hoolie and Policarpo were bent over hot tea at the table next to mine. I took the long way around. They hadn't seen me, and when I sat down, I realized they were speaking Spanish. I had nothing to say to them. I'd handle the cuts, I'd collect my money, and I'd go back home and start painting. That was my deal, and I'd do it. I was kicking my own ass for showing up, but now that I was here, I was going to get my other five hundred. It was a rule.

Hungry as I was, at first I didn't pay any attention to them. When I heard them scheming on million-dollar fights, I had to smile. Then I heard something about a two-hundred-thousand-dollar fight and realized they

Bad Ass

were talking about the fight with Big Willie Little. I turned up both my hearing aids.

"I know they take taxes, but I don't get what we do with what's left of the two hundred thousand," said Hoolie. "The promoter said we could cash his check here if we want to, but then what? I mean, we don't want to pack it to L.A., right?"

Policarpo said, "Two ways. First, we could trust the promoter, and cash his check in L.A. But what if the check bounces? I say cash it here, so we got it in our hands. Then have the casino transfer the money to banks in L.A., one third to me, two thirds to you, like the big guy said."

"How much we got left over from trainin-expense money?" asked Hoolie.

"About thirty-five hundred. One thousand for me and two for you, after the cut man gets his five."

"The cut man gets it in his ass," said Hoolie, "that's what he gets for hustlin me."

"He'll be pissed, *raza.*"

"*Son cosas de la vida*—that's life."

"Can we get away with that?"

"What's the old Paddy cunt gonna do?"

"You signed your name, *ese.*"

"What I signed was Julio Cercenar Bauzá, not Julio César Garza." They laughed about the one word, *cercenar*—to trim, to reduce. "Dumb old fuck didn't see the difference."

It was true. Because of Hoolie's scrawl and fancy whorls, I hadn't picked up the name switch.

"What if he says you signed it phony?" said Policarpo.

"I say I never signed it at all. He's the one who wrote the IOU, not me, right?"

"What, we just split his money, one third/two thirds?"

"No," said Hoolie, "half and half. After I kick the nig's ass, we'll go buy us some black pussy on the old man, eh?"

When they gave the high five, they saw me for the first time. I turned to one side and didn't make eye contact.

"Hey, man," said Hoolie, looking through the screen, "how long you been here?"

"Couple minutes," I said, shoveling rice into my face with chopsticks. "What's up?"

"We're gonna take a little walk, it's not too cold, and then maybe I'll have me a little siesta," said Hoolie as he and Policarpo came around the divider. "How come you don't say hello or nothin, man?"

"I was eatin. Didn't see you."

"Yeah, we didn't see you, too."

They stood there while I continued to eat.

Policarpo said, "You don't speak no ehSpanish, right?"

Hoolie's eyes flicked between Policarpo and me.

I shrugged, kept eating. "About like the rest of the California *gringos*," I said. "*Cerveza*, and *puta*, and *cuánto* — beer, and whore, and how much."

That got a laugh, and they left feeling satisfied. I went back for seconds, took my time, and chewed on the fact that I should be getting four thousand dollars, not one. There were 24-by-36-inch posters of Hoolie and Big Willie in the café. More were set up throughout the hotel. This was Big Willie's fourth defense of his title, and he hadn't looked good in his last fight. With his weight problem, and with Hoolie's speed and boxing ability, it figured that Big Willie was due to lose his title. But he was a durable little battler who loved being champ, and under pressure he was mean. He was big in the back and shoulders and neck. He would have gained weight and regained his fluids since the weigh-in, and Big Willie could bang, even when he was tired. Of course Señor Julio Cercenar Bauzá was known to bleed.

When I didn't see anyone around that was connected with the fight, I went into the casino and checked the line. Big Willie was a three-to-one underdog because of his weight problem. That's when I went to the nearest ATM and pulled some cash from three banks.

I looked for someone who knew me from nothing. There were hillbillies and bikers and college boys. There were sorority girls and telephone operators and welfare mothers. Old people and young. Sporting types, squares, drunks, and junkies. All colors. None looked right, so I waited.

I got a whore, a skin-and-bones Thai whore with frizzed hair, who was all knee bones, ankles, elbow joints, and skull. No ass left on her. She was maybe thirty but looked fifty. Nobody looked at her, neither males in lust nor females in sympathy. I wondered how she could make a dime much less pay the rent. I don't know if she was a crack-head or had AIDS, but for sure she had lived hard in the night. She made me for a typical old john, someone who wanted to feel her, not fuck her. I told her what I wanted and that I'd pay two hundred. I told her that I'd be right on her tail, that if she made a run with my money, I'd stab her. She understood. What I did was slip her 15 one-hundred-dollar bills in an envelope, and had her lay it all on Big Willie Little for me at the Sports Book. I win the bet, I pick up a fast forty-five hundred. Afterward, I tailed her to a video-game room. She gave me my fifteen-hundred-dollar printout, and I gave her 4 fifties. She shoved them into her training bra.

Bad Ass

She said, "You no wan' mo'? You no wan' bro jo? I goo'."

I gave the poor bitch another hundred and told her to go home. She squinted at me and gave me a tight little smile, maybe the first she'd given in a year, maybe her last ever.

In my room, like I always do, I opened my aluminum attaché case and spread my goods out to make sure everything was there. But this time, instead of reaching for a new bottle of adrenaline, I unsnapped a flap pocket and took out an old bottle I knew had gone bad, an outdated bottle I hadn't used from a couple of years before. I'd taped the lid so I wouldn't make a mistake, but kept it for when I needed a backup bottle with a rubber seal that would hold. When I twisted off the thin metal cap and poured the old stuff on a tissue, it was a pale piss-yellow. I mixed a fresh batch of salve, as I always do, using Vaseline and adrenaline. It smelled right, but the salve I prepared was from the piss-yellow stuff, not the clear. The salve's color wasn't affected. Once I made up the salve, I diluted the remaining outdated solution with water to lighten the color. Under the ring lights, no one would notice, especially since it still smelled legit.

Even though I'm no longer a trainer, I always walk off the size of the ring. I test to see how tight or loose the ropes are. I check how hard or soft the canvas is, which is to say how fast or slow it will be. I check the steps up to the ring, how solid and wide they are, and how much room there will be at ringside. This time I checked dick.

It was a twelve-round fight, and it went off on time. Hoolie and Big Willie split the first two rounds, but Hoolie came on in the third and fourth. In the fifth, each fighter knocked the other down, but neither could put the other away. Hoolie had planned to fight Big Willie from the outside, to keep him at the end of his punches, but Big Willie was a bull and wouldn't allow it, so Hoolie had to fight on Big Willie's terms. The fifth was even, but at the end of the round, Hoolie returned to the corner with a small laceration in his left eyelid. I was quick into the ring and used just enough fresh adrenaline, along with pressure, to temporarily stop the flow of blood. I also used the phony salve, which meant there would be no coagulant continually working in the wound.

Hoolie was winning the sixth easy. Near the end of the round, Big Willie countered, whacked Hoolie on the way in with a solid one-two, one-two combination to the face, the second left-right even harder than the first. Suddenly there was a deep cut above Hoolie's right eye, and the cut in the eyelid was split wide open. The ref called time and looked at the cuts, but he let the fight continue. By the bell, Hoolie was seeing black from the blood and scraping at both eyes to clear his vision. Once he was in the corner between the sixth and the seventh, I cleaned the wounds with sterile gauze and applied pressure with both thumbs. Once the cuts were clean, I applied my outdated-piss adrenaline with a swab and went back to more pressure.

Hoolie said, "You can fix it for me, right, homes?"

"No sweat, man."

"You're the best."

Because I had cleaned the cuts properly and because of the pressure I applied along with the swab, and because of the bogus salve I packed into the holes, it appeared that I had solved the problem. Policarpo and the other corner men were so busy giving Hoolie instructions and watering him that I could have used green paint and they wouldn't have noticed.

The bell for the seventh sounded. Big Willie and Hoolie fought like bats, each turning, each twisting and bending, each moving as if suspended in light, neither stepping back, and both wanting the title, both ripping mercilessly into the other. Both were splattered with Hoolie's blood. The head of each fighter was snapping back, and the ribs of both were creaking as each unleashed his force. Big Willie suffered a flash knockdown, but he was up again by the count of two. As he took the mandatory eight-count, his eyes were focused on Hoolie like a rattler's on a rat. The ref waved the fighters on. Big Willie stepped up and delivered a left-right-left combination, the second left snapping like it had come off a springboard. It would have destroyed most welterweights, but Hoolie grabbed Big Willie and held on.

The bell ended the round, and I cleaned the wounds and applied more pressure, temporarily stanching the red flow. I used more piss-yellow.

"I thought you fixed it, *ese*," said Hoolie, his voice coming out small between bruised lips.

"I did fix it," I said. "But you let him pop you, so it opened up on me. Be cool. Go with the flow."

In the eighth, Big Willie looked exhausted, but there was no quit in him. He sucked it up and concentrated his shots on Hoolie's cuts. Blood filled Hoolie's eyes until he was punching blindly and getting hit no matter how he tried to cover up. People at ringside were shielding themselves from the flying blood. Big Willie saw the ruined flesh, and his heart jacked as his own adrenaline pounded through him. Walking through Hoolie's wild punches, he drilled more shots into Hoolie's blood-blind eyes. Two more cuts opened in Hoolie's eyebrows. Veins weren't cut, but blood pumped down, and the fans were yelling to the ref to stop it. He called time and waved in the ring doctor, who immediately stopped the fight.

Big Willie Little was declared the winner, and still featherweight champion.

In the corner the doctor checked Hoolie's eyes. By then I had used fresh adrenaline, which stopped the blood cold. The cuts were an inch and a half,

Bad Ass

308 ◆ F. X. Toole

two inches long, which is big-time when it's around the eyes. But like I say, no vein was cut, and with the right stuff in there, Hoolie could have fought all night. Since Big Willie was sure to have run out of gas, and since I had no trouble stopping the cuts when I wanted to, I figure Hoolie should be the new champ. Except for me. *Son cosas de la* fucking *vida.*

Hoolie's corner men were washing him down with alcohol and the doctor had stitched up three of the cuts when the promoter came in with Hoolie's check. He was a big round Afrikaner from Johannesburg, with a walrus mustache and a huge Dutch gut. He had kind, wise eyes and seemed to float rather than walk.

"Too bad about the cuts," he said. "I thought Little was ready to go, there."

"I beat Big Willie's fuckin ass my eyes don't go," said Hoolie, who was desolate from the loss.

"You've got one of the best cut men I ever saw. Cool under fire, he was. I watched him. Did everything right." He sucked on his mustache. "What was the grease from the little container?"

I pulled out the flat plastic jar containing the piss salve. I unscrewed the wide lid. "Smell."

"Ahh, yes, good lad, you mix adrenaline right into the grease, yes? Keeps working, right?, during the round."

"That's it."

"Tough break, Hoolie being a bleeder."

"Sure is. Listen," I said. "I know it's not my place, but I'm not going back to L.A. with these guys. I'm wondering if there's some way they can cash out in the casino? So they can take care of me before they take off?"

The promoter looked at Hoolie. Neither he nor Policarpo said anything.

"I've got an IOU," I said.

Hoolie saw that the promoter realized something wasn't right. He played dumb. "But once we cash the check," he asked, "we can't have the money transferred to L.A., can we?"

"Certainly can. Like I previously explained, we can arrange the transfer of funds through the casino."

"Ah, yeah, I remember now. Cool."

At the cashier's window, Policarpo counted out my money in English. "One hundred, two hundred, three hundred, four hundred, five hundred."

As he handed the bills to me, I glanced at Hoolie, whose butterflied eyes were telling me he'd never use me in his corner again. I love a guy who says he's going to fuck you because you won't let him fuck you.

As I re-counted the first two bills in English, I decided to lay rotten eggs in Hoolie's mind. Without a break, I slipped into singsong Mexican street

Spanish. "*Trescientos, cuatrocientos, quinientos. Correcto, mano*—three hundred, four hundred, five hundred. Correct, my brother."

Hoolie remembered our conversation over my Chinese food. "Hey!, you speak ehSpanish?"

Now I went into a guttural, old-man Castillian. "*Pues, coño,* but only if it's to my advantage." *Pues, coño* is what nailed it—well, of course, cunt.

Hoolie blinked six times. Policarpo's jaw flopped open. For the first time I saw fear in Hoolie's eyes. *Did I fuck him or didn't I?* they screamed.

Riding the Rods

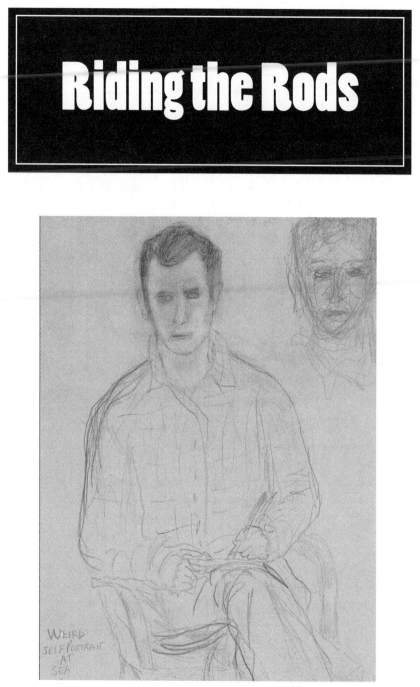

Jack Kerouac *Weird Self Portrait at Sea*

Boxcar Bertha

Sister of the Road

BIG OTTO HAD WRITTEN me a number of letters, but I hadn't heard from him for some time when a letter came from the Cook County Jail, in Chicago.

"I think I am settled and there is no need of your worrying about me any longer," he wrote. "I have reformed and will never steal again. If you want to see me this side of Hell, you had better come to Chicago before February 13th. Invitations are already out for my 'neck tie party.' "

I felt as though a cold hand had suddenly been laid on my heart! Otto a murderer! The neck about which my arms had been so many times—could it be possible that it was about to feel the choking clutch of a rope?

Without waiting for any preliminaries, I caught a Northern Pacific midnight freight with four men I made friends with at hobo college. They took good care of me. Mother fixed us a big batch of sandwiches. While we were rolling along through Idaho one of them pulled a candle out of his pocket, lit it and stuck it in the floor in the front end of the car and boiled coffee for me in a big cup. We had an army canteen with us. None of those men tried to make love to me. None of them mentioned the obvious fact that I was going to have a baby. Twice, once in Montana and once in Dakota, when the train hands started to get tough, they walked away as soon as they saw my condition.

The four men were going to Minneapolis to an employment agency that had called for hands in the western yards there, and each one soberly chipped in a dollar and handed the money to me as they put me on another freight car later, on the Chicago and Northwestern. The next morning I climbed out in the Kedzie yards and went into the city on a street car.

It was then February 11th. Otto was to be hanged on the thirteenth. He was already in the death cell. They would not allow anyone to see him but his relatives. I pleaded without success with the warden and the sheriff. A young newspaper man by the name of Hennessy heard me begging. He said, 'Sister, you come with me and I think I can make arrangements for you to see him.'

We sat in a little restaurant on Clark Street near Grand Avenue. "What is Otto to you, and why are you so anxious to see him?" he asked me. "Are you in the family way? Is it Otto?"

"He was formerly a very dear friend of mine," I told him, noncommittally.

"You mean he was your sweetheart and the father of your child and you are engaged to marry him. Now, you let me write the story just as I want it and I'll get you a pass to see him. I'll even do better than that. I'll get you a pass to see him hanged."

"Jesus!—Me see Otto hanged!" I felt as though I had been hit with a hammer, yet I knew that, if the man kept his word, I would go.

In less than an hour Hennessy came back with a pass and took me to the jail. We were admitted through a large iron gate and I was taken to the jailer's office and searched. The assistant jailer, a matron, and Hennessy walked in front of me as we passed through an iron door into the bundle cage. Then we went through another iron door along the first tier up a flight of iron steps into a big corridor, and to a large room at the front of the building.

"Just sit here, Miss Thompson. We'll call him."

They brought Otto from the death cell, handcuffed, with a guard on either side of him. He looked just the same as ever, except that his hair was a little greyer, and he was very pale. He spoke:

"Hello, beautiful. How are you?"

"Just hold that pose," said the photographer.

"Hurry up and snap it," said Hennessy. "I want to get a picture of Otto holding Miss Thompson in his arms."

I was too shocked to protest. The newspaper photographer snapped a picture of us shaking hands, of me embracing him, and then of him kissing me. I did everything Hennessy asked of me. None of it mattered.

"Boxcar, tell me, how've you been getting on?" Otto asked me, trying to be offhand about it. "What's your sister doing now? Do you ever see any of the old mob?"

But I could not talk to him of ordinary matters.

"Otto, aren't you afraid to die?" I found myself saying. "Doesn't the thought of being hanged bother you?"

"Well, I ain't hanged yet," he came back at me. "I've beat every rap so far. My lawyers are going to take this thing up to the Supreme Court, and I think the Governor will give me a stay of execution. You never say 'die' until you're dead, Bertha. I've been slated for an exit lots of times, but so far I've beaten every rap. In this game, the crooked live by faith."

Then his voice dropped to a whisper.

"On the level, Bertha, are you going to have a kid?" he asked. Then he added, "Say it's mine, will you?"

Tears sprang to my eyes as I heard him. Fifteen hundred lonely men! And now one man who might have been father to a child of mine, a man who was about to die, was pleading with me to say the nameless child within me was his. How could anyone ever explain the troubled hearts of men? How could any woman ever hope to give them peace?

But I wanted to talk about him.

"Tell me, Otto, what happened? I've hardly read the papers. How did you get into such a jam? I never thought you were a burglar or a highway robber. I always thought you were a first-class, gentle sneak-thief."

The guards, with an unusual show of consideration, had stepped away leaving us, for a moment, in a little world of our own.

"I was," he said, "but I got overly ambitious. If I had stuck to the trade my father had taught me, I'd have been all right. You see, Bertha, even in our racket we have our ups and downs. And ever since you left me I haven't amounted to much. I lost the courage to steal. I didn't have the training to work. I never dreamed, Bertha, that a woman could take so much out of a man when she left him as you did. Jesus, kid, I loved you. You're the only thing I ever loved in my life. I didn't want to live after you left me. I joined a cheap phoney mob of amateur hoodlums just because I thought I'd get croaked or the rope. You see, beautiful, you queered me. You made it impossible for me to be happy about stealing. There's nothing to it, Bertha; it was just a cheap cowboy drunken stunt.

"I was staying at a flop house, over on West Madison Street, and these other guys in the mob were taking a bath in a couple of gallons of Dago Red. One of them had been a bus-boy at the Drake Hotel. That's all they were, just cheap-skate, petty-larceny bus-boys. None of them had ever stolen anything more than an umbrella or a door mat in their lives. One of the guys said, and he was half stewed and the rest of us were soused, 'I'll tell you how we can make a touch for fifteen grand. It'll be a cinch. I used to work over in the Drake Hotel, and the fifth and twentieth they pay. The payroll is fifteen thousand dollars. All we need is five men. It'll be a cinch.' I don't know how the hell I ever got mixed up with those punks, but we got hold of a couple of gats, and stewed to the gills, we went over there like we was Jesse James. We killed the cashier. Two of our mob were killed. One got away. Woods and I were caught before we left the hotel. There's nothing to it, but it made a good newspaper story, and just another testimony for Dago Red."

Otto kept looking at me as if his eyes could never see enough of me. And when I had to go he whispered again, "Tell me, is it true you're going to have a kid? Please, beautiful, say it's mine."

Hennessy arranged that I was to see Otto an hour before the execution and also got me a press card admission to the hanging. An hour before the State took Otto's life, I stood before the door of the death cell and held his hand. I was half crazy with wanting to say something that would help, wanting to do something, and I didn't want Otto to see how scared I was.

"How's the weather out, Bertha?"

He seemed to be listening for something.

"Otto, I want you to do something for me," I said, to divert him.

"Will you?"

"Sure, beautiful, anything I can."

"All right, then. In about forty minutes you're going to say 'Good morning, God.' Otto, when you do that, how about asking Him something? First tell Him I loved you and that it's terrible the State hanged you and that it's awful that you killed a working man. Then ask Him if He can't do something to stop men killing each other. Ask Him if He won't fix things so it will be easier to go straight than crooked."

He was hearing me but his face was listening for something else, too. I tried to kid him, tried to keep him from thinking about the next few minutes.

"Otto, do you think it's true that from the world to which you're going you will be able to send back thoughts and inspiration? Will you think of me, will you try to tell me how to understand people like you, how to help them?"

But it was no use. Suddenly I was throwing my body against the bar close to his body, crying out to him to kiss me, to hurt me. I heard my own voice without any control, crying: "Bite me. Hurt me. Make me feel you after you're gone!"

He looked at me then, with pity and affection in his eyes, and tried to give me strength.

"Take it easy, kid," he said. "It ain't you that's goin'."

Then the guards came and took me away.

Promptly at 7:00 a.m. a hundred and fifty of us were allowed to file into the ground floor of the jail. A temporary gallows had been erected in the bull pen. All the cells that faced the gallows had been emptied and the prisoners taken to the other side of the prison.

"Here they come."

We knew almost before we heard them.

With their heads erect, cigarettes in their mouths and their hands manacled behind them, the men about to die walked to the scaffold. Otto looked quickly through the crowd, quickly recognized me, nodded, and twisted his lips into a ghastly smile. His face was listening. I knew what he was thinking. His eyes turned back toward the door. Every second he was expecting the telegraph boy to come in with a reprieve. He had beaten every rap in life so far. He had been in the Army for over a year and in the front line trenches for six months. German bullets and bombs and gas had missed him. He had been shot at by police and watchmen a dozen times. In drunken brawls he had been shot and stabbed, but had always escaped serious injury. By the look in his eye, I knew that he felt that he was going to beat this rap, also. He was listening when the guards tied a rope around his feet; placed a white hood over his head that extended to the middle of his body, put a rope around his neck so that the knot came at the back. Everything was peaceful, orderly.

Flop!

The floor under him dropped and he was swinging in the air. Otto swinging in the air. I tried to make myself remember him as I had been with him. I tried to remember his face before the hood was tied on. But I could not. Into my mind came only one thing, the lines of Oscar Wilde's, over and over again:

> It is sweet to dance to violins
> Where love and life are fair;
> To dance to flutes, to dance to lutes
> Is delicate and rare
> But it is not sweet with nimble feet
> To dance upon the air.

Then, there in the grey prison room with the white shrouded figures swinging slowly and more slowly, I felt deep within my body the first movements of my baby.

Woody Guthrie

Bound for Glory

THE WIND STRUCK AGAINST our boxcar and the rain beat itself to pieces and blew over our heads like a spray from a fire hose shooting sixty miles an hour. Every drop that blew against my skin stung and burned.

The colored rider was laughing and saying, "Man! Man! When th' good Lord was workin' makin' Minnesoty, He couldn' make up His mind whethah ta make anothah ocean or some mo' land, so He just got 'bout half done an' then He quit an' went home! Wowie!" He ducked his head and shook it and

Riding the Rods

kept laughing, and at the same time, almost without me noticing what he was doing, he had slipped his blue work shirt off and jammed it over into my hands. "One mo' shirt might keep yo' meal ticket a little bettah!"

"Don't you need a shirt to keep dry?"

I don't know why I asked him that. I was already dressing the guitar up in the shirt. He squared his shoulders back into the wind and rubbed the palms of his hands across his chest and shoulders, still laughing and talking, "You think dat little ole two-bit shirt's gonna keep out this cloudbu'st?"

When I looked back around at my guitar on my lap, I seen one more little filthy shirt piled up on top of it. I don't know exactly how I felt when my hands come down and touched this shirt. I looked around at the little tough guys and saw them humped up with their naked backs splitting the wind and the rain glancing six feet in the air off their shoulders. I didn't say a word. The little kid pooched his lips out so the water would run down into his mouth like a trough, and every little bit he'd save up a mouthful and spit it out in a long thin spray between his teeth. When he saw that I was keeping my eyes nailed on him, he spit the last of his rainwater out and said, "I ain't t'oisty."

"I'll wrap this one around the handle an' the strings will keep dry that way. If they get wet, you know, they rust out." I wound the last shirt around and around the neck of the guitar handle. Then I pulled the guitar over to where I was laying down. I tied the leather strap around a plank in the boardwalk, ducked my head down behind the guitar and tapped the runty kid on the shoulder.

"Hey, squirt!"

"Whaddaya want?"

"Not much of a windbreak, but it at least knocks a little of th' blister out of that rain! Roll yer head over here an' keep it ducked down behind this music box!"

"Yeeehh." He flipped over like a little frog and smiled all over his face and said, "Music's good fer somethin', ain't it?"

Both of us stretched out full length. I was laying on my back looking straight up into the sky all gray and tormented and blowing with low clouds that whined when they got sucked under the wheels. The wind whistled funeral songs for the railroad riders. Lightning struck and crackled in the air and sparks of electricity done little dances for us on the iron beams and fixtures. The flash of the lightning knocked the clouds full of holes and the rain hit down on us harder than before. "On th' desert, I use this here guitar fer a sun shade! Now I'm usin' the' dam thing fer a umbreller!"

"T'ink I could eva' play one uv dem?" The little kid was shaking and trembling all over, and I could hear his lips and nose blow the rain away, and his teeth chatter like a jack-hammer. He scooted his body closer to me, and I laid an arm down so he could rest his head. I asked him, "How's that fer a pillow?"

"Dat's betta." He trembled all over and moved a time or two. Then he got still and I didn't hear him say anything else. Both of us were soaked to the skin a hundred times. The wind and the rain was running a race to see which could whip us the hardest. I felt the roof of the car pounding me in the back of the head. I could stand a little of it, but not long at a time. The guitar hit against the raindrops and sounded like a nest of machine guns spitting out lead.

The force of the wind pushed the sound box against the tops of our heads, and the car jerked and buckled through the clouds like a coffin over a cliff.

I looked at the runt's head resting on my arm, and thought to myself, "Yeah, that's a little better."

My own head ached and pained inside. My brain felt like a crazy cloud of grasshoppers jumping over one another across a field. I held my neck stiff so my head was about two inches clear of the roof; but that didn't work. I got cold and cramped and a dozen kinks tied my whole body in a knot. The only way I could rest was to let my head and neck go limp; and when I did this, the jolt of the roof pounded the back of my head. The cloudbursts got madder and splashed through all of the lakes, laughing and singing, and then a wail in the wind would get a low start and cry in the timber like the cry for freedom of a conquered people.

Through the roof, down inside the car, I heard the voices of the sixty-six hoboes. There had been sixty-nine, the old man said, if he counted right. One threw his own self into the lake. He pushed two more out the door with him, but they lit easy and caught onto the ladder again. Then the two little windburnt, sunbaked brats had mounted the top of our car and were caught in the cloudburst like drowned rats. Men fighting against men. Color against color. Kin against kin. Race pushing against race. And all of us battling against the wind and the rain and that bright crackling lightning that booms and zooms, that bathes his eyes in the white sky, wrestles a river to a standstill, and spends the night drunk in a whorehouse.

What's that hitting me on the back of the head? Just bumping my head against the roof of the car. Hey! Goddam you! Who th' hell do you think you're a hittin', mister? What are you, anyhow, a dam bully? You cain't push that woman around! What's all of these folks in jail for? Believing in people? Where'd all of us come from? What did we do wrong? You low-down cur, if you hit me again, I'll tear your head off!

My eyes closed tight, quivering till they exploded like the rain when the lightning dumped a truckload of thunder down along the train. I was

Riding the Rods

whirling and floating and hugging the little runt around the belly, and my brain felt like a pot of hot lead bubbling over a flame. Who's all of these crazy men down there howling out at each other like hyenas? Are these men? Who am I? How come them here? How the hell come me here? What am I supposed to do here?

My ear flat against the tin roof soaked up some music and singing coming from down inside of the car:

> *This train don't carry no rustlers,*
> *Whores, pimps, or side-street hustlers;*
> *This train is bound for glory,*
> *This train.*

Can I remember? Remember back to where I was this morning? St. Paul. Yes. The morning before? Bismarck, North Dakota. And the morning before that? Miles City, Montana. Week ago, I was a piano player in Seattle.

Who's this kid? Where's he from and where's he headed for? Will he be me when he grows up? Was I like him when I was just his size? Let me remember. Let me go back. Let me get up and walk back down the road I come. This old hard rambling and hard graveling. This old chuck-luck traveling. My head ain't working right.

Where was I?

Where in the hell was I?

Where was I when I was a kid? Just as far, far, far back, on back, as I can remember?

Strike, lightning, strike!

Strike, Goddam you, strike!

There's lots of folks that you cain't hurt!

Strike, lightning!

See if I care!

Roar and rumble, twist and turn, the sky ain't never as crazy as the world.

Bound for glory? This train? Ha!

I wonder just where in the hell we're bound.

Rain on, little rain, rain on!

Blow on, little wind, keep blowin'!

'Cause them guys is a singin' that this train is bound for glory, an' I'm gonna hug her breast till I find out where she's bound.

Riding the Rods

Lee Stringer

Grand Central Winter

WHAT HAPPENED WAS I was digging around in my hole—there's this long, narrow, crawl space in Grand Central's lower regions, of which few people are aware and into which I moved some time ago. It is strung with lights and there is a water spigot just outside the cubbyhole through which I enter. It's on the chilly side in winter, and I baste down there in summer, but it is, as they say, home.

I have filled this place with blankets and books and have fortified it with enough cardboard baffles to hold any rats at bay (the secret being, of course, to never bring food down here. It's the food that attracts them). So, at the end of the day I come down here to polish off that last, lonely blast. Or just to sleep it off.

But as I said, I was digging around in this hole—lying flat on my back, reaching back and under the old blankets, newspapers, and clothes that I've amassed over time and that keep me insulated from the concrete floor, trying to find some small, dowellike instrument with which to push the screens from one end of my stem to the other, so that I could smoke the remaining resin caked up in the thing.

For those of you who have not had the pleasure, I point out that when you are piping up, the first thing to go is your patience. And I'm digging around under this mess, cursing and muttering under my breath like an old wino on a three-day drunk, when my fingers finally wrap around some sort of smooth, straight stick.

I pull it out and it's a pencil and it does the trick. I push my screens and take a hit and have a pleasurable half hour of sweaty trembling panic that at any second someone or something is going to jump out of the darkness—I get much too paranoid to smoke with the lights on—and stomp the living shit out of me or something.

That's the great thing about being a veteran crackhead.

Always a lot of fun.

Anyway the point is, I start carrying this pencil around with me because I really hate like hell to be caught without something to push with and then have to go searching or digging around like I was doing when I found the thing.

The good thing about carrying a pencil is that it's a pencil. And if I get stopped and searched for any reason, it's just a pencil. Of course I carry my stem around too. And there's no doubt about what that's for. But, hey I'm not looking to strain my cerebral cortex on the subject. It's all I can do just to hustle up enough scratch every day and go cop something decent—without getting beat, arrested, or shot—so I can have a lovely time cowering in the dark for a couple of hours.

So I have this pencil with me all the time and then one day I'm sitting there in my hole with nothing to smoke and nothing to do and I pull the pencil out just to look at the film of residue stuck to the sides—you do that sort of thing when you don't have any shit—and it dawns on me that it's a pencil. I mean it's got a lead in it and all, and you can write with the thing.

So now I'm at it again. Digging around in my hole. Because I know there's an old composition book down there somewhere and I figure maybe I can distract myself for a little while by writing something.

The things a person will do when he's not smoking.

The funny thing is, I get into it.

I mean really get into it.

I start off just writing about a friend of mine. Just describing his cluttered apartment. How I kind of like the clutter. How it gives the place a lived-in look. How you can just about read his life by looking around.

So I'm writing away, and the more I write, the easier it gets. And the easier it gets, the better the writing gets, until it's like I'm just taking dictation.

Pretty soon I forget all about hustling and getting a hit. I'm scribbling like a maniac; heart pumping, adrenaline rushing, hands trembling. I'm so excited I almost crap on myself.

It's just like taking a hit.

Before I know it, I have a whole story.

I go to read the thing and it's a mess. The pages are all out of order. Parts are scratched out. Other parts are written sideways in the margins. But what I can read looks pretty good.

Even great in parts.

By the time I go back and carefully rewrite the thing, it's too late at night for me to bother going out, which is a remarkable thing for me because I don't think there's been a day since I started that I have gone without at least one hit.

So I read the story over and over.

Fix a few things.

And what I end up with reads like Tennessee Williams (I have a paperback with all his short stories in it) in the way it kind of comes in through the side door. I mean, Williams will start off talking about, say, what it smells like to work in a shoe factory and before you know it, he's going on about wanting to kill his father or something like that.

That's how my story went.

It started with my friend's house and then I have a guy sitting there with him who wants to get some pills from him so he can take himself out before the AIDS virus gets him—you see, he is HIV-positive—and when he gets the pills, he goes over to the park to just lie down and fade away on the grass.

Only he feels the need to apologize to the world because he has to die in public. And someone will have to come along and pick up his sorry, dead ass and all. But he's homeless, there's no place for him to go.

I guess they'll never make a musical out of it.

But the thing is—and this is what gets me—when I read the story I can feel this guy's pain! I mean, I haven't been able to feel much of anything in years. And there I am, sitting down there under Grand Central, reading this thing scribbled in an old composition book, and I'm practically in tears.

The next day I take the story over to my friend's house and he reads it. All I'm expecting from him is a sarcastic remark because this guy is one of those snob alcoholics. He doesn't approve of anything.

Ever.

Least of all me.

But he just puts it down quietly when he finishes and gives me the slightest nod. Then he says,

"Do you love me?"

I know why he asks this.

Because in the story the two guys are friends but they would never admit it. They just hang around together putting each other down all the time—a lot like my friend and me—and in the end the one guy is sorry because he'll never have the chance to tell his buddy that he loves him—in a normal sort of way I mean—and that he'll miss him.

He never realizes this until he's dying.

The only real difference between the story and me and my friend, come to think of it, is that I'm not HIV-positive and I'm not dying.

But my friend is.

And when he asks me whether or not I love him, it gets to me because I would never have thought he gave a shit one way or the other. So I go over to him and hug him, and that weepy shit starts kicking up again.

What can I tell you?

It was one of those moments.

All because I sat in my hole and wrote this little story.

Next thing you know, I'm up at the *Street News* office with it, asking if anybody'd be interested in putting it in the paper, and—sure enough—damned if I don't open up the next issue and there's my story!

That's how I got my first thing published in *Street News*.

I think I called it "No Place to Call Home."

A couple of months later I had a regular column in there. And—one thing after the other—I had the writing bug.

After that there were *four* things I did every day. Hustle up money, cop some stuff, beam up, and write. And in the end I wound up dropping the other three.

JACK BLACK

You Can't Win

GEORGE SMILED AND TOOK a better grip on my hand. "Yes, I remember you, young fellow. You've grown some. Have you gathered any wisdom?"

"I've gathered enough to know that you are entitled to any part of this," I said, producing my small bankroll.

"This is payable to-morrow night," he said, taking twenty dollars.

The money was returned promptly and a bond of friendship and confidence was formed that remains unbroken. I came to know him as "Rebel George," prince of bunko men, the man who developed and perfected the "gold-brick" swindle. After stealing a fortune and losing it at faro bank, he quit in answer to the prayers of his faithful wife, who had for years shared his vicissitudes in and out of prison. At the age of sixty, prison bent and money broke, he started life on the level and when last I heard of him he was in a fair way to succeed in his small business.

From Butte I journeyed to Spokane, Washington, and then to Seattle. I marvel now that I did not stop in one of those spots of golden opportunity and go to work. With the money I would have saved in a couple of years I could have bought land or lots that would have made me independent in ten years. I think land hunger is inherited. I had no desire then, nor have I now, to own land. The desire to possess land, whether inherent or acquired, appears to me to be a sure safeguard against a wasted, dissolute, harmful life.

I had now become so saturated with the underworld atmosphere that no thought of any kind of honest endeavor entered my mind. Fully realizing their value I passed by many splendid opportunities in the booming Western towns; not that I was lazy or indolent, but that business and the hoarding of money had no attraction. I will leave it to the scientists and investigators to explain why Johnnie Jones lands in a pulpit, and his chum next door with equal opportunity, lands in a penitentiary. It's too deep for me. I know I never had any money sense and never will have, and I know that had I been blessed, or cursed, with land hunger and money sense I would to-day have more honest dollars than I ever had crooked dimes.

Twenty years of moderate application to his business will make most any man independent. In twenty years a journeyman mechanic will handle more money than a first-class burglar, and at the end of that time he will have a home and a family and a little money in the bank, while the most persistent, sober, and industrious burglar is lucky to have his liberty. He is too old to learn a trade, too old and broken from doing time to tackle hard labor. Nobody will give him work. He has the prison horrors and turns to cheap larcenies and spends the balance of his life doing short sentences in small jails.

In rare instances the broken thief finds friends, sympathetic, understanding, and ready to help him. Strong and kindly hands at his elbows ease him over the hard spots and direct him to some useful place in the world. Some understand such kindness and respond by breasting the current and battling upstream with their best strokes; others do not, or can not understand, and, like dead fish, float down and away forever.

My apprenticeship under the Sanctimonious Kid was all that could be desired by either of us, yet my education was far from finished. At Seattle, almost broke, and doubtful about being able to do anything worth while by myself, I cast about for a "sidekicker." Seattle was rebuilding after her big fire. Money was plentiful, and I never saw such an aggregation of beggars, tramps, thieves, and yeggs as were gathered there. Gambling, prostitution and the smuggling of opium flourished unmolested. The thieves hung out in Clancey's gambling house, and were protected and exploited by him. They thought Clancey was a little "Hinky Dink" in a little Chicago.

Every time a thief showed up with a hundred dollars he was "pinched," but Clancey took him out in an hour—for the hundred. When it was too late they found out that it was he who had them "pinched." Clancey died broke.

In Clancey's I found "St. Louis Frank," a product of Kerry Patch, a poor quarter of St. Louis, Missouri. I knew him from the bums' "convention" at Pocatello, where I met him first. He was clean looking and healthy and I liked him. About my own age, he was an honest, industrious, intelligent thief.

One night as we were looking around one of the smaller gambling houses, all the lights went out suddenly, but before we could get our hands on any of the money, they came on again. This started us to figuring a way to put them out at a given time when one of us could stand near a table and grab the bankroll. We found where the wires entered the building, and Frank volunteered to cut them if I would stand inside by the faro game and snatch the bankroll which was lying exposed in an open drawer beside the dealer. It looked so good that we enlisted two other "Johnsons," one to plant himself by the dice game, and the other by the roulette wheel. All three of us were to be in readiness to make a grab when the lights went out and make our way out of the building in the darkness.

Saturday night, when the biggest play was on, Frank made his way to the roof and we took up our posts inside.

I took a position by the faro game. The drawer that held the bankroll was so situated that a right-handed man would be handicapped in reaching for the money. Being left-handed, the spot fell to me. The drawer was open and the big leather pocketbook containing the money was lying in the bottom of it in plain sight, and not two feet from where I stood. The second man, in charge of the game, the "lookout," sat in a high chair at the dealers right. One of his feet was resting on the edge of the open drawer, and I saw at a glance that if he jammed the drawer shut with his foot when the lights went out he would trap my hand.

While I was thinking that over, Frank cut the wires and everybody in the big room did just what we expected; they remained perfectly still for a second waiting for the light to come on.

My hand was on the big fat "poke." I heard a jingle of gold coins across the room, and somebody shouted: "Thieves! Thieves!" The drawer was jammed shut on my hand.

Reaching down with my right hand I got the poke and tore my left hand out of its trap, leaving a piece of skin the size of a half dollar behind. There were three exits and we all got out safely in the scramble, and "weighed in" at my room.

Frank was there ahead of us. My grab yielded two thousand dollars in bills. The chap at the dice game put his hand on a stack of twenty twenty-dollar gold pieces, but it was too heavy and he fumbled it, getting only half. Our assistant at the roulette wheel got a couple of stacks of silver only.

The money was split at once, and our friends departed. Frank took most of our money out and left it with a saloon man we knew. I stayed in my room a couple of days waiting for my hand to heal.

One great failing of the thief is that when he gets money he immediately makes tracks for some hangout where he throws a few dollars on the bar just to "give the house a tumble" and let them guess where he "scored" and how much he got.

He looks wise, says nothing, spends a few dollars, and goes out. Then the guessing begins and it's surprising what good guessers some poor thieves are.

Frank insisted that we go downtown a few nights later. I took the bandage off my hand and went along. We dropped into "Billy, the Mug's," bought a few drinks, and departed. Half a block away we were pounced on by a couple of "dicks." One of them jerked my left hand out of my coat pocket where I had been keeping it to conceal the skinned place. "That's enough," he said, looking at it. They marched us down to the gambling house and showed us to the game keepers. They got no satisfaction there, the gamblers either could not or would not identify us. We were then taken down to the city "can," where they searched us thoroughly, finding nothing but a few dollars in silver. We were questioned separately and together, but refused to talk—a guilty man's only refuge. The officers ordered the man on the desk to put us on the "small book," meaning to hold us as suspicious characters. "Maybe Corbett can get something out of you," one of them said to us as they were leaving.

John Corbett was the officer in charge of the city jail. He was feared and hated from one end of the country to the other because of his brutality to prisoners. I doubt if a more brutal, bloodthirsty jailer ever flourished anywhere. He did not limit his beatings to underworld people. He beat up rich men, poor men, beggarmen, and thieves impartially. Anybody that didn't crawl for Corbett got a good "tamping." He was repeatedly brought before the commission for his cruelty to unfortunates falling into his hands, but for years mustered enough influence to hold his job. Corbett's treatment of prisoners was the shame and scandal of Seattle, and he kept it up until the women of that city got the right to vote. Then their clubs, in a body, went to the mayor and demanded Corbett's removal. He was removed.

Corbett appeared and took me downstairs where the cells were, in a moldy, damp, dark half basement. He was a powerful man, not tall, but thick and broad. He was black-browed, brutal-faced, heavy-jawed. He opened a cell door and I started to step in but he detained me. I sensed something wrong. His brownish-red eyes gleamed like a fanatic's. "You'd better tell me all about that robbery, young man." His voice was cold, level, and passionless.

"I know nothing about it, sir," I answered very decently; I was afraid. Like a flash one of his hands went to my throat. He pinned me to the wall, choking me, and brought something down on my head with the other hand that turned everything yellow and made my knees weaken. Still holding me by the throat he lifted me clear of the floor and threw me into the cell like a bundle of rags. There was about a half inch of water on the cell floor. I lay there in it, and looked about me by the dim light of a gas jet out in the corridor. There was nothing in the cell but a wooden bench.

After a few minutes I crawled over to it, and, pulling myself up, stretched out, more dead than alive. If people can be corrected by cruelty I would have left that cell a saint.

St. Louis Frank, in another part of the jail, got a worse beating than I did.

Our friends outside were busy. At ten o'clock next morning James Hamilton Lewis, affectionately called "Jim Ham," later United States senator from Illinois, then an ambitious fighting young lawyer who never "laid down" on a client, came to see us. At two that afternoon he had us out on a writ, free.

From that day on St. Louis Frank smiled no more. He became snarly, short spoken, and ugly. We got our money and parted. He went out on the road "bull simple," simple on the subject of shooting policemen. The stories told about him are almost unbelievable. Years later I saw him in the San Francisco county jail where he was waiting trial for the murder of a police officer in Valencia Street. The day he went to San Quentin where he was hanged, he sang out to me "So long, Blacky. If I could have got Corbett I wouldn't care."

All Corbett's beating did for me was to make me a little more careful. I got a boat to San Francisco, not knowing just what to do, but with a notion of killing time till old Foot-and-a-half George finished his time in Utah, and meeting him. I dug up the hotel keys Sanc and I had planted and experimented a little in hotel prowling. I hadn't the sure touch that came in later years with experience, and didn't do much good.

One night in the Baldwin Hotel Annex I got a roll of bills that rather surprised me, and I was still more surprised when I read in the next evening's paper that George Dixon, the little colored champion fighter, had lost his money to a burglar. At the Baldwin bar the next night somebody asked him what he would have done had he been awakened by the burglar.

Dixon, always a good loser, smiled. "I'd 'a' done just what you'd 'a' done. I'd 'a' gone right back to sleep till that man went on out."

JIM TULLY

Beggars of Life

I CLIMBED INTO AN empty gondola that had been used to carry coal, and the black dust was still in it. The trap-doors were open at the bottom, and I could see the road-bed below.

A weariness was on me, and I longed for a quiet harbor away from the jangle and hunger of the road. I wondered where I could get a coat to fit me. The subject of the coat fascinated me, and then my mind became braver, and dreamed of a whole suit.

A gust of wind came along and lifted my hat and carried it straight to the open trap-door. It rolled beneath the train.

Unmindful of the loss, I walked to the end of the car and dozed in the sun.

A rattling and bumping of the cars awoke me at a little town called Bryon. The sun was straight above me, and I decided to leave the train and hunt some dinner.

New switches were being installed along the road. The camp of a grading outfit was a few hundred yards away. Many mules stood about near the camp. Unhitched from the scrapers, they were enjoying the noon-day rest.

I walked straight for the camp and asked for something to eat. A round-shouldered man heard my request and seated me at a table around which the workmen were still gathered.

They stopped talking long enough to greet me, and placed the food near my reach.

The round-shouldered man had a head shaped like a canal boat. He had a long nose, very small ears, and eyes a washed-out blue. His suspender kept slipping off his round shoulder, and he seemed to be occupied half the time in putting it in place with his thumb.

While I was eating he asked, "Would you like to go to work, Kid?"

I thought of the new coat and answered, "Sure, what'll you gimme a day?"

"A dollar and your board," was the answer.

"All right. I'll take it."

When the noon hour was over, I was taken to a small team of mules that were already harnessed. I drove them to the grade, where a man hitched them to an iron instrument used to carry dirt from one point to another. This instrument was filled at one point and unloaded at another, so that my work consisted in driving the mules ten hours each day. The team could have almost made the trip without a driver, as I often held the lines an hour at a time without speaking to them.

When six o'clock came the first night, I ate a light supper from the tin dishes on the pine table, and dragged myself to bed.

The beds were old mattresses thrown upon the ground. Some of the men had wooden boxes near them. There were none of the ordinary necessities of civilized life. Neither tooth powder nor brush could be seen.

All used the same comb and towel. They washed in basins which were placed on a long wooden bench. As they dipped the water to their faces with cup-shaped hands, they would make loud spluttering noises.

None of the men had home ties, or anything to look forward to when the long grind of labor was over. The men talked of fine women as though they were far-off things, and not of this earth. Like most men, they idealized women too much. I did not learn until years later that both men and women were about the same either at the top or the bottom of society. But those poor devils have probably never learned it.

The fellow is always in demand who can talk about women among men on the ragged edge of life. The poor sentimentalists in the grading camp listened to stories about women told by the round-shouldered man, whose suspender would slip from his shoulder as he talked. They seemed to believe all the stories he told, as they believed the stories of the harlots who robbed them in an hour of the money they had earned by months of torturous labor.

On the third day, my body ached until I could hardly drag one foot after the other. My forehead was hot as I touched it. The team danced before my eyes as the trees had along the river.

The men were aroused each morning by the beating of a railroad spike upon a piece of iron hung from the branch of a tree near the kitchen.

When it rang the fourth morning, I clambered from my mattress on the ground, and fell dizzily back into it again.

The rest of the men answered the call to breakfast while I remained in bed. The round-shouldered man came in to see me. He looked to be twice as tall, and his shoulders were as broad as his length. My throbbing brain made my eyes flicker and caused the man to dance wildly before me. When he adjusted his suspender, his thumb seemed three feet long, and the suspender resembled the tug on a giant horse's harness.

He said, "Ain't shammin', are you, Kid? You'll be all right by noon," and danced out of the tent.

I dreamed feverishly till noon. I was an Irish general shot to death by the English and dying alone in my camp. I was a poet who recited many verses aloud.

Riding the Rods

As the trains thundered by, all the hoboes I knew waved wildly at me, and danced, a ragged crowd of madmen on top of the cars. I saw the top of a bridge dash their heads from the train. They still danced, ragged and headless, with immense eyes gazing fixedly from the centers of their breasts.

The round-shouldered man came at noon and at evening. He was convinced that I was not shamming the next day, so he gave me two dollars and told me to go to a doctor. Though scarcely able to stand, I managed to crawl to the man of medicine.

He gave me medicine, and talked of typhoid fever tactfully. I got his meaning. The round-shouldered man gave me another dollar, and I still had fifty cents left. Without bidding anyone good-bye, I boarded a freight for Chicago.

I craved water on top of the hot train. My throat burned and my jaws ached. My head was in a vise, and spikes were being driven through it. I screamed with pain. But the train rattled on through the hot day. My head whirled, and the train seemed to run in a wild circle. I became dizzy, and saw rainbows through which clear water gurgled. I reached for water, and grabbed but empty space.

Determined to leave the train and get a drink, I climbed down the iron ladder, each rung of which was as hot, burning steel.

Only one thing saved me jumping to my death—the train shrieked for a point called Davis Junction and slowed up ever so little. I did not know it then, nor did I stop to consider the speed of the train. I jumped, and rolled on the ground. How long I lay there I do not know. I found a saloon near the track. How—I know not. I thought about a new coat that dripped with water. I drank a large quantity of it in the saloon.

It nauseated me. The day wore on in blistering sun-scorched hours.

Burning with fever, I was thankful when the sun went down and the heat had subsided.

I still dreamed of the new coat, though my feet were on the ground, and my toes showed through the worn-out upper leather.

JAMES LEO HERLIHY

Midnight Cowboy

PASSING THE 8TH STREET Nedick's in Greenwich Village, he found a pair of large brown eyes looking at him from behind a coffee mug at the window counter.

Seeing Joe, Ratso closed his eyes quickly and remained as motionless as a person praying for invisibility.

But Joe, having wandered homeless and a stranger for three weeks, a long time by the clocks of limbo, was thrilled to see a face that was known to him. His whole being stopped short, accustoming itself to this keen, unexpected pleasure, and it took more than a moment to remember that Ratso Rizzo was an enemy. Joe went straight for the door and entered the place.

When Joe's hand landed on his shoulder, Ratso trembled, shriveling even farther into himself. "Don't hit me," he said, "I'm a cripple."

"Oh, I ain't gonna *hit* you," Joe said. "I'm gonna strangle you to death." The anger in his voice was the anger of an actor, for so acute had been his pleasure at seeing someone he knew, it would not leave him entirely. "Only first, I want you to turn your pockets inside out for me. Go ahead, start with that one."

Ratso complied without a whimper. The search yielded:

> 64 cents
> 2 1/2 sticks of Dentyne chewing gum
> 7 Raleigh's cork-tips, crushed flat
> 1 book of matches
> 2 pawn tickets

"What's in your sock?" Joe asked, remembering to snarl.

"Not a cent, I swear to God." Ratso raised his right hand and cast a quick glance toward heaven. "I swear on my mother's eyes.

"If I found out you was holdin' out on me," Joe said, "I'd kill you quick as look at you." He pushed the contents of the pockets across the counter toward Ratso. "Here, take this shee-it, I don't want it."

"You keep the sixty-four cents, Joe. Go 'head, it's yours, I want you to have it."

"Agh, them nickels is all sticky, what you do, slobber on 'em. I don't want to touch 'em. Put 'em back in your pocket."

At this point, having nothing to gain, Joe felt he should walk away from the filthy little rat altogether. But somehow he couldn't get his feet in motion. He was in a new quandary: Reason told him he was in the presence of an archenemy, and yet he had no appetite whatever for vengeance. Too much time alone had done something peculiar to his heart: A confused and unreliable organ at best, it now held something akin to joy.

Ratso was talking rapidly about that first night, saying I swear to God this and I didn't realize that, probably trying to lie his way out of the swindle he'd perpetrated.

Joe said, "You want some free medical advice, you'll shut y'goddam mouth about that night, hear?"

"Okay, right, right, okay!" Rizzo said. "Another subject: Where y'livin'? Y'still at the hotel?"

This question caused Joe to remember something he had been avoiding for days: his black-and-white horsehide suitcase locked up in that hotel room. Clearer than reality, it stood out now in his mind quivering with some quality of life it had never before possessed. At this moment he knew he would never see it again, and all the inappropriate joy he felt at seeing Ratso Rizzo turned suddenly to pain. He had to clench his teeth to keep his face in proper shape, and then he turned and hurried out of that Nedick's and across Sixth Avenue, headed uptown.

As he approached 9th Street, a voice called his name. He turned and found Ratso hurrying toward him, his body gyrating grotesquely with each step and his balance so precarious he seemed to be running the risk of a bad fall. Joe wanted to be alone, but he knew if he increased his pace, the runt would only hurry faster. In his present mood he had no stomach for such a spectacle; he slowed down.

When Ratso caught up with him, Joe said, "Listen, piss-ant, keep away from me. Now I mean it."

"Where you staying, Joe? You got a place?"

"You hear what I tole you?"

" 'Cause I have. I got a place."

"I mean it, Ratso. I ain't just talking. You come near me again, I'm gonna snatch you ball-headed."

"I'm inviting you, goddammit," said Ratso. "I mean I'm *inviting* you."

"You inviting shee-it."

"I *am*."

"Where is it?"

"Come on, I'll show you already."

They started to walk uptown together. Joe said, "I don't want to stay with you. You think I'm soft in the brain, stay with you?"

Ratso paid no attention to these protests. "It's got no heat," he said, "but by the time cold weather comes, I'll be in Florida. So what do I care, right?"

"I'd have to be out of my goddam mind," Joe said. "You'd sell the teeth right out o' my head while I'ze sleepin'."

"Actually, I don't have no beds either. But I got enough blankets to smother a horse."

'That how you gonna do it, eh, you crooked little turd? Smother me to death? Just you try it."

"An' I don't bother with no electric. To hell with it, I got candles. Right?"

Bit by bit, Joe began to understand Ratso's living conditions.

In New York there are always a large number of tenement buildings being emptied for eventual demolition. One by one the families are moved out, and as they leave, the owner, a great corporation, has a large white X taped across each window of the evacuated space. Ratso had been living in a series of these X-flats—as he called them—since he'd left home at the age of sixteen. In need of a place, he would walk the streets in search of a building on whose windows these white X's had begun to appear. Sometimes he had to break a lock, but more often the door had been left wide open. And occasionally he would even find that the departing tenant had left behind a few sticks of furniture for him. He would move his own meager belongings into the place and use it as his home until the management became aware of his presence, or until the last legitimate tenant had left and the water had been turned off.

His current dwelling was in a largely Puerto Rican block in the West Twenties. He took Joe there, led him up two flights of stairs to an otherwise vacant floor and down the hall to a little flat in the rear.

The late afternoon sun still gave some light to the room, and Joe found the place more welcoming than anything he'd slept in in weeks. Ratso's only furniture was a table and chair, but he had enough blankets to supply a rooming house. Joe's eyes were drawn to a thick stack of them in one corner near the window: every kind of blanket imaginable, comforters, quilts, army blankets, Indian blankets, all spread out neatly on the floor, making a good soft bed.

Ratso was eager to demonstrate the graces of his situation. He offered Joe a chair and then set to work with a saucepan of water and some canned heat to brew up powdered coffee for his guest. Joe headed for the chair but walked right past it and lowered himself onto the bed of blankets. He started mumbling something about how hard it was, but before he got the sentence out he had fallen into a deep dreamless sleep.

Some hours later, he awakened lost. He knew himself to be lying face to the wall in a strange, nearly dark room where a candle flame cast weird shadows on the walls and ceiling. But where? He turned slowly and found himself on a makeshift bed on the floor. Next to him, clad in corduroys, was a pair of poorly matched legs that he began to recognize.

Ratso was sitting there in the candlelight leaning against the wall, smoking, examining Joe's radio.

Joe sat up and snatched the radio from him. He turned it on to make certain it was undamaged. Then he switched it off again and held it close to his body.

"Where's my boots?" he said.

They were under the table. Ratso pointed at them.

"How'd they get off me?"

"I *took* 'em off ya."

Joe looked at the boots again, and then at Ratso. "What for?"

"So's you could sleep is all. I mean, *cripes!*"

Joe got to his feet and went to the table where his boots were. "I believe the smart thing for me is haul ass out of here." He sat on a chair and began pulling on the boots.

"Why? Why why why?" Ratso said. "What'sa matta?"

Joe held one of the boots between his forefinger and thumb, swinging it back and forth slowly, and in a sense he held Ratso in a similar fashion with his eyes. It was as if he were weighing one thing against the other.

Ratso was a thief, Joe thought, and only dangerous if you had something worth stealing. Now if he were to spend the night here, he could put the radio under his pillow—and as for the boots, what good would they be to somebody whose feet were of two different sizes? And what else could the kid be after? He didn't seem to be a fag. Looking at him now, Joe saw nothing more frightening than a puny crippled kid sitting on a pile of old blankets on the floor of a tenement flat afraid of being left alone. So why not stay? He didn't know a reason, but it seemed to him like every time he did something that looked simple, it ended up costing him his ass. Still, it wouldn't hurt to get one good night's sleep. But first he would scare hell out of the little sonofabitch on general principles.

Joe said, "Listen, I'm gonna tell you something, Ratso. Only first gimme cigarette."

Ratso gave him one of the crushed Raleighs and held the candle for him to light it with.

Riding the Rods

Then Joe looked squarely at Ratso and said: "It's this I want to tell you. For your own good. Now, um, you want me to stay here tonight, is that the idea?"

Ratso shrugged. "I ain't forcing you. I mean, like, you know, I ain't *forcing* you." His voice was lacking in conviction, and when he shrugged to demonstrate the quality of his indifference, his shoulders hardly moved at all. Joe knew that in spite of his actual words Ratso was pleading with him to stay, but still he felt the need to assert his control over the situation.

"Oh. Oh, I see." He put his foot inside his boot. "Hell, I had the 'pression you wanted me to stay here with you. But, uh, seems like I had the wrong 'pression."

"All right, I do," Ratso growled. "I want you to stay, you're invited. I tole you that already."

"You know what you're in for?"

"What?"

"If I stay? 'Cause I'm a very dangerous person, you didn't know that, did you? About all I think of is ways to kill people." He studied Ratso's face for a reaction. Ratso simply looked at him, betraying nothing. Joe continued: "It's a truth. Somebody does me bad like you done, all I do is think up ways to kill 'em. So now you been warned. Y'hear me, Ratso?"

"I hear you."

"You don't say that like you mean it. Maybe I better 'press you further."

"All right, I'm impressed already! You're dangerous, you're a killer!"

Joe nodded. "You goddam well better believe it." After a moment, he added, "So if you still want me to stay here for a day or two—I mean, is that what you want? or not?

Ratso frowned and growled, *"Yeah! Goddammit!"*

Joe held up his hand, satisfied. "Easy, easy." He dropped the boot and moved toward the pile of blankets. "Just want to be sure is all. 'Cause I'm not takin' any favors off anybody. Can't afford it."

When he was back on the blankets again, he looked around the place, accustoming himself to his new whereabouts. They smoked in silence for a moment. Then Ratso said, "You ever kill anybody?"

"Not yet," Joe said. "But I tore up this one fella something awful." He told the story of the night he gave Perry a beating in the whorehouse of Juanita Barefoot. "I couldn't control m'self. I get mad, I don't know m'own strength. If they had'en pull me off, that sombitch be a goner today. Same with you. I come after you with a knife that night. You didn't know that, did you? I'ze all set to use it, too." He stopped for a moment, thinking of a way to enrich the tale. "I spent the whole night in jail. It had'n been for them cops, they'd be one dead Ratso along about now."

"Ha! You think I'd mind that?"

"So," Joe went on, "ever' time you pass a cop f'm now on—you blow him a kiss, hear?"

He put out his cigarette on a jar lid Ratso maintained for this purpose.

"And while you're at it, Ratso," he said, lying down, "move the hell over. Y'crowdin' me."

Ratso moved over as far as he could, and then he said, "Joe?"

"Yeah?"

"In my own place, do me a favor, will you?"

"Nope. No favors. I ain't doin' no favors."

"No, I mean look, in my own goddam place—this is my place, am I wrong?"

"My favor days is all over," Joe said.

"Well, it's just, in my own goddam place, my name is not Ratso. You know? I mean it so happens my name is Enrico Salvatore. Enrico Salvatore Rizzo."

"Shee-it, man, I can't say all that."

"All right! *Rico* then! At least call me Rico in my own fucking place!"

"Go to sleep," Joe said.

"Okay, though?" the kid persisted.

Joe lifted his head and barked out: "*Rico! Rico! Rico!* Is that enough?" He turned his face to the wall. Then he said, "And keep your meathooks off my radio."

After a moment Ratso said, "Night," in a small, throaty voice. But Joe was far from ready to exchange any such niceties with this person. He pretended to be asleep.

This day in late September marked the beginning of Joe Buck's alliance with Ratso Rizzo. The pair of them became a familiar sight on certain New York streets that fall, the little blond runt, laboring like a broken grasshopper to keep pace with the six-foot tarnished cowboy, the two of them frowning their way through time like children with salt shakers stalking a bird, urgently intent on their task of finding something of worth in the streets of Manhattan.

Ratso chewed his fingernails, consumed all the coffee and tobacco he could get hold of, and lay awake nights frowning and gnawing at his lips. For he was the natural leader of the two, and upon his head rested the responsibility for thinking up new schemes for their survival.

Joe Buck, in the fashion of a follower, simply expressed his across-the-board pessimism about whatever was suggested, and then went along with it. Once, for instance, Ratso heard about a town in Jersey where the parking meters were said to be vulnerable to the common screwdriver. Joe Buck was skeptical and said so, often, but still he submitted to hocking his radio in order to raise bus fare for the trip across the river. When they got there it became clear at once that Ratso's information was out of date: the town had all new meters of a make no screwdriver could ever disturb. In the face of such a disappointment, Joe Buck was capable of behaving with magnanimity, at least to the extent of keeping his mouth shut while Ratso made excuses for the failure.

But on the whole this person with the sunburst on his boots remained cranky and disagreeable in his behavior toward the little blond runt. He realized it, too. Joe knew good and well he had become a pain in the neck, and what's more he was none too concerned about it. But there was a reason for his unconcern: He was happy.

For the first time in his life he felt himself released from the necessity of grinning and posturing and yearning for the attention of others. Nowadays he had, in the person of Ratso Rizzo, someone who needed his presence in an urgent, almost frantic way that was a balm to something in him that had long been exposed and enflamed and itching to be soothed. God alone knew how or why, but he had somehow actually stumbled upon a creature who seemed to worship him. Joe Buck had never before known such power and was therefore ill equipped to administer it. All he could do was taste it over and over again like a sugar-starved child on a sudden mountain of candy: cuss and frown and complain and bitch, and watch Ratso take it. For that's the way in which power is usually tasted, in the abuse of it. It was delicious and sickening and he couldn't stop himself. The only thing the runt seemed to demand was the privilege of occupying whatever space he could find in the tall cowboy's shadow. And casting such a shadow had become Joe Buck's special pleasure.

He enjoyed listening to Ratso, too. As they walked through the city, or shared a cup of coffee in a lunch stand or cafeteria, or shivered together in the progressively colder doorways of the waning year, he heard Ratso's views on many subjects. Bit by bit, he was able to piece together a picture of Ratso's early years in the Bronx.

Ratso was the thirteenth child of tired immigrant parents. He remembered his father as a hard-working bricklayer who in his off hours went to sleep whenever he found something even vaguely horizontal to lie upon. His mother, a burnt-out child bearer, usually sick, managed the family like a kindly, befuddled queen, issuing contradictory mandates from her bedroom. Occasionally she would pull a housecoat about her body and move through the flat trying to sort out the confusion she had wrought. On one such tour she found the seven-year-old Ratso under the kitchen stove in an advanced stage of pneumonia. Surviving this, he contracted infantile paralysis a few weeks later, and by the time he was discharged from the hospital the following year his mother was dead and gone. His three sisters and two of his nine brothers had left home, either for marriage or for other purposes. Of the eight remaining boys, none took any interest in cooking or housework; nor had Papa Rizzo ever given any special attention to the running of a family. When he thought of the job at all, it was in terms of supplying food. Therefore once a week he stocked the shelves with saltines and cans of pork and beans, the refrigerator with cheese and cold cuts and milk. For six days the boys would grab what they could, and on the seventh Papa Rizzo gave them a real Sunday dinner at a neighborhood spaghetti place. Occasionally in an earlier time—usually at Easter or on Mother's Day—he had hosted such dinners in this same restaurant, and the owner had always made him feel proud of his enormous brood by calling attention to the fact that he required the biggest table in the place. "*Ecco, che arriva Rizzo!*" he would say. "*Prende la tavola piu grande del locale!*" Even now, with only eight sons left, it was necessary to shove two regular tables together. But after the first month or so, these Sunday dinners were ill-attended, for the old bricklayer had developed a foul temper and took to using them as occasions for scolding and shouting. The boys, one by one, having learned to forage in ways they found easier than listening to the ravings of a disagreeable old man, wandered away from home altogether. Finally one Sunday afternoon at the family dinner there was only Ratso. When the owner led them to a table for two, the old man was shocked, and then embarrassed, and then chastened. He ate in silence, behaving with an almost ceremonial kindness toward the skinny, crippled, thirteen-year-old runt of his progeny. He also drank a good deal of wine, and then there came a moment in which he broke the silence and ended the meal by landing one tremendous wallop of his bare fist on the little formica-covered table, shouting his own name and reminding the world at large, and God, too, that he was accustomed to larger tables than this: "*Sono Rizzo! Io prendo la tavola piu grande del locale!*" The owner came over and the two old men wept together and embraced each other. Then Ratso led his father home. Entering the flat, the old man drew back and let out a dreadful howl. It was as if he had suddenly awakened from the longest of all of his naps and found his family wiped out by bandits and the walls of the flat all splattered with blood. Looking past Ratso as if the boy didn't exist, the bricklayer started to sob, asking over and over again the whereabouts of his sons. "*Dove sono i miei ragazzi terribili?*" Gradually, and perhaps only by default, Ratso became the favorite, and for a while life was better for him than for the others. He was given an allowance and was never scolded. The Sunday dinners continued. There was not much talk at the small table, but a silent intimacy had grown between them and the atmosphere was affectionate and peaceful. Papa Rizzo, by now a fat, benign, baldheaded old bear in his late sixties, drank a quart of Chianti all by himself, and on the way home from the restaurant he would find a number of opportunities to place his hand upon the head of his last remaining son, or, waiting for a traffic light, to wrap a heavy arm around his shoulder. On one such afternoon of a summer Sunday, Ratso was undermined by the great burden of weight his father placed upon him, and they both fell to the sidewalk. When Ratso was able to disengage himself, he found that the old man had died on him, right there in the crowded sunlight of the Bronx River Parkway.

From then on, Ratso was on his own. He was sixteen, with no special training for life. But he did have a quick natural intelligence, and, like most persons raised in large families, he was a good, fast liar. With these assets, he took to the streets.

Ratso could talk about the Bronx, and he could talk about Manhattan, and he could talk about nearly anything under the sun. But his best subject was Florida, and though he had never been there, he spoke more positively and with greater authority on this topic than on any other. He often studied folders in color put out by transportation companies or perused a stack of travel clippings collected from newspapers; he also owned a book called *Florida and the Caribbean.* In this splendid place (he claimed) the two basic items necessary for the sustenance of life—sunshine and coconut milk— were in such abundance that the only problem was in coping with their excess. For all that sunshine you needed wide-brimmed hats, special glasses and creams. As for coconuts, there were so many of these lying about in the streets that each Florida town had to commission great fleets of giant trucks to gather them up just so traffic could get through. And of course coconuts were the one complete food: This was common knowledge. Anytime you got hungry, all you had to do was pick one up and stab it with a pocketknife, and then hold it up to your mouth. Ratso was unable to tell about this without demonstrating with an invisible coconut. "Here your only problem is," he would say to Joe, sucking at the air between phrases, "—you want to know what your only problem is here, diet-wise? It's the warm milk running down your face and neck. Yeah, sometimes you got to exert yourself, you got to reach up and wipe off your chin. Tough, huh? You think you could stand that? I could. I could stand it." As for fishing, he made this sound so simple Joe actually got the impression you didn't need a rod and reel or even a pole. Without examining the picture too carefully for probability, he had formed a kind of cartoon image of the two of them standing near the water saying *here fishy-fishy*, at which point a pair of enormous finned creatures would jump into their arms precooked. A silly, happy thought, and he could smell the fish plain as day. Sometimes to keep this pleasant discussion going, Joe might feed a question: "But shee-it man, where in hell would you sleep? They got no X-flats down there, you can bet your smart ass on that." But Ratso had an answer for everything. At this cue he would begin to tell of the endless miles of public beaches on which had been built hundreds of pagodas and pergolas and gazebos; under these, on sun-warmed sand or softly padded benches, protected from rain and wind, one slept the sleep of Eden.

Most often under discussion, however, was the subject of their financial problem. Ratso was inclined to belittle any so-called honest solution. Neither of them was sufficiently presentable to get a job that would pay them at a worthwhile rate, nor had either of them been trained for such work. Besides, any course of action involving fulltime employment did not seem worthy of being called a solution; such talk Ratso considered frivolous and had no patience with. Of course, living by one's wits was just as problematical in its own way as legitimate work: Competition was overwhelming, one had constantly to be on the lookout for a new angle and, finding one, to be ready for its sudden obsolescence. ("For example, them goddam parking meters; right?") As for Joe Buck's earning potential, it was Ratso's considered opinion that he had not a hope in hell of making a living from women. Such a profession was extremely specialized, requiring a wardrobe, polish, and a front. The cowboy gambit wouldn't work on New York women. Not only was this costume an almost purely homosexual lure, it was severely specialized even within that group, attracting to it almost exclusively a very small masochistic element. ("Never mind *what* that is, you wouldn't believe it if I told you.") Sometimes, against his own better judgment, but in an extremity of hunger, he would arrange for Joe a fast five- or ten-dollar transaction in which little more was required of the cowboy than standing still for a few minutes with his trousers undone. But these unhappy conjunctions usually left Joe in a depressed and disturbed state of mind. He felt as though something invisible and dangerous had been exchanged, something that was neither stated in the bargain nor understood by either of the parties to it, and it left him sad and perplexed and with an anger he couldn't find any reasonable place for. Ratso agreed this was a poor way to earn a dollar. He claimed that prostitution had always been the hardest profession in the world as well as the most competitive—and even worse in today's world, where the commodity was being given away free in such liberal quantities. The only way to do really well at it was to rob the patron, but this required an adroitness and a sense of timing Ratso felt was lacking in his cowboy friend, and he did not encourage him to enter this extension of the market. Ratso did credit himself with the needed wit and cunning for it, but his chances of success were severely limited by the condition of his leg. ("Now you take your average fag: Very few of 'em want a cripple.")

Ratso had a specialty better suited to him: He was a pickpocket. But he wasn't very good at it. Too often he would be caught in the act by someone twice his size who could have hauled him off to a policeman with no trouble at all, and Ratso would then have to undergo the indignity of pleading for mercy on the basis of his crippled leg. He was more skilled at a variation of this form of theft, but this variation required a greater investment of time and was apt to be less lucrative as well: He would sit in a bar and strike up a conversation with a stranger, then watch for the moment at which he could steal the person's money. Sometimes he would lose up to an hour and come away with nothing more than a little change in his pocket and a beer or two under his belt.

Joe was disgusted by this kind of operation ("Makes me *puke!*") and would have nothing to do with the gains from it. Ratso would have to invent some cock-and-bull story to explain this kind of money, otherwise Joe would refuse to swallow so much as a hamburger purchased with it and would go around for days with a face as long as time.

But Joe was still in the first flush of his friendship with Ratso Rizzo, and during these weeks nothing that happened seemed quite so terrible to him as the prospect of being once again a totally alone person. Even though he had stepped free of those lone years and had entered upon this new time, they still existed somewhere, shadowing even the present like some creature of nightmares, black and ruthless and many-armed, ready to snatch him back into more and more and more solitude.

Riding the Rods

NELSON PEERY

Black Fire

"WHERE'S THAT MOTHERFUCKER?" His hand slid to his knife.

"Down in the yards. I knocked him out—kicked him. He's gonna try to kill me sure. Let me use your knife, Ace. He comes to, he'll kill me."

"We can't have no killin' here. That's all the cops want. We just have to run him off."

I stumbled to my shack, got the razor open, and fell asleep.

The next morning, Big John came into the jungle, the side of his face one big bloody abrasion. His parted swollen lips showed blood on his teeth.

"What you sayin'?" he greeted Ace.

"Get." Ace pulled his knife. "I don't want no rotten son of a bitch like you in this part. Now get."

John reached to his belt where he kept the razor. West Coast moved toward him. Ace shoved his knife to Big John's belly.

"Don't get no crazy ideas, ya low-down bastard. I'm countin' to three. If you ain't gone—you gonna stay."

West Coast moved closer.

"We don't want no wolves here, you rotten motherfucker. I knowed what you was up to all the time."

Big John was trembling. He narrowed his eyes at me. I knew that if we met again, one of us would die. I cursed myself for not having bought a knife. Big John turned and walked toward the yard. For a moment Ace watched him leave, then turned to me.

"I oughta slap your ass clean back to Minnesota."

"Thanks, Ace."

"Thank the Lord."

"Anybody can act a damn fool once," West Coast said. "You got to pay for your learnin'. You done paid. From now on don't never drink with no one person. If anybody tries to be so Goddamn sweet to you—take care."

I had to have a weapon. I looked over all the knives at the hardware store and bought an oversized linoleum knife. It handled easier than a dagger and could slash better.

The following week, Ace called the group together. We assembled around the food barrel. Ace stood up, concern and anxiety etched in his face.

"There's something you mens ought to know. I was talking to the boss up at the commissary. He told me that a dick by the name of Red Anderson been trans-ferred from the Southern Pacific up to here to clean the place up. Me and West Coast, we know this fuckin' guy from way back. He used to sit on the coal tender with a .30-06. When the train makes the hairpin curve crossin' the Sabine into Texas, he could look into and between every car. He'd shoot the bums off the train, or force 'em to jump into the gorge. Don't know how many he kilt."

"What must we do, Ace?"

"I don't rightly know. I suspect we just keep doin' what we doin' until somethin' happens."

"Jesus Christ," I mumbled, "this must be the dick I heard about in Kansas. Hear about him all over the country. He must be a killer."

It happened two days later. Four city cops with rifles, a fire engine with six firemen, and the new dick came to the jungle. The cops rounded us up and read the vagrancy law to us. Each of us had the necessary ten dollars. They couldn't arrest us. The firemen told us our shacks were a menace to public health. They gave us ten minutes to get out. I stuffed my belongings into the gunny-sack. It was fuller now than ever. The firemen doused the shacks with kerosene and set them on fire. I glanced over at the new dick. He was a red-neck if ever I saw one. The broad-rimmed, sweat-soaked felt hat shaded the perpetual scowl on his ruddy face. The warts on his neck stood out. Heavyset, with huge, thick hands, all he needed was a whip to become a picture of the driver man.

The shacks burned quickly. As we turned toward the skid row, Big Red walked over to Ace. "Listen, old niggah—I want you to stay outa here. I know all about your racket at the commissary. You lazy niggers try to live off the fat of the land. If I catch you on Great Northern territory, I'll kill you. You under-stand that?"

Ace glared back into the white man's eyes. "Fuck you, white man. I'm on city property—you ain't gonna kill nobody."

The jaw muscles trembled in Ace's black face. West Coast had tears of rage in his eyes. A feeling of rapport and unity swept through the hoboes. Red felt it too. He didn't reach for his gun.

"I ain't warnin' you no more." He turned and walked toward the com-missary. We watched until he was out of earshot.

"That white son of a bitch."

"Somebody ought to kill that bastard."

"I gets a chance, somebody will."

"What the hell we gonna do now, Ace?"

"I ain't sure. Looks like we better get. You can kill Red, but you can't kill Big G. They'd get somebody else."

Riding the Rods

We began to drift by ones and twos toward the end of the yard. We had to leave the city. Red wasn't playing and I knew he was a killer.

I heard there was work in San Francisco. It was the middle of September. If I couldn't find a job soon, I would have to decide to head back east or stay on this side of the Divide until spring. Until darkness would hide me, I waited for the evening freight in a dime-dinger, the ten-cent skid row movie.

The freight for Stockton was pulling out at 10:30. By walking slowly I could make the yards just in time and wouldn't take a chance on meeting Big Red.

The train hadn't made up. I climbed into a boxcar to wait. Both doors were open. As I began to close them, I saw Ace and West Coast four or five cars down from me. I saw someone else too. Red climbed between two cars. I started to yell a warning. Ace saw him too. West Coast turned to run between the cars. Ace stood there, refusing to run, giving West Coast a chance to get away.

It was a chilly, windy, cloudy night. The clouds raced beneath the moon and intermittently the scene was in darkness and then in the light of the bright September moon. West Coast stood hiding between two cars. He wasn't going to leave Ace. Red saw Ace, and his cold rasping white man's voice broke the night. "Halt! Heh—caught ya, huh?"

Ace didn't answer. Big Red's voice cut the night. "Put up your hands, nigger." Red pressed the gun against his chest.

"Bustin' into boxcars, huh?"

Ace raised his hands slowly. Red drew back his fist and, grunting with the effort, hit him in the face. Ace stumbled back against the tracks and fell.

"Get up, you old black bastard."

Holding his jaw, he got to his feet and raised his hands again. Big Red moved toward Ace, the blackjack dangling from his hand. West Coast swung from between the cars, the bowie knife dull in the moonlight. With the sixth sense of a cop, Red crouched and began to turn toward the danger. By crouching, the blow intended for his heart caught Red in the base of the skull. The blade crashed through and protruded from his mouth. Even in death, Red struggled for balance and then lunged headlong across the tracks. West Coast turned to steady Ace. I jumped from the car, wanting to run away. I couldn't leave Ace.

"Come on, Ace."

West Coast shoved me back.

"Get gone, boy. Hurry."

I glanced down at Big Red. I had never seen a man killed before. I had never seen a dead person except in a casket. The point of the knife jutted from the open mouth. The mean, brutal brains oozed from the other end. West Coast shoved me again.

"Go ahead, boy. Hurry."

The scene sank into my consciousness. A white man was dead. I saw it happen. I turned and ran in one direction; Ace and West Coast went the other way. The bright light of an engine shone down the eight-track right-of-way. In the dark it was impossible to tell which track the train was on. I crouched until the engine passed me. It was a fast rattler, an all-steel refrigerated train that ran the fruits and vegetables to Walla Walla. The topside catwalk was a part of the car and impossible to hold on to. The rear and side ladders were indented steps and impossible to hold. Between the cars was enough room for a man to stand on the coupling and hold on to two iron bars. The train, gathering speed, jerked me off the ground. The noise was deafening. The engine highballed its good-bye to Seattle.

MAGGIE ESTEP

Diary of an Emotional Idiot

DIRECTLY DOWNSTAIRS FROM ME lives Lonette, a woman with the lung power of Pavarotti. Every day, I hear her shouting at her kids, "You stupid idiots, get in the motherfucking house and shut up." The kids in turn call each other motherfucker in higher octaves. The seven-year-old calls the two-year-old motherfucker and the two-year-old runs down the hallway naked, smeared in dirt and yelling, "Motherfucker, motherfucker, motherfucker," in his soprano squeak.

A while back, after Jim the Painter but before the two loves that have brought me to you bleating and yelping, I had a boyfriend named Edgar. Edgar always said white people didn't say motherfucker right. White people, Edgar said, said "Motherrfuck-er" in a way that conveyed nothing but pure whiteness. He tried to teach me to say it right. I don't. I can't. I'm white.

Lonette, the lady downstairs, says it right and says it loud. So do her kids. Theirs is not a subtle familial love. But it is love.

When the mailman comes, Lonette sashays into the hall to watch him distribute the mail. She wears a large T-shirt that partially covers the way her fake designer jeans define each cheek of her ass. I hear her fifty-cent flip-flops whip the hallway floor as she goes to glare at the mailman. She doesn't trust him. I don't either. In fact, I like to think of the mailman as a vicious cyborg. He will kill us all if we're not careful.

The mailman has tiny rust-colored eyes and a doughy undefined face flecked with large freckles. He has a robotic way of flipping letters into each of the twenty-four slots for the twenty-four apartments in our building. He does not respond to my saying hello. He does not respond to anyone saying hello. When Lonette's kids say, "Hi, motherfuckin' mailman," he just looks right through them.

When I haven't had enough sleep, which is most of the time, I start to see the mailman as a product of the kind of government experiment we like to pretend doesn't exist. The mailman is a cantankerous cyborg and my taxes are paying for him.

Lonette doesn't pay taxes. She's on welfare and she gives blow jobs for ten dollars. This I know because she has sung it in a fevered contralto to her two-year-old son, Ralphie: "Motherfucker, I'm out there sucking dick for ten dollars and you gotta go and make noise when I come home? What the fuck is wrong with you, Ralphie? Shut up and get in the house."

Once in a while, Lonette gets a letter from a guy who lives in Montreal and this, I discovered, is what keeps her going. She cornered me by the mailbox one day. "Girl," she said, "did you get any of my mail in your box? I'm looking for my letter. I know that motherfuckin' mailman put it in the wrong box. Girl, look and see if you didn't get it." I hadn't. In my box were just the usual bills and threats. There are plenty of these right now. My current job is as a part-time receptionist at a dungeon. I take orders from a formidable dominatrix named Belle. I am not sufficiently versed in sadism to become an actual dominatrix but have enough of a fondness for it to answer a dungeon's phones.

The guy in Montreal is the father of at least one of Lonette's kids. I heard her telling this to Daisy, the stripper who lives upstairs. Lonette and Daisy frequently have voluble heart-to-hearts while standing in the stairwell a few feet away from my own door. Daisy and Lonette are my personal soap opera.

One day, Daisy told Lonette she was thinking about leaving New York. "I'm gettin' sick of this shithole, you know? I pay a fucking thousand dollars to live in cockroach soup, you know?"

"You pay a thousand dollars?" Lonette said.

"Yeah, a fucking thousand dollars, and the other night I'm making tomato soup and I go to stir it and there's fucking not one but THREE roaches in my soup."

"Girl, you're stupid, you paying too much rent. Last person lived in your apartment paid like seventy-five dollars or something. Old white guy. Had him a rabbit. Guy was a mothahfucken freak. But he didn't pay no thousand dollars."

"Yeah, well, what am I gonna do? You wanna tell me that? I mean this shit's better than *Florida*, you know?"

"I ain't been to Florida, but shit, they got sunshine there, right?"

"Yeah, sunshine. That doesn't do me any good. Gimme skin cancer. Make my fucking face fall off. Florida sucked. The only place to dance was this bar called Rudy's Booty. Nobody with teeth went in that place. I'd be dancing my fucking FACE off for these ninety-year-old guys that just grinned gums at me. No fun, right? Then I come up here but it's unreal, there's all these nineteen-year-olds with tits that stand up and say hello, and like I can't compete with that, so then I end up dancing out in fucking QUEENS and shit, like I get stuck with the day shift in QUEENS. I mean, what kind of shit is that?"

"Yeah, I hear you," Lonette said then, "but that ain't as bad as me. I'm in love with a guy that's got no ass and he lives in Montreal. He's my son Ralphie's daddy," she said.

This was as much of the exchange as I heard because then Lonette invited Daisy to come in and smoke a joint. I heard the metronomic clicking of Daisy's fuck-me pumps as she teetered into Lonette's hovel.

I am not, as I may have conveyed, a complete eavesdropping loner. I do have friends. I do have a lover: The Reader. This moniker because, the second time we slept together, right after we had had rigorous and delicious sex, I grabbed a book I was reading, showed it to The Reader, and asked, "Have you read this?" At which he flapped his beautiful blue eyes and said, "How would you feel if I told you I never read?" Not terribly surprised, I thought. But what I said was, "Oh, that's okay. I guess a lot of people don't read." When I relayed this to my closest friend, Jane, she said, "Ah, well, now we know what to call him. He is The Reader."

The Reader is physically beautiful but emotionally stunted, which is about all I can handle at this juncture. He is twenty-five and he is from a small town in Washington. His mother works in a candy store and, once a month, sends The Reader packages of candy. The Reader is a drummer. I am a bass player. I am a terrible bass player. In spite of this, I was briefly in a band that made money. It was a fluke, though. The Reader is a good drummer. All the same, he earns most of his living working as a busboy. The Reader is my lover. He is not really a friend. I have friends for that.

This might be a good moment to confess that I have literary ambitions. I write fuck books. Sort of high-minded porn. Occasionally, I even write poetry. About my neighbors. "The Decline of Eye Guy" is one I am working on. Eye Guy is the speed freak in the apartment directly next door to me. He lives with his girlfriend. Although her eyes don't bulge the way Eye Guy's do, for facility's sake, I call her Eye Girl. Eye Girl is very moody. She is always zooted up on some really foul combination of uppers and downers and Rollerblading. Her bouts of Rollerblading seem to coincide with fights with Eye Guy. I hear them scream at each other, and next thing, Eye Girl is on Rollerblades and making her way down the stairs. Eye Girl is friends with Lonette and Daisy. On good days, she sticks her head out the door of her and Eye Guy's apartment and screams: "LONETTE, GET YOUR UGLY ASS UP HERE AND GIVE ME FIVE DOLLARS, MY CHECK FROM MY MOTHER DIDN'T COME."

On bad days, she walks downstairs, bangs on Lonette's door, and says, "You fucking junkie cunt, open the fucking door right now."

I am not sure why Lonette, a welfare mother, gives Eye Girl, a trashy twentyish white girl, money. I don't think I want to understand that particular economy.

One day, the Cyborg Mailman did in fact put Lonette's letter from Montreal into the wrong box. The Cyborg Mailman put the letter from Montreal into the Heavy Metal Guitarist Upstairs's box.

I heard the very polite Japanese fashion students from upstairs standing in the stairwell telling it to Daisy the Stripper.

"Yes," the Japanese students were saying, "the man who play White Zombie over and over, that man he was very drunk and he defecate in hallway."

"Oh God, that's REALLY gross," Daisy said.

"Yes, and then he set fire to couch and firemen come and lady from downstairs came up to see what commotion was and see a letter for her is in apartment of Heavy Metal Guitarist and there is shit on letter."

"Oh my God. He SHIT on one of her precious letters from Montreal?" Daisy's voice rose an octave.

"Yes," the students said in unison. They are a boy and a girl and they often talk at the same time, as if they were the same person. As if they were Japanese Siamese Twin Fashion Students.

At this point I went out into the hall, said hello to Daisy, and nodded at the Japanese Siamese Twins. They nodded back in unison.

"You heard about how Mikey shit in the hall and set his couch on fire?" Daisy asked me then.

"Yeah, well, I just overheard you talking about it. That guy's nuts, man."

The Japanese Siamese Twins giggled.

"Oh, Mikey's not nuts, he's just drunk. I used to date him," Daisy said then.

"You did?" The twins and I in unison.

"Yeah, for two weeks. We were like sort of in love, but then he went on a bender and got like this HEAD WOUND from passing out at the Bronx Zoo because he gets drunk and he likes to go look at pandas and then he got too drunk and fell over and like crashed into some lady's wheelchair and hurt his head and then he broke up with me." She said it like it happens every day. Every day a guy drunkenly swoons for pandas and every day a guy gets a head wound and breaks up with a stripper who danced for toothless men in the Everglades.

Just as Daisy was nonchalantly relaying this detail of her lurid love life, Lonette emerged from her apartment. She was dragging two-year-old Ralphie by the arm. "Motherfucker, you're coming to the store with me," she was saying. Then she noticed all of us standing there and, at that very moment, the Cyborg Mailman came in and all hell broke loose.

The Cyborg Mailman saw us all standing there, but still he ignored us.

Lonette drew herself up to her full height and said, "MOTHER-FUCKER, YOU PUT MY MOTHERFUCKIN' LETTER IN FUCKIN' DRUNK MIKEY'S BOX AND HE FUCKIN' SHIT ON MY LETTER."

The mailman didn't say anything. He began to open up the mailboxes but he was shaken. You could see it. His eyes darted nervously.

"MOTHERFUCKER," Lonette wailed, "I'M TALKING TO YOU. LOOK AT ME WHEN I'M TALKING TO YOU."

"Please don't raise your voice at me," the mailman said then.

"DON'T RAISE MY VOICE? WHAT ABOUT DON'T PUT MY LETTER IN THE WRONG BOX, WHAT ABOUT THAT?"

"Listen, lady, I'm sorry, I'm only human."

"No you're not," Lonette said then, "you're like a fuckin' robot, and shit, you're like the terminator of mailmen. Used to be we had us a nice mailman, now we got you, fuckin' T2, man."

I couldn't believe it. Lonette also thought the mailman was a cyborg. I was not alone. She, too, wanted to shake that mailman, drive some heart into his circuitry, make him see how putting the letter from Montreal into Mikey the Heavy Metal Guitarist's box had almost ruined everything, how that letter was what the Lady Downstairs needed, that letter made it all worthwhile, a multitude of dicks to suck and a bunch of kids to yell "motherfucker" at.

And then the Cyborg Mailman melted. First, his hands began to shake uncontrollably, then he actually DROPPED a huge stack of mail. It went fanning out all over the floor as all of us stood dumb-foundedly witnessing the cracking of the cyborg facade. And then he started to cry. His puffy white features mushed together like malevolent cookie dough and tears came out of his rust-colored eyes.

Then he doubled over and wailed out, "I'M SORRY I'M SORRY I'M SORRY."

We were all shocked. Not one of us said a word. It was so uncharacteristic that we didn't have a clue as to what our lines should be.

And then the mailman just turned around and walked back down the greasy hall and out the door. He just left. He left the mailbag and everything. The mailman just walked out of the building.

We never found out what was wrong with him. We talked about it. Everyone did. Daisy and Lonette and the Japanese Siamese Twins and even Mikey the fecally fixated Heavy Metal Guitarist. We all wondered what went wrong. You always hear about mailmen going nuts. Postal psychopaths are perfectly commonplace. But now it had happened to us.

We never saw the Cyborg Mailman again. We have a new mailperson. A woman named Lucy. She is short, Puerto Rican, and loves to talk. She and Lonette talk about the Guy From Canada and how he has no ass. One day the Heavy Metal Guitarist asked Lucy what had happened to the old mailman but Lucy didn't know.

Last week, I came in and saw that Daisy had cornered Lucy the Mail-woman and was pouring her heart out to her: "Yeah, so then I was naked in front of these toothless guys in the Everglades, and they were like grinning GUMS at me and like . . ." she trailed on as Lucy the Mailwoman nodded sympathetically and continued to stick the mail in the slots. Maybe I should confide my heartaches to Lucy the Mailwoman. But I'm not like that. I'd rather tell them to you.

Sylvia Plath

The Bell Jar

JOAN'S ROOM, WITH ITS closet and bureau and table and chair and white blanket with the big blue C on it, was a mirror image of my own. It occurred to me that Joan, hearing where I was, had engaged a room at the asylum on pretense, simply as a joke. That would explain why she had told the nurse I was her friend. I had never known Joan, except at a cool distance.

"How did you get here?" I curled up on Joan's bed.

"I read about you," Joan said.

"What?"

"I read about you, and I ran away."

"How do you mean?" I said evenly.

"Well," Joan leaned back in the chintz-flowered asylum armchair, "I had a summer job working for the chapter head of some fraternity, like the Masons, you know, but not the Masons, and I felt terrible. I had these bunions, I could hardly walk—in the last days I had to wear rubber boots to work, instead of shoes, and you can imagine what *that* did to my morale. . . ."

I thought either Joan must be crazy—wearing rubber boots to work—or she must be trying to see how crazy I was, believing all that. Besides, only old people ever got bunions. I decided to pretend I thought she was crazy, and that I was only humoring her along.

"I always feel lousy without shoes," I said with an ambiguous smile. "Did your feet hurt much?"

"Terribly. And my boss—he'd just separated from his wife, he couldn't come right out and get a divorce, because that wouldn't go with this fraternal order—my boss kept buzzing me in every other minute, and each time I moved my feet hurt like the devil, but the second I'd sit down at my desk again, buzz went the buzzer, and he'd have something else he wanted to get off his chest. . . ."

"Why didn't you quit?"

"Oh, I did quit, more or less. I stayed off work on sick leave. I didn't go out. I didn't see anyone. I stowed the telephone in a drawer and never answered it. . . .

"Then my doctor sent me to a psychiatrist at this big hospital. I had an appointment for twelve o'clock, and I was in an awful state. Finally, at half past twelve, the receptionist came out and told me the doctor had gone to lunch. She asked me if I wanted to wait, and I said yes."

"Did he come back?" The story sounded rather involved for Joan to have made up out of whole cloth, but I led her on, to see what would come of it.

"Oh yes. I was going to kill myself, mind you. I said 'If this doctor doesn't do the trick, that's the end.' Well, the receptionist led me down a long hall, and just as we got to the door she turned to me and said, 'You don't mind if there are a few students with the doctor, will you?' What could I say? 'Oh no,' I said. I walked in and found nine pairs of eyes fixed on me. Nine! Eighteen separate eyes.

"Now, if that receptionist had told me there were going to be nine people in that room, I'd have walked out on the spot. But there I was, and it was too late to do a thing about it. Well, on this particular day I happened to be wearing a fur coat. . . ."

"In August?"

"Oh, it was one of those cold, wet days, and I thought, my first psychiatrist—you know. Anyway, this psychiatrist kept eyeing that fur coat the whole time I talked to him, and I could just see what he thought of my asking to pay the students' cut rate instead of the full fee. I could see the dollar signs in his eyes. Well, I told him I don't know whatall—about the bunions and the telephone in the drawer and how I wanted to kill myself—and then he asked me to wait outside while he discussed my case with the others, and when he called me back in, you know what he said?"

"What?"

"He folded his hands together and looked at me and said, 'Miss Gilling, we have decided that you would benefit by group therapy.'"

"*Group* therapy?" I thought I must sound phony as an echo chamber, but Joan didn't pay any notice.

"That's what he said. Can you imagine me wanting to kill myself, and coming round to chat about it with a whole pack of strangers, and most of them no better than myself. . . ."

"That's crazy." I was growing involved in spite of myself. "That's not even *human*."

"That's just what I said. I went straight home and wrote that doctor a letter. I wrote him one beautiful letter about how a man like that had no business setting himself up to help sick people. . . ."

"Did you get any answer?"

"I don't know. That was the day I read about you."

"How do you mean?"

"Oh," Joan said, "about how the police thought you were dead and all. I've got a pile of clippings somewhere." She heaved herself up, and I had a strong horsey whiff that made my nostrils prickle. Joan had been a champion horse-jumper at the annual college gymkhana, and I wondered if she had been sleeping in a stable.

Joan rummaged in her open suitcase and came up with a fistful of clippings. "Here, have a look."

The first clipping showed a big, blown-up picture of a girl with black-shadowed eyes and black lips spread in a grin. I couldn't imagine where such a tarty picture had been taken until I noticed the Bloomingdale earrings and the Bloomingdale necklace glinting out of it with bright, white highlights, like imitation stars.

SCHOLARSHIP GIRL MISSING. MOTHER WORRIED.

The article under the picture told how this girl had disappeared from her home on August 17th, wearing a green skirt and a white blouse, and had left a note saying she was taking a long walk. *When Miss Greenwood had not returned by midnight, it said, her mother called the town police.*

The next clipping showed a picture of my mother and brother and me grouped together in our backyard and smiling. I couldn't think who had taken that picture either, until I saw I was wearing dungarees and white sneakers and remembered that was what I wore in my spinach-picking summer, and how Dodo Conway had dropped by and taken some family snaps of the three of us one hot afternoon. *Mrs. Greenwood asked that this picture be printed in hopes that it will encourage her daughter to return home.*

SLEEPING PILLS FEARED MISSING WITH GIRL

A dark, midnight picture of about a dozen moon-faced people in a wood. I thought the people at the end of the row looked queer and unusually short until I realized they were not people, but dogs. *Bloodhounds used in search for missing girl. Police Sgt. Bill Hindly says: It doesn't look good.*

GIRL FOUND ALIVE!

The last picture showed policemen lifting a long, limp blanket roll with a featureless cabbage head into the back of an ambulance. Then it told how my mother had been down in the cellar, doing the week's laundry, when she heard faint groans coming from a disused hole. . . .

I laid the clippings on the white spread of the bed.

"You keep them," Joan said. "You ought to stick them in a scrapbook."

I folded the clippings and slipped them in my pocket.

"I read about you," Joan went on. "Not how they found you, but every-thing up to that, and I put all my money together and took the first plane to New York."

"Why New York?"

"Oh, I thought it would be easier to kill myself in New York."

"What did you do?"

Joan grinned sheepishly and stretched out her hands, palm up. Like a miniature mountain range, large, reddish weals upheaved across the white flesh of her wrists.

"How did you do that?" For the first time it occurred to me Joan and I might have something in common.

"I shoved my fists through my roommate's window."

Nuclear Family Nightmares

"My old college roommate. She was working in New York, and I couldn't think of anyplace else to stay, and besides, I'd hardly any money left, so I went to stay with her. My parents found me there—she'd written them I was acting funny—and my father flew straight down and brought me back."

"But you're all right now." I made it a statement.

Joan considered me with her bright, pebble-gray eyes. "I guess so," she said. "Aren't you?"

HUBERT SELBY JR.

Requiem for a Dream

THE PHONE RANG A second time and Sara Goldfarb leaned toward the phone as she continued to adjust the rabbit ears on her set, torn between the need to know who was calling and to get rid of the lines that darted, from time to time, across the picture, and she ooood as she tensed and squinted, leaning more and more toward the phone as it rang again, one hand reaching for the phone while the tips of the fingers of the other hand continued to tap the antenna over one centimeter at a time. Im coming, Im coming. Dont hang up, and she lunged at the phone, almost falling down in the middle of the sixth ring and flopping on the chair. Hello? Mrs. Goldfarb? Mrs. Sara Goldfarb? Its me. Speaking. The voice was so bright and cheery and so enthusiastic and real that she turned toward the TV set to see if the voice was coming from there. Mrs. Goldfarb, this is Lyle Russel of the McDick Corporation. She looked at the phone. She knew for real that his voice was coming from there, but it sounded just like a television announcer. She kept at least one eye on the television as she listened and spoke to Lyle Russel of the McDick Corporation. Mrs. Goldfarb, how would *you* like to be a contestant on one of televisions most *poignant*, most *heartwarming* programs? Oooo me? On the television???? She kept looking from the phone to the television, and back again, trying to look at both at the same time. Hahaha, I thought you would Mrs. Goldfarb. I can tell just by the warmth in your voice that you are just the kind of individual we want for our programs. Sara Goldfarb blushed and blinked, I never thought that maybe I would be on the television. Im just a— O haha, I know how you feel Mrs. Goldfarb. Believe me when I say I am just as thrilled as you to be a part of this fantastic industry. I consider myself one of the luckiest men in the world because every day I get a chance to help people just like yourself, Mrs. Goldfarb, to be a part of programming that not only are we proud of but the entire industry—no, the entire nation is proud of. Harrys mother was clutching the top of her dress, feeling her heart palpitate, her eyes blinking with excitement. O, I never dreamed . . . Lyle Russels voice became earnest. Very earnest. Mrs. Goldfarb, do you know what programs I am referring to? Do you have any idea? No . . . I a . . . Im watching an Ajax and Im not sure . . . On the television???? Mrs. Goldfarb, are you sitting down? If not, please sit down immediately because when I tell you what programs I am talking about you will be dizzy with joy. Im sitting. Im sitting already. Mrs. Goldfarb I'm talking about none other than . . . his voice suddenly stopped and Sara Goldfarb clutched even tighter at the top of her dress and stared wide-eyed at the phone and the television, not sure from which instrument his voice would come. When he spoke his voice was deep, low and full of feeling—Mrs. Goldfarb, we represent the quiz shows on television. Ooooooo . . . . He waited dramatically as Sara Goldfarb composed herself, her breathing audible over the voices from the television. Lyle Russels voice was authoritatively dramatic, Yes, Mrs. Goldfarb, plus— plus the brand new, I said, brand new, shows that will be on next season; the shows millions of Americans want to be on; *the* shows that are looked forward to anxiously by millions—Me . . . me . . . on the—O I cant—Yes, Mrs. Goldfarb you. I know how you feel, you are wondering why you should be so lucky when so many millions would give anything to be on one of these shows— O, I cant tell you . . . Well, Mrs. Goldfarb, I cant tell you why you are so lucky, I guess its just that God has a special place in his heart for you. Sara Goldfarb fell against the back of the viewing chair, one hand clutching desperately at the phone, the other the top of her dress. Her eyes bulged. Her mouth hung open. For the first time in memory she was unaware of the television. You will receive all necessary information in the mail Mrs. Goldfarb. Goodbye and . . . God bless. Click.

Visions of heavenly angels passed before Harrys mother as the psalmist sang so soothingly to her, before the buzzing of the phone in her hand, and the exploding of a bottle of cleaner into a white tornado, dispersed them. She breathed. Then exhaled. The phone. Yes. The phone goes on the hook. Gets hung gup. Aa haaaaaaa. Clunk, clunk. She missed the cradle. She looked at the phone for a minute then picked it up and put it gently on the cradle. On television. O my God, television. What will I wear???? What do I have to wear? I should be wearing a nice dress. Suppose the girdle doesnt fit? Its so hot. Sara looked at herself then rolled her eyes back and up. Maybe I/ll sweat a little bit but I need the girdle. Maybe I should diet? I wont eat. I/ll lose thirty pounds before Im on television. Then with a girdle Im looking like Spring Boyington . . . a little . . . sort of . . . Hair! I/ll get Ada to do my hair. Maybe they do it. Special. O . . . I should have asked . . . asked who? What was his name? I/ll remember, I/ll remember. It will come. He said they send me everything in the mail. I look good in the red dress with—No! Red doesnt come so good on the set. Isnt just right, kind of funny and blurred. And shoes and a pocketbook and earrings and necklace and a lace handkerchief O O O O, Sara nodding her head, grabbing her temples and rolling her eyes and lifting her arms, her palms turned upward, then closing her hands in a loose fist and tapping them against each other, then suddenly stopping all movements, sitting stiff in the chair for a moment, I/ll look in the closet. Thats what I/ll do. The closet. She nodded her head affirmatively and got up and out of her chair and went to the bedroom and started rummaging through her closets, taking dresses off hangers and holding them up in front of her then tossing them on the bed; crawling around on her hands and knees as she investigated the darkest and remotest corners of the closet, finding almost forgotten shoes and singing in a wordless and tuneless monotone as she dusted them off and tried pair after pair on, wobbling on some as her callused feet oozed over the sides, attacked the straps, then posed in front of the mirror looking at her shoes and her blue striped and stippled legs. . . . O, how she loved her gold shoes, all of them. Finally she couldn't resist. She put on the red dress. I know red doesnt come in so good on the set, but the red dress I like . . . I love. She posed, looked over her shoulder into the mirror . . . then the other shoulder, adjusted the length to various heights, started to try to zip it up but after half an inch and many minutes of exertion and squeezing and stuffing and adjusting she gave it up so she stood with it unzipped in front of her mirror, liking what she saw as she looked through eyes of many yesterdays at herself in the gorgeous red dress and gold shoes she wore when her Harry was bar mitzvahed . . . Seymour was alive then . . . and not even sick . . . and her boobala looked so nice in his—Ah, thats gone. No more. Seymours dead and her— Ah, I/ll show Ada how it looks. She held the unzipped back of her dress tightly as she waited for a station break, then went next door to her friend Ada. So wheres the party? Party, schmarty. This is like all the parties. When I tell you youll jump out the window. A basement window I hope. They sat down in the living room, strategically, so each could keep an eye, and ear, tuned to the television set while discussing the momentous occasion that brought Sara Goldfarb forth in the gorgeous red dress and gold shoes she wore the day her Harry, her boobala, was bar mitzvahed, an event so important and undreamed of that Sara was in such a state of shock, though ambulatory, she turned down a piece of halvah. Sara told Ada about the phone call and how she was going on television. She, Sara Goldfarb, was going on the television. Ada stared for a moment (with one ear she caught the end of the scene of the soap opera). For real? You wouldnt kid me? Why should I kid you? What am I dressing for, the supermarket? Ada continued to stare (the music told her they were fading out on the scene. She knew instinctively that a commercial was coming on even before there was that sudden increase in volume and explosion on the screen). You want a glass tea? She got up and started for the kitchen. Sara followed. The water was quickly boiled and each had a glass of tea when they returned to the living room, just at the end of the commercials, and sat in the same strategic positions, their ear and eye still tuned to the television, as they discussed and speculated on the enormity of the coming event in the life of Sara Goldfarb, an event of such prodigious proportions and importance that it infused her with a new will to live and materialized a dream that brightened her days and soothed her lonely nights.

MICHELLE TEA

The Passionate Mistakes and Intricate Corruption of One Girl in America

THIS WAS MY LIFE in Tucson. Early Tucson, before I was whoring, when I wasn't even working at all. What bliss. It seemed natural, Tucson so slow and lazy. Did anyone work? Not me. I was up with the sun in the toxic gold of my bedroom. It took 12 cans of spray paint to make the walls glow like that, my trigger finger cramped and sticky and I blew my nose gold for a week. Climb out of bed and yank down the black flannel curtains so the day could begin. Make some food in the little yellow kitchen, tea with honey, avocado on pita, bring it all into the backyard and eat naked on a towel in the sun. Whoever lived in the adobe before we did forgot to cancel their newspaper so I had that each morning, spread out on the dead needles that dripped off the Palo Verde tree, learning which Arizona politicians I was supposed to hate and which were good or at least hopeful. The backyard was marvelous. Small but fenced so you could get naked though I kept my panties on because I was afraid of that Arizona sun on my pussy. The Palo Verde tree hung over a rickety shed that certainly housed scorpions, and its needles would drop into piles on the roof, little nests for the cat to curl up and sleep in. The cat was slinky and quick, he'd bring Liz fear-frozen lizards, drop them by her head as she laid naked beside me. Oh Pal, I cooed, Don't You Love Me? Where Are My Lizards? The next night I found a caterpillar on my pillow, torn and leaking yellow. There were cactuses in the backyard, that happens in Tucson. They seemed alive to me in ways that other plants didn't, extra-terrestrial. A fat spiny pod with a crown of yellow blossoms. Another was so big it looked ancient, like a dinosaur plant. Someone told me it's where tequila comes from. The leaves, if that's what they were, curled into spears at the tip. I had cuts on my leg from walking too close. The desert was a ruthless place. All the animals were poison and even the plants had these weapons. There was a broken wooden swing hanging from the Palo Verde tree, rickety but you could sit in it if you were tiny like me. Hippies used to live there, we found chunks of their pottery jutting out of the dirt like ancient artifacts. I know I'm making this all sound so nice, but you have to know that the whole time I was in Tucson I was losing my mind. I was gone. Because of incest and male abuse. I had had some incest, though it wasn't the physical kind. It was holes cut into walls for my stepfather to attach his eyes to. I was a peepshow. Tucson was the aftermath. The horror of knowing someone and living with them and even thinking you're lucky and then wham and now you know that every person is really two people and how can you ever know what the other half is up to. At least with Liz it was obvious, mean and controlling most of the time but there was a nice Liz too and occasionally you caught a glimpse. Sometimes at bedtime, when she curled herself on top of me and was sweet. I could fall asleep like that and wake up with hope, and however the day destroyed it, it could be back in my arms at bedtime.

We went to Mexico when my sister Leicia came to visit. We'd been talking about it for a while — Liz wanted Mexican blankets, brightly striped and they would look beautiful in our golden bedroom, and I wanted to go to another country. I couldn't believe I was living so close to one, but then Tucson seemed entirely like another planet, with alien shrubbery and vicious little creatures. When I thought of Mexico I thought of fierce, angry color; Frida Kahlo's thick heart; chalky skeletons posed at an altar. The virgin of Guadeloupe draped in a robe of stars and shooting swords of light from her head. My sister's visit was a nightmare. She really should have spent her spring break in Miami or Daytona rather than vacationing at my nervous breakdown. Me and my mean girlfriend in a squat adobe, plotting the overthrow of the patriarchy and hating everyone. Of course Liz hated my sister and her long, polished hair, her bag of fruity toiletries. On her very first night in Tucson I sat Leicia down on the couch and told her that me and Liz were prostitutes. I figured why waste time. Why wait til the pager was sounding its shrill beep and Liz was tumbling through the house in a blonde wig and heels.

WANDA COLEMAN

In the City of Sleep

STILL I LOOK FOR love. It eludes me. Still I look in this haze/night settling over me . . . ever it eludes in this City of Sleep. There's no love, no hate. Only being and being healed.

There's a war going on. There is so much of everything going on and going and going. My man is a soldier in this war and I was waiting for him to come home so that we could be lovers again. So we could start to build a life together again. That life dismantled by the war in southeast Asia. The yellow war. The war for tungsten. The war I watched take seed after Korea, as a child in my parents' home while looking at the news on television. And at that time I wondered what the war could possibly mean to me. I was only nine years old and had no mind for men or the stuff of men. Laos was a funny word and its pronunciation eluded me.

He looked so tall and sad when we parted at the induction center. I still remember him standing there in his purple jumpsuit—that braid of gold hanging at his chest. God, he was so tall and bronze and *hey good lookin'*. And I had no idea why he was going or where. In a way I thought it was kind of nice—his going. This black man accepted into a military that had rejected my father in '42 as being "ground sick."

"What's ground sickness?"

"Hell if I know." And mother steered me discreetly aside. "They didn't like black men in the service."

And I understood. Somehow my questions to Daddy about what he did during World War II had hurt him. My curiosity had been prompted by the white chemistry teacher at school. He had told the class how he worked on top secret projects in the Army Air Corps and carried on daring correspondence with a Russian chemist. His children were very proud of him. I wanted to be proud of my dad too. Somehow I was denied and didn't understand why. Then I began to reason that perhaps it was a mistake to be proud of men who went to war and built death machines and had clandestine correspondences and killed other men. Men like my father, who didn't qualify for such activities, were superior. And my reasoning made me feel better. Now my lover was going off to war and I was going to be alone. I feared I couldn't handle the idea that he might never come back to me. Even if he lived to return home I knew he might not be returning to me. That knowledge made our last moments together very poignant. We both knew. It didn't stop me from babbling on about sending him "care packages" of homemade cookies, cigarettes, chocolate bars and stuff. We kept trying to make each other feel there was some possibility. It was possible he'd return home whole; that we'd marry and have children. It was possible we'd buy a home in the suburbs on his G.I. Bill. That he'd get a loan against the home and use it to go into business. It was possible that I'd help him turn that business into a corporation. It was possible that we'd be modestly wealthy. That we'd be able to send our children to good universities. That we would retire early and live comfortably off our earnings, perhaps travel and see the world as we've both longed to see it. It was possible I could be faithful to him every single day he was overseas.

> Dear Jane,
> You know I don't want to hold you back. And you were such a nice young brown-skinned lady with a big future ahead of you. And I'd hate to be a stumbling block for you. I'd hate to hold you to a promise you made at a weak moment. I'm releasing you from your promise so you can get on with your life. Here is a picture of me with my Vietnamese girlfriend. We have good times together. You should see the insects here—biggest suckers I've ever seen in my life. And you can turn a corner and suddenly you're face-to-face with an elephant. And this heat—this fuckin' heat makes the Mojave feel like a deep freeze. Anyway, this is quite a trip. I just wanted you to know. You are free to be whoever you want to be. And with whoever you want to be.
> Goodby. Good luck.

Whenever I am hurt I go to the City of Sleep. It is warm and welcoming and I can be there until the pain heals. I lay in the park under the trees that sing. I sit on a couch of stones that surround and soothe me. Or I enter the hushed halls of buildings eager to salve me in solitude. Or I watch the glistening passengerless autos that flow silently along crystal avenues like fish aswim in a stream. I curl up and I go there. Adrift on and above my pain. Until it disappears and is forgotten. Then I return to the world. I wake and go on. Until the next time I'm hurt.

When I was little I always went to the City of Sleep after a spanking. I'd go there until I felt loved again and that I had learned my lesson and that it was understood that I'd never be bad or make that mistake again. I'd sleep through the afternoon or morning. And when I woke mother always had something for me to eat. Or I could go and quietly watch television or play outside, understanding that the crisis had passed. After waking everything bad was gone. It was okay again.

I have thought about taking up permanent residence in that city. It's a wonderful, carefree place. But it's not enough to be free. Mere freedom carries with it the weight of responsibility. To be without care/responsibility/encumbrances. That is the ideal state. I've always thought of it in that way. I could always understand those who had to be free of caring about the world. Free of caring about what goes on in it. Or caring about things like skin color. In caring lies responsibility.

In my City of Sleep the days whiz by if I want them to. And to be free of care is also to be free of worry. I don't worry about what's at the end of my days, for example. I know what's at the end of my days—more sleep. Everlasting sleep. Lasting freedom from care.

When his letter came I read it and went into shock. I was hurt to the bone. I turned on television and curled up in bed and reread his letter, over and over until the pages were damp and I was exhausted with tears. I had to be sure I had read everything—had wrenched from it all possible meaning.

Here is a picture of me with my Vietnamese girlfriend.

Why don't they allow women to go to war? So we can be near our men. So that they won't forget us. So that we won't lose them. So that we can watch over them. So that we can care and feel responsible for them. So that if there's a change we can understand what brought about that change a whole lot better. We don't have to be on the battlefield or get in the way. We can be on the sidelines, nursing, mitigating, observing, rooting them on. . . .

I sound silly. I tend to get silly when I enter the City of Sleep. Things get distorted. Lines are no longer sharp or clear. Colors mute, fade, run into one another. And I have to really concentrate in order to bring objects into focus. Distinctions are blurry on sleepground.

She is a very pretty woman, this new girl, the one in the photograph. Very pretty. She's tiny—a much smaller woman than I am. She has long straight hair that almost reaches her waist. She has on a "Suzie Wong" dress of pink satin and there are elaborate stitchings on it in silver thread. And he is sitting

364 ◆ *Wanda Coleman*

there in his camouflage uniform, holding his helmet on one arm and her on the other. There are cards and cigarettes on the table next to them, a bottle and two glasses. It looks like a hut, but it could easily be a club.

I'd hate to hold you to a promise you made at a weak moment.

Was that a weak moment? Was giving myself to him done out of weakness? I had never felt so strong in my life at that moment. I felt I had the power to will away war. I felt my love was so powerful it protected him/would guide him safely through it and bring him back to me unharmed. Was that weakness? At that exact moment, when we lay naked and open to one another I felt armored by our love. When he kissed me I felt my own strength redoubled as his flowed into me on his tongue. And I felt so strong and secure in arousing his nature. Knowing he wanted me, feeling him hard against my thighs. Was that weakness? It's so confusing. When he entered me, that incredible joy I felt as we joined—all of that a weak moment? And as we lay together in the long peace afterwards, curled up and cooing in that delicious stink, clinging to each other as one. That was weakness? How could I mistake weakness for glory?

I'm missing something. What?

I'd hate to be a stumbling block for you.

He means love. Love is a stumbling block. Suppose he fell in love with her and wanted to marry her and bring her home. He knows I'll be here waiting. Or, suppose I met someone else and wanted to marry. I didn't realize it was possible for me to have that kind of joy with anyone else. I guess that's another way in which I'm silly. I believed all that stuff I was taught about love being eternal and unique. That once having loved it could never be the same again with anyone else. I guess I will soon find out. I will be free of caring for one man. Free of responsibility for seeing to one man's happiness. Free of one man's dreams. Our dreams.

In the City of Sleep there are no dreams. Sounds like a contradiction, but it's not. I just sleep. Dreams are full of cares and responsibilities. The City of Sleep is an alternate reality. There is nothing in that city that I don't want. No pain. No heartbreak. No people to involve myself with. Animals are decorative like shadows. They're quiet creatures—cats and birds. They ease round corners and flit from tree to tree. They enhance without creating disturbance. And that's very nice. I don't have to tend to them. They are a part of sleep.

In dreams I'm always busy doing things. My dreams are very exciting; they can be quite compelling—as compelling as reality—so compelling I often confuse the two. But when I don't enjoy the excitement, when I need a rest from them, when they turn into nightmares, I escape into the City of Sleep. The key word is excitement. There is no excitement in the City of Sleep. It

Nuclear Family Nightmares

is languid and tropical. The sky is forever blue. The houses are of white adobe. The sidewalks are of nephrite and marble. I waft along. I float. I'm just there. I never do anything. And nothing is done around me.

I want to release you from your promise so you can get on with your life.

I was getting on with my life. My life was structured around waiting for him to come back to me. I was making all these plans. He was going to be gone for two years. That's what he said—maybe three. Okay, so what was I going to do? Well, I was going to get a good job and work hard and save up as much money as I could. I was going to buy a new car. In two years, I'd have it just about paid for and it would be mine—ours. And I'd have enough money saved so that when we made the down payment on the house with his G.I. Bill we'd be able to furnish it to our taste. And if we decided to have children within a year or two of that, the money would cushion against my being unable to work while I carried our child. It would also give him enough time to readjust to civilian life. I've always heard that soldiers coming back from war have a difficult time readjusting even under ideal circumstances. And that people who love them never understand. But I would be ready to understand him. I'd spend two years working hard towards that understanding. And while he was going through his adjustment period, I'd still keep working, and be patient and allow him all the time and space he'd need. And then, when he gave word, we'd get married. Of course, I'd set aside a portion of my wages to cover the wedding. I've always wanted a big fantasy wedding, or a traditional church wedding. Or, if he wanted, something small and intimate—it wouldn't matter. Just as long as we married.

I *was* getting on with my life. I had determined to stay so preoccupied in my planning I wouldn't have time to miss him. Why would he say such a cruel thing in his letter. He was my life and I was getting on about him. And now it's all nothing. I certainly don't feel like getting up and going to work—ever again. I want to curl up in bed and sleep.

She's a very pretty girl. She has smooth yellow skin and bright white teeth. I've always heard that women in foreign countries have bad teeth. There's nothing wrong with her teeth. And her lips are very red and glossy. They shine. She looks as happy as I used to feel. Is it my imagination, or is that guilt I see in his eyes? His mouth is smiling. His eyes are not. They're narrowed and looking straight into the camera. He's trying to reach me.

Yeah, she kisses as good as you kiss, Babe. She's different not better. She's here and you're not. You think I'm a sonofabitch. And yes, I know you would have waited for me no matter how many women I had as long as I didn't fall for any of them. You can get past the sex. It's the love that makes you crazy. And you think I don't understand women, don't you, Babe.

Nuclear Family Nightmares

I'm getting sleepy. I can hardly keep my eyes open.

Thinking about something too much usually makes me sleepy even when I've had a cup of coffee. But that kind of sleep always brings dreams with it. When I sleep tonight I won't have any dreams.

You are free to be whoever you want to be.

That's outright a lie. I'm not free to be with him in Viet Nam. I'm not free to confront him and his new girlfriend and call her a tramp and call him a dirty lowdown two-timer. I'm not free to make a scene and try and fight her for my man. I'm not free to be his wife. I'm not free to have his child. That is the who I want to be and I'm not free to be any of it.

It hurts and makes me angry—both. Because he's lying to me. This is the first time he's ever lied to me about anything. Why is he lying when this photo makes lying so unnecessary?

I'm going in circles again. It's the sleepiness.

Let's see—how many pills did I take? I can't remember. But I think I took enough. Three and I could sleep through the atomic bomb. And the best thing to do now is sleep.

I wish I could visit my City of Sleep and never return. I wish that. Because if I wake up I'm going to have to do something. And at this moment I don't know what I'm going to do. Now that I'm free to do it. Now that he has freed me.

Upon waking I will have to take responsibility for myself. I will have to care for myself. I will have to find something to do. Damn it. I'll have to mother myself.

Can I?

I'll have to if I wake up. I'll have to.

Patti Smith

Complete

IN GRAMMAR SCHOOL MY classmates and I were wrenched from the wisdom of Uncle Wiggily and made to parade single-file into the depths of a makeshift fallout shelter. There we lay facedown among the stores of Spam, generic goods, and bottled water. It was peace, fifties fashion. Preparing for the bomb. Thus it was revealed our elders who had fought for our freedom had spent equal time inventing methods and self-annihilation.

As the decade rolled on, dressed in Davy Crockett gear, I clocked my world. *Life* magazine kept me posted. Picasso. Nazi war criminals. Jackson Pollock. Korea. The Beats. The death of Charlie Parker. The rise of Fidel Castro. By 1959, "Stagger Lee" was on the radio, *Naked Lunch* under the counter. Conformity was on the high rise. And cars looked just as ambitious.

As for me, I had turned in my coonskin cap and spent long hours in the library. I had discovered Tibet—the Dalai Lama, the great monasteries, and the prayer flags bracing the bright Himalayan wind. In March, while gathering material for a school paper, my Tibet was invaded by the Chinese. I was horrified to report the mass slaughter, imprisonment of monks and nuns, the burning of their temples, and the forced exile of their spiritual leader. At twelve years old I was unable to comprehend the public's disinterest. The general lack of outrage. Feeling helpless, I stood before my window at bedtime and said my prayers for the Dalai Lama and his people as wild-winged Chevrolets flew through the night.

KAREN FINLEY

A Different Kind of Intimacy

WHEN MY MOTHER, Mary Steinert, was six months old, the steering wheel came off into her father's lap while the family was out for a drive. My mother's arm was nearly severed, and a piece of the windshield embedded itself in her fontanelle. Her mother refused to let her arm be amputated. My mother was in a body cast for two years.

My maternal grandfather, Eddy, was a dashing gambler. He would take my mother with him on his gambling sprees to the Blackstone Hotel on Balboa Street, in Chicago. My grandfather's gambling addiction meant that it was not unusual for my mother to come home and find the furniture or other household items gone, sold, or repossessed. She lived with the awareness that everything might be gone at any time.

My father had red hair and freckled white skin, but my mother was olive-complexioned. Dark. My brothers believed that she was black when they were young. I remember going to Wisconsin to visit my father's family, and the people at restaurants asking the squaw with the long black braid to enter in the back. Sometimes, my mother was mistaken for a domestic, the nanny of her own children. She was constantly asked about her skin, about where she came from. How did she keep a tan all year?

On her father's side, my mother was Eastern-European, of Jewish descent (though her ancestors had converted to Catholicism). On her mother's side, in addition to being Hungarian Gypsy, my mother was American Indian. My mother did not appear to be white.

Because of that, she made sure that we lived in an integrated neighborhood. My mother felt more comfortable around people of color. And she blended in more in integrated neighborhoods than she did in WASPy ones. She wasn't stigmatized outright, because in society's eyes she occupied some fuzzy zone between "colored" and "white," but she lived with a shame of her skin, her darkness, and of being eroticized because of her "exotic" looks. The last thing she said to me, just before she died, was that the first thing she was going to talk to God about was "skin color."

Mental illness was present in my mother's family as well as my father's. My maternal grandmother suffered from depression and schizophrenia. On one visit to my grandmother's when I was very small, she insisted we all wear bathing caps to protect us from the rays of the aliens next door. Eventually my mother had to have her committed.

My mother's father died suddenly, of pneumonia, one weekend when she was ten. Her mother was five months pregnant. Mary soon went to work washing floors and working in a bakery. Her life was one of poverty and of too much responsibility for her age. It is her pain I have cried out in my art—the pain of the child who is not taken care of and so becomes the caretaker.

With great suffering comes either a bitterness or knowledge, a heightened sensitivity, a greater goodness. My mother had that sensitivity and goodness. If someone in our home kicked a door, she would say, "Don't kick the door. It is a tree."

She was an activist. On hot, windy nights, when trucks sprayed DDT on trees, my mother would stand outside measuring the winds, to gauge the amount of pesticide dispersed. She was insistent on the issue of civil rights, and if anyone ever made a racist remark, even in jest, they were immediately thrown out of our house.

I asked her once how she coped with missing my father, her husband, after his death. How she coped with being left alone.

"I would sit in restaurants and see families together. I would see families with fathers, in cars, on vacations, celebrating, and I would ask God why my family wasn't intact, why I couldn't be in one of those families. But finally I encountered my pain, my pride—the sin of pride. The sin of envy. And now when I see families—mothers and fathers—together, I am happy that that feeling of family exists, that it is out there. It isn't something I have to have, own. But it exists. And when I see people happy, I am not envious of their happiness. I feel happy for them and with them."

That became my motivation—the remarkable way in which my mother was able to transform her pain into compassion. That was what I wanted to do with my art.

The idea of turning pain into compassion was something that applied in a very direct way to my public sculpture, *The Black Sheep*. I wrote "The Black Sheep," the poem that concludes The Theory of Total Blame, as a prayer for the disenfranchised in society, for the Other. It is my version of "The Lord Is My Shepherd . . ."

At the opening of "The Black Sheep," on a corner at First and Houston Streets in lower Manhattan, a man came up to me and told me how much he liked the sculpture. "You know it is sitting right on top of my house? I wake up to it every day." I realized that this man lived in the subway. And I was overwhelmed by the realization that my art couldn't really do anything to fix his life—that life is more important than art, but life is meaningless without art.

According to my grandmother, Al Capone was present the night she went into labor with my father. My paternal grandfather was from a wealthy family that owned farms, dairies, orchards, department stores, gas stations. But he wasn't content just being a well-off Wisconsin gentleman. So, during Prohibition, he started a prosperous bootlegging concern and began doing business with Capone.

My father's family was a family of adventurers. When my grandfather was a child, he and his parents and sister were the first family to cross the United States in an automobile. The story was captured in *National Geographic*. These were people who did big things, took risks. They lived on a grand scale. They owned lakes and islands in northern Wisconsin, and they lived a lot of their lives outdoors, roughing it. The Finleys said that they were related to both the Barrymores and the Joyces (as in James Joyce). Whether it was true or not doesn't matter as much as the fact that they believed it.

And then there was the madness, the despair, the mania, the headaches—the intense headaches genetically related to bipolar disorder, headaches so maddening that they caused my great-grandfather to shoot himself in the head. My great-grandmother's depression in the wake of her husband's death was so great that she gave all of her property away. This depression, passed down through generations, has been a major ingredient of my own self-expression.

Like the rest of his family, my father, George Finley, was an adventurer, a boundary-pusher. He was extremely gifted, witty, charming, moody. In the 1950s, he was a professional jazz percussionist. He experimented with homosexual sex, drugs, and every other new experience that crossed his path. He developed a heroin addiction that was serious enough to land him in Lexington, the rehab center, after he stole my grandmother's checks and forged her signature in order to feed his habit.

With the emergence of rock and roll, and his illness, he gave up jazz. In order to make a living, he became a salesman. When he married my mother he "settled down," but he was never what you would call a conventional man.

My father inherited his family's illness, though not its money. He suffered from manic depression, or bipolar disorder, which is a genetic disease. Manic depression was not diagnosed during my father's lifetime. Those who suffered from it were often, disastrously, diagnosed as paranoid schizophrenic. That is the diagnosis my father received. He killed himself when he was forty-eight. I was twenty-one.

When I was fourteen, I had recurring dreams in which my father committed suicide. In the dream, my uncle came over with a Burger King dinner after my father killed himself, and I asked the police who was going to clean up the mess. This dream was upsetting both for its content and for the fact that it kept repeating itself—it recurred every night for a week. On the fourth night, I couldn't stand it anymore and I confronted my father about it. I still shudder when I recall telling him and him looking at me, emotionless and frozen, as if he was trying to hide something. He didn't deny the implication of the dream. Later, in real life, my uncle did come over with Burger King after the tragedy, and I did ask who was going to clean up the mess. In some ways this psychic premonition comforted me after the suicide. It seemed to indicate that there was some larger order to things, some explanation, and that thought gave me some relief.

Psychic phenomenon, predictions, omens, herbs, signs, tea leaves, auras, dreams, prophecies, and visions were all a part of my growing up. I was taught to read cards by my mother and her mother, who was Hungarian Gypsy. When my relatives visited, palms were read in a no-nonsense fashion. In 1978, when I went home for Christmas break, I read my father's palm. I looked for his lifeline and he said to me, "I don't have a lifeline, I have a deadline." He killed himself later that week.

He went into the garage, laid a piece of cardboard from a vacuum cleaner box on the floor, and put the gun to his temple. It was January, Friday the thirteenth. My ten-year-old brother, Brian, found my father dead in the garage. He had gone to get a shovel to clear a neighbor's walk. My forty-five-year-old mother was left with four sons and two daughters to bring up.

I went to our family seer, Harriet, the day my father died. He'd been acting angry and withdrawn, and none of the priests, doctors, and psychiatrists we'd gone to had been able to help. I didn't know what to do for him. When I entered Harriet's room and she looked up and saw me, she asked me to sit down and told everyone else in the room to leave. She poured me a brandy and told me that I couldn't help my father, that "everything" was "done." But she wouldn't tell me any more. I became agitated. She said that when I got home I would be greeted by a black man and a white woman. It was 3 p.m. She asked me to stay until 3:30.

When I got to my family's door, I was greeted by a black man and a white woman—the police. Seeing them standing there, just as Harriet had predicted, sent me into a state of shock. They told me that my father had committed suicide at 3:30.

My father's death gave me passion, an emotional indicator toward which to push the content of my work. It compelled me to take the unanswered grief, the terrible sadness that I lived with, and throw it at the world. It was the event that catapulted me into my heroic complex, my vision of myself as a kind of Joan of Arc. Because no one was able to protect me, I would protect others, be a do-gooder, lay the moral compass for others to live up to.

DONALD GOINES

Whoreson

WHEN MY FOURTEENTH YEAR on this bittersweet earth came, I felt as if I were a man. Jessie and I stood at just about the same height now. My hair was black, with thick curls that hung down upon my brow. Whenever I went up on the corner with Jessie, I could feel the admiring glances the whores would throw my way. A few would even joke with Jessie about when would be my coming-out date. On these occasions I would remark to Jessie that I was ready to pimp, but she would only laugh and cap:

"You think you know how to talk slick, boy, but that ain't the key. Anybody can talk out of the side of his neck. What you got to do is find the key, honey. I can't give it to you. I can only tell you where to look for it. You got to learn how to sell conversation, baby."

At this time I didn't know what she meant by finding the key. I knew I could think and talk fast, plus I knew all the latest slang. "You just ain't hip, mom," I'd cap. "I got some beef that sells better than hamburger." The first time I screamed this on Jessie, I don't know if she wanted to slap me or not. She had raised her hand, but I'd stepped back out of reach.

She looked at me sadly. Had I been older, I might have been able to read doubt in her eyes. "Pimping is an art, Whoreson," she told me seriously. "There are very few pimps in this world who can really take the title of being a pimp. Just because a man gets his money from a whore, that don't make him no true pimp. Real pimps are really rare."

To prove her point she reached down in her sweater and fumbled around. When she removed her hand she held a small roll of money. She put this into the palm of my hand, then closed my fingers over the bills.

"Count it," she said. "I'm going to continue working. When you think I've made enough money, tell me and we'll go home."

I counted the eighteen dollars on my way to the pigfoot joint on the corner. Tony and Milton were loitering around the jukebox. There was a booth full of young girls next to the jukebox, and they yelled at me playfully. I was in the process of convincing the girls to go up to my house, so that we could use the bedroom, when Jessie entered the restaurant. My back was turned to the door so I didn't notice her. The kids in the booth got quiet. I turned around to see what the matter was, only to find my mother bearing down on me. She stopped in front of me and held out a five dollar bill. I didn't know what to do so I took the money. Her eyes didn't hold a hint of a smile. Just as suddenly as she entered, she turned and retraced her steps without speaking.

I felt a little self-conscious so I stuffed the five dollar bill down into my pocket without flashing my roll. The last thing I wanted was for the kids to think I got my money from my mother. Tony would know where I got my bankroll at, but they wouldn't, and I had no desire for them to start getting wrong impressions. Had I really understood Jessie's intention I could have avoided the next incident just by going outside. But I was unprepared when she popped back in the door. She hadn't been gone ten minutes.

I stared at her coming across the floor. Bewilderedly, I held out my hand for the ten dollar bill she carried loosely. In a voice that sounded shriller than the one I normally used, I heard myself asking, "You ready to go in, Jessie?"

Jessie had never been ashamed of anything she did, to my knowledge. She knew that she was embarrassing me. This only aroused her sense of humor. "It's up to you, sweetmeat," she said, referring to the statement I'd made earlier. She ran her hand through my hair. "I'm ready whenever you're ready."

I really wanted to stay and shoot the bull with my school friends, but I was embarrassed by the way Jessie was acting. Given the choice of staying or leaving, I quickly accepted the latter. Had I been as old and wise as I thought I was, I would have realized that many people would get the wrong impression of our relationship. Being as naive as I was, the only thing that disturbed me was that people would think all the money I handled came from Jessie. Many sly looks were cast our way as we walked out of the restaurant, from the older people as well as from the young crowd.

Jessie had a way of walking that made people think a queen was going past. To carry myself with such pride was my desire. On our way home, Jessie started to cough. I held her arm, and she bent over and spit up a mouthful of blood. "You all right, Jessie?"

"I'm as well as any nigger woman can hope to be," she answered lightly. For the first time that night I was glad we were going home early.

When we got home Jessie slipped into a housecoat while I fixed some coffee. She came into the kitchen and sat down across from me. She had removed her makeup and, with it, the professional air she carried when she worked. I smiled with happiness. I realized that I loved this tall, strange, beautiful woman. She gave me one of her rare smiles. There was an understanding between us that was wonderful. Apparently, Jessie understood better than I that we were all each other had.

I went to the cupboard, removed two cups from the shelf, and rinsed them out in the sink. We always took this precaution so we wouldn't have to worry about drinking a roach. I poured us both some coffee before sitting back down. Without taking her eyes from mine Jessie placed a small bundle of reefer down beside my coffee cup.

It wasn't difficult for me to recognize the ten joints I had rolled that morning. They still had my blue rubber band around them. Leaving them under my pillow had been a mistake. I had meant to retrieve them earlier but had forgotten. To try and lie out of it would bring down instant punishment by whatever means lay near her at hand. From past experience I knew she wouldn't hesitate to throw the coffee cup at me if I lied. Jessie hated lies with a passion.

I stared at the reefer. Hoping that my hand wouldn't shake too bad, I reached boldly for the reefer. After removing one from the group, I tossed the rest on the table in front of her. Removing a book of matches from my pocket, I lit the joint and took a deep drag.

Jessie silently stared across the table at me. Neither of us had spoken yet, nor was I going to be the one to break the silence. She got up from the table and walked into the other room. Jessie returned and picked up a joint and lit it.

We sat at the table smoking reefer and talking till the sky began to get light outside.

Of the many things she warned me about that night, one was never to use any other drug but reefer. She made me promise that for no reason would I allow someone else, or myself, to shoot some heroin in my veins, or snort it up my nose. I wasn't worried about using horse. I had seen what shooting stuff did to Tony's mother, so I had no desire for that form of drug.

We were both lit up pretty well when we staggered up from the table that morning. Jessie had made a short trip down the street and got a bottle of wine to go with the weed, so we had become quite high. Her laughter rang out to welcome the sunrise as I helped her to stand. The flickering rays of the new day played tag across the wall as we staggered towards her bedroom with me holding her up.

After I had put her into her bed, I leaned down to kiss her on her lips, but she turned her head quickly to avoid it. I drew back and stared at her surprised. She drew my head back down and kissed me on the cheek.

"There, you're a big boy now, save your passionate kisses for your young girlfriends." Before I could tiptoe out of the room she had rolled over and gone to sleep.

The following weeks became difficult for me. Jessie continued to hunt me down in whatever restaurant, poolroom or doorway I happened to be loitering in.

It became so obvious that she was giving me her trap money that Tony remarked, "Man, why don't you tell Jessie what people are saying."

I stared at him amused. "If I knew what they were saying I'd tell her." He laughed at my reply. Time after time as we walked home from school, he'd look over at me and laugh. We continued down the street but soon I began to get weary of his humor. The more irked I became, the louder he laughed.

A group of boys came through a yard carrying a case of wine they had stolen. It was Head and his gang. He had received his nickname because of the size of his head. It was longer than a football, with lumps on the back of it. He was short and wide, with a flat nose from too many schoolyard fights. His gang was the only one in the neighborhood anywhere near as tough as ours, and because he was their leader, he was always trying to prove how mean he was.

They spotted us and stopped. All eight of them were roaring drunk. I realized that this could be trouble, so I watched Head closely. In school on many occasions we had started out joking only to end up talking about each other seriously. I knew that for some reason Head had a dislike for me.

He handed Tony his bottle. "I would offer you a drink, Whoreson, but I don't let white niggers drink out of my bottle."

All of us went to the neighborhood movie each weekend, and we had just seen a cowboy picture where an actor had made a similar remark. I grinned at what I thought was his idea of joking and remained silent.

Tony took a long drink and then handed me the bottle. "Man, didn't you hear what I said?" Head yelled angrily at Tony. The children in front of the broken-down houses stopped their playing to watch. Their mothers came out on the crumbling porches, like roaches flocking to garbage, drawn by the imminence of violence. It was in the air, something intangible, felt by all but seen by none.

"Fuck you, Head, in your big black ass," Tony replied quietly. I took a long drink from the bottle and then held it out towards Head. He knocked the bottle from my hand, breaking it on the ground.

"I wouldn't drink after no bastard that pimps off of his own mammy," he snorted loudly.

"Man, why don't you be cool," Tony said softly. "Anytime somebody's mama gives them some money, some ignorant sonofabitch could call it pimping."

"That's different," Head stated and stared at me with his beady red eyes. "This half-white freakish bastard is fucking his mammy."

Before the words had left his mouth, I'd reached across the narrow space and grabbed Head. My right hand seized his shirt, while my left exploded on his chin. I followed this with a knee to his groin, and when he bent over, I straightened him up with my knee. Blood shot all over my clothes and I busted his nose. With left and right hooks to the head, I knocked him out into the street. I ran after him and kicked him in the face. This is how the police caught me when they drove up behind us. I was still kicking him in the head and face. I had learned earlier in my childhood the art of street fighting. Violence was a way of life, and I was dedicated to being good in anything I participated in.

The police took us downtown. Before taking me to Juvenile they dropped Head off at receiving hospital. He was in need of medical treatment. I sat in a small room and waited for my mother to arrive. After what seemed like a two-hour wait, a tall white-haired man appeared and led me into another room, where my mother waited.

Jessie rushed over and examined me for any injuries. She seemed so concerned that I decided not to tell her what the fight had been about. I didn't want her to have any unnecessary worry, so I remained silent as we left the building. Evening had come over the city; dark clouds covered the sky as we walked down darkened streets in search of a cab. Jessie put her arm around my shoulder and spoke slowly.

"Not that I give a damn about what they say or think, Whoreson, but I just never realized what some low-minded bastards would think after seeing me give you my money every night."

We stopped walking for a moment while Jessie fumbled around in her purse. She removed a small notebook. Each page in the book was dated, with a notation in ink following each day as to how much money she had given me to hold that night. After each week, she had added the total for all seven days. I stared at the book in confusion. I still couldn't comprehend her reasons for keeping notes on the money. I returned the money to her every night after she quit work.

In a sudden fit of humor, she laughed at my perplexity. "Darling, this is just a record to show you what kind of whore money not to accept. If any of your girls should bring you this kind of money, it will mean you're not pimping, you're simping. Oh yes," she added, laughing rambunctiously, "thanks for giving me a vacation."

I have never known if she resorted to scorn intentionally that night, or if my ignorance really was that amusing. Whatever the reason, it got the job done. From that day on, I knew I would never accept schoolgirl money from a woman again.

When we continued walking, with her arm around my shoulder and her laughter ringing in my ear, I clutched the notebook tightly. It served its point. Besides teaching me what kind of trap money not to accept, it taught me that a woman would test her man at all times.

I knew then that I would one day pimp, and pimp good, because I was going to pimp with a passion.

John Waters

Shock Value

PARENTS SHOULD WORRY IF their children haven't been arrested by the time they turn sixteen. Being a juvenile delinquent is a birthright and as much a part of healthy adolescence as smoking cigarettes or getting pimples. If your kid is class president or an eager beaver in extracurricular activities, beware. These over-achievers usually reach their peak in high school, and from the day they graduate, it's downhill. If your kid is a terror and refuses to go along with any authority, he will be forced to hang around with social outcasts and learn early to sort out the exciting and original people from all the idiots. I'd never trust anyone who hadn't spent at least one night of his youth in the local jail. The more hell you raise as a teen-ager, the sweeter your memories will be.

As soon as I entered high school, I decided I was a beatnik and began wearing jeans with elaborate bleach stains and sandals that wrapped up to my knees. I never washed my hair and bleached the front of it a sickly orange. I sneaked into coffee houses and actually owned a pair of bongos. I created wild modern "art" that even the garbage man refused and began writing embarrassing poetry. None of this was done out of any deep social conviction, but in homage to my favorite beatnik TV character, Maynard G. Krebs, on *The Dobie Gillis Show.*

Naturally, none of this went over too well with the Christian Brothers at my Catholic high school. They forced me to cut my hair and dye it back to its natural color before I could attend classes. I went to great lengths to get revenge. Sneaking into the office files, I found out the real name and birthday of one of my teachers. I spread his real name all over the class and organized a mock child's birthday party in his honor. As he entered the classroom on this special day, the more nervy members of my class broke into a chorus of "Happy Birthday" and watched in terror as he spotted the pile of gaily wrapped children's birthday gifts on his desk. He realized his real name had been exposed to the entire class and went berserk. He looked directly into my eyes, knew I was responsible, and charged over to my desk and started beating me up with a rolled-up *Holiday* magazine.

You could really get the Brothers wild if you ever doubted their preposterous religious teachings. Once, my religion teacher told us with a straight face that it actually "rained bread," which, he explained, was "manna from heaven," or some such nonsense. Unable to control my laughter, I blurted out, "Oh, sure, I can hear the weather report now: partly cloudy with brief showers of bread," and the teacher lunged at me as if he had just discovered Martin Luther nailing his ninety-five points to the classroom door.

The brothers were really fanatics about sex. Every year our entire class was dragged off on an isolated religious retreat so they could brainwash us on this sticky subject. As soon as we arrived, we were forced to go to confession to cleanse ourselves of all sin, so our souls would be spotless for communion the next morning. The brothers warned us that since we were away from all temptation, the only possible sin we could commit during the night would be masturbation. Each classmate was given a religious scapular to wear around his waist, underneath his clothing. If you were ever tempted to masturbate, the saint's face would repel your hands when you reached down in much the same way that the ruby slippers gave off sparks when the Wicked Witch tried to get them off Dorothy's feet in *The Wizard of Oz*.

I soon stopped paying attention to anything the teachers said and learned to hook school. My father would drop me off in the morning and I'd watch him drive away and then hitchhike downtown, approach any woman in her early twenties (I soon learned that hairdressers were the best), and asked her to call the school and impersonate my mother. They always seemed to get a kick out of helping a kid hook school, and the principal always fell for the fake sick-call. I'd then run off and spend a happy day catching up on all the trashy films I had missed, carefully noting the running times so I could return home on schedule and not be caught.

On the days I attended classes, I tried my best to disrupt them. Many of the teachers gave up and agreed to give me the lowest possible passing grade if I'd just sit there and shut up. This sounded like a fair deal to me; I could finally do some interesting reading. Anything published by Grove Press was a must. Instead of boring biology and trigonometry lessons I could read the entire works of de Sade, William Burroughs, and Genet, and the Christian Brothers would never bother me. I moved on to all Freud's case histories of abnormal psychology and *The Erotic Minorities* and got through the school year with far less trouble.

I was never very close with my fellow classmates. They never hassled me but seemed to keep their distance. My real friends were from my own neighborhood and wanted to be just as rotten as I did.

My oldest friend is Mary Vivian Pearce, but she never uses her real name except in the credits of my films. Everyone has always called her Bonnie, and we've known each other ever since we were born. Bonnie's parents and my parents were best friends—until we started hanging around together as teen-agers; then they stopped speaking to each other until recently.

Bonnie loved to bleach her hair and hang around with the guys. She had been expelled from countless private schools and all she wanted to do was ride horses and gamble. We found all sorts of ways to entertain ourselves—doing an obscene dance called the "bodie green" at our local Catholic Youth Organization, barging into restaurants and unnerving the customers by "watching them eat," or stealing pocketbooks in after-school hangouts. We especially loved throwing snowballs at cars and became so notorious that a local columnist, Mr. Peep of the *Baltimore Sun*, gave us our first review:

> "Boys Will Be Boys and Girls Will Be Girls"[*]
> A young lady schoolteacher I know was briefly terrified by two strangers in Towson the other day. As she prepared to drive her station wagon away from a filling station near York Road and Pennsylvania Avenue, a youth accompanied by a girl pelted the machine with snowballs. Alone in her vehicle, the schoolteacher considered this a harmless, though slightly malicious tradition. The boy and the girl appeared "nice." But then the youth walked up to the car, opened the driver's door and poised to throw a firmly packed snowball into her face from a distant of about two feet. "Let her have it!" the moll behind him cried, utterly without humor. Neither of these charming children attends the school at which the teacher teaches Manners, as well as English.

We loved the article and clipped it for our scrapbook, but couldn't help wishing the columnist had known the rest of the story—he could have done a great follow-up article.

On the days when there was no snow, we'd buy boxes of Dot candies and throw these at cars instead. We called it "going Dotting." Since these little pel-lets were much smaller than snowballs and made a louder noise on impact, they actually were more effective in causing irate reactions from motorists.

Bonnie and I also loved to party, and once we discovered liquor, our social lives really took off. We'd crash every party we'd hear about, even if we had never laid eyes on the host. Usually these parties consisted of twenty or thirty teenage dates packed into a basement with nervous parents blinking on the lights to stifle any "making out." We'd barge right in and head straight for the parents' liquor cabinet and start guzzling. We'd always steal the best records,

---

[*] John Goodspeed, "Boys Will Be Boys and Girls Will Be Girls," *Baltimore Evening Sun*, 1961.

and sometimes we'd vomit. It didn't take long for word to spread on the teen-age party circuit that we were bad news as guests.

Once we were blackballed from social gatherings, Bonnie would take baby-sitting jobs so we'd have a place to run wild. The unsuspecting parents would carefully explain to Bonnie all the instructions for the evening as I hid on the lawn, waiting for them to leave. As soon as their car pulled out of the driveway, I'd invade the house and we'd drain the liquor supply and start snooping through their personal belongings. Sometimes we'd make random obscene phone calls to the operator so she'd cut off the phone. Then we'd eat all the food and sometimes pass out. If the parents ever came home unsus-pectedly, I would just run out the front door. Needless to say, Bonnie's baby-sitting career was short-lived.

By now word was getting back to our parents that we were a deadly duo. Her parents thought I was a bad influence and mine thought the same of her. We were forbidden to see each other, but that didn't stop us. Bonnie would accept straight dates so she could at least get out of the house. I would be waiting up the street at the stop sign, and when Bonnie and her "date" approached, she'd leap out of the car and jump into mine, and we'd pull away, leaving a very confused and disappointed young man idling in his car.

My favorite girl friend was Mona, a fifteen-year-old completely corrupted by *Vogue* magazine. Mona had a severe, one-sided Sassoon haircut and wore the most outrageous high fashion to her ninth-grade class. Her schoolmates were utterly confused by her. She hooked school so much that she was even-tually suspended from the entire Baltimore County School System.

We were the best shoplifting team operating. We'd walk right out of the store with the stuff in our hands and nobody would say anything. We'd charge luxury items in the best department stores to random names from the phone book when we discovered you didn't even need your parents' charge plate. We stole all the best hardback books and felt quite up-to-date on every-thing. We especially liked to steal signed pop-art pieces, even if we had to rip them out of the frames and fold the originals to get them under our coats.

Once, Mona got caught in a fancy department store and called me at my parents' house from the office where she was being held by an army of irate store detectives. They had discovered expensive cosmetics in her school note-book and layers of haute couture underneath her schoolgirl disguise. She pretended I was her psychiatrist. Quickly getting the message, I asked to speak to the head of security and gravely explained Mona's delicate psychiatric prob-lems and the mental harm of an arrest. After considering the medical advice, the detectives let her go with a stern lecture. Mona sobbed effectively, thanked them, hailed a cab, and, once home, ran from the driver without paying.

Mona and I loved to go to New York. To finance these trips, I'd type elaborate permission slips for nonexistent weekend sorority field trips, and Mona would give them to her mother, who would dutifully sign them and fork over the necessary expenses. My funds came from a settlement I received from Korvettes department store. Mona and I had been stealing records and I realized a store detective had seen me in the act. Since I knew he couldn't bust me until I left the store, I put the records back, but the store detective didn't see that. When he grabbed me, empty-handed, in the parking lot, I threw a fit and sued.

We'd either hitchhike to New York or hop the bus. On one trip, Mona horrified one fellow passenger by piercing my ear right on the Greyhound bus. As nauseated passengers stared in disbelief, Mona froze my ear lobe with an ice cube, heated a sewing needle over a match and jabbed it through my ear. I felt quite avant-garde arriving in New York with a stupid earring hanging from my ear, even if it was caked with blood.

Once we'd get to Greenwich Village, we'd boldly approach strangers on the street and ask for a place to stay. We met all sorts of interesting characters this way. Underground movies had just come out and *Film Culture* magazine was our bible. We saw them all—Kenneth Anger's *Scorpio Rising*; the Kuchar brothers' *Sins of the Fleshapoids*, *Hold Me While I'm Naked*, and *Teenage Rumpots*; Jack Smith's *Flaming Creatures* and *Blonde Cobra*; and early Warhol—*Couch*, *Blow Job*, and *Empire*. We also attended the most experimental "happenings" on the Lower East Side and always made a shoplifting visit to the newest boutiques for new outfits for Mona.

In 1964 drugs entered my life and it was a special new thrill that only added to my alienation from high school. None of my friends were experienced with drugs yet, so when a member of the student government offered me marijuana, I jumped at the chance and quickly got all my friends to try it. Since there was no talk of marijuana then, it seemed especially wicked, and we all became overnight potheads. I also got my hands on some LSD before it was even declared illegal and began tripping regularly with my friends, many of whom did LSD before they had a chance to try marijuana.

But thrilled as I was with my altered mind, reality soon reared its ugly head, and I had to go away to college. The Christian Brothers refused to let me graduate on the stage, but somehow NYU accepted me after a year of good grades at the University of Baltimore. I figured that if I was going to be forced to continue this charade of education, I might as well be in Greenwich Village. I was supposed to be taking film-making courses, but after attending a few classes and realizing that we'd have to watch the Odessa Steps sequence from *Potemkin* until it came out our ears, I immediately decided never to attend another class. Instead, I spent my days stealing textbooks from the university bookshop and selling them back as used books to finance endless trips to underground and exploitation movie houses. Sometimes I saw four movies a day and got a much better perspective on films than I would have got in the classroom. I eagerly came back to Baltimore and started tripping more than ever. The NYU staff had recommended to my parents that I undergo "extensive psychiatric treatment," so I put up with a psychiatrist, figuring I could at least beat the draft. When I finally got my induction papers, I showed them to the shrink and asked him to write me a note to get out of it. He smiled and said, "John, I think the Army would be the best thing in the world for you." I never went back to that quack.

I had absolutely no intention of going into the Army. I couldn't picture myself in green Army fatigues, bouncing along in the back of a jeep in Vietnam. As soon as I saw the forms they wanted me to fill out, I knew they'd never take me. I checked every box imaginable—alcoholic, junkie, homosexual, bed wetter—and waited in line with the other recruits. When I finally reached the head sergeant, I handed him the forms and held my breath.

"Is this all *true?*" he growled as his face turned beet red.

"Yes," I smiled.

I didn't even have to take the physical. I was dragged off to a paraplegic psychiatrist who sat in a wheelchair and panted in his most suggestive voice, "What do you like to do in bed?"

They sent me home in less than two hours. I was probably too skinny anyway.

DAVE EGGERS

A Heartbreaking Work of Staggering Genius

OF COURSE IT'S COLD. I knew it would be cold. I would have to have known it would be cold—why wouldn't it be cold, in late December, good god of course it's cold in Chicago in late December. I had lived here for a hundred years, knew the cold. I had loved the cold, embraced and mastered the cold, had raced with Pete to the lake when it was frozen, had studied the massive icicles, ice walls, waves frozen in mid-curl. I had objected when clumsy or

Nuclear Family Nightmares

cruel kids would break the formations, to hear the sound, to see them fall. I had brought my Walkman down, headphones under hat, piously learning the lessons of Echo and the Bunnymen while throwing rocks across the lake's ice, watching, listening to the beedlebeddlebeedlebeddle of the rocks hopping across the dull smoked glass, extending, the ice but not the rocks, endlessly, indistinguishable from the sky, the horizon vague, like a line erased or smudged. I knew the snow, the difference between pack and powder, how if you added some water to powder you could pack it, that if you packed a snow-ball and ran the hose over it and let it sit for a minute you'd have not a snow-ball but an ice-ball that if thrown accurately—all too accurately—would create a massive gash in the cheek of your brother Bill. I knew about the walls of my nose feeling like the hard frozen walls of a cave in a mountain in the arctic, toes frozen into pebbles, only dimly related to me, in my shoes, the sting of the wind against my legs, through my papery jeans. I knew all this.

So why why why didn't I bring a fucking coat? Sadder still, I didn't even think about bringing a coat. I did not forget, no, no. I never thought about it, not once.

I feel the cold when walking off the plane, and worse while thumping through that little hallway between airplane and terminal. Nothing can keep the cold away. I am cold already. I no longer have much use for the cold, will not be sledding this trip, and it hasn't even snowed. Its only use is as a forced and obvious metaphor, as foreshadowing. But I half-wish it were just raining. It is freezing and gray and night in Chicago, and I am wearing a pullover made of cellophane.

Toph is in L.A. with Bill and I am in Chicago. I will rent a car at the airport and will go back to my hometown, and will look up Sarah Mulhern, whose bed I ended up in one night a few weeks after I heard my mother would die, and will visit my father's friends, and the bar where my father (on the sly) used to go, and will maybe go to his office, and will go to the funeral home, and will go to my old house, ghosts in pocket, and will see my parents' oncologist, and will see worried friends, and go to the beach to remember what winter looks like there, and I will look and see if I can find their bodies.

No, no, I know I won't find their bodies—they were cremated, of course, eventually—but I have long dreamed, because I am misshapen and think it might be an interesting story to tell, of coming closer to finding them, at least seeing the building where they were brought, the medical school—you know what I really want to see? I want to see the face of the doctor or doctoral student or nurse or whoever it was who used my parents as cadavers. I have pictures of them, not real pictures but images in my mind of them, in a great, armory-sized room, its floors shiny, dotted with stainless steel tables, all with tools, small machines for picking and drilling and extracting, with long thin cords, and there are medical students, five to a table, the tables spread out in a way that is perhaps too spread out, not cozy but overly spacious, gridlike, eerie by way of rigidity. God knows what they do with two cancer-ridden bodies like that—if they're used as tumor case studies or examined for their parts, like rusted cars on blocks, stripped, their colonized areas ignored in favor of their comparatively benign legs, arms, hands—oh God, my dad used to do a trick at Halloween, with a hand. We had a realistic-looking rubber hand, had had it for ten years, it was always around, and at Halloween he would scrinch his own arm into his sleeve, then put the rubber hand where his own hand should be. When a trick-or-treater would come to the door, he would open the child's sack and drop first candy, and then the hand, into the bag. It was great.

Oh my gosh! he would bellow, waving around his handless arm. *Oh my gosh!* The child would be terrified, speechless. Then my dad would compose himself, and calmly reach into the bag. *Let me get that . . .*

So I plan to find out which medical school received them, and then I will go to the medical school, and will find the teacher who at the time was in charge of the use of cadavers, and I will knock on his door. I will. I have no courage for such things but in this case I will, I will surmount my—This is what I will say, brightly, when he opens the door, the doctor, when he cracks his door to see who has knocked:

I don't know what I'll say. Something scary. But I won't be angry about it. I want only to take a look at the man. Offer greetings. I want him to be shorter than me, in his late thirties, forties, fifties, frail, bald, with glasses. He will be dumbstruck by my introduction, afraid for his life, my shadow darkening him, and then I will close in on him, all casual confidence, and will ask something, something like:

"So tell me. What did it look like?"

"Excuse me?" he'll say.

"Was it like caviar? Was it like a little city, with one big gleaming eye? A thousand little eyes? Or was it empty, like a dried gourd? See, I have a feeling it might have been like a dried gourd, empty and light, because when I carried her, she was so light, much lighter than I expected. When you're carrying a person, I just thought of this, when you're carrying a person, why is it easier to carry them when they hold tight around your neck? Like, you're supporting their full weight no matter what, correct? But then they grab you around the neck and suddenly it's easier, like they're pulling up on you, but either way you're still carrying them, right? Why should it make a difference that they're holding you, too—The point is that at the time, before when I was carrying her, when she was reclining on the couch and watching TV, in general I was kind of thinking that the thing in her stomach might be terribly heavy. And then I lifted her, and the weird thing was that she was so light! Which would mean that it was something hollow maybe, not the writhing nest of worms, the churning caviar, but just something dry, empty. So which was it? Was it the dried gourd, or the festering cabal of tiny gleaming pods?"

"Well—"

"I have been wondering for many years."

He will tell me. And I will know.

And then I will be at peace.

Oh I'm kidding. I kid you. About being at peace. This trip is about the fact that things have been much too calm in San Francisco—I am making enough money, Toph is doing well at school—and thus completely intolerable. I will return home and look for ugly things and chaos. I want to be shot at, want to fall into a hole, want to be dragged from my car and beaten. Also, I have a wedding to go to.

BETH LISICK

Monkey Girl

OH, MONKEY GIRL. OH yeah, Monkey Girl. Gung Hay Fat Choy! I was born in the year of the monkey.

I was walking around the Chinese New Year parade. There I am drinking a warm beer, I had my paycheck in my sock, and this old lady I'm standing next to asks me what year I was born.

"1968," I tell her. "The year of the monkey." That much I'm sure of.

"Oh. Monkey is naughty!" she tells me and clucks her tongue. "Monkey is sneaky. You are naughty monkey, I know."

Well, oh yeah, Monkey Girl. Gung Hay Fat Choy, Monkey Girl! "I know all about you."

Then one of those guys, the kind working for the environmentally progressive energy corporations in between getting his master's and his bachelor's, approaches me, his gigantic hand extended. "Hi! I'm Steve! I'm a rat."

Nuclear Family Nightmares

"Rat is clever," the old lady says. "Rat work hard. Rat make good mate."

"So, why don't we blow this teriyaki stand and get a drink," he says.

I tell him teriyaki is Japanese. Mr. Stanford Rat Boy is not so smart after all. "Yeah. I'll let you buy me a drink."

So I go along with this for a couple of . . . months. And I can't even think of my own excuses why at this point I just keep thinking, monkey is naughty. But he's a rat, and I have to keep reminding myself of that.

I have two recurring nightmares: one about my dad's '77 Pinto and another about rats. I'm naked in my bed and there are big lumps moving underneath my skin. They're rats that have burrowed there except there are no entry or exit wounds. They're just crawling between muscle and skin up my thighs, up my stomach and then busting out where my collarbone breaks. Their hideous yellow-tooth faces look a lot like mine.

The last rat I saw before this guy was in an East Village garbage can snorfling through a bag of used Pampers. The rat before that crawled up my pajama leg as I slept in a smelly, drafty studio in Santa Cruz. And then there was Pippin, the only pet that was ever all mine. She choked to death in my fourth grade bedroom on a tennis ped I gave her to sleep in while I was away at my family reunion in the Ozarks.

Gung hey you, you fat choy! You were born in the year of the rat?

Now sometimes I read my horoscope and if I don't like it I can just pretend I'm the self-involved Cancer, the brooding Scorpio, instead of the happy-go-lucky Sagittarius. However, for some reason, I deeply believe in this rat thing. This Chinese lunar calendar business. It must be all that advertising about the mystique of the Orient. Ancient Chinese secret, huh?

Just give me a horse. 1954. 1966. I'll gladly swat the flies from his butt.

Or a snake. 1965. I have no problem sucking poison.

Rooster. '69. I've been known to enjoy a cock.

Dragons. Tigers. Oxen. Cool!

Dogs. Pigs. Rabbits. Sheep. Cute. Kind of '80s country kitchen wallpaper material, but cute enough.

This monkey girl just wants to go to the monkey bars, hanging upside down while all the blood pools inside my head and I think I'm somewhere else. Somewhere far away from Pintos and tennis peds, family reunions, the Ozarks and this dirty, clever, hardworking rat with the six figure income who only wants me because I'm naughty.

Jessica Tarahata Hagedorn

Dogeaters

JOEY WOKE IN A pool of sweat. The light bulb dangling from a cord above his head glimmered faintly. In Uncle's hot, windowless room, Joey had no sense of whether it was day or night. He sat up panting heavily, jolted from his dreamless sleep by the dog's incessant barking outside the door. Joey's head was still sore, a dry metallic taste in his mouth. Unbearably thirsty, he reached for a dirty glass half-filled with water on the floor beside him.

He looked slowly around the room, trying to remember and rearrange events in his dazed mind. A collage of pornographic centerfolds covered Uncle's walls, making the room feel even smaller and more claustrophobic. Joey shut his eyes to close out the sprawling, leering images of painted girls and blank-eyed boys with erect penises fondling each other without enthusiasm. Joey knew he was one of them—the ominous and holy children of the streets. "Scintillating Sabrina and Gigi." "Boys at Play." "Bangkok Bombshells." "Lovely Tanya and Her Sister."

He reached up and unscrewed the light bulb. No light came in from two rectangular openings Uncle had sawed near the ceiling, the only sources of ventilation in the small room. It was definitely night, Joey decided, unnaturally quiet except for the dog's rustling movements outside the front door. How long had he been asleep? In the distance, Joey heard the sound of a man's voice calling out to someone. Then laughter, followed by the buzz of more male voices and footsteps walking by Uncle's shack. The dog barked; a man laughed again. It could've been one of the gangs out for the night, on their way to hang out in front of the *sari-sari* store to drink *tuba* or *basi* and exchange stories about ghosts and women. It could've been Jojo or Junior, gang boys who sometimes bought dope from Joey and Uncle. Through Uncle's paper-thin walls, all sounds seemed to come from the same darkness Joey was sitting in. The dog was restless; Joey could hear every panting breath and low growl as if the animal was in the room with him. The footsteps and voices faded away. Joey was overwhelmed by loneliness.

He bit down hard on his lower lip, wanting to cry out for help but restraining himself. He knew the friendly sounds outside could just as well have come from Metrocom or Special Squadron agents sent to find him. He realized the old man had tied the dog up outside to prevent him from leaving. *Fucking Uncle*, Joey cursed—the old man was always one step ahead of him. The adrenalin coursing through his body made him want to jump up and run. Fucking Uncle, fuck it. He could just say *fuck it*, take his chances with the damn dog and run. Joey gulped at dry, dead air. He felt sick but there was nothing left to vomit.

He crawled to the chair in the center of the room, clutching it for support as he pulled himself up to his feet. His hand brushed over the objects scattered on the table next to the chair, finally curling around Uncle's Eveready flashlight. Exhaling with relief, Joey switched it on. A path of dim light opened up in the stifling darkness. Without being seen from the street, Joey had to find Uncle's cache of drugs and whatever cash he might have lying around before making his escape.

The old man was going to kill him, or have him killed. Joey felt too weak to laugh. He had been waiting for this all his life—this moment of betrayal from Uncle. It had been his destiny, and he welcomed it. He wondered how the old man had figured it all out. Uncle never ceased to amaze him. For the right price, he was capable of anything. Who would he blackmail, now? The man with the lean, pockmarked face? The bait, as usual, would be Joey. Uncle was more than willing to sacrifice his surrogate son.

The revelation was almost a relief, but in spite of himself, Joey felt hurt. He had expected betrayal, but was not ready for despair and anger at being betrayed. In his way, he loved the old man. *Zenaida, Zenaida,* Joey whispered to himself, *Mother of God, my god, the bastard buried you.* He had not said his mother's name in years, and steeled himself against the tears welling up inside him. He was disgusted by his own sentimentality; he had never considered himself capable of self-pity, terror, or yearning for his long-deceased mother. He had always felt cheapened and humiliated by the memory of her, Zenaida, and his unknown father. And so his litany went: *GI baby, black boy, I am the son of rock'n'roll, I am the son of R and B, I can dance well, you can all go to hell! Putang Ina Ko!*

Mother of a whore, his phantoms chanted, whore of a mother, son of a whore! They beckoned to him: Once a whore, always a whore! Was the German home in Germany, safe in his warehouse full of art and cats? Joey's tears were blocked by the force of his growing rage. He knew he had to escape, somehow. Past the growling dog to somewhere safe, somewhere safe and anonymous. He needed food and shelter—for how long wasn't important. He knew he wanted to live: it was that simple and basic. Joey was not going to let the old man or anyone else kill him.

There was no time to lose. Joey ransacked the room, flipping through Uncle's neatly folded clothes, overturning the cardboard boxes Uncle used for storage. He found a case of bullets, but no gun. Joey whimpered and cursed in frustration, flinging Uncle's possessions around him: a useless iron with no plug, two towels, a black rosary, letters bound in twine and addressed to "Ismael Silos" in beautiful, faded handwriting, a water-stained photo album with all the pictures removed, three cans of Vienna sausages and one tin of Spam, one black Converse sneaker without shoelaces, and a pile of Uncle's treasured collection of foreign magazines. The old man had paid a small fortune for black-market copies of *Hustler, Lolita, Spartacus, Penthouse,* and *High Society*—some still unopened and wrapped in plastic. The raunchier, the better. "You know I like to look," Uncle used to gloat. The sight of Uncle poring over glossy pictures of naked white women had always made Joey feel ashamed and sad. Feeling ludicrous, he tore up as many magazines as he could; in a final fit of malice, he unzipped his jeans and pissed all over Uncle's strewn possessions.

Joey never found money or Uncle's cache of drugs, but inside the Converse shoe he came upon the sleek butterfly switchblade Uncle had brought back years ago from Batangas. "Guns are efficient," Uncle used to say, "but knives give you more satisfaction." He preferred knives, he said, because sometimes things got personal; you simply had to make that kind of grisly contact with your victim's flesh and bone. "When you stab someone, you look him in the eye. Always look him in the eye," Uncle told him, "and let him know exactly who you are . . . It's a way of paying your final respects."

Joey had never killed anyone. There had been a moment once, with a customer. Joey had been thirteen, wise enough to carry a knife for protection. The man had gotten out of hand, and things had threatened to get ugly. Something sparked in Joey's eyes; his body tensed and shifted. The man realized he'd gone too far; he backed off, murmuring apologies. Nothing else had to be said. Joey was paid a little extra. The moment passed quickly, and was just as soon forgotten. He never saw the man again.

It was extraordinary, how Joey had managed to sidestep the violent encounters common in the lives of everyone else around him. He'd never been arrested or had to pay a bribe to get himself out of a jam. "You're a lucky boy," Uncle often marveled, "I knew it when I first took you in. You bring *me* luck."

Joey pressed himself against the door and softly called the dog's name, "Ta-ruk," imitating the coaxing tone the old man used to lure his pet. Cautiously, Joey opened the door just wide enough for the dog to see and smell the piece of Spam he held in one hand. The dog whined in anticipation, wagging his tail as Joey undid his chain and let him inside the shack, bolting the door carefully behind him. Joey watched as the animal lunged at the canned meat thrown on the floor.

There was nothing to keep Joey from escaping now. The dog was preoc-cupied; Joey could easily slip out the door. But he felt another rush of anger; the switchblade opened like a gleaming fan in his hand. Omens, signs, Uncle's language of the spirits . . . He had to leave a message the old man would understand.

It was essential to act immediately, without thinking. Emitting a muffled scream, Joey grabbed the scruffy fur at the back of the dog's neck and held on for dear life, thrusting the sharp blade below the dog's right ear. Blood spurted everywhere as the dog jerked in response. Joey kept stabbing the animal, the queasiness in the pit of his stomach rising to his throat. Once again he tasted metal on his tongue. The dog yelped and whined with each thrust of the knife, horrifying Joey. He began to weep, furious with the dog for not dying quickly. His anguished cries and the animal's became one and the same. His arm grew numb with the effort of killing, but Joey wouldn't stop until the shuddering dog finally lay still.

The smell of blood in the dark, airless room was unbearable. Joey stripped off his T-shirt but kept on his jeans, now stained and splattered black with gore. He wiped the sticky knife blade on his shirt, then folded and slipped the *balisong* into his back pocket. Using water from the giant oil drum Uncle kept in a corner, Joey washed up hurriedly. Shivering in his damp jeans, he bent down to lap at the water in the drum, trying to quench his terrible thirst. That done, he took a clean T-shirt from one of the over-turned cartons. It was the best he could do; Uncle's pants would never fit him. Leaving his bloody shirt and the butchered carcass of Uncle's dog behind as souvenirs, Joey slipped out the door.

Katherine Dunn

Geek Love

"WHEN YOUR MAMA WAS the geek, my dreamlets," Papa would say, "she made the nipping off of noggins such a crystal mystery that the hens them-selves yearned toward her, waltzing around her, hypnotized with longing. 'Spread your lips, sweet Lil,' they'd cluck, 'and show us your choppers!' "

This same Crystal Lil, our star-haired mama, sitting snug on the built-in sofa that was Arty's bed at night, would chuckle at the sewing in her lap and shake her head. "Don't piffle to the children, Al. Those hens ran like whiteheads."

Nights on the road this would be, between shows and towns in some camp-ground or pull-off, with the other vans and trucks and trailers of Binewski's Carnival Fabulon ranged up around us, safe in our portable village.

After supper, sitting with full bellies in the lamp glow, we Binewskis were supposed to read and study. But if it rained the story mood would sneak up on Papa. The hiss and tick on the metal of our big living van distracted him from his papers. Rain on a show night was catastrophe. Rain on the road meant talk, which, for Papa, was pure pleasure.

"It's a shame and a pity, Lil," he'd say, "that these offspring of yours should only know the slumming summer geeks from Yale."

"Princeton, dear," Mama would correct him mildly. "Randall will be a sophomore this fall. I believe he's our first Princeton boy."

We children would sense our story slipping away to trivia. Arty would nudge me and I'd pipe up with, "Tell about the time when Mama was the geek!" and Arty and Elly and Iphy and Chick would all slide into line with me on the floor between Papa's chair and Mama.

Mama would pretend to be fascinated by her sewing and Papa would tweak his swooping mustache and vibrate his tangled eyebrows, pretending reluctance. "Welllll . . ." he'd begin, "it was a long time ago . . ."

"Before we were born!"

"Before . . ." he'd proclaim, waving an arm in his grandest ringmaster style, "before I even dreamed you, my dreamlets!"

"I was still Lillian Hinchcliff in those days," mused Mama. "And when your father spoke to me, which was seldom and reluctantly, he called me 'Miss.' "

"Miss!" we would giggle. Papa would whisper to us loudly, as though Mama couldn't hear, "Terrified! I was so smitten I'd stutter when I tried to talk to her. 'M-M-M-Miss . . .' I'd say."

We'd giggle helplessly at the idea of Papa, the GREAT TALKER, so flummoxed.

"I, of course, addressed your father as *Mister* Binewski."

"There I was," said Papa, "hosing the old chicken blood and feathers out of the geek pit on the morning of July 3rd and congratulating myself for having good geek posters, telling myself I was going to sell tickets by the bale because the weekend of the Fourth is the hottest time for geeks and I had a fine, brawny geek that year. Enthusiastic about the work, he was. So I'm hosing away, feeling very comfortable and proud of myself, when up trips your mama, looking like angelfood, and tells me my geek has done a flit in the night, folded his rags as you might say, and hailed a taxi for the airport. He leaves a note claiming his pop is very sick and he, the geek, must retire from the pit and take his fangs home to Philadelphia to run the family bank."

"Brokerage, dear," corrects Mama.

"And with your mama, Miss Hinchcliff, standing there like three scoops of vanilla I can't even cuss! What am I gonna do? The geek posters are all over town!"

"It was during a war, darlings," explains Mama. "I forget which one precisely. Your father had difficulty getting help at that time or he never would have hired me, even to make costumes, as inexperienced as I was."

"So I'm standing there fuddled from breathing Miss Hinchcliff's Midnight Marzipan perfume and cross-eyed with figuring. I couldn't climb into the pit myself because I was doing twenty jobs already. I couldn't ask Horst the Cat Man because he was a vegetarian to begin with, and his dentures would disintegrate the first time he hit a chicken neck anyhow. Suddenly your mama pops up for all the world like she was offering me sherry and biscuits. 'I'll do it, Mr. Binewski,' she says, and I just about sent a present to my laundryman."

Mama smiled sweetly into her sewing and nodded. "I was anxious to prove myself useful to the show. I'd been with Binewski's Fabulon only two weeks at the time and I felt very keenly that I was on trial."

"So I says," interrupts Papa, " 'But, miss, what about your teeth?' Meaning she might break 'em or chip 'em, and she smiles wide, just like she's smiling now, and says, 'They're sharp enough, I think!' "

We looked at Mama and her teeth were white and straight, but of course by that time they were all false.

"I looked at her delicate little jaw and I just groaned. 'No,' I says, 'I couldn't ask you to . . .' but it did flash into my mind that a blonde and lovely geek with legs—I mean your mama has what we refer to in the trade as LEGS—would do the business no real harm. I'd never heard of a girl geek before and the poster possibilities were glorious. Then I thought again, No . . . she couldn't . . ."

"What your papa didn't know was that I'd watched the geek several times and of course I'd often helped Minna, our cook at home, when she slaughtered a fowl for the table. I had him. He had no choice but to give me a try."

"Oh, but I was scared spitless when her first show came up that afternoon! Scared she'd be disgusted and go home to Boston. Scared she'd flub the deal and have the crowd screaming for their money back. Scared she'd get hurt . . . A chicken could scratch her or peck an eye out quick as a blink."

"I was quite nervous myself," nodded Mama.

"The crowd was good. A hot Saturday that was, and the Fourth of July was the Sunday. I was running like a geeked bird the whole day myself, and just had time to duck behind the pit for one second before I stood up front to lead in the mugs. There she was like a butterfly . . ."

"I wore tatters really, white because it shows the blood so well even in the dark of the pit."

"But such artful tatters! Such low-necked, slit-to-the-thigh, silky tatters! So I took a deep breath and went out to talk 'em in. And in they went. A lot of soldiers in the crowd. I was still selling tickets when the cheers and whistles started inside and the whooping and stomping on those old wood bleachers drew even more people. I finally grabbed a popcorn kid to sell tickets and went inside to see for myself."

Papa grinned at Mama and twiddled his mustache.

"I'll never forget," he chuckled.

"I couldn't growl, you see, or snarl convincingly. So I sang," explained Mama.

"Happy little German songs! In a high, thin voice!"

"Franz Schubert, my dears."

"She fluttered around like a dainty bird, and when she caught those ugly squawking hens you couldn't believe she'd actually do anything. When she went right ahead and geeked 'em that whole larruping crowd went bonzo wild. There never was such a snap and twist of the wrist, such a vampire flick of the jaws over a neck or such a champagne approach to the blood. She'd shake her star-white hair and the bitten-off chicken head would skew off into the corner while she dug her rosy little fingernails in and lifted the flopping, jittering carcass like a golden goblet, and sipped! Absolutely sipped at the wriggling guts! She was magnificent, a princess, a Cleopatra, an elfin queen! That was your mama in the geek pit.

"People swarmed her act. We built more bleachers, moved her into the biggest top we had, eleven hundred capacity, and it was always jammed."

"It was fun." Lil nodded. "But I felt that it wasn't my true métier."

"Yeah." Papa would half frown, looking down at his hands, quieted suddenly.

Feeling the story mood evaporate, one of us children would coax, "What made you quit, Mama?"

She would sigh and look up from under her spun-glass eyebrows at Papa and then turn to where we were huddled on the floor in a heap and say softly, "I had always dreamed of flying. The Antifermos, the Italian trapeze clan, joined the show in Abilene and I begged them to teach me." Then she wasn't talking to us anymore but to Papa. "And, Al, you know you would never have got up the nerve to ask for my hand if I hadn't fallen and got so bunged up. Where would we be now if I hadn't?"

Papa nodded, "Yes, yes, and I made you walk again just fine, didn't I?" But his face went flat and smileless and his eyes went to the poster on the sliding door to their bedroom. It was old silvered paper, expensive, with the lone lush figure of Mama in spangles and smile, high-stepping with arms thrown up so her fingers, in red elbow-length gloves, touched the starry letters arching "CRYSTAL LIL" above her.

My father's name was Aloysius Binewski. He was raised in a traveling carnival owned by his father and called "Binewski's Fabulon." Papa was twenty-four years old when Grandpa died and the carnival fell into his hands. Al carefully bolted the silver urn containing his father's ashes to the hood of the generator truck that powered the midway. The old man had wandered with the show for so long that his dust would have been miserable left behind in some stationary vault.

Times were hard and, through no fault of young Al's, business began to decline. Five years after Grandpa died, the once flourishing carnival was fading.

The show was burdened with an aging lion that repeatedly broke expensive dentures by gnawing the bars of his cage; demands for cost-of-living increases from the fat lady, whose food supply was written into her contract; and the midnight defection of an entire family of animal eroticists, taking their donkey, goat, and Great Dane with them.

The fat lady eventually jumped ship to become a model for a magazine called *Chubby Chaser*. My father was left with a cut-rate, diesel-fueled fire-eater and the prospect of a very long stretch in a trailer park outside of Fort Lauderdale.

Al was a standard-issue Yankee, set on self-determination and independence, but in that crisis his core of genius revealed itself. He decided to breed his own freak show.

My mother, Lillian Hinchcliff, was a water-cool aristocrat from the fastidious side of Boston's Beacon Hill, who had abandoned her heritage and joined the carnival to become an aerialist. Nineteen is late to learn to fly and Lillian fell, smashing her elegant nose and her collarbones. She lost her nerve but not her lust for sawdust and honky-tonk lights. It was this passion that made her an eager partner in Al's scheme. She was willing to chip in on any effort to renew public interest in the show. Then, too, the idea of inherited security was ingrained from her childhood. As she often said, "What greater gift could you offer your children than an inherent ability to earn a living just by being themselves?"

The resourceful pair began experimenting with illicit and prescription drugs, insecticides, and eventually radioisotopes. My mother developed a complex dependency on various drugs during this process, but she didn't mind. Relying on Papa's ingenuity to keep her supplied, Lily seemed to view her addiction as a minor by-product of their creative collaboration.

Their firstborn was my brother Arturo, usually known as Aqua Boy. His hands and feet were in the form of flippers that sprouted directly from his torso without intervening arms or legs. He was taught to swim in infancy and was displayed nude in a big clear-sided tank like an aquarium. His favorite trick at the ages of three and four was to put his face close to the glass, bulging his eyes out at the audience, opening and closing his mouth like a river bass, and then to turn his back and paddle off, revealing the turd trailing from his muscular little buttocks. Al and Lil laughed about it later, but at the time it caused them great consternation as well as the nuisance of sterilizing the tank more often than usual. As the years passed, Arty donned trunks and became more sophisticated, but it's been said, with some truth, that his attitude never really changed.

My sisters, Electra and Iphigenia, were born when Arturo was two years old and starting to haul in crowds. The girls were Siamese twins with perfect upper bodies joined at the waist and sharing one set of hips and legs. They usually sat and walked and slept with their long arms around each other. They were, however, able to face directly forward by allowing the shoulder of one to overlap the other. They were always beautiful, slim, and huge-eyed. They studied the piano and began performing piano duets at an early age. Their compositions for four hands were thought by some to have revolutionized the twelve-tone scale.

I was born three years after my sisters. My father spared no expense in these experiments. My mother had been liberally dosed with cocaine, amphetamines, and arsenic during her ovulation and throughout her pregnancy with me. It was a disappointment when I emerged with such commonplace deformities. My albinism is the regular pink-eyed variety and my hump, though pronounced, is not remarkable in size or shape as humps go. My situation was far too humdrum to be marketable on the same scale as my brother's and sisters'. Still, my parents noted that I had a strong voice and decided I might be an appropriate shill and talker for the business. A bald albino hunchback seemed the right enticement toward the esoteric talents of the rest of the family. The dwarfism, which was very apparent by my third birthday, came as a pleasant surprise to the patient pair and increased my value. From the beginning I slept in the built-in cupboard beneath the sink in the family living van, and had a collection of exotic sunglasses to shield my sensitive eyes.

Nuclear Family Nightmares

Despite the expensive radium treatments incorporated in his design, my younger brother, Fortunato, had a close call in being born to apparent normalcy. That drab state so depressed my enterprising parents that they immediately prepared to abandon him on the doorstep of a closed service station as we passed through Green River, Wyoming, late one night. My father had actually parked the van for a quick getaway and had stepped down to help my mother deposit the baby in the cardboard box on some safe part of the pavement. At that precise moment the two-week-old baby stared vaguely at my mother and in a matter of seconds revealed himself as not a failure at all, but in fact my parents' masterwork. It was lucky, so they named him Fortunato. For one reason and another we always called him Chick.

"Papa," said Iphy. "Yes," said Elly. They were behind his big chair, four arms sliding to tangle his neck, two faces framed in smooth black hair peering at him from either side.

"What are you up to, girlies?" He would laugh and put his magazine down.

"Tell us how you thought of us," they demanded.

I leaned on his knee and looked into his good heavy face. "Please, Papa," I begged, "tell us the Rose Garden."

He would puff and tease and refuse and we would coax. Finally Arty would be sitting in his lap with Papa's arms around him and Chick would be in Lily's lap, and I would lean against Lily's shoulder while Elly and Iphy sat cross-legged on the floor with their four arms behind them like Gothic struts supporting their hunched shoulders, and Al would laugh and tell the story.

"It was in Oregon, up in Portland, which they call the Rose City, though I never got in gear to do anything about it until a year or so later when we were stuck in Fort Lauderdale."

He had been restless one day, troubled by business boondoggles. He drove up into a park on a hillside and got out for a walk. "You could see for miles from up there. And there was a big rose garden with arbors and trellises and fountains. The paths were brick and wound in and out." He sat on a step leading from one terrace to another and stared listlessly at the experimental roses. "It was a test garden, and the colors were . . . designed. Striped and layered. One color inside the petal and another color outside.

"I was mad at Maribelle. She was a pinhead who'd been with your mother and me for a long while. She was trying to hold me up for a raise I couldn't afford."

The roses started him thinking, how the oddity of them was beautiful and how that oddity was contrived to give them value. "It just struck me—clear and complete all at once—no long figuring about it." He realized that children could be designed. "And I thought to myself, now *that* would be a rose garden worthy of a man's interest!"

We children would smile and hug him and he would grin around at us and send the twins for a pot of cocoa from the drink wagon and me for a bag of popcorn because the red-haired girls would just throw it out when they finished closing the concession anyway. And we would all be cozy in the warm booth of the van, eating popcorn and drinking cocoa and feeling like Papa's roses.

OBEY

Ray Bradbury

Fahrenheit 451

MONTAG LOOKED AT THESE men whose faces were sunburnt by a thousand real and ten thousand imaginary fires, whose work flushed their cheeks and fevered their eyes. These men who looked steadily into their platinum igniter flames as they lit their eternally burning black pipes. They and their charcoal hair and soot-colored brows and bluish-ash-smeared cheeks where they had shaven close; but their heritage showed. Montag started up, his mouth opened. Had he ever seen a fireman that *didn't* have black hair, black brows, a fiery face, and a blue-steel shaved but unshaved look? These men were all mirror images of himself! Were all firemen picked then for their looks as well as their proclivities? The color of cinders and ash about them, and the continual smell of burning from their pipes. Captain Beatty there, rising in thunderheads of tobacco smoke. Beatty opening a fresh tobacco packet, crumpling the cellophane into a sound of fire.

Montag looked at the cards in his own hands. "I—I've been thinking. About the fire last week. About the man whose library we fixed. What happened to him?"

"They took him screaming off to the asylum."

"He wasn't insane."

Beatty arranged his cards quietly. "Any man's insane who thinks he can fool the government and us."

"I've tried to imagine," said Montag, "just how it would feel. I mean, to have firemen burn *our* houses and *our* books."

"We haven't any books."

"But if we did have some."

"You *got* some?"

Beatty blinked slowly.

"No." Montag gazed beyond them to the wall with the typed lists of a million forbidden books. Their names leapt in fire, burning down the years under his ax and his hose which sprayed not water but kerosene. "No." But in his mind, a cool wind started up and blew out of the ventilator grille at home, softly, softly, chilling his face. And, again, he saw himself in a green park talking to an old man, a very old man, and the wind from the park was cold, too.

Montag hesitated. "Was—was it always like this? The firehouse, our work? I mean, well, once upon a time . . ."

"Once upon a time!" Beatty said. "What kind of talk is *that?*"

Fool, thought Montag to himself, you'll give it away. At the last fire, a book of fairy tales, he'd glanced at a single line. "I mean," he said, "in the old days, before homes were completely fireproofed—" Suddenly it seemed a much younger voice was speaking for him. He opened his mouth and it was Clarisse McClellan saying, "Didn't firemen *prevent* fires rather than stoke them up and get them going?"

"That's rich!" Stoneman and Black drew forth their rule books, which also contained brief histories of the Firemen of America, and laid them out where Montag, though long familiar with them, might read:

"Established, 1790, to burn English-influenced books in the Colonies. First Fireman: Benjamin Franklin."

RULE 1. Answer the alarm quickly.

2. Start the fire swiftly.

3. Burn everything.

4. Report back to firehouse immediately.

5. Stand alert for other Alarms.

Everyone watched Montag. He did not move.

The alarm sounded.

The bell in the ceiling kicked itself two hundred times. Suddenly there were four empty chairs. The cards fell in a flurry of snow. The brass pole shivered. The men were gone.

Montag sat in his chair. Below, the orange dragon coughed to life.

Montag slid down the pole like a man in a dream.

The Mechanical Hound leapt up in its kennel, its eyes all green flame.

"Montag, you forgot your helmet!"

He seized it off the wall behind him, ran, leapt, and they were off, the night wind hammering about their siren scream and their mighty metal thunder!

It was a flaking three-story house in the ancient part of the city, a century old if it was a day, but like all houses it had been given a fireproof plastic sheath many years ago, and this preservative shell seemed to be the only thing holding it in the sky.

"Here we are!"

The engine slammed to a stop. Beatty, Stoneman, and Black ran up the sidewalk, suddenly odious and fat in their plump fireproof slickers. Montag followed.

They crashed the front door and grabbed at a woman, though she was not running, she was not trying to escape. She was only standing, weaving from side to side, her eyes fixed upon a nothingness in the wall, as if they had struck her a terrible blow upon the head. Her tongue was moving in her mouth, and her eyes seemed to be trying to remember something and then they remembered and her tongue moved again:

" 'Play the man, Master Ridley; we shall this day light such a candle, by God's grace, in England, as I trust shall never be put out.' "

"Enough of that!" said Beatty. "Where are they?"

He slapped her face with amazing objectivity and repeated the question. The old woman's eyes came to a focus upon Beatty. "You know where they are or you wouldn't be here," she said.

Stoneman held out the telephone alarm card with the complaint signed in telephone duplicate on the back:

> "Have reason to suspect attic; 11 No. Elm, City.
> E. B."

"That would be Mrs. Blake, my neighbor," said the woman, reading the initials.

"All right, men, let's get 'em!"

Next thing they were up in musty blackness swinging silver hatchets at doors that were, after all, unlocked, tumbling through like boys all rollick and shout. "Hey!" A fountain of books sprang down upon Montag as he climbed shuddering up the sheer stair well. How inconvenient! Always before it had been like snuffing a candle. The police went first and adhesive-taped the victim's mouth and bandaged him off into their glittering beetle

OBEY

cars, so when you arrived you found an empty house. You weren't hurting anyone, you were hurting only *things!* And since things really couldn't be hurt, since things felt nothing, and things don't scream or whimper, as this woman might begin to scream and cry out, there was nothing to tease your conscience later. You were simply cleaning up. Janitorial work, essentially. Everything to its proper place. Quick with the kerosene! Who's got a match!

But now, tonight, someone had slipped. This woman was spoiling the ritual. The men were making too much noise, laughing, joking, to cover her terrible accusing silence below. She made the empty rooms roar with accusation and shake down a fine dust of guilt that was sucked in their nostrils as they plunged about. It was neither cricket nor correct. Montag felt an immense irritation. She shouldn't be here, on top of everything!

Books bombarded his shoulders, his arms, his upturned face. A book lit, almost obediently, like a white pigeon, in his hands, wings fluttering. In the dim, wavering light, a page hung open and it was like a snowy feather, the words delicately painted thereon. In all the rush and fervor, Montag had only an instant to read a line, but it blazed in his mind for the next minute as if stamped there with fiery steel. "Time has fallen asleep in the afternoon sunshine." He dropped the book. Immediately, another fell into his arms.

"Montag, up here!"

Montag's hand closed like a mouth, crushed the book with wild devotion, with an insanity of mindlessness to his chest. The men above were hurling shovelfuls of magazines into the dusty air. They fell like slaughtered birds and the woman stood below, like a small girl, among the bodies.

Montag had done nothing. His hand had done it all, his hand, with a brain of its own, with a conscience and a curiosity in each trembling finger, had turned thief. Now, it plunged the book back under his arm, pressed it tight to sweating armpit, rushed out empty, with a magician's flourish! Look here! Innocent! Look!

He gazed, shaken, at that white hand. He held it way out, as if he were farsighted. He held it close, as if he were blind.

"Montag!"

He jerked about.

"Don't stand there, idiot!"

The books lay like great mounds of fishes left to dry. The men danced and slipped and fell over them. Titles glittered their golden eyes, falling, gone.

"Kerosene!"

They pumped the cold fluid from the numeraled 451 tanks strapped to their shoulders. They coated each book, they pumped rooms full of it.

They hurried downstairs, Montag staggering after them in the kerosene fumes.

"Come on, woman!"

The woman knelt among the books, touching the drenched leather and cardboard, reading the gilt titles with her fingers while her eyes accused Montag.

"You can't ever have my books," she said.

"You know the law," said Beatty. "Where's your common sense? None of those books agree with each other. You've been locked up here for years with a regular Tower of Babel. Snap out of it! The people in those books never lived. Come on now!"

She shook her head.

"The whole house is going up," said Beatty.

The men walked clumsily to the door. They glanced back at Montag, who stood near the woman.

"You're not leaving her here?" he protested.

"She won't come."

"Force her, then!"

Beatty raised his hand in which was concealed the igniter. "We're due back at the House. Besides, these fanatics always try suicide; the pattern's familiar."

Montag placed his hand on the woman's elbow. "You can come with me."

"No," she said. "Thank you, anyway."

"I'm counting to ten," said Beatty. "One. Two."

"Please," said Montag.

"Go on," said the woman.

"Three. Four."

"Here." Montag pulled at the woman.

The woman replied quietly, "I want to stay here."

"Five. Six."

"You can stop counting," she said. She opened the fingers of one hand slightly and in the palm of the hand was a single slender object.

An ordinary kitchen match.

The sight of it rushed the men out and down away from the house. Captain Beatty, keeping his dignity, backed slowly through the front door, his pink face burnt and shiny from a thousand fires and night excitements. Montag thought, how true! Always at night the alarm comes. Never by day! Is it because fire is prettier by night? More spectacle, a better show? The pink face of Beatty now showed the faintest panic in the door. The woman's hand twitched on the single matchstick. The fumes of kerosene bloomed up about her. Montag felt the hidden book pound like a heart against his chest.

"Go on," said the woman, and Montag felt himself back away and away out the door, after Beatty, down the steps, across the lawn, where the path of kerosene lay like the track of some evil snail.

On the front porch where she had come to weigh them quietly with her eyes, her quietness a condemnation, the woman stood motionless.

Beatty flicked his fingers to spark the kerosene.

He was too late. Montag gasped.

The woman on the porch reached out with contempt to them all, and struck the kitchen match against the railing.

People ran out of houses all down the street.

JACK KETCHUM

The Lost

> . . . *Jennifer saw Ray falling, cursing and twisting and firing again twice and saw Katherine crash to the floor with a bloom of red spreading across the back of her shirt like red ink spilled from an inkwell, Katherine jerking facedown on the bare wood floor, jerking and then still.*

SHE SAW THIS ALL in an instant and couldn't understand how these things could happen, how they could be *accomplished* and so suddenly. The moment had changed everything and astonished her, left her quivering, twitching in its wake as though her body were crawling with spiders. She couldn't have moved from where she was in a million years. *Let alone hit him with a chair. Let alone run.* She was aware of the tangy metallic smell of *gun* and the echo in her ears which blotted out all other sound, aware that at some point during this brief lightning flash of time she'd peed her pants, a sudden voiding, she didn't even know it had happened.

The wife *Elizabeth, her name's Elizabeth for godsakes can't you remember?* was down on her knees on the floor with her husband. She had her hands to his wound, *in* his wound, like she was trying to hold some lost part of him inside. She was shaking her head and sobbing and Jennifer could dimly make out the sounds of her hysterical grief over the roar in her ears.

She heard Ray say something to the woman but she couldn't make that out either.

She watched him glance slowly from one of them to the other. *His glance lingering on each.* Katherine didn't move. She lay on her side still cuffed and tied to the chair, one leg bent at the knee as though frozen in the act of running. The two middle spindles had snapped at the base during her fall.

Sally lay half propped against the wall. There was blood on her forehead.

When he looked at Jennifer she saw him notice how she'd wet herself and saw his lip curl in disgust and realized that she felt no shame in it, no thoughts about it at all, the peeing didn't matter.

He turned abruptly and walked away down the hall—that choppy, jerky walk of his—digging into his jeans for bullets to reload the gun and disappeared.

She still couldn't move.

She wasn't like the others. The others didn't know him.

They did now.

She was pinned to the spot.

The woman Elizabeth didn't seem to be aware of his leaving. Her eyes were shut against the steady flow of tears and she was shaking with hysteria and her hands were red with blood nearly to the elbow. She kept rocking him. Holding on to the ruined head. *Holding him in.*

Her skirt was sodden.

He was gone just a moment.

When he returned his eyes were wide and seemed to focus *outside* the room, not on her or any of them or anything in the room in particular but beyond or maybe inward, she didn't know. He drifted into the room like a ghost and his head turned for a long moment to where the circular mirror had left its clean impression on the wall and he had the gun in one fist and a serrated steel carving knife in the other.

He stared at the spot like there still was a mirror there and then he turned.

Light and dark swam together the second time for her that night and she clutched at the arms of the chair knowing she could not lose consciousness, not now or else she might never wake up again so she gripped the chair until her fingers ached and slowly the room and everything in it returned to her the way she needed it to return, blank pale walls and covered furniture. Sally against the wall. Katherine in the hall. She saw that he'd drifted past her, was moving slowly past to stand behind the woman kneeling with her husband on the floor. He shoved the revolver into his belt.

He raised the knife and held it above her pointed down and her hearing had returned enough by then for her to hear him mutter *do her just like Sharon, he was talking about Sharon Tate* and if the woman even knew he was standing there she didn't show it, she just kept holding on to her husband's head until the knife came down and entered her just above the collarbone and she yelped like a struck dog and blood spurted up and out and Ray pushed the entire length of the blade down into her.

Her arms flew up and clutched his fists on the handle of the knife and he pulled it out, a rough sawing motion and he reached for her shoulder and pushed her face-first across her husband, her blood already pooling on the floor as now the hands went to her own pulsing wound as before they bad gone to his, *holding it in, holding in the life.* A high mewling and a gurgling sound were coming out of her and blood ran down her chin and Jennifer looked away, just closed her eyes and looked away until she heard a thump on the floor beside her.

She looked down startled by the sound and saw that Ray had rolled the woman over on her back and pushed her again so that she lay sprawled right at her feet, the thump was the back of her head against the floor. Instinctively she drew her feet in beneath the chair seat as though away from something dirty and polluted flowing toward her, away from what he was doing, cutting through the buttons of her blouse and unzipping the skirt and pulling it down around her thighs, cutting through the white padded bra while the woman choked on her blood, the woman staring up at the ceiling and coughing a thin, bloody spray at him up into his face which he wiped away with the back of his hand, the one that held the knife which then cut through the panties too, and Jennifer closed her eyes a second time.

She had to.

She was going to be sick. She was going to throw up again.

She knew what they'd done to Sharon Tate.

They'd cut out her baby.

And that's what Ray was mumbling about, that and all the other filthy things they did to her, toneless, mild, talking about *cutting her tits off and carving these words in her belly and blood on the walls and that'll give 'em something to think about absolutely, cut out the baby and put it in her lap, wrap the cord around her neck* and telling the woman to beg, *beg* for her baby and meantime he was stabbing her over and over god knows how many times she could hear the woman's tiny cries deep in her throat and thumping sounds like melons dropping, heard every impact, she could smell the blood in the air thick as the smell in a butcher shop, she could hear it fall like heavy raindrops on the floor, imagine it flowing pooling toward her feet.

Please stop you have to stop! she thought, *she was going to go crazy if he didn't, she was going to, it was going to happen, please, what you heard could drive you insane* and heard two footfalls and a crash, glass breaking and she opened her eyes and saw Sally standing over him, blood running down her cheek and holding the finial and harp and socket and part of the broken base of a white china lamp in her hands. She saw Ray covered with shards and china dust reel across the glistening naked body beneath him and throw out his hand for balance, saw it slide across the blood-soaked floor so that he came down hard on his elbow and she felt a wild surge of pleasure at his pain.

"BIIITCH!" he roared and reached for the pistol in his belt, the rifle slung over his back clattering against the floor as he rolled but Sally just took another step forward. She could see that Sally was terrified to move anywhere near him but she did, *she did it anyway!* and shoved the jagged base of porcelain into his face, hard against his forehead and cheek so she heard it scrape bone and suddenly he was screaming and bleeding, *Ray* was bleeding *not* somebody else, bleeding from his head and from his face, and Jennifer brought both her legs out from under the chair as fast and hard as she could and kicked him in the back of the head, aiming for the blood that already welled there.

The effort almost toppled the chair and her with it. She didn't care. It felt good. *It felt wonderful!*

She watched him fall forward over the woman's body, fall face-to-face with the woman, Ray staring down into her open dead eyes and open mouth just a moment before what was left of the lamp came down on him again, Sally not finished, not finished with him yet, going after him—then his hand shot out and gripped the base of the lamp and pulled it from her hands and sailed it across the room over his head and he staggered dazed to his feet. She saw Sally backing away and looking for something else to hurt him with but there was nothing, only boxes and crates and chairs and then the pistol was out of his belt and pointing at her ending all bravery and all resistance.

In the silence she heard two women cry out, a dissonant two-part harmony. One of the voices was hers.

Philip K. Dick

Sales Pitch

IN THE EVENING DARKNESS the robot was a silent, unmoving figure. A cold wind blew around it and into the house. Morris shivered and moved back from the door. "What do you want?" he demanded. A strange fear licked at him. "What is it?"

The robot was larger than any he had seen. Tall and broad, with heavy metallic grippers and elongated eye-lenses. Its upper trunk was a square tank instead of the usual cone. It rested on four treads, not the customary two. It towered over Morris, almost seven feet high. Massive and solid.

"Good evening," it said calmly. Its voice was whipped around by the night wind; it mixed with the dismal noises of evening, the echoes of traffic and the clang of distant street signals. A few vague shapes hurried through the gloom. The world was black and hostile.

"Evening," Morris responded automatically. He found himself trembling. "What are you selling?"

"I would like to show you a fasrad," the robot said.

Morris' mind was numb; it refused to respond. What was a *fasrad?* There was something dreamlike and nightmarish going on. He struggled to get his mind and body together. "A what?" he croaked.

"A fasrad." The robot made no effort to explain. It regarded him without emotion, as if it was not its responsibility to explain anything. "It will take only a moment."

"I—" Morris began. He moved back, out of the wind. And the robot, without change of expression, glided past him and into the house.

"Thank you," it said. It halted in the middle of the living room. "Would you call your wife, please? I would like to show her the fasrad, also."

"Sally," Morris muttered helplessly. "Come here."

Sally swept breathlessly into the living room, her breasts quivering with excitement. "What is it? Oh!" She saw the robot and halted uncertainly. "Ed, did you order something? Are we buying something?"

"Good evening," the robot said to her. "I am going to show you the fasrad. Please be seated. On the couch, if you will. Both together."

Sally sat down expectantly, her cheeks flushed, eyes bright with wonder and bewilderment. Numbly, Ed seated himself beside her. "Look," he muttered thickly. "What the hell is a fasrad? *What's going on?* I don't want to buy anything!"

"What is your name?" the robot asked him.

"Morris." He almost choked. "Ed Morris."

The robot turned to Sally. "Mrs. Morris." It bowed slightly. "I'm glad to meet you, Mr. and Mrs. Morris. You are the first persons in your neighborhood to see the fasrad. This is the initial demonstration in this area." Its cold eyes swept the room. "Mr. Morris, you are employed, I assume. Where are you employed?"

"He works on Ganymede," Sally said dutifully, like a little girl in school. "For the Terran Metals Development Co."

The robot digested this information. "A fasrad will be of value to you." It eyed Sally. "What do you do?"

"I'm a tape transcriber at Histo-Research."

"A fasrad will be of no value in your professional work, but it will be helpful here in the home." It picked up a table in its powerful steel grippers. "For example, sometimes an attractive piece of furniture is damaged by a clumsy guest." The robot smashed the table to bits; fragments of wood and plastic rained down. "A fasrad is needed."

Morris leaped helplessly to his feet. He was powerless to halt events; a numbing weight hung over him, as the robot tossed the fragments of table away and selected a heavy floor lamp.

"Oh dear," Sally gasped. "That's my best lamp."

"When a fasrad is possessed, there is nothing to fear." The robot seized the lamp and twisted it grotesquely. It ripped the shade, smashed the bulbs, then threw away the remnants. "A situation of this kind can occur from some violent explosion, such as an H-Bomb."

"For God's sake," Morris muttered. "We—"

"An H-Bomb attack may never occur," the robot continued, "but in such an event a fasrad is indispensable." It knelt down and pulled an intricate tube from its waist. Aiming the tube at the floor it atomized a hole five feet in diameter. It stepped back from the yawning pocket. "I have not extended this tunnel, but you can see a fasrad would save your life in case of attack."

The word *attack* seemed to set off a new train of reactions in its metal brain.

"Sometimes a thug or hood will attack a person at night," it continued. Without warning it whirled and drove its fist through the wall. A section of the wall collapsed in a heap of powder and debris. "That takes care of the thug." The robot straightened out and peered around the room. "Often you are too tired in the evening to manipulate the buttons on the stove." It strode into the kitchen and began punching the stove controls; immense quantities of food spilled in all directions.

"Stop!" Sally cried. "Get away from my stove!"

"You may be too weary to run water for your bath." The robot tripped the controls of the tub and water poured down. "Or you may wish to go right to bed." It yanked the bed from its concealment and threw it flat. Sally retreated in fright as the robot advanced toward her. "Sometimes after a hard day at work you are too tired to remove your clothing. In that event—"

"Get out of here!" Morris shouted at it. "Sally, run and get the cops. The thing's gone crazy. *Hurry.*"

"The fasrad is a necessity in all modern homes," the robot continued. "For example, an appliance may break down. The fasrad repairs it instantly." It seized the automatic humidity control and tore the wiring and replaced it on the wall. "Sometimes you would prefer not to go to work. The fasrad is permitted by law to occupy your position for a consecutive period not to exceed ten days. If, after that period—"

"Good God," Morris said, as understanding finally came. "You're the fasrad."

"That's right," the robot agreed. "Fully Automatic Self-Regulating Android (Domestic). There is also the fasrac (Construction), the fasram (Managerial), the fasras (Soldier), and the fasrab (Bureaucrat). I am designed for home use."

"You—" Sally gasped. "You're for sale. You're selling yourself."

"I am demonstrating myself," the fasrad, the robot, answered. Its impassive metal eyes were fixed intently on Morris as it continued, "I am sure, Mr. Morris, you would like to own me. I am reasonably priced and fully guaranteed. A full book of instructions is included. I cannot conceive of taking *no* for an answer."

Clive Barker

The Hellbound Heart

AND THEN, LIGHT.

It came from *them:* from the quartet of Cenobites who now, with the wall sealed behind them, occupied the room. A fitful phosphorescence, like the glow of deep-sea fishes: blue, cold, charmless. It struck Frank that he had never once wondered what they would look like. His imagination, though fertile when it came to trickery and theft, was impoverished in other regards. The skill to picture these eminences was beyond him, so he had not even tried.

Why then was he so distressed to set eyes upon them? Was it the scars that covered every inch of their bodies, the flesh cosmetically punctured and sliced and infibulated, then dusted down with ash? Was it the smell of vanilla they brought with them, the sweetness of which did little to disguise the stench beneath? Or was it that as the light grew, and he scanned them more closely, he saw nothing of joy, or even humanity, in their maimed faces: only desperation, and an appetite that made his bowels ache to be voided.

"What city is this?" one of the four enquired. Frank had difficulty guessing the speaker's gender with any certainty. Its clothes, some of which were sewn *to* and *through* its skin, hid its private parts, and there was nothing in the dregs of its voice, or in its willfully disfigured features that offered the least clue. When it spoke, the hooks that transfixed the flaps of its eyes and were wed, by an intricate system of chains passed through flesh and bone alike, to similar hooks through the lower lip, were teased by the motion, exposing the glistening meat beneath.

"I asked you a question," it said. Frank made no reply. The name of this city was the last thing on his mind.

"Do you understand?" the figure beside the first speaker demanded. Its voice, unlike that of its companion, was light and breathy—the voice of an excited girl. Every inch of its head had been tattooed with an intricate grid, and at every intersection of horizontal and vertical axes a jeweled pin driven through to the bone. Its tongue was similarly decorated. "Do you even know who we are?" it asked.

"Yes." Frank said at last. "I know."

Of course he knew; he and Kircher had spent long nights talking of hints gleaned from the diaries of Bolingbroke and Gilles de Rais. All that mankind knew of the Order of the Gash, he knew.

And yet . . . he had expected something different. Expected some sign of the numberless splendors they had access to. He had thought they would come with women, at least; oiled women, milked women; women shaved and muscled for the act of love: their lips perfumed, their thighs trembling to spread, their buttocks weighty, the way he liked them. He had expected sighs, and languid bodies spread on the floor underfoot like a living carpet; had expected virgin whores whose every crevice was his for the asking and whose skills would press him—*upward, upward*—to undreamed-of ecstasies. The world would be forgotten in their arms. He would be exalted by his lust, instead of despised for it.

OBEY

But no. No women, no sighs. Only these sexless *things*, with their corrugated flesh.

Now the third spoke. Its features were so heavily scarified—the wounds nurtured until they ballooned—that its eyes were invisible and its words corrupted by the disfigurement of its mouth.

"What do you want?" it asked him.

He perused this questioner more confidently than he had the other two. His fear was draining away with every second that passed. Memories of the terrifying place beyond the wall were already receding. He was left with these decrepit decadents, with their stench, their queer deformity, their self-evident frailty. The only thing he had to fear was nausea.

"Kircher told me there would be five of you," Frank said.

"The Engineer will arrive should the moment merit," came the reply. "Now again, we ask you: *What do you want?*"

Why should he not answer them straight? "Pleasure," he replied. "Kircher said you know about pleasure."

"Oh we do," said the first of them. "Everything you ever wanted."

"Yes?"

"Of course. Of course." It stared at him with its all-too-naked eyes. "What have you dreamed?" it said.

The question, put so baldly, confounded him. How could he hope to articulate the nature of the phantasms his libido had created? He was still searching for words when one of them said:

"This world . . . it disappoints you?"

"Pretty much," he replied.

"You're not the first to tire of its trivialities," came the response. "There have been others."

"Not many," the gridded face put in.

"True. A handful at best. But a few have dared to use Lemarchand's Configuration. Men like yourself, hungry for new possibilities, who've heard that we have skills unknown in your region."

"I'd expected—" Frank began.

"We *know* what you expected," the Cenobite replied. "We understand to its breadth and depth the nature of your frenzy. It is utterly familiar to us."

Frank grunted. "So," he said, "you know what I've dreamed about. You can supply the pleasure."

The thing's face broke open, its lips curling back: a baboon's smile. "Not as you understand it," came the reply.

Frank made to interrupt, but the creature raised a silencing hand.

OBEY

"There are conditions of the nerve endings," it said, "the like of which your imagination, however fevered, could not hope to evoke."

". . . yes?"

"Oh yes. Oh most certainly. Your most treasured depravity is child's play beside the experiences we offer."

"Will you partake of them?" said the second Cenobite.

Frank looked at the scars and the hooks. Again, his tongue was deficient. *"Will you?"*

Outside, somewhere near, the world would soon be waking. He had watched it wake from the window of this very room, day after day, stirring itself to another round of fruitless pursuits, and he'd known, *known*, that there was nothing left out there to excite him. No heat, only sweat. No passion, only sudden lust, and just as sudden indifference. He had turned his back on such dissatisfaction. If in doing so he had to interpret the signs these creatures brought him, then that was the price of ambition. He was ready to pay it.

"Show me," he said.

"There's no going back. You do understand that?"

"Show me."

They needed no further invitation to raise the curtain. He heard the door creak as it was opened, and turned to see that the world beyond the threshold had disappeared, to be replaced by the same panic-filled darkness from which the members of the Order had stepped. He looked back towards the Cenobites, seeking some explanation for this. But they'd disappeared. Their passing had not gone unrecorded however. They'd taken the flowers with them, leaving only bare boards, and on the wall the offerings he had assembled were blackening, as if in the heat of some fierce but invisible flame. He smelled the bitterness of their consumption; it pricked his nostrils so acutely he was certain they would bleed.

But the smell of burning was only the beginning. No sooner had he registered it than half a dozen other scents filled his head. Perfumes he had scarcely noticed until now were suddenly overpoweringly strong. The lingering scent of filched blossoms; the smell of the paint on the ceiling and the sap in the wood beneath his feet—all filled his head. He could even smell the darkness outside the door, and in it, the ordure of a hundred thousand birds.

He put his hand to his mouth and nose, to stop the onslaught from overcoming him, but the stench of perspiration on his fingers made him giddy. He might have been driven to nausea had there not been fresh sensations flooding his system from each nerve ending and taste bud.

It seemed he could suddenly feel the collision of the dust motes with his skin. Every drawn breath chafed his lips; every blink, his eyes. Bile burned in the back of his throat, and a morsel of yesterday's beef that had lodged between his teeth sent spasms through his system as it exuded a droplet of gravy upon his tongue.

His ears were no less sensitive. His head was filled with a thousand dins, some of which he himself was father to. The air that broke against his eardrums was a hurricane; the flatulence in his bowels was thunder. But there were other sounds—innumerable sounds—which assailed him from somewhere beyond himself. Voices raised in anger, whispered professions of love, roars and rattlings, snatches of song, tears.

Was it the world he was hearing—morning breaking in a thousand homes? He had no chance to listen closely; the cacophony drove any power of analysis from his head.

But there was worse. The eyes! Oh god in heaven, he had never guessed that they could be such torment; he, who'd thought there was nothing on earth left to startle him. Now he reeled! Everywhere, *sight!*

The plain plaster of the ceiling was an awesome geography of brush strokes. The weave of his plain shirt an unbearable elaboration of threads. In the corner he saw a mite move on a dead dove's head, and wink its eyes at him, seeing that he saw. Too much! *Too much!*

Appalled, he shut his eyes. But there was more *inside* than out; memories whose violence shook him to the verge of senselessness. He sucked his mother's milk, and choked; felt his sibling's arms around him (a fight, was it, or a brotherly embrace? Either way, it suffocated). And more; so much more. A short lifetime of sensations, all writ in a perfect hand upon his cortex, and breaking him with their insistence that they be remembered.

He felt close to exploding. Surely the world outside his head—the room, and the birds beyond the door—they, for all their shrieking excesses, could not be as overwhelming as his memories. Better that, he thought, and tried to open his eyes. But they wouldn't unglue. Tears or pus or needle and thread had sealed them up.

He thought of the faces of the Cenobites: the hooks, the chains. Had they worked some similar surgery upon him, locking him up behind his eyes with the parade of his history?

In fear for his sanity, he began to address them, though he was no longer certain that they were even within earshot.

"Why?" he asked. "Why are you doing this to me?"

The echo of his words roared in his ears, but he scarcely attended to it. More sense impressions were swimming up from the past to torment him. Childhood still lingered on his tongue (milk and frustration) but there were

OBEY

adult feelings joining it now. He was grown! He was mustached and mighty, hands heavy, gut large.

Youthful pleasures had possessed the appeal of newness, but as the years had crept on, and mild sensation lost its potency, stronger and stronger experiences had been called for. And here they came again, more pungent for being laid in the darkness at the back of his head.

He felt untold tastes upon his tongue: bitter, sweet, sour, salty; smelled spice and shit and his mother's hair; saw cities and skies; saw speed, saw deeps; broke bread with men now dead and was scalded by the heat of their spittle on his cheek.

And of course there were women.

Always, amid the flurry and confusion, memories of women appeared, assaulting him with their scents, their textures, their tastes.

The proximity of this harem aroused him, despite circumstances. He opened his trousers and caressed his cock, more eager to have the seed spilled and so be freed of these creatures than for the pleasure of it.

He was dimly aware, as he worked his inches, that he must make a pitiful sight: a blind man in an empty room, aroused for a dream's sake. But the wracking, joyless orgasm failed to even slow the relentless display. His knees buckled, and his body collapsed to the boards where his spunk had fallen. There was a spasm of pain as he hit the floor, but the response was washed away before another wave of memories.

He rolled onto his back, and screamed; screamed and begged for an end to it, but the sensations only rose higher still, whipped to fresh heights with every prayer for cessation he offered up.

The pleas became a single sound, words and sense eclipsed by panic. It seemed there was no end to this, but madness. No hope but to be lost to hope.

As he formulated this last, despairing thought, the torment stopped.

All at once; all of it. Gone. Sight, sound, touch, taste, smell. He was abruptly bereft of them all. There were seconds then, when he doubted his very existence. Two heartbeats, three, four.

On the fifth beat, he opened his eyes. The room was empty, the doves and the piss-pot gone. The door was closed.

Gingerly, he sat up. His limbs were tingling; his head, wrist, and bladder ached.

And then—a movement at the other end of the room drew his attention.

Where, two moments before, there had been an empty space, there was now a figure. It was the fourth Cenobite, the one that had never spoken, nor shown its face. Not *it*, he now saw: but *she*. The hood it had worn had been discarded, as had the robes. The woman beneath was gray yet

OBEY

gleaming, her lips bloody, her legs parted so that the elaborate scarification of her pubis was displayed. She sat on a pile of rotting human heads, and smiled in welcome.

The collision of sensuality and death appalled him. Could he have any doubt that she had personally dispatched these victims? Their rot was beneath her nails, and their tongues—twenty or more—lay out in ranks on her oiled thighs, as if awaiting entrance. Nor did he doubt that the brains now seeping from their ears and nostrils had been driven to insanity before a blow or a kiss had stopped their hearts.

Kircher had lied to him—either that or he'd been horribly deceived. There was no pleasure in the air; or at least not as humankind understood it.

He had made a mistake opening Lemarchand's box. A very terrible mistake.

"Oh, so you've finished dreaming," said the Cenobite, perusing him as he lay panting on the bare boards. "Good."

She stood up. The tongues fell to the floor, like a rain of slugs.

"Now we can begin," she said.

WILLIAM S. BURROUGHS

Naked Lunch

THE EXAMINATION

CARL PETERSON FOUND A postcard in his box requesting him to report for a ten o'clock appointment with Doctor Benway in the Ministry of Mental Hygiene and Prophylaxis. . . .

"What on earth could they want with me?" he thought irritably. . . . "A mistake most likely." But he knew they didn't make mistakes. . . . Certainly not mistakes of identity. . . .

It would not have occurred to Carl to disregard the appointment even though failure to appear entailed no penalty. . . . Freeland was a welfare state. If a citizen wanted anything from a load of bone meal to a sexual partner some department was ready to offer effective aid. The threat implicit in this enveloping benevolence stifled the concept of rebellion. . . .

Carl walked through the Town Hall Square. . . . Nickel nudes sixty feet high with brass genitals soaped themselves under gleaming showers. . . . The Town Hall cupola, of glass brick and copper, crashed into the sky.

Carl stared back at a homosexual American tourist who dropped his eyes and fumbled with the light filters of his Leica. . . .

Carl entered the steel enamel labyrinth of the Ministry, strode to the information desk . . . and presented his card.

"Fifth floor . . . Room twenty-six . . ."

In room twenty-six a nurse looked at him with cold undersea eyes.

"Doctor Benway is expecting you," she said smiling. "Go right in."

"As if he had nothing to do but wait for me," thought Carl. . . .

The office was completely silent, and filled with milky light. The doctor shook Carl's hand, keeping his eyes on the young man's chest. . . .

"I've seen this man before," Carl thought. . . . "But where?"

He sat down and crossed his legs. He glanced at an ashtray on the desk and lit a cigarette. . . . He turned to the doctor a steady inquiring gaze in which there was more than a touch of insolence.

The doctor seemed embarrassed. . . . He fidgeted and coughed . . . and fumbled with papers. . . .

"Hurumph," he said finally. . . . "Your name is Carl Peterson I believe. . . ." His glasses slid down into his nose in parody of the academic manner. . . . Carl nodded silently. . . . The doctor did not look at him but seemed none the less to register the acknowledgment. . . . He pushed his glasses back into place with one finger and opened a file on the white enamelled desk.

"Mmmmmmmm. Carl Peterson," he repeated the name caressingly, pursed his lips and nodded several times. He spoke again abruptly: "You know of course that we are trying. We are all trying. Sometimes of course we don't succeed." His voice trailed off thin and tenuous. He put a hand to his forehead. "To adjust the state—simply a tool—to the needs of each individual citizen." His voice boomed out so unexpectedly deep and loud that Carl started. "That is the only function of the state as we see it. Our knowledge . . . incomplete, of course," he made a slight gesture of depreciation. . . . "For example . . . *for example* . . . take the matter of uh *sexual deviation*." The doctor rocked back and forth in his chair. His glasses slid down onto his nose. Carl felt suddenly uncomfortable.

"We regard it as a misfortune . . . a sickness . . . certainly nothing to be censored or uh sanctioned any more than say . . . tuberculosis. . . . Yes," he repeated firmly as if Carl had raised an objection. . . . "Tuberculosis. On the other hand you can readily see that *any* illness imposes certain, should we say *obligations*, certain *necessities* of a prophylactic nature on the authorities concerned with public health, such necessities to be imposed, needless to say,

OBEY

with a minimum of inconvenience and hardship to the unfortunate individual who has, through no fault of his own, become uh infected. . . . That is to say, of course, the minimum hardship compatible with adequate protection of other individuals who are not so infected. . . . We do not find obligatory vaccination for smallpox an unreasonable measure. . . . Nor isolation for certain contagious diseases. . . . I am sure you will agree that individuals infected with hurumph what the French call '*les malades gallants*' heh heh heh should be compelled to undergo treatment if they do not report voluntarily." The doctor went on chuckling and rocking in his chair like a mechanical toy. . . . Carl realized that he was expected to say something.

"That seems reasonable," he said.

The doctor stopped chuckling. He was suddenly motionless. "Now to get back to this uh matter of sexual deviation. Frankly we don't pretend to understand—at least not completely—why some men and women prefer the uh sexual company of their own sex. We do know that the uh phenomena is common enough, and, under certain circumstances a matter of uh concern to this department."

For the first time the doctor's eyes flickered across Carl's face. Eyes without a trace of warmth or hate or any emotion that Carl had ever experienced in himself or seen in another, at once cold and intense, predatory and impersonal. Carl suddenly felt trapped in this silent underwater cave of a room, cut off from all sources of warmth and certainty. His picture of himself sitting there calm, alert with a trace of well mannered contempt went dim, as if vitality were draining out of him to mix with the milky grey medium of the room.

"Treatment of these disorders is, at the present time, hurumph symptomatic." The doctor suddenly threw himself back in his chair and burst into peals of metallic laughter. Carl watched him appalled. . . . "The man is insane," he thought. The doctor's face went blank as a gambler's. Carl felt an odd sensation in his stomach like the sudden stopping of an elevator.

The doctor was studying the file in front of him. He spoke in a tone of slightly condescending amusement:

"Don't look so frightened, young man. Just a professional joke. To say treatment is symptomatic means there is none, except to make the patient feel as comfortable as possible. And that is precisely what we attempt to do in these cases." Once again Carl felt the impact of that cold interest on his face. "That is to say reassurance when reassurance is necessary . . . and, of course, suitable outlets with other individuals of similar tendencies. No isolation is indicated . . . the condition is no more directly contagious than cancer. Cancer, my first love," the doctor's voice receded. He seemed actually to have gone away through an invisible door leaving his empty body sitting there at the desk.

Suddenly he spoke again in a crisp voice. "And so you may well wonder why we concern ourselves with the matter at all?" He flashed a smile bright and cold as snow in sunlight.

Carl shrugged: "That is not my business . . . what I am wondering is why you have asked me to come here and why you tell me all this . . . this . . ."

"Nonsense?"

Carl was annoyed to find himself blushing.

The doctor leaned back and placed the ends of his fingers together:

"The young," he said indulgently. "Always they are in a hurry. One day perhaps you will learn the meaning of patience. No, Carl. . . . I may call you Carl? I am not evading your question. In cases of suspected tuberculosis we—that is the appropriate department—may ask, even *request*, someone to appear for a fluoroscopic examination. This is routine, you understand. Most such examinations turn up negative. So you have been asked to report here for, should I say a psychic fluoroscope???? I may add that after talking with you I feel *relatively* sure that the result will be, for practical purposes, negative. . . ."

"But the whole thing is ridiculous. I have always interested myself only in girls. I have a steady girl now and we plan to marry."

"Yes Carl, I know. And that is why you are here. A blood test prior to marriage, this is reasonable, no?"

"Please doctor, speak directly."

The doctor did not seem to hear. He drifted out of his chair and began walking around behind Carl, his voice languid and intermittent like music down a windy street.

"I may tell you in strictest confidence that there is definite evidence of a hereditary factor. Social pressure. Many homosexuals latent and overt do, unfortunately, marry. Such marriages often result in . . . Factor of infantile environment." The doctor's voice went on and on. He was talking about schizophrenia, cancer, hereditary dysfunction of the hypothalamus.

Carl dozed off. He was opening a green door. A horrible smell grabbed his lungs and he woke up with a shock. The doctor's voice was strangely flat and lifeless, a whispering junky voice:

"The Kleiberg-Stanislouski semen floculation test . . . a diagnostic tool . . . indicative at least in a negative sense. In certain cases useful—taken as part of the whole picture. . . . Perhaps under the uh *circumstances*." The doctor's voice shot up to a pathic scream. "The nurse will take your uh *specimen*."

"This way please. . . ." The nurse opened the door into a bare white walled cubicle. She handed him a jar.

OBEY

"Use this please. Just yell when you're ready."

There was a jar of K. Y. on a glass shelf. Carl felt ashamed as if his mother had laid out a handkerchief for him. Some coy little message stitched on like: "If I was a cunt we could open a dry goods store."

Ignoring the K.Y., he ejaculated into the jar, a cold brutal fuck of the nurse standing her up against a glass brick wall. "Old Glass Cunt," he sneered, and saw a cunt full of colored glass splinters under the Northern Lights.

He washed his penis and buttoned up his pants.

Something was watching his every thought and movement with cold, sneering hate, the shifting of his testes, the contractions of his rectum. He was in a room filled with green light. There was a stained wood double bed, a black wardrobe with full length mirror. Carl could not see his face. Someone was sitting in a black hotel chair. He was wearing a stiff bosomed white shirt and a dirty paper tie. The face swollen, skull-less, eyes like burning pus.

"Something wrong?" said the nurse indifferently. She was holding a glass of water out to him. She watched him drink with aloof contempt. She turned and picked up the jar with obvious distaste.

The nurse turned to him: "Are you waiting for something special?" she snapped. Carl had never been spoken to like that in his adult life. "Why no. . . ." "You can go then," she turned back to the jar. With a little exclamation of disgust she wiped a gob of semen off her hand. Carl crossed the room and stood at the door.

"Do I have another appointment?"

She looked at him in disapproving surprise: "You'll be notified *of course*." She stood in the doorway of the cubicle and watched him walk through the outer office and open the door. He turned and attempted a jaunty wave. The nurse did not move or change her expression. As he walked down the stairs the broken, false grin burned his face with shame. A homosexual tourist looked at him and raised a knowing eyebrow. "Something *wrong?*"

Carl ran into a park and found an empty bench beside a bronze faun with cymbals.

"Let your hair down, chicken. You'll feel better." The tourist was leaning over him, his camera swinging in Carl's face like a great dangling tit.

"Fuck off you!"

Carl saw something ignoble and hideous reflected back in the queen's spayed animal brown eyes.

"Oh! I wouldn't be calling any names if I were you, chicken. You're hooked too. I saw you coming out of The Institute."

OBEY

"What do you mean by that?" Carl demanded.

"Oh nothing. Nothing at all."

"Well, Carl," the doctor began smiling and keeping his eyes on a level with Carl's mouth. "I have some good news for you." He picked up a slip of blue paper off the desk and went through an elaborate pantomime of focusing his eyes on it. "Your uh test . . . the Robinson-Kleiberg floculation test . . ."

"I thought it was a Blomberg-Stanlouski test."

The doctor tittered. "Oh dear no. . . . You are getting ahead of me young man. You might have misunderstood. The Blomberg-Stanlouski, weeell that's a different sort of test altogether. I *do hope* . . . not necessary. . . ." He tittered again: "But as I was saying before I was so charmingly interrupted . . . by my hurumph learned young colleague. Your KS seems to be . . ." He held the slip at arm's length. ". . . completely uh negative. So perhaps we won't be troubling you any further. And so . . ." He folded the slip carefully into a file. He leafed through the file. Finally he stopped and frowned and pursed his lips. He closed the file and put his hand flat on it and leaned forward.

"Carl, when you were doing your military service . . . There must have been . . . in fact there *were* long periods when you found yourself deprived of the uh consolations and uh *facilities* of the fair sex. During these no doubt trying and difficult periods you had perhaps a pin up girl?? Or more likely a pin up harem?? Heh heh heh . . ."

Carl looked at the doctor with overt distaste. "Yes, of course," he said. "We all did."

"And now, Carl, I would like to show you some pin up girls." He pulled an envelope out of a drawer. "And ask you to please pick out the one you would most like to uh make heh heh heh. . . ." He suddenly leaned forward fanning the photographs in front of Carl's face. "Pick a girl, any girl!"

Carl reached out with numb fingers and touched one of the photographs. The doctor put the photo back into the pack and shuffled and cut and he placed the pack on Carl's file and slapped it smartly. He spread the photos face up in front of Carl. "Is she there?"

Carl shook his head.

"Of course not. She is in here where she belongs. A woman's place what???" He opened the file and held out the girl's photo attached to a Rorschach plate.

"Is that her?"

Carl nodded silently.

"You have good taste, my boy. I may tell you in strictest confidence that some of these girls . . ." with gambler fingers he shifts the photos in Three

OBEY

Card Monte Passes—"are really *boys*. In uh *drag* I believe is the word???" His eyebrows shot up and down with incredible speed. Carl could not be sure he had seen anything unusual. The doctor's face opposite him was absolutely immobile and expressionless. Once again Carl experienced the floating sensation in his stomach and genitals of a sudden elevator stop.

"Yes, Carl, you seem to be running our little obstacle course with flying colors. . . . I guess you think this is all pretty silly don't you now . . . ???"

"Well, to tell the truth . . . Yes . . ."

"You are frank, Carl. . . . This is good. . . . And now . . . Carl . . ." He dragged the name out caressingly like a sweet con dick about to offer you an Old Gold—(just like a cop to smoke Old Golds somehow) and go into his act. . . .

The con dick does a little dance step.

"Why don't you make The Man a proposition?" he jerks a head towards his glowering super-ego who is always referred to in the third person as "The Man" or "The Lieutenant."

"That's the way the Lieutenant is, you play fair with him and he'll play fair with you. . . . We'd like to go light on you. . . . If you could help us in some way." His words open out into a desolate waste of cafeterias and street corners and lunch rooms. Junkies look the other way munching pound cake.

"The Fag is wrong."

The Fag slumps in a hotel chair knocked out on goof balls with his tongue lolling out.

He gets up in a goof ball trance, hangs himself without altering his expression or pulling his tongue in.

The dick is diddling on a pad.

"Know Marty Steel?" Diddle.

"Yes."

"Can you score off him?" Diddle? Diddle?

"He's skeptical."

"But you can score." Diddle diddle "You scored off him last week didn't you?" Diddle???

"Yes."

"Well you can score off him this week." Diddle . . . Diddle . . . Diddle . . . "You can score off him today." No diddle.

"No! No! Not that!!"

"Now look are you going to cooperate"—three vicious diddles—"or does the . . . does the Man cornhole you???" He raises a fay eyebrow.

"And so Carl you will please oblige to tell me how many times and under what circumstances you have uh indulged in homosexual acts???" His voice drifts away. "If you have never done so I shall be inclined to think of you as a

OBEY

somewhat atypical young man." The doctor raises a coy admonishing finger. "In any case . . ." He tapped the file and flashed a hideous leer. Carl noticed that the file was six inches thick. In fact it seemed to have thickened enormously since he entered the room.

"Well, when I was doing my military service . . . These queers used to proposition me and sometimes . . . when I was blank . . ."

"Yes, of course, Carl," the doctor brayed heartily. "In your position I would have done the same I don't mind telling you heh heh heh. . . . Well, I guess we can uh *dismiss as irrelevant* these uh understandable means of replenishing the uh *exchequer.* And now, Carl, there were perhaps"—one finger tapped the file which gave out a faint effluvia of moldy jock straps and chlorine—"occasions. When no uh economic factors were involved."

A green flare exploded in Carl's brain. He saw Hans' lean brown body—twisting towards him, quick breath on his shoulder. The flare went out. Some huge insect was squirming in his hand.

His whole being jerked away in an electric spasm of revulsion.

Carl got to his feet shaking with rage.

"What are you writing there?" he demanded.

"Do you often doze off like that? In the middle of a conversation . . . ?"

"I wasn't asleep that is."

"You weren't?"

"It's just that the *whole thing* is unreal. . . . I'm going now. I don't care. You can't force me to stay."

He was walking across the room towards the door. He had been walking a long time. A creeping numbness dragged his legs. The door seemed to recede.

"Where can you go, Carl?" The doctor's voice reached him from a great distance.

"Out . . . Away . . . Through the door . . ."

"The Green Door, Carl?"

The doctor's voice was barely audible. The whole room was exploding out into space.

POPPY Z. BRITE

Drawing Blood

ONE OF THE TAPS twisted on.

Hot liquid gushed into the sink, splashed up onto his belly, his chest, his hands and arms. Zach jumped back, looked down at himself, and felt his well-trained gag reflex try to trigger for the second time that night.

He was covered with dark streaks and splotches of the blood that was still globbing out of the faucet, pooling in the sink. But this was no fresh vivid crimson like the blood from his lip yesterday. This blood was thick and rank, already half-clotted. Its color was the red-black of a scab, and it stank of decaying meat.

As he watched, the other tap turned slowly on. A second fluid began to mingle with the rotting blood, a thinner fluid, viscous and milky-white. The odor of decay was suddenly laced with the raw fresh smell of semen. As they came out of the faucet, the two streams twisted together like some sort of devil's candy cane, red and white (and Black all over . . . wouldn't Trevor love to put *this* in a story?).

Zach felt hysterical laughter bubbling up in his throat. Tom Waits's drunken piano had nothing on this bathroom. The sink was bleeding and ejaculating: great. Maybe next the toilet would decide to take a shit or the bathtub would begin to drool.

He looked back up at the mirror and felt the laughter turn sour, caustic, like harsh vomit on the back of his tongue.

But for certain familiar landmarks—his green eyes, the dark tangle of his hair—Zach barely knew his own reflection in the glass. It was as if a sculptor had taken a plane to his face and shaved layers of flesh from the already-prominent bones. His forehead and cheekbones and chin were carved in stark relief, the skin stretched over them like parchment, sickly white and dry, as if the lightest touch would start it sifting from the bones. His nostrils and eye sockets seemed too large, too deep. The shadowy smudges beneath his eyes had become enormous dark hollows in which his pupils glittered feverishly. The skin around his mouth looked desiccated, the lips cracked and peeling.

It was not the face of a nineteen-year-old boy in any kind of health. It was the face of the skull hiding beneath his skin, waiting to be revealed. Zach suddenly understood that the skull always grinned because it knew it would emerge triumphant, that it would comprise the sole identity of the face long after vain baubles like lips and skin and eyes were gone.

He stared at his wasted image in fascination. There was a certain consumptive beauty to it, a certain dark flame like that which burns in the eyes of mad poets or starving children.

He put out his hand to touch the mirror, and the lesions began to appear.

Just a few tiny purplish spots at first, one on the stark jut of his cheekbone, one bisecting the dark curve of his eyebrow, one nestled in the small hollow at the corner of his mouth. But they began to spread, deepening like enormous bruises, like a stop-motion film of blighted orchids blooming beneath the surface of his skin. Now nearly half his face was suffused with the purple rot, tinged necrotic blue at the edges and shot through with a scarlet web of burst capillaries, and there was no semblance of beauty to it, no dark flame, nothing but corruption and despair and the promise of death.

Zach felt his stomach churning, his chest constricting. He had never obsessed about his looks, had never needed to. His parents had usually avoided fucking up his face too badly because it might be noticed. He still had faint belt marks on his back and two lumpy finger joints on his left hand from breaks that had healed badly, but no facial scars. He'd never even had zits to speak of. He had grown up with no particular awareness of his own beauty, and once he realized he had it and learned what it was good for, he had taken it for granted.

Now watching it rot away was like feeling the ground disappear from under his feet, like having a limb severed, like watching the knife descend for the final stroke of the lobotomy.

(*Or like watching a loved one die, and knowing you had a hand in that death . . . Zach, do you love yourself?*)

The faucet was still gushing, the sink clogged nearly to overflowing with the twin fluids. A small black pinhole had appeared in the center of each lesion on his face. As he watched, the dots swelled and erupted. Pain zigzagged across the network of his facial nerves. Beads of greasy glistening whiteness welled from the tiny wounds.

Zach felt a sudden, blinding flash of rage. What the hell was the white stuff supposed to be? Maggots? Pus? More come? What kind of cheap morality play was this, anyway?

"*FUCK IT!*" he yelled, and seized the edges of the mirror and ripped it off its loose moorings and flung it into the bathtub. It shattered with a sound that could have awoken all of St. Louis Cemetery. The faucet slowed to a trickle, then stopped.

OBEY

RICHARD CONDON

The Manchurian Candidate

IN AUGUST, 1944, JOHNNY came limping home to take up his part in the red-hot campaign that "friends" (meaning Raymond's mother and, to a conclusive extent, even though it seems absolutely impossible in retrospect, the Communist party) had been carrying forward since the day he had gone off to war. All Johnny had to do was to wear his uniform, his crutches, and his bandaged foot and shout out a few hundred topical exaggerations that Raymond's mother had written up and catalogued over the years to evade any conceivable demand. Because of the clear call from the people of his state, Johnny was permitted to resign from the armed forces on August 11, 1944.

He was elected governor of his state in the elections of 1944 and re-elected in 1948. As he entered his second term he was forty-one years old; Raymond's mother was thirty-eight. Raymond was twenty-one and was working as a district man for the *Journal*, having graduated from the state university at the head of his class.

At forty-one, Governor Iselin was a plain, aggressively humble man, five feet eight inches tall in specially shod elevator shoes. There was a fleshiness of the nose to mark him for the memory. His hair was thin and, under certain lighting, appeared to have been painted in fine, single lines across his scalp over rosettes and cabbages of two-dimensional liver spots. His clothes, from a time shortly after his marriage to Raymond's mother, were of homespun material but they had been run up by the hands of a terribly good and quite wealthy tailor in New York. Raymond's mother had Johnny's valet shine only the lower half of his high black shoes so that it would seem, to people who thought about those things, that he managed to shine his own shoes between visits of the Strawberry Lobby and the refusal of pardons to the condemned. An abiding mark of the degree of Johnny's elemental friendliness shone from the fact that he could look no one in the eye and that when he talked he would switch syntax in seeming horror of what he had almost said to his listener. The governor never shaved from Friday night to Monday morning, no matter what function might be scheduled, as though he were a part-time Sikh. He would explain that this gave his skin a rest. Raymond's mother had invented that one, as she had invented very nearly everything else about him excepting his digestive system (and if she had invented that it would have functioned a great deal better), because not shaving "made him like some slob, like a farm hand or some Hunky factory worker." It is certain that over a weekend, when Big John was generating noise out of every body orifice, switching syntax, darting his eyes about, and flashing that meaty nose in his unshaven face, he was the commonest kind of common man forty ways to the ace. However, he had been custom-made by Raymond's mother. She had developed Johnny (as José Raoul Capablanca had developed his chess play; as Marie Antoine Carême had folded herbs into a sauce for Talleyrand) into the model governor, on paper that is, of all the states of the United States, and in some of those other states the constituents read more about Jolly Johnny than about their own men. She had riveted into the public memory these immutable facts: John Yerkes Iselin was a formidable administrator; a conserver who could dare; an honest, courageous, conscience-thrilled, God-fearing public servant; a jolly, jovial, generous, gentling, humorous, amiable, good-natured, witty big brother; a wow of a husband and a true-blue pal of a father; a fussin', fumin', fightin', soldier boy, all heart; a simple country judge with the savvy of Solomon; and an American, which was the most fortuitous circumstance of all.

Raymond's mother hardly showed one flicker of chagrin when General Eisenhower was persuaded to make the stroll for the nomination in 1952, the one unexpected accident that could have blocked her John from the White House. She broke a few little things at the Mansion when she heard the news: mirrors, lamps, vases, and other replaceable bric-a-brac. She was entitled to a flash of violence, one little demonstration that she could feel passion, and it harmed no one because Johnny was dead drunk and Raymond had marched off to the Korean War.

In the Autumn of 1952, two weeks before Raymond's return from Korea to receive the Congressional Medal of Honor, almost two months before the end of Big John's statutory final term as governor, U.S. Senator Ole Banstoffsen, the grand old man who had represented his state in Washington for six consecutive terms, succumbed to a heart attack almost immediately after a small dinner with his oldest and dearest friends, Governor and Mrs. John Iselin, and died in the governor's arms in the manner of a dinner guest of the Empress Livia's some time before in ancient Rome. The exchange of last words made their bid to become part of American history, for through them Big John found his life's mission, and the words are set down herewith to complete the record.

SENATOR BANSTOFFSEN

John—Johnny, boy—are you there?

GOVERNOR ISELIN

Ole! Ole, old friend. Don't try to speak! Eleanor! *Where is that doctor!*

SENATOR BANSTOFFSEN
(his last words)

Johnny—you must—carry on. Please, please, Johnny swear to me as I lay dying that you will fight to save Our Country—from the Communist peril.

GOVERNOR ISELIN
(greatly moved)

I pledge to you, with my soul, that I will fight to keep Communists from dominating our institutions to the last breath of my life, dear friend.
(Senator Banstoffsen slumps into death, made happy.)

GOVERNOR ISELIN

He's gone! Oh, Eleanor, he's gone. A great fighter has gone on to his rest.

The verbatim record must have been set down by Raymond's mother, as she was the only other person present at the senator's death, and she undoubtedly found time to make notes while they waited for the doctor and while the words were still so fresh in her mind, but Johnny did not use them for almost three years, during which time they had undoubtedly been carefully filed for their value as Americana and as a source of inspiration to others.

Governor Iselin appointed himself to succeed Senator Banstoffsen, to fight the good fight, and his re-election followed. He was sworn in on March 18, 1953, by Justice Krushen, after his wife had insisted that he take The Cure for two and a half months at a reliable, discreet, and medically sound ranch for alcoholics and drug addicts in sun-drenched New Mexico, following the booze-drenched Christmas holidays of 1952.

OBEY

Hardboiled

JIM THOMPSON

The Grifters

BOBO JUSTUS HAD WAVY, iron-gray hair and a deeply tanned, chiseled-looking face. He was a small man, short that is, but he had the head and torso of a six-footer. Knowing his sensitivity about his height, Lilly was grateful for her flat-heeled shoes. That was one thing in her favor at least. But she doubted that it would count for much, judging by his expression.

He addressed her tonelessly, his lips barely moving.

"You goddamned silly-looking pig! Driving a goddamned circus wagon! Why don't you paint a bull's-eye on it? Hang a couple of cowbells on the bumper?"

"Now, Bo. Convertibles are quite common in California."

"Convertibles are quite common in California," he mimicked her, weaving his shoulders prissily. "Are they as common as two-timing, double-crossing whores? Hah? Are they, you sneaky little slut?"

"Bo"—she looked around quickly. "Hadn't we better go some place private?"

He drew back a hand as though to slap her, then gave her a shove toward the car. "Get with it," he said. "The Beverly Hills. I get you alone, and I'm going to pop every pimple on your pretty pink butt!"

She started the car and drove out through the gate. As they joined the stream of town-bound traffic, he resumed his tight-lipped abuse.

Lilly listened attentively, trying to decide whether he was building up steam or letting it off. Probably the last, she guessed, since it had been almost three weeks since her blunder. Murderously angry, he probably would have taken action before this.

429

Most of the time she was silent, making no response except when it was asked for or seemed urgently indicated.

". . . told you to watch that fifth race, didn't I? And, by God, you really watched it, didn't you? I bet you stood there grinning clear to your ankles while the dog comes in at a hundred-and-forty per!"

"Bo, I—"

"How much did your pals cut you in for, huh? Or did they give you the same kind of screwing you gave me? What the hell are you, anyway—a stud-horse with tits?"

"I was down on the nag," Lilly said quietly. "You know I was, Bo. After all, you wouldn't have wanted me to bet it off the board."

"You were down on it, huh? Now, I'll ask you just one question. Do you want to stick to that story, or do you want to keep your teeth?"

"I want to keep my teeth."

"Now, I'll ask you one more question. Do you think I got no contacts out here? You think I couldn't get a report on the play on that horse?"

"No, I don't think that. I'm sure you could, Bo."

"That nag paid off at just the opening price. There wasn't hardly a flutter on the tote board from the time the odds were posted." He lit a cigarette, took a couple of quick angry puffs. "What kind of crap you handing me anyway, Lilly? There ain't enough action to tickle the tote, but you claim a five-grand win! Now, how about it, huh? You ready to fly straight or not?"

She drew in a deep breath. Hesitated. Nodded. There was only one thing to do now, to tell the truth and hope for the best.

She did so. Justus sat turned in the seat; studying, analyzing her expression throughout the recital. When she had finished, he faced back around again, sat in deadpan silence for several minutes.

"So you were just stupid," he said. "Asleep at the switch. You think I'm going to buy that?"

Lilly nodded evenly. He'd already bought it, she said, three weeks ago; suspected the truth before he was told. "You know you did, Bo. If you hadn't, I'd be dead by now."

"Maybe you will be yet, sister! Maybe you'll wish you was dead."

"Maybe."

"I laid out better than a hundred yards for a screwing. Just about the highest-priced piece of tail in history. I figure on getting what I paid for."

"Then you'd better do some more figuring," Lilly said. "I'm not that kind of punching bag."

"Real sure about that, are you?"

"Positive. Give me a cigarette, please."

He took a cigarette from his package, and tossed it across the seat. She picked it up, and tossed it back to him.

"Light it please, Bo? I need both hands in this traffic."

She heard a sound, something between a laugh and a snort, anger and admiration. Then, he lit the cigarette and placed it between her lips.

As they rode on, she could sense the looks he slanted at her, almost see the workings of his mind. She was a problem to him. A very special and valued employee, one whom he actually liked, had yet erred badly. It was unintentional, her one serious mistake in more than twenty years of faithful service. So there was strong argument for forgiveness. On the other hand, he was showing unusual forbearance in allowing her to live, and more hardly seemed to be indicated.

Obviously, there was much to be said for both sides of the debate. Having forgiven so much, he could forgive completely. Or having forgiven so much, he need forgive no more.

They were almost at the hotel before he reached his decision.

"I got a lot of people working for me, Lilly. I can't have things like this happening."

"It never happened before, Bo." She fought to keep her voice level, free of any hint of begging. "It won't happen again."

"It happened once," he said. "With me, that's practically making a habit of it."

"All right," she said. "You're calling the shots."

"You got any kind of long coat in the car? Anything you can wear home over your clothes?"

"No." A dull ache came into her stomach.

He hesitated, then said it didn't matter. He'd lend her his raincoat. "Ought to be right in style out here. Goddamnedest sloppiest-looking women I ever seen."

She stopped the car at the hotel entrance, and an attendant took charge of it. Bobo handed her out to the steps, then courteously gave her his arm as they entered the building. They crossed the lobby, Bobo holding himself very erect, and entered the elevator.

He had a suite on the fourth floor. Unlocking the door, he motioned for her to precede him. She did so, letting her body go limp, preparing herself for what she knew was coming. But you could never prepare for a thing like that—not fully. The sudden shove-blow sent her hurtling into the room, stumbling and tripping over her own feet. And finally landing in a skidding sprawl on the floor.

As she slowly picked herself up, he locked the door, drew the shades, and entered the bathroom, emerging immediately with a large towel. Crossing to the sideboard, he took a number of oranges from a bowl of fruit, dropped them in the towel and pulled up its ends to form a bag. He came toward her, swinging it loosely. Again, Lilly tried to brace herself with limpness.

She knew *the oranges*. She knew all such gimmicks, though never before had she been the victim of any. The oranges was an item from the dummy-chuckers' workbag, a frammis of the professional accident fakers.

Beaten with the fruit, a person sustained bruises far out of proportion to his actual injuries. He looked badly hurt when he was hardly hurt at all.

But he could be hurt. If he was hit hard enough and in certain areas of his body. Without feeling much pain at the time, he could have his internal organs smashed. Used in just the right way (or the wrong way), the oranges produced much the same effect as an enema or douche of plaster-of-paris.

Bobo drew closer. He stopped in front of her. He moved to one side and little behind her.

He gripped the towel with both hands. And swung.

And let the oranges spill harmlessly to the floor.

He gestured.

She bent to pick up the fruit. And then again she was sprawling. And his knees were in her back and his hand was against her head. And she was pinned spreadeagled, against the carpet.

A couple passed in the hallway, laughing and talking. A couple from another planet. From the dining room—from another world—came the faint sound of music.

There was the click of a cigarette lighter, the smell of smoke. Then, the smell of burning flesh as he held the glowing coal against the back of her right hand. He held it with measured firmness, just enough to keep it burning without crushing it out.

His knees worked with expert cruelty.

The cigarette burned into her hand, and his knees probed the sensitive nerves of her spine.

It was a timeless world, an endless hell. There was no escape from it. There was no relief in it. She couldn't cry out. It was impossible even to squirm. The world was at once to be endured and unendurable. And the one possible relief was within her own small body.

Scalding urine spurted from her loins. It seemed to pour from her in a flood.

And Bobo stood up, releasing her, and she got up and went into the bathroom.

She held her hand under the ice-water tap, then patted it with a towel and examined it. The burn was ugly, but it didn't appear to be serious. None of the large veins were affected. She lowered her slacks and swabbed herself with a slightly moistened towel. That was about as much as could be done here. The raincoat would cover up her stained clothes.

She left the bathroom, crossed to the lounge where Bobo was seated, and accepted the drink he gave her. He took out his wallet, and extended a thick sheaf of new bills.

"Your five grand, Lilly. I almost forgot."

"Thanks, Bo."

"How you making out these days, anyway? Stealing much from me?"

"Not much. My folks didn't raise any stupid kids," Lilly said. "I just clip a buck here and a buck there. It mounts up, but nobody gets hurt."

"That's right," Justus nodded approvingly. "Take a little, leave a little."

"I look on it this way," Lilly said, shrewdly enunciating his own philosophy. "A person that don't look out for himself is too dumb to look out for anyone else. He's a liability, right, Bo?"

"Absolutely! You're a thousand percent right, Lil!"

"Or else he's working an angle. If he doesn't steal a little, he's stealing big."

"Right!"

"I like that suit, Bo. I don't know what there is about it, but somehow it makes you look so much taller."

"Yeah?" He beamed at her. "You really think so? You know a lot of people been telling me the same thing."

Their amiable talk continued as twilight slid into the room. And Lilly's hand ached, and the wet clothes burned and chafed her flesh. She had to leave him feeling good about her. She had to make sure that the score between them was settled, and that he was actually letting her off so lightly.

They discussed several business matters she had handled for him in Detroit and the Twin Cities on her circuitous way to the coast. Bobo revealed that he was only in town for the day. Tomorrow he was heading back east via Vegas, Galveston, and Miami.

"Another drink, Lilly?"

"Well, just a short one. I've got to be running along pretty soon."

"What's the hurry? I thought maybe we could have dinner together."

"I'd like to, but . . ."

It was best not to stay, best to quit while she was ahead. She'd been very, very lucky apparently, but luck could run out on you.

"I've got a son living here, Bo. A salesman. I don't get to see him very often, so . . ."

"Well, sure, sure," he nodded. "How's he making out?"

"He's in the hospital. Some kind of stomach trouble. I usually visit him every night."

"Sure, naturally," he frowned. "Gettin' everything he needs? Anything I can do?"

Lilly thanked him, shaking her head. "He's doing fine. I think he'll be getting out in a day or two."

"Well, you'd better run along," Bobo said. "A boy's sick, he wants his mother."

She got the raincoat out of the closet, and belted it around her. They said good night, and she left.

A little urine had trickled down her legs, making them itch and sting, and leaving an unpleasant sogginess in her shoes. Her underpants chafed and stung, and the seat of the slacks seemed to have soaked through. The ache in her right hand grew, spread slowly up into her wrist and arm.

She hoped she hadn't soiled Bobo's lounge. She'd been very lucky, considering the amount her blunder must have cost him, but a little thing like that might spoil it.

She picked up her car, and drove away from the hotel.

As she entered her apartment, she kicked out of her shoes, began flinging her clothes from her; leaving them in a trail behind her as she hurried toward the bathroom. She closed its door. Kneeling, she went down in front of the toilet as though it were an altar, and a great sob shook her body.

Weeping hysterically, laughing and crying, she began to vomit.

Lucky . . .

Got off easy . . .

Boy, am I lucky!

MICKEY SPILLANE

The Big Kill

ALL THAT PENT-UP hate on her face turned into a cunning sneer and she said, "He's here, Mike."

I started to move the same time she started to talk and I wasn't fast enough. I had a glimpse of something white streaking toward my head just before it smashed the consciousness from my body.

Hardboiled

Long before my eyes could see again I knew what would be there when I opened them. I heard the kid crying, a series of terror-stricken gasps because the world was too much for him. I pushed up from the floor, forced my eyes open and saw him huddled there in the corner, his thin body shivering. Whatever I did with my face made him stop, and with the quick switch of emotions a child is capable of, he laughed. He climbed to his feet and held on to the arm of the chair babbling nonsense at the wall.

I raised my head and caught her looking at me, a spiteful smile creasing her face. She was a big beautiful evil goddess with a gun in her hand ready to take a victim and there wasn't a thing I could do about it. My .45 was over there on the table and I didn't have the strength to go for it.

Jerry was in a chair holding his broken arm to his chest, rocking back and forth from the pain in it. One side of the cast was split halfway.

Then I saw the junk on the floor. The suit I had thrown away and the kid's overalls that had been stuffed in the bottom of the can. And Marsha smiled. She opened her palm and there were the films, four thin strips of them. "They were in the pocket of the overalls." She seemed amazed at the simplicity of it.

"They won't do you any good, Marsha. Teen's finished and so are they. Your little racket's over." I had to stop for breath. Something sticky ran down my neck.

"They'll serve their purpose," she said. "Somebody else might guess like you did, but they'll never know now. Those Toady had I destroyed. These will go too and only you will be left, Mike. I really hate having to kill you, but it's necessary, you know."

There was none of the actress in her voice now. There was only death. She had finished acting. The play was over and she could put away the smiles and tears until the next time.

I swung my head around until my eyes were fixed on Jerry. He stopped rocking. I said, "Then I guess you'll have to marry Jerry, won't you? He'll have you trapped like you had Ed and Lou trapped. He'll have something you'll pay dearly for, won't he?"

I think she laughed again. It was a cold laugh. "No, Mike. Poor Jerry will have to go too. You see, he's my alibi." Her hand went out and picked up my gun. "Everyone knows how crazy he is about me. And he's so jealous he's liable to do anything . . . especially if he came up here and caught us together . . . like tonight. There would have been gunplay. Unfortunately, you killed each other. The nurse was in the way and she died too. Doesn't that make a good story, Mike?"

Jerry came out of his chair slowly. He had time to whisper incredulously,

"Marsha!" The .45 slammed in her hand and blasted the night to bits. She watched the guy jerking on the floor and threw the gun back on the table. The rod she held on me was a long-barreled revolver and it didn't tremble in her hand at all. She held it at her hip slanting it down enough to catch me in the chest.

She was going to get that shot off fast for the benefit of the people who were listening. She was killing again because murder breeds murder and when she had killed she was going to put the guns in dead hands and go into her act. She'd be all faints and tears and everyone would console her and tell her how brave she was and damn it all to hell, her story would stand up! There wouldn't be a hole in it because everything was working in her favor just like when she killed her secretary! It would be a splash in the papers and she could afford that.

The hate was all there in my face now and she must have known what I was thinking. She gave me a full extra second to see her smile for the last time, but I didn't waste it on the face of evil.

I saw the kid grab the edge of the table and reach up for the thing he had wanted for so long, and in that extra second of time she gave me his fingers closed around the butt safety and trigger at the same instant and the tongue of flame that blasted from the muzzle seemed to lick out across the room with a horrible vengeance that ripped all the evil from her face, turning it into a ghastly wet red mask that was really no face at all.

Paul Schrader

Taxi Driver

The Traveling Salesman

Brooklyn street corner—day.
TRAVIS *stands near the corner wearing his boots, jeans, western shirt and army jacket.*

He pulls his aspirin bottle out of his pocket, shakes three or four into his palm, pops them into his mouth and chews.

An "Off Duty" taxi pulls up to the kerb. TRAVIS *gets in.*

Hardboiled

DOUGH-BOY *leans back from the wheel and greets* TRAVIS *as he enters.*

DOUGH-BOY
Hey Travis. This here's Easy Andy. He's a traveling salesman.

(*In the back seat, beside* TRAVIS, *sits* ANDY, *an attractive young man of about twenty-nine. He wears a pin-striped suit, white shirt and floral tie. His hair is modishly long.*)

ANDY
Hello, Travis.

(TRAVIS *nods as the taxi speeds off.* DOUGH-BOY *slows down near an economy hotel. Not a flophouse, but not so fancy they care what the guests do in the privacy of their rooms.*)

ANDY
This is fine, Dough-Boy. (*To* TRAVIS.) Pay Dough-Boy here.

(TRAVIS *pulls a twenty-dollar bill out of his pocket and gives it to* DOUGH-BOY.)

TRAVIS
Twenty bucks?

DOUGH-BOY
(*Takes bill*)
Yeah. Hey thanks. That's real nice, Travis.

(TRAVIS *and* ANDY *get out of the cab and walk towards the hotel.* DOUGH-BOY *pulls away. As they enter the hotel, they pass a junkie, stoned out and spread-eagled across the hood of a derelict old blue Dodge. Inside the hotel,* TRAVIS *follows* ANDY *up the worn carpeted stairs and down the hallway.* ANDY *unlocks the door to one of the rooms. The hotel room is barren and clean; there's no sign anyone is staying in it. The fire-escape is appropriately near.* ANDY *locks the door behind them, steps over to the closet, unlocks it and pulls out two grey Samsonite suitcases—the kind you can drive a truck over.*)

ANDY
Dough-Boy probably told you I don't carry any Saturday Night Specials or crap like that. It's all out of State, clean, brand new, top-of-the-line stuff.

(ANDY *places the suitcases on the white bedspread. The suitcases are equipped with special locks, which he quickly opens. Stacked in grey packing foam are rows and rows of brand-new hand guns.*)

TRAVIS

You got a .44 Magnum?

ANDY

That's an expensive gun.

TRAVIS

I got money.

(ANDY *unzips a cowhide leather pouch to reveal a .44 Magnum pistol. He holds it gingerly, as if it were a precious treasure.* ANDY *opens the chambers and cradles the long eight-inch barrel in his palm. The .44 is a huge, oversized, inhuman gun.*)

ANDY
(Admiringly)

It's a monster. Can stop a car—put a bullet right into the block. A premium high resale gun. $350—that's only a hundred over list.

(EASY ANDY *is a later version of the fast-talking, good-looking kid in college who was always making money on one scheme or another. In high school he sold lottery tickets, in college he scored dope, and now he's hustling hand guns.*

ANDY *holds the Magnum out for* TRAVIS's *inspection. There's a worshipful close-up of the .44 Magnum. It is a monster.*

TRAVIS *hefts the huge gun. It seems out of place in his hand. It is built on Michelangelo's scale. The Magnum belongs in the hand of a marble god, not a slight taxi-driver.* TRAVIS *hands the gun back to* ANDY.)

I could sell this gun in Harlem for $500 today—but I just deal high quality goods to high quality people. *(Pause.)* Now this may be a little big for practical use, in which case I'd recommend the .38 Smith and Wesson Special. Fine solid gun—nickel plated. Snub-nosed, otherwise the same as the service revolver. Now that'll stop anything that moves and it's handy, flexible. The Magnum, you know, that's only if you want to splatter it against the wall. The movies have driven up the price of the Magnum anyway. Everybody wants them now. But the Wesson .38—only $250—and worth every dime of it. *(He hefts .38.)* Throw in a holster for $10.

(TRAVIS *hefts the nickel-plated .38, points it out the window.*)

Some of these guns are like toys, but a Smith and Wesson, man, you can hit somebody over the head with it and it will still come back dead on. Nothing beats quality. *(Pause.)* You interested in an automatic?

TRAVIS

I want a .32. Revolver. And a palm gun. That .22 there.

ANDY

That's the Colt .25—a fine little gun. Don't do a lotta damage, but it's as fast as the Devil. Handy little gun, you can carry it almost anywhere. I'll throw it in for another $125.

(TRAVIS *holds the .32 revolver, hefts it, slips it under his belt and pulls his shirt over it. He turns from side to side, to see how it rides in his waist.*)

TRAVIS

How much for everything?

ANDY

The .32's $150—and you're really getting a good deal now—and all together it comes to, ah, seven eighty-five for four pieces and a holster. Hell, I'll give you the holster, we'll make it seven seventy-five and you've got a deal—a good one.

TRAVIS

How much to get a permit to carry?

ANDY

Well, you're talking big money now. I'd say at least five grand, maybe more, and it would take a while to check it out. The way things are going now $5,000 is probably low. You see, I try not to fool with the small-time crap. Too risky, too little bread. Say 6 G's, but if I get the permit it'll be as solid as the Empire State Building.

TRAVIS

Nah, this'll be fine.

ANDY

You can't carry in a cab even with a permit—so why bother?

Hardboiled

TRAVIS

Is there a firing range around?

ANDY

Sure, here, take this card. Go to this place and give 'em the card. They'll charge you, but there won't be any hassle.

(TRAVIS *pulls out a roll of crisp one-hundred-dollar bills and counts off eight.*)

You in 'Nam? Can't help but notice your jacket?

TRAVIS
(*Looking up*)

Huh?

ANDY

Vietnam? I saw it on your jacket. Where were you? Bet you got to handle a lot of weapons out there.

(TRAVIS *hands* ANDY *the bills.* ANDY *counts them and gives* TRAVIS *a twenty and a five.*)

TRAVIS

Yeah. I was all around. One hospital, then the next.

ANDY
(*As he counts*)

It's hell out there all right. A real shit-eatin' war. I'll say this, though: it's bringing back a lot of fantastic guns. The market's flooded. Colt automatics are all over. (*Pockets the money.*)

TRAVIS
(*Intensely*)

They'd never get me to go back. They'd have to shoot me first. (*Pause.*) You got anything to carry these in? (*Gestures to pistols.*)
(TRAVIS *is like a light-switch: for long periods he goes along dark and silent, saying nothing; then suddenly, the current is turned on and the air is filled with the electricity of his personality.* TRAVIS's *inner intensity sets* ANDY *back a bit, but he quickly recovers.*)

ANDY

Sure.

(ANDY *pulls a gym bag from under the bed. He wraps the guns in the sheet in the bag and zips it up. An identical gym bag can be partially seen under the bed. He hands* TRAVIS *the bag.*)

You like ball games?

TRAVIS

Huh?

ANDY

I can get you front and center. What do you like? I can get you Mets, Yankees, Knicks, Rangers? Hell, I can get you the Mayor's box.

TRAVIS

Nah. I ain't interested.

(ANDY *closes and locks the suitcases.*)

ANDY

OK, OK.

(TRAVIS *turns to leave.*)

Wait a second, Travis. I'll walk you out.

Travis Gets Organized

Several weeks later. The face of Travis's apartment has changed. The long, blank wall behind the table is now covered with tacked-up charts, pictures, newspaper clippings, maps. Camera does not come close enough to discern the exact contents of these clippings. Close-up of TRAVIS *in the middle of the floor doing push-ups. He is bareback, wearing only his jeans. There is a long scar across his left side.*

TRAVIS
(Voice over)
May 29, 1972. I must get in shape. Too much sitting has ruined my body.

Twenty-five push-ups each morning, one hundred sit-ups, one hundred knee-bends. I have quit smoking.

(TRAVIS *still bareback, passes his stiff arm through the flame of a gas burner without flinching a muscle.*)

Total organization is necessary. Every muscle must be tight.

(*At the firing range. The cracking sound of rapid-fire pistol shots fills the musty air of the firing range. The walls are heavily soundproofed, and saw-dust is spread over the floor.* TRAVIS *stands rock solid, firing the .44 Magnum at an arm's length. With each blasting discharge from the Magnum, Travis's body shudders and shakes, his arm rippling back.* travis *quickly bolts himself upright, as if each recoil from the giant gun was a direct attack on his masculinity.*

TRAVIS *fires the Magnum as quickly as he can re-set, re-aim and re-fire. The Magnum empty, he sets it down, picks up the .38 Special and begins firing as soon as he can aim. After the .38 comes the .25: it is as if he were in a contest to see how quickly he can fire the pistols. After all the guns are discharged, he begins reloading them without a moment's hesitation. Downrange, the red and white targets have the black outline of a human figure drawn over them. The contour-man convulses under the steady barrage of Travis's rapid-fire shots.*)

(*Inside the apartment.* TRAVIS, *now wearing an unfastened green plaid western shirt, sits at the table writing in his diary. The vial of Bennies rests on the table.*)

My body fights me always. It won't work, it won't sleep, it won't shit, it won't eat.

(*Later.* TRAVIS, *his shirt still open revealing his bare chest, sits on his straight-backed chair watching the TV. The .44 Magnum rests on his lap.*

The TV is broadcasting Rock Time, *a late-afternoon local teenage dance and rock show. On screen young teenyboppers are dancing, and the TV cam-eraman, as any devotee of the genre knows, is relentlessly zooming-in on their firm young breasts, fannies and crotches—a sensibility which reflects* TRAVIS's *own. These supper-hour rock dance shows are the most unabashedly voyeuristic form of broadcasting the medium has yet developed.*

The hard rock number ends, and the TV camera cuts to the local DISC JOCKEY, *a hirsute plastic-looking man of about thirty-five. Five scrumptious teenyboppers are literally hanging on his shoulders and arms, their faces turned up to him in droolish awe. Out of his mouth comes an incessant stream of disc jockey blather. He is the complete asshole.)*

TV DISC JOCKEY: Freshingly, fantastic, freaked-out dance time. Can you dig it? Dig on it. You got it, flaunt it.

(TRAVIS *watches the show, his face hard and unmoving. He is as the Scriptures would say, pondering all these things in his heart. Why is it the assholes get all the beautiful young chicks? He takes a swig of peach brandy.)*

A. I. BEZZERIDES

Thieves' Market

THEY WALKED PAST BUILDINGS and dark spaces where slips opened to the harbor. Men lay on loading docks, huddled against bulkheads and piles, waiting for daylight, hours away. Some walked with their collars up and their arms clasped tightly to their bodies. The fog horn made a great sound and in the spasms of silence Nick could hear the smashing and washing of the surf against pilings. Waves rolling in, carrying on them the scum and sewage of the harbor, and when the wind shifted, a smell rose from it, the giant bad breath of the city.

Nick wanted to sleep, but I can't, he thought. If I sleep now I'll never wake up, I'll never be there to cash Figlia's check in the morning.

He felt someone shake his arm. Tex. She said, "How about a cup of coffee?" and when he looked up he saw they had come to a greasy-spoon restaurant built into a corner of one of the warehouses, its lights smothered in the fog.

"Doesn't all this walking make you hungry?" Tex said. "All of a sudden I'm hungry."

They went into the restaurant and sat down. After the waiter had gone, Tex had a sudden quiet compulsion to look over her shoulder. She knew someone was standing outside, beyond the window, watching her and all she had to do was turn swiftly and she would catch him, but not yet, she told herself, not now. Then instantly she thought, Now, and she turned and saw Frenchy. He was an apparition, gone the instant she turned, but she had seen him, she knew she had, it did not surprise her that she had.

Nick was observing her with narrowed eyes.

"You really ought to eat something," Tex said.

Nick turned to the window too. The juke box had stopped playing and the sound of surf came up, smashing against the pilings beneath the restaurant so the floor shook. Fog pressed against the windows and the room was like a ship at sea. The ham and eggs sizzled on the grill. The waiter was leaning over the counter, talking soundlessly in pantomime, with one of the men. The juke box played again, the same tune.

"What's on your mind?" Tex said.

"For two bits I'd go back to the truck," Nick said.

"Good idea," Tex said. "If you're tired, you could get some sleep."

She could see Nick going angry and she removed a cigarette from her purse and pretended to look for a match. "Got a light?" she said.

"You're nothing but a two buck whore," Nick said.

"Five bucks," Tex said. "The cost of loving's gone up."

"You God damned whore."

"Go ahead, honey, give it to me, tell me what a bad girl I am."

"I don't have to tell you, you know what you are. You're a rotten whore."

"Oh, yes, I've led a wicked life and I'm going straight to hell, that's for sure now, unless you step in and save me. Save me, lover."

"Save yourself, you whore."

"Don't get any idea you're calling me any names, brother. Sure I'm a whore. I could be a secretary or a sales girl or a file clerk or a soda jerk, but I'm a whore. I like being a whore."

"That's because you don't know any better."

"I know where I stand. That's more than you'll ever know."

"What's wrong with where I stand? I'm on my own. I've got a truck. I just sold a hot load and I'm going to sell a lot more. With a little luck, I'll buy me a couple more rigs and I'm on my way, but you'll still be a whore."

"The difference between you and me is we're both flat on our backs, but you don't know it."

"Jesus, what ever soured you up that way? Did you ever try getting a job and doing something decent for a living?"

"Sure, I got me a job once punching a typewriter, took dictation, made eighteen a week. Couldn't begin to keep myself in nylons. The boss tried to get me to go out nights. Wasn't he being nice to me, letting me work? If I'd be nice to him, I could work steady, extra money if I would, but I wouldn't. So I got me a job working counter in a store, sold ties and shirts. Employment agent wanted a commission for finding me the position and the manager wanted a commission because he gave it. So I got me a job working as a file clerk in an insurance office. Three hundred women doing nothing but make files on a lot of folks who were dead or going to die, twenty two fifty a week, work thirty years and you get a pension. We used to call it the big lay. So I got me a job jerking sodas, sixteen a week, the boss kept all the tips, but I got to drink all the malts I could hold and wrestle with the comptometer jockeys on the make."

"Maybe you weren't cut out to work," Nick said. "Maybe what you need is somebody to take care of you. Why don't you get married?"

"I tried that too," Tex said.

Nick looked at Tex and Tex said, "Well, aren't you going to ask me about marriage? Marriage is so nice. You fall in love with a fine upstanding young man and you marry him. After two weeks in bed, you come to."

Nick looked away and Tex said, "Aren't you going to ask me about my baby?" She opened her purse and brought out a picture of a young man holding a child and handed it to Nick. "Paul writes to me about her all the time. Shirley is four years old today, he writes, and she wants to know when she's going to see her mama. When are we going to see you, Hazel?"

"She looks like you," Nick said.

"Sure, she looks like me. Wish her luck."

"What made you walk out on them?"

"I got sick of being broke in this land of plenty. I couldn't take it no more. I wouldn't mind if there was nothing and you with plenty of nothing, but when they dangle plenty in your face and say this is yours if you'll pay, I couldn't take it. None of that ten percent down and untie the knots in your head the rest of your life for little old Tex, none of that *for richer, for poorer* stuff for her. I couldn't go for the long hard life."

"You walked out because he was broke," Nick said. "You were born a whore."

"Sure, and you were born a sucker. You're the one I feel sorry for. You still think you're going to pay your way with nickels."

"Don't kid yourself, I know how tough it is."

"It's tougher on you than it is on me," Tex said. "I've got something to peddle. They beat a path to my bed. I don't have to lay up with no bald-headed pot-bellied slob to hold down my job or trade a free piece now and then to get a square meal. I don't have to kiss nobody's pratt. You're trying to get on your own, but you never will, but I am. I'm strictly on my own."

Nick shook his head. "You sound so bad, I don't believe it. You're just talking."

Tex smiled. "You'd better drink your coffee before it gets cold."

"I wish I hadn't met you," Nick said. "I wish I hadn't come out after you. Why did I come out after you?"

"I don't know, why did you?" Tex said.

Nick stood up ready to go and Tex raised the cup to her lip again. She could feel Frenchy watching her. It sang in her, knowing he was out there watching.

They had been walking along the docks for a long distance and when Nick looked at Tex, he could see her attention was on something ahead in the fog, far away. I know why I came out, he thought. I want her. He remembered himself with her in the room, the way everything in her jumped when he touched her and he knew he had to come out. I had to, he thought.

What the hell are we doing out here when we could be in the room? he thought. A while ago I was carrying her to bed and nothing happened and now here we are, wasting time. Pretty soon it'll be daylight and it'll be too late. Why don't we go up now, while there's time? He looked again at Tex and again he felt the crippling pain of longing. He wanted to open her dress and run his hands over the rounds of her shoulders and into the warmth of her neck. He wanted to remove her clothes and make her stand freezing in the wind that carried on it all the sounds of the harbor. When he kissed her, her lips would be cold and behind them he would feel her teeth chattering. How light and strong she would be in his arms, when he carried her to bed. He would lay her down and look at her, his eyes hooded with longing. But there was no time, scarcely an hour until daybreak, and here he was tormenting himself with waiting. Why don't we go to your room, he wanted to say, but a shyness came over him and he could hardly look at her. She must know how I feel, he thought.

Tex stopped walking. Behind them the freight train had finished switching its cars and was returning, its lantern swinging. The tracks which crossed and crisscrossed the smooth belly of the pavement glistened in the red light. The train bore down upon them and Nick held Tex's arm and led her onto a dock. She shivered and drew against Nick, her face against his chest.

Nick turned Tex in his arms. He saw her glance past him, the look swift and furtive. Behind him, beyond the sound of the scummy surf that smashed through barnacled piles and spilled itself in a yeasty foam onto the mucky shore beneath the dock, he heard the stealthy scuffle of a step. He had to see, but when he tried to turn, Tex's arms were like steel around his neck.

"Nick!" he heard her say, and he tore himself free but before he could turn, something cracked into his skull and he went numb and blind. He felt himself go; I'm going, he thought, and he tried to hold himself. He felt a hand forcing his pocket where the wallet was and he tried to seize it, but he sensed another blow coming and he clawed out, encountering face, eyes and mouth, and far off he heard someone screaming and he clutched the face until he felt an arm encircle and tighten against his neck, garroting him, and he tried to squirm free, but he was caught, his arms were caught, and he felt himself reeling; but he twisted and with all his remaining strength he bit the arm just above the wrist, hard. But there was another blow, after which there was nothing.

DAVID GOODIS

Dark Passage

COLEY POINTED TO THE ancient barber's chair. Parry sat down in it and Coley began working a pedal and the chair began going down. The chair went down to a shallow oblique and Coley pulled a lamp toward the chair, aimed the lamp at Parry's face and tugged at a short chain. The lamp stabbed a pearly ray at Parry's face.

Parry closed his eyes. The towel-covered headrest felt too hard against his skull. The chair was uncomfortable. He felt as if he was on a rack. He heard water running and he opened his eyes and saw Coley standing at the sink and working up a lather on white hands. Coley stood there at the sink for fully five minutes. Then he waved his hands to get some of the water off and he held his hands up in the air with the fingers drooping toward him as he came back to the chair and looked at Parry's face.

"Will it take long?" Parry said.

"Ninety minutes," Coley said. "No more."

"I thought it took much longer than that," Parry said. Coley bent lower to study Parry's face and said, "I have my own method. I perfected it twelve years ago. It's based on the idea of calling a spade a spade. I don't monkey around. You have the money?"

"Yes."

"Sam said you can afford two hundred dollars."

"You want it now?"

Coley nodded. Parry took bills from his pocket, selected two one-hundred dollar bills, placed them on the top of a cabinet neighboring the chair. Coley looked at the money. Then he looked at Parry's face.

Parry said, "I'm a coward. I don't like pain."

"We're all cowards," Coley said. "There's no such thing as courage. There's only fear. A fear of getting hurt and a fear of dying. That's why the human race has lasted so long. You won't have any pain with this. I'm going to freeze your face. Do you want to see yourself now?"

"Yes," Parry said.

"Sit up and take a look in that mirror." Coley pointed to a mirror that topped one of the cabinets.

Parry looked at himself.

"It's a fairly good face," Coley said. "It'll be even better when I'm done with it. And it'll be very different."

Parry relaxed in the chair. He closed his eyes again. He heard water running. He didn't open his eyes. He heard the sound of metal getting moved around, the sound of a cabinet drawer opening and shutting, the clink of steel against steel, the water running again. He kept his eyes closed. Then things were happening to his face. Some kind of oil was getting rubbed into his face, rubbed in thoroughly all over his face and then wiped off thoroughly. He smelled alcohol, felt the alcohol being dabbed onto his face. Then water running again. More clinking of steel, more cabinet drawers in action. He tried to make himself comfortable in the chair. He decided it was impossible for Coley to do this job in ninety minutes. He decided it was impossible for Coley to change the face so that people wouldn't recognize it as belonging to Vincent Parry. He decided there wasn't any sense to this, and the only thing he would get out of it was something horrible happening to his face and he would be a freak for the rest of his life. He wondered how many faces Coley had ruined. He decided his face was going to look horrible but people would recognize him anyway and he wondered what he was doing up here in this quack set-up in San Francisco when he should be riding far away from San Francisco. He decided his only move was to jump out of the chair and run out of the office and keep on running.

He stayed there in the chair. He felt a needle going into his face. Then it went into his face again in another place. It kept jabbing deep into his face. His face began to feel odd. Metal was coming up against the flesh, pressing into the flesh, cutting into the flesh. There was no pain, there was no sensation except the metal going into his flesh. Different shapes of metal. He couldn't understand why he preferred to keep his eyes closed while this was going on.

It went on. With every minute that passed something new was happening to his face. Gradually he became accustomed to it—the entrance of steel into his flesh. He had the feeling he had gone through this sort of thing many times before. Now he was beginning to get some comfort out of the chair and there was a somewhat luxurious heaviness in his head and it became heavier and heavier and he knew he was falling asleep. He didn't mind. The manipulation of steel against his face and into his face took on a rhythm that mixed with the heaviness and formed a big, heavy ball that rolled down and rolled up and took him along with it, first on the top of it, on the outside, then getting him inside, rolling him around as it went up and down on its rolling path. And he was asleep.

He had a dream.

He dreamed he was a boy again in Maricopa, Arizona. A boy of fifteen running along a blackened street. He was running alone and eventually he came to a place where a woman was performing on a trapeze. From neck to ankles the woman was garbed in a skin-tight costume of bright orange satin. The woman's hair was darkish orange. The woman had drab brown eyes and her skin was tanned. It was the artificial tan that came from a violet-ray lamp. The woman was about five feet four inches tall and she was very thin and she was not at all pretty but there was nothing in her face to suggest ugliness. It was just that she was not a pretty woman. But she was a wonderful acrobat. She smiled at him. She took the trapeze way up high and sailed away from it. She described three slow somersaults going backwards, going up, going over and coming down on the trapeze again as it whizzed back. Elephants in the three rings far below lifted their trunks and lifted their eyes and watched her admiringly. The trapeze whizzed again and she left the trapeze again, going up and up and up, almost to the top of the tent until she described the wonderful series of backward somersaults that brought her down again to the trapeze. She was tiny way up there and then she grew as she came down. She stepped off the trapeze and came sliding down a rope. She bowed to the elephants. She bowed to everybody. She came over to him. He told her she was wonderful on the trapeze. She said it was really not at all difficult and anyone could do it. He could do it. He said he couldn't do it. He told her he was afraid. She laughed and told him he was silly to be afraid. She took his arm and led him toward the rope. The bright orange satin was flesh of flame on her thin body. She opened her mouth to laugh at him and he saw many gold inlays among her teeth. He pleaded with her to take him away from this high, dizzy place, this swirling peril. The trapeze came up to the limit of its whizzing arc and she left the trapeze, took him with her and they went up, somersaulting backward together, going up and over and he fought to get away from her and she laughed at him and he fought and fought until he got away from her. He went down alone. Down fast, face foremost, watching the sawdust and the faces and the colossal dull green elephants coming toward him. Down there they were attempting to do something for him. They were trying to arrange a net to catch him. Before they could get the net connected he was in amongst them, plunging past them and landing on his face. He felt the impact hammering into his face, the pain tearing through his face, hitting the back of his head and bouncing back and running all over his face. He was flat on his back, his arms wide, his legs spread wide as he looked up at the faces looking down on him. The pain was fierce and he moaned and the mob stood there and pitied him. He could see her high up there. The orange satin twirled and glimmered as she went away from the trapeze in another backward somersault. She came down wonderfully on the trapeze and although she was way up there her face was very close to his eyes and she was laughing at him and the gold inlays were dazzling in her laughing mouth.

The pain was fierce. It was a burning pain and there was something above the pain that felt very heavy on his face. He opened his eyes. He looked up at Coley.

"All over," Coley said.

Mezz Mezzrow

Really the Blues

I'D HAD A BELLYFUL of gangsters and muscle men by that time. They'd always been luring me on, trying to win me away from the music to their loutish way of life—all of them, from the gamblers and pimps in the Chicago syndicate to Frank Hitchcock's boys at Burnham and the hophead mugs over in Detroit. Our whole jazz music was, in a way, practically the theme-song of the underworld because, thanks to prohibition, about the only places we could play like we wanted were illegal dives. The gangsters had their dirty grabbers on our music too, just like they kept a death grip on everything else in this booby-hatch of a country. If I resisted their come-on even a little, it was only because of my obsession with the music. Every time I got in trouble, it was because I strayed away from the music. Whenever I latched on solid to the music, I flew right. I was beginning to sense a heap of moral in all this, but my hot instincts to stick with the music and keep straight were all frustrated now. I saw these white gangsters ruling the roost in Harlem, so I blamed them for it. I kept sinking lower and lower. Every night I would wind up in Harlem with nothing to do but wolf down a mess of barbequed ribs smothered in red-hot tabasco sauce and swill terrible rotgut by the barrel. That didn't soothe my jumpy stomach much either. At first my digestion was just nervous; pretty soon it stopped altogether.

I even made myself lose that Woodmansten Inn job, along with Eddie Condon and Sullivan, but still the jitters wouldn't quit me. The last night there I was blowing real hard, really reciting out in front of the band, when suddenly I went all shatter-brained. A bunch of ugly-looking gangsters had taken the joint over for a big party, and they were all wobbling around the floor with their floozies, so drunk they could hardly stand. One of these mugs danced right up under the bandstand and just stood there, staring at me. When I swayed, he swayed. When I stomped, he stomped. Suddenly I began to shake so bad I could hardly hold my clarinet. I had just remembered something that froze my spine. Joe E. Lewis had been working in a Chicago night-club run by some gangsters, and one night he mentioned to his bosses that he was thinking about changing jobs because he had got a much better offer. Those hoodlums didn't argue with him. They didn't bargain. They just smiled, and paid him a visit and slit his throat from ear to ear. It happened in his hotel, just around the corner from where I was living.

I watched that yegg while my clarinet weaved a spell around him, and I thought, Jesus, this music sure has got a hold of him. Suppose he owns some club and likes my playing so much he wants me to go to work for him? Maybe he's thinking it over right now, while he's casing me. If I have to work for him I'll really be under his thumb, and if I try to make a move they'll just cut me open like they did poor Joe E. Lewis. . . . Right quick I changed the phrasing and meter of my improvisation, fading all the way into the background. The audience felt the let-down and yelled, "Come on, get hot," but I didn't feel like reciting any more—I'd lost all voice for it.

That same night I quit the job and rushed home. I sprinted all the way from the bus stop to my house, and took those stairs three at a time. I heard footsteps dogging me all the way, right up the stairs and into the house. They were slow and dragging, in gimp-time. They sounded like Johnny Powell's drums.

My mind was a cistern, clogged with maggoty memories. I remembered that just before I left Chicago, in the same apartment house where Tesch and I lived, right over my head, some dame had been strangled with a lamp cord. Then came the Saint Valentine's Day massacre, when a bunch of Capone's gangsters got dressed up like cops and drove up in a police wagon and lined another mob against the wall and mowed them down with machine guns, leaving the mangled bodies all crumpled up on the floor like some soggy lumber. Then, right after I hit New York, Arnold Rothstein the gambler was strolling down the stairs at the Park Central and came somersaulting down with a load of lead in his hide. And there was that subway train that got derailed at Times Square, leaving over two hundred bodies of dead and near-dead piled up ready for the dustbins. All that came flooding up in my mind, and plenty more. I remembered the way Legs Diamond wrecked the Castilian Gardens just for kicks one night, and the nightmares I had after that other party of his. I remembered Frank Hitchcock piled in a ditch, and Capone's wife masquerading out at the Martinique, and Bow Gistensohn on a cold marble slab and Emil Burbacher in Joliet, the frightened girls trying to run away from the syndicate whorehouses and their pimps coming after them, the opium-smoking bigshots of the Purple Gang whose pictures were beginning to pop up in the papers because, one by one, they were being wheeled into the morgue icebox. Ten solid years of murder and riot. Ten years of a bloody showerbath. They kept unwinding in my head.

It looked to me like the whole continent was being drowned in a bath of blood, from coast to coast. The nation was committing mass suicide—it was like a slimy snake blowing its top, writhing and wriggling with the fits, beginning to chew up its own tail. Sure, I was surrounded by a race of gangsters running amuck, a hundred million blowtops, born with icecubes for hearts and the appetites of a cannibal. "They devour one another, and cannot even digest themselves." Nietzsche said that. "See them clamber, these nimble apes! They clamber over one another, and thus scuffle into the mud and the abyss." They were sure clambering some in the U.S. of A. Nobody was safe in this funky jungle. It was all one great big underworld, and they'd put their dirty grabbers on the one good thing left on earth, our music, and sucked it down into the mud with them.

PETER PLATE

Angels of Catastrophe

THE HOTELS ON MISSION Street were a coda for the seventh ring of oblivion. An underworld where landlords evicted tenants by setting their rooms on fire. The tête-a-tête with Kulak at the Federal Building left Durrutti unsettled. He couldn't stop trembling; his left arm shook uncontrollably. Lounging in his room at the El Capitán didn't make things any easier.

He went to see Jackie and Arlo, thinking they might soothe him. The door to their room was ajar when he knocked on it. Arlo was pulling on a pair of white silk stockings over her pale unshaved legs. She looked up at Durrutti with eyes that were soaked in barbiturates and whinnied, "Hey, baby cakes. Where have you been keeping yourself? Come in, come in. I ain't seen you in ages."

Durrutti hesitated. Jackie was behind the door with a .38 Ruger semi-automatic in her hand. Her hair was quarantined under a row of plastic curlers. Her face was slathered with Vaseline. A silk bathrobe hung undone, exposing her mammoth belly, and beneath it her cock, which she had tied back with a baby blue thong. She said, miffed by the intrusion, "Shit, it's Ricky Durrutti. What do you need, man?"

He wasn't sure. He walked into the room and over to the bed, tested the mattress with his hand, scattering the silverfish, then sat down on a hill of soiled red satin sheets and looked around him. Arlo had covered the walls and ceiling with Indian fabric. Durrutti answered Jackie, saying, "Ah, I don't know. I just want something to take the edge off things. I need to fucking mellow out. I'm losing it."

Arlo was quick to fathom Durrutti. She minced toward him with one silk stocking dangling from her hand; the rest of her was stark naked. Her thin hairless concave chest was postmortem white and her penis was jet black. Her hair, wet from a shower, was parted down the middle and hung in two wings to her shoulders. She asked, "What's wrong? You tripping? Shit bugging you? You can tell mama, can't you?"

Arlo's high lilting voice was designed to do two things in life. To make Jackie jealous and to flirt with other men. While Durrutti basked in the warmth of Arlo's mock solicitude, he didn't want to tangle with her spouse. Nor did he want to talk about his recent visit to Kulak. Disclosure would be premature. He replied, "You guys seen Jimmy Ramirez yet?"

Hardboiled

Jackie fumed as she pointed the Ruger at Durrutti's head, unconscious of what she was doing. Her torso was marked with faded tattoos from her stint in the Marines. Her cock drooped like fruit under her open robe. "Jimmy is gonna get his ass kicked. I fronted him some sherms to sell for me. And do you know what he did? He smoked them. Then he told me he lost the money. That liar is gonna come to no good."

The revelation didn't shock Durrutti. The Mexican's reputation was on the skids in every quarter. He was becoming the prince of unpopularity. "Yeah, well, if you hear anything about him, tell me."

"You still looking for him?" Jackie asked.

Durrutti was noncommittal. "Yeah."

"How come?"

He didn't know how much he could trust Arlo and Jackie. They didn't like pressure. If they knew Kulak was asking about them, they might turn on him. Like most dope dealers, they'd snitch on anyone who compromised their safety and their enterprise. Durrutti was not exempt. Recognition of this sobered him and he said, "It ain't nothing. Speaking of Jimmy, you got any more sherms?"

Arlo changed voices, trading in her street whore dialect for the prim and efficient clucking of a retail clerk at Woolworth's. "Sure do, darling. You want a two dollar joint or the five dollar kind?"

"Give me a five dollar one, please."

Jackie plucked a two paper joint from a pocket in her bathrobe and handed it to Durrutti. The misshapen sherm stank of parsley and was warm from having nestled against Jackie's groin. Durrutti threw a handful of one-dollar bills on the bed sheets and pocketed the thing, asking Arlo, "This shit decent?"

Arlo stepped into a Vivienne Westwood shift, a prize from the Goodwill box in Pacific Heights, and trilled for Durrutti's benefit, fabricating an assertion that was part sales pitch and part religious zeal. "Honey, it ain't just good. We're talking about a whole other dimension here. This here angel dust is pharmaceutical. It's gonna tear your brain apart."

Arlo's enthusiasm echoed in his ears when Durrutti sat down on the floor in his room. The angel dust was going to take him to a higher ground, money-back guaranteed. He put an ashtray beside him on the rug, then lit the sherm and took a drag. Five seconds passed. Ten more seconds went by and the room began to spin.

Before he could exhale a parade of hallucinations began their attack on his brain. His face ran down his chest in a sheet of melting skin, bubbling like molten taffy. He thought to himself, Thank the Lord I don't have a mirror around.

The doorframe bulged as if someone was going to pop through it. The unlocked door gaped wide—and Lonely Boy stepped inside. "I came to see you, homes."

The *vato loco* was unarmed and alone. He gave the room a haunted glance, looked in the armoire and under the piss-stained porcelain sink. He got down on his knees and checked under the bed, sneezing on the dust balls. Convinced he was safe from ambush, Lonely Boy then padded over to the window and peeked out from behind the chintz curtains at Mission Street.

He stood there for a long while, staring at the sidewalk. The sun had passed over the building and the street was bathed in shade, cooling the air. He watched the hookers, the school kids and the fishmongers with the scrutiny of a mad scientist—Mission Street was his laboratory. His grand experiment. His final stand. Satisfied his cosmos was in order, Lonely Boy closed the curtains and sat down on the floor next to Durrutti.

His freshly sunburned open face had a large suppurating zit on his right cheek. He was wearing a black Hanes T-shirt, a pair of blue Dickies cut off two inches below the knees and white Nike trainers. He stretched out his legs and clasped his hands behind his neck and inspected the room again. "So this is your crib, huh? Stark, ain't it? I guess you don't believe in furniture."

It took everything Durrutti had to get his tongue to work. The struggle to do it made him sweat. The yield was marginal. "Yeah."

"You ain't got much, do you?"

"Nope."

Lonely Boy was full of opinions. "You look goofy, dude." His voice resembled a bullfrog on helium. "You loaded?"

Durrutti let the words roll out of his mouth like fresh cement. "Well . . . uh, I'm wasted. You want to smoke some sherms?"

"No, homie, I don't do that stuff no more. It's bad for my lungs. I've got to think of my future."

Lonely Boy helped himself to one of Durrutti's Marlboros and puffed on it, lost in contemplation. He had burdens all up and down the hemisphere. His family depended on him to become a success for them in America. They wanted him to go to school and get an education. His homeboys needed him to fight the Sureños and the Norteños and the cops. Lonely Boy wanted to do it all.

He looked older than his years with his clean shaven scalp, the two tattooed teardrops under his left eye that signified time served in the California Youth Authority system, and the tattoo with his mother's name on his forearm. He poked at the zit on his cheek, letting his eyes go faraway, as he said, "You know *mi ruca?*"

That was Spooky from Shotwell Street, a tiny girl who wore her hair in a foot-high bouffant girded by a blue bandanna. A *huera* with vivid black eyes. She worked at Whiz Burger, an easy walk from her house. Tattooed in old-school gothic script on her neck was the phrase: *mi amor por vida*—Lonely Boy.

"Your girlfriend?" Durrutti asked. "How is she?"

"She's cool, man. Me and her, we've been together for two years. We been to jail together and all over the place, you know? We've seen a lot and yeah, she's knocked up."

"She's pregnant? Jesus Christ."

"You know it. Three months now. First of the new year, she's gonna bring me a big strong *hijo.*"

The angel dust had left Durrutti color blind and effusive. "That's great. Congratulations."

"Ain't no thing. It was easy. I could do it every day if I had to. You know what else?"

"What's that?"

Lonely Boy hotboxed the cigarette and exhaled three perfectly symmetrical smoke rings, working his jaw like a locomotive to execute the trick. "I told you I knew who killed the cop on Mission Street, didn't I?"

"No, you didn't."

"No? Don't bullshit me," Lonely Boy said. "I didn't? Well, fuck me. I thought I did. But you know Chamorro had to go, don't you? The backstabbing motherfucker. It's like he forgot his arithmetic, that if he tried to rip us off, we wouldn't do anything to retaliate. He was stupid, that's for sure. He fucked up and when you do that, you don't get no second chances."

Lonely Boy jiggled his head up and down, his eyes brooding and hooded, his jug-handled ears flushed scarlet. He seemed distant and slightly vacant. What he'd confessed made Durrutti cringe as if a furry long-legged tarantula was walking on his face. He didn't want to be the recipient of information like that. On the other hand, his survival depended on it. The paradox was making him crazy. The angel dust made him even crazier. He asked him, "Who did the shooting?"

Lonely Boy whispered with sadness, a tad offended, "You think I'm going to tell you? No way, *cabron.* This ain't about you. This is about me and that shit is confidential."

"But the cops are fucking with me."

"So? What can I do about that? Clap my hands and make them go away? If it were only that easy, I would have done it yesterday."

"I need your help."

"What do you want, charity? Ain't nothing for free."

"No, I don't want your goddamn charity. I need advice."

"Don't be asking me. This ain't no welfare office. Figure it out for yourself. Be a man."

He made a quarterturn and stared at Durrutti. The angel dust was taking apart his face. There was a swirling maw where Lonely Boy's mouth should have been. His eyes evaporated into viscous steam. His head went up in a column of smoke. The rest of him disintegrated geometrically; first his arms, then his legs. His dimmed voice crackled. "It's all uphill from here, so you better watch your shit." He got to his feet and walked out of the room. The next thing Durrutti knew the sky was black and it was raining, unusual for the summer months. Sheets of ocean-driven water washed over Mission Street, drowning the sidewalks. He went to the window, cranked it open and stuck his neck outside; a pre-autumnal wind whipped across his face, plastering his hair to his scalp. The traffic lights, a red line of them, blinked on and off like fireflies. An unerring flow of people scurried down the street with newspapers held over their heads, looking lost in the rain. But that was only the beginning; the weather was going to get a lot worse before it got any better.

NELSON ALGREN

The Man with the Golden Arm

THE CAPTAIN FELT IMPALED. It had been a bit too long since he had laughed. Felt joy or sorrow or simple wonder. When a light ripple, half protest and half mockery, moved down the other side of the wall he felt somehow appalled that caged men should laugh at anything. The ragged edge of that careless laughter hung like a ripped scarf upon an iron corner of his heart.

An iron heart, an iron life. Laughter and tears had corroded in his breast. In the whitish light of the query room a tic took a corner of his mouth and his lips worked trying to stop it, like a drunk trying to work off a fly.

For something had happened to the captain's lips as well as to his heart. All his honest policeman's life he had guarded both so well, knowing how

Hardboiled

little time there was, in the roistering world, for pity and loose talk and always too much traffic in the sort of thing anyhow. Too many women holding out pity like a day-old sweet roll out of a greasy bag—"We are all members of one another"—what had that half-crazed priest of the line-up meant by *that?*

Something that even the punk had seemed to know when he'd said, "Everybody's a habitual in his heart"? What did it mean that all the guilty felt so certain of their own innocence while he felt so uncertain of his own? It was patently wrong that men locked up by the law should laugh while the man who locked them there no longer felt able even to cry. As if those caged there had learned secretly that all men are innocent in a way no captain might ever understand.

"I know you," Bednar assured them quietly, "I know you all. You think you're all members of one another, somethin' like that."

They thought they were putting something over on him in there; while all the while it was himself who was putting it over on them.

Yet the glare in his eyes seemed to fill some small part of a need he had never felt before. And the unrecorded arrest slips littering his desk seemed written in a code devised by ancestral enemies.

"If you don't pull out of the blues you'll be writin' your own name on the sheet," Cousin Kvorka had joked with him that forenoon. Since that moment Bednar had been trying to rid himself of a compulsive yearning to write his name there where for so long he had written only the names of the guilty and the doomed.

The guilty and the doomed. He saw that steerer's small white face, exhausted like a child's from crying in his cell, and in one moment his own heart seemed a bloodstained charge sheet with space left upon it for but one more name.

In a suffocating need of absolution he took the pen and wrote, in a steady hand, corner to corner across the sheet, the meaningless indictment: *Guilty.*

Immediately he had done that through his mind there careened a carnival of rogues he had long forgotten. All those he'd disposed of, one way or another, from behind this same scarred desk. A shambling gallery of the utterly condemned. With that same exhausted small white face following everyone so anxiously, from so far behind. "I only done my honest copper's duty," the captain defended himself against the steerer and against them all, his fingers spreading involuntarily to conceal the word written across the sheet.

Yet somewhere along the line a light in his heart had gone out like an overcharged light bulb, leaving only some sort of brittle husk for a heart; a husk ready to crumble to a handful of dust. "My honest copper's duty," he repeated like a man trying to work a charm which had once worked for someone else: to cast out blue-moon moods, low-hanging memories and all bad dreams.

He said it twice and yet guilt like a dark bird perched forever near, so bald and wingless and cold and old, preening its dirty feathers with an obscene beak. "I'm one sick bull," Bednar decided, "it's time to go home." But it had been time to go home for hours and yet he sat on as though manacled to his unfiled arrest slips and that single word so firmly written beneath his hand.

He dried the sweat off his forehead with a blood-red bandanna, then tossed the rag aside as if he had touched his temples with the blood of others. "He wasn't nothin' to nobody, the punk," the captain recalled.

Then why did it feel like turning informer, why did he feel he had sold out a son, like being paid off in gold? For if everyone were members of one another—he put the notion down. That would mean those on the other side of the wall were his own kind.

It could not be. For if they were anything less than enemies he had betrayed himself a thousandfold. It would be too much to make a traitor out of a man for having done his simple duty. But what if he had done traitor's work all his life without realizing it? He tried to rise, for he had to find out, he had to find out what he had done to himself by doing his simple captain's duty.

"Cut out that racket in there," he warned the ceaseless murmur behind the wall: for a moment he had the delusion that they were examining his anguish through some peephole, nudging each other and winking, as convicts do, as they watched. "I never hated a man of you," he tried to appease them. And heard a knowing reply: "Nor loved any man at all."

Heard his own lips say that and felt himself growing angry. What ghostly kind of good would it have done a soul if he had? What except to delay justice awhile? For every man of them, he knew, had been guilty to the hilt, guilty of every sort of malice of which the human heart is capable. What they hadn't done to others had been only through indolence and lack of a proper chance.

For every man was secretly against the law in his heart, the captain knew; and it was the heart that mattered. There were no men innocent of intent to transgress. If they were human—look out. What was needed, he had learned long ago, was higher walls and stronger bars—there was no limit to what they were capable of.

Somewhere along the line he had learned, too, that not one was worth the saving. So he'd been right in saving none but himself. And if that had left them all to be members of one another, then it had left him to be a member of no one at all. Had, indeed, left him feeling tonight like the most fallen of anybody.

Hardboiled

The captain realized vaguely that the thing he had held secretly in his heart for so long against them all was simply nothing more than a hostility toward men and women as men and women.

And now so lost to all men and women that the murmur beyond the walls troubled him like the voices of friends he had denied ever having known. "The bums 'r gettin' my goat, that's all," he decided, pulling himself together. They had begun by stealing his sleep. He listened in fevered hope of hearing them call out to all the world that he was no better than the very worst of them. That he knew as well as themselves who was guiltiest tonight.

Silence. They blamed no one. They had the brassbound nerve to take the rap and forgive him for everything. Everything.

So that suddenly the captain wished to do something so conspicuously noble, something at once so foolish and so kind, so full of a perfectly useless mercifulness toward the most undeserving of all, that prisoners and police alike would laugh openly at him. Would laugh without pity as at an old enemy gone balmy at last.

He wished them all to speak to him directly, without trace of respect, make some sort of obscene joke out of his uniform and his badge and his unassailable record—he wished suddenly to be insulted so grievously and accused so unjustly that there would be no use of defending himself: so hopelessly misunderstood by everyone that there would be nothing left to do but keep his silence while everything he had labored so long and so faithfully to build was torn down, overnight, right before his eyes.

His heart paced with the prospect of such a fall as if in anticipation of an orgy. Then slowed, stanching its own excitement. "It sounds like they're all on their knees prayin' for me in there," he fancied. And did not wish to be prayed for.

For it was time to be stoned. He had been so proud to be an enforcer of the laws men fell by, of being the kind of man who tempered Justice with Mercy. Now it was time to see himself whether there were any such things at all. If there were neither one nor the other for himself, he would do without. An iron life, an iron heart, he could wish for an iron death.

Alone below the glare lamp in the abandoned query room, stifled by a ravaging guilt, he knew now those whom he had denied, those beyond the wall, had all along been members of himself. Theirs had been the common humanity, the common weakness and the common failure which was all that now could offer fresh hope to his heart.

Yet he had betrayed them for so long he could not go to them for redemption. He was unworthy of the lowliest—and there was no court to try any captain for doing his simple duty. No place was provided, by church or state, where such a captain might atone for everything he had committed in his heart. No judge had been appointed to pass sentence upon such a captain. He had been left to judge himself.

All debts had to be paid. Yet for his own there was no currency. All errors must ultimately be punished. Yet for his own, that of saving himself at the cost of others less cunning than himself, the punishment must be simply this: more lost, more fallen and more alone than any man at all.

Thieves, embezzlers and coneroos, all might redeem themselves in time. But himself, who had played the spiritual con game, there was no such redemption. There was no salvation for such self-saviors.

Only his own heart might redeem him: through tears or laughter. His heart that felt stopped by dust.

It had been too long since the captain had laughed. Even longer since he had wept.

Someone—could it still be that steerer?—cried out in sleep on the other side of the wall—bringing him, out of the wisdom of some ancestral dream, news of salvation to policemen and prisoners, dealers and steerers and captains, blind men and hustling girls, cripples and priestlike coneroos alike.

To the hunter as well as the hunted.

The captain wept.

Crocodile tears: he belonged to no man at all.

JOHN FANTE

The Big Hunger

WITH WRITERS, SLEEP AND prose are brothers. If the stuff comes, if it moves across the page, the nights are serene. If there are no words, there is no sleep. It was one of those times. I couldn't sleep.

It was also the time of Roseville's strangest bandit. Every day the *Tribune* had a fresh report of his crimes. Housewives were furious. The baffled police added an extra car to the night patrol, but the thief struck again and again. He was a panty thief. His plunder never varied. He showed no interest in shirts, dresses or overalls. Every night, now on the Northside, now on the South, the thief stripped some clothesline of a pair of ladies' panties. In despair the police asked the women of the town to bring in their washing at night. But there was always someone who forgot, and it was into her yard that the scoundrel crept, snatched a pair of panties off the line, and vanished into the night.

In my sleeplessness I mused about this exotic bandit. Polishing my gun, I pondered his curious depredations and contrived to find ways of capturing him. All at once I arrived upon a scheme.

I put on a robe and tiptoed into the room where my wife slept. Opening her dresser, I removed three pairs of her silk panties. Without a sound I went downstairs and through the house to the backyard. Our clothesline ran parallel with the back fence along the alley. There in the moonlight I hung the panties, one black, one white, one pink. A soft breeze lifted them to irresistible proportions. Now I hurried back to my room, turned off the lights, and sat at my window awaiting developments. I was there ten minutes before I realized my scheme was mad and worthless. In the first place my gun was not loaded, nor had I any desire to shoot the famous thief. In the second place, should he arrive on the scene, he would simply snatch the panties and be off, for I certainly had no intention of rushing out and grappling with him.

Alert as a wound, I smoked cigarettes and listened to the night noises. It was late summer and warm. Beyond my window an elm spread itself, luminous in the moonlight. Already the leaves were falling. We lived on a quiet tree-lined street. Approaching footsteps were audible two blocks away, and that was a rare sound, for everyone in the district went to town by car.

But now I heard footsteps. They were very near, in our yard, swishing through the dead leaves. The steps began in the front yard and moved around to the side of the house. I unhooked the screen and looked out the window. All was clear and bright, no movement, no sound. I locked the screen and sat back. Once more I heard the footsteps. This time I snapped on the light, opened the screen and called out, "Who's there?" No answer. I snapped off the light.

Instantly the leaves rustled, the steps moving around the house to the side door. Now I was certain of it: someone was in our yard, a tramp, a prowler, a thief. A man's home was about to be invaded. The situation called for action. I picked up my gun. In the yard the invader's feet plowed through the leaves defiantly.

Alarmed and angry I stood with the gun in my hand, the bullets buried in a sack of silk stockings downstairs on the back porch. I cursed my wife and tiptoed down the staircase. I needed ammunition. The moon lit up the living room, and I crouched low at the foot of the stairs, for the curtains were apart and I could be seen from the outside.

Hardboiled

Sprawled flat on my stomach, I crawled through the dining room to the kitchen. My heart banged against the floor, the gun in my hand was sticky with perspiration, and I felt hot and suffocating in the flannel robe. The hiss of leaves told me the intruder was at the side door between the kitchen and the dining room. This was no panty thief, this was a burglar.

An inch at a time, I dragged myself across the linoleum in the kitchen. By now I had reached the door to the back porch. Raising my arm, I turned the lock. There was a sharp click. Instantly the noise outside stopped. Sweat poured from me. I lay prostrate, panting and waiting. Another weary twenty feet lay between me and the broom closet. Again there was activity at the side door, and I thought I heard the knob turn. I kept going, dragging myself along the floor of the back porch to the broom closet. With both hands I reached up and tore the stocking sack from a hook.

Feverish with excitement, I clawed through the stockings, cursing my wife and all women, my fingers snagging the silk as they searched for the elusive box of cartridges. At last I found it and loaded the gun. Now I was unafraid. With six bullets in the .38 I got to my feet and walked boldly through the kitchen to the side door. For hair-trigger action I cocked the gun. The situation was well in hand. I was aware of the consequences. I knew no jury would convict me.

I flung open the door.

"Stay where you are," I said.

He didn't. It was Heinrich, the long brown Dachshund belonging to the Richardsons, our next-door neighbors. Heinrich yelped and skittered through the leaves and under the hedge.

I sat on the doorstep. I was utterly exhausted, my whole body bathed in sweat, my face and robe smeared with dust and lint picked up on the long crawl across the floor. Tangled silk stockings draped my arms and ankles. It had been a terrifying night, and the less my wife knew of it the better. I unloaded the gun, replaced the cartridges in the stocking bag, mopped up the sweaty streak across the linoleum, put everything in order, and took a shower.

Then I remembered the panties out on the clothesline. They had to be returned. Disgusted with myself, I went downstairs once more and into the backyard. It was two o'clock. As I gathered the panties, I heard a voice behind me, and the voice said;

"For lord's sake."

It was Richardson. He was a railroad engineer. He went to work at insane hours, and he was on his way to work now, opening the doors to his garage.

I said, "Hi, neighbor."

But there was a sickening feeling in the pit of my stomach as I walked back to the house, for I knew Richardson stood in his driveway looking at me and thinking of the zany wanted by the police.

W. R. Burnett

The Asphalt Jungle

COBBY WAS PLAYING POKER in the middle cardroom when Timmons opened the door and motioned that he wanted to speak to him. Cobby was immediately worried, because Timmons never broke in on a big game unless there was something mighty important going on. Cobby felt his nerves beginning to jump. In fact they'd been jumping intermittently ever since the big deal blew up.

All the same, he had three jacks, which he was pretty sure was the winning hand, and he was anxious to play it out. He motioned for Timmons to wait. But Timmons shook his head warningly and showed some distress. Still Cobby couldn't give up. Turning to the players, he said: "Check!"

"It's not your bet, Cobby," cried one of the players. "What the Jesus kind of poker is this!"

"Okay, okay!" said the opener wearily. "Since it's all loused up now, I'll check."

Everybody checked, complaining, and the hands were laid down. Cobby ran third, much to his surprise; then he got up, laughing a little in spite of his apprehension. At least this interruption had saved him some money.

He left the cardroom, followed by sour looks. Timmons whispered in his ear: "Dietrich!"

"You mean they got the drag out again?"

"No," said Timmons. "That's what *I* thought. But he don't want me for nothing. He wants you. I put him in room one."

Cobby cleared his throat nervously, swallowed a couple of times; then, arranging his features into what he thought was a pleasant, easy smile, he opened the door of room one and went in. Big Dietrich looked up with a grin. He had a highball in front of him and he was smoking one of Cobby's best cigars. Cobby relaxed a little and sat down opposite the hulking Sergeant of Police.

"Crooked Ear fixed me up," said Dietrich. "I hope you don't mind, Cobby, my boy."

"No. Not at all, Monk," said Cobby, thawing more and more. "The place belongs to you. You know that."

"Thanks. Well, here's to you and yours." Dietrich drank, draining the glass; then he sat puffing for a moment on his cigar, eying Cobby, who began to fidget. "You know, Cobby," he said finally, "things were a little slow tonight; so I got to thinking about you, and I said to myself: 'I'll just drop down and talk to my old friend Cobby.' You see, I been worrying about you, Cobby. You're a nice little guy, with a nice big, semi-legitimate racket—doing all right. But sometimes guys get hungry, and they branch out, and then they get themselves in a lot of trouble."

"What are you talking about, Monk? Me—I don't branch out." A nerve in Cobby's back began to twitch, and he shifted about nervously, trying to ease himself.

"Yes, sir," said Dietrich, ignoring what Cobby had said. "They branch out—and then, wham! they get it. Every man should stick to his own racket. Why, Cobby—did you know for instance that a guy who helps to plan a robbery is as guilty as the guys who actually pull the job?"

"Never thought about it one way or another," mumbled Cobby. "How about another drink, Monk?"

"No, thanks. Not tonight, Cobby. Take it another way. Suppose these guys who are pulling a robbery get themselves in a corner—you know—and they have to set a guy over. Well . . . the fellow sitting cozy at home who helped plan the robbery, he's equally guilty. They can burn him—in the chair. Now what do you think of that, Cobby?"

"Never thought about it at all. Why should I?"

The smile faded from Dietrich's big, fat, tough face, and, reaching a powerful paw across the table, he seized Cobby by the lapels and shook him violently.

"Well . . . you better think about it, and think about it hard and fast. If you don't, you're going to see what the death cells at the Walls look like!"

"Monk! Wait!" cried Cobby. "What goes here? Are you drunk, or pulling another one of your ribs—like the last time?"

Dietrich shouted in his face.

"Where's Riemenschneider?"

Cobby started violently, and his face began to turn deathly pale. Dietrich let go of him all of a sudden, and he fell back into his chair, limp. Nerves were twitching all over him now.

Leaning forward, Dietrich hit him a hard, sudden backhand blow that

Hardboiled

spun him out of his chair and onto the floor, where he crouched, shaking his head, his mind void of all thought, his body quaking with fear.

Dietrich got up, walked over to him, and raised his huge, heavily shod foot as if to give him the boot. Cobby jumped to his feet immediately and tried to get behind the table, but Dietrich clouted him again and he fell over backwards, taking a chair with him this time.

Cobby began to plead with tears in his eyes as he crouched in front of Dietrich, torn with fear. If he stayed down, Dietrich might kick him and break his ribs. If he got up, Dietrich might knock him down again. Cobby was so sensitive to pain that he could scarcely bear the thought of it, let alone endure it.

"Monk! Monk! Have you gone crazy? Look. It's me. Cobby! For the love of God, Monk . . . !"

"Where's Riemenschneider?" cried Dietrich, staring down ferociously at Cobby. "I want answers, or I'm going to kick your teeth out."

Cobby jumped up in a panic, putting his hand over his mouth; and Dietrich belted him again, slamming him back against the wall, where his head knocked a sporting print to the floor, breaking the glass.

"He's gone," cried Cobby. "He holed up here. But now he's gone. I don't know where he is."

Dietrich had been using his open hand. He now doubled up his big, beefy fist and advanced on Cobby.

"Maybe you'd like to do a little talking," cried Dietrich. "Or should I fracture your skull?"

"Monk! For God's sake . . . !" gasped Cobby, hysterical with the fear of a beating. "What do you want me to talk about? I came clean on the doctor. He's gone. Swear to God, that's the truth!"

Dietrich stared at him, hard-eyed, menacing, for a long time, paying no attention to the fact that Cobby was wilting to such an extent that he had to grab the table for support and even so could barely stand upright.

Finally Dietrich spoke in a surprisingly gentle voice.

"Maybe it is, Cobby. Maybe it is. Now let's get down to the Pelletier business. How would you like to go down to Headquarters with me and make a statement in front of the Commissioner?"

"A statement . . . ?" stammered Cobby, hope beginning to show in his terrified eyes. "What . . . what about?"

"About who engineered the robbery, who pulled it off—who shot Brannom. Things like that."

Cobby nodded, unable to speak; then tears began to run down his cheeks, and, going to pieces completely, he fell into a chair and, putting his head on the card table, sobbed like a six-year-old kid.

Hardboiled

Dietrich laid a heavy hand on his shoulder.

"That's my boy!" he said. "We'll make ourselves a little deal, Cobby. With the Commissioner, I mean. You turn state's—and maybe we can rig up a suspended sentence."

Without looking up, Cobby nodded again. Dietrich sat down at the table, picked up his cigar, and began to puff on it. Then he laughed coarsely.

"Remember what I told you, Cobby, about this case? Didn't I tell you some fink would blow it sky high?"

Cobby looked up at him with dead eyes; then he straightened in his chair and tried to get himself together.

"It . . . it's not that I'm a fink . . ." he began slowly and confusedly; then he broke off, turned away, and fumbled ineptly for a cigar.

"No, no; of course not!" said Dietrich, patting him on the shoulder. "It's just a manner of speaking."

ANDREW VACHSS

The Getaway Man

AFTER THAT FIRST TIME, we didn't do any more test runs. Everything was for real.

One job was a post office. We went at night. Virgil was dressed in one of those padded suits people who work in meat lockers wear. Tim swung the sledgehammer against the glass. Virgil put his arms over his head and jumped right on through where it was smashed in. The alarm went off, loud.

Virgil ran around and opened the door from the inside, so Tim could help him.

The alarm kept ringing. Tim said we had to keep everything under three minutes. He told me to keep watch, but not to make any noise unless the cops showed up.

Tim and Virgil came out. They were hauling a big gray post office bag. They heaved it into the trunk and jumped in with me.

"Drive like the Devil's behind you, Eddie," Tim said.

The bag was full of all kinds of stuff. Mostly stamps. There was a little cash, not much. The big score was all the blank money orders. Tim said he knew a guy who would give us a good deal on them, but we had to turn them over fast, before the feds got the list out.

One thing I learned from Tim: It was better to take a long time planning a big job than to do a lot of little ones in a hurry. After a while, I got to be in on the planning. Just the driving part, but that was very important, Tim said. Mostly the route for the getaway, but also what car to use, too.

Mr. Clanton's junkyard was so big, you could make a new car out of the parts of old ones. He showed me how to cut license plates in half and make new ones out of the pieces. Ones that wouldn't come up stolen if a cop looked at them.

"Can you get us something *really* fast?" Tim asked me one night.

"Fast top end? Or off the line?" I said. There's a big difference, but most people never think about that.

"We're *gonna* be chased, Eddie," he said. "Count on it."

"How could the cops—?"

"Not the cops," he said. "It's going to be a race. If we win, we get a *lot* of money. And nobody's going to call the cops."

"What happens if we—?"

"We get dead," Virgil said. He had a big grin on his face.

Mr. Clanton had an old Chevy stock car at his place. It used to run in Sportsman Modified over at the Speedway a few years ago. "The owner got sick of throwing away money," Mr. Clanton told us. "The fool he had for a driver spent more time on the wall than he did on the track. They never could get themselves a decent sponsor, so I took it in trade for some motors. It's just been sitting around here, ever since."

I spent a lot of time with that car. Putting in a new engine was easy—the whole front end tilted up and there was plenty of room to work. The suspension was the problem.

"This one was set up to go roundy-round," Mr. Clanton said. "Spent its whole sad life making left turns. It's geared real short, too."

I told him I was sure I could fix it, and he let me use his shop to try. Every time I made a change, I took it out and tried it, to make sure it worked.

One night, Virgil asked me what the hell was taking me so long. Before I could say anything, Tim said, "Eddie knows what he's doing."

That made me even more determined to do it perfect.

When I was done, the car looked like it was normal, if you didn't get too close. I even got the lights hooked up. There was only the one seat in the front, but we weren't going any long distance. The bad thing about it for a getaway car was that it only had two doors. If you've got more than one man coming, it takes longer to jump into that kind of car. But Tim said he had a plan for that, too.

The building was against the side of a hill, so you had to climb a long flight of outside stairs to get to the door on the second floor. That was around the side; the front was the same level as the ground—that's where they had the strip club.

"The game's upstairs," Tim said, "but the chase is going to come from around the front. They'll have to call down for help."

"What about doing their tires?" I asked him. "So they can't chase us."

"You see how many cars there are in the lot, Eddie? We don't know which ones the bouncers drive. We'd have to do them all. Anyway, there's way too much traffic in the lot, people coming in and out all the time. Anybody spots us doing the tires, we're done. You've got to *drive*, kid. All right?"

"I got it," I said. My chest felt big with what Tim had called me. Same as Virgil.

I started the engine. We rolled over to a spot right next to the bottom of the stairs. Tim and Virgil got out.

They climbed up the stairs. I lost sight of them when they went in the door.

I closed my eyes for a second, to fix the road I'd have to drive in my mind. Then I waited.

Somebody came charging down the stairs. Virgil. He grabbed the wide-mouth can he had stashed at the bottom, ran about halfway back up, and started splashing gas all over the steps as he backed down again.

Three shots blasted. Tim came flying down the stairs, a laundry sack in one hand. When he got to where the gas was, he threw down the sack and vaulted off. Soon as he was in the air, Virgil lit the whole thing up.

I revved the engine, put the car in first, held the clutch down.

Virgil threw the laundry sack in the side window. It landed right next to me. He crawled in behind; Tim jumped in the front. They pulled their masks off.

The flames were swallowing the stairs. I dropped the clutch. We came out of that lot like a shotgun blast. The stock car got a little sideways on the dirt, but I was ready for it to do that, and I never had to let off the gas.

The road went straight as a string for about five miles before there was any chance to turn off. I couldn't see any lights behind us.

"We're gone!" Tim said, looking over his shoulder.

We were almost to the first turnoff when I saw a pair of pickups coming toward us. Suddenly, they slammed on their brakes, blocking the road.

Hardboiled

"Well, look at that. Hillbillies got themselves a CB radio, huh?" Virgil said. I couldn't see his face behind me, but I knew he was grinning.

I stabbed the brakes as I gunned the engine and downshifted all the way to second. As we started to skid, I cranked the wheel hard over, and floored it. The stock car got sideways, powersliding right at the two pickups. I whipped the wheel back to the left and we slipped around them with about a yard to spare.

A big chunk of the windshield disappeared just before I heard the shots.

"Come on, cocksuckers!" Virgil yelled right in my ear, blasting his pistol out the window.

Tim was somewhere under all that glass, but I could see him moving.

Everything slowed down then. I could see it all happening, like we were underwater. I felt a couple of shots go into the rear of the car, like they were going into me. Tim's face was all bloody. He was trying to get his gun up. One of the pickups wheeled around behind us. It had a row of bright lights in a bar across the top of its roof, blazing.

"Drive us, Eddie!" Tim said. Real soft, but it was like a shout to me.

I bent the stock car into that first corner, and put my right foot through the floorboard. I'd been over those roads dozens of times, practicing. It felt like there was a wire running from my hands direct into the front wheels, like I was bending my own body around those curves. Once in a while I could catch a flash of the pickup's lights on an angle, but they never got close enough to fire any more shots. At least, none I could hear.

When I spotted the big tree with the giant white "X" I had spray-painted on it, I knew we were nearly home. Just up the road a piece from the "X" was a tight hairpin curve around a mass of rocks. I could hear the pickup coming on. I braked deep, sliding just a little bit. Then I slowed down even more, so we were just barely moving. I could hear Virgil slam another clip in his pistol.

I looked over at Tim. He finally had his gun up, but he couldn't turn enough to aim back out his window.

The pickup came closer. I goosed the throttle with the clutch in, making sure the carburetor was clean. The second I saw the wash of the pickup's lights, we took off again. The stock car slipped around that hairpin like water through a pipe.

The pickup thought we were going much faster than we really were. By then, it was too late for them to slow down. I couldn't see the crash, but I heard it.

"They ain't got no more!" Virgil yelled.

PINCKNEY BENEDICT

Dogs of God

INCHCAPE TOLD IT THIS WAY:

"We're going down the long slope on Little Allegheny Mountain. Three of us have got our trucks in a line: Looney Martin in the front, then me, and Asa Boggs bringing up the back door. It's eight, nine miles long, the stretch of mountain highway we're on, and better than an eight percent grade for most of its length, with a steep drop-off on either side, so it's got a pretty wicked reputation. A lot of guys have gone over on that grade, burned out their brakes, rolled their rigs. It's a killer.

"Most all of the trucking companies won't even let their haulers use it anymore, because so many people have pitched over the edge and took their trucks with them. That gets to be expensive after a while. You have to go the long way if you don't use it, though, around by the Henderson Gap, so there's some of us that still take the old route. You can carry a lot more loads in a day that way, if you don't screw it up.

"So we're going down the slope, and Asa's on the radio telling us about some guy who fell asleep and ran his rig full tilt into a bridge stanchion. *Did you hear about that, Inchworm?* he asks me. Inchworm is my handle. Asa says it was a Transtar eighteen-wheeler semi, going like the hammers of hell, and the trailer snapped like a whip, flipped up over the top of the cab. He says it looked just like some kind of a giant metal scorpion, waving its tail up over its back.

"While Asa's going on, I smell a terrible smell. Looking, I see Looney's got

471

smoke boiling out from his brakes. He's got a real load on, probably seventy thousand pounds gross or more, loaded with twenty-five tons of gravel anyway, and he's pulling away from us down the hill. I've got the same load, and Asa the same as me, but I've got it in the low range, just creeping down the hill. I get on the radio and tell Looney to let up on the brakes or he'll burn them out. Maybe he don't know the smoke he's laying down. He can't hear me, though, because Asa's still talking, and I imagine he's walking on my signal pretty good, and me on his, so Looney's probably just getting noise.

"*Clear the channel,* I tell Asa, and he says, *Come again?* and goes right on back into his story. He hasn't smelled Looney's cooking brakes yet, and he can't see Looney because my truck's in the way. *Get off the radio, goddamnit,* I say, and this time he does it. I listen to see if Looney's broadcasting any-thing, though if he is I don't know what I can do. He's as far beyond my help as if he was on the moon, and all I can do is watch whatever's going to happen. Still, it seems to me like it would be good to hear his voice. There's nothing on the CB but static, and way back in the background some voices that you can hear but you can't tell at all what they're saying, like they might be in the next county over or the next state and their signal just getting to you by taking a freak bounce off the clouds.

"Finally I say, *Looney. Breaker, Looney-tune. How about you?* His truck's way out ahead now, rolling down the slope, getting faster, and I wonder if his brakes could be gone already. If so, there's nothing holding him back. His truck's older and badly outfitted, so he's got no jake brake on the engine to shut him down if he gets in trouble. Asa's on the air again, wanting to know what's wrong. Finally I get him to clear, and I give Looney another shout. *Looney, Looney, you got your ears on?* I say, but I'm starting to think he must of shut the radio off so he wouldn't have to listen to Asa tell his story.

"By this time he's losing control, but he rolls right on by the first runaway truck ramp like he hasn't seen it. I don't blame him, because if I was in trouble but figured I could hold out for the second one a few miles on down, I'd do it that way too. The second ramp is a kind of upward corkscrew, a dirt track; up and up it goes, and you're losing speed all the time until you're stopped right there at the top. But the first one—the first one's just a straight single lane that leads off the highway at an angle, runs for a couple hundred yards, and drops sheer into the ravine. Nothing to stop you at the end but a mound of crushed limestone. It's got a carpet of deep gravel covering it that's supposed to wear away your speed, but if I've got to trust my life to gravel stopping me, thirty-five tons of truck haring along at eighty or ninety miles an hour, I'll take another choice, thank you very much.

"So Looney skips the first ramp and heads on down the mountain. I pick up my speed a little to keep him in sight, but I don't want to end up where it looks like he's going, so I keep my eye on my velocity, just using the brakes as much as I need them, testing the pedal to make sure they don't fade. Asa's crowding me, because he wants to see what's up, and because he hasn't got much in the way of brains. And all I can think is *How did you let it get away from you, Loon. Weren't you watching?*

"It surprises me to hear him on the citizen's band. He's shouting. *Hey, hey, hey,* he yells, and then there's a sound like he's banging the mike against the dashboard. Hammering it. Then he's yelling, *Hey, hey,* again. He's keeping the mike keyed, so it's no use to try to talk to him. He won't hear anything through his own transmission. His truck's just screaming along the grade now, brakes gone for sure, and it sounds through the radio like a plane that's on its way down. This awful rising rattling pitch that you know has got to end in a smash. He goes around a curve, out of my sight for a few seconds until I round the turn myself. He's still on the CB, talking now, and I try to pay attention to what he's saying. It may be all that he gets to say. He's shouting, but still it's hard to hear him over the noise of his truck. *Maketh me to lie down,* he says. *Valley of the shadow,* he says, and *death.*

"We're still a couple of miles above the second truck ramp, which is near the bottom of the grade, and he's starting to weave with the speed; the truck's sloshing back and forth over the center line, and the few cars that are coming the other way, up the grade, have scattered off to the edges of the road one side and the other. He sideswipes one of them and it spins in place and winds up sitting on the guardrail. The impact doesn't slow him down a bit. Over the radio I hear him hit the car. It sounds like he has crushed a tin can in his fist. *You're killing people, Looney,* I shout, but into the air, into the windshield, not into the radio. A couple of seconds later I'm going past the car he hit, a big Buick, its front end and driver's side crushed, and nobody's getting out of it or even moving so far as I can tell.

"*My head with oil,* he says, his voice over the radio as clear as though he is sitting next to me in the cab of my own truck. He begins to say something else, but his voice is cut off by a loud cracking noise. It sounds like he has been shot. His voice, and the sounds from his truck, are gone from the radio. It's just static again. It takes me a second to recognize that popping sound: one of his front tires has blown out.

"You don't try to steer or brake when that happens; you just ride it on down. We're nearly to the second truck ramp now, the better one, but he won't make it. The tire has gone, and he's rolling on the rim, throwing up a trail of bright sparks like it's some kind of a light show under his truck, like he's an electric trolley following along a high-tension wire. The other front tire goes pretty soon after, and the fuel tanks rip loose from under the tractor's running boards. The tanks carry back into the rear wheels, the wheels under the load, and all eight of them go at once. It's like watching a drunk stagger down the street though traffic, seeing Looney's truck with all its tires gone, wandering over the road. It swerves and then it tips over onto its side. The load of gravel washes out onto the road, a little rock slide right there on the highway.

"I'm into the junk trail that Looney's truck is leaving behind it as it dies, and I'm spending all my time trying not to hit nothing, dodging axle parts and bouncing fuel tanks and riding over all the rocks and pieces of scrap that I couldn't tell you what they are. It scares me to think I might lose a tire and go down myself, and I think that's the first time I've been scared during this whole experience. I throttle back, looking to pull over onto the berm, hoping Asa's giving me enough room that he won't smash into the back of my truck.

"By the time I look up, Looney's about six feet from hitting a milk tanker that has just started the climb up Little Allegheny, and still sliding. The tanker's got a blue tractor with a big sleeping compartment behind the cab, and I can't help but wonder if there's anyone napping back there. Then I close my eyes, even though my truck is still under way, because those two vehicles colliding is something that I simply do not want to see.

"The sound of it—the sound of it I'm unable to describe. A giant man digging his thumbs deep into your ears, way back in where it is waxy and dark and it is so sensitive that you can't bear anyone to touch. Or that same place, if a bug were in there, a big black beetle, and its wings were beating against your eardrum a hundred times a second, and there was no way to get it out but to go in after it with something long and thin and pointed, something sharp made out of steel. It's a sound I can hear in my head perfectly, but one I cannot imitate and wouldn't like to. Right at the last, I hear Looney's mike key on, and I hear him screaming, and then stop screaming. But there is no way that could happen, and no way I could hear his voice over the sound of the grinding metal and busting glass."

Inchcape took a breath.

"Afterward, there's a lot of cleaning up to do. Asa and I are the first men on the spot, and then some people from cars that have stopped on both sides of the road. Twenty-five tons of gravel seems like a lot when it is riding just back of you in the dump bed of your truck, but when it is all on the road it don't seem like so much. Just a thin covering is all, and our feet are crunching through it all the rest of that afternoon.

"The milk is everywhere too, and I'm sure it was a lot of money's worth of milk, thin blue-looking stuff, but before long it has streamed down the hill and ran into the culverts, mixed with the diesel that is draining from both trucks, and down the drains with it and it is gone. It has been a dry season, and whatever liquid leaves the hardtop road is sucked down into the dirt in no time at all. Flies collect on the shredded metal of the milk tanker's container.

"The results are pretty much what you might expect of such a thing. The folks in the Buick have been injured but not killed, although one of them dies in the hospital later that night. Looney is dead as a mackerel, we can see that right away; it takes a rescue squad a couple of hours to cut his body out with acetylene torches and power saws and the Jaws of Life gadget that they got.

"In the end, the wrecker crew that comes to pick up the two trucks can't get them apart. They have hit so hard they are practically welded together at their cabs. I heard later that they took both of them down to the salvage yard in one piece, dragging them behind a couple of their heaviest wreckers. At the yard, they got a couple of those big Komatsu crawlers to come in and cut the trucks apart from each other. It was the only way they could do it.

"One surprising thing: the driver of the tanker is alive. A long breaker bar slid out from a toolbox behind the seat and cracked him on the leg, and he's got a knot there the size of a football. But overall he's pretty happy when we drag him out of the wreck and set him by the side of the road. We tell him to take it easy, sit quiet and wait for the ambulance because the leg might be busted, or he could have other injuries that we can't see, and he just doesn't feel it because he is jazzed up. But he won't listen, goes gimping around the wreck, marveling at the whole thing with this silly grin on his face. He even grins when he looks into the dump truck's cab and sees what's left of Looney.

"Asa goes over to him. I go over there too, because I don't like the way Asa's walking, got his shoulders hunched and his arms held tight against his sides like he wants a fight. Asa puts a hand on this guy's shoulder—he's still staring in there at Looney—and spins him around so the guy nearly folds up on his bad leg. The seam of his trouser leg is splitting over the swelling, and I can see the skin in there's a bad color, got to be a fracture of some kind. I saw guys that got injuries like that when they were playing football and they never knew it for hours, high on winning and the game. This guy's just like that.

"Asa says to him, *Get that look off your damn face. A man has died here.*

"And the guy says, *Look?*

"Asa says, *You're smiling. Why the hell would you be smiling?* Other people are drifting over to watch what's happening, but nobody interferes. They've had enough excitement for a while, maybe. I'll step in if it gets any worse than it is, but I'm holding off for the minute.

"The guy holds up his hands and says, *I'm not smiling.* At the same time there's this big grin on his face. When he says that about not smiling, the grin gets even wider. He's showing all his teeth, and he has nice white even teeth. From drinking a lot of milk, maybe. His teeth are beginning to chatter together a little, and his lips are going blue, but altogether he looks very merry.

"*You're looking in there at my dead friend's corpse and you're smiling,* Asa says. I can tell he's about to go in swinging, so I take him by the arm. He doesn't want to come at first, but I manage to lead him away. Behind us, the other folks are gathered around the tanker driver, and I can hear his voice. He's saying, *I'm not smiling, I'm not smiling,* over and over again. Asa and I go over to my truck, and we get up into the cab, and we tune in an FM station to listen to a few songs, and we smoke a couple of cigarettes, waiting for the police and the ambulance to show up.

"*He was smiling,* Asa says. He's got a cigarette in his hand, but he's not smoking it. He's just letting it burn down toward his fingers. *I didn't like to see that.*

"*I know it, Asa,* I say. *I know exactly what you mean. But listen: I think the guy is in shock.*

"He looks over at me, and I wonder for a second if he's going to take a swing at me. Then he laughs, and he says to me in this angry voice, *Shock, hell. That man's as happy as a clam.*

"The guy has gotten away from the people who were trying to tend him, and he's hobbling around, really moving like a cripple, twisting on that busted leg. He's going from place to place on the road around the two wrecked trucks, pointing at the mashed pieces that are laying everywhere on the ground, telling their names in this big loud voice that carries to us even in the closed cab. *Looney's dead,* is all I can think, and this injured guy's climbing on his truck, sounding glad and excited and calling out the details of his survival to anybody in the crowd around him that'll listen."

Pleasant Gehman

Escape from Houdini Mountain

BABY, YOU'VE GOT IT all. You've got the dull eyes, glassy stare, complete with dark circles and bags the size of steamer trunks beneath them. You've got the smeared lipstick applied from a nearly empty tube, the push-up bra with the old, worn-out elastic, and cheap trendy slut clothes with a tiny but noticeable rip under the arm.

Worn-down heels, the sides of the shoes streaked with scuff marks, runs in your hose. Bitten-down cuticles, chipped toenail polish. A purse with the lining half ripped out with not too much cash inside but plenty of pills and shreds of tobacco mingling in the bottom next to the loose change, mostly pennies.

Hair dull from ratting it up and too much cut-rate bargain bin hairspray, generic-brand shampoo. The fun-fur coat that's never once been dry-cleaned. Faint frown lines, deep smile lines and a complexion that's slightly sallow.

Plastic earrings from the 99-Cent store highlighting your faint desperation. I'm asking you, is it an accident or is it art? It's definitely a look, and you've got it down. As a matter of fact, you've gone above and beyond the call of duty, with dutiful attention to every last detail! I'm telling you, nothing, but *nothing* says "cheap bar trash" like those scarred and bruised knees.

How do you do it?

HARRY CREWS

The Car

THE OTHER DAY, THERE arrived in the mail a clipping sent by a friend of mine. It had been cut from a Long Beach, California, newspaper and dealt with a young man who had eluded police for fifty-five minutes while he raced over freeways and through city streets at speeds up to 130 miles per hour. During the entire time, he ripped his clothes off and threw them out the window bit by bit. It finally took twenty-five patrol cars and a helicopter to catch him. When they did, he said that God had given him the car, and that he had "found God."

I don't want to hit too hard on a young man who obviously has his own troubles, maybe even is a little sick with it all, but when I read that he had found God in the car, my response was: *So say we all.* We have found God in cars, or if not the true God, one so satisfying, so powerful and awe-inspiring that the distinction is too fine to matter. Except perhaps ultimately, but pray we must not think too much on that.

The operative word in all this is *we*. It will not do for me to maintain that I have been above it all, that somehow I've managed to remain aloof from the national love affair with cars. It is true that I got a late start. I did not learn to drive until I was twenty-one; my brother was twenty-five before he learned. The reason is simple enough. In Macon County, Georgia, where I grew up, many families had nothing with a motor in it. Ours was one such family. But starting as late as I did, I still had my share, and I've remembered them all, the cars I've owned. I remember them in just the concrete specific way you remember anything that changed your life. Especially I remember the early ones.

The first car I ever owned was a 1938 Ford coupe. It had no low gear and the door on the passenger side wouldn't open. I eventually put a low gear in it, but I never did get the door to work. One hot summer night on a clay road a young lady whom I'll never forget had herself braced and ready with one foot on the rearview mirror and the other foot on the wing vent. In the first few lovely frantic moments, she pushed out the wing vent, broke off the rearview mirror and left her little footprints all over the ceiling. The memory of it was so affecting that I could never bring myself to repair the vent or replace the headliner she had walked all over upside down.

Eight months later I lost the car on a rain-slick road between Folkston, Georgia, and Waycross. I'd just stopped to buy a stalk of bananas (to a boy raised in the hookworm and rickets belt of the South, bananas will always remain an incredibly exotic fruit, causing him to buy whole stalks at a time), and back on the road again I was only going about fifty in a misting rain when I looked over to say something to my buddy, whose nickname was Bonehead and who was half drunk in the seat beside me. For some reason I'll never understand, I felt the back end of the car get loose and start to come up on us in the other lane. Not having driven very long, I overcorrected and stepped on the brake. We turned over four times. Bonehead flew out of the car and shot down a muddy ditch about forty yards before he stopped, sober and unhurt. I ended up under the front seat, thinking I was covered with gouts of blood. As it turned out, I didn't have much wrong with me and what I was covered with was gouts of mashed banana.

The second car I had was a 1940 Buick, square, impossibly heavy, built like a Sherman tank, but it had a '52 engine in it. Even though it took about ten miles to get her open full bore, she'd do over a hundred miles an hour on flat ground. It was so big inside that in an emergency it could sleep six. I tended to live in that Buick for almost a year and no telling how long I would have kept it if a boy who was not a friend of mine and who owned an International Harvester pickup truck hadn't said in mixed company that he could make the run from New Lacy in Coffee County, Georgia, to Jacksonville, Florida, quicker than I could. He lost the bet, but I wrung the speedometer off the Buick, and also—since the run was made on a blistering day in July—melted four inner tubes, causing them to fuse with the tires, which were already slick when the run started. Four new tires and tubes cost more money than I had or expected to have anytime soon, so I sadly put that old honey up on blocks until I could sell it to a boy who lived up toward Macon.

After the Buick, I owned a 1953 Mercury with three-inch lowering blocks, fender skirts, twin aerials, and custom upholstering made of rolled Naugahyde. Staring into the bathroom mirror for long periods of time I practiced expressions to drive it with. It was that kind of car. It looked mean, and it was mean. Consequently, it had to be handled with a certain style. One-handing it through a ninety-degree turn on city streets in a power slide where you were in danger of losing your ass as well as the car, you were obligated to have your left arm hanging half out the window and a very *bored* expression on your face. That kind of thing.

Those were the sweetest cars I was ever to know because they were my first. I remember them like people—like long-ago lovers—their idiosyncrasies, what they liked and what they didn't. With my hands deep in crankcases, I was initiated into their warm greasy mysteries. Nothing in the world was more satisfying than winching the front end up under the shade of a chinaberry tree and sliding under the chassis on a burlap sack with a few tools to see if the car would not yield to me and my expert ways.

The only thing that approached working on a car was talking about one. We'd stand about for hours, hustling our balls and spitting, telling stories about how it had been somewhere, sometime, with the car we were driving. It gave our lives a little focus and our talk a little credibility, if only because we could point to the evidence.

"But, hell, don't it rain in with that wing vent broke out like that?"

"Don't mean nothing to me. Soon's Shirley kicked it out, I known I was in love. I ain't about to put it back."

Usually we met to talk at night behind the A&W Root Beer stand, with the air heavy with the smell of grease and just a hint of burned French fries and burned hamburgers and burned hot dogs. It remains one of the most sensuous, erotic smells in my memory because through it, their tight little asses ticking like clocks, walked the sweetest softest short-skirted carhops in the world. I knew what it was to stand for hours with my buddies, leaning nonchalant as hell on a fender, pretending not to look at the carhops, and saying things like: "This little baby don't look like much, but she'll git rubber in three gears." And when I said it, it was somehow my own body I was talking about. It was *my* speed and *my* strength that got rubber in three gears. In the mystery of that love affair, the car and I merged.

But, like many another love affair, it has soured considerably. Maybe it would have been different if I had known cars sooner. I was already out of the Marine Corps and twenty-two years old before I could stand behind the A&W Root Beer and lean on the fender of a 1938 coupe. That seems pretty old to me to be talking about getting rubber in three gears, and I'm certain it is *very* old to feel your own muscle tingle and flush with blood when you say it. As is obvious, I was what used to be charitably called a late bloomer. But at some point I did become just perceptive enough to recognize bullshit when I was neck deep in it.

The 1953 Mercury was responsible for my ultimate disenchantment with cars. I had already bored and stroked the engine and contrived to place a six-speaker sound system in it when I finally started to paint it. I spent the better half of a year painting that car. A friend of mine owned a body shop and he let me use the shop on weekends. I sanded the Mercury down to raw metal, primed it, and painted it. Then I painted it again. And again. And then again. I went a little nuts, as I am prone to do, because I'm the kind of guy who if he can't have too much of a thing doesn't want any at all. So one day I came out of the house (I was in college then) and saw it, the '53 Mercury, the car upon which I had heaped more attention and time and love than I had ever given a human being. It sat at the curb, its black surface a shimmering of the air, like hundreds of mirrors turned to catch the sun. It had twenty-seven coats of paint, each coat laboriously hand-rubbed. It seemed to glow, not with reflected light, but with some internal light of its own.

I stood staring, and it turned into one of three great scary rare moments when you are privileged to see into your own predicament. Clearly, there were two ways I could go. I could sell the car, or I could keep on painting it for the rest of my life. If twenty-seven coats of paint, why not a hundred and twenty-seven? The moment was brief and I understand it better now than I did then, but I did realize, if imperfectly, that something was dreadfully wrong, that the car owned me much more than I would ever own the car, no matter how long I kept it. The next day I drove to Jacksonville and left the Mercury on a used-car lot. It was an easy thing to do.

Since that day, I've never confused myself with a car, a confusion common everywhere about us—or so it seems to me. I have a car now, but I use it like a beast, the way I've used all cars since the Mercury, like a beast unlovely and unlikable but necessary. True as all that is, though, God knows I'm in the car's debt for that blistering winning July run to Jacksonville, and the pushed-out wing vent, and finally for that greasy air heavy with the odor of burned meat and potatoes there behind the A&W Root Beer. I'll never smell anything that good again.

JAMES FOGLE

Drugstore Cowboy

RICK SAT SLUMPED IN the front seat of the car and watched Bob drag the suit carrier with Nadine's body in it out of the car and off into the brush. Rick wondered how she had done it, whether she had meant to, or if she had just accidentally put too much in the spoon. She really hadn't seemed all that depressed. She didn't like the way things were going, but that in itself didn't seem excuse enough for such a drastic move. She must have just been ignorant and used too much, Rick decided. Powdered Dilaudid was pretty deadly stuff to fool around with, especially if you didn't know what you were doing.

Now it seemed that Bob blamed him for it, and by rights, he probably was to blame, at least more than anybody else. A dope fiend or thief was supposed to take care of his old lady, watch out for her, see that she didn't get hurt, that she didn't speak at the wrong moment or snitch or ever threaten to. It was funny, the relationship between a doper and his old lady. Old ladies were considered a luxury among dopers who could afford them, for what could they do for you besides offer a little companionship? If they didn't keep their mouths shut and their business straight, nothing! And if they ran their heads a lot, like most of them do, they were a bitch.

Rick's thoughts turned again to Bob. Jesus, the guy sure was acting funny. Looks as though he's really going to throw up his hands and go out on his own. Something sure was going on in his head.

Rick remembered the first time he had met Bob and Diane. He had just gotten out of the joint in California, and had headed north because he'd heard it was better up there and also because he just didn't think he could stand another jolt in those California prisons.

When he had gotten off the bus in the city, he'd checked into a fleabag hotel and then just wandered the streets looking for someone he might know. It took him a week to do just that. And the guy he found was no prize either, and besides that, he didn't even know the guy very well. He had just seen him around the prison yard. They got to talking anyway, and it seemed that this guy didn't have any more going for him than Rick, and he'd been out for six months.

He partnered up with his acquaintance and began shoplifting, and that's how he met Bob and Diane. His friend had taken him over to Bob's to try to make a trade, some clothes for some narcotics. Bob was arrogant as hell and Rick hated him at first. Bob seemed to come on so strong and so shitty. He acted like everyone else in the world was below him and had to do what Bob wanted or they weren't any good. This went on for some time until one day Bob asked Rick to stay behind when he and Tommy had come by for a trade. Bob was just as abrupt as ever, but when the door closed on Tommy's heels, Bob turned with a complete change of mood and asked, "Say, Rick, you want to go to work for me and get your ass off the streets for a while?"

Bob had somehow turned that little phrase into a challenge with a little respect for Rick as a person thrown in, as if he were actually saying, "You're a good man and I know you'll work out. All you need is a little help and advice and we can make a great team and take on the whole goddamn world."

Rick said yes, but with misgivings. He could hardly say he liked Bob at this point and he wasn't sure he could do what Bob would no doubt ask of him. He soon found out that Bob's act was all a sham, that he acted nasty to outsiders because he was so good to those he associated with, and that he just couldn't stand to have too many friends. It wasn't long before Rick realized that he'd been hearing about Bob all his life, even way down in Southern California. They talked about the heeler who'd try anything, about the guy who had raided more drugstores on the West Coast than anyone else, the dude who, even when he held big stuff, still wouldn't sell narcotics to anyone.

Then Rick got to thinking about how he had met Nadine. He had entered a small drugstore at closing time with Bob and Diane, and there was no one in the store but the girl at the cash register in the main part of the store and the druggist in the back. Rick was supposed to engage the girl in conversation, distracting her until Bob and Diane were ready to make their move. And the strangest thing happened. Rick and that sexy blond girl hit it off not more than ten seconds into their conversation. The blood rushed to Rick's head as he decided right there on the spot that before him was the nicest, cutest, cuddliest young thing he had ever laid eyes on. And he could tell she was getting just as excited as he was, the way she moved forward ever so slightly with the warmth literally leaping out of her bosom, the way she smiled, pleased with the size and strength and looks of the man before her.

By the time it was Rick's duty to put a hammerlock on her, while Diane held a gun on the pharmacist and Bob dived for the drawers, Rick felt peculiar touching, moving against this sweet girl, but in such a grossly crude manner, as she looked up at him weakly, more puzzled than scared, almost embarrassing him, not for being a brute but for not trusting her. And finally Rick could stand it no longer and he hollered over to Bob, "Bob, she's coming with me." Bob had looked up, his hands full of bottles, with the most incredulous look on his face, and said, "What?" Rick had gone on, "You heard me, Bob, I want this woman. You got a woman, why can't I have one?" And Bob had stood there with a pained and bewildered look on his face, almost forgetting what he was doing, and Diane had started laughing so hard that she nearly dropped the gun and fell to the floor in a fit. But Nadine, she just looked up at Rick, and rather than being surprised or outraged by his presumption, told him with her soft eyes, That's more like it, you're my man.

And now she was dead. Nadine was gone. Would there ever be another like her, Rick wondered.

Bob was digging well out of sight of the road. The sod and roots almost beat him at first, but he kept chopping and hacking and digging and chopping until he finally had a shallow grave about two feet deep. Then he dragged the plastic carrier with Nadine's body in it to the hole and slid it in. At the last moment, he unzipped the end of the carrier and looked down. Nadine lay there with a surprised look on her face and her eyes open, staring back. Bob shuddered, zipped the case shut, and began to fill in the hole. When he was through, he absently stumbled around the area picking up random sticks and breaking off parts of bushes to use in covering the newly disturbed earth. Diane finally put an end to this by demanding, "Let's go, Bob. That's enough."

Bob then turned, almost as if he had no will of his own left and had been awaiting the command to send him back to the car.

Once there, he got his suitcases and clothes out of the car, put them in the rear of the pickup, and without another word or even so much as a glance at his friends, got behind the wheel, started the engine, turned in the seat to see out the rear window, and began backing out along the narrow country road.

Diane watched from the weeds beside the road. She watched him disappear from sight and kept standing there as if waiting for him to change his mind at the last minute and return. Fifteen minutes passed and finally Rick stirred in the front seat of the car and stuck his head out the window. "What's happening? Why all the fuss?" he asked her.

Diane shrugged her shoulders and dropped her eyes. "Hell, I don't know."

"Do you think he's really going to do all that stuff, withdraw and everything?"

Diane's body seemed to sag from the weight of her head and shoulders as she slowly made her way to the passenger's side of the car. "Yeah, I suppose he is," she said. "If there's one thing I've never heard, it was Bob tell me he was going to do something that he didn't at least try."

"Shit, how long do you think he'll last? A week, a month, a few days?"

"You got a lot to learn yet, buster," Diane said, looking directly at Rick as she climbed in the car. "But if you're careful, got the guts, and really want to become a thief, just maybe I'll be able to teach you how. Quit worrying about Bob. He'll do his own thing and whichever way it turns out, it will be right for him. You just start worrying about us. Now, I know you're ten years younger than I am, but I'm not looking for romance anyway. I'm looking for someone with guts. You had it easy with Bob, too easy, in fact. You'd have never learned nothing with him, really. Oh, you'd have saw how it was done, all right, but that ain't nothing like having to go in and lead the charge yourself. So if you think you can handle all that, we'll team up here and now. You get you an old lady and I'll get me an old man, and we won't pick them because they're beautiful people, we'll pick the ones that will make the best thieves in our heeling crew, and, baby, everyone will dive on this crew. It won't be no one-man show. Whoever gets lined up first will do the thing, and no slipping and sliding either, or down the road they go. We'll drive them crazy. We'll give those druggists a show that will keep them entertained for weeks while they sit around telling their friends about it. Hell, they probably won't even mind losing their little bit of stuff. You just stick with me, Rick, and I'll show you what it's all about. Bob was too soft anyway. He couldn't hurt a flea, you know, and couldn't fight a lick. Damn near every pharmacist on the coast has beaten him up at one time or another. Jesus, he sure could take a whipping, though."

WAYLON JENNINGS

This Outlaw Shit

BEYOND THE LAW. OUTSIDERS. A whip and a gun, head 'em off at the pass, and good guys don't wear black.

If you look through the scrapbook of any kid who grew up in the forties and fifties, male or female, you'll find a frayed sepia photograph of the child dressed like a cowboy, down to the spurs, six-gallon hat, six-guns drawn, looking about as tough as any six-year-old has a right to be. The great American hero, as filtered through the movies and popular lore, and now, in the hands of a ragged assortment of Hillbilly Central characters, country music.

Excuse me; make that Pop music. Capital P, as in platinum.

On January 12, in the bicentennial year of 1976, RCA released *Wanted: The Outlaws*. It was a compilation of mostly previously released tracks, starring myself, Willie, Jessi, and Tompall. The cover was pure Old West, a yellowed reward poster with the stagecoach air of the nineteenth-century frontier, Dodge City to Tombstone.

We weren't just playing bad guys. We took our stand outside country music's rules, its set ways, locking the door on its own jail cell. We looked like tramps, Willie in overalls, me with my hair slicked back and Levis, fringe sprouting on our cheeks and chins. I'd begun growing my face fur in the early seventies, when I was down with hepatitis. I thought, hell, I'm not going anywhere. I think I'll grow a mustache. Next I moved on to the beard.

Jessi's mom came to watch out for me when I returned home from the hospital. Her name was Helen, and she thought I hung the moon. I might be a wild man, but she'd had a vision about me a long time before and knew I didn't mean Jessi any harm. Myself was another matter.

"How's my good-looking king of the road doing? Is my daughter treating you right?"

She inspected my new facial growth, scraggly and scruffy as it was. It takes me a long time to grow anything. I don't get a five o'clock shadow until two o'clock the following afternoon, and my face seems dirty for a month. I still don't have any hair on my chest; it must be the Indian in me.

"Son," said Jessi's momma, "that beard and mustache sure looks like a bunch of piss-ants going to a funeral."

"I don't believe the way she talks in front of you," said Jessi.

I had grown it just for kicks, but when I looked in the mirror, it was like I was starting to look like myself. We all were undergoing transformations. I mean, can you imagine Willie without a beard and those braids? If we took on the guise of cowboys, it was because we couldn't escape the pioneer spirit, the restlessness that forces you to keep pushing at the horizon, seeing what's over the next ridge. When I put the black hat on and walked to the stage, carrying my Telecaster, I was staking my own piece of land where the buffalo roam. Don't fuck with me, was what we were saying.

We knew we were good. We loved the energy of rock and roll, but rock had self-destructed. Country had gone syrupy, dripping honey all over its sentimentality. Progressive country? Any music had better progress or it'll get left behind.

We were loose. Nothing to prove. I never believed you could tell people you were great; you had to show them. And increasingly, on the radio, at the concerts and festivals, we were getting our chance. We could see we were gathering a new audience, with their own shape and personality. A lot of times, they weren't country music fans, but they weren't asking us to change. They liked us the way we were. Country fans, maybe because they'd known me for longer, could sometimes give us a hard time. One night in Atlanta, some guy yelled at me, "Take that damn hat off, shave that face and do 'Waltz Across Texas.' "

I said, "You come around after the show and I'll waltz you right up against the side of the wall." I liked to challenge the audience.

We were walking contradictions, and we didn't mind. We were rebels, but we didn't want to dismantle the system. We just wanted our own patch. In the South, especially, they try to live by the rules; it's the legacy of the Bible Belt. Anybody that breaks the rules is a sinner. When you come into a working system, and start trying to change it, you are regarded as the Devil.

Anybody can think whatever they want to think, but don't try to tell me how to go about my "bidness." It's hard to tell a Texan what to do. We accepted the way people were and hoped they'd accept who we were. What we talked about was real, the truth. You could depend on it.

Outlaw music.

Hazel Smith, the great Nashville media specialist, writer, ultimate fan, and publicist for Hillbilly Central, christened it when asked by a disc jockey from WCSE in Ashboro, North Carolina, what to call the renegade sound that was bubbling out of Nineteenth Avenue South. He wanted to base a show around me, Willie, Kris, Tompall, and all the others who were making a name for themselves going up against the Nashville establishment. Other stations, one in Flint, Michigan, and another in Austin aptly named KOKE, were also starting to herald the new breed of rogue hillbilly.

"Hillbilly Central" was the name of the column Hazel wrote for *Country Music* magazine. She had a bird's-eye view of all the frantic comings and goings as she sat out in the front office and directed some of the stranger traffic that started dropping by. The building was open twenty-four hours, and she'd sometimes come in to work and find people strewn about the offices, passed out next to an empty wine bottle or an open bottle of pills. Another night of "losing weight."

I'd done a song of Lee Clayton's titled "Ladies Love Outlaws," about how women don't look at a wild man and see someone hard. Like Jessi when she saw me on television, they think an Outlaw just needs somebody gentle to settle him down. Either they're not scared or they're just as wild as you are; I ran into quite a few like that.

There was a verse about Jessi and me in it—"Jessi liked Cadillacs and diamonds on her hands / Waymore had a reputation as a ladies' man," which was only partly true—but the song's larger insight was the attraction we all feel for those who move against society's grain. Bob Dylan sang "To live outside the law you must be honest" in "Absolutely Sweet Marie"; the Shangri-Las liked their Leader of the Pack "good-bad, but not evil." It's a common theme, dating back to Robin Hood and forward through Jesse James to Thelma and Louise.

To us, Outlaw meant standing up for your rights, your own way of doing things. Most lawbreakers are common criminals. Bonnie and Clyde were nothing but a couple of idiots. So was Billy the Kid; you can look and tell he wasn't all there. They got attention by killing people. The ones who shot them, heroes like Wyatt Earp or Bat Masterson, weren't any better. Those lawmen didn't want to walk the same side of the street when Johnny Ringo or Clay Allison came to town. The ones that got killed were those who couldn't aim, farmers with rusty guns they used for shooting snakes, innocent bystanders.

If I had an Outlaw hero, someone to set my standard and measure my progress, it was Hank Williams. He had touched me way back in Littlefield, through the strength of his songs and the soul of his voice. I especially loved his Luke the Drifter recitations, morality tales like "Pictures from Life's Other Side" or "Too Many Parties and Too Many Pals," usually recorded the Morning After the Night Before. Everything I did in Nashville, anything *anyone* did, was measured against Hank's long, lanky shadow.

You'd hear all these stories, how he pulled a jukebox that didn't have his records on it out to the street and shot it full of holes, or ran around all night dead drunk and pilled out and still gave the greatest show you ever saw. We thought that was the way to do it. Does your wife cheat on you? Well, I heard Hank's wife did, if only in all them lonesome blues. Did Hank miss concerts? We could, too. Did Hank write great songs and read funny books and take pills and swarm?

I wanted to be like him. We all did. Even his contemporaries held Hank in awe. Faron Young brought Billie Jean, Hank's last wife, to town for the first time. She was young and beautiful, and Hank liked her immediately. He took a loaded gun and pointed it to Faron's temple, cocked it, and said, "Boy, I love that woman. Now you can either give her to me or I'm going to kill you."

Faron sat there and thought it over for a minute. "Wouldn't that be great? To be killed by Hank Williams!"

He wound up driving Hank and Billie Jean around in Hank's Cadillac, with the two of them loving it up in the back seat. All of a sudden, it got very quiet in the car. Faron thought he should say something. "Hey, Hank, that left fender got a little rattle in it."

"Shut up, boy," said Hank. "Watch the road and keep driving. I bet you wish you had one that rattled like that."

Hank loved Audrey, his "main" wife, though life between them was unbearable. The night he married Billie Jean, on stage in New Orleans, he turned around to his steel player, Don Helms, and said, "Shag, I'm gonna marry Billie Jean tonight. Audrey be up to get me tomorrow." He worshipped Audrey, he really did. They both were screwing around, and he was surely a woman hound, but I think in some of his songs, like "Your Cheating Heart," Hank was really writing about himself.

After Hank died, it became almost an unwritten law in Nashville to try and put the make on Hank's Old Lady. Audrey always liked her boyfriends to have coal-black hair. One night, when Hank Jr. was on the show, I was walking from the bus with her, and she said, "Darling, have you ever thought about dyeing your hair black?" I told her I liked it fine the way it was, thank you. I may have laid down in the back seat of the Cadillac Hank died in when Hank Jr. showed it to me, but I wasn't about to try any of his other sleeping positions.

Both Hank's ex-wives said I reminded them of Hank. Billie Jean, who later married Johnny Horton, came to town one time and wanted to meet me, so Harlan brought her over to the office. Johnny had been killed in an auto accident. She asked me, "What are you doing later when you get off?"

"Look, lady," I said, "you killed Hank Williams and you killed Johnny Horton and you stunted Faron Young's growth. So you just leave me alone." We both laughed, me a little nervously.

If we were all walking around trying to fill Hank's boots, for me, it was literally. Hank Jr. gave me a pair of Hank Sr.'s cowboy boots, and sometimes, late at night, I'd put them on and stroll around the house. They fit pretty well. I could feel his presence hovering over me. I wore them to the studio one midnight, and while we were recording, a big lightning storm blew up. It hit a tree out in the parking lot, which then fell over my brand new El Dorado. We went out to look at it and sure enough, the tree was fully covering the car. We raised one branch, and then another, and backed the car out. There wasn't a scratch on it.

We went back to the studio and started recording again. While we were out in the room, lightning struck the building, overloading the recorder, scoring the black facing off the tape. They made me take the boots off after that.

Another night, I was upstairs in the office with my feet up on the desk. I had the boots on and I was talking about them, and about Hank. All of a sudden, the pictures on the right-hand side of the wall slid off their hooks, crashing to the floor. Everybody left in a hurry.

"Are you sure Hank done it this way?" Each time the bus would break down, or you'd get stranded, or drive five hundred miles to a gig only to find it had been cancelled, we'd compare our troubles to Hank's. We wanted to be like him, romanticizing his faults, fantasizing ourselves lying in a hotel room sick and going out to sing, racked with pain, a wild man running loose even if it meant dying in the back seat of a blue Cadillac on the way to greet the new year in Canton, Ohio. That was part of being a legend.

Driving to Hillbilly Central one morning during the *Dreaming My Dreams* sessions, I was thinking about Hank's influence and the example he'd set for us, both good and bad. I grabbed an envelope from the seat and started writing, one hand on the wheel, the other balancing pencil and paper on my knee. When I got to the studio, we immediately recorded it—me and Richie managed to turn the beat completely around—and I read it off the envelope. Two weeks later, our bus driver, Billy, came to me and asked if he could have the envelope with the original lyrics. He'd found it on my music stand. I looked at it and I swear I couldn't read a word. It was just scribbling.

> *Lord it's the same old tune, fiddle and guitar*
> *Where do we take it from here?*
> *Rhinestone suits and big shiny cars, Lord*
> *It's been the same way for years.*
> *We need a change.*
> *Somebody told me, when I came to Nashville*
> *Son, you finally got it made*

Old Hank made it here, and we're all sure that you will
But I don't think Hank done it this way
I don't think Hank done it this way
Ten years on the road pickin' one-night stands
Speeding my young life away.
Tell me one more time just so's I understand
Are you sure Hank done it this way
Did old Hank really do it this way
Lord I've seen the world with a five-piece band
Looking at the back side of me
Singing my songs, one of his now and then
But I don't think Hank done 'em this way
I don't think Hank done 'em this way.

BILL HICKS

Love All the People

WELL, FOLKS, THIS IS kind of a sentimental evening for me because . . . this is my final live performance I'll ever do, ever. No biggie, no, no, no, no, no hard feelings, no sour grapes whatsoever. I've been doing this sixteen years, enjoyed every second of it — every plane flight, every [. . .], every delay, every cancelled flight, every lost luggage, living in hotel rooms, every broken relationship, playing the Comedy Pouch in Possum Ridge, Arkansas, every fucking year. It's been great, don't get me wrong.

But the fact of the matter is, the reason I'm gonna quit performing is I finally got my own TV show coming out next fall on CBS. So — thank you. I know. It is *not* a talk show. *(heavy breathing)* Dear God, thank you, thank Jesus, thank Buddha, thank Mohammad, thank Allah, thank Krishna, thank every fucking god in the book. *(heavy breathing)* Please rela — *(heavy breathing)* No, it's not a talk show: it's a half-hour weekly show that I will host, entitled "Let's Hunt and Kill Billy Ray Cyrus." So y'all be tuning in? Cool, cool. Cool, it's a fairly self-explanatory plot, ah . . . Each week we let the hounds of hell loose and we chase that jar-head, no-talent, cracker asshole all over the globe . . . till I finally catch that fruity little ponytail of his in the

White Line Fever

back, pull him to his knees, put a shotgun in his mouth like a big black cock of death *(shotgun boom)* and we'll be back in '95 with "Let's Hunt and Kill Michael Bolton." So.

Thank you very much. I'm just trying to rid the world of all these fevered egos that are tainting our collective unconscious and making us pay a higher psychic price than we imagine. In fact, that's how I pitched it to the networks exactly, I said ah . . . "I'd like to do a show where I rid the world of all these fevered egos that are tainting our collective unconscious," and the guy at CBS said, "Will there be titty?" And ah I said, "Sure, I don't know, sure." Boom! A check falls in my lap and ah . . . I'm a producer. I never knew it was that easy. All these years I been trying to write scripts and characters and plots and stories that had meaning. "Will there be titty?" Sure. Boom! I'm a . . . I'm a producer now. "Where've you been all our life, boy? We been lookin' for you in Hollywood. What are these titties gonna do? Jiggle? You're a fuckin' genius. Give him another check. I can't write enough checks for you. You've answered our prayers in Hollywood. Jiggling titties, who would have thunk of it?"

I was over in Australia during Easter, which was interesting. Interesting to note they celebrate Easter the same way we do, commemorating the death and resurrection of Jesus . . . by telling our children a giant bunny-rabbit . . . left chocolate eggs in the night. Now . . . I wonder why we're fucked up as a race. Anybody? Anybody got any clues out there? Where do you get this shit from, you know? Why those two things, you know? Why not goldfish left Lincoln Logs in your sock drawer, you know? As long as we're making shit up, go hog-wild, you know? At least a goldfish with a Lincoln Log on its back, going across your floor to your sock drawer, has a miraculous connotation to it.

> "Mommy, I woke up today and there was a Lincoln Log in me sock drawer." "That's the story of Jesus."

Who comes up with this shit? I read the Bible, I can't find the word "bunny" or "chocolate" anywhere in that fucking book.

D'y'all have different books of the Bible than I do? Are y'all Gideons? Who *are* the fucking Gideons? Ever met one? No! Ever seen one? No! But they're all over the fucking world, putting Bibles in hotel rooms. Every hotel room: "This Bible was placed here by a Gideon." When? I've been here all day. I ain't seen shit. I saw the housekeeper come and go, I saw the minibar guy come and go, I've never laid eyes on a fucking Gideon. What are they—

Ninjas? Where are they? Where're they from—Gidea? What the fuck are these people? I'm gonna capture a Gideon. I'm gonna make that my hobby. I am. I'm gonna call the front desk one day: "Yeah, I don't seem to have a Bible in my room."

People suck and that's my contention. I can prove it on scratch paper and a pen. Give me a fucking Etch-A-Sketch, I'll do it in three minutes to prove the fact, the factorum, I'll show my work, case closed. I'm tired of this backslapping, aren't humanity neat bullshit. We're a virus with shoes, OK? That's all we are.

What do you say we ah . . . lighten things up and talk about abortion. You know . . . I feel like I'm losing some of you here and I wanna win all of you back with this one. Let's talk about abortion. Let's talk about child-killing, and see if we can't get some chuckles rippling through the room here. Let's talk about mass murder of young, unborn children, see if we can't coalesce into one big healthy gut-laugh. Ha ha ha ha ha ha ha! Boy, I've never seen an issue so divisive. You ever seen—it's like a civil war, in'it? Even among my friends, who are all very intelligent, they are totally divided on abortion. It's unbelievable. Some of my friends, for instance, think these pro-life people are annoying idiots. Other of my friends think these pro-life people are evil fucks . . . How are we gonna come to a consensus? You oughta hear the arguments around my house. They're annoying, they're idiots, they're evil, they're FUCKS! Brothers, sisters, come together. Can't we once just join hands and think of them as evil, annoying idiot-fucks? I beseech you.

BREECE D'J PANCAKE

The Way It Has to Be

ALENA STEPPED UNDER THE awning of the Tastee Freeze and looked out at the rain draining into the dust, splattering craters with little clouds. When it stopped, cars hissed along the highway in whorls of mist. She stood by the slotted window, peering through the dirty glass to empty freezers and sills speckled with the crisp skeletons of flies. Far down the parking lot stood a phone booth, but as she stirred circles in the bottle caps and gravel, she knew she could not call home.

She sat on a lip of step by the porcelain drinking fountain and watched Harvey's head lolling against the car window, his holster straps arching slack above his shoulders. She felt her stomach twitch, and tried to rub her eyes without smearing. She didn't want it this way, but knew Harvey would never change. She laughed a little; she had only come from West Virginia to see the cowboys, but all this range was farmed and fenced. The openness freed and frightened her.

Harvey jostled, rolled down the window. There was a white dust of drool on his chin. "Wanna drive?" he said.

She started toward the car. "All last night I worried. Momma's cannin' stuff today."

"Lay off," he said. "You gotta right to get out." He tightened his holster and pulled on his jacket.

"You love that thing?"

"He's got it comin'."

"Parole catches you, you got lots more."

"Lay off, it's too early," he said, reaching for a cigarette.

While she drove, Alena saw the haze lift, but not like a dew. Instead, it left a dust film and far ahead there was always more haze. As they skirted Oklahoma City, it thickened, and the heat stuck to their skin. She pulled off at a hamburger stand and Harvey got out while she looked at the map. In a side panel, a picture of the Cowboy Hall of Fame called her away from the route. Harvey came back with a bag of sandwiches and coffee.

"Harv, let's go here," she said, offering the picture.

He looked, then grabbed her thigh just below the crotch and kissed her. "There'll be plenty of time after this."

As they ate, Harvey took a slip of paper from his shirt pocket and checked the map. He stared at the dashboard for a long time, thinking. Alena watched his brow draw tight, but she could not ask him to give it up. She hoped Harvey was not dumb enough to kill him.

Harvey took the wheel and they drove down a small secondary toward a farm. Alena watched the land slip by, growing flatter, longer in the new heat. Always the steady haze hid the horizon, and she wished she would see a cowboy.

The stairwell was empty, quiet, yet Alena's nerves twisted again as she looked at Harvey. He walked uneasily and his eyes were crossed from the whiskey.

Two flights up and they opened their door. The room was small and old-fashioned, and opened to the street, where the dust storm turned the streetlights yellow. Harvey took off his jacket, opened his satchel and got out the whiskey. He was shaking, and his gun flapped loosely in its holster.

"Jesus, Harvey," she said, sitting on the bed.

"Will you shut up?"

She could still see it: the man reached out to shake and Harvey handed him three in the chest. "I'm afraid," she said, and could not forget the old woman sitting on the porch, stringing beans. Alena wondered if she still sat there, her mouth open, her son dead in the yard.

"Have a drink," Harvey said. He had stopped shaking.

"I'm gonna barf."

"Barf then, dammit." He rubbed his neck hard.

She stood by the sink and looked into the drain, but nothing would come up. "What're we gonna do?"

"Stay here," he said, finishing the pint, looking for another.

"I'm sorry I'm scared," she said, and turned on the water to wash her face.

"Lay down," Harvey said, standing by the window.

Alena sat in the chair by the sink, watching Harvey. His pint half gone, he leaned against the window casement. Not the man she knew in the hills, he looked skinny and meaner to her, and now she knew he was a murderer, that the gun he always carried had worked. She was not part of him now; it was over so easily she wondered if they had ever loved.

"We'll go to Mexico and get married," he said.

"I can't, I'm too scared."

Harvey turned toward her, the yellow light of the street glowing against his face and chest.

"The whole time I was in," he said, "I waited for two things: to kill him, and to marry you."

"I can't, Harvey. I didn't know."

"What? That I love you?"

"No, the other. I thought it was talk."

"I don't talk," he said, and took a drink.

"God, I wish you hadn't."

"Whadaya want? To be back in the hills?"

"Yes, I don't want this anymore. I hate this."

He pulled his gun and pointed it at her. She sat, looking at him, his eyes wide with fear, and she leaned over the chair and threw up a stream of yellow bile. When she stopped coughing and wiped her chin, Harvey sat slumped in the corner, the pistol dangling in his hand.

White Line Fever

"You goddamned bitch," he muttered. "Now I need you and you're a god-damned bitch." He lifted the pistol to his temple, but Alena saw him smile. A puff of air came from his lips, and he put the gun in its holster.

"I'm gonna get drunk," he said, standing up. "You suit yourself. I'm not comin' back." Down the hall, she could hear him bumping against the walls.

Alena washed herself, then turned on the light. Her eyes were circled and red, her lips chapped. She put on makeup and went out.

As she walked down the street, the dust blew papers against her ankles, and she went into a café with a Help Wanted sign. The girl behind the counter looked bored when Alena ordered a beer.

"You need help?"

"Not now, only in the morning. Come in the morning and ask for Pete. He'll probably put you on."

"Thanks," she said, and sipped.

In the back was a phone booth, and Alena carried her beer to it. She made the call, and the phone rang twice.

"Hello, Momma."

"Alena," her voice trembled.

"I'm in Texas, Momma. I come with Harvey."

"Stringin' round with trash. We spoiled you rotten, that's what we done."

"I just didn't want you all to worry."

There was a long quiet. "Come on back, Alena."

"I can't, Momma. I got a job. Ain't that great?"

"Top shelf in the cupboard fell down and made a awful mess. I been worried it's a token."

"No, Momma, it's all right, you hear? I got a job."

"All that jelly we put up is busted."

"It's all right, Momma, you got a bunch left."

"I reckon."

"I gotta go, Momma. I love you."

The phone clicked.

The night calmed, and most of the dust settled in eddies by the curb. As she walked along to the hotel, Alena felt better. Harvey was gone, but it didn't matter. She had a job, and she was in Texas.

As she passed through the lobby of the hotel, the clerk smiled at her, and she liked it. But on the landing to the room, Harvey waited. Cigarette butts were all around his feet, and he was rumpled, cripple-looking.

"I come back to apologize," he said, standing to hold her. She fell against him.

"Nothin's changed," she said. "I'm stayin' here."

White Line Fever

"That's it?"

She nodded. "I got a job, so I called home. Everything's okay."

"Can we talk upstairs?"

"Sure," she said.

"Then let's talk," and his hand brushed against the revolver as he reached for another cigarette.

Don De Grazia

American Skin

BEFORE GOING TO SLEEP that night, Tim and I sat with Zack for a while by a small, three-log fire at the rear of all the neat little rows of two-man tents. This was about as far away as we could get from the Drills' tent, which was the size of a small house and hooked up with electricity to boot. Behind us and our tiny fire was the woodline—miles and miles of forest filled with every poisonous snake in North America and, adding to my morbid, sullen mood, packs of wild dogs that yelped and howled through the night.

Though we'd been there less than a week, Zack was already on every Drill Sergeant's shit list, which made sense, as his sole reason for joining had been to antagonize authority. He dosed up on acid one night in his Evanston dorm room at Northwestern University and watched on TV how Bill Murray's wisecracking supposedly turned the Army on its ear in the movie *Stripes*. The next day, before he even came down fully from the trip, he went to the recruiter and signed up.

Now, after just four days, the novelty had worn off pretty good. That night, after they gassed us, the Drills decided to put Zack on fire-guard duty all night long as an example of what happens to wiseacres in the United States Army. He said he was just waiting for the Drills to doze off, though—then he was going to hide somewhere and go to sleep anyway.

We sat in silence by the fire for a while, reading the letters we'd gotten at evening mail call. Marie wrote me a quick note filled with meaningless street gossip and anecdotes of Jason's latest scrapes with the law and references to new hardcore punk bands I'd never heard of and it nearly made me weep with depression at a Gorgon life so hollow I couldn't even miss it.

White Line Fever

The gas attack had been a hard blow for me. I'd lived through worse things, of course, and I was destined for worse things, but I don't think I ever felt as low and weak and without hope as I did right then.

"I'm getting out of here, man," Zack suddenly said, staring into the little fire that each of us periodically fed with tiny twigs and pine needles. Hot as the days were, it got near to freezing there at night, and my toes were aching beneath the stiff, thin leather of my new combat boots.

"Where you gonna go, Mustafa?" Tim asked, stretching his field jacket over his broad shoulders and pulling up the hood. Unlike most of the recruits, his camouflage BDUs seemed to *fit* him right; he looked like a soldier should. Tim was starting to actually take a semi-liking to Zack, it seemed, but he harassed the hell out of him. "Where you gonna go, Zack? Out there?" Tim pointed towards the deep black woods where the dogs howled. Even further out you could hear the steady dull pounding of practice mortar rounds. Boom . . . Boom . . . Boom. . . .

"I'm *thinking*, man. I don't know *how* yet, but I'm getting out. Frankly, that gas thing was the final straw."

For the first time that night I felt the urge to speak.

"They tried to kill us, man," I said with quivering lips.

"They didn't try and *kill* us," Tim scoffed. He was sitting furthest from the fire with his hands buried in his coat, and his words came out in white puffs, like tiny smoke signals. 'How else are they supposed to get us ready for war?'

"What war?" Zack asked.

"There could be one, man," Tim said. "In South America . . . or, I don't know . . ."

"The Mideast," Zack offered. "Eastern Europe. Korea again. So what? Would you go and fight?"

"Right now? Yeah, I'd have to."

"Why? To die protecting your homeland when it isn't in danger in the first place? That would be a *shameful* way to die."

"It's a *duty*, dude. Besides, I got no choice. I signed a paper."

"A *duty*? Listen," Zack said, "you gotta read Ayn Rand, friend: '*I swear on my life that I will live for no man, nor will I ask any man to live for me.*' That's her most famous character's credo. I'm telling you this, friend, because right when I met you, you reminded me of an Ayn Rand character. Seriously, like an updated Ayn Rand character. And here you are, a *skinhead*, saying you'd let your government treat you like a bitch."

Tim grinned, but I saw his lean face get that reddish soak of anger. People didn't generally talk to him like that. He pulled his hood back down and pointed a long, pale finger at Zack.

"Mustafa, first of all, you don't know me."

"No, you don't know yourself."

The grin vanished from Tim's face and his gray eyes went hard.

"I know my dad went to Viet Nam and came back with a metal plate in his head. And I don't think it's 'shameful.' I'm proud of what he did."

I had never known this before. I looked over at Zack, who nodded vigorously.

"You *should* be, man. He didn't have a choice in the matter and he survived it."

"He had a choice. He volunteered for the Marines."

"Well . . . then it's a moot point. He voluntarily put himself at risk for a cause he believed in. If *I* was old enough then, I would have disagreed with the cause, but I *still* probably would have had to either go fight, or go to prison, or become some kind of a fugitive. Listen, the government exists to enslave its people—the draft is just another form of slavery."

I thought of Nuccio recalling when he and my dad got their draft notices for Korea, and for the first time saw my dad's Captain's bars in a new context. To avoid the fighting Nuccio used his connections. My dad became an officer.

"Slavery?" Tim scoffed. "Why? Just because *you* didn't believe in the fuckin' cause? What about World War Two? Hitler's gassing Jews like dogs. Would you have gone?"

Zack shrugged.

"Tim, are you familiar with the term 'Red herring'?" A faint smile reappeared on Timmy's lips, and his eyes widened a bit in warning, as if he gave Zack credit for having the balls to talk down to him like that, but might just have to kill him anyway.

"I asked you a fuckin' question, Mustafa . . ."

"You ask me what I would have done in World War Two and the answer is, I would have fought against Hitler *if I fucking felt like it*. But as far as 'duty' goes? Again, like John Galt said: 'I swear on my life that I will live for no man, nor . . .' "

"Oh, that's cool," Tim said, suddenly leaning his face in closer to Zack's. "You're born lucky, so fuck the little Jew girl, *let* 'em stick her in an oven."

Though I was actually reveling in the energy of their debate, I was starting to get a little nervous, but Zack just gave a blink that seemed to say "you can hit me, but I won't shut up," and continued:

" 'Born lucky?' Bullshit. People who are born lucky don't go to war. They have their well-connected daddies make a few phone calls so they can stay at home. You've got a sucker mentality, Penn. You wanna fight somebody else's battles, go ahead, but don't force me—at the barrel of a gun—to go with you."

"Pff, Mustafa, you don't even know what the fuck you're talking about. Did you know a bunch of hard-ons from your squad were talkin' about giving you a blanket-party when we get back to the barracks? Talkin' about putting on their gas masks to disguise themselves and holding you down in your bunk and beating your ass 'cause you keep fucking up. Yeah . . . it ain't gonna happen, though, because I *told* them it ain't gonna happen. And I don't even *like* you. You won't *ever* see anybody here even *think* about pullin' shit like that with Alex or me, because we're skins, and we watch each other's backs . . ."

With that Tim leaned back again and shoved his fists back into the pockets of his field jacket. Zack held up a hand in protest.

"Well, I thank you for that . . . even though I never asked for your help. But, frankly, you're confusing the issue! Look what you're defending. The fact is that the government could send you *anywhere* right now and get you killed for any reason. You're their *property*, and you didn't *ask* to be here. You didn't volunteer like your dad. All you were doing was watching Alex's back in a bar. You were *screwed* into joining the Army. You guys told me that yourself!"

His words—and even more so the bitterly sympathetic *tone* of his words—felt like a slap in the face, a wake-up call of some sort. I looked at Tim who stared now at the coals of the campfire, his face pulled tight. He nodded vaguely to acknowledge that Zack was right, then exploded:

"But nobody made *you* sign up, ya fuckin' goofball!"

"It was a mistake," Zack conceded. "But I'm getting out." He reached down, grabbed a big manila envelope that he'd been sitting on, and started pulling out sheets of onion-skin paper and throwing them on the fire. They were pages of a long, rambling letter from his mom, written in Turkish. Just after mailcall he'd translated a couple of passages for us which described, in hilarious detail, what a disappointing loser he'd turned out to be in her eyes. After the letter was burned he pulled out a thin newspaper, but before he could toss that into the flames too, I grabbed it. I'd been dying for something to read. It was a copy of *The Daily Northwestern*.

"Whattya gonna do?" Tim persisted. "Run away? The FBI will track you down. Punch a Drill? They'll put you in Leavenworth, breaking rocks."

"I could say I'm a fag."

"Well, they *knew* you were Turkish when you signed up."

Their conversation had been filling me with unfocused rage, which, strangely, made me feel better, stronger. But now the talk was taking a futile turn, so I read the college newspaper backwards from the Sports section, describing how NU's teams had all been trounced, walloped, shellacked, etc., through the classified rooms for rent, and the features, to the front page. And there I saw a picture. Not just any picture, mind you. It was a picture that would change my life. Mere ink and paper, yes, but . . . well. But it's true.

It showed two girls standing on a lawn before an old, whitestone building with two pillars and a wide stone staircase. One girl wore a loose and flowery dress. She stood with her legs spread and bent and stared with crossed eyes at a little beanbag ball she had balanced on her forehead. She had kind of a big schnozz, so it was pretty funny looking. At least the other girl thought so. She wore jeans and a T-shirt. Thin. Brown, bobbed hair. Very pretty, yes, but it was something else that sucked the breath out of me. Let's see, she was laughing—but you could tell the sound of her laugh wasn't mean or sarcastic at all. It was a wide-eyed, open-mouthed, surprised laugh. And she was clapping. She had her fingers clasped to her chest, and her wrists were limp, bent to one side. She seemed so genuinely *happy*. I looked to the caption for a name, but all it said was:

> At Deering Meadow Friday students took advantage of unseason-
> ably warm weather.

I interrupted their argument to ask Zack if he knew the girl in the picture. He squinted in the firelight and shook his head.

"No . . . wait," he said, pointing to the girl with the Hackey-Sack on her nose. "I know that one, a little. I sold her a bag of weed once and she bitched that it was light."

"What about her?" I asked, pointing to the other girl.

"It *was* light, though. Her? Nah. Wait a minute . . . no. Probably some sorority slut. I gotta get outta here, man."

Tim stood up to stretch his long legs. His knee had been bothering him ever since the night we got arrested. As he walked a few steps towards the woodline to take a piss, he looked back at Zack and sneered: 'Deal with it.' That was the Delta Company's motto—"DEAL WITH IT!" It was painted on our barracks wall above a mural showing a huge hand of cards. The hand was a pair of deuces.

"Fuck 'Deal With It,'" Zack snapped. "That's such typical American shit—'Deal With It.' Do what you're told. Toe the line . . . right face, halt. It's the American Way."

"Pfff . . . you're high, dude," Tim said, disgusted, then sat down by the fire again and pulled his hood back up.

"Oh, come on Tim," Zack said. "Don't tell me a skinhead's going to defend the *system* here in America . . . Come *on*."

Though I was still lost in the picture, I felt compelled to join in at this point. Though it may seem strange—highly ironic, even—I, like Tim, felt a strong, unshaped patriotism in my skinhead bones; one that had absolutely nothing to do with government.

"It is *not* the American Way," I said, folding up the newspaper and sliding it into my cargo pocket. That picture had filled me with a strange, intense vigor. "It's not the American Way at all."

"Yeah . . ." Tim said.

"It *is*, though," Zack sighed.

"Would you rather be in Turkey?" Tim asked. "There something so great about the Turkish Way? Is that why you live in America?"

"I'm not Turkish," Zack said. "I was born here. I'm American. I'm an American citizen. I can criticize my country."

Tim looked at me knowingly, then narrowed his gray eyes to slits and looked back at Zack, shaking his head with disgust.

"Your people come to this country because it's the *best* fuckin' country in the whole world, and the free-est, with the most opportunity, and then American colleges teach their kids—like you—that the American Way Sucks."

"I'm not even passing judgment," Zack said. "I'm just saying that the American Way is to conform."

"Ah, bullshit," I said. I felt challenged, especially with Tim there. I had always been considered the intellectual of the skinheads. Did this guy think that just because he went to some fancy college . . . ?

"You're talking about every *other* way," I informed him, and Tim leaned over and looked into the fire again, letting me take over. "How about fuckin' whatshisname from Greek . . . *Greek* mythology. Him and his old man are escaping an island on mechanical wings, and the father says: 'Don't fly too close to the sun, son.' "

"Icarus," Zack said.

"Yeah, *I know* it's Icarus," I said, "and . . ."

"And Icarus doesn't listen," Zack said, his voice filled with boredom, "and the sun burns his wings and he dies and I am so fucking sick of hearing that cliché shit."

"So am I!" I said, slapping the anarchy tattoo beneath my BDU blouse. "But don't go sayin' it's the American Way."

"I don't care what way it is. You know what it fucking reminds me of?" he said. "That Icarus shit reminds me of those beer commercials that say: 'And remember, please don't drink too much.' "

"Fuckin' A," I agreed. I had no idea what he was talking about.

"Because I'll tell you something, friend," he continued. "No matter what anybody says otherwise, I'll tell you what the old men have always dreamed of and the old ladies have always prayed for and the best girls in every grass hut and every skyscraper since time began have pined for, and that's an Icarus who *makes it.*"

And every sorority house, I added silently.

"You're goddamn right," I said. *"That's* the American Way, friend."

"All right, fine. Then why don't we act like Americans and get the hell out of here?"

"Because this isn't America," Tim said, spitting on the dying fire. "It's the Army."

WELDON KEES

The Ceremony

WHEN THE PHONE RANG, Hollenbeck was leaning over his desk looking at a blueprint, his eyes tracing the network of white lines. He let it ring again, and then he looked up, frowning, and resignedly lifted the receiver. Never a moment's peace, he said to himself, never a minute without some sort of interruption. Try to get something done, just try.

"Hello," he said gruffly into the mouthpiece.

"That you, Floyd?" a voice came.

It was Kinnaman. What the hell did he want now? "Yeh," he said.

"Floyd," the voice on the phone whined, "out here a—"

"Yeh," he said helplessly "What is it? What's the trouble now?"

"You better come out here, Floyd. Murdock and Janss—"

"What about 'em? What's the trouble? Can't you look after that job or do I have to be there every goddamn minute?"

The half-burned cigarette fell off the ashtray. He picked it up from the desk and threw it on the floor and stepped on it.

"Murdock and Janss—"

"Yeh?"

"They won't dig no more. They said—"

"What?" Hollenbeck said. "And just why won't they dig any more?"

"You better come out here. These guys. They said they won't dig no more the way the setup is. You ought to—"

"Well, what's the matter with 'em? For God's sake. They were all right when I left." Hollenbeck paused, staring for a moment at a fly that was buzzing around an apple core on his desk. "Listen, Kinnaman, can't you take care of things? Do I have to look after everything?"

"You better come out here, Floyd," Kinnaman went on. "I can't do nothing with them guys. After they struck the first one—"

"The first one? What're you talking about?"

The phone sounded dead.

"Hey. Hey, Kinnaman."

"Yeh?"

"You there?"

"Yeh, sure. What's the matter?"

"Sounded like the phone was dead."

"No, it's okay. I can hear you fine."

"It just sounded like it was dead for a minute there." He scratched his leg. The fly was still buzzing.

"I'm just telling you, Floyd, I can't argue with these here guys. You better hop in the car and run out here. Janss said—"

"All right, all right," said Hollenbeck. "I'll be out. Keep your shirt on." One thing after another, he thought.

"I just thought," Kinnaman began.

Hollenbeck put down the receiver and lit another cigarette. He just thought, he said to himself. He just thought, did he? Well. He just thought. He stared at the blueprint, thinking: Just when I was beginning to accomplish something. Just when I was getting something done. The fly buzzed near his head and lit on his ear. He swung at it and missed.

Getting up, he put on his hat and coat and went out to the curb where the car was parked. It started easily and he threw it into second and pulled away from the curb. A car with a Florida license plate went by and he looked at it wishing that he was out of the goddamned town and through with it for good. To get away to Florida; fishing. That was the life. Not this. He bore down on the footfeed and turned the corner, heading towards the highway. By the time he struck the gravel, he was doing fifty-five.

He pulled the car into the lot and turned off the ignition and coasted up to the place where they were digging the basement for the barbecue joint. Kinnaman came over to the car and put his foot on the runningboard.

"Well, what's the matter this time?" Hollenbeck said. He saw Janss and Murdock sitting on the ground, their shovels beside them.

"Get out and take a look."

"What's up?"

Kinnaman didn't answer for a minute. Hollenbeck waited impatiently. I haven't got all day, he thought. They think I've got all the time in the world.

"There's bodies here," Kinnaman said finally.

"What?"

"Bodies. Indian bodies. Petrified."

"What the hell are you talking about, Kinnaman?"

"It's a fact. They're petrified. There used to be an Indian cemetery or something around here. We struck one of them while we was digging and now Janss and Murdock don't want to dig no more."

"What the hell's the matter with 'em. Why won't they dig?"

"They're scared," Kinnaman said. "Don't ask me. Hell, it ain't no fault of mine, Floyd."

"What are they scared of?" Hollenbeck said. Damned ignorant fools, he thought. Those things wouldn't hurt them. Vaguely he remembered that someone had told him once of an Indian burial ground someplace in the vicinity.

"Those guys," Kinnaman said. "They say you shouldn't go fooling around with dead bodies, even if they're petrified. I can't do nothing with 'em."

"Jesus Christ," Hollenbeck said. But he didn't feel like getting out of the car. "Listen, Kinnaman, can't you take care of things? Can't I leave for a couple of minutes without something going haywire out here? Or do I have to stand over you guys every minute?"

Kinnaman shrugged his shoulders. "You better talk to 'em. Maybe you can do something with 'em."

"I'll do something with them, all right." He got out of the car and slammed the door. Kicking at the sandy soil, he walked beside Kinnaman to where the two men were sitting. He stared at the flat landscape, wondering what new grief he would have to put up with tomorrow. There was always something.

When they came up, Janss and Murdock stood and nodded to Hollenbeck.

"Well, what's the matter with you guys?" Hollenbeck said.

Janss looked up at him as if he didn't want to say anything. He was a short man with a scar on his forehead. "It's them bodies. We don't want to fool with them."

"Yeh," Murdock said. "That monkeying around with dead people. You can't ask a guy to do that, Mr. Hollenbeck."

What am I paying you guys for, that's what I want to know, Hollenbeck thought. Not to sit around and beef. "Where is this body, anyway?" he asked.

"Over there."

They went over to where they had been digging. Murdock pointed at something that looked to Hollenbeck like a slab of stone.

He got down on his haunches and looked at it closely. It was a petrified man, all right. The first he'd ever seen, except for one in a museum, years ago in Chicago. He felt of the thing, and it gave him a queer sensation when his hands touched it. Like death. He looked up, trying to shake off the feeling he had, trying to appear as tough as he could, and said, "Well, what of it? Break it up and get it out of here. What am I paying you guys for?"

The men didn't answer him. He stood up and looked angrily at their faces, thinking: Say something, one of you guys, say something.

"Break it up and get it out of here, I said. You guys want these jobs, don't you? Or maybe I got you all wrong. Maybe you'd like to find something else that'd be more genteel or something. Come on, get going."

Janss cleared his throat and looked at Murdock. There was a long silence, and then both of them began to speak at once. They looked at each other confusedly and stopped.

"Well, how about it? If you lay down on this, I'll promise you that you'll never get any work from me or anybody else in this town. Get that? Know what I mean?"

"But dead people," Janss said. Murdock stared at the ground.

"So damn dead they've turned to stone," Hollenbeck said. "Come on, break the thing up and get it out of here."

No answer.

"I got better things to do than run out here every ten minutes to straighten out things like this. Well, you going to get back to work, or not?"

Janss and Murdock exchanged glances.

"Okay," Murdock said. "All right with you, Janss?"

"Yeh."

"I hate to beg you," Hollenbeck said sarcastically. "There's plenty of guys who wouldn't put up with such a goddamn fuss about some piece of rock. But we got a barbecue stand to put up here. Maybe you forgot about that?"

"Okay, okay," Murdock said. "Where's them sledgehammers?"

Hollenbeck watched the men as they went over to the truck to get them. "Crazy bastards," he said to Kinnaman.

"Yeh."

"Scared of a piece of rock. Imagine."

"Yeh."

"It's really funny."

"Yeh, it is, kind of."

The men returned, lugging the heavy hammers. They carried them over to the petrified Indian.

"Now break it up good," said Hollenbeck. They were nuts the fuss they made. Wasting all this time of his.

White Line Fever

506 ◆ *John Sayles*

"Yeh, break it up good," Kinnaman repeated.

The men raised their hammers and swung them down. At the first blow, the body cracked. Hollenbeck stood there, shading his eyes from the sun with his hand. One less petrified Indian. The next time the hammers descended there were four large pieces and other little ones, crumbling.

"The vanishing American," Hollenbeck said.

"Huh?" said Kinnaman.

Hollenbeck laughed. That was good, really good. It hadn't sounded so funny until he said it. And it had come out, just like that, all of a sudden.

"The vanishing American," Hollenbeck said again. "Get it?"

Kinnamen laughed too. "Say, that's good!" he said. "That's all right. That's really all right, boss."

Hollenbeck couldn't get over how funny it was. He laughed harder. The vanishing American. And it had come to him, just like that. Without thinking about it at all.

"Jesus, that's really good, Floyd!" Kinnamon said.

The blows of the hammers kept coming down, even, regular, on the crumbling pieces of stone. Dust rose in the air in a little cloud, drifting slowly down.

"That's really good, Floyd," said Kinnaman, his sides shaking.

"That's about the funniest thing I've heard in a long time."

JOHN SAYLES

Terminal Lounge

WHEN TOMMY PULLS THE cord for the first Rush the train is just leaving the station. The before-dinner drinkers are in for a quick one, the Mighty Sparrow is chattering on the box, and after he knocks back his own shot Tommy can feel the floor starting to move under his feet, that trick of the senses where it's not clear if the platform is moving or the train, the ground never quite where you expect it when you put your next foot down.

Bethany asks where Donna is when she comes up for hers.

"She might be in and she might not," says Tommy, checking out her face jewelry. It used to gross him out, especially the nose things that looked like boogers, but now he thinks it's kind of sexy, like the whole bare-belly thing and the ones with the tattoos in the small of their backs. "You card that bunch by the door?"

"They checked out okay."

Tommy hates wearing his glasses and can't read print on a driver's license without them, so he puts the girls on it. "Look like they're fifteen, max."

Nick and Nora come in then, Nick with the junior wise-guy chain hanging down and his shirt open a couple buttons too many and his tanning-salon bronze skin, giving his little chin jerk of a greeting to Tommy as he slides onto the stool. Nora has brought a package into the place, already wobbly on her heels. Nora is maybe five years older than Nick and does the full-frontal makeup thing, her nails always matching her eye shadow and her hair tortured into tight little ringlets that look like they hurt. She sits hard and looks not quite at Tommy.

"L.I.T.," she says.

Tommy looks to Nick, who just holds his hands out as if to say, Don't ask.

"I should ask for a doctor's report, serving one of those."

Nora is usually a white-wine gal. She doesn't acknowledge the joke.

"Gin and tonic," says Nick.

Tommy turns to assemble the ingredients for Nora, splashing gin, vodka, rum, and tequila into the blender, measuring out white crème de menthe. Nora was a clerk at Public Works, and one day Nick was behind with his utilities and came in person to squawk over the penalty. They'd been coming in together for six months or so, lots of knee hockey on the stools till there was a booth free and they could put their heads together. They were always out the door, Nora stuck to Nick like a barnacle, by half past ten. Tommy dumps a can of sour mix in, fills with cola to the line, and flicks the machine on. He prefers working with a shaker, the whole Chiquita Banana rumba of the movement, but there isn't time when the Lounge is filling up.

"I don't see why not," says Nick, as if continuing a conversation.

"What're you, kidding?" Nora avoids her own eyes in the mirror, won't look at Nick.

"It's how we started. Why not—"

"Go out with a bang."

"Don't be that way."

"What way should I be?"

"You never had any complaints."

"Right."

"I mean we're both adults. We came into this thing with open eyes. I don't see why we can't—"

"Because you're marrying some cunt tomorrow, that's why."

"Watch the mouth." Nick looks to Tommy as if for moral support.

Tommy lays the drinks in front of them. "One Long Island Iced Tea for the lady." He smiles. "One G and T for the gentleman—and I use the term loosely."

Nick is not amused. She isn't the only one he brings in—Nora—but with the others he doesn't linger. Just a leg opener at the bar, maybe something stronger if he can get them to go for it, and then out. A clean operator, though, never a scene. There have been a few in the Lounge already, slaps and shouts, engagement rings thrown, that one crazy Puerto Rican girl, Dominican, whatever, waving one stiletto heel around like an ice pick while she stalked the poor shlub she was mad at with the other one still on, a hobbling little cyclone of fury. And the one with Donna—which was highly unprofessional of her—but that was family business and there was no breakage. Tommy's mother threw plates, God knows with plenty of reason, and he would make a joke of it with Mike Delahanty from the apartment downstairs, who could hear everything.

"Wasn't too bad," Tommy would say. "Three plates, a coffee mug, and a cereal bowl."

"You should buy the plastic ones," Delahanty would say, smug, as if his father hadn't gone out for the famous pack of cigarettes and never come back. "You can pitch a double-header with 'em, they won't bust."

The stools were all taken now, each passenger with a destination in mind, the whiskey sippers, the imported-draft drinkers, the ones who upped the ante with each round ordered and the cautious ones who tapered off. A few might miss their stop, lulled by the ride, but most pushed back from the counter right on schedule. Brewster, who never slouched or rested his elbows on the counter, was a Grey Goose martini man, just that single silver bullet and then home to the wife. Zigliewicz, Mr. Z from the Department of Human Services, drank Manhattans, constantly pinching the bridge of his nose, as if testing it for numbness until it told him it was time to go. A few, like Overholt and Spacy Stacy and sometimes Tyler, were there for the whole ride.

"Baseball," says Tyler, working on his second, just sipping now, "you hit sixty home runs one year, whatever the record is, you've always got that. Maybe the next year you lose a step, eyesight diminishes, can't hit the curveball—"

"They send you to Paducah." Overholt proclaims it like a sentence of death.

"You're out of the game. But that accomplishment, that record, they can't take that away. My racket, you have a shit day, a shit week, it's like you've always *been* shit. It erases what you've done in the past."

"You've done that well? The Market version of sixty home runs?"

"Not my point. My point is there's no *closure*. Every day you start from scratch—"

"A Sisyphean task."

"He at least had a big rock to push against. All I've got is the damn telephone, some numbers."

"You got to bank your best years."

"My *ex* got to bank my best years. It's like putting Babe Ruth's first wife in the Hall of Fame."

"Athletes are an exception. The rest of us—"

"The rest of us are only as good as our last twenty-four hours."

"There's a depressing thought," says Tommy, replacing Overholt's drink with a new one, a bit heavier on the Sprite. "You make your fortune a drop at a time," Pete Koenig, who he broke in under at the old Wharf Rat, used to say. "The drops add up to drams, the drams to pints, the pints to barrels, and pretty soon you're swimming in it." Not that he shorted anybody seriously or switched labels. Tending bar was psychology, not chemistry, and they could always buy it at the liquor store and pour their own if they had a complaint.

"The numbers will always catch up with you." Tyler was a tireless purveyor of statistical doom. The rate at which the ozone layer and rain forests were disappearing. The odds in favor of plane crashes. The probability that you already had prostate cancer. "You study the actuarial tables, it's never a question *if* they catch up, only *when*."

"We're all born behind the eight-ball." Overholt, holding his rye up to the light to appreciate its color.

"And the people I'm surrounded with. You ever watch seagulls?"

"Spiraling aimlessly at the mighty ocean's edge." Overholt has been known to stand and recite from memory.

"I see them in the landfills on the way to work. They call it a flock, as if they cooperate with each other, when it's only just a mob of predators out to feed their own faces and to hell with the other guy."

"A cutthroat business."

"But even seagulls only want what the other bird has in its mouth."

"Beak. Winged creatures have a beak."

"They never attack another gull just to see him go down. I swear I'd chuck the whole thing in a minute, but at my age—"

"You're a stripling."

"In your twenties, you make a lateral move, no big deal. You can shop around for a few years. Employer looks at me on his carpet, thirty-eight with my hat in my hand, he thinks one thing: This guy crapped out. Couldn't cut it."

"You wear a hat?" Overholt looks around for evidence.

"An expression."

"Used to be an American man would not venture forth with his head uncovered. Newsboy cap, pearl-gray fedora—an entire industry was devoted to it. Haberdashery. Be glad that's not your game. You wouldn't have a job left to be disgusted with."

Tyler makes a trembling fist, squeezing till his knuckles go white. "That's my stomach, six-forty-five every weekday, when I roll out of bed."

"We seek transcendence," says Overholt, "but we settle for numbness."

"Transcendence."

"To rise above our worldly lot. To soar."

Tyler unclenches the fist. "I work on the eighty-fifth floor, got a window, look down on the whole city. But I never feel like I'm soaring."

The Joint

Ken Kesey *Sketch*

MALCOLM BRALY

On the Yard

ONE MORE MORNING — A few days before Christmas — and as always Chilly Willy stood in the big yard with Nunn and Society Red. The rain was bad, coming down in gray sheets whipped by the wind, and they were under the rain shed at a particular spot they thought of as Chilly's Other Office. Experienced cons avoided this spot on a rainy day and should a fish blunder into it he was invited to move on. It was a small alcove that held the back door to the bakery, but it offered enough shelter to make book.

The three friends were silent. Action was slow, and Chilly was in a grim mood. They had already talked bad about the weather and discussed the opinion, an article of faith to many, that the big yard was probably the only place on earth where the wind blew from all four directions at once. Except naturally in the summer when the asphalt topping was about to boil, and old cons were falling out from the heat, then the wind would come straight and cool from the bay only to pass about twenty feet above their heads. The wind, they decided, confirmed the conspiracy that all nature joined — to screw them around whenever possible. And while Chilly Willy was willing to agree that the big yard was probably the most miserable stretch of real estate in the western hemisphere, he privately couldn't lay it all to the weather.

They had tried to remember what was for chow and then had been sorry they were able to because it was one-eyed hash, a scoop of hash which looked at if it might have already been digested, at least once, half hidden under a chill and rubbery fried egg.

The goon squad had gone by, buttoned to their chins in green foul weather gear, on one of their mysterious errands, and they had told each other what a dog sonofabitch the guard they called the Indian was, and how the Farmer was all right if you didn't try to shuck him, but if you did shuck him and he caught you, you might as well try to climb the wall. And the Spook — no one could hope to understand the Spook, they could only hope to avoid him. Chilly thought of some half-wild thing driven mad by the daily burden of its own pain, but he also considered that the Spook might be playing a part, as all the goon squad might, to make their jobs easier. He tried to picture them at the end of the day sitting in some bar, drinking beer and laughing over how they put the convicts on. Nice guys really, family men — Chilly smiled. The picture wouldn't quite come clear.

And they had talked about who was stuff and who wasn't. Stuff was anything of value and faggots and sissies were of great value to many, and it was a treasure hunt of sorts to search for the signs, the revealing and half-unconscious gestures, that sped the word of fresh stuff on the yard. And they talked about others they thought might be stuff, but who for one reason or another were pretending not to be, and no one was entirely free from these speculations, which even penetrated the circle of their closest buddies.

Chilly had said, "I don't play that game, but if I ever start I'm going to have to try old Red here."

And Society Red had answered, 'Tough enough, if you got eyes to swap out. A little tit for tat and you promise to let me go first."

And Nunn, "You're so anxious to go first, Red, makes me wonder if you haven't been cheated before."

"Yeah, your old mother cheated me. You know I don't play that stuff. I've been known to pitch, but I'm no catcher."

"No one cops to playing it, but there's sure a whole lot of suckers going around talking it."

And Chilly Willy had said, "It's something to talk about."

They had talked about everything else and now they were just standing around half hoping something would happen so they could talk about that.

Chilly knew the rain in the big yard was different from that which fell in the free world. Once in a while you might have to run a half a block in the rain, maybe get your top-coat wet, and you might have to stand a few minutes waiting for a bus, or a taxi, but you never had to walk miles in it, or stand for hours watching it come down, imagining every few minutes that it was letting up a little when it was only getting ready to rain harder. Rain served to turn a day which might have just been dull into one that was actively miserable.

The rain shed could have housed a dozen locomotives, but so acute was the overcrowding that even packed in nearly solid only about two-thirds of the inmate population were able to find shelter under the shed. The rest were left to tough out the rain the best way they could. A few walked the yard ignoring the rain. A small cluster sheltered in each of the block doorways. And one isolated man stood on the wooden bench that lined the far side of the yard. He stood hunched, unmoving, letting the rain run down the sides of his face. No one paid any attention because he was a known psych case who most days carried a large bundle of ragged newspapers and had his shirt pocket stuffed to straining with the stubs of lead pencils, all sharpened to needle points. He hadn't dared to risk his precious papers in the rain, but his freshly sharpened pencils saved him from the day's worst terrors. If he stood quite still, dared nothing, avoided any notice, he might be able to survive until lockup and the safety of his cell.

Those who had been quick enough had found seats in one of the chapels and sat there listlessly, listening to one of the inmate organists practicing the selections he would play during the Christmas services. Some in an agony of boredom might even read the Christian literature put out for them.

Others waited out the rain in the library sitting at the reading table leafing through the back issues of the *National Geographic* looking for the occasional photographs of native women posed with uncovered breasts.

Chilly Willy, though he could ease many of the discomforts of the prison, couldn't do anything about the rain. He and his friends bore it with the rest. Except they wore yellow oilcloth raincoats and rainhats, like those the old fisherman wears in the tuna ad, and this rain gear was boneroo, which meant the average mainline inmate could be in water up to his ass seven days a week, and still stand no chance whatever of being issued a raincoat. The control of raincoats verged on high politics, and like, say, the baton of the French Academy they were the symbol—more symbol than actual protection against the weather—of power, position, influence, even honor in their society. The yellow raincoats were worn by their proud owners on days when there was even the barest chance of rain, and frequently they blazed to full sunlight standing out against the faded denim of the mainline inmate with the relentless authority of ermine.

Nunn and Society Red owed their raincoats to Chilly Willy. Red had attempted to block his rainhat into a style currently in vogue with pimps and hustlers called the Apple, but the heavy oilcloth, stubborn and style-blind, was reasserting its former shape. One of the woolen earflaps, intended to button under the chin but folded by Red into the crown, had slipped loose to dangle unnoticed. Nunn pulled at it, extracting its full length, fusty as long-handled underwear.

"That's very sharp," Nunn mocked approval. "Makes you look real clean."

Red tucked the earflap back out of sight. "I'm known to be clean, lean and clean, like your old mom."

"That's right," Nunn agreed. "Mom was clean."

"Clean out of her skull. Otherwise she'd have done you up as soon as she dropped you."

Chilly stared out at the space beyond the rain shed where he could see the water striking against the glistening blacktop. The only sign that he had been listening at all was that he began to tap one highly polished and expensive shoe against its mate. He watched the men walking in the rain—nuts, exercise freaks, claustrophobes—they dug their chins into their upturned collars, and plunged their hands into their pockets. The wind whipped the bottoms of their pants around their ankles. Chilly noted scornfully that a good third of these aggressive outdoorsmen wore sunglasses.

Then he saw Juleson, also walking in the rain, with his library books, wrapped in plastic, dangling from a belt as kids dangled their readers. The books looked thick and dense.

Who's he trying to shuck, Chilly wondered.

Chilly did a lot of reading on his own, but he would have been quicker to parade the yard in lace trick pants than to make a show of himself carrying books. Big thinker, he told himself contemptuously. And deadbeat, he added.

Chilly chose his reading material from the select books that never saw light on the mainline shelves, but were hidden in the back room as a rental library operated by the head inmate librarian, who charged from a pack to five packs a week depending upon the demand for a specific book. Most of these books were L and L's, derived from Lewd and Lascivious Conduct, hotdog books heavy with sex, and they were always in demand. But unless they were brand-new, most of the L and L books in the institution had suffered a specific mutilation. An unwary reader would pursue a slow and artfully constructed fictional seduction, feeling the real and tightening clutch of his own excitement, turn the page and fall into an impossible abberation of context. He would discover several pages missing, sliced out of the book so neatly it was difficult to detect even when the page numbers clearly indicated they were gone, and almost impossible to detect before actually reading the book.

Most of the big yard thought it was probably some rapist turned hank freak who was cutting the sex scenes from the L and L books, that somewhere in one of the blocks there was a hidden scrapbook filled with the erotic passages removed from the hundreds of novels found mutilated, and nightly the hank freak would read of one coupling after another while he masturbated.

It was a natural theory to evolve since many of them had done the same thing—reading late at night, with their cell partners already asleep, they might come on a vivid cartoon of perfect sexual encounter, no tumblings, no failures, no fizzles, and their hips would unconsciously begin to work in sympathetic rhythm until they seemed to join the glorious phantoms rolling like colored shadows cast on the page below, and labored far above them until they spilled their own strength across the page like a solitary god who, unable to form the conception, might still know loneliness, and even in the rush of final white light sense his purpose pushing unconnected against the emptiness around him.

But Chilly didn't support the hank freak theory—on one count of evidence—the work was too neatly done, it was surgical, and he couldn't picture the hank freak taking the pains. No, Chilly thought, here was the hand of a puritan, a censor, working with the antiseptic precision of righteousness.

Chilly was still watching Juleson, and his restless displeasure had found a focus. Most of the things Chilly hated were safe from his anger, but here was this superior fool walking the yard like he was no part of it. Chilly walked over to the edge of the rain shed, and when Juleson went by again he called him. Then he worked his way back to the bakery door, aware that Juleson was about twenty feet behind him. He turned around to catch Juleson's expression of uneasiness, and he felt, without seeing them, that Nunn and Society Red had automatically moved to back him up.

"I've been meaning to see you, Oberholster—" Juleson began.

"You got my stuff?" Chilly asked, automatically falling into the tone and vocabulary he used for these exchanges.

"Well, no, as a matter of fact I haven't. That's what I wanted to see you about."

"How would it do you any good to see me if you ain't got my stuff? If you can't come up, I'm the last guy you want to see. You didn't draw?"

"No. I'm sorry. I was expecting some money for my birthday, but it . . . it hasn't come yet."

"You know how many times I hear that?"

'This is the first time you've heard it from me."

"All right, when do I get my stuff?"

Juleson shrugged, meeting Chilly's level gaze with difficulty. "To be honest with you, I don't know."

"You be honest. That's a keen virtue. But I can't smoke it, and I can't pay the people I owe with it. How much you figure you'll owe me next month?"

"Why fifteen packs, a box at three-for-two. That's right, isn't it?"

"No, that isn't right," Chilly repeated with satirical patience. "You had *one* month to get up fifteen packs. Now it's twenty-two packs. Another month and it's three cartons. Are you following me?"

Juleson took a half-step back, his face flushing. "Nothing was said—" He paused and then continued in a more reasonable tone, "You're defeating your own purpose. I can probably scrape together fifteen packs."

"What do you know about my purpose?" Chilly asked. "You pick up mind reading out of one of them books of yours?"

"I assume you want your cigarettes back."

"I'm going to get my cigarettes back. If it were a gambling debt, some bet you lost, I might lighten up. I write off a lot of bad paper. But I handed you a box cash, three-for-two, and you're no fish, you know three-for-two figures every month, or did you think you were dealing with the Bank of America? Now I want my stuff, or I'm going to get in your ass."

Juleson started to walk away. He turned after a few steps. "I'll pay you the fifteen packs I agreed to pay you as soon as I can."

"You'll pay what *I* think you owe, not what *you* think you owe, and I'm telling you like it is. You got any weird ideas you can handle me, forget it, I don't bother with collecting. That's Gasolino's speciality."

Juleson was clearly growing angry. "Why do you have to pull this sort of thing?" he asked. "You're not one of these brainless assholes. You surely don't need the cigarettes. What do you get out of it?"

Chilly turned to Nunn. "You notice how this joint is beginning to crawl with amateur psychs?"

Nunn smiled tightly. "As one of the brainless assholes I hope you don't expect an intelligent comment from me."

Society Red started laughing, like water collapsing deep in a drain.

Juleson stared at them white-faced. "Sure, I know. Big joke. Catch some guy short and scare him blue just to be getting a little of your own back. But sometime you're going to pick the wrong man, and you'll be the one who ends up with the shank in him. Then I'll do the laughing, me and everyone else who tries to do his own time and get along without turning this place into a jungle."

Chilly had listened to this, his face quiet and still, but now he stepped forward and began to tap the air an inch from Juleson's chest. "Now, you listen. You're digging a hole with your own fat jaw. You want to pay fifteen packs? All right, you got one week to come up with fifteen packs. That's it. Otherwise I turn the debt over to Gasolino. Now, get in the wind."

They watched Juleson walk away. "There goes a mad sucker," Nunn said.

"What's he going to do?" Chilly wanted to know. "Write a letter to the warden?"

"You really going to put Gasolino on him?"

"I didn't creep up and slip that box in his back pocket. He came and asked for it."

"Yeah, but a lousy box?"

"It's principle." Chilly smiled thinly. "That's something he'd understand."

They finally booked a bet. A man whose hair and jacket looked like animal pelt, so solidly were they matted with the white cotton lint from the textile mill, stopped to bet a single pack on the outcome of the Cotton Bowl game. Then feeling around in his jacket pocket he came out with a cigarette holder that appeared to have been made from a toothbrush handle and some scraps of abalone.

"Three packs and it's yours," he said.

"I'd give three packs to get rid of it," Nunn said.

Society Red took the cigarette holder and waved it with his notion of elegance. "Pretty smooth pimp stick for only three packs."

"Red," Chilly said, "you'd go for fried ice cream." He took the holder from Red and returned it. "We make book. We don't collect handicraft."

The man studied the cigarette holder for a minute, then looked up doubtfully. "Think she's worth three packs? I give two."

"Old buddy," Nunn said, "they saw you coming."

"Yeah, I'm beginning to think so."

The man moved on.

"Where do fools like that come from?" Chilly asked in a tone that didn't suppose an answer.

Nunn answered anyway. "From all over. He figures he's going to work his way out of the textile mill and go into the King business."

"What was wrong with him?" Red wanted to know.

"He was taking up space," Nunn said.

"Your mammy takes up space."

"Knock it off," Chilly ordered. "Give mom a rest."

After this they fell silent again. They would have preferred to pass the time talking, but for a while each of them before saying anything considered that he already knew exactly what the others would find to answer to it, and what he would say to that . . . and it didn't seem worth the effort.

Chilly saw Charlie Wong, the warden's houseboy, coming down the yard in a yellow slicker, probably making a run on the hospital. On impulse, Chilly stepped out and intercepted him.

"Hey, Wong, I want to talk to you."

Wong nodded, smiling, his dark eyes bland as he watched Chilly with a show of polite interest.

"I hear you're getting some pot in," Chilly said.

"Pot?" Wong grinned. "You catch cook. Plenty pot."

"Marijuana," Chilly said.

"Ah, velly bad!" Wong made a swift clawing gesture across his forehead. "Plenty devils."

"You can drop the Oriental Uncle Tom," Chilly said quietly. "I don't buy it."

Wong drew back and studied Chilly alertly. "Uncle Tom?" he asked.

"I've talked to someone who knew you on the streets."

Wong smiled thinly, his eyes suddenly wise. "And you would expose this poor Chinaboy?"

"Did anyone ever tell you I was a cop?"

"Hardly."

"What about the pot? I'd like a piece of it."

"Have you ever heard of a Chinese smoking pot?"

"My information was pretty good."

"I hope you didn't pay for it. I never bring anything through that gate, and I don't intend to start."

"Is that the way you want to play it?" Chilly asked.

"It's the way it is."

"All right," Chilly said mildly. "It was just a notion I had."

Wong's eyes went bland again like a picture going out of focus, and he reached out to tap his finger against the air a half-inch from Chilly's forehead. "Many wheels," he said. "You catch plenty notions."

Chilly smiled. "You're something else, Chinaman."

Wong gave a slight bow and turned to continue down the yard, while Chilly walked thoughtfully towards Nunn and Red.

"What've you got going with that nut?" Nunn asked.

"Nothing. He's in a good spot to hear things."

"Yeah, if you could understand the sucker when he tried to repeat it."

'That's a problem," Chilly said without emphasis.

The crowd under the rain shed began to shift and there was the sudden silence they all knew too well. They turned to watch a pair of hospital attendants pushing a gurney through a corridor forming for them in the crowd. They moved at a quick trot. The inmate stretched out on the gurney trailed his hand, wet with blood, over the side. Red stains like a trail of irregular poker chips marked the path the gurney had taken.

"Another cutting," Nunn said. "That's three just since I came back."

"It's gang action," Chilly said. "They're not looking to kill. They want to make their mark, get blood on their knife. The Chingaderos. The No Names. The Flower Street Gang. Someone was telling me a new bunch was beginning to come in—the Vampires."

"They got their mark all over the joint," Red said. "Must be a hundred of them kids to draw all them bastards with fangs."

"Shit, there's three of them," Nunn said. "Two little punks and a duke, who could probably cause some trouble if he wasn't a stone nut. Big, tall, skinny-assed kid, who thinks he's Genghis Khan, or something. They were in the county with me, came to the joint on the same chain. The nut made the shelf before he even got inside the walls. He didn't want to flash his prune for a skin shake."

That's what we need here," Chilly said. "More nuts."

Again they fell silent. This time it was almost ten minutes before anyone spoke, then Chilly said, in his educational voice, "The problem for today is— why does shit stink?"

"Who says it does?" Nunn offered in immediate contrary motion.

"That Lola Peterson," Red said, naming a starlet in the last movie they'd seen. "I'll bet hers don't stink."

"I'm serious," Chilly said. "Why does it?"

"It just does."

"Nothing *just* happens," Chilly began to educate. "There's always causation."

"Chilly, you've been reading again."

"It wouldn't hurt you none. Maybe you could figure how to stay out of these joints. How many times have I seen you come back? Three?"

"Two," Nunn said, half angry. "Just two."

"Just two," Chilly repeated mockingly.

"Two times is nothing," Red said. "This is my fourth fall."

"Radio, Red," Chilly ordered. "You're a special case, all heart and no brain, but Nunn here he's supposed to be a schooled hustler, down with all games, so how come he lets a bunch of numb-brained fuzz catch him time after time?"

Nunn was hot. "Because some lousy rat mother fucker always splits on me. That's why. Every other stud you meet on the streets belongs to the bottles. They got four snitches on each block. Every morning the heat knows what you had for dinner the night before, whether or not you took a crap and how many times you made it with your old lady. Studs who used to be solid regulars are out there giving up their own mothers, and that ain't—"

"Hang up," Chilly broke in. "Hang up a minute. Say that's all true, you still knew it when you hit the streets last time. You were down with it. If a snitch gets close enough to turn you that's still your goof. Snitches snitch just like snakes bite and you're still left to do your own dying. The point is, they're whipping you to death out there and you're not even trying to figure out why. If you got your ass torn up every time you shot craps, after a while you'd put craps down and maybe try low ball. Now you tell me why you haven't got sense enough to do at least that much when you're out there on those streets?"

"All right, Chilly," Nunn said, no longer angry. "You made your point. You win, man, as usual. Why does shit stink?"

For a moment Chilly stared at his friend. Then he smiled.

"That's easy. It stinks so you won't eat it."

ELDRIDGE CLEAVER

Soul on Ice

BLACK BEAUTY, IN IMPOTENT silence I listen, as if to a symphony of sorrows, to your screams for help, anguished pleas of terror that echo still throughout the Universe and through the mind, a million scattered screams across the painful years that merged into a single sound of pain to haunt and bleed the soul, a white-hot sound to char the brain and blow the fuse of thought, a sound of fangs and teeth sharp to eat the heart, a sound of moving fire, a sound of frozen heat, a sound of licking flames, a fiery-fiery sound, a sound of fire to burn the steel out of my Balls, a sound of Blue fire, a Bluesy sound, the sound of dying, the sound of my woman in pain, *the sound of my woman's pain*, THE SOUND OF MY WOMAN CALLING ME, ME, I HEARD HER CALL FOR HELP, I HEARD THAT MOURNFUL SOUND BUT HUNG MY HEAD AND FAILED TO HEED IT, I HEARD MY WOMAN'S CRY, I HEARD MY WOMAN'S SCREAM, I HEARD MY WOMAN BEG THE BEAST FOR MERCY, I HEARD HER BEG FOR ME, I HEARD MY WOMAN BEG THE BEAST FOR MERCY FOR ME, I HEARD MY WOMAN DIE, I HEARD THE SOUND OF HER DEATH, A SNAPPING SOUND, A BREAKING SOUND, A SOUND THAT SOUNDED FINAL, THE LAST SOUND, THE ULTIMATE SOUND, THE SOUND OF DEATH, ME, I HEARD, I HEAR IT EVERY DAY, I HEAR HER NOW . . . I HEAR YOU NOW . . . I HEAR YOU. . . . I heard you then . . . your scream came like a searing bolt of lightning that blazed a white streak down my black back. In a cowardly stupor, with a palpitating heart and quivering knees, I watched the Slaver's lash of death slash through the opposing air and bite with teeth of fire into your delicate flesh, the black and tender flesh of African Motherhood, forcing the startled Life untimely from your torn and outraged womb, the sacred womb that cradled primal man, the womb that incubated Ethiopia and populated Nubia and gave forth Pharaohs unto Egypt, the womb that painted the Congo black and mothered Zulu, the womb of Mero, the womb of the Nile, of the Niger, the womb of Songhay, of Mali, of Ghana, the womb that felt the might of Chaka before he saw the Sun, the Holy Womb, the womb that knew the future form of Jomo Kenyatta, the womb of Mau Mau, the womb of the blacks, the womb that nurtured Toussaint L'Ouverture, that warmed Nat Turner, and Gabriel Prosser, and Denmark Vesey, the black womb that surrendered up in tears that nameless and endless chain of Africa's Cream, the Black Cream of the Earth, that nameless and endless black chain that sank in heavy groans into oblivion in the great abyss, the womb that received and nourished and held firm the seed and gave back Sojourner Truth, and Sister Tubman, and Rosa Parks, and Bird, and Richard Wright, and your other works of art who wore and wear such names as Marcus Garvey and DuBois and Kwame Nkrumah and Paul Robeson and Malcolm X and Robert Williams, and the one you bore in pain and called Elijah Muhammad, but most of all that nameless one they tore out of your womb in a flood of murdered blood that splashed upon and seeped into the mud. And Patrice Lumumba, and Emmett Till, and Mack Parker.

O, My Soul! I became a sniveling craven, a funky punk, a vile, groveling bootlicker, with my will to oppose petrified by a cosmic fear of the Slavemaster. Instead of inciting the Slaves to rebellion with eloquent oratory, I soothed their hurt and eloquently sang the Blues! Instead of hurling my life with contempt into the face of my Tormentor, *I shed your precious blood!* When Nat Turner sought to free me from my Fear, my Fear delivered him up unto the Butcher—a martyred monument to my Emasculation. My spirit was unwilling and my flesh was weak. Ah, eternal ignominy!

I, the Black Eunuch, divested of my Balls, walked the earth with my mind locked in Cold Storage. I would kill a black man or woman quicker than I'd smash a fly, while for the white man I would pick a thousand pounds of cotton a day. What profit is there in the blind, frenzied efforts of the (Guilty!) Black Eunuchs (Justifiers!) who hide their wounds and scorn the truth to mitigate their culpability through the pallid sophistry of postulating a Universal Democracy of Cowards, pointing out that in history no one can hide, that if not at one time then surely at another the iron heel of the Conqueror has ground into the mud the Balls of Everyman? Memories of yesterday will not assuage the torrents of blood that flow today from my crotch. Yes, History could pass for a scarlet text, its jot and tittle graven red in human blood. More armies than shown in the books have planted flags on foreign soil leaving Castration in their wake. But no Slave should die a natural death. There is a point where Caution ends and Cowardice begins. Give me a bullet through the brain from the gun of the beleaguered oppressor on the night of seige. Why is there dancing and singing in the Slave Quarters? A Slave who dies of natural causes cannot balance two dead flies in the Scales of Eternity. Such a one deserves rather to be pitied than mourned.

Black woman, without asking how, just say that we survived our forced march and travail through the Valley of Slavery, Suffering, and Death— there, that Valley there beneath us hidden by that drifting mist. Ah, what sights and sounds and pain lie beneath that mist! And we had thought that our hard climb out of that cruel valley led to some cool, green and peaceful, sunlit place—but it's all jungle here, a wild and savage wilderness that's overrun with ruins.

But put on your crown, my Queen, and we will build a New City on these ruins.

JACK HENRY ABBOTT

In the Belly of the Beast

. . . YOU SIT IN solitary confinement stewing in nothingness, not merely your own nothingness but the nothingness of society, others, the world. The lethargy of months that add up to years in a cell, alone, entwines itself about every "physical" activity of the living body and strangles it slowly to death, the horrible decay of truly living death. You no longer do push-ups or other physical exercises in your small cell, you no longer pace the four steps back and forth across your cell. You no longer masturbate, you can call forth no vision of eroticism in any form, and your genitals, like the limbs of your body, function only to keep your body alive.

Time descends in your cell like the lid of a coffin in which you lie and watch it as it slowly closes over you. When you neither move nor think in your cell, you are awash in pure nothingness.

Solitary confinement in prison can alter the ontological makeup of a stone.

. . . My years in solitary confinement altered me more than I care to admit, even to myself. But I will try to relate the experience, because you're understanding, and what you do not understand is only what you cannot because *you* have not experienced the hole for years. You *listen* and that is all that counts.

It is hard for me to begin. Beginnings are like that for me now.

But something happens down there in the hole, something like an event, but this event can only occur over a span of years. It cannot take place in time and space the way we ordinarily know them.

Not many prisoners have experienced this event. It *never* fails: most prisoners I know who have been in prison off and on all their lives will tell you they have served *five years* in the hole. Everyone is lying, and I do not know why they must say they served *five years* in the hole. Why *five years?* I cannot understand why that particular duration occurs to all of them. They do not say "I served *four years* or *three years*" — nor even six or seven years. It is *always* five years. I *do* know perhaps a half dozen who *have* indeed served five years or six years, but they are so few and so far between.

At any rate, let me return to the point. Let us say you are in a cell ten feet long and seven feet wide. That means seventy feet of *floor* space. But your bunk is just over three feet wide and six and a half feet long. Your iron toilet and sink combination covers a floor space of at least three feet by two feet. All tallied, you have approximately forty-seven square feet of space on the floor. It works out to a pathway seven feet long and about three feet wide — the excess is taken up by odd spaces between your commode and wall, between the foot of the bunk and the wall.

If I were an animal housed in a zoo in quarters of these dimensions, the Humane Society would have the zookeeper arrested for cruelty. It is illegal to house an animal in such confines.

But I am not an animal, so I do not insist on such rights.

My body communicates with the cell. We exchange temperatures and air currents, smells and leavings on the floor and walls. I try to keep it clean, to wash away my evidence, for the first year or two, then let it go at that.

I have experienced everything possible to experience in a cell in a short time — a day or so if I'm active, a week or two if I'm sluggish.

I must fight, from that point on, the routine, the monotony that will bury me alive if I am not careful. I must do that, and do it without losing my mind. So I read, read anything and everything. So I mutter to myself sometimes; sometimes recite poetry.

I have my memories. I have the good ones, the bad ones, the ones that are neither of these. So I have *myself.*

I have my seven-by-three-feet pathway, and I pace, at various speeds, depending on my mood. I think. I remember. I think. I remember.

Memory is arrested in the hole. I think about each remembered thing, study it in detail, over and over. I unite it with others, under headings for how I feel about it. Finally it changes and begins to tear itself free from facts and joins my imagination. Someone said *being is memory.*

It travels the terrain of time in a pure way, unfettered by what is, reckless of what was, what will become of it. Memory is not enriched by any further experience. It is *deprived* memory, memory deprived of every movement but the isolated body traveling thousands of miles in the confines of my prison cell.

The Joint

My body plays with my mind; my mind plays with my body; the further I go into that terrain of time, into my memories, the more they enter my imagination. The imagination—bringing this memory into that, and that into this, every possible permutation and combination—replaces further experience, which would, if not enhance it, at least leave it intact.

I remember well, with such clarity, I am blinded by the memory. It is as if I had forgotten—but it is that I remember so well, too well.

Why am I here? Because I needed the money? Or was it the palmprint on the counter? What was it—a theft? Or was it that girl by the pond in the flowery dress who smiled at me . . . ?

Where was I?

Every memory has an element of pain or disappointment. It scolds a little and in its own way. These elements are normally overshadowed by a familiarity we can live with—we happily forget the rest. The rest: there is no rest—but a quality we can live with in comfort, a degree of quietude.

In the hole after a while the painful elements begin to throw out shoots and sprout like brittle weeds in the garden of memory—until finally, after so long, they choke to death everything else in the garden.

You are left with a wild wasteland of scrubby weeds and flinty stone and dusty soil. They call it *psyche-pain*.

It is the same with ideals. Everyone has a few: a touch of idealism, a little of passion. As life in the hole, in the pure terrain of time, continues, your passions are aroused less and less with the help of memories and more and more by your ideals. Love, Hate, Equality, Justice, Freedom, War, Peace, Beauty, Truth—they all eventually become Idols, pure and empty abstract gods that demand your fealty, your undying obedience. Little Hitlers come from every precious feeling, every innocent notion you ever entertained, every thought about yourself, your people, the world—all become so many idols, oblivious to each other, that stridently dictate to you in the prison hole.

You cannot fill them up with your days, your years, for they are empty too. But you try—God, how you try.

The wasteland that is your memory now comes under the absolute dictatorship of idols too terrible to envision.

They are the hard, driving winds that torture the tumbleweeds across the prairie desert of memory—the crazy, hard winds that whip up smaller chaotic columns of dust that twist a few feet in the air like little tornadoes. They are the scorching suns that wither the scrubby vegetation and torture the air that shimmers in waves of suffocating heat that rises from the dead, hard stone. They are the cold, merciless nights of the desert that offer surcease only to the fanged serpents: the *punishment* unfolds.

Don't go near yourself.

Then the mirages in the wasteland. You are far from insanity; you are only living through an experience, an event. The mirages are real reflections of how far you have journeyed into that pure terrain of time. They *are* real. They bring the now out-of-place things back into the desert that was once the felicitous garden of your memory. *There a cherished woman passes into existence and you approach, draw close to her, and you touch her and she caresses you and then she vanishes in a shimmer to reveal the man masturbating that you have become and are caressing so tenderly. A beautiful flower is seen at a small distance and opens its radiant wings in a promise of spring among the dusty weeds. More suddenly than it appeared, it disappears to reveal a dark sploth on the wall in the fetid, musky cell. A brook bubbles over the dusty pebbles of the wasteland, promising to quench, to quench—and as you turn, it disappears in a flush of the toilet.*

Ken Kesey

Sketches

PSYCHEDELIC SIXTIES. God knows that whatever that means it certainly meant far more than drugs, though drugs still work as a pretty good handle to the phenomena.

I grabbed that handle. Legally, too, I might add. Almost patriotically, in fact. Early psychedelic sixties . . .

Eight o'clock every Tuesday morning I showed up at the vets' hospital in Menlo Park, ready to roll. The doctor deposited me in a little room on his ward, dealt me a couple of pills or a shot or a little glass of bitter juice, then locked the door. He checked back every forty minutes to see if I was still alive, took some tests, asked some questions, left again. The rest of the time I spent studying the inside of my forehead, or looking out the one little window in the door. It was six inches wide and eight inches high, and it had heavy chicken wire inside the glass.

You get your visions through whatever gate you're granted.

Patients straggled by in the hall outside, their faces all ghastly confessions. Sometimes I looked at them and sometimes they looked at me, but rarely did we look at one another. It was too naked and painful. More was revealed in a human face than a human being can bear, face-to-face.

Sometimes the nurse came by and checked on me. Her face was different. It was painful business, but not naked. This was not a person you could allow yourself to be naked in front of.

Six months or so later I had finished the drug experiments and applied for a job. I was taken on as a nurse's aide, in the same ward, with the same doctor, under the same nurse—and you must understand we're talking about a huge hospital here! It was weird.

But, as I said, this was the sixties.

Those faces were still there, still painfully naked. To ward them off my case I very prudently took to carrying around a little notebook, to scribble notes. I got a lot of compliments from nurses: "Good for you, Mr. Kesey. That's the spirit. Get to know these men."

I also scribbled faces. No, that's not correct. As I prowl through this stack of sketches I can see that these faces bored their way behind my forehead and scribbled themselves. I just held the pen and waited for the magic to happen.

This was, after all, the sixties.

Stanley "Tookie" Williams

Life in Prison

SPENDING DAY AFTER DAY in prison can cause strange things to happen to a person's sanity. It's easy to lose touch with reality. Some men become claustrophobic while in prison, meaning they fear being stuck in closed and narrow spaces, such as being locked in a cell. If it gets too bad, they can become stir-crazy—which means the mental pain of living in a cell for so long becomes more than they can bear.

Prisoners who are stir-crazy are insane. We call these men "J-Cats." It's slang for Category J, the official term used by prison staff to identify inmates in need of mental-health care. There are a lot of J-Cats here on death row. These men have retreated so far from reality, they don't even know they're in prison. Some of them curse at anyone who walks by their cells. Others scream and shout all night long to no one in particular. Many of them are so out of their minds that they don't take showers, comb their hair, brush their teeth, or change their clothes. They smell so bad that no one wants to be near them. Stir-crazy prisoners also urinate on themselves and smear feces all over their bodies, as well as on the walls and the floors. They may even sling human waste at you, if you're unlucky enough to be within range of their cells.

I admit that after several years here, I began to feel claustrophobic. At times I thought that I was about to go crazy. It felt like the walls were closing in on me and that if I didn't get out of the cell right then and there I would lose my mind. Sometimes my feelings of claustrophobia would last for about a minute or two. But it felt like hours. It was very frightening. I would think, Hey, wait a minute. I'm Tookie. This isn't supposed to be happening to me. But it was.

I used to get claustrophobic feelings every several months. Then, once or twice a year. Now I don't experience them at all. In fact, the last time I feared the cell was going to collapse on me was in 1989—and I had good reason to be afraid. On that day, October 17, 1989, as I sat in my cell drawing a picture, baseball's World Series was on both the television and radio. The third game was about to begin at Candlestick Park in nearby San Francisco. Excitement about the game could be heard in the voices of inmates cheering from their cells here on The Row.

I remember dropping my pencil on the floor, and at that moment, when I reached down to pick it up, the entire building began to shake. I tried to stand up, but it was hard to do—like trying to stand on top of a water bed. The motions of the floor were like the waves of an ocean.

It was an earthquake. And it was scary.

The inmates started hollering. We all felt like trapped animals. Moving as quickly as I could, I got to the front of the cell. Then I prayed that the barred door would swing open. The building was rocking so severely, I thought it might crumble. And I didn't want to be smashed under a pile of bricks. I wanted out. But there wasn't a thing I could do.

I knew that screaming would not change what was happening to me. So I just stood there, gripping the bars with all my might. I longed for the shaking to stop before San Quentin—the state's oldest in-use prison, built in 1852—collapsed. I had read that in California there would one day be an earthquake so destructive it would destroy most, if not all, of the state. With that in mind, I prepared myself for what I believed would be the end of my life.

I'll never forget how I felt that day. This is the end, I thought. I won't ever see my family again. My feelings went beyond the fear caused by claustrophobia. I didn't worry about losing my mind, because I was more concerned with remaining alive. I didn't want to die in a prison cell. But the bars remained locked. I was trapped.

The quake seemed to last forever. And there was nowhere I could run. I had never felt so helpless in my entire life. All of the big muscles I had worked so hard to develop over the years could not help me.

When the earthquake finally stopped, there was an electrical problem. So, for many hours after the quake, we had no electricity and had to sit in the dark. When the electrical power was restored, I was able to turn on the television and find out exactly how much damage the earthquake had caused. This was the worst earthquake in San Francisco since 1906.

Imagine being in your bathroom at home with the lock jammed when an earthquake hit. Picture yourself pounding on the door, screaming for your parents — for anyone — to get you out of there. Then think about how it would feel to be in that position and know that your parents were gone for the day, your neighbors were on vacation, and that no one was coming to your rescue. I'll bet you would feel abandoned, afraid, alone in the world. Most inmates carry that aching feeling inside of them virtually every single day of their incarceration.

Some of us manage to live with that pain. Some of us don't. Those of us who cannot tolerate the pain go stir-crazy.

I've kept from going stir-crazy by realizing I have only two choices: I can allow the pain to destroy me, or I can fight it. I've chosen to fight it by staying as active as possible. I write, draw, read, study, exercise, meditate, and pray. I find my greatest peace through meditation and prayer. But I'm still only tolerating a pain that never goes away.

I know several inmates who have tried to kill themselves. They say they would rather be dead than continue to live in a cell on death row.

Two inmates on The Row did kill themselves. Both were found hanging in their cells. It was hard for me to believe. For years, neither one showed any sign that he did not want to live. They saw themselves as tough guys, and they appeared to be smart and strong. They liked to exercise. Nothing seemed to trouble them, except the fact that they were on death row, which, I admit, is plenty to be troubled about.

One of them had been a Crip member for years. He had a big rep — or reputation — for himself on the streets. Back in the hood — or neighborhood — there were youngsters who looked up to him and wanted to be like him. People respected him. This man used to lift weights and was fairly big. When he walked, he had that swagger that meant, I'm tough, so everybody had better leave me alone. Now he's dead.

Fortunately for me, thoughts of killing myself have never entered my mind. But living in prison does have a strange effect on each person here. For some people, such as J-Cats, insanity takes over. Other men, like the Crip who hanged himself, choose death.

There is much sadness behind these prison walls.

Prison life is boring—and fiercely lonely. Some inmates have relatives who will have nothing to do with them now that they're in prison. I know death-row inmates who have gone as long as ten years without visitation from any family member. Only their lawyers have come to San Quentin to see them. But when you're in prison, sometimes even your legal team won't come through for you. My attorney once went seven years without visiting me.

I'm fortunate that my mother has always been in my corner. We talk on the telephone and write to each other, and she often visits me. But there are inmates whose mothers and fathers have told them never to call or write.

Also, many of the men here used to have wives or girlfriends, as well as buddies, back home. But no more. After several months in prison, many of the people I cared about were gone from my life, too.

When you're in prison, there are no guarantees that the people you know—relatives, friends, or spouses—will remain in your life. In prison, you're out of sight and out of mind.

Years spent in a cell, by yourself and with no one to care about you, can cause an inmate to act real strange. Inmates overwhelmed by loneliness behave in ways that aren't connected to reality. If someone pays attention to them, they may start to believe that the person has romantic feelings for them. For example, a female prison professional might say only "hello" to a lonely inmate for that man to fall in love.

One of the inmates here, nicknamed Black, misunderstood a simple greeting for something more meaningful. A female nurse would from time to time ask, "How are you doing today, Black?" And because of that, Black wrote a poem for her. He would desperately try to recite the love poem during the seconds it took her to walk past his cell. First, the nurse talked to one of Black's friends on The Row about the problem she was having. She told the friend to inform Black that she was not interested in a romantic relationship with him. But Black kept writing and reciting love poetry to her. Eventually, that nurse obtained a transfer to another part of the prison to get away from Black.

Other men in prison are so crazy from their loneliness that they get angry if a female guard or nurse does not greet them or talk to them. Those inmates will yell foul language down the tiers at such women.

Loneliness is a painful feeling for everyone here. Even for me. Nothing in this cell can take away my loneliness. I can stay as busy as ever, but the loneliness of being confined to a cell never goes away.

Fortunately for me, I have not gone stir-crazy or crazy lonely, where I've completely lost control of my actions and of my mind. And my bouts with claustrophobia have ceased. But I know better than to take for granted a relatively okay state of mind, because I know that prison life is madness.

DONN PEARCE

Cool Hand Luke

BUT AS TIME WENT on Luke gained a reputation of being not only one of the best poker players in Camp but also one of the biggest eaters. He could put away an incredible pile of beans and corn bread. And when Rabbit took up a Store Order Luke would buy all sorts of Free World groceries with his poker winnings—apples, bananas and cookies, raw carrots and sardines. Every day he bought a quart of milk. He'd spread his jacket out on the ground, lay down on his back, open the container and drink the whole quart at once, gulping it down in one long, bubbling draught.

He was a natural. But in addition to his native aptitude he was given valuable lessons in technique from Curly. Recognizing Luke as a talented challenger to his position as the camp's biggest eater, Curly taught him all sorts of esoteric tricks of the trade. It was Curly who gave him the extra-large tablespoon that he carried, digging it out of his locker where he had it stashed away as a spare, giving it to Luke with a big grin.

Here, Luke. Use this. That little toy you got there ain't big enough to keep a man alive.

Curly could eat. But he could work too. This is what kept him out of the Box in the old days when he would eat so much supper that the count was held up when the men checked into the Building for the night. Carr and the Wicker Man stood outside on the porch. The guards sat on the gun platforms. The captain was rocking and spitting in front of his Office. The cooks and trustees stood by in the kitchen. The Walking Boss sat in the Messhall, standing guard over Curly who sat there all alone—eating.

That was how he won the unique distinction of having the legal right to get in at the head of the chow line, this privilege granted by personal orders of the Captain himself.

It was inevitable that the day should come. It was hot and the Bull Gang had spent all day in a drainage ditch in water up to their waists, cutting out the dense undergrowth of briars and willows and palmettos with bush axes. Luke had worked like a fiend, slashing away at twice the speed of anyone else, lopping off the fronds and branches with forehand and backhand strokes of ferocity. But because of the temperature and because we weren't very far from Camp, the Bull Gang was the first squad to check in from the road.

Luke was the first man to reach the Messhall door, limping and staggering, his pants and shoes soaking wet with mud and slime. Everyone waited for the other squads to come in. Finally the Patch Squad arrived and then Curly came up, stepping right in front of Luke with a grin.

Everybody made jokes and wisecracks. The two double-gut giants stood by the screen door, grinding their teeth and stomping their feet, their spoons held in their hands at the ready, glittering in the sunset.

Boss Higgins was the Walking Boss in charge of the Messhall that night. He went inside. Taking his position by the kitchen door, he gave the signal.

Curly and Luke each grabbed a plate and leaped to the line of pots where one trustee was serving the scrap of fat back and another the catheads. On this particular night the Dog Boy ladled up the main dish, a concoction of stewed potatoes. It was a soft, overcooked mess but not really bad at all. But for the big eaters it was a pure blessing. Ordinarily they always chewed a mouthful of food just twice and then swallowed. But on this night they didn't have to chew at all.

Before the sixth man had filed inside Curly and Luke were standing by the door, their empty plates dangling in bored, innocent hands. They ignored our grins, scowls and insulting whispers, calmly waiting there for the end of the line to come through so they could get seconds.

Then again they leaped to their places with over-heaped plates, their spoons scooping in a whipped blur as they slopped, slurped and swallowed and jumped up neck and neck to go back for more. This time the Dog Boy stacked up their plates with a mountainous heap, never believing they could finish it and getting a vicious thrill out of the Heat he imagined they were bringing down upon themselves from the Free Man.

But they polished off that serving in less than sixty seconds and returned once again. And then we knew. For the first time in over three years, Curly's title was being seriously challenged.

The whole drama was acted out in silent pantomime. We couldn't cheer, shout or make bets. But we expressed our glee and our befuddlement with our eyes, our nods, fingers and smiles.

Reluctantly we finished up our own pitifully small portions. One by one we got up and stepped outside to wash off our spoons under the faucet, to take off our shoes and empty our pockets to allow the Floorwalker to shake us down. Inside the Messhall, a few brave ones were still dawdling, risking the wrath of the Free Man in order to witness at first hand this incredible contest.

Four plates and then five. The Dog Boy's remarks became louder and more cutting. Being a trustee he had the right to speak aloud in the Messhall. And being a Judas whose job was to train the bloodhounds and to chase escaping convicts, and being a natural son of a bitch besides, he tried his very best to put the Heat on the gulping, swelling duet.

Damn. Ain't never seen such gluttons. Keep on and the State's liable to go broke feedin' 'em. Here boy! Soooooeeeee! You want some more slops? *Soooeeeee!*

But the Free Man simply observed the proceedings from his chair in the corner, clutching his ulcered stomach with his fingers. Then he growled out impatiently.

Them two are the best Rollers in Camp. Boss Godfrey says Luke's able to do more work than any man in the Bull Gang. A man sure as hell cain't work if he don't eat right. Ah only wish ah could eat like that. Ah'd give anything.

And that shut up the Dog Boy who had come dangerously close to putting the Finger on himself.

After six plates of stewed potatoes each, the pot was empty. With a sigh of regret, Curly started to rise. But then Jabo the Cook came out with two aluminum bowls of stewed prunes that were left over from the guards' table at breakfast. He offered them to Curly and Luke and then sat down on the bench opposite them, holding his chin in his hand and watching. Babalugats was the last Gunman left in the Messhall. But then he could tarry no longer and came out to break the news to the rest of us who were clinging to the bars and wire of the windows, waiting for some word.

They both spit out the last pit at the same time to set the metal bowls ringing in an affirmative major chord. Sardonically the Cook offered to get them still another bowl but Curly was too cunning. He realized that if they ran the thing into the ground there was a serious risk of getting into trouble. They had had their fun. But they didn't want to become Wise Guys.

They left the Messhall, waddling with short, stiff-legged steps, their bellies swollen painfully. Then Curly stopped and twisted his big torso on his hips, letting go with a truly magnificent fart. Luke grinned, raised his right leg and answered the call, trumpeting far over the distant groves dim with the shadows of dusk.

It was a draw.

But to have eaten Curly to a draw was such an outstanding accomplishment that Luke's fame was immediately established. Shortly afterwards, Curly was made a trustee. No longer working under the gun, his appetite fell off considerably and although he had retired undefeated, Luke became the new Intestinal Champion.

And then one night while playing poker he managed to bluff his way into stealing a pot of a dollar and sixty-five cents. Everyone else had thrown in his hand except Bullshit Bill who was holding a pair of aces. But when Luke raised the last bet a dollar he refused to call the raise. After dragging in the nickels, dimes and quarters, Luke showed his hand to Bullshit Bill. He had a pair of nothing. Smiling, he murmured softly.

Just remember, man. Wherever you go and whatever you do. Always play a real cool hand.

And from that night on he always answered to the name of Cool Hand Luke.

ED SANDERS

The Family

FOR MOST OF THE 1960s Manson sat in jail. Through the tumult of the various liberation movements outside in America, through riots, through assassinations, the beginning of Vietnam, peace rallies, sexual liberation, rock and roll, the Beatles For Sale, the Beach Boys, napalm, Hare Krishna, and the growing refusal of women to be victimized—a movement of which he had little awareness—through all this sat Manson monitoring reality through magazines and hearsay conversation.

It was while counting the days at McNeil Island that Manson began studying magic, warlockry, hypnotism, astral projection, Masonic lore, scientology, ego games, subliminal motivation, music and perhaps Rosicrucianism.

Especially hypnotism and subliminal motivation. He seemed determined to use it to effect control over others, to his benefit.

One prison mate of Manson at McNeil Island recalls vividly the great Charlie Manson Headphones Caper.

Utilizing the prison radio station, Manson planted what his cell partner called "posthypnotic suggestions" in all the prisoners at McNeil Island Penitentiary.

Each prisoner had access to the station by means of headphones hanging on the bunk beds in the cells. Manson set up a clandestine scheme whereby the radio station would broadcast messages at 3 a.m. over the earphones. The message or instruction was repeated over and over.

The prisoners were required to hang their headsets at night on the bedsteads so that the messages were picked up by the sleepers but were not loud enough to attract the guards.

The story continues that McNeil Island had a basketball team that rarely won any games. Manson beamed messages to the sleeping inmates urging them to get out and to root for the McNeil Island team.

Charlie then placed bets with the zealous new fans that the opposing teams would win and quickly won himself two hundred packs of cigarettes, the medium of exchange in U.S. prisons.

Another was the applause caper: he planted suggestions over the earphones that everyone should keep applauding for Manson when he sang at a particular prison talent contest. Manson won the contest earphones-down, evidently receiving a standing ovation of some duration.

Of irony, Manson seems to have become a protégé in prison of prohibition gangster Alvin Karpis, a member of the evil Ma Barker gang, which left fourteen victims dead.

Alvin "Old Creepy" Karpis taught Charlie to play the steel guitar and seems to have been a general counselor to the young man, although when interviewed after Manson's arrest, Karpis said that he had considered Manson the last man on earth "to go into the mass murder business."

"Charlie was hooked on this new thing called 'scientology,'" says Karpis. "He figured it would enable him to do anything or be anything. Maybe he was right. The kid tried to sell a lot of other cons on scientology but got strictly nowhere."

Scientology is a reincarnationist religion that claims to train individuals to experience past lives, to leave their bodies—i.e., "exteriorize"—and to achieve great power and immortality, among other things. Manson learned about scientology from one Lanier Ramer, from Gene Deaton and from Jerry Milman, who was Manson's roommate at McNeil Island Penitentiary.

Lanier Ramer, according to Manson's followers, had been active in the study of scientology and had become a Doctor of Scientology, an early rank in the movement, now abolished.

Ramer broke away from scientology and formed his own group. He was apprehended for armed holdup and was sent to McNeil Island.

Manson has told a jailhouse visitor that he received 150 sessions of "processing" in jail, evidently from Lanier Ramer.

Manson has contended that he learned scientology methods very quickly because his "mind wasn't programmed." But Manson was not a "product" of scientology in any way; he merely borrowed a few ideas from it. The scientologists call it "squirreling"—that is, borrowing and mutating scientology practices or methods.

Manson picked up a fair number of scientology phrases, neologisms and practices that he put to his own use when he began to reorganize the minds of his young followers.

Phrases like "to mock up" and "cease to exist" and "to come to Now" and the concept of "putting up pictures" all seem to have their origin in Manson's McNeil Island sessions with Lanier Ramer.

Manson also studied Masonic lore and picked up some knowledge of Masonic hand signals (which later he would flash to judges during court appearances).

He evidently learned something about scientology recognition signals also. Later, in the era of creepy crawlie, Manson would develop his own complex system of hand and body signals—really a whole language of chopnotation—among his followers.

For someone so unskilled in reading and writing, Manson took a high interest in certain books on hypnotism and psychiatry. According to a friend, he was interested particularly in a book called *Transactional Analysis* by Dr. Eric Berne, the author of *Games People Play*. Charlie, ever the proselytizer, urged his friends to read his discovered books.

From his study of *Transactional Analysis*, Manson may have developed his perverse doctrine of Child Mind. Certainly he borrowed lots of ideas from the pioneer work in group therapy.

He had a friend, one Marvin White, who appears to have been released from McNeil Island and then to have made arrangements to mail Charlie books on black magic and related subjects.

Another book that helped provide a theoretical basis for Manson's Family was *Stranger in a Strange Land* by Robert Heinlein, the story of a power-hungry telepathic Martian roaming the earth with a harem and a quenchless sexual thirst while proselytizing for a new religious movement. Initially, Manson borrowed a lot of terminology and ideas from this book— not, hopefully, including the ritual cannibalism described therein.

Manson was, however, to identify with the hero of the book, one Valentine

Michael Smith (Manson's first follower's child was named Valentine Michael Manson)—a person who, in the course of building a religious movement, took to killing or "discorporating" his enemies. Smith, in the book, ultimately was beaten to death by an angry mob and ascended to the Sky.

During his later murder trial, Manson's followers held water-sharing ceremonies where Manson, in jail, magically took a long-distance hit off a glass of water which was being stared at by a circle of sitting adepts.

What he seems to have known most intimately though was the Bible, which he was able to quote at great length.

MARVIN FELIX CAMILLO

Introduction to Short Eyes

IT SEEMS LIKE ONLY yesterday that Miguel Piñero spoke to me about one of several plays he was writing. He seemed more pleased with *Short Eyes* than with any of his other plays. We had met in Sing Sing (where I was working as an actor-in-residence and assistant to Mr. Clay Stevenson) in the spring of 1972. By early summer of 1973 we had developed a friendship in which little thought was given to the fact that we were living in different worlds: mine, the free world; his, the prison.

We considered several projects that never got off the ground or through the bars. Our only successful project while Miky was incarcerated was winning an award for one of his poems, "Black Woman with the Blonde Wig On." I submitted the poem to a contest while working as Special Programs Consultant to the Council on the Arts in Westchester County. The poem won an award and I almost won a little vacation in the "joint" with Miky. In the May 27, 1971, issue of *The New York Times*, Mel Gussow had reviewed our show *Prison Sounds*, which included "Black Woman with the Blonde Wig On," and in recognition of Miky's promise he acknowledged his poetic ability and mentioned the poetry award. The warden at Sing Sing read Gussow's article, called us into his office, and read us the Riot Act. He called it contraband. I called it good poetry.

• • •

The Joint

I urge the readers of *Short Eyes* not to search for some great social reform message or to analyze the personal motives of the original cast or to fall into the trap of feeling this play can be done only by ex-inmates or people from a subculture. Read it as a play that can and should be acted by any serious-minded group of people wishing to do a play that appeals to them.

Miguel Piñero is no more a playwright because he went to jail than Tennessee Williams is a playwright because he came from the South. Tito Goya (Cupcakes) is not a "sweet kid," Ben Jefferson (Ice) never masturbated to Jane Fonda's picture, and J. J. Johnson (El Raheem) has never been a Muslim or a porter. When the prisoners enter the dayroom, we are witnessing not a prison play but a play about human relationships. We see Omar, a perennial prisoner, doing his bid, being concerned primarily about "getting on the help" so he can benefit from the extra cigarettes or whatever little goodies he can get from the commissary and, of course, the favors others render him—especially the "sweet kids" (those considered "stuff").

Murphy, the tough Irishman, becomes tougher in order to survive in a world of Puerto Ricans and blacks, where he controls the flow of drugs and homemade wine inside the "joint." Murphy has more resentment for the alleged child rapist, Clark Davis, than anyone else in the prison.

Clark Davis represents an emotionally disturbed man from an emotionally disturbed society. His death is the result of the rigidity of social values and morals in the prison world, because the values we witness in the play are the same as those of the outside world, but more intensified. Prison is a society within a society, and Clark Davis's life and death are the result of both societies. Juan's judgment of Davis's death in his rap to Cupcakes is meant to reach the other participants in Davis's murder, as well as everyone in the theater audience: "You blew it because you placed yourself above understanding." Juan is the outlaw who makes no excuses.

Paco is the dope fiend and *bugarrón*, the *payaso*, moving with quick, loud, tropical rhythms, laughing on the outside while he searches for love to help him through his bid. "Willing to go both ways," he even makes an unsuccessful attempt to conquer Cupcakes sexually.

Cupcakes is our youth, our hope, and very vulnerable because of his own fears. But at the same time he enjoys all the attention that he receives from the other love-starved prisoners. His beauty and innocence become their shot of dope.

El Raheem represents a search for self through an original religion. He is definitely not a Muslim or a Black Panther. He is a man choosing to do his bid by studying and teaching *his* truth about the original black man. His not being able to kill someone "looking up at me helpless" is not an act of cowardice but a very touching element of humanity.

When the critics reviewed the audience's reaction to the play as well as the play itself, we all knew that we were involved in something more than a prison drama or a slice of life by an ex-convict. We were involved in a human story. Miguel Piñero, this "saintly outlaw," this *espiritista* of words, has given birth to a play that has poetry which can be trusted and respected.

MIGUEL PIÑERO

Short Eyes

CLARK

You know, somehow it seems like there's no beginning. Seems like I've always been in there all my life. I have like little picture incidents running across my mind . . . I remember being . . . fifteen or sixteen years old

(JUAN *crosses upstage center to clean toilet*)

or something around that age, waking up to the sound of voices coming from the living room . . . cartoons on the TV . . . They were watching cartoons on the TV, two little girls. One was my sister, and her friend . . . And you know how it is when you get up in the morning, the inevitable hard-on is getting up with you. I draped the sheet around my shoulders . . . Everyone else was sleeping . . . The girl watching TV with my sister . . . yes . . . Hispanic . . . pale-looking skin . . . She was eight . . . nine . . . ten . . . what the difference, she was a child . . . She was very pretty—high cheekbones, flashing black eyes . . . She was wearing blue short pants . . . tight-fitting . . . a white blouse, or shirt . . . My sister . . . she left to do number two . . .

(JUAN *returns to stage right*)

She told her friend wait for me, I'm going to do number two, and they laughed about it. I sneaked in standing a little behind her . . . She felt me standing there and turned to me . . . She smiled such a pretty little smile . . . I told her I was a vampire and she laughed . . . I spread the sheets apart and she suddenly stopped laughing . . . She just stood there staring at me . . .

The Joint

Shocked? surprised? intrigued? Don't know . . . don't know . . . She just stood and stared . . .

(JUAN *crosses to downstage left*)

I came closer like a vampire . . . She started backing away . . . ran toward the door . . . stopped, looked at me again. Never at my face . . . my body . . . I couldn't really tell whether or not the look on her face was one of fear . . . but I'll never forget that look.

(BROWN *crosses on catwalk from left to right with a banana. Stands at right*)

I was really scared that she'd tell her parents. Weeks passed without confrontation . . . and I was feeling less and less afraid . . . But that's not my thing, showing myself naked to little girls in schoolyards.

(JUAN *crosses to downstage right corner and begins to mop from downstage right to downstage left*)

One time . . . no, it was the first time . . . the very first time. I was alone watching TV . . . Was I in school or out . . . And there was this little Puerto Rican girl from next door . . . Her father was the new janitor . . . I had seen her before . . . many times . . . sliding down the banister . . . Always her panties looked dirty . . . She was . . . oh, why do I always try to make their age higher than it really was . . . even to myself. She was young, much too young . . . Why did she come there? For who? Hundred questions. Not one small answer . . . not even a lie flickers across my brain.

OFFSTAGE VOICE

All right, listen up. The following inmates report for sanitation duty: Smalls, Gary; Medena, James; Pfeifer, Willis; Martinez, Raul. Report to C.O. grounds for sanitation duty.

CLARK

How did I get to the bathroom with her? Don't know. I was standing there with her, I was combing her hair. I was combing her hair. Her curly reddish hair . . .

(JUAN *crosses upstage right, starts to mop upstage right to upstage left*)

I was naked . . . naked . . . except for these flower-printed cotton underwears . . . No slippers, barefooted . . . Suddenly I get this feeling over me . . . like a flash fever . . . and I'm hard . . . I placed my hands on her small shoulders . . . and pressed her hand and placed it on my penis . . . Did she know what to do? Or did I coerce her? I pulled down my drawers . . . But then I felt too naked, so I put them back on . . . My eyes were closed . . . but I felt as if there was this giant eye off in space staring at me . . .

(JUAN *stops upstage left and listens to* CLARK, *who is unaware* JUAN *is in back of him*)

I opened them and saw her staring at me in the cabinet mirror. I pulled her back away from the view of the mirror . . . My hands up her dress, feeling her underdeveloped body . . . I . . . I . . . I began pulling her underwear down on the bowl . . . She resisted . . . slightly, just a moment . . . I sat on the bowl . . . She turned and threw her arms around my neck and kissed me on the lips . . . She gave a small nervous giggle . . . I couldn't look at her . . . I closed my eyes . . . turned her body . . . to face away from me . . . I lubricated myself . . . and . . . I hear a scream, my own . . . there was a spot of blood on my drawers . . . I took them off right then and there . . . ripped them up and flushed them down the toilet . . . She had dressed herself up and asked me if we could do it again tomorrow . . . and was I her boyfriend now . . . I said yes, yes . . .

(JUAN *goes to center stage, starts mopping center stage right to stage left.* BROWN *exits from catwalk above right*)

I couldn't sit still that whole morning, I just couldn't relax. I dressed and took a walk . . . Next thing I know I was running—out of breath . . . I had run over twenty blocks . . . twenty blocks blind . . . without knowing . . . I was running . . . Juan, was it my conscious or subconscious that my rest stop was a children's playground . . . Coincidence perhaps . . . But why did I run in that direction, no, better still, why did I start walking in that direction . . . Coincidence? Why didn't my breath give out elsewhere . . . Coincidence?

(JUAN *moves to downstage left,* CLARK *moves to upstage center and sits on window ledge*)

I sat on the park bench and watched the little girls swing . . . slide . . . run . . . jump rope . . . Fat . . . skinny . . . black . . . white . . . Chinese . . . I sat there until the next morning . . . The next day I went home and met the little

Puerto Rican girl again . . . Almost three times a week . . . The rest of the time I would be in the playground or in the children's section of the movies . . . But you know something? Er, er . . .

(CLARK *moves toward* JUAN, *who is downstage left corner*)

JUAN

Juan.

CLARK

Yes, Juan . . . Juan the listener . . . the compassionate . . . you know something, Juan . . . I soon became . . . became . . . what? A pro? A professional degenerate?

(The sound of garbage cans banging together is heard offstage)

I don't know if you can call it a second insight on children. But . . . I would go to the park . . . and sit there for hours and talk with a little girl and know if I would do it or not with her . . . Just a few words was all needed . . . Talk stupid things they consider grownup talk . . . Soon my hand would hold hers, then I would caress her face . . . Next her thighs . . . under their dress . . . I never took any of them home or drove away with them in my car . . . I always told them to meet me in the very same building they lived in . . .

OFFSTAGE VOICE

On the sanitation gate.

(Sound of gate opening)

CLARK

On the roof or their basements under the stairs . . . Sometimes in their own home if the parents were out . . . The easiest ones were the Puerto Ricans and the black girls . . . Little white ones would masturbate you right there in the park for a dollar or a quarter . . . depending on how much emphasis their parents put in their heads on making money . . . I felt ashamed at first . . . But then I would rehearse at nights what to do the next time . . . planning . . . I

(JUAN *starts moving slowly from downstage left to upstage left*)

couldn't help myself . . . I couldn't help myself . . . Something drove me to it . . . I thought of killing myself . . . but I just couldn't go through with it . . . I don't really wanna die . . . I wanted to stop, really I did . . . I just didn't know how. I thought maybe I was crazy . . . but I read all types of psychology books . . . I heard or read somewhere that crazy people can't distinguish right from wrong . . . Yet I can . . . I know what's right and I know what I'm doing is wrong, yet I can't stop myself . . .

JUAN

Why didn't you go to the police or a psychiatrist . . .

(JUAN *crosses to shower room upstage left*)

CLARK

I wanted to many a time . . . But I know that the police would find some pretext to kill me . . . And a psychiatrist . . . well, if he thought he couldn't help me he'd turn me over to them or commit me to some nut ward . . . Juan, try to understand me.

(JUAN *comes out of shower room and starts putting away his cleaning equipment*)

JUAN

Motherfucker, try to understand you . . . if I wasn't trying to, I would have killed you . . . stone dead, punk . . .

JOHN RECHY

The Sexual Outlaw

VOICE OVER: HUSTLERS, CLIENTS, AND EMINENT PSYCHIATRISTS

"MALEHUSTLERS . . . DRIFTERS, TOUGH, STREET-smart. And smarter, but pretending, sometimes, to be dumb. Students and middle-class youngmen, though on the rough streets not as many as, briefly too, become callboys (the callboy faction being safer, more 'conservative'—only muted revolution there). A precarious existence—you're new one day, old another. The clients remain, the sellers are pushed aside; a fresh wave of hustling outlaws flows regularly into the city.

"The customers. . . . The myth says they're all middle-aged or older, probably married, shy. But that's not true. Those exist, yes, abundantly; there are, too—though far, far fewer—the attractive and the young who merely prefer to pay, especially among those who want to cling to the myth that masculine hustlers are 'straight.' "

I'm speaking about male streethustling to a group of eminent California psychiatrists and psychologists who meet irregularly. I sit at one end of the table and face about twenty men and women. Occasionally they will whisper briefly among each other.

With as much defiance as honesty I say:

The world of streethustling holds great power over me, and the others in it, a world we love; I've experienced it—survived it—for years—much longer, I'm proud to say, than most. It's a world clouded in generalities. Hustling is one of those activities that has to be experienced first-hand to be fully understood; sociology doesn't work.

The first man who picked me up while I was hustling—the very day I arrived in New York—approached me with these words: "I'll give you ten and I don't give a damn for you." That was a good street price at that time. His words—and, as it turned out, he *did* give a damn; a very moving, tough man—opened up a world of sexual power through being paid, and they took me to streets in New York, Los Angeles, San Francisco, New Orleans, Chicago, St. Louis, Dallas—even, to smash my sheltered childhood, in El Paso, my hometown, where I was picked up by a junior-high teacher of mine, who didn't recognize me.

Even when I had good jobs, I was on the streets recurrently, pulled back as if by a powerful lover. Even when *City of Night* was riding the best-seller lists. I've seen copies of my books in the houses of people who have picked me up anonymously. At times just the offer of sexmoney is enough. Those times I don't need, actually, to go with anyone.

There is a terrific, terrible excitement in getting paid by another man for sex. A great psychological release, a feeling that this is where real sexual power lies—not only to be desired by one's own sex but to be paid for being desired, and if one chooses that strict role, not to reciprocate in those encounters, a feeling of emotional detachment as freedom—these are some of the lures; lures implicitly acknowledged as desirable by the very special place the male-hustler occupies in the gay world, entirely different from that of the female prostitute in the straight. Even when he is disdained by those who would never pay for sex, he is still an object of admiration to most, at times an object of jealousy. To "look like a hustler" in gay jargon is to look very, very good.

One of the myths of the hustler is that he is actually looking for love. Perhaps, under the surface, deeply. On the surface there is too often contempt for the client, yes, at best pity—sometimes, seldom and at times only fleetingly, affection; yes, I have felt that. The client, too, at times resents the hustler because he desires him. I think of the hustling streets as a battlefield; two armies, the hustler and the client, warring, yet needing each other.

Outside of a busy coffeeshop where hustlers gather in clusters throughout the night, an older man in a bright-new car parked and waited during a recent buyers' night. Youngmen solicited him anxiously in turns, stepping into the car, being rejected grandly by him, stepping out, replaced by another eager or desperate youngman. Smiling meanly, the older man—one of that breed of corrupted, corrupt, corrupting old men—turned down one after the other, finally driving off contemptuously alone, leaving behind raised middle fingers and a squad of deliberately rejected hustlers—some skinny, desolate little teenagers among the more experienced, cocky, older others; skinny boys, yes, sadly, progressively younger, lining the hustling streets; prostitutes before their boyhood has been played out, some still exhibiting the vestiges of innocence, some already corrupted, corrupt, corrupting—an increasing breed of the young, with no options but the streets—which is when it is all mean and ugly, when it is not a matter of choice; wanted for no other reason than their youth, their boyhood. . . . And yet, later that very night, I met a man as old as the contemptuous other one—but, this one, sweet, sweet, eager to be "liked," just liked, desperate for whatever warmth he might squeeze out, if only in his imagination, in a paid encounter, eager to "pay more"—to elicit it—simply for being allowed to suck a cock. . . . Hustling is all too often involved in mutual exploitation and slaughter, of the young and the old, the beautiful and the unattractive.

The standard street price is twenty dollars—but this fluctuates; you ask for as much as you can get (and designate what for). You go for less depending on your needs—bartering is not rare. Another lucky day you'll go for more—$25, $30, more. Like the stock market, streethustling has daily highs and lows.

The relationship among masculine hustlers is a very delicate one. It relies on repression. A fantasy in the gay world is of two street hustlers making it with each other. There's the notion that today's hustlers are tomorrow's payers. Both concepts are largely inaccurate. Many masculine streethustlers still think of themselves defensively as "straight," a role those attracted to them expect, even at times demand, they play. Often girls hang around necking with hustlers on the street until a client for their boyfriends appears. Though some hustlers may move back and forth into a cruising area for an unpaid contact of mutual attraction, in hustling turf among other masculine hustlers they must remain, rigidly, "buddies" (like Paul Newman and Robert Redford).

Now about hustlers becoming payers later on: Perhaps that's true of callboys with notoriously less hangups. I'm talking about the masculine, straightplaying streethustler; he knows, from his vast experience and those shared by others like him, of the hustler's contempt, pity—at times even hatred—for the client. It would require a psychic upheaval for him to be able to shift roles masochistically. And the malehustler is a proud creature, though less so now.

A few years back, he was almost without exception masculine; it was almost always assumed he would "do nothing back." Within the past few years—drugs, gay liberation—two other breeds have thrived—the masculine bisexual and the androgynous, usually willowy but not effeminate, young hustler. Of course, the queens have existed since the time of the dinosaurs.

Street techniques vary, but there are general aspects. The hustler usually stands on one of several known corners, or walks idly along the streets, or mills with other hustlers outside known food stands, coffeeshops. Steady hustlers have their favorite corners. A client will stop his car and signal a hustler. Depending on his style or lack of it, the hustler will then stand by the car until the man speaks first or will just hop in.

Fantasy is important on the streets. If a client asks whether you're married, you say yes if you're smart, because he wants that. If he asks if you've been in the marines, or the army, or the navy (curiously never the air force), yes. If he asks if you've ever worked in a carnival, or posed for pictures, or been in a rodeo, yes, yes, yes.

Danger of course is always present, a constant factor. Plainclothes cops offer money, make the entrapping proposition, then bust. There are the marauding gangs of hoods who raid hustling streets. And the psychotic figures attracted and repelled by hustlers . . . The psychic danger of constant loneliness.

For many drifting youngmen, hustling is their only means of experiencing worlds otherwise totally locked to them. For moments their desired young bodies are the keys to those worlds. Their fleeting youth is their one bid for attention. Beyond that, their lives will fade. But during those moments, hustling, they matter, importantly. The drabness lifts.

Postscript

Recently *Time* magazine created a new style of male-hustling. A story on "pornography" referred to the thriving heterosexual massage parlors lining the south side of a certain Los Angeles boulevard, and to the male prostitutes hustling on the north side. The latter was not true. There had existed, yes, a "limbo" section on that thoroughfare, where one stood or hitchhiked along certain blocks or lingered outside an all-night coffeehouse. Although occasionally you might find a client there, it was not a hustling area, more mutual cruising than anything else. Days after the *Time* mistake, the area conducive to hitchhiking was suddenly converted into a hustling turf rivaling that on Selma—at a time when the arrests were decimating hustlers on that street.

Now, on weekends, malehustlers—thumbs held out in varying personal styles—stand at virtually every parking meter along the newly thriving thoroughfare, sometimes so busy now you have to walk for blocks to find a place for yourself. Cars drive around the blocks slowly, choosing.

This new style has the advantage that you're there legally—hitchhiking, not "loitering" (though cops have already begun their jealous harassment). The disadvantage is that you often get a ride from someone who doesn't know, or more often pretends not to know, that the hitchhikers are hustlers— a situation that has given rise to a breed of men who get off simply on giving hustlers a ride. You will see the same hustler a few minutes later hitchhiking back to the first turf—two small islands at the end of a stretch of a mile-and-a-half of street.

In summer especially, the heavy influx of drifters creates a sad spectacle. Goodlooking anxious youngmen—a whole spectrum, from the slender and blond to the tough and dark—wait eagerly, even signaling cars on slow nights, buyers' nights—eager youngmen being driven up and down the same street and hoping for a firm connection for the night.

And another change, this one internal—call it the subtle stirring of the radicalization of the malehustling contingent. Existing on the fringes of the gay world, male hustlers have always been dual outsiders, outlaws from the main society, and outcasts within the main gay world of hostile non-payers and non-sellers. Desired abundantly, and envied, they are nonetheless the least cared about. Routine mass roundups of hustlers occur with no outcry, virtually no manifestation of concern within the vast gay world—while a comparable gay roundup anywhere else will see mushrooming conferences called by ever-ready gay "spokesmen" before television cameras. An attorney points out that, compared to non-commercial gays, a disproportionate number of arrested hustlers will actually be jailed—because few can afford to pay for representation—hustlers are easy spenders, living from day to day—and because hustler arrests bring no free publicity for the lawyer who might defend them.

Still, during a gay parade on Hollywood Boulevard, groups of malehustlers of a breed notorious for their posture that they are not gay—"just hustling for bread"—cheered marching contingents of open homosexuals. When three hustlers were arrested for popping firecrackers near invading cops, a pressurized anger stirred palpably among the others. That very night on Selma, a group of girls sped by in a car and yelled, "Queers! Queers!" at the masculine, toughlooking hustlers milling about on the streets. Only a few years earlier that breed would have answered with a ball-wounded, "Come back and I'll show you who's queer!" Not that night. There was an almost total indifference. One of the most masculine of the streethustlers southerndrawled at the shouting women: "Yeah, we queer, so what?" It was as radical a statement as had ever been voiced on that street.

Concurrently, the camaraderie—an increasing camaraderie—among hustlers is easing in its strict role-playing, slowly but perceptibly. Unacceptable before—disastrous to one's masculine hustling image—comments are now lightly exchanged routinely admiring of each other's attractiveness or specialty—muscles, handsome faces, unique clothes style, even reputed cock size. There is still the uneasiness, the sexual uneasiness, among masculine hustlers, but more and more cross turfs back and forth, from hustling to mutual cruising of other males; indeed, a type of non-hustling, non-paying goodlooking youngmen now roam the hustling streets attracting equally goodlooking malehustlers, not with money but with their own good looks.

What remains unchanged are the lurking dangers of cop entrapment—and the brevity of the life on the hustling streets. A hustler's life *is* brief. Some hustlers begin in their young teens. New hustlers still arrive almost daily and find favorite spots nightly, on Selma or on the new turf *Time* created. The first weeks you won't wait around long, stepping in and out of cars friskily, waving back at your friends still waiting. Abruptly, the time of waiting stretches, the number of rides diminishes. You meet each other on the street and one of you asks, "What's happenin?" and the other answers noncommittally, shrugging, and asks back and the answer comes, "Not doin too good tonight, slow night." Even as you speak, fresh competition hops into cars, waving back at you. There is the awareness—perceived as yet by only the two of you—that on the street you're becoming a has-been before you ever were, really a "has."

On Selma late one night a young hustler, there week after week, passes, nods in the easy camaraderie that happens among street hustlers recognizing each other. "How's it goin?" "All right—with you?" He shrugs, "Could be better," and adds quickly, boosting himself, "Just made five bucks, the guy just played with my cock for a couple of minutes in his car, said he didn't have no place, I didn't even have to take my dick out—yeah, I made five bucks in a couple of minutes," spotting the same man still driving around the block choosing, "five bucks for a couple of minutes, can't beat that."

He was right—you couldn't beat five bucks for two minutes, that's $150 an hour! Right up there. More than psychiatrists make, at least now.

Unfortunately his clients, and the world that crowns youth only briefly, will make it impossible for him—unlike psychiatrists—to hook his clients for years.

Another night. Another corner. And a young hustler comes by; perhaps eighteen, wearing that beauty that exists only because it *is* eighteen. But wait: the special street-youthfulness is tattered. He's perhaps nineteen; perhaps even twenty. He recognizes me from other streets. "Hey, man, can I ask you a question?" I pull back in panic. I know what he's going to ask, he's already verbalizing it: "How old are you?"

I lie outrageously—but even the fake age makes him react—in implied admiration, yes, of my street survival, but his reaction wounds anyway, deeply: "Wow!—and you *still* got a good hustle." He's congratulating my survival, perhaps even envying it a tiny bit: For him at that age, what? "Am I dressed okay?" he asks me abruptly, nervously opening his shirt an extra button. "I mean, I'm not making it like I used to. I've been hanging around three hours today—and nothing!"

I'm still wounded by his question, his reaction—the specter of age is floating under the street light. But I feel wounded for him, too. I have my body cunningly constructed for street survival, and I have options—but he, at nineteen or twenty, the freshness of his youth is already tarnished. He's a thin, no-longer-boy.

Exploited? Oh, yes, unquestionably. Just as later tonight he may exploit; he may rob and beat up the next man who picks him up, or—but this is less likely—be robbed and beaten up himself. Most probably, both will make a bargain and go through with it.

And the influx will continue, the new faces and young bodies fresh among the straining older ones; an influx created at least in part—and hypocritically—by grotesquely bloated cop reports issued periodically and aimed, despite disclaimers, at making all homosexuals look like rich predators luring innocent youths. Because: A twelve-year-old boy can earn up to $1000 a day as a prostitute, a recent, incredibly absurd cop report—front-paged rashly without questioning by Los Angeles newspapers—claimed (imagine!—a new upper-class!—aging rock stars and twelve-year-old male prostitutes in Gucci gear!); a report issued in the wake of a sex scandal involving underage scout girls and cops and in the face of threats to cut the vice division's budget. A thousand dollars a day, hustling! That means there are many rich perverts just waiting to molest your little boy unless you give us a lot of money to bust them wherever they hang out, the insidious message is conveyed.

Left out is the fact that most of the men who pick up the very young on the streets (and unlike many who prefer the older ones) do not belong to the so-called "gay community" of upfront homosexuals, those who frequent gay bars, parks; no, they are loners, closeted victims of repression, quite often married, having children of their own, leading otherwise "straight" lives.

A thousand bucks a day hustling, man!

So dozens of boys line the streets, going for ten bucks on a slow night, even less when you're desperate for a place to sleep; finding kindness sometimes, yes, often, but just as often finding contemptuous men; and realizing that, finally, it's a buyer's market on the streets because the number of men who pick up hustlers remains relatively stable—they own cars, homes, have jobs, businesses, do not form a floating group—whereas the hustlers arrive in waves; new ones for the same buyers, the "older" hustlers thrust aside in as little as a few weeks.

Old youngmen and boys haunt the streets.

Then the cops raid the hustling turfs.

XXX HARDCORE

Netted, trapped, the youngest and most frightened of the hustlers will tell their captors whatever they want to hear. One thousand dollars a day? Yes, sure—a lot of rich fags out there. (But you have no money to get a lawyer.) A customer every fifteen minutes? Oh, yeah. (But the familiar corner became your enemy.) Thousands of customers? Yes—and all rich, famous, powerful, on TV. (But you can't call one to bail you out.) And so the terrified boys are offered up in sacrifice to exaggerated reports and shrieking headlines: HOMOSEXUALS PREYING ON INNOCENT BOYS!

Getting attention. These often lost, pitiful youngmen. Getting attention only when they're busted—and in order to whip up the frothing homophobia whenever the cops need it. Only then. Not before—or even after—when the options might be opened by genuine official concern for the young—the money-sucking agencies, bureaus, divisions, departments vomiting rancid sociologese and pieties; spewing nonsense; extending no real options to these boys (if they *want* options—because choice must be respected—and the psychic lure of the streets is strong, the life even glamorous in its trashy way, and you're a special, desired survivor—if you last) against whatever existence may bring about—unhappiness and exploitation, whether in the farm fields, dingy restaurant kitchens, or on the mean hustling streets.

The explosive, self-serving cop report issued, the citizens quivering anew over the "gay threat"—the boys will probably be back on the enticing streets, because, ultimately, nobody cared otherwise in the hypocritical agencies, bureaus, divisions, departments. Still young, many too young; boys and youngmen more knowledgeable now—because youth is no guarantee of innocence (as bands of preteenagers increasingly preying violently on the lame old attest), just as age is no affirmation of corruption.

Mutual exploitation—the old corrupt, the young corrupt. That is the nature of the ugly, devouring, beautiful, lonely, exciting, devastating, dead-end, glorious hustling streets.

No, you don't get rich on the streets—though you have good periods and at first it seems you might. True, a few hustlers will find one person who genuinely cares for them, even helps them into another life. But that's rare on the streets. Other hustlers will drop out, when the intervals of waiting stretch into nights—get jobs, marry, have children, perhaps even be relatively happy, more than likely eke out lives of screaming frustration. Others may move into the vaster gay world of non-commercial encounters, even form relationships. Some are only summer hustlers, returning "home" when the season is over. But the resourceless ones—yes, most of them—what happens when they're through on the exciting, tough streets, those once-good-looking, once-youngmen cocky in their desirability, remembering the cars that braked eagerly, the often-beautiful homes their looks opened so easily? They disappear.

And on skid row—if you care to look—you may now and then see among the others a singularly doomed old man. Something makes you look again. Lurking in the weather-scorched brown face is the lingering breath of a special magic, the thin, sad ghost of the conquering youngman he was.

ANNIE SPRINKLE

Hardcore from the Heart

California Lawyer magazine invited me to write an article for them. I was delighted to reach a new audience and to get to tell war stories of my legal battles, both in my sex work and my performance art work. Also I was dating a lawyer at the time and I wanted to impress her. I wrote this piece during the heat of the O.J. Simpson trial.

My FIRST BRUSH WITH the law was when I was an eighteen-year-old hippie in Tucson, Arizona. I got a job selling popcorn at a theater that was showing a new movie called *Deep Throat*. The XXX-rated movie was immensely popular: college students, married couples, and all kinds of folk lined up alongside the raincoat brigade to buy their tickets. After several prosperous months, the theater where I worked was shut down and the film confiscated by police. An obscenity trial ensued. I was subpoenaed as a witness for the prosecution and was ordered to hang out in the witness room for two weeks with Linda Lovelace and the film's director Gerard Damiano (a handsome and charming 46-year-old Italian gentleman). Waiting around to be called to the stand was a bit dull, so to pass the time, Damiano gave me "deep throat lessons." I had to take the stand briefly, which I consider my first public performance. Fortunately, lawyer Louis Nizer won this important case for freedom of expression, and Damiano and I won each other's hearts.

I moved to New York City to be Gerard's mistress and got a job as an apprentice in film-making at Kirt Films, a company which created dozens of 16mm porn films. The apprenticeship didn't pay anything, so I worked weekends at Spartacus Spa, which in the late 1970s was Manhattan's fanciest "massage parlor" (legal jargon for whorehouse). I entertained and had sex with all kinds of men, from the rich and famous, to Hassidic Jewish businessmen, from Mafia gangsters, to police officers. Naturally I had quite a few clients who worked as judges and lawyers. The men of the legal profession were generally respectful, good tippers (often we made about the same hourly wage), and always in a hurry to get back to work. They came to me racked with stress and tension, and left feeling relaxed and blissful. I could take pride in my work. I'm convinced that without prostitution, the legal system could not function.

Being that prostitution was/is illegal, it was reassuring to know I always had a lawyer to defend me if need be. Often there were busts and arrests, but lucky for me they always came down on my days off. I continued to do prostitution for twenty years. I've always been involved in the grass-roots movement to decriminalize prostitution—the political cause which is most near and dear to my heart. We've made some baby steps. It's really about time that someone, somehow, challenged the prostitution laws and got them thrown in the garbage where they belong. It is absurd and mean-spirited to make consensual sex a crime.

After several months of working behind the cameras at Kirt Films, I decided it looked like more fun to be in front, so someone wrote me a two-page script called *Teenage Deviate*. After the eighteen hours it took to complete the shooting of this not-so-major motion picture, a porn star was born. I went on to make 150 features and fifty 8mm loops, and have my name in lights on Broadway. Sometimes my films got into legal conflicts. Mostly the film's distributors and producers dealt with these problems, which was great, but I did pay a price. My biggest hit was *Deep Inside Annie Sprinkle* (the number two biggest-selling video in 1982), which I not only starred in, but wrote and directed. The producers and distributors decided to self-censor the film because theaters where the film was shown (mostly the Pussycat chain in California) were taking a lot of heat (no pun intended). I was disappointed with the final censored version of my movie, which became known as "the California version."

For a couple years I did a stint as a stripper. Traveling the bumpy burlesque trail I got to see just how ridiculous laws could be, and how clever the lawyers could be in helping us get around those laws. For example, in one city the law demanded "no full nudity." So we simply kept our g-strings on when we took our bras off, and put our bras back on before we took off our g-strings. It was full nudity, but not all at once. In another city, the law said "no nudity and liquor allowed at the same address," so a glass wall was built between the bar and the stage, and each side of the glass was given a different address. In yet another city, the law insisted that "dancer's nipples had to be covered." So dancers had to paint them over with clear liquid latex which kept us legal, but made our nipples painfully irritated. Doesn't anyone see how silly this all is? Why do "citizens have to be protected" from dancing nude women?

Miraculously the only time I was ever actually arrested was in Jamestown, Rhode Island. I was at the home of my friends, erotic entrepreneurs Mickey and Susan Leblovic and Dutch artist Willem de Ridder. We were putting together a little, avant-gardish, one-shot sex magazine, with my diary excerpts and various photos. It was a labor of love, as we had no hopes of making much money from it, if any. We needed a typesetter, so we placed a help wanted ad in the local newspaper. Little did we know we'd hired an undercover police woman, who cheerfully worked side by side with us for a month. To create something extra special for the climax, my friend, amputee centerfold, Long Jean Silver, came up from New York and we did a playful photo shoot, thoroughly enjoying each other's bodies, including her penetrating me with her sexy 16" stump leg. I was delighted by our efforts. The moment our masterpiece was completed, twenty-five state police (one-third of their entire department), along with our "typesetter," entered the house, guns drawn and pointed, wielding search and arrest warrants. Seems we had been under surveillance for a month, wire taps and all. We were charged with over a hundred felony counts combined: "conspiracy to make and distribute obscene material," "sodomy," and my personal favorite, "conspiracy to commit sodomy." In Rhode Island, sodomy is defined as "an abominable, detestable act against nature," which is apparently what some folks consider sex with amputees. My experience with Jean felt loving and liberating, and I assure you, nature was not offended at all.

We were thrown into freezing cold jail cells with no blankets or toothbrushes for forty-eight hours, treated like murderers by police officers and portrayed that way by the press. We gained comfort by planning a massive demonstration with hundreds of amputees and people in wheelchairs on the steps of the courthouse and by making up our own lyrics to famous protest songs like "We Shall Overcum."

Finally we were released on bail. Our friends in New York threw a benefit for us to raise funds to pay our lawyers, William Kunstler and Paul DeMaio. It was of course a sex party, held at Plato's Retreat (Manhattan's infamous sex club). The who's who of the sex world was there. Mickey even invited several vice officers from the Rhode Island police department and they came (no pun intended) and even paid for their tickets. (A week later internal affairs held an investigation and some were suspended from their jobs!) Paul DeMaio, who was also a judge at the time, came, and almost got thrown off his bench after his photo appeared on the front page of the *Providence Journal* surrounded by a bevy of unauthorized women.

Eventually all our charges were dropped except for poor Mickey Leblovic's, who was found guilty of two counts of conspiracy to publish and distribute obscene material, and was sentenced to four years in prison (he served eighteen months). Now that's truly obscene! It was totally unjust. I was never able to recover my seized belongings—all my favorite sex toys, my bras and panties, the dog's leash, my toothbrush, a box of Tampax, my douche bag, or my personal nude snapshots of a lover who happened to be a New York City police officer. (He got in big trouble at his job. Oops.)

The arrest only fueled the flames of my desire to help make the world a more sexually mature and compassionate place. I continued to explore the vast frontiers of sexuality and to share and document my experiences and findings with explicit films, photography, writing and performance. However, being in jail did scare the shit out of me (although in actual fact, I got horribly constipated), so I took refuge in the art world where surprisingly I was made to feel quite welcome and found that I could be more myself and have a more eclectic aesthetic. There was much more creative freedom, less censorship, and more legal protection. For example, in various prestigious art theaters, I did a performance art piece where I inserted a speculum and invited the audience members to line up and each individually have a look at my cervix with the aid of a flashlight. Then I followed it up with a beautiful "sacred sex magic, masturbation ritual." If I had done the same thing at 42nd Street's Show World Center, not only would the audience not have liked or appreciated it, but I would have quickly been arrested, found guilty of breaking some silly law, and could possibly have gone to jail.

Of course artists do have their legal battles as well. There was never any problem anywhere in Europe, but in the US, every theater where I performed my controversial one-woman show *Annie Sprinkle, Post-Porn Modernist* had its lawyers standing by ready to bail me out of jail and fight the good fight. Although I came close many times, I was never arrested. Guess I had "socially redeeming value" on my side. My name did get dragged through the mud on the US senate floor, by that adorable Senator Jesse Helms, in the debate over government funding for the arts. (All of the theaters where I had performed received some of the government's measly stipends.) For me, dealing with censorship and anti-sex laws is a way of life, something I deal with on a daily basis. I, and my peers, have experienced enormous amounts of harassment and abuse from bigoted, ignorant, sex-phobic people with their archaic, classist, misogynist laws.

There is a bright side. At a Chicago conference on Censorship in the Arts I fell madly in love with one of the lawyers who fought, and won, the "NEA 4 case" against the National Endowment for the Arts. She was absolutely brilliant, charismatic, charming, and had a passion for women and their rights. We were lovers for almost a year.

Thus began my uncontrollable romantic obsession and intense sexual fetish for female lawyers. I absolutely melt next to someone wearing a grey pin-striped suit, with big hard law books, carrying a soft leather case over-flowing with important briefs. I adore a lover who speaks Latin, can litigate, draft petitions, has the power to sue, and get someone out of a death sentence. Give me a stuffy, conservative office to make love in after hours. Give me a person who works out on the stairmaster of their mind, deconstructing and reconstructing contracts. Give me a lawyer whose job creates lots of stress and tension which I can lovingly and passionately relieve. Give me love letters on legal pads. Give me lesbian lawyer love.

I do hope that all my future brushes with the law, of which there will no doubt be many more, are primarily of a romantic, sensual nature. Lawyers do make the best motions.

TERRY SOUTHERN AND MASON HOFFENBERG

Candy

THE HUNCHBACK HAD A sip of the wine and spat it in the towel.

Through the open door of the kitchen, Candy could be seen moving about, and now she was bending over to put something into the oven. In the tight jeans, her round little buttocks looked so firm and ripe that any straight-thinking man would have rushed in at once to squeeze and bite them; but the hunchback's mind was filled with freakish thoughts. From an emotional standpoint, he would rather have been in the men's room down at Jack's Bar on the Bowery, eating a piece of urine-soaked bread while thrusting his hump against someone from the Vice Squad. And yet, though he had decided that she was nutty (and because of this she was of no use to his ego), he was also vaguely aware that she was a mark; and, in an obscure, obstacle-strewn way, he was trying to think about this now: *how to get the money.* He wasn't too good at it, however, for his sincerity of thought was not direct enough: he didn't really feel he *needed* money, but rather that he *should* feel he needed it. It was perhaps the last vestige of normalcy in the hunchback's values; it only cropped up now and then.

"Onion omelet," Candy announced with a flourish as she entered, "hope you like tarragon and lots of garlic," and she put it on the table. "Looks good, doesn't it?" She felt she could say this last with a certain innocent candor, because her friends assured her she was a very good cook.

Aside from an occasional grunt and snort, the hunchback kept silent throughout the meal and during Candy's lively commentary, while into his image-laden brain now and then shot the primal questions: "*Where? No kill! How? Without kill! Where?*"

This silence of his impressed Candy all the more, making her doubly anxious to win his approval. "Oh, but here I'm talking away a mile, and you can't get in a single word!" She beamed, and nodded with a show of wisdom, "Or isn't it really that there's nothing to say—'would it have been worth while *after all*, et cetera, et cetera.' Yes, *I* know . . . oh, there's the tea now. *Tea!* Good night, *I'm* still on Eliot—the darling old fuddy, don't you *love* him? It's coffee, of course. Espresso. I won't be a minute. . . . Have some of the Camembert, not too *bien fait*, I'm afraid, but . . ." She rushed out to the kitchen, still holding her napkin, while the hunchback sat quietly, munching his bread. It was hardly the first time he had been involved in affairs of this sort.

When the darling girl returned, she suggested they move over to the couch to have their coffee. There she sat close beside him and leafed through a book of Blake's reproductions.

"Aren't they a *groove*," she was saying, "they're *so* funny! Most people don't get it at all!" She looked up at the wall opposite, where another print was hanging, and said gleefully: "And don't you just love *that* one? The details, I mean, did you ever look at it closely? Let me get it."

The print was hanging by a wire placed high, and Candy had to reach. She couldn't quite get it at first, and for a long moment she was standing there, lithe and lovely, stretching upward, standing on the tiptoes of one foot, the other out like a ballet-dancer's. As she strained higher, she felt the sinews of her calf rounding firmly and the edge of her flannel shirt lifting gently above her waist and upward across her bare back, while the muscles of her darling little buttocks tightened and thrust out taut beneath the jeans. Oh, I *shouldn't!* she thought, making another last effort to reach the print. What if he thinks I'm . . . well, it's *my* fault, darn it!

As it happened, the hunchback *was* watching her and, with the glimpse of her bare waist, it occurred to him suddenly, as though the gray sky itself had fallen, that, as for the other girls who had trafficked with him, what they had wanted was to be ravenously desired—to be so overwhelmingly physically needed that, despite their every effort to the contrary for a real and spiritual rapport, their beauty so powerfully, undeniably asserted itself as to reduce the complex man to simple beast . . . who must be fed.

By the time Candy had the print down and had reached the couch with it, the eyes of the hunchback were quite changed; they seemed to be streaked with red now, and they were very bright. The precious girl noticed it at once, and she was a little flustered as she sat down, speaking rapidly, pointing to the print: "Isn't this too *much?* Look at this figure, here in the corner, most people don't even . . ." She broke off for a moment to cough and blush terribly as the hunchback's eyes devoured her, glistening. In an effort to regain composure, she touched her lovely curls and gave a little toss of her head. 'What *can* he be thinking?' she asked herself. 'Well, it's my own fault, darn it!' The small eyes of the hunchback blazed; he was thinking of *money*. "I love you!" he said then quickly, the phrase sounding odd indeed.

"Oh, darling, *don't* say that!" said Candy, imploring, as though she had been quite prepared, yet keeping her eyes down on the book.

"I want very much!" he said, touching her arm at the elbow.

She shivered just imperceptibly and covered his hand with her own. "You mustn't say that," she said with softness and dignity.

"*I want fuck you!*" he said, putting his other hand on her pert left breast.

She clasped his hand, holding it firmly, as she turned to him, her eyes closed, a look of suffering on her face. "No, darling, please" she murmured and she was quite firm.

"I want fuck—suck you!" he said, squeezing the breast while she felt the sweet little nipple reaching out like a tiny mushroom.

She stood up abruptly, putting her hands to her face. "Don't. Please don't," she said. She stood there a moment, then walked to the window. "Oh why must it be like this?" she beseeched the dark sky of the failing day. "Why? Why?" She turned and was about to repeat it, but the voice of the hunchback came first.

"Is because of *this?*" he demanded. "Because of *this?*" He was sitting there with a wretched expression on his face, and one arm raised and curled behind his head, pointing at his hump.

Candy came forward quickly, like a nurse in emergency. "No, you poor darling, of course it isn't! *No, no,*" and the impetus of her flight carried her down beside him again and put him in her arms. "You silly darling!" She closed her eyes, leaning her face against his as she stroked his head. "I hadn't even noticed," she said.

"Why, then?" he wanted to know. "*Why?*"

Now that she had actually touched him, she seemed more at ease. "*Why?*" she sighed. "Oh, I don't know. Girls are like that, never quite knowing what they want—or need. Oh, I don't know, I want it to be *perfect,* I guess."

"Because of *this,*" repeated the hunchback, shrugging heavily.

"No, you darling," she cooed, insisting, closed-eyed again, nudging his cheek with her nose, "no, no, no. What earthly *difference* does it make! I have blue eyes—you have that. What possible earthly difference does it make?"

"*Why?*" he demanded, reaching up under her shirt to grasp one of her breasts, then suddenly pulling her brassiere up and her shoulder back, and thrusting forward to cover the breast with his mouth. Candy sobbed, "*Oh darling, no,*" but allowed her head to recline gently against the couch. "Why does it have to be like this?" she pleaded. "Why? Oh, I know it's my own fault, darn it." And she let him kiss and suck her breast, until the nipple became terribly taut and she began to tingle all down through her precious tummy, then she pulled his head away, cradling it in her arms, her own eyes shimmering with tears behind a brave smile. "No, darling," she implored, "*please* . . . not now.*"

"Because of *this,*" said the hunchback bitterly.

"No, no, no," she cried, closing her eyes and hugging the head to her breast, holding his cheek against it, but trying to keep his mouth from the proud little nipple, "no, no, *not* because of that!"

"I want!" said the hunchback, with one hand on her hip now undoing the side buttons of her jeans; then he swiftly forced the hand across the panty sheen of her rounded tummy and down into the sweet damp.

"Oh, darling, no!" cried the girl, but it was too late, without making a scene, for anything to be done; his stubby fingers were rolling the little clitoris like a marble in oil. Candy leaned back in resignation, her heart too big to deprive him of this if it meant so much. With her head closed-eyed, resting again on the couch, she would endure it as long as she could. But, before she reached the saturation point, he had nuzzled his face down from her breast across her bare stomach and into her lap, bending his arm forward to force down her jeans and panties as he did, pulling at them on the side with his other hand.

"No, no, darling!" she sighed, but he soon had them down below her knees, at least enough so to replace his fingers with his tongue.

It means so much to him, Candy kept thinking, *so* much, as he meanwhile got her jeans and panties down completely so that they dangled now from one slender ankle as he adjusted her legs and was at last on the floor himself in front of her, with her legs around his neck, and his mouth very deep inside the fabulous honeypot.

"If it means so much," Candy kept repeating to herself, until she didn't think she could bear it another second, and she wrenched herself free, saying *"Darling, oh darling,"* and seized his head in her hands with a great show of passion.

"Oh, why?" she begged, holding his face in her hands, looking at him mournfully. "Why?"

"I *need fuck you!"* said the hunchback huskily. He put his face against the upper softness of her marvelous bare leg. Small, strange sounds came from his throat.

"Oh, darling, darling," the girl keened pitifully, "I can't bear your crying." She sighed, and smiled tenderly, stroking his head.

"I *think* we'd better go into the bedroom," she said then, her manner suddenly prim and efficient.

In the bathroom, standing before the glass, Candy finished undressing—unbuttoning her shirt, slowly, carefully, a lamb resigned to the slaughter, dropping the shirt to the floor, and taking off her brassiere, gradually revealing her nakedness to herself, with a little sigh, almost of wistful regret, at how *very* lovely she was, and at how her nipples grew and stood out like cherrystones, as they always did when she watched herself undress. How he *wants* me! she thought. Well, it's my own fault, darn it! And she tried to imagine the raging lust that the hunchback felt for her as she touched her curls lightly. Then she cast a last glimpse at herself in the glass, blushing at her own loveliness, and trembling slightly at the very secret notion of this beauty-and-beast sacrifice, she went back into the bedroom.

The hunchback was lying naked, curled on his side like a big foetus, when Candy appeared before him, standing for a moment in full lush radiance, a naked angel bearing the supreme gift. Then, she got into bed quickly, under the sheet, almost soundlessly, saying, *"Darling, darling,"* and cuddling him to her at once, while he, his head filled with the most freakish thoughts imaginable—all about tubs of living and broken toys, every manner of excrement, scorpions, steelwool, pig-masks, odd metal harness, etc.—tried desperately to pry into the images a single reminder: *the money!*

"Do you want to kiss me some more, darling?" asked the girl with deadly soft seriousness, her eyes wide, searching his own as one would a child's.

XXX HARDCORE

Then she sighed and lay back, slowly taking the sheet from her, again to make him the gift of all her wet, throbbing treasures, as he, glazed-eyed and grunting, slithered down beside her.

"Don't hurt me, darling," she murmured, as in a dream, while he parted the exquisitely warm round thighs with his great head, his mouth opening the slick lips all sugar and glue, and his quick tongue finding her pink candy clit at once.

"Oh, darling, darling," she said, stroking his head gently, watching him, a tender courageous smile on her face.

The hunchback put his hands under her, gripping the foam-rubber balls of her buttocks, and sucked and nibbled her tiny clit with increasing vigor. Candy closed her eyes and gradually raised her legs, straining gently upward now, dropping her arms back by her head, one to each side, pretending they were pinioned there, writhing slowly, sobbing—until she felt she was no longer giving, but was on the verge of taking, and, as with an effort, she broke her hands from above her and grasped the hunchback's head and lifted it to her mouth, coming forward to meet him, kissing him deeply. "Come inside me, darling," she whispered urgently, "I want you *inside* me!"

The hunchback, his brain seething with pure strangeness, hardly heard her. He had forgotten about the money, but did know that *something* was at stake, and his head was about to burst in trying to recall what it was. Inside his mind was like a gigantic landslide of black eels, billions of them, surging past, one of which held the answer. His job: *catch it!* Catch it, and chew off the top of its head; and there, in the gurgling cup, would be . . . the *message*: "You have forgotten about . . . ?"

But which eel was it? While his eyes grew wilder and rolled back until only the whites showed, Candy, thinking that he was beside himself with desire for her, covered his face with sweet wet kisses, until he suddenly went stiff in her arms as his racing look stopped abruptly on the floor near the bed: it was a coat hanger, an ordinary wire coat hanger, which had fallen from the closet, and the hunchback flung himself out of the bed and onto the floor, clutching the hanger to him feverishly. Then, as in a fit of bitter triumph, he twisted it savagely into a single length of coiled black wire, and gripping it so tightly that his entire body shook for a moment, he lunged forward, one end of it locked between his teeth. *He thought it was the eel.*

Candy had started up, half sitting now, one hand instinctively to her pert, pulsating breast.

"Darling, what is it?" she cried. "Darling, you *aren't* going to . . ."

The hunchback slowly rose, as one recovered from a seizure of apoplexy, seeming to take account of his surroundings anew, and, just as he had learned from the eel's head that the forgotten issue was money, so too he believed now that the girl wanted to be beaten.

"*Why*, darling?" pleaded Candy, curling her lovely legs as the hunchback slowly raised the black wire snake above his head. "*Why? Why?*" she cried.

And as he began to strike her across the back of her legs, she sobbed, "Oh, why, darling, why?" her long round limbs twisting, as she turned and writhed, her arms back beside her head as before, moving too except at the wrist where they were as stiff as though clamped there with steel, and she was saying: "Yes! *Hurt* me! Yes, yes! Hurt me as *they* have hurt you!" and now her ankles as well seemed secured, shackled to the spot, as she lay, spread-eagled, sobbing piteously, straining against her invisible bonds, her lithe round body arching upward, hips circling slowly, mouth wet, nipples taut, her teeny piping clitoris distended and throbbing, and her eyes glistening like fire, as she devoured all the penitence for each injustice ever done to hunchbacks of the world; and as it continued she slowly opened her eyes, that all the world might see the tears there—but instead she herself saw, through the rise and fall of the wire lash—the hunchback's white gleaming hump! The *hump*, the white, unsunned forever, radish-root white of hump, and it struck her, more sharply than the wire whip, as something she had seen before—the naked, jutting buttocks, upraised in a sexual thrust, not a thrust of taking, but of *giving*, for it had been an image in a hospital room mirror, of her own precious buttocks, naked and upraised, gleaming white, and thrusting downwards, as she had been made to do in giving herself to her Uncle Jack!

With a wild impulsive cry, she shrieked: "*Give me your hump!*"

The hunchback was startled for a moment, not comprehending.

"Your *hump*, your *hump*!" cried the girl, "GIVE ME YOUR HUMP!"

The hunchback hesitated, and then lunged headlong toward her, burying his hump between Candy's legs as she hunched wildly, pulling open her little labias in an absurd effort to get it in her.

"Your hump! Your hump!" she kept crying, scratching and clawing at it now.

"Fuck! Shit! Piss!" she screamed. "Cunt! Cock! Crap! Prick! Kike! Nigger! Wop! *Hump!* HUMP!" and she teetered on the blazing peak of pure madness for an instant . . . and then dropped down, slowly, through gray and grayer clouds into a deep, soft, black, night.

XXX HARDCORE

Dennis Cooper

Period

With a jab of his elbow, Nate broke the store's window. No alarm, nothing. Leon reached through the uneven star and came back with a shit-load of jewelry.

They ran until they'd reached that weird place only they recognized.

Leon was so spent, he couldn't think shit. The necklaces, watches, and pins formed a garish-ass pile in the grass. It looked for all the world like Satan's hatchet face laughing or yelling in profile, from their angle at least.

The sky was so muggy and black they could barely stand up. They'd been snorting crystal meth every hour for hours. Leon felt nothing but horny for Nate by this point. That hurt. Everything was hateful apart from how wildly he longed for the fucker.

Leon shut his eyes, reopened them, and made himself look available. He never could figure out how he did that. Except that it came maybe ninety per-cent from the way he was built.

Nate removed article after article of clothing until there was technical human perfection, as far as Leon was concerned. There shouldn't have been anyone in the world that important. It killed him.

John Rechy

City of Night

Among the bands of malehustlers that hang out in downtown Los Angeles, there are often a few stray girls: They are quite young, usually pre-maturely hardened, toughlooking even when theyre pretty. They know all about the youngmen they make it with and sometimes live with: that those youngmen hustle and clip other males. And aware of this, they dont seem to care. Occasionally, one of those girls will go into the park with a malehus-tler, sitting there until he will maybe spot a score; and then, as if by tacit agreement, theyll split: the youngman going off with the score, the girl back to Hooper's coffee-and-donuts, where, in the afternoons at that time, they usually hung out.

One among them intrigued me especially. She was the prettiest—about 19, with long ashblonde hair and hypnotic eyes. She always looked at you with a half-smile that was somehow wistful, as if for her the world, though sad, still amused her. I knew from Buddy, who had been with her and who dug her ("But shes kinda strange," he said, "like she aint always there"), that she lived with three malehustlers in a small downtown apartment—one of them the squarefaced youngman I had been interrogated with that afternoon in Pershing Square. . . . She was very hip—she talked like all the rest, and very tough. But with her, somehow, it all seemed wrong, incongruous in a way I couldnt really understand. It wasnt only that she was so pretty; some of the others were too. It was something else, something altogether different about her from the others. . . . A kind of toughmasked lonesomeness.

One afternoon, at Hooper's, I sat near her at the counter. Outside, the cops had stopped a madeup queen. The girl next to me smiles and says: "Oh, oh, another queen busted—for 'jay-walking.'" I moved next to her, and for the next few minutes we spoke easily. Then I caught her looking at me very strangely. She says unexpectedly: "You know, man, theres something that bugs me about you. Ive seen you in the park and around here, and you look like all the others—but theres something else." I was surprised to hear her say about me precisely what I thought about her. At the same time, I panicked: I don't like people to know me too well. . . . "I mean," she went on, "like you never really hang around too much with the others—and you dont talk to anyone too much." . . .

We left Hooper's and went into the park, sitting there briefly, listening to the afternoon preachers. It felt good to be sitting here with this girl, to be seen with her by some of the men I had scored from.

Abruptly, as if suddenly bugged by the park, she asked me to come up to her place. "I live with three guys," she said, "but they're always out here in the afternoon."

The door to the apartment is open. "It's always unlocked," she said. "If you ever need a pad, come up—we got lots of room."

The cramped apartment is completely disheveled—unwashed dishes piled in the sink, frozen-food trays and beer cans discarded on the floor—her clothes and those of the others strewn all over the rooms. There were two beds in the one bedroom, a couch, and a mattress on the floor.

Again I catch her looking at me in that strange way—and she said—just like this—just as abruptly and unexpectedly at this: "I bet you dig Bartok."

XXX HARDCORE

I told her yes.

"Me, too, man," she said. "See, I knew it . . . Thats what I meant when I said something about you bugged me. I mean, you *look* like you belong but— . . . Why do you hang around this scene?" she asked me.

"I dont know," I answered her.

"I dont really know why I hang around either," she said.

From under one bed, she pulls out a cheap record-player, and there was a record already on the turntable. "It's the only one Ive got," she said. It begins to play: Bartok's *Music for Strings, Percussion and Celesta*. Scratchily on the cheap machine—but still beautifully—it plays the haunting, haunted music.

I lay beside her on the rumpled bed, and I hold her hand—which is very cold—while the music played; and she pressed herself suddenly against me with a huge lost franticness.

"Man," she said, "I know the scene: Youve got to pretend you dont give a damn and swing along with those that really dont—or you go under. . . ."

Startlingly, as I rolled over on her, she gets up suddenly. Suddenly she looks mean. "Why dont you get out of that scene?" she snaps. "All of you keep telling yourselves youre straight—and you make it with chicks to prove it—and when you make it with other guys, you say it's only for the bread—and besides, with them, you dont do anything back in bed—if you dont! . . . Sure, maybe it's true—Now!" She turns the record off. "Why dont you split the scene, man—*if you really want to!*" she said. Then in a tone that was as much bitter as mean, she challenged: "I bet youve never even clipped a wallet from those guys you go with."

I remember the almost-time. . . . "No."

"Get out of it—now!" she said. "Get a job!"

"I've worked more than you think," I said, strangely defensive.

"But you always come back," she thrust at me quickly.

"Yes."

"Then why?"

"I dont know," I said again.

She returns to the bed. And now she begins to remove her clothes. . . . As we clung to each other in a kind of franticness, she said:

"My name is Barbara."

I would meet her at Hooper's after that, and later we'd go to her apartment. Always, she plays that one record. I would hold her while the music played. And yet, always, the meanness would recur. "Cool it," she said once, when I was coming on with her. She went into the bathroom, returned with a rubber. "You never know what the hell you guys have had your pricks in," she said brutally.

"What about you?" I came back at her just as brutally. "Every hustler in the park's had you—several times." I regretted it instantly.

"I know," she sighs almost sadly. . . .

Afterwards, for those times I was with her, she would lie like a lost child, huddled and small and warm now. And somehow terrified. . . .

Then for several days she didnt show at Hooper's. Buddy told me she'd asked the three malehustlers she had been living with to move out. "You getting hung up on that chick, or something?" he asked me. I told him no. But the next day, when she didnt turn up, I went to the apartment.

For the first time, the door is locked. I knocked very long before anyone answered. Now the door opens. She stood there in her slip—and she looks strangely prettier than I had ever seen her: those strange eyes staring at me, into me.

"Im sorry," she said hurriedly, breathlessly, "I cant see you now." She was about to close the door.

"Now or later," another voice said—a woman's voice. I looked beyond the door, and a tall, slender girl I had never seen before is standing there, dressed in black slacks. She looked at me with almost-hatred. "Shag, man," she said roughly, "I mean, split—Barbara dont need you guys any more. . . . Shes got me."

And she put her arm intimately about the other's bare shoulders.

Now, seized by a feeling of loss which had to do with Barbara—but also with something unrecognized which extended beyond her—I went to clean-aired San Francisco (where I would return—later—and stay much longer)—but soon I was back in Los Angeles.

The park, then, was hot with cops. Days earlier, a young vagrant had murdered a girl who had just arrived in town—and during the time that followed—vengefully—vengefully for not having spotted the psyched-up stud before the papers implicated them—the bulls stormed the park. And all the young drifters stayed away.

And Main Street, though also fuzzhot, is even more crowded now.

When the bars close on Main Street, their world spills into the streets. Malehustlers, queens, scores—all those who havent made it yet in one way or another—or have made it and are trying again—disperse into the night, squeezing every inch of nightlife from the streets.

They stand pretending to be looking into store windows—continue their searches into the all-night moviehouses—the burlesque-movie theaters, where along the dark rows, in the early jammed hours of the morning on weekends, men sit, fly open, pulling off. . . . Or the scattered army goes to Hooper's on Main Street—where periodically the cops come in, walk up and down the counter sullenly, picking you out at random—and youre suddenly intensely studying the cup of coffee before you.

Life is lived on the brink of panic on the streets, intensifying the immediate experience—the realness of Today, of This Moment—Now!—and panic is generated by the threat of the vice-squad (plainclothesmen sitting in the known heads licking their lips; sometimes roaming the streets, even offering you money before they bust you); by the copcar driving along the streets—a slowly moving hearse. Like a gang looking for a rumble from a rival gang, cops haunt this area, personally vindictive. . . .

And for the homeless drifters there is also the panic that one day youll wake up to the fact that youre through on the streets, in the bars—that everyone has had you, that those who havent have lost Interest—that youve been replaced by the fresher faces that come daily into the city in that shifting wave of vagrants—younger than you now (and Youth is at a premium), and now the interest you once felt is focused on someone else. One day someone will say about you: "I had him when he was young and pretty."

And as a reminder of this, beyond Los Angeles Street, in the same area of the world of Main Street but not really a part of it, is Skid Row—and you see prematurely old defeated men, flying on Thunderbird or Gallo wine, lost in this sunny rosy haven—hanging shaggily like zombies waiting for the Mission to open; folded over in a pool of their own urine where theyve passed out along the alleys. . . .

If youre young, you avoid that street, you concentrate on Today.

Tomorrow, like Death, is inevitable but not thought of. . . .

At night, the fat Negro woman sprawled like chocolate pudding between Harry's Bar and Wally's mumblingly coaxes you to take a copy from the slender stack of religious magazines falling from her lap to her fat tired feet. The magazine shouts: AWAKE!

And along that strip, the gray hotels welcome the scores and malehustlers: No Questions Asked. For a few minutes—unless you havent got another place and stay all night—you occupy the fleetingly rented room, where inevitably a neonlight outside will wink off and on feebly like exhausted but persistent lightning. . . . Throughout the night there are sounds of rapid footsteps running down the stairs.

In the morning, if you stay, you walk out into the harsh daylight. The sun bursts cruelly in your eyes. For one blinding instant you see yourself clearly.

The day begins again. . . . The same.

Today!

XXX HARDCORE

TIM MILLER

Shirts & Skin

I HAD A CLUTCHING-at-straws faith in safe sex, and I convinced myself that I could trust its principles. I structured my understanding of the world around its precepts. It behooved me to have that faith because I was having sex with a *lot* of people in the early '90s. I had to believe in safe sex just like I had to believe in other forces essential for life: gravity, photosynthesis, friction. I felt compelled to be a party-liner about safe sex because this system helped me to keep my fears at bay. That faith allowed me to get up in the morning, make my breakfast, and not have a nervous breakdown.

Since Andrew and I had been careful in our sex, according to the accepted mores of the time, this was a perfectly responsible time to have a discussion, if indeed we even needed to have it. The subject came up on its own, as it so often does.

I said, "Andrew, it's intense to be here, lying in a bed on East Sixth Street, talking about all this relationship material. My boyfriend John, the guy I told you about who died of AIDS, he used to live on Sixth, just down the block."

"Ouch," Andrew said, hugging his arms around me. We breathed together for a bit. "It sucks, I know. My ex-boyfriend back in California is pretty sick right now. I worry about him a lot."

We held this close between us as we circled the subject like hunters tracking a wild animal. The about-to-stampede elephant was in bed with us now.

"So, Andrew . . . um . . ." I hemmed and hawed, trying to spit out the obvious question. "Where are you in all of this AIDS stuff?"

"I'm positive," Andrew said, looking directly at me. "I just found out a little while ago. What about you?"

"I'm negative," I replied after an exhale whistled between my front teeth. "The one time I checked, anyway. I could hardly believe it, considering my history. You know . . . John and all."

Well, the cards were on the table: It was a full house. The cameras zoomed in for the close-up. Everything was going real slow, spooky and sci-fi. At this point there was a hydrogen bomb blast over the East River. This explosion blared through the windows onto our bodies, burning away the bullshit between Andrew and me. I witnessed a powerful moment between two human faggots at the end of the twentieth century.

I felt as if a strange bird, strange as the subject at hand, had flown into Andrew's bedroom. This creature was a little clumsy, like Big Bird, as it broke through the glass and flapped around Andrew's room, knocking his high school graduation pictures off the wall. This bird landed at the end of Andrew's futon and looked at us. This bird, like this moment between us, could be fierce or friendly. It was totally up to us.

I looked Andrew in the eye. I had nothing useful to say, nothing that wouldn't collapse under the weight of its own structure of obvious verbs and insufficient adjectives. I felt our fates float around us for a moment. There was a hurt that hovered over Andrew's face for an even tinier instant.

"I hope you're not freaked out that I didn't tell you earlier," Andrew said quietly, looking down toward our feet.

"No." I said the right thing, though I knew no single word could describe the snarl of feelings that were revving up inside me. Without thinking, I quickly toured the inside of my mouth with my tongue to see if I had any canker sores there. Everything seemed okay. "I'm a big boy. I know how to take care of myself."

Then I put my lips on Andrew's. Our tongues touched, and it was like a promise, eyes open, hearts too. Andrew and I started to make love again. We moved our hands over the hills and valleys of our bodies just as we had a few hours before. Our fingers sketched across the details and limits of our skin and shape, and I felt a powerful mix of excitement and fear. What was different now? There was an honest thrill in knowing who we really are.

I knew something special had happened. I didn't want to make it into a big deal. In a way it was just how things were, our lives as we need to live them. I wasn't even sure what any of this positive/negative information meant anymore. But if I tried to say it meant nothing to me at that moment, that would have been a lie, a whopper of a lie. I was so tired of lying.

I had been in this situation before, of course, with other men who were positive. There was a guy from Cedar Rapids. And a fellow from Spokane. One man was white. Another man was black. I confess they were all cute. All dear. All very hot. I am weak.

One of these men used to lead workshops in Texas for ex-gay born-again Christians. That didn't last too long before he met a nice boy at a gay bar in Tulsa. They moved to San Francisco, and he now works in a card shop in the Castro.

Another man won a scholarship to Princeton, where he pored over medieval texts while eyeing the water polo players with his feet propped up on the back of the swimming-arena bleachers.

One man escaped the death squads in San Salvador and walked all the way through Guatemala and Mexico to make a new life in Los Angeles. He sent money each week to his family.

Another man went home with Jeffrey Dahmer yet managed to live and tell the tale. (If that's not a fucking success story, I don't know what is.)

I put my skin next to the skin of each of these men. I needed their touch, maybe more than they needed mine. I loved one man's crazy Brillo hair, his crooked smile, his deeply, dimpled ass. I loved another man's wild courage at his job, his scary family story, his dick that veered to the left like a stretch of road.

All of these men were positive. They told me this. They knew. I'm negative. I was pretty surprised that the coin flipped that way. It always scares me to tell people this. I worry that they'll think I'm a lightweight know-nothing who-said-you-could-talk-about-AIDS-from-your-position-of-negative-privilege? queen.

I worry that mentioning being negative is a kind of a social faux pas, a breach in etiquette. I should probably just keep quiet about my status since I don't get tested very often anyway. Some experts suggest a person should be tested every six months. For me, it's more like every six years, 1990 and 1996. I worry that talking too much about being negative might jinx it, make it somehow not true, make it somehow pop like a dreamy soap bubble when the alarm rings at 6 A.M. All it takes is a snap of the fingers, and suddenly I become a superstitious old Italian woman in Bari worried about the evil eye. It's best to shut up.

Andrew and I made love that morning in the light of day in the eleventh year of the plague. I heard his housemates stirring in the other room and their raised-eyebrow comments about the two pairs of Doc Martens in a pile outside of Andrew's wedged-shut bedroom door. As usual my thoughts while we fucked were honking their horns like a traffic jam at the psychic corner of Hollywood Boulevard and 42nd Street:

Oh, that feels nice. His kisses, so sweet. Those kisses, so wet. Well, they're not really that wet, not in the big scheme of wetness. I can't be bothered worrying about saliva anyway. I can't live in a world where we can't kiss. Does he feel me holding back? No, I think it's okay. He knows I'm a little nervous, I think.

Hey, now Andrew's sucking my dick. Ooh, that's nice. He can do the thing with his throat with such ease, the thing that always makes me gag when I try it. Wait, if Andrew's sucking my dick, does that mean I have to suck his dick? No, I'm an adult. I took that workshop about boundary drawing. I can own that I won't be comfortable with that. I can say yes and no in my life. Well, maybe I'll just lick his balls some. That would be a friendly gesture. Well, maybe up the shaft for a bit. It couldn't hurt to just lick across the head of his dick for a bit, could it? No, better not. If I do, I'll have an anxiety attack tomorrow.

Fuck, this is why so many HIV-positive men I know don't want to be bothered dealing with fucked-up negative dudes' panic attacks like mine. Oh, but his asshole feels so nice on my fingertip. Does he have condoms beside the bed? If we're gonna fuck, I have to fuck him. The man who's negative becomes insta-top, right? Well, that's cool; I've really gotten more into my top energy lately anyhow. It's really who I am, my deepest self, right?

But what if tomorrow it's been a long day and I'm tired and I don't have the yang savings account to smack his butt and lift those legs and huff and puff and blow my load up the boy-pussy-man-cunt-hothole of my desire? What will I do then? One finger, two fingers, three fingers. It's like a song on Sesame Street.

I gotta fuck him. It feels too nice. Where's a rubber? Wait, maybe I can fuck him without a rubber. Shoot my HIV-negative come up him? The man who fucks isn't at risk, right? Well, it depends what country you're in, doesn't it? No, better use a condom. Gotta stay safe, right? Right?

But what about that big Wuthering Heights mansion inside me that wants to put my come in my lover's mouth and asshole? I want to get him pregnant. That's biological, right? What about that part of me that wants to eat up that come and stuff it up my butt and feel that skin-to-skin contact?

What's safe, anyway? You can never be totally safe. You would have to never get out of bed. That might be safe. You should never cross the street against the signal. Never climb on slippery rocks just for the seashore thrill. It would be much safer never to get close to anybody ever again, not close enough to touch.

Put the damn condom on!

My cock is slipping into Andrew's asshole. That feels so nice. He's kissing me now, telling me he likes my dick inside him. C'mon, this kiss, I gotta have it. It's that simple. It's that necessary. I gotta have it if this nice man Andrew lets me.

Where am I on my map now? Where did I put my compass? Here I am, right here by this winding river! I can't stand on one side of the water and only wave a clumsy oar. I can't let this kiss not happen. And I want to know its whole story.

Hey, my brain is quieting down! I'm actually in the experience of fucking another man! I'm not looking over my shoulder, waiting for the police siren! Andrew turns over, and I see his beautiful back and skin and ass as we fuck. I feel his hipbones inside his body in the palms of my hands. He's slapping my chest as we fuck. This is great! Wow, look at me, Mom! Here's your HIV-negative son confronting his fears and having hot sex with a man who's positive! Aren't you proud of me, Mom? Mom?

My mom appears inside my head with gobs of leftover filling from Taco Night dripping through her fingers. "Didn't you read all those Los Angeles Times articles I've been sending you for years? Aren't you scared, you dirty faggot son o' mine who will never give me grandchildren?"

(Oh, God, I'm going to lose my hard-on, I know! This always happens when I think of my mom while I'm having sex. Quick, Tim, think of smooth-skinned English boys in wet underwear, splashing in the fountains of Trafalgar Square. That always helps.)

"Scared, Mom? Oh, I guess once in a while I worry sometimes for a second or two. Okay, I go mad with crazy worry, wildfire fear. All the fear you gave me. All the fear you had in your life. Sometimes I fear everything. I fear getting on airplanes. I fear that I left the stove on. I fear that I said the wrong thing. But in this Museum of Fear, I have a special wing, about the size of the Louvre, dedicated to all the things that I might get, from the men I get close to. Have sex with.

"Clap! Warts! Hepatitis! Crabs! Amoebas! HIV!

"Okay, Mom, this fear sometimes chews me up for breakfast. This terror is a tidal wave hovering above me. It whirls, and I feel like I'm going to scream. This crazy fear is a virus too. It's a fierce enemy, completely merciless. It takes no prisoners.

"This fear can haunt my dreams when I have sex that is not so safe, like that time in London. It kept me sleepless and tortured an entire night in a crummy hotel in South Kensington, London. I replayed my judgment lapse a thousand times, watched it in slow motion. I had to feel my body swell up with dead bodies, then a horrible beast pulled them out of my asshole. Spinning in my bed, I was spitting distance from the gloriously tacky memorial to Prince Albert, who long before he was a dick piercing was the beloved of Victoria. When he died Victoria (that queen) took whatever was good and hot in her woman's body and entombed it with Albert, her dead husband, and worshiped it all as a dead thing! Mom, she gave that fear to you and to me, okay? Fuck all that! I'm pretty busy right now, so, Mom, get out of my head!"

Andrew spits in my mouth. Pulls my dick hard into him. Does he want me to shoot inside him? I wonder. Andrew's about to come. I can see his dick getting bigger. The head of his cock looks like the face of someone about to sneeze. I'm getting close too. Maybe I should pull out? We can shoot together. He wants me to come inside him, in the rubber, I know it. Should I ask him? Maybe I'll just tell him. Then the ball is in his court.

We turn the fuck upside down. He moves onto his back, his legs up where I *can lick them. Top to bottom, I want to turn this fear in my life around too. I want to flip the scary meaning of that word get upside down like a fried egg. Over. Easy. I need to understand what I get in a different way. Oh, fuck, I have to remember both sides of the things I get from the men in my life: We get close. We get hurt. We get touched. We get left. We get laid. We get scared. We get held. We get Dad. We get love. We . . .*

TERRY SOUTHERN

Now Dig This

> *This piece was written in the '70s in response to a form letter from George Plimpton requesting submissions for the ultimate "sports-death fantasy."*

My dear George

Many thanks for your very kind "letter" [if, indeed, a scrap of ragscap in memeo may be so construed—in which case old values are not merely crumbling, but have actually buried us more dead than alive. If there *is* a god (type) in heaven, it is my one hope and prayer to same that your Dad was spared the sight or knowledge of that heinously gross format!]

What then, running a bit *short*, are you? A bit of the old skimp-oh-roo, is it? Well, I am pleased to say that a certain yrs tly is delighted, indeed *flattered*, to serve as "FILLER"—that *you* may meet your professional obligations and continue to "walk tall" in the Quality-Lit World which we both know and love so well. So let's just give this one a couple of strokes and see if we don't get what Big Bill Becker used to call "a touch of the old tumescence."

Now then, my own "sports-death fantasy" has always seemed to me a bit odd and perhaps even somewhat impressionistic. From what I have been able to learn so far (through hypnosis and drug-recall sessions, including the usual truth-serums, E-Meter, polygraph and various lie-detector type tests) as to the origin of the fantasy, it seems to have stemmed from early visits to *China*—not your mainland China, mind, but your tiny offland China. This was during the wondrous halcyon days of the perennially unbeatable Little

League team of Taiwan (unbeaten in over 3000 games, unscored on in almost as many).

I would go there each year—"just for the ride," you might say—in the company of Larry Rivers and Gore Vidal, who made this annual "trip to our own little Mecca," as they called it, under the rather shabby (in my view) guise of "scouting 13-year-old lads for the majors."

While Gore and Lar were "doing their thing" with the lads, a certain yrs tly was into—or shall we say *trying* to get into, hee-hee—something quite different (namely, reportage for one of the quality slicks—*Pubes*, it was, if memory serves) covering the highly touted, though short lived, "Great Ice Ping Pong Tournament." As sports buffs will recall, the sport did not differ from ordinary ping pong so much *en principe* as in the actual mechanics of the game—making use as they did of rounded ice-cubes instead of the con-ventional hollow plastic-balls, and using foam-rubber padding on both table and paddle surfaces to afford the necessary resilience for the bouncing cubes.

I was attending the "Young Ladies Finals" when the incident in question occurred. The contestants, ages 15 to 21, were clad, ostensibly to give them "the maximum in freedom of movement," in what can only be termed the "scantiest attire." In fact, there was a thinly veiled aura *of pure sexuality* sur-rounding the entire proceedings, so it did not come as a total surprise when I was approached by one of the "Officials," a Mr. "Wong Dong," if one may believe him, who, with a broad grin and a great deal of ceremonious bowing and scraping, asked if I would care to meet one of the competitors. "Very interesting," he insisted, "a top contender."

I agreed, and soon found myself in an open alcove with "Kim," a most attractive girl of 18 or so—attractive except for what I first thought of as "rather puffy cheeks." I soon learned, however, that the "puffiness" was caused merely by the presence and pressure of an ice-cube in each cheek—this being the technique of preparing the ice-balls *("le preparation des boules")* for play, holding the cubes in the cheeks until they melted slightly to a roundness.

The girl seemed extremely friendly, and Mr. D. now asked to examine the cubes. "Ah," he said, beaming, when she produced them—two glittering golf-ball size pieces of ice—one in each upturned hand. "We have arrived at a propitious moment," he continued, turning to me again, "the *boules* are now of ideal proportion for . . . '*la grande exstase du boules du glace*'!"

Not entirely devoid of a certain worldliness, I had heard of the infamous "ice-cube job" as it was commonly known—the damnable practise, in my view, of *fellatio interruptus*, or according to other sources, *"fellatio prolongata"*—

XXX HARDCORE

whereby, at the moment of climax, the party rendering fellatio, with an ice-cube in each cheek, presses them vigorously against the member, producing a dramatic counter-effect to the ejaculation in progress. As I say, I was aware of the so-called *"extase du boule du glace,"* but had never experienced it—nor, and I would be less than candid if I did not say so, was I particularly keen—though, of course, I did not wish to offend my host—who then spoke to the girl, in Chinese, before turning to me.

"It is arranged," he exclaimed happily. "Allow her to grasp and caress your genitalia." And returning the cubes to her mouth, she extended her hand in a manner at once both coy and compelling, and with a grace charming to behold. Even so, I was not prepared to respond to this gesture without first working up a bit of heft.

I adroitly stepped just beyond her reach, though quite without ostentation so as not to offend. "Perhaps we should, uh, wait," I said, glancing about the room as though wanting more privacy.

"Ah," observed Mr. D., with a most perceptive smile, "you shall be quite comfortable here, I assure you." And so saying, he drew closed a beaded curtain, and then stepped through it, bowing graciously as he departed.

Alone with Miss Kim I felt immediately more secure, and a slight, unobtrusive squeeze assured me that a fairly respectable tumess was near at hand.

"Very well, Miss Kim," I told her, "you may, uh, proceed . . ." which she did, with, I can assure you, the utmost art and ardor. We had been thus engaged for several moments, and I was just approaching a tremendous crescendo—indeed was actually into it, when the beaded veil was burst asunder and in rushed the two madcaps, Vidal and Rivers!

"Get cracking, you oafish rake!" shrieked Vidal with a cackle of glee and inserted two large amyl nitrate ampules, one in each of my nostrils, and then popped them in double quick order. Simultaneous to this, Miss Kim pressed with great vigor the two ice cubes against my pulsating member, and the diabolic Rivers injected a heady potion of Amphetamine laced with Spanish Fly into my templer vein. The confluence, and outrageous conflict, of these various stimuli threw my senses into such monstrous turmoil that I was sent reeling backwards as from the impact of an electric shock, torn from the avid embrace of the fabulous Miss Kim, who bounded after me in hotly voracious pursuit, screaming: "Wait! *L'exstase du boules du glace* COMMENCE!" I now lay supine as she swooped down to resume her carnivorous devastation, while around us, obviously themselves in the crazed throes of sense-derangement, Vidal and Rivers pranced and cavorted as though obsessed by some mad dervish or tarantella of the Damned! Thus, my monumental and unleashed orgasm, prolonged

(throughout eternity it seemed!) by the pressure of the *boules*, and intensified beyond endurance by *drogues variées*, caused me to expire, in a shuddering spasm of delirium and delight. Ecstasy beyond all bearing! Death
beyond all caring! "I die!" I shouted (as I still do when I relive the experience), ". . . *FULFILLED!!!*"

Of course I did not die (oh no, Vidal and Rivers had *other* plans!) and persuaded a newly arrived member of our party, the near legendary "Dr.
Benway" (who later gained certain prominence as author using the name
William S. Burroughs) to administer certain so-called "remedial elixirs" (the
exact nature of which I have never ascertained) and brought me around. In
any event, I continue to relive (almost nightly, in fact) the sensations of that
most memorable experience.

yrs as per,
[signed] T.

Best to the fab missus.

PAT CALIFIA

Public Sex

THE NECESSITY OF EXCESS

> *Love comes with a knife, not some shy question,*
> *and not with fears for its reputation!*
> —*Jelaluddin Rumi, "Which Way Does the Night Go?"*

IT'S JUST AN ILLUSION, but it makes all the hairs on my body stand straight
up in awe: that sensation of holding another person's beating heart in the palm
of my cupped hand. The first time this happened to me, I was very stoned and
following the terse directions of a thoroughly debauched fag who thought it
would be a giggle to see the look on my face when my whole hand went up
his asshole. So many contradictory insights washed over me, I could barely
keep my forearm moving in its hot sheath of Crisco and intestinal mem-
branes. I knew that without the MDA, pot, acid, and poppers I'd ingested, this
never would have happened. But I also knew there was something sacred

about the deep intimacy of this experience that was higher than any chemical could ever get me, perhaps as high as heaven itself.

The man I was fucking was not a nice person, nor did he have any particular affection for me; after we were done, he would move on to someone with a bigger fist and a thicker arm, or simply line up dildos in order (from "large" to "gargantuan") and perch on them till daybreak. And yet I felt such great love, flowing from me to his body, which had opened, accepted and blessed me; and from his body to mine, waves of gratitude for the pleasure it was experiencing. I was utterly aware of the vulnerability of the man whose legs were locked up and back, his feet waving around his ears, but I was also in thrall to the power of his piggishness, enslaved by the aggressive strength of his wanton hole. And there we were, one man and one woman, locked in sexual congress, fulfilling the demographics of a heterosexual fuck—but nothing could possibly be queerer than each of us or the act of penetration we engaged in.

I've told this story many times before, but I find myself thinking about those days, that decade, more and more of late, as we enter one more round of controversy about AIDS, the bathhouses, anonymous public sex, gay marriage and monogamy. During the late '70s and early '80s, I was privileged to hang out with Steve McEachern, who ran The Catacombs, a fist-fucking club, held in the basement of his Victorian house every Saturday night. This connection was made through a bisexual woman who was a lover of mine, Cynthia Slater. Gay leathermen took pity on her and included her in some of their games because they recognized her appetites as being kindred to their own. Her prodigious boozing and drugging, outrageous masochism, tiny hands, gutter-gums style of dirty-talk topping, and shameless exhibitionism were legendary. The straight S/M scene barely existed then, and it certainly wasn't a playground big enough for Slater's dramatic abilities. To some, not all, leathermen of that era, the fact that a few women shared their predilections was just affirmation. When you've had your pick of hundreds of the most gorgeous men in the world for all your adult life, a girl or two at your elbow in the Eagle or up to her elbow in your ass was simply not a big deal. The consensus then was that if you tried a new drug or a new kink and you didn't like it, you should probably just try it again under slightly different circumstances.

I was a lesbian with separatist tendencies, but I found myself in a quandary similar to Slater's. There was a group, Samois, for leather dykes, which I had started, and there were women-only S/M play parties, which I ran, but I needed a place to go where I was not managing everything. Even though I kept myself in school and earned a living, being able to have the kind of sex I wanted was my true obsession. I found myself hunting along the fringes of leathermen's territory because they shared that obsession. The stark extremism of gay-male S/M iconography echoed my own fantasies and freed me to write them down. The ethos of erotic risk-taking helped me to escape from feminine conditioning to see every sexual opportunity or invitation as a threat. I learned that lust had both everything and nothing to do with love, and that love had a million equally alluring faces. The tidy practicality of trick towels and no-spill popper bottles was endearing. Along with the orgiastic encouragement, a firm sense of balance existed: You could be as big a sexual outlaw as you liked on Saturday night, but come Sunday morning, cooking a fabulous brunch was every bit as important.

And so I am puzzled by that demagogic playwright who urges gay men to be more like lesbians. Perhaps his experience does not embrace lesbians like me, who envy and emulate the outrageous, go-for-broke quality of the unfettered gay male libido. I and a handful of other women have been cherished and enriched by the love and encouragement of our gay male partners in debauchery. The sad fact is that if all gay men settled down into pairs like animals clambering into Noah's ark, a whole world of possibilities would disappear for dykes and for straight people. A culture which embraces nonmonogamy, casual public sex, erotic art, sex toys, costuming, and a playful, theatrical attitude toward pleasure is a national treasure, not a shameful anachronism.

Twenty years ago, who could have predicted that any gay activist worthy of the name would be preaching the same values as Anita Bryant? It was a mad time, both wonderful and terrible. Gay men had decided they were not going to repress themselves any more; they were so sick of being discriminated against, beaten up, ridiculed, pathologized, murdered, arrested, excommunicated, and disowned that they rose up like fireworks. This was a frenzied period of creativity, lust, intoxication, activism, and brotherhood. Sadly, there was fierce opposition to this struggle for liberation, and many of us who were starving for freedom could not allow ourselves to eat and drink at the table of self-acceptance. So it was also a time of violence, disease, and suicide in all its urban guises.

Gay bars and bathhouses were a key part of this burgeoning homosexual culture. I believe it was Jack Fritscher, *Drummer* editor, author, and prophet of homomasculinity, who said, "Gay liberation began because we wanted the right to party without getting arrested." Disenfranchised people lack, first and foremost, a homeland. Fags and dykes, bis and trannies, are like gypsies or the Lost Ten Tribes of Israel, a people without a place to park our lives. Moralists who wax indignant about the mess and intrusiveness of queer public sex miss its key subversive value as a means of staking, even on a temporary basis, some territory within which gay desire might safely flourish. We could not have a radical politic that affirmed our right to be until we had places to go where we could be reassured that we did indeed exist in sufficient numbers to help one another, and could form bonds that could move us as a bloc to the voting booth, a meeting, or a riot. Promiscuity was the root of early gay activism. Sex is, after all, the only thing that we have in common. And desire is notorious for leaping fences. If we will let it, it can connect us despite obstacles of class, race, age . . . or gender.

AIDS has erased the vibrancy and beauty of that time, and left us ashamed of the place where we came from. I don't think we could help but interpret something this devastating as a punishment that we perhaps deserved. We all grew up being told that homosexuality was a sin and a sickness. It's easier to believe there's a reason why we've died in such huge numbers, even if it reinforces our self-hatred, than to comprehend the fact that we were mowed down by a force of nature that has no intention or purpose. Human beings seem able to cope with just about anything as long as we think we know why it happened. And so now there are gay activists who say that we need to close down the bathhouses, stop partying, and devote our efforts instead to winning a legal right to gay marriage. They tout self-control, monogamy, and membership in the mainstream as our escape route from the epidemic, not condoms or safer sex or a vaccine. This strategy has been bolstered by recent reports that STD statistics are on the rise once again, the result of a large-scale return to unsafe sex by people who falsely believe AIDS is no longer a terminal illness.

Same-sex couples absolutely ought to be allowed to marry. And for those who choose it, monogamy is a valid boundary to set. But gay activists who are telling us that marriage and monogamy are our only hope of salvation from the scourge of AIDS simply haven't done their homework. They are behaving as if AIDS is the only sexually transmitted, fatal disease that ever existed. But what about syphilis? This disease, once epidemic and always fatal, ravaged Europe and America a mere century ago. Feminist scholars like Judith Walkowitz and medical historians such as William Brandt have documented the shortcomings in public policy and treatment which allowed syphilis to flourish.

Take note: Syphilis cut a deep swath through the heterosexual population. Easy access to legal marriage was no barrier to the spirochete. No one made a more vigorous attempt to control disease with the braided flail of self-control, monogamy, and marriage than the Victorians. In England, the Contagious Diseases Act allowed police to detain any woman suspected of being infected for an indefinite period of time. In America, police departments tried to eliminate prostitution by cracking down on red-light districts. Even after a primitive form of treatment for the disease became available and latex condoms were invented which could prevent its transmission, the epidemic continued because religious organizations lobbied to prevent large-scale public education about prevention and treatment. Why? To protect the sacred state of matrimony. Syphilis was seen as the just punishment of the rake; the fact that he would also infect his innocent wife was widely ignored. When penicillin was discovered, it took a fierce battle before health departments were widely authorized to test and treat venereal disease. Moralists feared that without the threat of illness, sterility, and death, people would become licentious.

The American gay men who are advocating marriage and monogamy as our front-line defense against AIDS also seem woefully ignorant of the course this disease has taken in Africa, where HIV Type D has felled heterosexual victims for the most part. Marriage hasn't done a damn thing to protect public health there. Nor has it stemmed the tide of the disease among heterosexual IV drug users in America and Europe. Moral panics do not prevent disease. Instead, they hamper public health education about preventing disease transmission, and they derail funding for medically-based cures. Syphilis was taken down by penicillin, not by romantic love or antiprostitution campaigns or fear of insanity and premature death. And AIDS has killed millions more people than it had to because we continue to allow what should be private moral standards to dictate public policy.

Queers have more reason than anybody to be suspicious of heterosexuals' claims to virtue. We all know how many "straight" boys love to get another man to suck their dicks—as long as they think they won't get caught. It's amazing to see so many gay men and lesbians fall prey to a communal rose-tinted delusion about the warty institution of marriage. Marriage works for heterosexuals because a thriving sex industry provides entertainment for husbands who otherwise could not tolerate their responsibilities. Gay marriage isn't going to shut down any bathhouses; it's going to fund more of them. Nobody who rhapsodizes about gay marriage seems prepared to talk about its inevitable sequel—gay divorce. Are we ready for these rancorous and expensive events, complete with public battles over child custody and alimony? We already have a huge body of experience in our own community about long-term same-sex relationships and how to make them work. At least 90 percent of the gay couples I know who have been together for more than five years, and are still happy, have made some accommodation for sex outside the relationship. The other 10 percent are pantomiming *Who's Afraid of Virginia Woolf?*

The AIDS epidemic will not be over until we find a vaccine that prevents infection and a treatment that eliminates the virus from the body of an infected person. Until then, our best bet is to saturate every at-risk population with explicit, sexy, and humorous prevention education and lobby for an end to restrictions on needle exchange programs. When there is a vaccine or an effective treatment or, please Goddess, both, people will return to pre-AIDS sexual behavior. *And that's as it should be.* Because there was nothing wrong with that behavior in the first place. In fact, sexual excess has intrinsic value and a spiritual meaning that makes it a vital part of the human experience.

The body is like the "you are here" X on a map of a shopping mall. It is the place where we have to begin. Despite our mortality, the flesh is the only route we can take to glimpse eternity. Desire for another's touch is our first protest against the existential loneliness that inexorably dogs human consciousness. We reach for another person to provide us with reassurance, distraction, the wince of erotic gratification. For a few seconds, perhaps, we sense what it might be to welcome Another. And then we return to a state of longing and emptiness. And we repeat the cycle, again and again, until perhaps we also begin to look for a more sublime partnership with our creator, who has the power to turn our most painful questions into peace and meet our anger and fear with unflinching love. Lily Tomlin jokes, "When we talk to God, we're praying, but when God talks to us, we're psychotic." In a world driven mad by materialism, by a determination to derive meaning and value solely from temporal things, of course we appear to be insane when we attend to the voice of the Spirit. Desire was made a part of our nature not only to draw us closer to one another but to urge us on to our ultimate source and resting place. It is, or can be, a divine madness indeed.

When we shelter one another's desires, even those that are strange or degrading, we borrow a little divine grace and provide a smaller version of the shelter of that transcendental love. After all, is this not where life began, in mud and blood, spit and cum? If a deity fashioned us, these were the building blocks She chose to use. Are they not therefore holy? The man who arranges himself in a sling or a bathtub, awaiting anointing with Crisco or piss, has come in perfect love and perfect trust like a child awaiting baptism. Lust can be a sacrament that washes us clean of envy, pride, and anomie, and returns us to daily life with a satisfied heart, renewed hope, and greater compassion. The mouth is not the only orifice that generates poetry; we must learn to listen to the hymns of our other openings; other lips. If our literature, "gay literature," did no more than this, rescue our genitals from revulsion and celebrate them instead, it would be heroic.

The impulse to create life and to give birth motivates every form of sexuality, not merely the union between man and woman. The poet Muriel Rukeyser captured this perfectly when she praised "the homosexual who goes building another/with touch with touch . . . each like himself, like herself each," and urges us "not to despise any touch." Most of us, gay men and lesbians, bisexual and transgendered people, have experienced the rejection of our families. We are often told that they wish we had never been born. And so we must give birth to one another, become the midwives and mothers and fathers that welcome each other into new lives as queer people. We create a new country within each other's arms.

My friend Skip Aiken, an Old Guard leatherman if there ever was one, used to say, "Men ought to share cum with one another." (He also used to say, "I never knew what I wanted in bed until I had sex with three hundred different people.") His doctor would claim that Skip died of a heart attack, not AIDS, but I think his heart broke from too much loss and grief. Yet he never altered his conviction that there was something important about that exchange, beyond the climax it betokened. Who else, other than gay and bisexual men, are capable of loving men enough to patiently and carefully change them? We will probably always be a selfish and aggressive species, capable of cannibalism, genocide, and rape. But is there no way to channel that aggression, transmute it so that it provides passion and pleasure instead of destruction and death? The heterosexual male's just fear of other men's violence has created millennia of suffering. The hatred of homosexuality is twined with violence down to its root. Someday, a spatter of semen will be a kiss of benediction, not a curse. Let a thousand of those white flowers bloom, I say.

KEN KESEY

One Flew Over the Cuckoo's Nest

THEY'RE OUT THERE.

Black boys in white suits up before me to commit sex acts in the hall and get it mopped up before I can catch them.

They're mopping when I come out the dorm, all three of them sulky and hating everything, the time of day, the place they're at here, the people they got to work around. When they hate like this, better if they don't see me. I creep along the wall quiet as dust in my canvas shoes, but they got special sensitive equipment detects my fear and they all look up, all three at once, eyes glittering out of the black faces like the hard glitter of radio tubes out of the back of an old radio.

"Here's the Chief. The *soo*-pah Chief, fellas. Ol' Chief Broom. Here you go, Chief Broom. . . ."

Stick a mop in my hand and motion to the spot they aim for me to clean today, and I go. One swats the backs of my legs with a broom handle to hurry me past.

"Haw, you look at 'im shag it? Big enough to eat apples off my head an' he mine me like a baby."

They laugh and then I hear them mumbling behind me, heads close together. Hum of black machinery, humming hate and death and other hospital secrets. They don't bother not talking out loud about their hate secrets when I'm nearby because they think I'm deaf and dumb. Everybody think so. I'm cagey enough to fool them that much. If my being half Indian ever helped me in any way in this dirty life, it helped me being cagey, helped me all these years.

I'm mopping near the ward door when a key hits it from the other side and I know it's the Big Nurse by the way the lockworks cleave to the key, soft and swift and familiar she been around locks so long. She slides through the door with a gust of cold and locks the door behind her and I see her fingers trail across the polished steel—tip of each finger the same color as her lips. Funny orange. Like the tip of a soldering iron. Color so hot or so cold if she touches you with it you can't tell which.

She's carrying her woven wicker bag like the ones the Umpqua tribe sells out along the hot August highway, a bag shape of a tool box with a hemp handle. She's had it all the years I been here. It's a loose weave and I can see inside it, there's no compact or lipstick or woman stuff, she's got that bag full of a thousand parts she aims to use in her duties today—wheels and gears, cogs polished to a hard glitter, tiny pills that gleam like porcelain, needles, forceps, watchmakers' pliers, rolls of copper wire . . .

She dips a nod at me as she goes past. I let the mop push me back to the wall and smile and try to foul her equipment up as much as possible by not letting her see my eyes—they can't tell so much about you if you got your eyes closed.

In my dark I hear her rubber heels hit the tile and the stuff in her wicker bag clash with the jar of her walking as she passes me in the hall. She walks stiff. When I open my eyes she's down the hall about to turn into the glass Nurses' Station where she'll spend the day sitting at her desk and looking out her window and making notes on what goes on out in front of her in the day room during the next eight hours. Her face looks pleased and peaceful with the thought.

Then . . . she sights those black boys. They're still down there together, mumbling to one another. They didn't hear her come on the ward. They sense she's glaring down at them now, but it's too late. They should of knew better'n to group up and mumble together when she was due on the ward. Their faces bob apart, confused. She goes into a crouch and advances on where they're trapped in a huddle at the end of the corridor. She knows what they been saying, and I can see she's furious clean out of control. She's going to tear the black bastards limb from limb, she's so furious. She's swelling up, swells till her back's splitting out the white uniform and she's let her arms section out long enough to wrap around the three of them five, six times. She looks around her with a swivel of her huge head. Nobody up to see, just old Broom Bromden the half-breed Indian back there hiding behind his mop and can't talk to call for help. So she really lets herself go and her painted smile twists, stretches to an open snarl, and she blows up bigger and bigger, big as a tractor, so big I can smell the machinery inside the way you smell a motor pulling too big a load. I hold my breath and figure, My God this time they're gonna do it! This time they let the hate build up too high and over-loaded and they're gonna tear one another to pieces before they realize what they're doing!

But just as she starts crooking those sectioned arms around the black boys and they go to ripping at her underside with the mop handles, all the patients start coming out of the dorms to check on what's the hullabaloo, and she has to change back before she's caught in the shape of her hideous real self. By the time the patients get their eyes rubbed to where they can halfway see what the racket's about, all they see is the head nurse, smiling and calm and cold as usual, telling the black boys they'd best not stand in a group gossiping when it *is* Monday morning and there *is* such a lot to get done on the first morning of the week . . .

". . . mean old Monday morning, you know, boys . . ."

"Yeah, Miz Ratched . . ."

". . . and we have quite a number of appointments this morning, so per-haps, if your standing here in a group talking isn't *too* urgent . . ."

"Yeah, Miz Ratched . . ."

She stops and nods at some of the patients come to stand around and stare out of eyes all red and puffy with sleep. She nods once to each. Precise, automatic gesture. Her face is smooth, calculated, and precision-made, like an expensive baby doll, skin like flesh-colored enamel, blend of white and cream and baby-blue eyes, small nose, pink little nostrils—everything working together except the color on her lips and fingernails, and the size of her bosom. A mistake was made somehow in manufacturing, putting those big, womanly breasts on what would of otherwise been a perfect work, and you can see how bitter she is about it.

The men are still standing and waiting to see what she was onto the black boys about, so she remembers seeing me and says, "And since it *is* Monday, boys, why don't we get a good head start on the week by shaving poor Mr. Bromden first this morning, before the after-breakfast rush on the shaving room, and see if we can't avoid some of the—ah—disturbance he tends to cause, don't you think?"

Before anybody can turn to look for me I duck back in the mop closet, jerk the door shut dark after me, hold my breath. Shaving before you get breakfast is the worst time. When you got something under your belt you're stronger and more wide awake, and the bastards who work for the Combine aren't so apt to slip one of their machines in on you in place of an electric shaver. But when you shave *before* breakfast like she has me do some mornings —six-thirty in the morning in a room all white walls and white basins, and long tube-lights in the ceiling making sure there aren't any shadows, and faces all round you trapped screaming behind the mirrors—then what chance you got against one of their machines?

I hide in the mop closet and listen, my heart beating in the dark, and I try to keep from getting scared, try to get my thoughts off someplace else— try to think back and remember things about the village and the big Columbia River, think about ah one time Papa and me were hunting birds in a stand of cedar trees near The Dalles. . . . But like always when I try to place my thoughts in the past and hide there, the fear close at hand seeps in through the memory. I can feel that least black boy out there coming up the hall, smelling out for my fear. He opens out his nostrils like black funnels, his out-sized head bobbing this way and that as he sniffs, and he sucks in fear from all over the ward. He's smelling me now, I can hear him snort. He don't know where I'm hid, but he's smelling and he's hunting around. I try to keep still. . . .

(Papa tells me to keep still, tells me that the dog senses a bird somewheres right close. We borrowed a pointer dog from a man in The Dalles. All the village dogs are no-'count mongrels, Papa says, fish-gut eaters and no class a-tall; this here dog, he got *insteek!* I don't say anything, but I already see the bird up in a scrub cedar, hunched in a gray knot of feathers. Dog running in circles underneath, too much smell around for him to point for sure. The bird safe as long as he keeps still. He's holding out pretty good, but the dog keeps sniffing and circling, louder and closer. Then the bird breaks, feathers springing, jumps out of the cedar into the birdshot from Papa's gun.)

The least black boy and one of the bigger ones catch me before I get ten steps out of the mop closet, and drag me back to the shaving room. I don't fight or make any noise. If you yell it's just tougher on you. I hold back the yelling. I hold back till they get to my temples. I'm not sure it's one of those substitute machines and not a shaver till it gets to my temples; then I can't hold back. It's not a will-power thing any more when they get to my temples. It's a . . . *button,* pushed, says Air Raid Air Raid, turns me on so loud it's like no sound, everybody yelling at me hands over their ears from behind a glass wall, faces working around in talk circles but no sound from the mouths. My sound soaks up all other sound. They start the fog machine again and it's snowing down cold and white all over me like skim milk, so thick I might even be able to hide in it if they didn't have a hold on me. I can't see six inches in front of me through the fog and the only thing I can hear over the wail I'm making is the Big Nurse whoop and charge up the hall while she crashes patients outta her way with that wicker bag. I hear her coming but I still can't hush my hollering. I holler till she gets there. They hold me down while she jams wicker bag and all into my mouth and shoves it down with a mop handle.

(A bluetick hound bays out there in the fog, running scared and lost because he can't see. No tracks on the ground but the ones he's making, and he sniffs in every direction with his cold red-rubber nose and picks up no scent but his own fear, fear burning down into him like steam.) It's gonna burn me just that way, finally telling about all this, about the hospital, and her, and the guys—and about McMurphy. I been silent so long now it's gonna roar out of me like floodwaters and you think the guy telling this is ranting and raving my *God*; you think this is too horrible to have really happened, this is too awful to be the truth! But, please. It's still hard for me to have a clear mind thinking on it. But it's the truth even if it didn't happen.

When the fog clears to where I can see, I'm sitting in the day room. They didn't take me to the Shock Shop this time. I remember they took me out of the shaving room and locked me in Seclusion. I don't remember if I got breakfast or not. Probably not. I can call to mind some mornings locked in Seclusion the black boys keep bringing seconds of everything—supposed to be for me, but they eat it instead—till all three of them get breakfast while I lie there on that pee-stinking mattress, watching them wipe up egg with toast. I can smell the grease and hear them chew the toast. Other mornings they bring me cold mush and force me to eat it without it even being salted.

This morning I plain don't remember. They got enough of those things they call pills down me so I don't know a thing till I hear the ward door open. That ward door opening means it's at least eight o'clock, means there's been maybe an hour and a half I was out cold in that Seclusion Room when the technicians could of come in and installed anything the Big Nurse ordered and I wouldn't have the slightest notion what.

I hear noise at the ward door, off up the hall out of my sight. That ward door starts opening at eight and opens and closes a thousand times a day, kashash, *click*. Every morning we sit lined up on each side of the day room, mixing jigsaw puzzles after breakfast, listen for a key to hit the lock, and wait to see what's coming in. There's not a whole lot else to do. Sometimes, at the door, it's a young resident in early so he can watch what we're like Before Medication. BM, they call it. Sometimes it's a wife visiting there on high heels with her purse held tight over her belly. Sometimes it's a clutch of grade-school teachers being led on a tour by that fool Public Relation man who's always clapping his wet hands together and saying how overjoyed he is that mental hospitals have eliminated all the old-fashioned cruelty: "What a *cheery* atmosphere, don't you agree?" He'll bustle around the schoolteachers, who are bunched together for safety, clapping his hands together. "Oh, when I think back on the old days, on the filth, the bad food, even, yes, brutality, oh, I realize ladies that we have come a long way in our campaign!" Whoever comes in the door is usually somebody disappointing, but there's always a chance otherwise, and when a key hits the lock all the heads come up like there's strings on them.

This morning the lockworks rattle strange; it's not a regular visitor at the door. An Escort Man's voice calls down, edgy and impatient, "Admission, come sign for him," and the black boys go.

Admission. Everybody stops playing cards and Monopoly, turns toward the day-room door. Most days I'd be out sweeping the hall and see who they're signing in, but this morning, like I explain to you, the Big Nurse put a thousand pounds down me and I can't budge out of the chair. Most days I'm the first one to see the Admission, watch him creep in the door and slide along the wall and stand scared till the black boys come sign for him and take him into the shower room, where they strip him and leave him shivering with the door open while they all three run grinning up and down the halls looking for the Vaseline. "We *need* that Vaseline," they'll tell the Big Nurse, "for the thermometer." She looks from one to the other: "I'm *sure* you do," and hands them a jar holds at least a gallon, "but mind you boys don't group up in there." Then I see two, maybe all three of them in there, in that shower room with the Admission, running that thermometer around in the grease till it's coated the size of your finger, crooning, "Tha's right, mothah, tha's right," and then shut the door and turn all the showers up to where you can't hear anything but the vicious hiss of water on the green tile. I'm out there most days, and I see it like that.

But this morning I have to sit in the chair and only listen to them bring him in. Still, even though I can't see him, I know he's no ordinary Admission. I don't hear him slide scared along the wall, and when they tell him about the shower he don't just submit with a weak little yes, he tells them right back in a loud, brassy voice that he's already plenty damn clean, thank you.

"They showered me this morning at the courthouse and last night at the jail. And I *swear* I believe they'd of washed my ears for me on the taxi ride over if they coulda found the vacilities. Hoo boy, seems like everytime they ship me someplace I gotta get scrubbed down before, after, and during the operation. I'm gettin' so the sound of water makes me start gathering up my belongings. And *get* back away from me with that thermometer, Sam, and give me a minute to look my new home over; I never been in a Institute of Psychology before."

Playing in the Apocalypse

The patients look at one another's puzzled faces, then back to the door, where his voice is still coming in. Talking louder'n you'd think he needed to if the black boys were anywhere near him. He sounds like he's way above them, talking down, like he's sailing fifty yards overhead, hollering at those below on the ground. He sounds big. I hear him coming down the hall, and he sounds big in the way he walks, and he sure don't slide; he's got iron on his heels and he rings it on the floor like horseshoes. He shows up in the door and stops and hitches his thumbs in his pockets, boots wide apart, and stands there with the guys looking at him.

"Good *morn*in', buddies."

There's a paper Halloween bat hanging on a string above his head; he reaches up and flicks it so it spins around.

"Mighty nice fall day."

He talks a little the way Papa used to, voice loud and full of hell, but he doesn't look like Papa; Papa was a full-blood Columbia Indian—a chief—and hard and shiny as a gunstock. This guy is redheaded with long red sideburns and a tangle of curls out from under his cap, been needing cut a long time, and he's broad as Papa was tall, broad across the jaw and shoulders and chest, a broad white devilish grin, and he's hard in a different kind of way from Papa, kind of the way a baseball is hard under the scuffed leather. A seam runs across his nose and one cheekbone where somebody laid him a good one in a fight, and the stitches are still in the seam. He stands there waiting, and when nobody makes a move to say anything to him he commences to laugh. Nobody can tell exactly why he laughs; there's nothing funny going on. But it's not the way that Public Relation laughs, it's free and loud and it comes out of his wide grinning mouth and spreads in rings bigger and bigger till it's lapping against the walls all over the ward. Not like that fat Public Relation laugh. This sounds real. I realize all of a sudden it's the first laugh I've heard in years.

He stands looking at us, rocking back in his boots, and he laughs and laughs. He laces his fingers over his belly without taking his thumbs out of his pockets. I see how big and beat up his hands are. Everybody on the ward, patients, staff, and all, is stunned dumb by him and his laughing. There's no move to stop him, no move to say anything. He laughs till he's finished for a time, and he walks on into the day room. Even when he isn't laughing, that laughing sound hovers around him, the way the sound hovers around a big bell just quit ringing—it's in his eyes, in the way he smiles and swaggers, in the way he talks.

"My name is McMurphy, buddies, R. P. McMurphy, and I'm a gambling fool." He winks and sings a little piece of a song: " '. . . and whenever I meet with a deck a cards I lays . . . my money . . . down,' " and laughs again.

Playing in the Apocalypse

He walks to one of the card games, tips an Acute's cards up with a thick, heavy finger, and squints at the hand and shakes his head.

"Yessir, that's what I came to this establishment for, to bring you birds fun an' entertainment around the gamin' table. Nobody left in that Pendleton Work Farm to make my days interesting any more, so I requested a *transfer*, ya see. Needed some new blood. Hooee, look at the way this bird holds his cards, showin' to everybody in a block; man! I'll trim you babies like little lambs."

Cheswick gathers his cards together. The redheaded man sticks his hand out for Cheswick to shake.

"Hello, buddy, what's that you're playin'? Pinochle? Jesus, no wonder you don't care nothin' about showing your hand. Don't you have a straight deck around here? Well say, here we go, I brought along my own deck, just in case, has something in it other than face cards—and check the pictures, huh? Every one different. Fifty-two positions."

Cheswick is pop-eyed already, and what he sees on those cards don't help his condition.

"Easy now, don't smudge em; we got lots of time, lots of games ahead of us. I like to use my deck here because it takes at least a week for the other players to get to where they can even see the *suit. . . .*"

He's got on work-farm pants and shirt, sunned out till they're the color of watered milk. His face and neck and arms are the color of oxblood leather from working long in the fields. He's got a primer-black motorcycle cap stuck in his hair and a leather jacket over one arm, and he's got on boots gray and dusty and heavy enough to kick a man half in two. He walks away from Cheswick and takes off the cap and goes to beating a dust storm out of his thigh. One of the black boys circles him with the thermometer, but he's too quick for them; he slips in among the Acutes and starts moving around shaking hands before the black boy can take good aim. The way he talks, his wink, his loud talk, his swagger all remind me of a car salesman or a stock auctioneer—or one of those pitchmen you see on a side-show stage, out in front of his flapping banners, standing there in a striped shirt with yellow buttons, drawing the faces off the sawdust like a magnet.

"What happened, you see, was I got in a couple of hassles at the work farm, to tell the pure truth, and the court ruled that I'm a psychopath. And do you think I'm gonna argue with the court? Shoo, you can bet your bottom dollar I don't. If its gets me outta those damned pea fields I'll be whatever their little heart desires, be it psychopath or mad dog or werewolf, because I don't care if I never see another weedin' hoe to my dying day. Now they tell me a psychopath's a guy fights too much and fucks too much, but they ain't wholly right, do you think? I mean, whoever heard tell of a man gettin' too much poozle? Hello, buddy, what do they call you? My name's McMurphy and I'll bet you two dollars here and now that you can't tell me how many spots are in that pinochle hand you're holding *don't* look. Two dollars; what d'ya say? God *damn*, Sam! can't you wait half a minute to prod me with that damn thermometer of yours?"

Dick Gregory

Nigger

In November of 1962 I was sitting on the stage of a jam-packed auditorium in Jackson, Mississippi, with Roy Wilkins, waiting to go on. I was a little restless. I had flown in just for that night, and I wanted to make my speech and get out of town. And now I had to sit up there and wait while they were introducing some old Negro who had just gotten out of jail. I hardly listened. He had killed a man, they said, another Negro who had been sent by the whites to burn the old man's house down. The old man had been leading a voter registration drive. I should have listened carefully. But I had no way of knowing that old man was going to change my entire life.

The old man shuffled out to the microphone. I think he said he was seventy-eight years old. I'll never forget what he said next.

"I didn't mind going to jail for freedom, no, I wouldn't even mind being killed for freedom. But my wife and I was married a long time, and, well, you know I ain't never spent a night away from home. While I was in jail, my wife died."

That destroyed me. I sat there, and my stomach turned around, and I couldn't have stood up if I had to. Here's this little old Mississippi Negro, the kind of big-lipped, kinky-haired, black-faced verb-buster every other Negro in America looks down on. And this man bucked and rose up and fought the system for me, and he went to jail for me, and he lost his wife for me. He had gone out on the battle lines and demonstrated for a tomorrow he would never see, for jobs and rights he might not even be qualified to benefit from. A little old man from a country town who never spent a night away from his wife in his married life. And he went to jail for me and being away killed her.

Playing in the Apocalypse

After the old man finished speaking, I went to him and told him thanks. I told him that I hated to come to him with money after what had happened to him, but if he had a child or loved one anywhere in the world he wanted to see on Christmas, I wanted the privilege of sending him there. He said he had a son in California, and later I gave Medgar Evers a train ticket and a check for the old man.

I don't remember what I spoke about that night, I was so upset. As I came off the stage, Medgar introduced me to a woman named Leona Smith as if I should know her. When I didn't react, he said she was the mother of Clyde Kennard. That name didn't mean anything to me either. So Medgar told me a story that made me sick.

Clyde Kennard was thirty-five years old, and for the past three years he had been in jail. The charge was stealing five bags of chicken feed. But the real reason was that he had tried to enroll in Mississippi Southern College. Before I left Jackson that night, I promised Mrs. Smith that I would do everything in my power to get her son out of jail. When I got back to Chicago, Medgar started calling me about the case and sending me more information. I couldn't believe it.

Kennard was born in Mississippi, and he attended the University of Chicago. When he got out of the paratroopers after Korea, he bought his parents a farm in Mississippi. His stepfather got sick, and Clyde went down to run the farm. He wanted to finish his college education, so in 1959 he applied to the nearest school, Mississippi Southern. He was turned down and harassed by the police, and finally somebody planted five stolen bags of chicken feed on his farm. The price of feed was raised to make the charge a felony, and Kennard was sentenced to seven years at hard labor. When another Negro admitted stealing the feed, the white authorities told him to shut up.

On New Year's Eve, from the stage of Mister Kelley's in Chicago, I made a resolution for 1963: Get Kennard out of jail. I thought that if all the facts were dug up and printed in the newspapers, America would get Kennard out of jail. A white UPI reporter who came by to interview me was so upset by the story that he volunteered to go into Mississippi and gather more information. The first bit of information he dug up was that Clyde Kennard was dying of cancer.

Irv Kupcinet, the famous Chicago columnist, broke the Kennard story. My new researcher came up with Kennard's medical records, and gave them to the press. Kennard was transferred to the prison hospital. Then a Chicago millionaire called business connections in Mississippi, and Kennard was released from jail. He was thirty-five years old when we flew him to Chicago to start cancer treatments, but he looked eighty-five. And it was too late. He died six months later.

I met James Meredith that year, too—one of the most brilliant and courageous men in America, a man who gave dignity to every Negro in the country, who put every Negro in college, who played one of the biggest parts in setting up the revolution in the history of the American Negro struggle. Negroes looked a little different and acted a little different when James Meredith was graduated because they all were graduated with him, graduated from the derogatory stigma that all Negroes are ignorant, that all Negroes are lazy, that all Negroes stink.

I was different, too. An old man's wife had died. Two young men had tried to integrate schools that the biggest fools wouldn't want to go to. One had failed and died, and the other had succeeded and suffered. For the first time, I was involved. There was a battle going on, there was a war shaping up, and somehow writing checks and giving speeches didn't seem enough.

Made in the shade? Hell, as long as any man, white or black, isn't getting his rights in America I'm in danger. Sure I could stay in the night clubs and say clever things. But if America goes to war tomorrow would I stay home and satirize it at the Blue Angel? No, I'd go overseas and lay on some cold dirt, taking the chance of dying to guarantee a bunch of foreigners a better life than my own Momma got in America.

I wanted a piece of the action now, I wanted to get in this thing. I got my chance sooner than I expected.

Some people in Mississippi were having problems with food. A guy came by the night club one evening in Chicago and asked me to sign a fundraising letter. I told him I never lend my name to anything. If it's an organization I can work with, I'll work. I told him I didn't get through at the night club until 4 a.m. but if he'd leave some literature under my apartment door I'd read it before I went to sleep. He did. I got another lesson on how dirty this situation was.

Leflore County in Mississippi had cut off its shipments of federal surplus foods, most of which went to Negroes. This was in retaliation for voter registration drives in Greenwood, the county seat. The white authorities claimed they couldn't afford the $37,000 a year it cost them to store and distribute the free food to the poor people. I endorsed the letter that morning and sent a check for $100.

Later that day, the fund-raisers called me and asked if I would come by for a press conference. I asked for more information so I could answer questions intelligently. And I sent my new researcher down to Greenwood. Then I went into the streets of Chicago. Daddy-O Dayley, the disc jockey, and I collected

14,000 pounds of food. I chartered a plane, and on February 11, 1963, we flew the food into Memphis. We loaded it into trucks there, and drove 134 miles to Clarksdale. From there it was taken to Greenwood. I was still afraid of the South, and I wanted to leave that night. That's why I picked February 11 to go to Mississippi. The next day was Lincoln's Birthday and President Kennedy had invited Lil and me and 800 other people to a celebration at the White House. So we handed out the food, and I promised the voter registration workers from SNCC—the Student Non-Violent Coordinating Committee— that I'd come back when the demonstrations began. Then I headed back to Memphis, flew to Chicago to pick up Lil, and flew on to Washington.

It was a wonderful affair. We shook hands with President Kennedy, and with Lyndon Johnson. Lil was almost nine months pregnant at the time, and I was hoping she'd give birth right in the White House. Waited around as long as we could, but the party was over and she didn't even feel labor pains. So we went back to Chicago.

I started getting reports from my researcher. Through February and March there was violence in Greenwood. Cars were wrecked, a Negro regis- tration worker was shot in the back of the neck, the SNCC headquarters was set on fire. Bullets were fired into Negro homes. SNCC workers were beaten up. When Negroes marched in protest, the police put the dogs on them. They arrested the eleven top registration workers. And I had promised to go down to Greenwood.

I was scared to death. Making speeches, giving money, even going down South for a night or two at a time—that was one thing. But getting out on those streets and marching against bullets and dogs and water hoses and cattle prods . . .

I knew they were laying for me down there. The Mississippi newspapers and public officials were on me for the food lift. They claimed that I hadn't brought down 14,000 pounds of food after all, that it had been much less. They said that if Dick Gregory was going to take care of their poor Negroes, let's send them all up to Chicago. They said I was just doing it for publicity.

And then the time came to make up my mind. The big push for voter reg- istration was scheduled to start on April 1. Most of the SNCC people were in jail, and they needed leaders in Greenwood. And they needed a well-known name that would bring the situation national attention. On Sunday, March 31, I lay on a hotel bed in Philadelphia and changed my mind a hundred times. I thought of a lot of good reasons for not going.

They'll kill me down there, those rednecks, they'll call me an outside agi- tator and pull me into an alley and beat my head in, they'll shoot me down in the street. What's that going to prove? And what about Michele and Lynne and Lil, lying in a hospital right now with Dick, Jr., my son, who's going to grow up with nothing but some press clippings for a Daddy?

If Whitey down South doesn't kill me in Greenwood then Whitey up North will kill me in show business. Everybody I talked to but Lil told me not to go. It would ruin me as a comic. Nobody's going to come to laugh at an entertainer who goes marching and demonstrating and getting himself arrested.

I had two airline tickets in my room, one for me and one for James Sanders, a brilliant young Negro comedy writer. I dropped them in the waste-basket. I'll call SNCC headquarters, tell them I'm sick, I've changed my mind, I can't break my contract and leave town. I called Lil instead, at the hospital. She told me not to worry about anything, to go down if I wanted to, and suddenly I was telling her about that Mississippi Negro, the man that other Negroes called nigger, that cotton-picker in his tarpaper shack who could rip this thing, who could give courage to every Negro in America, who could wake up the nation. I had faith then that when America saw what was happening in Greenwood, it would make sure that it never happened again, anywhere. I wanted to be a part of this thing, but I was scared.

Sure, I had made speeches that every door of racial prejudice I can kick down is one less door that my children have to kick down. But, hell, my kids don't have to worry. . . .

I lay there all that night, into the morning, going, not going, picking the tickets out of the wastebasket, throwing them back in, but never tearing them up. And as I lay there my own life started spinning around in my mind, and my stomach turned over, and I thought about St. Louis and Momma and Richard, running off to buy himself a dinner of a Twinkie Cupcake and a bottle of Pepsi-Cola, little Richard whose Daddy was so broken by the system that he ran away and came back just to take the rent money out of the jar in the kitchen. Goddamn, we're always running and hiding, and then I thought about an old man whose wife had died, and about Clyde Kennard, and about James Meredith, they didn't run away, and now it was almost dawn in Philadelphia and there was a familiar dry taste in my mouth, and that old hot water was seeping into a cold body and my room was the grandstand of the biggest stadium in the world—America—and the race was for survival and the monster said go.

Playing in the Apocalypse

Assata Shakur

Assata

ONE YEAR EVERYBODY WAS wearing buttons on their coats. Some had writing on them and others had pictures of movie stars. I went somewhere with my mother and my aunt, and they asked me if i wanted a button. I picked out one with Elvis Presley on it. All the kids at school thought Elvis Presley was cool. I wore that button religiously, all winter, and that summer, when i went down South, i went to see one of Elvis Presley's movies.

In Wilmington, at that time, there was only one movie theater where Black people were allowed to go. It was called the Bailey Theater. Once you bought your ticket, you went up a long staircase on the side of the theater to the second balcony, the "colored" section. Shame on you if you were nearsighted. The movie was like all the rest of Elvis's movies—forgettable! When it was over, i went downstairs. All the white kids were leaving with pictures of Elvis Presley that they had bought. I started to walk to my grandparents' restaurant on Red Cross Street, but then i turned around and walked back. If the white kids could have a picture of Elvis, then so could i. At least i was gonna try. I knew it would be absolutely no use to go to the ticket booth and ask the woman anything. She would most assuredly say no. So i walked right on past her, straight into the white section of the theater. What a surprise it was! It was just like the movies in New York. They had soda machines, a butter popcorn machine, and all kinds of candy and potato chips and things. Upstairs in the "colored" section, they had some old, stale plain popcorn and a few candy bars and that was it.

The moment i walked in, all the action stopped. Everybody's eyes were on me. I walked over to the counter where they were selling the pictures. Before i could open my mouth, the salesgirl told me, "You're in the wrong section; just go outside and go up the stairs on the side."

"I want to buy a picture of Elvis Presley," i said.

"What'd you say, again?" she drawled.

"I want to buy a picture of Elvis Presley," i repeated. "They don't have any upstairs."

"Well, I don't know," she said. "I'll have to get the manager." She said something to the other woman behind the counter and then left. By this time a crowd had gathered around me.

"What's she doing in here?" they kept asking each other. "Now, she knows better," somebody was saying. "Look, Ma, a colored girl." "Ya get lost, honey?" "What's she want?" "Don't they have no pictures in the colored sec-tion?" "What's she need with a picture anyway?"

The crowd was all around me, gawking. It seemed like the manager would never come.

"Can't she read? Don't she know that we don't allow no colored in here?" "I don't know what it's about. Something about a picture." "Came walking right in here bold as day."

Finally the salesgirl came back. A man was with her. All eyes were fixed on the manager. He took one look at me and another at the crowd forming around me.

"Give her the picture and get'er out of here," he told the salesgirl. Hur-riedly, she sold me the picture.

"All right, folks, it's all over now. Go on about your business."

I took my picture and went prancing out into the daylight. I was feeling good. It seemed funny when i thought about it. The looks on those crakas' faces, all puffed up like balloons. I had a good time, laughing all the way to my grandparents' restaurant. And of course the minute i got there, i told everybody what happened. I was just so proud. I took my picture and put it on the back counter right next to the funeral parlor calendar. The picture stayed there a few days until Johnnie from the cab stand across the street came and told me that Elvis had said the only thing a Black person could do for him was to buy his records and shine his shoes. Quietly, i slid the picture into obscurity, then oblivion. (Later i read that Elvis had given Spiro Agnew a gold-plated .357 Magnum and had volunteered to work for the FBI.)

TIMOTHY LEARY

The Delicious Grace of Moving One's Hand

MYTHS ABOUT LSD

The First Myth: IT'S OKAY TO TAKE PSYCHEDELIC DRUGS IF YOU'RE SERIOUS-MINDED BUT YOU SHOULDN'T TAKE THEM FOR KICKS.

True or false? I think my answer to this myth is fairly obvious. I think that you should take psychedelic drugs for kicks. There's this weird illusion that dope should have a practical reward. Marijuana's all right, for example, if it can reduce alcoholism and raise your income. We're just beginning the neurological revolution. We know now that we can change consciousness. It doesn't make any difference what you've got going in space if you don't control, manage, and direct your own consciousness toward natural freedom.

I had an interesting experience once on a stage like this at MIT. I was having a debate with Professor Letvin. He's a psychiatrist I had been somewhat friendly with when I was at Harvard. He stood on a stage and said that he didn't want to debate on the dangers of LSD and marijuana because there was nothing to be worried about. The main issue was moral—was I the devil?—and that's pretty far out for an MIT psychiatrist in 1967 or whenever it was to stand there and talk to MIT people and talk about the devil. That was the saddest moment of my life. I felt for the first time that I had met someone who understood at least what the issue was about. He said that good was the logical, rational mind and anything that threatened to loosen or divert or turn off for one minute this divine manifestation of two billion revolutions was the devil.

Another myth: LSD WILL STOP THE REVOLUTION.
   Now the facts of the matter are that I consider the psychedelic drugs plus electric rock and roll to be the most powerful revolutionary agents man has ever known. It's so obvious and so logical and empirically demonstrable. When anyone in any country in the world today—including America, Europe, Western Europe, Eastern Europe, anyone who turns on today is automatically doing something that is illegal. That means that the person who is going to turn on must, in his own mind, and eventually in his own behavior, say to the government in Peking or in Moscow or in Stockholm or in Washington, "I don't believe the government has the right to control my mind or pass laws against my changing my consciousness."
   Turning on is a political act. It's the kind of political act that is most characteristic of the new revolution which is the *hedonic* revolution. The weapons here are not Molotov bombs. The weapons are the radiant eye and the smiling face, the holy orgasm—as a revolutionary weapon it can never be overlooked.
   A second fascinating thing about psychedelic drugs as revolutionary agents is that they put you into a conspiracy immediately. If you want to turn on you can't go to the drugstore, right, and mail in a coupon to get your dope. You have to engage in a rather risky contract with someone that you trust enough and that trusts you enough. Now this loving, benevolent network does not work in a perfect way. But still I would say that the dope network does exist and

the efficiency and the loyalty and the brotherhood and sisterhood it develops is a socioeconomic fact that has been overlooked by most of our scholars.

Now there's a third political aspect to turning on that is extremely important. It immediately puts you on the right side in the cowboys and Indians game or the cops and robbers game or whatever they called it in your neighborhood when you were a kid. Imagine, for example, *Das Kapital*. And just suppose Rosemary and I could get in our time machine and go back and knock on his door and we'd walk in and say, "Karl, baby, I've got something here for you, something that is guaranteed within six months to turn 75 percent of the student body, the aristocratic student body of the University of St. Petersburg on the right side of the Cossacks and into the free man game."

Another, fourth, and the most important revolutionary aspect of the psychedelic strength is that it does internally, neurologically, what it is doing outside, symbolically. You see, the symbolic forms or the behavioral forms of revolution are placards and picketing and demonstrations, storming the Bastille, and burning draft cards, and these are important and necessary at a particular moment. But they're short-lived. And they really don't change a lot of minds. They tend to solidify a position: You burn your draft card and it solidifies everyone a little more seriously. These are symbolic acts, but the revolutionary act of taking a psychedelic drug is very important because it *anarchizes your nervous system*. It does the same thing inside that you want to do outside, that is liberate.

Now that we're on this topic—The Fifth Myth: I'm frequently counted upon to say this: BLACKS DON'T SEEM TO TURN ON. THE BLACKS DON'T LIKE TO TAKE LSD.

Well, I don't know about that. I have talked to most of the black militant leaders in the country and not one of them said he'd throw me in jail when he took over. As a matter of fact, most of them turn on. As a matter of fact, a good way of defining the psychedelic experience is to say that blacks are more turned on than whites. Now I'm not going into any liberal, masochistic routine here. I don't feel badly about this because I can say flatly that almost everything important I've learned in the last eight years about how to live a life of joy and increasing love and beauty and sensuality and freedom I've learned from colored people. That is, I went to India and studied with brown people over there. And I've listened to the rhythms and to the messages and to the teachings of the black Americans. *Soul on Ice* is a very powerful statement of the turned on position and of course, the red Indians are here to teach us a great deal. The psychedelic movement is a technicolor movement and there ain't no pure whites. The Tao-dye is always blending.

Another interesting thing about the black movement: It's very important that we're clear about what's happening. The blacks are in favor of *dropping out*. What did you say? Well, that's exactly what the black movement is. Blacks are saying, We're dropping out of the American system of reward and punishment, that they're completely irrelevant and ridiculous. We want our own school, we want our own department, we want our own thing. That's all that is meant by the term drop out. You drop out and do your own thing. We have a tremendous amount to learn from our black prophets and our black gurus.

Now the Sixth Myth has to do with research. It's the liberal kind of *Harper's, New Republic, New York Times, San Francisco Chronicle* position to say, "DRUGS LIKE LSD AND MARIJUANA SHOULD BE AVAILABLE TO RESEARCH — SERIOUS-MINDED, APPROVED, FEDERALLY FUNDED RESEARCH . . ."

Well, I want to say right here for the record, here and now, that if anyone is going to have control over the chemicals which can change my mind, the last person I want to have control over these chemicals is a serious-minded government agent. I want Rosemary to have those drugs and I want my brothers and sisters at the ranch to have control over my mind and I want you to, too. You control these things yourself with the help of your wife and your husband and your friends. The whole thing about research, of course, is that research is a new, white elephant in this country. Research . . . can you do research on happiness, can you do research on ecstasy, can you do research on your spiritual experience?

Obviously you can't.

Well, yes you can. If you want to and if that's your thing, do it. Maybe we'll learn something from it. I'm very impressed, for example, by the research that **Johnson and Matthews** did on the sexual experience. It's perfectly analogous if it's different at all from the psychedelic experience. **Houston and Matthews** hooked up many women and they recorded all the physiological events that occurred during, before, and after orgasm and it's a great deal. I think maybe a lot of people can benefit by reading that book but I don't think that the only time you should have sex is when it's research. I can just imagine that if you get some government psychiatrists studying the sexual response, you'd really have a heavy thing. We gave this couple

---

Masters and Johnson: Virginia Johnson and William Masters (humorously referred to here as Houston and Matthews, and Johnson and Matthews?) are best known for their investigation of the physiology of sexual intercourse using volunteers at the Reproductive Biological Research Foundation in St. Louis. Their reports, *Human Sexual Response* and *Human Sexual Inadequacy*, were wildly popular in the late '60s and early '70s.

intelligence tests during the event and their IQ dropped. They can't even divide 7 into 100 backwards. Matter of fact they can't even hold a normal conversation while they're copulating. The social intelligence is destroyed completely. They knock over vases and make grunting noises. And what it does to the heart rate. Clearly sex should be under the auspices of government scientists only. Laymen are not allowed.

The Seventh Myth. A seventh frequently appearing comment is that IT'S TOO BAD THAT PSYCHEDELIC DRUGS ARE ILLEGAL.

True or False? Well, I don't worry about it at all. Matter of fact, I just know that psychedelic drugs have to be *a-legal.* How can you have an uptight repressive controlled government licensing a hedonic, spiritual chemical?

You know that sex is illegal—you have to have a special license to do it. I sent this back to my planet. I said, "Lovemaking down here, you have to have a government license to do it." And it really blew their minds up there. Now you know you're on the right track in the pursuit of freedom and ecstatic pleasure and God if you're in trouble with the law, and if you're not you have to worry a little bit.

If you have any messianic or visionary solution to make everyone happy and joyous and loving and you start talking about it and set up a little shop or start a little institute and you do it and so forth the government is not going to bother you unless it starts to work.

No, I don't think that we can expect that a controlled society can legalize freedom. You can't expect it. There *is* a risk involved. Well, so what? I'm glad there is a risk. I'm glad the psychedelic experience is something that you just can't sign up on the easy pay card plan. I'm glad you have to put your chips out—your spiritual and your emotional and your realistic chips. If the game isn't a risk what are you playing for?

Now another myth, the Eighth Myth, constantly debated back and forth, is that LSD CHANGES YOU FOR BETTER OR FOR WORSE.

I'm not sure whether LSD does change you. I think it may unfold you. It may bring to the surface things that you weren't aware of and again we've got to be realistic about this. They can't be good or bad in the social sense or even the psychological sense.

I'm not sure that anything happens during or after LSD that wouldn't have happened anyway. It may have speeded it up. A lot of people were confronted with their inevitable psychosis at the age of eighteen instead of the age of fifty when they're running for Congress.

Now in the early days the hoax was that LSD made people crazy, so that people took LSD and something strange was happening. Well, after eight or ten years of it, I can only conclude that LSD probably *prevents* the number of inevitable psychoses. Where it does help them unfold, it does it under a voluntary circumstance where you know it's the drug that's doing it.

Now in Myth Number Nine we have here the statement that LSD BREAKS CHROMOSOMES.

Well, you know, I wish they did. But, unfortunately for our visionary hopes, LSD does not break chromosomes. This was a hoax. That's a pretty heavy thing to say—that something will affect your unborn children. The anti-pleasure forces have run through a series of dire warnings.

Interestingly enough they ran through exactly the same warnings that the AMA was running through a hundred years ago. Rosemary brought back from a swap meet—she's addicted to swap meets—anyhow, a book leather-bound and gold. I opened it up. It was the most impressive book I'd ever seen, parchment paper. And it was written by an MD who lived in Boston one hundred years ago and it had the imprimatur and the stamp of the Massachusetts Medical Society, and the Congregational Church Medical Society, and the *Boston Globe*, and the *New York Times*. Everyone said "Read this book." And I opened it up and I read the chapter on self-abuse. It was titled *Self-Abuse: How It Rises and Is Maintained.* I realized that I was in the hands of either a great humorist or a terribly guilty masturbator. It was really unbelievable. He laid down a whole trip on masturbation and it was exactly what they're saying about psychedelic drugs today. He said, you know, first of all it makes you crazy. You can always tell one when you see them. They have a kind of an easy, shiftless look about them. He said in particular you can tell how the female masturbator walks because she kind of slinks. Not only will it put you in a mental hospital—you'll be absolutely certain to go to a mental hospital—but that's not the worst part of it. Really, it's a disease. And there are all sorts of diagnostic clues as to how to pick one out. He says, "I don't care how much the boy or girl lies to me, I can tell one when I see them." The worst thing about it is . . . well, not the worst thing . . . but one of the worst things is that masturbation is a disease which is really worse than typhoid because with typhoid maybe a cure can get you back on your feet but once a masturbator is on the road to pleasure, hedonism, and sexuality there's no ending except the mental hospital or the house of ill shame. Then you had: It rots your brain and it's bad for your digestion and it loosens the will. There's just no power at all. The masturbator just won't buckle down to the Protestant Ethic at all. But worst of all, if you don't care about going to the mental hospital, if you don't care about your body, your parents, your country, and so forth, think of our children. *Masturbation leads to monsters.*

Now I'll run through briefly some of these other myths. There's a Tenth Myth that IT'S ALL RIGHT IF COLLEGE KIDS EXPERIMENT WITH DRUGS A LITTLE, THAT'S NATURAL. They're growing up, it's like going off to the whorehouse in Atlantic City so let them have their fun, that the real menaces here are the dealers.

Well, the medium is the message, and I will predict flatly that if we have television—hedonic youth of the television waves of the future—the great heroes, the mythic heroes of our times are going to be the rock and roll musicians and the dealers. I know that human nature is frail and that there are a lot of unloving things that happen in an economic society like our own. And money is involved in many transactions with drugs although increasingly less with LSD but still I would say that all of the economic groups who are out making money in this country, the holiest I know, and I've met and talked to many of them, are dealers.

This was taught out in the Catholic Church which is a very very sophisticated psychedelic organization. The Catholic Church had a big heresy controversy. They said that the holy host, the sacrament of the Catholic Church, once it was consecrated, is supposed to be the body and blood of God. Now if that host is given to you by a priest who is a sinner, who has taken money on the side, does it still work? And the answer came down: "Yes, you've got to believe that the medium is the message." And the message can pass through the hands of CBS or NBC or ABC and the soap salesmen but still it's happening and it's happening in an electronic flashing way. I believe another group that's very misunderstood are the rock and roll promoters. Well, you say, they're having a festival and they brought in all these rock and roll bands and 50,000 kids came out but somebody made a lot of money on it. It's unfortunate if that happens but still 50,000 kids had their conditioning and their reflexes and their reward and punishment system shaken up a little by the Rolling Stones.

Now another myth, the Eleventh Myth: PSYCHEDELIC DRUGS MAY BE OKAY FOR RESPONSIBLE ADULTS BUT CERTAINLY NOT FOR YOUNG PEOPLE.

Of course, it's a biological fact that young people are closer to the divine process than old people, closer to their bodies, to their senses, to their DNA code and the whole thing. The whole revolution, everything that is happening today, comes from exactly the people that supposedly are not ready or mature or serious enough to discover heaven on earth.

MALCOLM X

The Autobiography of Malcolm X

EVERY MORNING WHEN I wake up, now, I regard it as having another borrowed day. In any city, wherever I go, making speeches, holding meetings of my organization, or attending to other business, black men are watching every move I make, awaiting their chance to kill me. I have said publicly many times that I know that they have their orders. Anyone who chooses not to believe what I am saying doesn't know the Muslims in the Nation of Islam.

But I am also blessed with faithful followers who are, I believe, as dedicated to me as I once was to Mr. Elijah Muhamad. Those who would hunt a man need to remember that a jungle also contains those who hunt the hunters.

I know, too, that I could suddenly die at the hands of some white racists. Or I could die at the hands of some Negro hired by the white man. Or it could be some brainwashed Negro acting on his own idea that by eliminating me he would be helping out the white man, because I talk about the white man the way I do.

Anyway, now, each day I live as if I am already dead, and I tell you what I would like for you to do. When I *am* dead—I say it that way because from the things I *know*, I do not expect to live long enough to read this book in its finished form—I want you to just watch and see if I'm not right in what I say: that the white man, in his press, is going to identify me with "hate."

He will make use of me dead, as he has made use of me alive, as a convenient symbol of "hatred"—and that will help him to escape facing the truth that all I have been doing is holding up a mirror to reflect, to show, the history of unspeakable crimes that his race has committed against my race.

You watch. I will be labeled as, at best, an "irresponsible" black man. I have always felt about this accusation that the black "leader" whom white men consider to be "responsible" is invariably the black "leader" who never gets any results. You only get action as a black man if you are regarded by the white man as "irresponsible." In fact, this much I had learned when I was just a little boy. And since I have been some kind of a "leader" of black people here in the racist society of America, I have been more reassured each time the white man resisted me, or attacked me harder—because each time made me more certain that I was on the right track in the American black man's best interests.

The racist white man's opposition automatically made me know that I did offer the black man something worthwhile.

Yes, I have cherished my "demagogue" role. I know that societies often have killed the people who have helped to change those societies. And if I can die having brought any light, having exposed any meaningful truth that will help to destroy the racist cancer that is malignant in the body of America — then, all of the credit is due to Allah. Only the mistakes have been mine.

LENNY BRUCE

How to Talk Dirty and Influence People

WHEN I RETURNED to New York, it turned out that the police didn't have complete tapes of the shows I was arrested for, so they actually had a guy in court *imitating my act* — a License Department Inspector who was formerly a CIA agent in Vietnam — and in his courtroom impersonation of me, he was saying things that I had never said in my *life*, on stage or off.

Witnesses for the prosecution included *New York Daily News* columnist Robert Sylvester, Marya Mannes from *The Reporter*, John Fischer, editor of *Harper's* magazine, and a minister.

Witnesses for the defense included Jules Feiffer, Nat Hentoff, Dorothy Kilgallen, and *two* ministers.

"Sitting in on Lenny Bruce's current New York 'obscenity' trial," Stephanie Gervis Harrington wrote in the *Village Voice*, "one gets the feeling of being present at an historical event — the birth of the courtroom of the absurd. Of course, if you sit through it long enough, you gradually adjust to the fact that eight grown men are actually spending weeks of their time and an unreckoned amount of the taxpayers' money in deliberation — passionate deliberation on the prosecutor's good days — over whether another grown man should be able to use four-letter words in public without going to jail."

The ludicrousness of it all was inadvertently summed up by my attorney, Ephraim London, when he asked a witness who had been at my performance at the Café Au Go Go: "Did you see Mr. Crotch touch his Bruce?"

On reporting the incident, *The Realist* predicted, "Henceforth and forevermore, we shall have had at that precise moment a meaningful new synonym added to our language." And the magazine's editorial proceeded to demonstrate its use:

"Mommy, look, there's a man sitting over there with his bruce hanging out."

"Beverly Schmidlap is a real bruceteaser, y'know?"

"Kiss my bruce, baby."

And a cartoon by Ed Fisher had a judge saying, "Before I pass sentence on you, Lenny Bruce, is there anything you wish to say—anything printable, that is?"

Meanwhile, back in real life, a three-judge Criminal Court, in a 2–1 split vote, sentenced me to three four-month terms in the workhouse, to be served concurrently. But the State Supreme Court has granted me a certificate of reasonable doubt and—at this writing—the case is on appeal.

What does it mean for a man to be found obscene in New York? This is the most sophisticated city in the country. This is where they play Genet's *The Balcony.* If anyone is the first person to be found obscene in New York, he must feel utterly depraved.

I was so sure I could reach those judges if they'd just let me tell them what I try to do. It was like I was on trial for rape and there I was crying, "But, Judge, I can't rape anybody, I haven't got the wherewithal," but nobody was listening, and my lawyers were saying, "Don't worry, Lenny, you got a right to rape anyone you please, we'll beat 'em in the appellate court."

The *New York Law Journal* pleaded guilty to not publishing the lower court's statement, with an explanation: "The majority opinion, of necessity, cited in detail the language used by Bruce in his night-club act, and also described gestures and routines which the majority found to be obscene and indecent. The *Law Journal* decided against publication, even edited, on the grounds that deletions would destroy the opinion, and without the deletions publication was impossible within the *Law Journal* standards."

Among the examples of my "obscene references" that the court had quoted in its opinion, the very first was this: "Eleanor Roosevelt and her display of 'tits.' "

Now, in the course of my research I obtained the legislative history from Albany of the statute under which I had been arrested, and I discovered back in 1931 there was added to that statute an amendment which *excludes from arrest* stagehands, spectators, musicians and *actors.* The amendment was finally signed into law by Governor Roosevelt. The court refused to be influenced by this information.

Well, I believe that ignoring the mandate of Franklin D. Roosevelt is a great deal more offensive than saying that Eleanor had lovely nay-nays.

● ● ●

June 1964—graduation time—honorary degrees were being handed out all over the place. The TV show, *That Was the Week That Was*, bestowed on me—or rather upon a photograph of me with a graduation cap superimposed on my head—an honorary Doctor of Letters: "To the man who won fame using them four at a time."

I'm really so fed up with the "dirty word" thing. People think, Christ, I'm *obsessed* with that. But I just *have* to defend myself because you don't know how much I'm attacked on it. Every new time I go on the road, the papers are filled with it.

Now I'll say "a Jew" and just the word *Jew* sounds like a dirty word, and people don't know whether to laugh or not. They'll seem so brazen. So there's just silence until they know I'm kidding, and then they'll break through.

A Jew.

In the dictionary, a Jew is one who is descended from the ancient tribe of Judea, but—I'll say to an audience—you and I know what a Jew is: one who killed our Lord. Now there's dead silence there after that.

When I did this in England, I said, "I don't know if you know that over here, but it got a lot of press in the States." Now the laughs start to break through. "We did it about two thousand years ago, and there should be a statute of limitations with that crime." Now they know—the laughter's all there—but I'm *not* kidding, because there *should* be a statute of limitations for that crime, and those who pose as Christians—paraphrasing Shakespeare—neither having the gait of Christians nor the actions of Christians—still make the Jews pay their dues.

I go from a pedantry (Shakespeare) to the hip argot (pay their dues) for another deuce.

Then I ask, why should Jews pay these dues? Granted that we killed him and he was a nice guy; although there was even some talk that we didn't kill Christ, we killed Gesmas, the one on the left. (There were, you recall, three who got done in that day.) But I confess that we killed him, despite those who said that Roman soldiers did it.

Yes, we did it. I did it. My family. I found a note in my basement: "We killed him—signed, Morty."

"Why did you kill Christ, Jew?"

"We killed him because he didn't want to become a doctor, that's why."

Now sometimes I'll get sort of philosophical with it and maybe a little maudlin: "We killed him at his own request, because he was sad—he knew that people would use him."

Or sometimes I will tag it with, "Not only did we kill him, but we're gonna kill him again when he comes back."

I suppose that if *I* were Christlike, I would turn the other cheek and keep letting you punch me out and even kill me, because what the hell, I'm God's son, and it's not so bad dying when you know that you've got a pass to come back indefinitely. All right, so you have to take a little crap when you come home and you have to "get it" from your Father . . .

"Oh, you started again, you can't get along. Who was it this time? The Jews, eh? Why can't you stop preaching? Look, this is the last time I'm telling you, the next time you get killed, you're *staying* there. I've had enough aggravation with your mother."

Of all the comedians I have ever met, Steve Allen is not only the most literate, but also the most moral. He not only talks about society's problems, but he *does* things about them. He's a good person, without being all sugar and showbiz, and I really dig him for that.

I was on the *Steve Allen Show* twice. Now, if I work for an hour in a night club, out of that hour I will ad-lib perhaps four minutes; sometimes, if I'm really fertile, ten minutes. But for me ever to have to come out and open with the same word and finish with the same word and do the same bits in the same order in each show, then I wouldn't feel like a comic at all. But you have to do this for television. And it bugs me.

They sat me down there, and I'm doing the bit for 15 guys. And I got into material that they wouldn't let me do on the *Allen Show*. I have a tattoo on my arm, and because of this tattoo, I can never be buried in a Jewish cemetery. That's the Orthodox law. You have to go out of the world the same way you came in—no marks, no changes.

Anyway, I told how, when I got back from Malta and went home to Long Island, I was in the kitchen, washing with soap, and my Aunt Mema saw the tattoo. So she flips. A real Jewish yell.

"Look what you did! You ruined your arm! You're no better than a gypsy!"

So the producer says that I can't do this on the show because it would definitely be offensive to the Jewish people.

"You're out of your *nut*," I responded.

No, he said, every time we get into a satire of any ethnic group, we get a lot of mail. You can't talk about that.

I argued with them. I said if they wouldn't let me do that, I wouldn't do the show. Now, I'll never use four-letter words for shock value—it has to fit and swing with the character whom I want to say it—but I know I can't use four-letter words on television in *any* case. But here, I wasn't making any such references, I was just doing a true bit.

They had a meeting about it. They argued for about an hour while I was kept waiting in a corner, like a leper with a bell on my neck.

Playing in the Apocalypse

"We talked it over, Lenny. You know, it's not only offensive to the Jewish people, but it's definitely offensive to the Gentile people too."

"Oh, yeah—how do you figure that?"

"Well, what you're saying in essence is that the Gentiles don't *care* what they bury."

The funny thing is, friends of mine are always showing me anti-Semitic articles. "Look at what this bigoted bastard wrote!" And then I dug something. Liberals will buy anything a bigot writes.

In fact, they really *support* hatemongers.

George Lincoln Rockwell, head of the American Nazi Party, is probably a very knowledgeable businessman with no political convictions whatsoever. He gets three bucks a head and works the mass rallies consisting of nothing but angry Jews, shaking their fists and wondering why there are so many Jews there.

And Rockwell probably has only two *real* followers—and they're deaf. They think the swastika is merely an Aztec symbol.

PAUL KRASSNER

My Acid Trip with Groucho Marx

EACH TABLET OF OWSLEY White Lightning contained 300 micrograms of LSD. I had purchased a large enough supply from Dick Alpert to finance his trip to India. The day before he left to meditate for six months, we sat in a restaurant discussing the concept of choiceless awareness while trying to decide what to order on the menu.

In India, he gave his guru three tablets and apparently nothing happened.

"Come fuck the universe with me," Alpert's postcard beckoned. Instead, I stayed tripping in America, where I kept my entire stash of acid in a bank vault deposit box.

LSD was influencing music, painting, spirituality, and the stock market. Tim Leary once let me listen in on a call from a Wall Street broker thanking him for turning him onto acid because it gave him the courage to sell short. Leary had a certain sense of pride about the famous folks he and his associates had introduced to the drug.

"But," he told me, "I consider Otto Preminger one of our failures."

I first met Preminger in 1960 while I was conducting a panel on censorship for *Playboy*. He had defied Hollywood's official seal of approval by refusing to change the script of *The Moon Is Blue*. He wouldn't take out the word *virgin*. At the end of our interview, he asked, "Ven you tronscripe dis, vill you fix op my Henglish?"

"Oh, sure," I replied quickly. "Of course."

"Vy? Vot's drong viz my Henglish?"

I saw Otto Preminger again in 1968. He was making a movie called *Skidoo*, starring Jackie Gleason as a retired criminal. Preminger told me he had originally intended the role for Frank Sinatra. I was hanging around with friends from the Hog Farm, who were extras in the movie. *Skidoo* was proacid propaganda thinly disguised as a comedy adventure. However, LSD was not why the FBI was annoyed with the film. Rather, according to Gleason's FBI files, the FBI objected to one scene in the script where a file cabinet is stolen from an FBI building. Gleason was later approved as a special FBI contact in the entertainment business.

One of the characters in *Skidoo* was a Mafia chieftain named God. Screenwriter Bill Cannon had suggested Groucho Marx for the part. Preminger said it wasn't a good idea, but since they were already shooting, and that particular character was needed on the set in three days, Groucho would be playing God after all. I had dinner with Groucho. He was concerned about the script of *Skidoo* because it pretty much advocated LSD, which he had never tried, but he was curious. Moreover, he felt a certain responsibility to his young audience not to steer them wrong, so could I possibly get him some pure stuff and would I care to accompany him on a trip? I did not play hard to get. We arranged to ingest those little white tablets one afternoon at the home of an actress in Beverly Hills.

Groucho was especially interested in the counter-cultural aspects of LSD. I mentioned a couple of incidents that particularly tickled him, and his eyes sparkled with delight. One was about how, on Haight Street, runaway youngsters —refugees from their own families—had stood outside a special tourist bus— guided by a driver "trained in sociological significance"—and held mirrors up to the cameras pointing at them from the windows, so that the tourists would get photos of themselves trying to take photos. The other was about the day that LSD became illegal. In San Francisco, at precisely two o'clock in the afternoon, a cross-fertilization of mass protest and tribal celebration had taken place, as several hundred young people simultaneously swallowed tabs of acid while the police stood by helplessly. "Internal possession wasn't against the law," I explained to Groucho.

"And they trusted their friends more than they trusted the government," he said. "I like that."

We had a period of silence and a period of listening to music. I was accustomed to playing rock and roll while tripping, but the record collection at this house consisted entirely of classical music and Broadway show albums. First, we listened to the Bach Cantata No. 7. "I'm supposed to be Jewish," Groucho said, "but I was seeing the most beautiful visions of Gothic cathedrals. Do you think Bach *knew* he was doing that?"

"I don't know. I was seeing beehives and honeycombs myself."

Later, we were listening to the score of a musical comedy, *Fanny*. There was one song called "Welcome Home," where the lyrics go something like, "Welcome home, says the clock," and the chair says, "Welcome home," and so do various other pieces of furniture. Groucho started acting out each line, as though he were actually *being* greeted by the clock, the chair, and the rest of the furniture. He was like a child, charmed by his own ability to respond to the music that way.

There was a bowl of fruit on the dining room table. During a snack, he said, "I never thought eating a nice juicy plum would be the biggest thrill of my life."

Then we talked about the sexual revolution. Groucho asked, "Have you ever laid two ladies together?" I told him about the time that I was being interviewed by a couple of students from a Catholic girls' school. Suddenly Sheila Campion, *The Realist*'s Scapegoat, and Marcia Ridge, the Shit-On—she had given herself that title because "What could be lower than a Scapegoat?"—walked out of their office totally nude. "Sorry to interrupt, Paul," said Sheila, "but it's Wednesday—time for our weekly orgy." The interviewers left in a hurry. Sheila and Marcia led me up the stairs to my loft bed, and we had a delicious threesome. It had never happened before and it would never happen again.

At one point in our conversation, Groucho somehow got into a negative space. He was equally cynical about institutions, such as marriage—"legal quicksand"—and individuals, such as Lyndon Johnson—"that potato-head."

Eventually, I asked, "What gives you hope?"

He thought for a moment. Then he just said one word: "People."

He told me about one of his favorite contestants on *You Bet Your Life*. "He was an elderly gentleman with white hair, but quite a chipper fellow. I asked him what he did to retain his sunny disposition. 'Well, I'll tell you,' he said. 'Every morning I get up and I *make a choice* to be happy that day.' "

Groucho was holding on to his cigar for a long time, but he never smoked it, he only sniffed it occasionally. "Everybody has their own Laurel and

Hardy," he mused. "A miniature Laurel and Hardy, one on each shoulder. Your little Oliver Hardy bawls you out—he says, 'Well, this is a *fine mess* you've gotten us into.' And your little Stan Laurel gets all weepy—'Oh, Ollie, I couldn't help it. I'm sorry, I did the best I *could.* . . .' "

Later, when Groucho started chuckling to himself, I hesitated to interrupt his reverie, but I had to ask, "What struck you funny?"

"I was thinking about this movie, *Skidoo*," he said. "I mean some of it is just plain ridiculous. This kid puts his stationery, which is soaked in LSD, into the water supply of the prison, and suddenly everybody gets completely reformed. There's a prisoner who says, 'Oh, gosh, now I don't have to be a rapist any more!' But it's also sophisticated in its own way. I like how Jackie Gleason, the character he plays, *accepts* the fact that he's not the biological father of his daughter."

"Oh, yeah? That sounds like the ultimate ego loss."

"But I'm really getting a big kick out of playing somebody named God like a dirty old man. You wanna know why?"

"Type casting?"

"No, no—it's because—do you realize that irreverence and reverence are the *same thing?*"

"Always?"

"If they're not, then it's a misuse of your power to make people laugh." His eyes began to tear. "That's funny," he said. "I'm not even sad."

Then he went to urinate. When he came back, he said, "You know, everybody is waiting for *miracles* to happen. But the whole *human body* is a goddamn miracle."

He recalled Otto Preminger telling him about his own response to taking LSD and then he mimicked Preminger's accent: "I saw *tings*, bot I did not zee myself." Groucho was looking in a mirror on the dining room wall, and he said, "Well, I can see *myself*, but I still don't understand what the hell I'm *doing* here. . . ."

A week later, Groucho told me that the Hog Farm had turned him on with marijuana on the set of *Skidoo*.

"You know," I said, "my mother once warned me that LSD would lead to pot."

"Well, your mother was right."

When *Skidoo* was released, Tim Leary saw it, and he cheerfully admitted, "I was fooled by Otto Preminger. He's much hipper than me."

I met Otto Preminger again in 1969, when we were both guests on the *Merv Griffin Show*, guest-hosted by Orson Bean.

Black Panther Eldridge Cleaver had gone underground to avoid being tried for a shootout with police in Oakland, and I mentioned on the show that I had interviewed him, which wasn't true, although Stew Albert was indeed trying to arrange just such an interview.

Deadpan comedian Jackie Vernon was also a guest on the show. He reacted to my long hair. "Why don't you take a bath?" he said. Nobody had ever asked me that on network television before. Later, I would have a Monday-morning-quarterback session with George Carlin, who applied a kind of Aikido to life as well as to comedy, turning negative energy into positive energy. He suggested, "You should've said, 'Why, thank you, Jackie, I hadn't considered that.' " But when it happened on TV, I was caught off guard and just kept silent. So did the audience. The tension was broken by Preminger.

"Dot iss duh seekness ov our society, dis stereo-typical ottitood."

Then the audience applauded, and we went to a commercial.

Over dinner, Preminger told me that his father was the equivalent of the attorney general in Austria before Hitler's conquest. And he said that someday he wanted to direct a film about Julius and Ethel Rosenberg.

"They were lynch victims of the cold war," he said. "The law says spies can be executed during *wartime*. If Eisenhower had commuted their sentences to life, a less hysterical review of their case could later have resulted in their freedom."

The next day, a pair of FBI agents showed up at my door. They wanted to know where Eldridge Cleaver was. I refused to let them in. "Why should I cooperate with you? The FBI continually hassles people who haven't broken the law."

"Come on, now. That's the FBI. We're individuals."

"I don't believe it—this is just great—here's the FBI warning me about the danger of guilt by association."

In 1971, during an interview with *Flash* magazine, Groucho Marx said, "I think the only hope this country has is Nixon's assassination." Yet he wasn't subsequently arrested for threatening the life of a president. In view of the indictment against Black Panther David Hilliard for using similar rhetoric, I wrote to the Justice Department to find out the status of their case against Groucho, and received this reply:

> Dear Mr. Krassner:
>   Responding to your inquiry, the Supreme Court has held that Title 18 U.S.C., Section 871, prohibits only "true" threats. It is one thing to say that "I (or *we*) will kill Richard Nixon"

when you are the leader of an organization which advocates killing people and overthrowing the Government; it is quite another to utter the words which are attributed to Mr. Marx, an alleged comedian. It was the opinion of both myself and the United States Attorney in Los Angeles (where Marx's words were alleged to have been uttered) that the latter utterance did not constitute a "true" threat.

Very truly yours,

James L. Browning, Jr.
United States Attorney

It would later be revealed that the FBI had published pamphlets in the name of the Black Panthers, advocating the killing of cops, and that an FBI file on Groucho Marx had indeed been started, and he actually *was* labeled a "national security risk." I phoned Groucho to tell him the good news.

"I deny everything," he said, "because I lie about everything." He paused, then added, "And everything I *deny* is a lie."

The last time I saw Groucho was in 1976. He was speaking at the Los Angeles Book Fair. He looked frail and unsmiling, but he was alert and irascible as ever. He took questions from the audience.

"Are you working on a film now?"

"No, I'm answering silly questions."

"What are your favorite films?"

"*Duck Soup. Night at the Opera.*"

"What do you think about Richard Nixon?"

"He should be in jail."

"Is humor an important issue in the presidential campaign?"

"Get your finger out of your mouth."

"What do you dream about?"

"Not about you."

"What inspired you to write?"

"A fountain pen. A piece of paper."

Then I called out a question: "What gives you the most optimism?"

I expected him to say "People" again, but this time he said, "The world."

There was hardly any standing room left in the auditorium, yet one fellow was sitting on the floor rather than take the aisle seat occupied by a large Groucho Marx doll.

CARLOS CASTANEDA

The Teachings of Don Juan

IN THE EVENING OF Saturday, September 5, the old man sang his peyote song to start the cycle once more. During this session I chewed only one button and did not listen to any of the songs, nor did I pay attention to anything that went on. From the first moment my whole being was uniquely concentrated on one point. I knew something terribly important for my well-being was missing.

While the men sang I asked Mescalito, in a loud voice, to teach me a song. My pleading mingled with the men's loud singing. Immediately I heard a song in my ears. I turned around and sat with my back to the group and listened. I heard the words and the tune over and over, and I repeated them until I had learned the whole song. It was a long song in Spanish. Then I sang it to the group several times. And soon afterward a new song came to my ears. By morning I had sung both songs countless times. I felt I had been renewed, fortified.

After the water was given to us, don Juan gave me a bag, and we all went into the hills. It was a long, strenuous walk to a low mesa. There I saw several peyote plants. But for some reason I did not want to look at them. After we had crossed the mesa, the group broke up. Don Juan and I walked back, collecting peyote buttons just as we had done the first time I helped him.

We returned in the late afternoon of Sunday, September 6. In the evening the leader opened the cycle again. Nobody had said a word but I knew perfectly well it was the last gathering. This time the old man sang a new song. A sack with fresh peyote buttons was passed around. This was the first time I had tasted a fresh button. It was pulpy but hard to chew. It resembled a hard, green fruit, and was sharper and more bitter than the dried buttons. Personally, I found the fresh peyote infinitely more alive.

I chewed fourteen buttons. I counted them carefully. I did not finish the last one, for I heard the familiar rumble that marked the presence of Mescalito. Everybody sang frantically, and I knew that don Juan, and everybody else, had actually heard the noise. I refused to think that their reaction was a response to a cue given by one of them merely to deceive me.

At that moment I felt a great surge of wisdom engulfing me. A conjecture I had played with for three years turned then into a certainty. It had taken me three years to realize, or rather to find out, that whatever is contained in the cactus

Lophophora williamsii had nothing to do with me in order to exist as an entity; it existed by itself out there, at large. I knew it then.

I sang feverishly until I could no longer voice the words. I felt as if my songs were inside my body, shaking me uncontrollably. I needed to go out and find Mescalito, or I would explode. I walked toward the peyote field. I kept on singing my songs. I knew they were individually mine—the unquestionable proof of my singleness. I sensed each one of my steps. They resounded on the ground; their echo produced the indescribable euphoria of being a man.

RICHARD BRAUTIGAN

The Abortion

AH, IT FEELS SO good to sit here in the darkness of these books. I'm not tired. This has been an average evening for books being brought in: with 23 finding their welcomed ways onto our shelves.

I wrote their titles and authors and a little about the receiving of each book down in the Library Contents Ledger. I think the first book came in around 6:30.

MY TRIKE by Chuck. The author was five years old and had a face that looked as if it had been struck by a tornado of freckles. There was no title on the book and no words inside, just pictures.

"What's the name of your book?" I said.

The little boy opened the book and showed me the drawing of a tricycle. It looked more like a giraffe standing upside down in an elevator.

"That's my trike," he said.

"Beautiful," I said. "And what's your name?"

"That's my trike."

"Yes," I said. "Very nice, but what's your name?"

"Chuck."

He reached the book up onto the desk and then headed for the door, saying, "I have to go now. My mother's outside with my sister."

I was going to tell him that he could put the book on any shelf he wanted to, but then he was gone in his small way.

Playing in the Apocalypse

• • •

LEATHER CLOTHES AND THE HISTORY OF MAN by S. M. Justice. The author was quite motorcyclish and wearing an awful lot of leather clothes. His book was made entirely of leather. Somehow the book was printed. I had never seen a 290-page book printed on leather before.

When the author turned the book over to the library, he said, "I like a man who likes leather."

LOVE ALWAYS BEAUTIFUL by Charles Green. The author was about fifty years old and said he had been trying to find a publisher for his book since he was seventeen years old when he wrote the book.

"This book has set the world's record for rejections," he said. "It has been rejected 459 times and now I am an old man."

THE STEREO AND GOD by the Reverend Lincoln Lincoln. The author said that God was keeping his eye on our stereophonic phonographs. I don't know what he meant by that but he slammed the book down very hard on the desk.

PANCAKE PRETTY by Barbara Jones. The author was seven years old and wearing a pretty white dress. "This book is about a pancake," she said.

SAM SAM SAM by Patricia Evens Summers. "It's a book of literary essays," she said. "I've always admired Alfred Kazin and Edmund Wilson, especially Wilson's theories on *The Turn of the Screw*." She was a woman in her late fifties who looked a great deal like Edmund Wilson.

A HISTORY OF NEBRASKA by Clinton York. The author was a gentleman about forty-seven who said he had never been to Nebraska but he had always been interested in the state.

"Ever since I was a child it's been Nebraska for me. Other kids listened to the radio or raved on about their bicycles. I read everything I could find on Nebraska. I don't know what got me started on the thing. But, any way, this is the most complete history ever written about Nebraska."

The book was in seven volumes and he had them in a shopping bag when he came into the library.

HE KISSED ALL NIGHT by Susan Margar. The author was a very plain middle-aged woman who looked as if she had never been kissed. You had to look twice to see if she had any lips on her face. It was a surprise to find her mouth almost totally hidden beneath her nose.

"It's about kissing," she said.

I guess she was too old for any subterfuge now.

MOOSE by Richard Brautigan. The author was tall and blond and had a long yellow mustache that gave him an anachronistic appearance. He looked as if he would be more at home in another era.

This was the third or fourth book he had brought to the library. Every time he brought in a new book he looked a little older, a little more tired. He looked quite young when he brought in his first book. I can't remember the title of it, but it seems to me the book had something to do with America.

"What's this one about?" I asked, because he looked as if he wanted me to ask him something.

"Just another book," he said.

I guess I was wrong about him wanting me to ask him something.

IT'S THE QUEEN OF DARKNESS, PAL by Rod Keen. The author was wearing overalls and had on a pair of rubber boots.

"I work in the city sewers," he said, handing the book to me. "It's science-fiction."

YOUR CLOTHES ARE DEAD by Les Steinman. The author looked like an ancient Jewish tailor. He was very old and looked as if he had made some shirts for Don Quixote.

"They are, you know," he said, showing the book to me as if it were a piece of cloth, a leg from a pair of trousers.

JACK, THE STORY OF A CAT by Hilda Simpson. The author was a girl about twelve years old, just entering into puberty. She had lemon-sized breasts against a green sweater. She was awakening to adolescence in a delightful way.

"What do you have with you this evening?" I said.

Hilda had brought in five or six books previously.

"It's a book about my cat Jack. He's really a noble animal. I thought I would put him down in a book, bring it here and make him famous," she said, smiling.

THE CULINARY DOSTOEVSKI by James Fallon. The author said the book was a cookbook of recipes he had found in Dostoevski's novels.

"Some of them are very good," he said. "I've eaten everything Dostoevski ever cooked."

MY DOG by Bill Lewis. The author was seven years old and said thank you when he put his book on a shelf.

HOMBRE by Canton Lee. The author was a Chinese gentleman about seventy.
"It's a Western," he said. "About a horse thief. Reading Westerns is my hobby, so I decided to write one myself. Why not? I spent thirty years cooking in a restaurant in Phoenix."

VIETNAM VICTORY by Edward Fox. The author was a very serious young man who said that victory could only be achieved in Vietnam by killing everybody there. He recommended that after we had killed everybody there we turn the country over to Chiang Kaishek, so he could attack Red China, then.
"It's only a matter of time," he said.

PRINTER'S INK by Fred Sinkus. The author was a former journalist whose book was almost illegibly written in longhand with his words wrapped around whiskey.
"That's it," he said, handing the book to me. "Twenty years." He left the library unevenly, barely under his own power.
I stood there looking down at twenty years in my hands.

BACON DEATH by Marsha Paterson. The author was a totally nondescript young woman except for a look of anguish on her face. She handed me this fantastically greasy book and fled the library in terror. The book actually looked like a pound of bacon. I was going to open it and see what it was about, but I changed my mind. I didn't know whether to fry the book or put it on the shelf.
Being a librarian here is sometimes a challenge.

UFO VERSUS CBS by Susan DeWitt. The author was an old woman who told me that her book, which was written in Santa Barbara at her sister's house, was about a Martian conspiracy to take over the Columbia Broadcasting System.
"It's all here in my book," she said. "Remember all those flying saucers last summer?"
"I think so," I said.
"They're all in here," she said. The book looked quite handsome and I'm certain they were all in there.

THE EGG LAYED TWICE by Beatrice Quinn Porter. The author said this collection of poetry summed up the wisdom she had found while living twenty-six years on a chicken ranch in San Jose.

"It may not be poetry," she said. "I never went to college, but it's sure as hell about chickens."

BREAKFAST FIRST by Samuel Humber. The author said that breakfast was an absolute requisite for traveling and was overlooked in too many travel books, so he decided that he would write a book about how important breakfast was in traveling.

THE QUICK FOREST by Thomas Funnell. The author was about thirty years old and looked scientific. His hair was thinning and he seemed eager to talk about the book.

"This forest is quicker than an ordinary forest." he said.

"How long did it take you to write it?" I said, knowing that authors seem to like that question.

"I didn't write it," he said. "I stole it from my mother. Serves her right, too. The God-damn bitch."

THE NEED FOR LEGALIZED ABORTION by Doctor O. The author was doctory and very nervous in his late 30s. The book had no title on the cover. The contents were very neatly typed, about 300 pages long.

"It's all I can do," he said.

"Do you want to put it on a shelf yourself?" I said.

"No," he said. "You take care of that yourself. There's nothing else that I can do. It's all a God-damn shame."

It has just started to rain now outside the library. I can hear it splash against the windows and echo among the books. They seem to know it's raining here in the beautiful darkness of lives as I wait for Vida.

WE SLOWLY, CAREFULLY AND abortively made our way back to downtown Tijuana surrounded and bombarded by people trying to sell us things that we did not want to buy.

Playing in the Apocalypse

We had already gotten what we'd come to Tijuana for. I had my arm around Vida. She was all right but she was a little weak.

"How do you feel, honey?" I said.

"I feel all right," she said. "But I'm a little weak."

We saw an old man crouching like a small gum-like piece of death beside an old dilapidated filling station.

"HEY, a pretty, pretty girl!"

Mexican men kept reacting to Vida's now pale beauty.

Vida smiled faintly at me as a taxicab driver dramatically stopped his cab in front of us and leaned out the window and gave a gigantic wolf whistle and said, "WOW! You need a taxi, honey!"

We made our way to the Main Street of Tijuana and found ourselves in front of Woolworth's again and the bunnies in the window.

"I'm hungry," Vida said. She was tired. "So hungry."

"You need something to eat," I said. "Let's go inside and see if we can get you some soup."

"That would be good," she said. "I need something."

We went off the confused dirty Main Street of Tijuana into the clean modern incongruity of Woolworth's. A very pretty Mexican girl took our order at the counter. She asked us what we wanted.

"What would you like?" she said.

"She'd like some soup," I said. "Some clam chowder."

"Yes," Vida said.

"What would you like?" the waitress said in very good Woolworth's English.

"I guess a banana split," I said.

I held Vida's hand while the waitress got our orders. She leaned her head against my shoulder. Then she smiled and said, "You're looking at the future biggest fan The Pill ever had."

"How do you feel?" I said.

"Just like I've had an abortion."

Then the waitress brought us our food. While Vida slowly worked her soup, I worked my banana split. It was the first banana split I'd had in years.

It was unusual fare for the day, but it was no different from anything else that had happened since we'd come to the Kingdom of Tijuana to avail ourselves of the local recreational facilities.

The taxicab driver never took his eyes off Vida as we drove back to America. His eyes looked at us from the rear-view mirror as if he had another face and it was a mirror.

"Did you have a good time in Tijuana?" he said.

"Lovely," I said.
"What did you do?" he said.
"We had an abortion," I said.
"HAHAHAHAHAHAHAVERYFUNNYJOKE!"

the driver laughed.
Vida smiled.
Farewell, Tijuana.
Kingdom of Fire and Water.

HUNTER S. THOMPSON

Fear and Loathing in Las Vegas

MAINLINE GAMBLING IS A very heavy business—and Las Vegas makes Reno seem like your friendly neighborhood grocery store. For a loser, Vegas is the meanest town on earth. Until about a year ago, there was a giant billboard on the outskirts of Las Vegas, saying:

DON'T GAMBLE WITH MARIJUANA!
IN NEVADA: POSSESSION—20 YEARS
SALE—LIFE!

So I was not entirely at ease drifting around the casinos on this Saturday night with a car full of marijuana and head full of acid. We had several narrow escapes: at one point I tried to drive the Great Red Shark into the laundry room of the Landmark Hotel—but the door was too narrow, and the people inside seemed dangerously excited.

We drove over to the Desert Inn, to catch the Debbie Reynolds/Harry James show. "I don't know about you," I told my attorney, "but in my line of business it's important to be Hep."

"Mine too," he said. "But as your attorney I advise you to drive over to the Tropicana and pick up on Guy Lombardo. He's in the Blue Room with his Royal Canadians."

"Why?" I asked.

"Why *what?*"

"Why should I pay out my hard-earned dollars to watch a fucking corpse?"

"Look," he said. "Why are we out here? To entertain ourselves, or to *do the job?*"

"The job, of course," I replied. We were driving around in circles, weaving through the parking lot of a place I thought was the Dunes, but it turned out to be the Thunderbird . . . or maybe it was the Hacienda . . .

My attorney was scanning *The Vegas Visitor*, looking for hints of action. "How about 'Nickel Nick's Slot Arcade?'" he said. "'Hot Slots,' that sounds heavy . . . Twenty-nine cent hotdogs . . ."

Suddenly people were screaming at us. We were in trouble. Two thugs wearing red-gold military overcoats were looming over the hood: "What the hell are you doing?" one screamed. "You can't park *here!*"

"Why not?" I said. It seemed like a reasonable place to park, plenty of space. I'd been looking for a parking spot for what seemed like a very long time. Too long. I was about ready to abandon the car and call a taxi . . . but then, yes, we found this *space.*

Which turned out to be the sidewalk in front of the main entrance to the Desert Inn. I had run over so many curbs by this time, that I hadn't even noticed this last one. But now we found ourselves in a position that was hard to explain . . . blocking the entrance, thugs yelling at us, bad confusion. . . .

My attorney was out of the car in a flash, waving a five-dollar bill. "We want this car parked! I'm an old friend of Debbie's. I used to *romp* with her."

For a moment I thought he had blown it . . . then one of the doormen reached out for the bill, saying: "OK, OK. I'll take care of it, sir." And he tore off a parking stub.

"Holy shit!" I said, as we hurried through the lobby. "They almost had us there. That was quick thinking."

"What do you expect?" he said. "I'm your attorney . . . and you owe me five bucks. I want it now."

I shrugged and gave him a bill. This garish, deep-Orlon carpeted lobby of the Desert Inn seemed an inappropriate place to be haggling about nickel/dime bribes for the parking lot attendant. This was Bob Hope's turf. Frank Sinatra's. Spiro Agnew's. The lobby fairly reeked of high-grade formica and plastic palm trees—it was clearly a high-class refuge for Big Spenders.

We approached the grand ballroom full of confidence, but they refused to let us in. We were too late, said a man in a wine-colored tuxedo; the house was already full—no seats left, at *any* price.

Playing in the Apocalypse

"Fuck seats," said my attorney. "We're old friends of Debbie's. We drove all the way from L.A. for this show, and we're goddamn well going in."

The tux-man began jabbering about "fire regulations," but my attorney refused to listen. Finally, after a lot of bad noise, he let us in for nothing—provided we would stand quietly in back and not smoke.

We promised, but the moment we got inside we lost control. The tension had been too great. Debbie Reynolds was yukking across the stage in a silver Afro wig . . . to the tune of "Sergeant Pepper," from the golden trumpet of Harry James.

"Jesus creeping shit!" said my attorney. "We've wandered into a time capsule!"

Heavy hands grabbed our shoulders. I jammed the hash pipe back into my pocket just in time. We were dragged across the lobby and held against the front door by goons until our car was fetched up. "OK, get lost," said the wine-tux-man. "We're giving you a break. If Debbie has friends like you guys, she's in worse trouble than I thought."

"We'll see about this!" my attorney shouted as we drove away. "You paranoid scum!"

I drove around to the Circus-Circus Casino and parked near the back door. "This is the place," I said. "They'll never fuck with us here."

"Where's the ether?" said my attorney. "This mescaline isn't working."

I gave him the key to the trunk while I lit up the hash pipe. He came back with the ether-bottle, un-capped it, then poured some into a kleenex and mashed it under his nose, breathing heavily. I soaked another kleenex and fouled my own nose. The smell was overwhelming, even with the top down. Soon we were staggering up the stairs towards the entrance, laughing stupidly and dragging each other along, like drunks.

This is the main advantage of ether: it makes you behave like the village drunkard in some early Irish novel . . . total loss of all basic motor skills: blurred vision, no balance, numb tongue—severance of all connection between the body and the brain. Which is interesting, because the brain continues to function more or less normally . . . you can actually *watch* yourself behaving in this terrible way, but you can't control it.

You approach the turnstiles leading into the Circus-Circus and you know that when you get there, you have to give the man two dollars or he won't let you inside . . . but when you get there, everything goes wrong: you misjudge the distance to the turnstile and slam against it, bounce off and grab hold of an old woman to keep from falling, some angry Rotarian shoves you and you think: What's happening here? What's going on? Then you hear yourself mumbling: "Dogs fucked the Pope, no fault of mine. Watch out! . . . Why money? My name is Brinks; I was born . . . born? Get sheep over side . . . women and children to armored car . . . orders from Captain Zeep."

Ah, devil ether—a total body drug. The mind recoils in horror, unable to communicate with the spinal column. The hands flap crazily, unable to get money out of the pocket . . . garbled laughter and hissing from the mouth . . . always smiling.

Ether is the perfect drug for Las Vegas. In this town they love a drunk. Fresh meat. So they put us through the turnstiles and turned us loose inside.

The Circus-Circus is what the whole hep world would be doing on Saturday night if the Nazis had won the war. This is the Sixth Reich. The ground floor is full of gambling tables, like all the other casinos . . . but the place is about four stories high, in the style of a circus tent, and all manner of strange County-Fair/Polish Carnival madness is going on up in this space. Right above the gambling tables the Forty Flying Carazito Brothers are doing a high-wire trapeze act, along with four muzzled Wolverines and the Six Nymphet Sisters from San Diego . . . so you're down on the main floor playing blackjack, and the stakes are getting high when suddenly you chance to look up, and there, right smack above your head is a half-naked fourteen-year-old girl being chased through the air by a snarling wolverine, which is suddenly locked in a death battle with two silver-painted Polacks who come swinging down from opposite balconies and meet in mid-air on the wolverine's neck . . . both Polacks seize the animal as they fall straight down towards the crap tables—but they bounce off the net; they separate and spring back up towards the roof in three different directions, and just as they're about to fall again they are grabbed out of the air by three Korean Kittens and trapezed off to one of the balconies.

This madness goes on and on, but nobody seems to notice. The gambling action runs twenty-four hours a day on the main floor, and the circus never ends. Meanwhile, on all the upstairs balconies, the customers are being hustled by every conceivable kind of bizarre shuck. All kinds of funhouse-type booths. Shoot the pasties off the nipples of a ten-foot bull-dyke and win a cotton-candy goat. Stand in front of this fantastic machine, my friend, and for just 99¢ your likeness will appear, two hundred feet tall, on a screen above downtown Las Vegas. Ninety-nine cents more for a voice message. "Say whatever you want, fella. They'll hear you, don't worry about that. Remember you'll be two hundred feet tall."

Jesus Christ. I could see myself lying in bed in the Mint Hotel, half-asleep and staring idly out the window, when suddenly a vicious Nazi drunkard appears two hundred feet tall in the midnight sky, screaming gibberish at the world: "*Woodstock Über Alles!*"

We will close the drapes tonight. A thing like that could send a drug person careening around the room like a ping-pong ball. Hallucinations are bad enough. But after a while you learn to cope with things like seeing your dead grandmother crawling up your leg with a knife in her teeth. Most acid fanciers can handle this sort of thing.

But *nobody* can handle that other trip—the possibility that any freak with $1.98 can walk into the Circus-Circus, and suddenly appear in the sky over downtown Las Vegas twelve times the size of God, howling anything that comes into his head. No, this is not a good town for psychedelic drugs. Reality itself is too twisted.

Ralph Steadman *Vintage Dr. Gonzo*

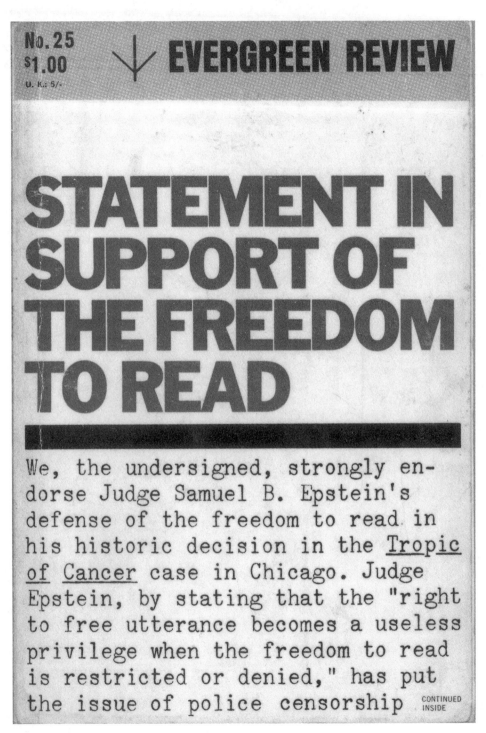

No. 25
$1.00
U. K.: 5/-

EVERGREEN REVIEW

STATEMENT IN SUPPORT OF THE FREEDOM TO READ

We, the undersigned, strongly endorse Judge Samuel B. Epstein's defense of the freedom to read in his historic decision in the <u>Tropic of Cancer</u> case in Chicago. Judge Epstein, by stating that the "right to free utterance becomes a useless privilege when the freedom to read is restricted or denied," has put the issue of police censorship CONTINUED INSIDE

Cover of *Evergreen Review* Volume 6, Number 25, July–August 1962

(CONT. FROM FRONT COVER)

squarely before the public. In recent months, policemen, encouraged by certain minority pressure groups, have succeeded in forcing their own narrow-minded literary tastes upon many communities.

We believe with Judge Epstein that neither the police nor the courts should be allowed to dictate the reading matter of a free people. The issue is not whether <u>Tropic of Cancer</u> is a masterpiece of American literature; rather, it is whether an author of Henry Miller's artistic integrity is entitled to the protections afforded by the Constitution of the United States.

This is an issue of immediate and serious concern to every citizen who holds dear the traditions of our democracy, and who abhors the intrusion of official censorship into the vital area of artistic and literary expression. It is an issue to which we are especially sensitive.

Judge Epstein's ruling against book banning has reaffirmed the right of a free people to decide for itself what it may or may not read. Beyond that, it sounds a clear warning to all of us to guard the principles upon which our country was built.

We urge all who, along with Judge Epstein, resent police censorship in the area of literature and the arts to make their voices heard in their own communities and to defeat any attempts at repression before they are allowed to erode our most precious freedoms.

Inside Cover of *Evergreen Review* Volume 6, Number 25, July–August 1962

Contributors

Jack Henry Abbott hanged himself on February 10, 2002, at the Wende Correctional Facility in Alden, New York, at the age of fifty-eight. Behind bars since late childhood, Abbott was a self-educated exceptional writer who published his best-selling correspondences with Norman Mailer, titled *In the Belly of the Beast*. This collection remains one of the most powerful and visionary works of American prison literature ever written. Six weeks after Mailer helped Abbott secure temporary residence at a halfway house, Abbott found himself back in prison after stabbing a waiter in New York City, ending his chances of ever again being a free man.

Mumia Abu-Jamal, author of *Live from Death Row*, was convicted of killing a policeman in 1982 and was sentenced to death. In December 2001 a federal judge upheld his conviction but ruled that Abu-Jamal should either receive a new sentencing hearing or have his sentence commuted to life in prison, given the many unresolved conflicts surrounding the trial. Before his conviction, he was an outspoken outlaw journalist, member of the Black Panther Party, active supporter of the group MOVE, and head of the Philadelphia Association of Black Journalists.

Kathy Acker invented the postmodern novel with genius and aplomb. Her books include *Hannibal Lecter, My Father; Blood and Guts in High School; Don Quixote; Great Expectations; and Pussy, King of the Pirates.* Amy Scholder wrote, "Acker is a one way street, and if you've learned anything from this writer, it's to be fearless enough to go down it with her. Once you do, there's no turning back." Writers and readers around the world mourned her death in Mexico from cancer on November 30, 1997.

Nelson Algren, one of the most original writers ever to come out of Chicago, is best known for *The Man with the Golden Arm*, which won the National Book Award in 1950, and *A Walk on the Wild Side*. Said Simone de Beauvoir of Algren: "Through his stories, you got the feeling that he claimed no rights to life and that nevertheless he had always had a passionate desire to live. I liked that mixture of modesty and eagerness." He died in 1981 after profoundly changing the landscape of American literature with his nonconformist intensity and brutally honest depictions of immigrant life in Chicago.

Lester Bangs, the most influential critic of rock and roll ever to appear in newsprint, wrote more like a rock star than a critic. His music essays for *Creem,* a sixties underground zine, are legend. Recently he was portrayed in Cameron Crowe's film *Almost Famous.* His books include *Mainlines, Blood Feasts and Bad Taste,* and *Psychotic Reactions and Carburetor Dung.*

Sonny Barger is the world's most famous Hell's Angel, having been in and out of prison for the last forty-seven years. The federal government considers him "the most powerful and well-known outlaw motorcyclist in the country." *Hell's Angel* was cowritten with Keith and Kent Zimmerman.

Clive Barker has extended the horror genre into a new surreal form of demonic American pop cultural gore-fest, while climbing up the best-seller lists. His novels include *Books of Blood, The Damnation Game, Weaveworld,* and *The Great and Secret Show.* His novella *The Hellbound Heart* inspired *Hellraiser,* a cinematic cult classic. The film *Candyman* is also based on his work.

Paul Beatty, the first spoken-word poet to be crowned Slam Champion at the Nuyorican Poets Cafe in Manhattan's East Village, swept the poetry world with the publication of his debut book of poems, *Big Bank Take Little Bank.* This was followed by a second collection, *Joker, Joker, Deuce.* Beatty then turned his energies to fiction, with instant success. His first novel, *White Boy Shuffle,* a dazzling debut, was quickly followed by a second novel, *Tuff.*

Pinckney Benedict, author of the novel *Dogs of God* and of two collections of short fiction—*Town Smokes* and *The Wrecking Yard*—frequently appears as an essayist on National Public Radio's "All Things Considered" and is the recipient of several prizes and awards, including the *Chicago Tribune's* Nelson Algren Award.

Boxcar Bertha described herself as a "hobo, a radical, a prostitute, a thief, a reformer, a social worker and a revolutionist." Spending most of her life on the road, she was the subject of an over-the-top 1972 film by Martin Scorsese.

A. I. Bezzerides's two-fisted screenplays include *On Dangerous Ground* (directed by Nicholas Ray in 1951) and *Kiss Me Deadly* (directed by Robert

Aldrich in 1955). A superb novelist, his book *Thieves' Market* is a classic example of the genre of noir fiction.

Jack Black was a hobo, a member of the "yegg" (criminal) brotherhood, and a highwayman. His autobiography, *You Can't Win*, a bestseller in 1926, was recently reissued.

Paul Bowles was a novelist and essayist who spent most of his life as a New York expatriate in Tangier, Morocco, traveling extensively across Europe while writing and recording music. Among his notable works are *The Sheltering Sky* and *Let It Come Down*. He died in Tangier on November 18, 1999.

Ray Bradbury, author of more than five hundred published works, including *The Martian Chronicles, The Illustrated Man, Fahrenheit 451*, and *Something Wicked This Way Comes*, is, for many, the defining figure of twentieth-century science fiction. Bradbury has been awarded the National Book Foundation's 2000 Medal for Distinguished Contribution to American Letters.

Malcolm Braly served time in various prisons, including San Quentin, and began to write in the shadow of his guards. When *Felony Tank*, his first novel, appeared he was still behind bars. Two more novels appeared upon his release: *Shake Him Till He Rattles* and *It's Cold Out There*. *On the Yard*, considered by many his masterpiece, was begun during his confinement and finished once off parole. His autobiography, *False Starts: A Memoir of San Quentin and Other Prisons*, earned high praise when it appeared.

Richard Brautigan first became involved in the late 1950s San Francisco Beat scene and during this time published *Lay the Marble Tea*, a collection of twenty-four poems. But it is for his emergence as a prose writer emblematic of the San Francisco hippie and psychedelic movement in the 1960s that he is best known. Brautigan gained a national following through such titles as *Trout Fishing in America, All Watched Over by Machines of Loving Grace,* and *In Watermelon Sugar,* unconventional tongue-in-cheek prose works underscored by a subtle sense of sadness, even grief. From 1966 to 1967 he served as the poet-in-residence at California Institute of Technology. He later moved to Pine Creek, Montana, and refused to grant interviews or give lectures. In 1982 *So the Wind Won't Blow It All Away* was published. In 1984 Brautigan died of a self-inflicted gunshot wound.

Bonnie Bremser, born as Brenda Frazer, began her association with the Beat Generation at nineteen when she met the poet Ray Bremser. After splitting from her husband, she lived for some time on Allen Ginsberg's farm in Cherry Hill, New York, while writing her autobiography. She began working for the U.S. Department of Agriculture during the 1990s, apparently "having left her Beat life far behind."

Poppy Z. Brite's books have been described as "a spicy gumbo of subcultural hipness simmered in a cauldron of modern horror fiction" *(Fangoria)*. Such books as *Drawing Blood, Lost Souls,* and *Wormwood.* have earned her a cult following, particularly among gothic youth with black lipstick and bruised eyes.

James Brown single-handedly created soul and funk by pushing the boundaries of gospel and rhythm-and-blues music, coming up with a style whose influence and innovations can be seen reflected on everything from jazz to hip-hop and rock and roll. The "hardest working man in show business" is an equally talented singer, dancer, and bandleader, as was evidenced by the power and energy of his unforgettable live concerts. By the mid-1970s, Brown's creative well started to run dry, culminating in his much-publicized 1988 interstate car chase with police and eventual conviction for firearms and drug possession. His autobiography was cowritten with Bruce Tucker.

Lenny Bruce rose to the heights of the comedy profession during the fifties and sixties, but he was much more than a comedian. He was a brilliant artist and passionate champion of personal freedoms who, through largely improvised monologues purposely peppered with "obscene" language, both challenged restrictive mores and laws and deflated the sacred cows and pompous taboos of the day. For this he underwent a brutal regimen of arrests and trials that contributed to his decline and undoubtedly hastened his eventual death from a heroin overdose in 1966.

Eric Burdon's life has been a musical journey unmatched by many other performers in rock music history. He has gone from the driving force of the grittiest British Invasion band, to pioneering the San Francisco psychedelic rock scene, to fronting WAR—the biggest funk band of the 1970s—to eventually reuniting his original band, The Animals, for a worldwide tour. He wrote a memoir called *Please Don't Let Me Be Misunderstood,* tours frequently with the New Animals, and is completing work for an upcoming studio CD, *The Coat of Many Colors.*

Bestriding both the worlds of the pulp novel and the gangster flick, the legendary bare-fisted writer **W. R. Burnett** made his start while still working for the Ohio Bureau of Workmen's Compensation, authoring five novels, several plays, and numerous short stories. He later fled to California, where he continued to bang out full-length fictions as well as many screenplays. His novels

Little Caesar, High Sierra, and *The Asphalt Jungle* were made into major motion pictures that are considered high points of hard-boiled cinema.

William S. Burroughs was the dark genius of the classic Beat group that included Allen Ginsberg, Jack Kerouac, and Gregory Corso. Among his best-known books are *Junky, Naked Lunch, The Soft Machine, The Ticket That Exploded, Nova Express, The Wild Boys, Exterminator,* and *Yage Letters,* his collected correspondences with Ginsberg. Terry Southern wrote of *Naked Lunch:* "An absolutely devastating ridicule of all that is false, primitive, and vicious in current American life: the abuses of power, hero worship, aimless violence, materialistic obsession, intolerance, and every form of hypocrisy."

Pat Califia has written prolifically about queer theory, gender identity, and women's sexuality. Being a transgendered bisexual, Califia rebelled against a Mormon family and worked actively to raise sexual awareness in San Francisco during the 1970s. Now known as Patrick, he has suffered from a medical problem causing extensive nerve damage to his body since the 1990s, but he continues to publish work, including the recent vampire novel *Mortal Companion.*

Marvin Felix Camillo conducted a drama workshop at Sing Sing, where Miguel Piñero served time. Camillo's workshop grew into an acting company of ex-convicts called "The Family," members of which made up most of the cast in the production of *Short Eyes.*

Jim Carroll, a poet, musician, and diarist was born and grew up in New York City. Talented at both basketball and writing, he attended Trinity High School in Manhattan on a scholarship and was an All-City basketball star—a period in his life vividly described in his widely praised book *The Basketball Diaries.* Carroll's first collection of poetry, *Living at the Movies,* was published in 1973 when he was twenty-two. His other books include *The Book of Nods, Forced Entries,* and *Fear of Dreaming.* As leader of the Jim Carroll Band, he has recorded several albums, including *Catholic Boy, Dry Dreams,* and *I Write Your Name. Praying Mantis,* a spoken-word recording, was released in 1991, while the acclaimed record *Pools of Mercury* came out in 1998.

While studying for her M.A. at the University of Denver, **Carolyn Cassady** met Neal Cassady, Jack Kerouac, and Allen Ginsberg. She married Neal, had three children by him, and carried on a long affair with Jack Kerouac, at her husband's suggestion. *Off the Road* is her account of those years.

Neal Cassady served as the model for Dean Moriarity, the legendary hero of Jack Kerouac's *On the Road.* Later, he drove the bus for Ken Kesey's Merry

Pranksters. His rapturous, nonstop monologues and sporadic writings artistically and spiritually influenced both Kerouac and poet Allen Ginsberg. By the time of his death in Mexico in 1968, just four days short of his forty-second birthday, he had already entered the annals of American folklore forever. His final hours are described in Kesey's short story *The Day After Superman Died*, where Cassady is quoted slurring his final words, "sixty-four thousand nine hundred and twenty-eight," the number of nails he had counted thus far while walking along a desolate railroad track.

Between 1960 and 1965, **Carlos Casteneda,** a young graduate student in anthropology at the University of California, Los Angeles, studied closely with Don Juan Matus, a Yaqui Indian sorcerer from Sonoro, Mexico. The record of this experience, set down in *The Teachings of Don Juan: A Yaqui Way of Knowledge*, was an immediate hit when it appeared, regarded as a key contribution to the countercultural dialogues about reality perception that underscored early drug experimentation in the 1960s. Thereafter followed three more volumes: *A Separate Reality, Journey to Ixtlan*, and *Tales of Power*.

One of the first Hispanic American women to achieve international acclaim as a writer, **Sandra Cisneros** is the distinguished author of numerous books, including *Woman Hollering Creek and Other Stories; My Wicked, Wicked Ways;* and *Loose Woman.* She has worked as a teacher to high school dropouts, a poet-in-the-schools, and is the recipient of numerous awards.

Eldridge Cleaver was a veteran of some of the worst prisons in California's harsh state penal system, including San Quentin, Folsom, and Soledad. He served as minister of information for the Black Panther Party for Self-Defense, and as a staff writer for *Ramparts*, the famed sixties magazine of New Left politics and literature. His 1968 book *Soul on Ice* elevated Cleaver to a national spokesman for Black Power. That same year he was wounded in a Panther shoot-out with Oakland police. Cleaver jumped bail, fled to Algeria, and lived in exile there and in Paris. He returned to America in 1975 and died in 1998.

Born and raised in the Watts slums of Los Angeles, **Wanda Coleman** is the widely acclaimed author of numerous books, including *A War of Eyes & Other Stories, Mad Dog Black Lady, Imagoes* and *Heavy Daughter Blues: Poems and Stories 1968–1986.*

Richard Condon was a novelist who wrote the 1959 political conspiracy thriller *The Manchurian Candidate.* It became the subject of two major motion pictures starring Frank Sinatra and Denzel Washington, respectively. He died in Texas on April 9, 1996.

For a time in the late 1950s **Clarence Cooper Jr.** worked as an editor for the *Chicago Messenger*. He authored six books of fiction but was disillusioned by the hostile reaction to them. Struggling with a severe heroin habit, increasingly alienated from those around him, he died broke and alone in New York City in 1978.

Dennis Cooper was born on January 10, 1953, in Pasadena, California. His literary aspirations were explored early on and often took the form of imitations of Rimbaud, Verlaine, De Sade, and Baudelaire. He has written a series of immensely successful novels, including *Period* and *Closer,* and is presently the editor of Akashic Books' groundbreaking *Little House on the Bowery* series, which he describes as "an oasis for people who have come to see contemporary literature as a spotty, conservative medium."

Gregory Corso was part of the cultural revolution known as the Beat Generation. Allen Ginsberg called him "a rascal poet Villonesque and Rimbaudian." His books include *The Happy Birthday of Death, Elegiac Feelings American, Mindfield: New and Selected Poems, Long Live Man,* and *An Accidental Autobiography.* He died on January 17, 2001. Patti Smith wrote upon his death: "The fresh light pours. The boys from the road steer him on. But before he ascends into some holy card glow, Gregory, being himself, lifts his overcoat, drops his trousers, and as he exposes his poet's rump one last time, cries, 'Hey man, kiss my daisy.' Ahh Gregory, the years and petals fly."

Jeff Craig is the coauthor with Eric Burdon of *Please Don't Let Me Be Misunderstood.*

Harry Crews, born during the Great Depression in rural Georgia, portrays the sensibilities of southern life with empathy and understanding. He also has a keen interest in sporting activities and physical prowess, which he has addressed in a number of novels, including the well-received title *Body.*

Miles Davis was one of the most innovative, original, and influential musicians of the twentieth century. As a jazz composer and multitalented trumpeter, Davis cannot be matched in terms of sheer importance to the development of the genre he helped define and expand. While *Kind of Blue* revolutionized jazz in 1959, it remains impossible to narrow his vast genius to a single record or musical period. Miles died on September 28, 1991. *Miles* was cowritten with poet Quincy Troupe.

Don De Grazia, a fiction writing department member at Columbia College in Chicago, submitted *American Skin* as his master's thesis. His debut work has been hailed as an American classic, and plans have been made for its adaptation as a feature film. He is at work on his second novel.

Philip K. Dick, regarded by many as the quintessential sub-cult science fiction writer of the postwar era, was the author of over fifty novels, including *Martian Time-Slip, A Scanner Darkly,* and *Flow My Tears, the Policeman Said.* The motion pictures *Minority Report, Total Recall,* and most famously, *Blade Runner* are based upon his short stories.

Before his suicide at the age of twenty-six, **Breece D'J Pancake** studied in the creative writing program at the University of Virginia and published his short fiction in *The Atlantic.* The posthumous publication of his collected stories electrified the literary world.

DMX, born as Earl Simmons, grew up in the projects of Yonkers, New York, served multiple jail terms, and had little prospects for his future. Now an actor and one of the best-selling hip-hop artists ever, his bleak lyrical content reflects the struggles he has managed to overcome over the course of his life. As he writes: "To live is to suffer, but to survive, well, that's to find meaning in the suffering." In June 2004 he was arrested for auto theft.

Roxanne Dunbar-Ortiz is a historian and professor in the Department of Ethnic Studies at California State University, Hayward. She is the author of *Red Dirt: Growing Up Okie, The Great Sioux Nation,* and *Roots of Resistance,* among other books. A scholar and activist on indigenous issues, she has been a consultant for the UN's Committee on International Humanitarian Issues.

Katherine Dunn, a journalist and novelist from Oregon, was a nominee for the National Book Award with her 1989 novel *Geek Love,* describing the life of a freakish and grotesque carnival family. Her dark humor and masterful control of narrative and language work to overturn accepted conceptions of "family values."

Andrea Dworkin, a radical feminist writer, writes prolifically about male violence toward women through pornography, prostitution, and what she perceives as other institutionalized mechanisms of subjugation. Dworkin made enemies across political lines by drafting a law that defined pornography as a civil rights violation against women, which was briefly passed in Indianapolis before ultimately being ruled as unconstitutional. She lives in Brooklyn, New York.

Bob Dylan is the major poet/songwriter of our time. He was born in 1941 in Hibbing, Minnesota, and continues to record and tour consistently.

Dave Eggers is author of the groundbreaking memoir *A Heartbreaking Work of Staggering Genius* and of a novel, *You Shall Know Our Velocity!* Eggers helped start *Might* magazine and then went on to establish McSweeney's, a firm devoted to publishing avant-garde literary journals and cutting-edge books. He is also a gifted visual artist and the founder of 826 Valencia in San Francisco, a nonprofit writing center for youth.

Maggie Estep's first novel, *Diary of an Emotional Idiot*, was published in 1997. She has recorded spoken-word CDs, and her writing has appeared in various magazines, including *Spin, Harper's Bazaar*, the *Village Voice*, and the *New Yorker*. Described by Jonathan Ames as "the bastard daughter of Raymond Chandler and Anais Nin," her most recent novel, *Gargantuan: A Ruby Murphy Mystery*, was published in 2004. She lives in New York City.

Evergreen Review has been hailed as one of the most provocative magazines ever. Under the steerage of its founder, publisher, and editor, Barney Rosset, *Evergreen* was the outlaw bible for a generation of free-thinking radicals and activists. Championing everything from Beckett to Brautigan, erotica to the arts, its no-nonsense attitude confronted and challenged the conventions of the day. Rosset brought together the most adventurous photographers, artists, and writers of the generation to push the boundaries of cultural and political discourse in the United States.

Acknowledged by Charles Bukowski to have been a key influence on his career, **John Fante** was in many regards the classic hard-boiled Los Angeles fiction writer. His books include *Wait Until Spring, Bandini; Ask the Dust;* and *Dreams from Bunker Hill*, which he dictated to his wife, Joyce, when he lost his eyesight to diabetes. Fante died in 1983. His posthumous works include *Wine of Youth, The Road to Los Angeles*, and *1933 Was a Bad Year*.

Karen Finley is a world-renowned performance artist. Her infamous performances brought her to the Supreme Court in Finley v. NEA, the Waterloo of the culture wars. She has acted in films and authored five books, including her first book, *Shock Treatment*, which was published by City Lights.

James Fogle's compelling novel, *Drugstore Cowboy*, tells the story of four traveling junkies who loot narcotics from local pharmacies. Based on personal experience (the author has spent over thirty-five years in prison), Fogle takes his addiction and uses it as a metaphor for modern-day alienation and aimlessness. The film version was voted Best Picture of 1989 by the National Society of Film Critics.

Pleasant Gehman's writing has appeared in *Spin, Genre, Bikini, Los Angeles*

Magazine, and *L.A. Weekly*. She is editor of *The Underground Guide to Los Angeles*.

Barry Gifford is a contemporary novelist whom Americans can be proud of. His novels have been translated into twenty-five languages, and he has received awards from PEN and the National Endowment for the Arts, among many others. Gifford cowrote with David Lynch the screenplay for *Lost Highway* and with Matt Dillon the script for *City of Ghosts*. His writings include *Wyoming*, *American Falls*, *The Rooster Trapped in the Reptile Room*, *Do the Blind Dream?*, and *Wild at Heart*.

Author **Donald Goines** lived the desperate life that he portrayed in his many razor-edged novels. At various times a pimp, thief, armed robber, dope dealer, and operator of corn liquor houses, Goines, at thirty-nine, was shot dead at his typewriter by an unknown assailant, in what some believe was an underworld hit. He left behind an astonishing body of work, seventeen novels in all—a Balzacian underclass panorama of the street jungle and its predators. One of the most widely read black authors in America, his best known works include the novels *Dopefiend*, *Black Gangster*, *Whoreson*, and *Never Die Alone*, which has been made into a major motion picture starring DMX.

Emma Goldman was a Russian-born anarchist who was a loud feminist voice and radical libertarian. Her subversive politics brought her into conflict with the United States government on many occasions, most famously when a follower of hers, Leon Czolgosz, shot President McKinley and she found herself facing conspiracy charges. Undeterred, "Red Emma" continued to agitate and disturb the status quo, and was eventually deported to Russia, where she experienced the Russian Revolution firsthand. At her deportation hearing, J. Edgar Hoover called her "one of the most dangerous women in America." She died on May 14, 1940, and her outlaw legacy has had a profound impact on progressive political discourse since that time.

David Goodis wrote some of the most powerful pulp fiction novels of the postwar era. Yet his name might have disappeared altogether had it not been for French publishers who reissued his works with much fanfare, long after these titles had vanished from American bookshelves. Some of the giants of French avant-garde cinema also showed their devotion, including Jean-Luc Godard and François Truffaut, who adapted his work for the motion picture screen. The best known of these adaptations is Truffaut's *Shoot the Piano Player*, based on Goodis's novel of the same name.

When **Dick Gregory** rose to stardom as a stage comedian, and then reached further heights with the publication of his autobiography, *Nigger*, he used his newfound fame to march in the front lines of the civil rights and Vietnam antiwar movements of the 1960s. Gregory has been at the forefront of social activism ever since, including his own one-man campaign to revolutionize the unhealthy eating habits of his fellow Americans. His other books include *Callus on My Soul: A Memoir* and *The Shadow That Scares Me*.

The Guerrilla Girls have been reinventing the word "feminism" since 1985, fighting discrimination with facts, humor, and fake fur: "Still going strong in the twenty-first century, we're a bunch of anonymous females who take the names of dead women artists as pseudonyms and appear in public wearing gorilla masks. In nineteen years we have produced over a hundred posters, stickers, books, printed projects, and actions that expose sexism and racism in politics, the art world, film and the culture at large."

Woody Guthrie lived the life described in his songs, from Dust Bowl wanderer to labor union man, simultaneously creating some of the most authentic folk songs ever put to wax. His influence resonates in the music of everyone from Bob Dylan to Bruce Springsteen.

Jessica Tarahata Hagedorn is a novelist, poet, and multimedia and performance artist. Among her notable works are the novels *Dogeaters* and *The Gangster of Love*, both of which harness her cross-cultural experience as a Philippine-born American.

James Leo Herlihy was a novelist and playwright as well as an actor who had roles in over fifty plays. The first two plays he authored, *Streetlight Sonata* and *Moon in Capricorn*, were successfully produced, followed by *Blue Denim*, coauthored with William Noble, which enjoyed a lucrative run on Broadway. But it is for his fiction that he is best known. *All Fall Down*, a novel and his first critically acclaimed work, was later adapted as a film. In 1965 he published *Midnight Cowboy*, which became a film starring Dustin Hoffman and John Voight. Withdrawing from the notoriety brought about by his success, Herlihy spent some years teaching, first at the City College of New York, then at the University of Arkansas, and later at the University of Southern California. Before his death, he wrote only one other novel, *Season of the Witch*. He died in Los Angeles in 1993, from an overdose of sleeping pills.

Larry Hester is a reporter for *Vibe* Online.

Bill Hicks was a controversial comedian known for voicing his outspoken political issues on stage, addressing such topics as the Gulf War and the Los Angeles riots. His rising stardom coincided with his increased dependency on drugs and alcohol, both of which he battled throughout the 1980s. He died on February 26, 1994, from pancreatic cancer.

Chester Himes, a contemporary of Richard Wright and James Baldwin, was a novelist who confronted his readers with the harsh truths of racism directly through his realist writing style. Living as an expatriate in Paris during the mid-1950s, he published a series of highly acclaimed black detective novels, as well as the race novel *If He Hollers Let Him Go.* He died on November 12, 1984, in Spain.

John Clellon Holmes was an essayist, poet, novelist, and associate of the Beats. He described the characters of its most important figures well before *On the Road* was published in his 1952 novel, *Go.* His final book of poems, *Dire Coasts,* was published in 1988, the year he died.

Waylon Jennings was one of the most popular and influential country music singers and guitarists. His collaborations with Willie Nelson are now legendary, among them *Wanted: The Outlaws!* and *Waylon and Willie.* He died in 2002 after an immensely successful musical career.

In addition to her award-winning memoir, *Minor Characters* (an account of her on-again, off-again relationship with Jack Kerouac), **Joyce Johnson** is the author of *What Lisa Knew: The Truths and Lies of the Steinberg Case* and the novels *In the Night Café, Bad Connections,* and *Come and Join the Dance.*

Alan Kaufman, editor of *The Outlaw Bible of American Poetry* and author of *Jew Boy,* a memoir, attended the graduate writing program at Columbia University and later got his start as a spoken-word poet in the scenes that sprang up in Manhattan's Nuyorican Poet's Cafe and Cafe Babar in San Francisco. His other books include *The New Generation: Fiction for Our Time from America's Writing Programs* and *Who Are We?,* a collection of poems. He has just completed *Matches,* a fictional work based upon his experiences as an infantryman in the Israeli army.

Weldon Kees was a successful short-fiction writer who published over forty short stories from 1934 to 1945. Kees also began to write poetry and took up painting, filmmaking, and music after World War II, and was a journalist and reviewer for a number of major national publications. His car was found near the Golden Gate Bridge on July 18, 1955, and he has not been seen since.

Jack Kerouac's *On the Road* is one of the greatest American novels of the postwar era. Although he is widely identified as a fiction writer, he was really a poet in prose. Considered the father of the Beat Generation, Kerouac cut a solitary, beautiful figure in the sterile landscape of the Eisenhower era, living the occasional hobo life of hitchhiking and hopping freights with a backpack loaded down with manuscripts, Buddhist prayer books, and canned foods. A prodigious writer, his other books include *The Dharma Bums, Desolation Angels,* and *The Subterraneans.* His first book was *The Town and the City.*

Jan Kerouac first met her father, Jack, when she was nine years old. He arrived at her mother's apartment in the East Village and immediately asked: "Where's the liquor store?" Jan took his hand and led him to the shop. He bought some Harvey's Bristol Cream sherry and drank the entire bottle that afternoon in their living room. She is also the author of *Trainsong,* published before her death to wide critical praise. Despite the physical hardship imposed by kidney failure in 1991, she continued to work on a third novel, *Parrot Fever,* which was never published. She died in Albuquerque, New Mexico, in June 1996 at the age of forty-four.

Ken Kesey, one of the outlaw legends of the sixties psychedelic revolution, led his Merry Pranksters on a bus steered by Neal Cassady with a payload of acid. He is the author of the critically acclaimed *One Flew Over the Cuckoo's Nest* and *Sometimes a Great Notion.* He spent the rest of his life in Oregon's Willamette Valley on his family's farm and died on November 10, 2001.

Jack Ketchum's novels of horror include *Off Season, Hide and Seek, Cover, The Girl Next Door,* and *Stranglehold.*

Callie Khouri is a writer-director who, while working as a secretary at a music video production company, received an Oscar for her first screenplay, Ridley Scott's *Thelma & Louise,* starring Geena Davis and Susan Sarandon. Since then, she wrote *Something to Talk About* in 1995 and made her directorial debut in 2002 with an adaptation of Rebecca Wells's *Divine Secrets of the Ya-Ya Sisterhood.*

Paul Krassner, a prolific writer and comedian, received his grounding in prankster activism from Lenny Bruce. He edited *The Realist* (published from 1958 through 2001), serving as an early example of a counterculture magazine in the United States, and as this book confirms, dropped acid with Groucho Marx.

Timothy Leary, a one-time professor at Harvard University, was an established psychologist, writer, and advocate of LSD. His work as a drug campaigner on campus led to his dismissal from Harvard in 1963, at which point he moved with Dr. Richard Alpert to a mansion in Milbrook, New York, where they created a drug colony and continued to conduct experiments before repeated FBI raids landed him in jail. The Weather Underground broke him out of prison, and he ended up in Switzerland before being eventually extradited to the United States. He died from prostate cancer on May 31, 1996. The final words he uttered were "Why not?"

Meridel Le Sueur was at her most productive in the 1930s, churning out short stories for magazines. Her career rose around 1940 with the anthology *Salute to Spring*, although she enjoyed a resurgence of interest later in the century. She is the author of numerous books, and in the 1950s she was blacklisted for writing material that the U.S. government considered subversive. She died in 1996.

Beth Lisick's books include *This Too Can Be Yours* and *Monkey Girl*. She writes the column "Buzz Town" for SF Gate, the online version of the *San Francisco Chronicle*. She was the knock-kneed, impossibly beautiful spoken-word lead artist of the band The Beth Lisick Ordeal, which broke up in 2000.

Lydia Lunch was one of the founding members of Teenage Jesus and The Jerks, a 1970s "no-wave" band. In the 1980s Lunch released a spoken-word cassette, *The Uncensored Lydia Lunch*, which heralded a new form of in-your-face, truth-spitting performance. There followed rich collaborations with Hubert Selby Jr., Henry Rollins, and Don Bajema. She is coauthor, with Exene Cervenka, of *Adulterers Anonymous*.

Norman Mailer, acknowledged to be one of the most controversial American writers of the last half century, has walked a tightrope over public opinion, often with a dagger in his teeth. From his hipster manifesto *The White Negro* to his literary sponsorship of the criminal Jack Henry Abbott, Mailer has fascinated and outraged bourgeois sensibilities, examining hysteria, confusion, crime, and violence across America.

Greil Marcus, one of the preeminent cultural critics in America today, is the author of *Double Trouble, Dead Elvis, Lipstick Traces,* and *Mystery Train*.

Gillian McCain is the coeditor of *Please Kill Me: The Uncensored Oral History of Punk*. She is the author of *Tilt*, a collection of prose poems.

Michael McClure, reading in 1955 at the Six Gallery, joined with Allen Ginsberg, Phil Whalen, Philip Lamentia, and Gary Snyder to launch the San Francisco renaissance. During the "Summer of Love," he composed the original words on which Janis Joplin's song "Oh Lord, Won't You Buy Me a Mercedes Benz" was based. A prolific writer, his books include *A Fist Full, Jaguar Skies,* and *Selected Poems*.

Legs McNeil is the coeditor of *Please Kill Me: The Uncensored Oral History of Punk*, a book widely hailed as the definitive work on the subject. The founder of the seminal magazine that gave punk its name, he is a former editor at *Spin* and editor in chief of *Nerve*.

Mezz Mezzrow was a professional jazz clarinetist and the author of an auto-biography, *Really the Blues*. Though a white man, Mezzrow rejected white society and embraced African American culture to the extent of regarding himself as black. In this regard, he was an early forerunner of the Beats. An integral part of the Chicago jazz scene, Mezzrow played with the Austin High Gang and recorded with the Jungle Kings and the Chicago Rhythm Kings. Later he moved to New York and played with Eddie Condon. In the 1930s he led a few swing-oriented dates with his integrated band, The Disciples of Swing.

Henry Miller is the crawdaddy of American literary outlaws. His poetic novel *Tropic of Cancer* was smuggled into the United States by GIs returning from World War II. Publisher Barney Rosset of Grove Press issued the first American edition, which led to a Supreme Court ruling that eventually overturned its ban, morphing the unassuming Miller into a cause celebre for free-speech champions everywhere. Also an accomplished watercolorist, his other books include *Black Spring, Tropic of Capricorn, The Air-Conditioned Nightmare*, and his epic masterpiece trilogy, *The Rosy Crucifixion*. Often calling himself "the happiest man alive," Miller passed peacefully on June 7, 1980, but not before establishing himself as one of the most important American writers of his generation.

Tim Miller has been writing solo theater works since 1980 and became a cultural hero after successfully suing the NEA for withdrawing a grant under political pressure.

Cookie Mueller, says filmmaker John Waters, "was a writer, a mother, an outlaw, an actress, a fashion designer, a go-go dancer, a witch-doctor, an art-hag, and above all, a goddess. Boy, do I miss that girl." She wrote prolifically and died from AIDS-related causes in 1989. Most of her writings are collected in the anthology *Ask Dr. Mueller*.

Eileen Myles has been reading and performing her work locally, nationally, and internationally since 1974. A 1997 book of poems, *School of Fish*, was awarded a Lambda Literary Award, and her autobiographical novel *Cool for You* also received wide critical praise. The *Village Voice* called her book *Not Me* "the most poignantly tough-minded collection of visionary smut ever published." She was artistic director of St. Mark's Poetry Project from 1984 to

1986 and has written about art and literature for *Art in America*, *The Nation*, *The Stranger*, *Out*, and numerous other publications.

John O'Brien authored, among other books, the autobiographical novel *Leaving Las Vegas*. He committed suicide two weeks after the movie version went into production, but director Mike Figgis dedicated the film as a good tribute to O'Brien, after briefly contemplating abandoning the project.

Neil Ortenberg is a publisher, editor, writer, and founder of Insurgent Communicatons. The *New York Times* called him "a publisher with a rock 'n' roll heart." He serves on the board of Barney Rosset's legendary *Evergreen Review* and is currently working on a screenplay based on the life of Dee Dee Ramone.

Chuck Palahniuk is a novelist best known for *Fight Club*, later adapted into a blockbuster motion picture. His wry and aggressive humor is also apparent in other works like *Survivor*. He resides in Portland, Oregon.

Grace Paley is the author of three highly acclaimed collections of short fiction — *The Little Disturbances of Man*, *Enormous Changes at the Last Minute*, and *Later the Same Day* — as well as three collections of poetry. She has been involved in antiwar, feminist, and antinuclear movements, was a member of the War Resisters' League and Women's Pentagon Action, and was one of the founders of the Greenwich Village Peace Center in 1961.

Kenneth Patchen wrote more than forty raging and delicate books of poetry, prose, and drama, including *Before the Brave*, *First Will and Testament*, and *Journal of Albion Moonlight*. In 1942 he published *The Dark Kingdom* in a limited edition of seventy-five copies and painted each cover individually in watercolor. He was a phenomenal visual artist and poetry performer as well. He died in 1972.

Donn Pearce wrote the novel *Cool Hand Luke*, which he helped adapt into a 1967 film with Paul Newman starring as the lead character. For his efforts, he was nominated by the Academy for Best Adapted Screenplay that year.

Nelson Peery, the son of a postal worker, hopped freight trains in his youth and later labored for many years as a bricklayer. Through all this time, he was an active and dedicated political revolutionary. In World War II he served in the all-black 93rd Infantry Division. He learned to write while taking evening classes in Minneapolis with Meridel Le Sueur.

Harvey Pekar is best known for his autobiographical comic book series

American Splendor, a first-person account of his troubled life that was recently adapted into a successful film. The series was published on an approximately annual basis from 1976 through the early 1990s, illustrated by high-profile artists such as R. Crumb, Frank Stack, and Joe Sacco.

Miguel Piñero was cofounder of the Nuyorican Poets Café with Miguel Algarin. He won a Guggenheim and acted in television and movies. His 1974 play about life in prison, *Short Eyes,* is a theatrical landmark. He wrote twelve full-length plays.

During eight years spent living in abandoned buildings in San Francisco's Mission District, **Peter Plate** taught himself to write and has since emerged as an important novelist and spoken-word performer. *Angels of Catastrophe* is part of Plate's Mission Quartet, which includes the novels *Police and Thieves, One Foot Off the Gutter,* and *Snitch Factory.*

Sylvia Plath was an acclaimed author, poet, and essayist who posthumously won the Pulitzer Prize for poetry in 1983 for *The Collected Poems.* Though she had two children with Ted Hughes, their marriage eventually failed and contributed to her feelings of depression before her suicide on February 11, 1963. Her autobiographical novel, *The Bell Jar,* remains one of the darkest and most powerful accounts of a gradual slide into insanity ever written.

Dee Dee Ramone is the founding bassist of the massively influential New York City punk band The Ramones. Born Douglas Colvin, he established for the band a unique musical style and public image while recording such seminal records as *Leave Home, Rocket to Russia,* and *Road to Ruin.* He was found dead in his Hollywood home on June 5, 2002, shortly after being inducted into the Rock and Roll Hall of Fame. Dee Dee was also a poet, artist, and solo performer. His books include *Lobotomy, Legend of a Rock Star,* and *Chelsea Horror Hotel.* He was the subject of a documentary film called *Hey, Is Dee Dee Home?*

The publication of **John Rechy**'s *City of Night* in 1963 was a landmark in American literature and sent shockwaves throughout the literary establishment, for it was the author's largely autobiographical account of his life as a gay street hustler. Despite his newfound role as a respected literary figure, Rechy openly continued to work in the sex trade for a number of years. His other novels include *Rushes, The Sexual Outlaw,* and *Numbers.* Rechy is a recipient of the PEN Center USA West Lifetime Achievement Award and winner of the William Whitehead Award for Lifetime Achievement.

Lou Reed is rock's answer to Charles Baudelaire. Reed is a street-smart, sexually ambiguous paradigm of cool who first studied under the poet Delmore Schwartz before teaming up with the Andy Warhol–anointed band, Velvet Underground, in the mid-sixties. Since leaving them in 1970, he has launched a hugely successful solo career and released innumerable albums over the decades, including *Transformer* and *Berlin*. His most recent studio record, eponymously inspired by Poe's *The Raven*, was released in 2003. His own self-regenerating one-man revolution, Reed continues to perform, and his lyrics are collected in *Between Thought and Expression*.

Frank Reynolds was the secretary of the San Francisco Hell's Angels in the 1960s, and in his middle years began practicing Zen meditation. He died peacefully in Northern California on January 30, 2003, at the age of sixty.

Larry Rivers was a leading American painter associated with abstract expressionism and pop art. Before launching his artistic career, he studied at the Juilliard School in New York and was a professional jazz saxophonist. He died on August 14, 2002.

Luis Rodriguez's widely acclaimed memoir of L.A. gang life, *Always Running*, was the focus of a national debate over the banning of books deemed controversial by public schools. He is the author of several collections of poetry and is presently working on *Music of the Mill: A Novel*. He is also founder-director of Tia Chucha Press in Chicago, a publisher of cross-cultural, socially engaged poetry.

In 1951 **Barney Rosset** bought a fledgling literary publishing company, Grove Press, named after the Greenwich Village street where it began. For the next thirty-three years he ran it from various locations in the same neighborhood, developing Grove into a critical part of the downtown New York firmament and one of the most influential publishers of its day. Writers came to Grove because it championed their work in an often hostile environment. In the fifties, Rosset published D. H. Lawrence's *Lady Chatterley's Lover* and Henry Miller's *Tropic of Cancer*, defending these books and others in court when they were attacked. Over the years Grove took on hundreds of lawsuits, in the process of expanding the range of public discourse. Following his strong personal tastes, Rosset developed an impressive list of authors. Indeed many Grove writers, who were considered iconoclasts in their day, are now regarded as central figures in our culture, such as: Samuel Beckett, William S. Burroughs, Frantz Fanon, Octavio Paz, Pablo Neruda, Alain Robbe-Grillet, Marguerite Duras, Jean Genet, Eugene Ionesco, Harold Pinter, Tom Stoppard, Hubert Selby Jr., Kenzaburo Oe, Kathy Acker, and David Mamet. In 1988 the PEN American Center presented Rosset with its Publisher Citation for "distinctive and continuous service to international letters, to the freedom and dignity of writers, and for the free transmission of the printed word across the barriers of poverty, ignorance, censorship, and repression."

Ed Sanders, often considered to be the link between the Beat and hippie generations, is a versatile poet, singer, activist, and novelist who wrote his first celebrated work, *Poem from Jail,* on prison toilet paper after being arrested at an antinuke rally in 1961. He opened the Peace Eye Bookstore in the Lower East Side and founded the journal *Fuck You: A Magazine of the Arts* in 1962. He presently publishes the *Woodstock Journal* from his hometown in upstate New York with wife Miriam Sanders. His books include *Tales of Beatnik Glory.*

Margaret Sanger's influence on bringing birth control information to American women cannot be understated, nor can her steadfast opposition to conservative organized religion or her outspoken opposition to censorship be denied. Trained as a nurse, she was forced to flee the country in 1914 to avoid prosecution resulting from her proactive reproductive literacy campaigns. Now an iconic figure of the pro-choice movement, she founded the American Birth Control League in 1921 and the Birth Control Federation of America, which would become Planned Parenthood of America in 1939. After eventually returning to the United States, she died on September 6, 1966.

Sapphire (Ramona Lofton) is the author of two collections of poems: *American Dreams* and *Black Wings and Blind Angels.* Her novel, *Push,* won the Black Caucus of the American Library Association's First Novelist Award for 1997 and the Book-of-the-Month Club Stephen Crane Award for First Fiction.

John Sayles, the epitome of the American indie filmmaker, began his career writing B-films for Roger Corman in the mid-1970s before his directing first feature in 1980, *The Return of the Secaucus Seven.* A recipient of the MacArthur Fellowship, Sayles continues to make critically acclaimed films completely removed from mainstream outlets, notably *Passion Fish* and *Lone Star* in the 1990s. His collection of short stories, *Dillinger in Hollywood,* was published by Nation Books in 2004.

Paul Schrader is an acclaimed screenwriter and director, influenced by the likes of Bresson and Dreyer. His script of Martin Scorsese's *Taxi Driver* was nominated for a Golden Globe Award for its grim depiction of self-destructive urban life. He has also written the screenplays for *Raging Bull, The Last Temptation of Christ,* and *Bringing out the Dead,* all of which are Scorcese productions. Schrader directed *Mishima* in 1985, which was nominated for the Palme d'Or at Cannes that year.

Gil Scott-Heron, writer, poet, and musician, influenced an entire generation of rap musicians through his attitude, poetry, and "bluesology." Renowned in the seventies and eighties as the "Minister of Information," he is one of the most outspoken commentators on politics, race, and culture of the postwar era. Among his most vital recordings are *Small Talk at 125th and Lenox* and *Pieces of a Man.*

Hubert Selby Jr.'s first novel, *Last Exit to Brooklyn,* incited shock, admiration, and controversy for its stark portrayal of people driven to extremes of violence and desperation, upon its release in 1964. The novel was the subject of an obscenity trial in England. His other novels include *The Room, The Demon, Requiem for a Dream*—which was made into a powerful film by Darren Aronofsky—and *Song of the Silent Snow.* Selby died on April 26, 2004, of chronic lung disease at age seventy-five, outliving the wildest expectations of his doctors and family.

Assata Shakur, a revolutionary leader of the Black Liberation movement in the United States, still lives in political exile in Cuba more than twenty-five years after escaping from prison.

Tupac Shakur has been called the black James Dean. His discography includes *Me Against the World, Strictly 4 My N.I.G.G.A.Z., All Eyez on Me, Thug Life, 2Pacalypse Now,* and *Don Killuminati: The Seven Day Theory.* His films include *Juice, Above the Rim,* and *Gang Related.* On September 7, 1996, after leaving the Mike Tyson fight in Las Vegas, Shakur was shot four times in the chest by an assailant in a white Cadillac. On Friday, September 13, after six days in critical condition, Shakur was pronounced dead. Quincy Jones said of Tupac: "Tupac was a fighter, a young man who constantly sought out demons and battled them to his death. Tupac's life embodied the spirit of hip-hop, the music of America's youth."

Playwright and actor **Sam Shepard**'s numerous plays include *True West* and *Paris, Texas* (both have been made into motion pictures). His other plays include *La Turista, Forensic and the Navigators,* and *The Tooth of Crime.* In 1975 Shepard joined Bob Dylan's Rolling Thunder Revue and kept a private record of his experiences, later published as *Rolling Thunder Logbook.*

Iceberg Slim was the professional pseudonym used by by Robert Beck during his years as a successful pimp. When Beck turned his hand to writing, his first book, the autobiography *Pimp,* rocked respectable America, but sales were brisk and Beck's place was assured. *Pimp* was followed by other books, including *The Naked Soul of Iceberg Slim, Mama Black Widow, Trick Baby,* and *Death Wish.*

Patti Smith has become the emblematic avant-garde figure of our time, moving easily between the worlds of literature, performance art, and rock. Her debut single, *Piss Factory/Hey Joe*, funded by her then-partner Robert Mapplethorpe, signaled the arrival of a major talent. The brilliantly cathartic *Horses* followed this. Her other albums include *Ain't Nuthin' But a She Thing*, *Gone Again*, *Peace and Noise*, and *Masters*, a boxed set of six CDs released in 1996. Her most recent book is *Strange Messenger: The Work of Patti Smith*.

Snoop Dogg, aka Calvin Broadus, is one of the few living embodiments of nineties gangsta rap. With the help of Dr. Dre, with whom he had previously collaborated, Snoop was able to release an incendiary solo debut with the multiplatinum *Doggystyle*. His autobiography, *The Doggfather*, recounts the struggles he faced growing up in the South Bay 'hoods of Los Angeles, while ruminating on the rise and fall of gangsta rap.

Valerie Solanas was a radical feminist and author of the *S.C.U.M. (Society for Cutting Up Men) Manifesto*. She is best remembered for pumping bullets through Andy Warhol's left lung, spleen, stomach, liver, esophagus, and right lung on June 3, 1968. After spending years between prison and mental institutions, Solanas was released on September 1971 from the New York State Prison for Women at Bedford Hills. She was arrested again in November 1971 for threatening letters and calls to numerous people, including Andy Warhol. She died of emphysema and pneumonia on April 26, 1988.

From his controversial novel *Candy* (cowritten with Messon Hoeffenberg) to his screenplays for the film classics *Easy Rider* and *Dr. Strangelove* to his spearheading of the New Journalism, **Terry Southern** was one of the seminal behind-the-scenes innovators of 1960s counterculture. He appears on the cover of the Beatles' album *Sgt. Pepper's Lonely Hearts Club Band* wearing sunglasses.

Mickey Spillane is an American thriller writer, master of the "hard-boiled" style peppered with sex and sadism. Spillane is best known for his private detective Mike Hammer, who appeared in his first published book, *I, the Jury*, in 1947. His novel *Kiss Me Deadly* was turned into a successful film in 1955, and he also enjoyed a brief career as an actor.

Annie Sprinkle, a self-described "post-porn modernist," is North America's first sex icon, having worked as a porn star, stripper, prostitute, television host, porn magazine editor, performance artist, and writer.

Ralph Steadman is a legendary cartoonist and illustrator. His partnership with Hunter S. Thompson started a new style of reportage that captured the imagination of a generation. They first teamed up to cover the Kentucky Derby in May 1970. His books include *The Grapes of Ralph* and *Gonzo: The Art*.

Lee Stringer is one of the most authentic and original writers living today. *Grand Central Winter* tells of his life on the streets while residing in a small crawlspace under Grand Central Station, addicted equally to crack as to writing. Seven Stories Press published his meditation on childhood, *Sleepaway School*, in 2004.

Michelle Tea is a prolific writer, spoken-word performer, and an innovative arts organizer who created Sister Spit, an all-girl open-mic event that earned a *San Francisco Bay Guardian* "Best of the Bay" award. Her most recent works are *Rent Girl*, an illustrated graphic novel, and a collection of poems titled *The Beautiful*.

Piri Thomas was born in New York City's Spanish Harlem. Despite his furious struggle to escape from poverty, racism, crime, and drug addiction, he served seven years of incarceration at hard labor. In 1967 he attained national fame as the author of the autobiography *Down These Mean Streets*, today regarded as a pivotal work of American literature. His other works include *Savior, Savior Hold My Hand; Seven Long Times*; and *Stories from El Barrio*.

Hunter S. Thompson is a supreme prose stylist and the undisputed king of gonzo journalism. As the chronicler of an American soul ravaged by its own excesses, Thompson has been a one-man counterculture, riding with Hell's Angels, running for sheriff, serving time in a Louisville jail, and numbing his speed-typist hands while fist-fighting in Greenwich Village. His books include *Fear and Loathing in Las Vegas*, *Hell's Angels: A Strange and Terrible Saga* and *Great Shark Hunt: Strange Tales from a Strange Time*.

Jim Thompson sold his first story to *True Detective* when he was just fourteen. He then went on to produce twenty-nine novels as well as screenplays for the Stanley Kubrick films *The Killing* and *Paths of Glory*. Movies based on his novels include *The Getaway, The Killer Inside Me, The Grifters,* and *After Dark, My Sweet*.

After two decades spent as a licensed cut man and trainer in the world of professional boxing, and another forty years collecting rejection slips from clueless literary mags, **F. X. Toole** (Jerry Boyd) turned the literary world on its head with his first and only book, *Rope Burns: Stories from the Corner*. Many hailed this first collection of boxing short fiction as the best work ever done on the subject. He was seventy years old at his moment of triumph. Two years later, he died.

Jim Tully, like his contemporary Dashiell Hammett, helped develop the hard-boiled novel. He was a journalist, lecturer, road kid, boxer, and circus handyman who floated in and out of prison throughout much of his early life. A true literary wanderer, Tully died from a heart ailment in Hollywood on June 22, 1947.

Andrew Vachss is not only one of the leading crime novel practitioners in America today but also a crusading attorney who retains an individual practice limited to matters concerning abused, neglected, or delinquent youth. Among his best-known novels are *Flood, Blue Belle, Strega, Down in the Zero,* and *Footsteps of the Hawk.*

Melvin Van Peebles is a novelist, screenwriter, director, songwriter, and actor known best for his films *Watermelon Man* and *Sweet Sweetback's Baadasssss Song.* He also authored *Panther: The Pictorial History of the Black Panthers and the Story Behind the Film.* The recent film *Baadasssss,* directed by his son Mario Van Peebles, was based on the making of *Sweet Sweetback.*

John Waters, as William Burroughs maintained, is the "Pope of Trash," given his propensity to obsess over violence and gore in his fringe cinema. Directing films for the sole purpose of overturning the accepted moral principles of filmmaking, Waters has turned into a cult icon for his depiction of American subculture in films like *Pink Flamingos, Hairspray,* and most recently, the NC-17-rated *A Dirty Shame,* which explores the world of sex addicts in Baltimore.

Arnold Weinstein collaborated with Larry Rivers on *What Did I Do?* He is a playwright, lyricist, poet, translator, and stage director.

Stanley "Tookie" Williams, one of the founding members of the notorious "Crips" gang, is a death-row inmate at San Quentin State Prison. He is the author of the memoir *Life in Prison* and of *Tookie Speaks Out Against Violence,* an eight-book violence prevention series for students from five to ten years old. He has also launched the Internet Project for Street Peace, a program that links at-risk youth from the United States to youth in Zurich, Switzerland. His educational website can be found at http://www.tookie.com

David Wojnarowicz, who was hailed during his brief life as a visionary genius, rose from being a hard-bitten street hustler to a major visual artist and equally powerful memoirist (*Close to the Knives, Memories that Smell Like*

Gasoline). Launched through his graffiti art collaborations with Keith Haring, Wojnarowicz's fight for free expression sparked high-profile face-offs with everyone from the NEA to New York's Cardinal John O'Connor. Yet, in his art, as in his writings, he was intensely tender and elegiac, a poignancy earned, in part, through battling AIDS, which killed him

In 1965, while serving as a reporter for the *New York Herald*, **Tom Wolfe** published *The Kandy-Kolored Tangerine-Flake Streamline Baby*. An immediate hit, it heralded the New Journalism, a type of irreverent and shamelessly witty reportage particularly suited to the upstart sensibilities of the emerging counterculture. This was followed in 1968 by *The Pump House Gang*, made up of more articles about life in the sixties, and *The Electric Kool-Aid Acid Test*, a nonfiction account of Ken Kesey and the Merry Pranksters. He has since become a best-selling author and novelist. His other works include *From Bauhaus To Our House*, *The Right Stuff*, *Bonfire of the Vanities*, and *A Man In Full*.

Born Malcolm Little, the black nationalist leader **Malcolm X** rose from a life of drug addiction, crime, and incarceration to become one of the most powerful, articulate, and possibly the most admired African American political activists of the twentieth century. He served for a time as a spokesman for the Nation of Islam before breaking with them bitterly and founding his own religious organization, The Muslim Mosque, Inc. There followed repeated attempts to murder him and for the rest of his brief life, Malcolm X had bodyguards close by at all times. At first he opposed the kind of integration politics espoused by leaders such as Martin Luther King, in favor of complete separation of the races with total black autonomy. But after his departure from the Nation of Islam and following a life-changing visit to Mecca, Saudi Arabia, Malcolm X broadened his views to include a more pragmatic concept of racial integration as well as of spiritual and political liberation for everyone, whites included. On February 21, 1965, in Manhattan's famed Audubon Ballroom, the thirty-nine-year-old was gunned down by assassins of the Nation of Islam. His life story is the subject of an Oscar-winning film by Spike Lee. His *Autobiography* was cowritten with Alex Haley.

Chuck Zito is a tough, uncompromising, stand-up guy. A former celebrity bodyguard, Golden Gloves boxer, martial arts expert, past president of the N.Y. Nomads chapter of the Hell's Angels, and actor on the HBO drama *Oz*, Zito is the star of the upcoming USA Network series *Chuck Zito's Street Justice*. His memoir was cowritten with Joe Layden.

Permissions

S. Burroughs. Excerpt from *Naked Lunch*. © 1959 by William Burroughs. Used by permission of Grove/Atlantic, Inc. • William S. Burroughs. Excerpt from *Junky*. © 2003 by William Burroughs. Reprinted with permission of the Wylie Agency, Inc. • Pat Califia. "The Necessity of Excess" from *Public Sex: The Culture of Radical Sex*. © 1994 by Pat Califia. Reprinted by permission of Cleis Press. • Jim Carroll. Excerpt from *The Basketball Diaries*. © 1978 by Jim Carroll. Reprinted by permission of the Gernert Company. • Carolyn Cassady. Excerpt from *Off the Road*. © 1990 by Carolyn Cassady. Reprinted by permission of HarperCollins Publishers, Inc. • Neal Cassady. Excerpt from *The First Third and Other Writings*. © 1971, 1981 by the Estate of Neal Cassady. Reprinted by permission of City Lights Books. • Carlos Castenada. Excerpt from *The Teachings Of Don Juan: A Yaqui Way of Knowledge*. © 1968 by the Regents of the University of California. Used by permission of the Regents of the University of California. • Sandra Cisneros. Excerpt from *The House on Mango Street*. © 1984 by Sandra Cisneros. Reprinted by permission of Susan Bergholz Literary Services, New York. All rights reserved. • Eldridge Cleaver. Excerpt from *Soul on Ice*. © 1968 by Eldridge Cleaver. Used by permission of McGraw Hill. • Wanda Coleman. "In The City of Sleep" from *A War of Eyes & Other Stories*. © 1988 by Wanda Coleman. Reprinted by permission of the author. • Richard Condon. Excerpt from *The Manchurian Candidate*. © 1959, 1987 by Richard Condon. Used by permission of Harold Matson Co., Inc. • Dennis Cooper. Excerpt from *Period*. © 2000 by Dennis Cooper. Used by permission of Grove/Atlantic, Inc. • Gregory Corso. Excerpt from *An Accidental Autobiography*. © 2003 by New Directions Publishing Corp. Reprinted by permission of New Directions Publishing Corp. • Harry Crews. "The Car" from *Classic Crews*. © 1972 by Harry Crews. Reprinted by permission of John Hawkins & Associates, Inc. • Miles Davis with Quincy Troupe. Excerpt from *Miles: The Autobiography*. © 1989 by Miles Davis. Reprinted by permission of Simon & Schuster Adult Publishing Group. • Don De Grazia. Excerpt from *American Skin*. © 1998 by Don De Grazia. Reprinted with the permission of Scribner, an imprint of Simon & Schuster Adult Publishing Group. • Philip K. Dick. "Sales Pitch" from *The Philip K. Dick Reader*. © 1987 by Philip K. Dick. Reprinted by arrangement with Kensington Publishing Corp. All rights reserved. www.kensingtonbooks.com. • Snoop Dogg and Davin Seay. Excerpt from *Tha Doggfather*. © by Calvin Broadus. Reprinted by permission of HarperCollins Publishers, Inc. • Roxanne Dunbar-Ortiz. Excerpt from *Outlaw Woman*. © 2001 by Roxanne Dunbar-Ortiz. Reprinted by permission of City Lights Books. • Katherine Dunn. Excerpt from *Geek Love*. © 1989 by Katherine Dunn. Used by permission of Alfred A. Knopf, a division of Random House, Inc. • Andrea Dworkin. "Virginity" from *Intercourse*. © 1987 by Andrea Dworkin. Reprinted with permission of The Free Press, a division of Simon & Schuster Adult Publishing Group and The Elaine Markson Agency. • Bob Dylan. Excerpt from *Tarantula*. © 1971 by Bob Dylan. Used by permission of the author. • Dave Eggers. Excerpt from *A Heartbreaking Work of Staggering Genius*. © 2001 by Dave Eggers. Reprinted by permission of Simon & Schuster. • Maggie Estep. Excerpt from *Diary of an Emotional Idiot*. © 1997 by Maggie Estep. Used by permission of Soft Skull Press, Inc. • *Evergreen Review* cover. Cover © 2004 by Barney Rosset. Used by permission. • John Fante. Excerpt from *The Big Hunger: Stories 1932–1959*. © 2000 by Joyce Fante. Reprinted by permission of HarperCollins Publishers, Inc. • Karen Finley. Excerpt from *A Different Kind of Intimacy*. © 2000 by Karen Finley. Reprinted by permission

Golden Mayer. Used by permission of Grove/Atlantic, Inc. • Paul Krassner. "My Acid Trip with Groucho Marx" from *Confessions of a Raving, Unconfined Nut.* © 1993 by Paul Krassner. Used by permission of the author. • Timothy Leary. Excerpt from *The Delicious Grace of Moving One's Hand.* © 1998 by Futique Trust. Appears by permission the publisher, Thunder's Mouth Press, a division of Avalon Publishing Group. • Meridel Le Sueur. Excerpt from *Ripening.* © 1982 by Meridel Le Sueur. Used by permission of The Feminist Press. • Beth Lisick. Excerpt from *Monkey Girl.* © 1997 by Beth Lisick. Reprinted by permission of Manic D. Press. • Lydia Lunch. Excerpt from *Paradoxia: A Predator's Diary.* © 1999 by Lydia Lunch. Reprinted by permission of Creation Books. • Norman Mailer. Excerpt from *An American Dream.* © 1965 by Norman Mailer. Used by permission of The Wylie Agency, Inc. • Greil Marcus. "The Old, Weird America" from *Bob Dylan's Basement Tapes.* © 1997 by Greil Marcus. Reprinted by permission of Henry Holt, LLC. • Legs McNeil and Gillian McCain. Excerpt from *Please Kill Me.* © 1996 by Legs McNeil and Gillian McCain. Used by permission of Grove/Atlantic, Inc. • Mezz Mezzrow. Excerpt from *Really the Blues.* © 1964 by Mezz Mezzrow. Reprinted by arrangement with Kensington Publishing Corp. All rights reserved. www.kensingtonbooks.com. • Henry Miller. Excerpt from *Tropic of Cancer.* © 1934 by Henry Miller. Used by permission of Grove/Atlantic, Inc. • Tim Miller. Excerpt from *Shirts & Skins.* © 1997 by Tim Miller. Used by permission of Alyson Books. • Cookie Mueller. Excerpt from *Ask Dr. Mueller.* © 1997 by Cookie Mueller. Used by permission of Serpent's Tail, Ltd. • Eileen Myles. Excerpt from *Cool for You.* © 2000 by Eileen Myles. Used by permission of Soft Skull Press, Inc. • John O'Brien. Excerpt from *Leaving Las Vegas.* © 1990 by John O'Brien. Used by permission of Grove/Atlantic, Inc. • Chuck Palahniuk. Excerpt from *Fight Club: A Novel.* © 1996 by Chuck Palahniuk. Used by permission of W.W. Norton & Company, Inc. • Grace Paley. "The Illegal Days" from *Just As I Thought.* © 1998 by Grace Paley. Reprinted by permission of Farrar, Straus and Giroux, LLC. • Breece D'J Pancake. "The Way It Has To Be" from *The Stories of Breece D'J Pancake.* © 1977, 1978, 1979, 1981, 1982, 1983 by Helen Pancake. Used by permission of Little, Brown and Company, Inc. • Kenneth Patchen. Excerpt from *The Journal of Albion Moonlight.* © 1941 by Kenneth Patchen. Reprinted by permission of New Directions Publishing Corp. • Donn Pearce. Excerpt from *Cool Hand Luke.* © 1965 by Donn Pearce. Appears by permission of the publisher, Thunder's Mouth Press, a division of Avalon Publishing Goup. • Nelson Peery. Excerpt from *Black Fire.* © 1999 by Nelson Peery. Used by permission of the New Press. • Harvey Pekar. Excerpt from *The New American Splendor Anthology.* © 1991 by Harvey Pekar. Appears by permission of the publisher, Thunder's Mouth Press, a division of Avalon Publishing Goup. • Miguel Piñero. Excerpt from *Short Eyes.* ©1974, 1975 by Miguel Piñero. Reprinted by permission of Hill and Wang, a division of Farrar, Straus and Giroux, LLC. • Peter Plate. Excerpt from *Angels of Catastrophe.* © 2001 by Peter Plate. Used by permission of Seven Stories Press. • Sylvia Plath. Excerpt from *The Bell Jar.* © 1971 by Harper & Row, Publishers, Inc. Reprinted by permission of HarperCollins Publishers, Inc. • Dee Dee Ramone. Excerpt from *Legend of a Rock Star* and Paintings. © 2002 by Dee Dee Ramone. Appears by permission of the publisher, Thunder's Mouth Press, a division of Avalon Publishing Group. • John Rechy. Excerpt from *City of Night.* © 1963 by John Rechy. Used by permission of Grove/Atlantic, Inc. • John Rechy. Excerpts from *The Sexual Outlaw.* © 1977 by John

Rechy. Used by permission of Grove/ Atlantic, Inc. • Lou Reed. "To Do the Right Thing" from *Lou Reed: Emotion in Action.* © 1991 by Lou Reed. Reprinted by permission from Hyperion. • Frank Reynolds and Michael McClure. Excerpt from *Freewheelin' Frank.* © 1967 by Frank Reynolds and Michael McClure. Used by permission of Grove/Atlantic, Inc. • Larry Rivers and Arnold Weinstein. Excerpt from *What Did I Do?* © 2001 by Larry Rivers and Arnold Weinstein. Used by permission of Arnold Weinstein. • Luis J. Rodriguez. Excerpt from *Always Running—La Vida Loca, Gang Days in L.A.* © 1993 by Luis J. Rodriguez. Reprinted with permission of Curbstone Press. Distributed by Consortium. • Barney Rosset. "Tin Pan Alley" © 2004 by Barney Rosset. Used by permission of the author. • Ed Sanders. Excerpt *The Family.* © 2002. Appears by permission of the publisher, Thunder's Mouth Press, a division of Avalon Publishing Group. • Margaret Sanger. "The Woman Rebel" from *The Selected Papers of Margaret Sanger.* © 1003 by Margaret Sanger. Reprinted by permission of the author. • Sapphire. Excerpt from *Push: A Novel.* © 1997 by Sapphire. Used by permission of the author. • John Sayles. Excerpt from "Terminal Lounge" from *Dillinger in Hollywood.* © 2004 by John Sayles. Used by permission of Nation Books, a division of Avalon Publishing, Inc. • Paul Schrader. Excerpt from *Taxi Driver.* © 1990 by Paul Schrader. Used by permission of Faber and Faber, Inc. • Gil Scott-Heron. Excerpt from *The Vulture.* © Gil Scott-Heron. Reprinted by permission of Canongate Books Ltd. • Hubert Selby Jr. Excerpt from *Last Exit to Brooklyn.* © 1957 by Hubert Selby Jr. Used by permission of Sterling Lord Literistic, Inc. • Hubert Selby Jr. Excerpt from *Requiem for a Dream.* © 1978, 1988 by Hubert Selby Jr. Appears by permission of the publisher, Thunder's Mouth Press, a division of Avalon Publishing Group. • Assata Shakur. Excerpt from *Assata: An Autobiography.* © 1987 by Assata Shakur. Used with permission of Lawrence Hill Books. • Sam Shepard. Excerpt from *Rolling Thunder Logbook.* © 1977 by Sam Shepard. Used by permission of Viking Penguin, a division of Penguin Group (USA) Inc. • Earl Simmons and Smokey D. Fontaine. Excerpt from *E.A.R.L.: The Autobiography of D.M.X.* © 2003 by Earl Simmons. Reprinted by permission of HarperCollins Publishers, Inc. • Patti Smith. Excerpts from *Complete.* © 1998 by Patti Smith. Used by permission of the author. • Valerie Solanas. Excerpt from *SCUM Manifesto.* © 1997 by AK Press. Reprinted by permission of AK Press, www.akpress.org. • Terry Southern and Mason Hoffenberg. Excerpt from *Candy.* © Estate of Terry Southern. Reprinted by permission of Sterling Lord Literistic, Inc. • Terry Southern, edited by Nile Southern. Excerpt from *Now Dig This: The Unspeakable Writings of Terry Southern.* © 2001 by The Terry Southern Literary trust. Used by permission of Grove/Atlantic, Inc. • Mickey Spillane. Excerpt from *The Big Kill.* © 1951 by E.P. Dutton, renewed © 1979 by Mickey Spillane. Used by permission of Dutton, a division of Penguin Group (USA) Inc. • Annie Sprinkle. Excerpt from *Hardcore from the Heart.* © 2001 by Annie Sprinkle. Used by permission of Continuum. • Ralph Steadman. *Vintage Dr. Gonzo.* © Ralph Steadman, www.ralphsteadman.com. Used by permission of Sobel Weber Associates, Inc. • Lee Stringer. Excerpt from *Grand Central Winter.* © 1998 by Lee Stringer. Used by permission of Seven Stories Press. • Michelle Tea. Excerpt from *The Passionate Mistakes and Intimate Corruptions of One Girl in America.* © 1998 by Michelle Tea. Reprinted courtesy of Semiotext(e) Native Agents / Smart Art Press. • Piri Thomas. Excerpt from *Down These Mean Streets.* © 1967, 1995 by Piri Thomas. Used by permission of Alfred A. Knopf, a division of Random House, Inc. • Hunter

ALAN KAUFMAN, NEIL ORTENBERG, and BARNEY ROSSET are the reputed ring-leaders of the Outlaw Liberation Army (OLA), an illegal underground cadre responsible for dozens of literary crimes. Kaufman, the gang's founder, is author of the highly acclaimed memoir *Jew Boy*, editor of the best-selling *The Outlaw Bible of American Poetry*, and a member of PEN American Center. His novel *Matches: Tales of an Israeli Soldier* will be published in 2005 by Little Brown and Company. The last confirmed sighting of him, captured on a San Francisco surveillance camera, shows him backing out of a book store, bandit-masked, clutching a briefcase filled with Marvel comics. Ortenberg, purportedly the gang's feared enforcer, has been a publisher, editor, writer, and founder of Insurgent Communications. *Newsweek* called him "a gonzo publisher," and he is currently working on a screenplay based on the life of Dee Dee Ramone, and is sought for questioning in the recent spray painting of "OLA" over the entire facade of Manhattan's Lincoln Center. He has published such authors as Gregory Corso, Gore Vidal, John Waters, Chester Himes, Hubert Selby Jr., and Melvin Van Peebles. Barney Rosset, legendary founder of Grove Press, is widely regarded as the most important literary publisher of the post-war era. The list of his authors includes Samuel Beckett, William S. Burroughs, Jean Genet, Henry Miller, Jack Kerouac, Kathy Acker, and David Mamet. In 1988, PEN American Center presented Rosset with its prestigious Publisher Citation. Allegedly the OLA's master-mind, Rosset was last seen hustling tourists in a Thai pool hall.